SOUTH ASIAN ARCHAEOLOGY SERIES

EDITED BY ALOK K. KANUNGO No. 5

Excavating Waves and Winds of (Ex)change

A Study of Maritime Trade in Early Bengal

Shahnaj Husne Jahan

BAR International Series 1533
2006

Published in 2019 by
BAR Publishing, Oxford

BAR International Series 1533

South Asian Archaeology Series 5
Excavating Waves and Winds of (Ex)change

ISBN 9781841717531 paperback
ISBN 9781407329895 e-book

DOI https://doi.org/10.30861/9781841717531

A catalogue record for this book is available from the British Library

This book is available at www.barpublishing.com

BAR Publishing is the trading name of British Archaeological Reports (Oxford) Ltd. British Archaeological Reports was first incorporated in 1974 to publish the BAR Series, International and British. In 1992 Hadrian Books Ltd became part of the BAR group. This volume was originally published by John and Erica Hedges in conjunction with British Archaeological Reports (Oxford) Ltd / Hadrian Books Ltd, the Series principal publisher, in 2006. This present volume is published by BAR Publishing, 2019.

BAR
PUBLISHING
BAR titles are available from:

BAR Publishing
122 Banbury Rd, Oxford, OX2 7BP, UK
EMAIL info@barpublishing.com
PHONE +44 (0)1865 310431
FAX +44 (0)1865 316916
www.barpublishing.com

Foreword

Alok Kumar Kanungo
Series Editor, South Asian Archaeology Series
International Series of British Reports

The International Series of British Archaeological Reports, with its 1500 titles to the present time, is undoubtedly one of the most important places of publication in the discipline of Archaeology. But it is a pity that works on the archaeology of South Asia have been less represented in the series than their interest and value deserves.

The archaeological record of South Asia (comprising India, Pakistan, Nepal, Bhutan, Bangladesh, Sri Lanka and the Maldives) is extremely rich. This wealth begins in the Lower Palaeolithic period and includes, for example, the Harappan Civilization, one of the oldest in the world (covering a very large area and having many unique features -- the most ancient known town planning, its architecture and high standards of civic hygiene, its art, iconography, paleography, numismatics and international trade). South Asia also has a large number of earlier, contemporary, and later Neolithic and Chalcolithic cultures. Moreover, what makes South Asia particularly significant for the study of past human behaviour is the survival of many traditional modes of life, like hunting-gathering, pastoralism, shifting cultivation, fishing, and fowling, the study of which throws valuable light on the reconstruction of past cultures. In the region there are a large number of government and semi-government institutions devoted to archaeological teaching and/or research in archaeology and a large and professionally trained body of researchers.

Of course, a number of universities and other institutions, in the area do have their own publication programmes and there are also reputed private publishing houses. However, British Archaeological Reports, a series of 30 years standing, has an international reputation and distribution system. In order to take advantage of the latter – to bring archaeological researches in South Asia to the notice of scholars in the western academic world – the South Asian Archaeology Series has been instituted within the International Series of British Archaeological Reports. This series (which it is hoped to associate with an institution of organization in the area) aims at publishing original research works of international interest in all branches of archaeology of South Asia.

Those wishing to submit books for inclusion in the South Asian Archaeology Series should contact the South Asian Archaeology Series Editor, who will mediate with the BAR Editors and publishers of BAR, in Oxford. The subject has to be appropriate and of the correct academic standard (*curriculum vitae* are requested and books may be referred); instructions for formatting will be given, as necessary.

Dr. Alok Kumar Kanungo
Department of Archaeology
Deccan College Post-Graduate & Research Institute
Pune 411006
INDIA
email: alok_kanungo@yahoo.com

... Dwelling on this feeling of happiness,
I adopt it wholeheartedly
as the sole object of my pursuit.
(Lalan Shah, 1774-1890)

Contents

List of Figures and Tables

FIGURES

[All the photographs and maps produced in this volume, unless mentioned otherwise, are by the author.]

TABLES

Acknowledgements

The Deccan College Post-Graduate and Research Institute in Pune taught me how to excavate. The milieu of the college and the numerous sites I excavated in Rajasthan and Karnataka, always and unfailingly offered me shades of solitude in scorching heat where I learnt to listen to silences. With each dig as a trench would imperceptibly sink, I would weave my construction of the past and wonder yet again how unfailingly life changes. Now, as I sit excavating memories, ex-changing the present of the past, or, if you will, the past for the present, I feel most honoured that I was initiated into the craft of listening to the past, by a host of distinguished scholars. It was at Deccan College that I was introduced to ancient history, culture and archaeology. I bow with reverence to Professor K. Paddayya, Professor V.N. Misra, Dr. S.N. Rajaguru, Dr. V.S. Shinde, Dr. V.D. Gogte, Dr. S.J. Mangalam, Dr. P.K. Thomas, Dr. P.P. Joglekar, Dr. S.R. Walimbe, Dr. M.D. Kajle, Dr. B.C. Deotare, Dr. R.K. Mohanty and Dr. Gouri Lad for all their wisdom and kindness. I am deeply indebted to Dr. Pratibha Pingle and Dr. Asha Gurjar of the Sanskrit Dictionary Project, Deccan College and Pandit Chandra Shekhar Bhattacharyya of Dinajpur for translating Pali and Sanskrit texts and thank them sincerely for their invaluable help.

This monograph – or if I may call it my voyage across the waves and winds of exchange that brings change – would never have been possible if I had not been fortunate to have the kindness, generosity and support of numerous individuals and institutions. They are Professor Bratindranath Mukherjee, University of Calcutta, Dr. Kishor K. Basa, Utkal University, Bhubaneshwar, Dr. Gautam Sengupta, Director, the Department of Archaeology and Museums, West Bengal, Pranab K. Chattapadhya, Centre for Archaeological Study and Training, Eastern India and Md. Mosharraf Hossain, Deputy Director, Department of Archaeology and Museums, Government of Bangladesh, for their valuable suggestions? I offer my profuse gratitude to you all. I would also like to record my gratefulness to Dr. S. U. Deraniyagala, ex-Director General of the Department of Archaeology, Sri Lanka, Ms. Janya Manavid, Head of the Department of Archaeology and National Museum, Bangkok, Ms. Patcharee, Director of the National Museum Bangkok for making it possible for me to visit archaeological sites, take photographs and study the collections of their respective museums. Beyond and above customary acknowledgement, I offer my most sincere gratitude to Professor Firdous Azim, BRAC University, Dhaka, for her patient reading of the final draft of this monograph, and the criticism that she offered. Without her help, this work would have been smeared with numerous slips and mistakes.

My research led me to a number of libraries whose staff have kindly provided all possible assistance in my work. Although the list is long, it would be ethically incorrect if I do not mention the following libraries by name: Deccan College Post-Graduate and Research Institute, Pune, the Indian Museum and the National Library, Kolkata, in India, the University of Dhaka in Bangladesh, the Department of Archaeology, Yangon and the Department of Archaeology, Mandalay in Myanmar, the Department of Archaeology, Sri Lanka and the National Library, Colombo, the Silpakorn University, the SEAMEO-SPAFA Regional Centre for Archaeology and Fine Arts, and the Siam Society, Bangkok in Thailand. Some of the rare publications that I have been able to access were because of these dedicated persons who maintain some of the best collections I have come across. I would like to thank them all not only for their assistance but also for the valuable labour that they put in maintaining these storehouses of wisdom.

As storehouses of wisdom, libraries complement museums and I have been fortunate in having been able to visit some rare collections held in a number of museums. I offer my heartfelt gratitude to the authorities and staff of the following museums for granting permission to study their collection. These are the site museums of the Department of Archaeology at Mahāsthāngarh, Mainamati, and Pāhāḍpur in Bangladesh; the Asutosh Museum of Indian Art and the Indian Museum, Kolkata in West Bengal, India; the National Museum, Yangon, the Bagan Archaeological Museum, the collection held by the Department of Archaeology, Mandalay, Śrīkshetra Archaeological Museum in Myanmar; the National Museum, Bangkok and the Ban Kao National Museum, Kanchanaburi province in Thailand; the National Museum, Colombo, the Archaeological Museum of Anuradhapura, the Data Processing Centre, Anuradhapura in Sri Lanka; the Singapore History Museum, the Asian Civilisations Museum in Singapore; and the National Museum of the Philippines, Manila.

I have had the privilege of observing the operation of the port of Chittagong and hence I offer my gratitude to the Chittagong Port Authorities. Satellite images have been a boon for solving a few problems that no other source could. I offer my sincere gratitude to the authorities and staff of the National Data Centre, NRSA, Hyderabad in India and SPARRSO, Dhaka in Bangladesh for allowing me to study satellite images of Bangladesh and West Bengal. I gratefully acknowledge the assistance provided to me for archaeological and ethnographic fieldwork in Bangladesh by Mohammad Zulfekar Hossain, Hossain Mohammad Zubair, Mohammad Zakaria Hai Badhan, Mr. Swarup Hasan Shahin, Mr. and Mrs. Khairat Hossain Choudhury, Milton, Ayub Bachchu, Shahed and Mr. Bishwanath Banik. I am also thankful to Ms. Tripti Rani and Ms. Shamima Sultana for their kindness and full cooperation.

In this large list of names and institution, I want to set aside this little corner for expressing my profound gratitude to my parents Advocate Md. Abdul Hai and Mrs. Julekha Usmani for their unconditional love, support and encouragement. Without your faith and shelter, this research would have remained incomplete. Perhaps you will never know what your warmth and affection has meant for me.

Having worked on this volume for over eight years, voyaging across routes to my roots and reconstructing pieces of my identity, my mind is crowded now with distant images of the past – of the endless and tumultuous waves of the Bay of Bengal, innumerable ships and sails, pilgrims, mariners and merchants. The salted wind, a domed sky and vast stretches of murmuring and shimmering waves all around are fascinating beyond description. I feel, as though, I have voyaged across the seven seas to pre-modern Bengal. On the northernmost tip of the Bay, one of the seven seas, there still live voyagers – perhaps descendants of the mariners who accompanied C̃ād Saodāgar and Dhanapati Datta and whose distant forefathers must have accompanied Vijaya. My ethnographic fieldwork would not have been possible without the kindness and warm hospitality that I received from all these voyagers who live and toil on the shores of Bangladesh and West Bengal. But more than that, these people have shown me what it means to sail in the open seas. It is only befitting that I dedicate this work to these anonymous seafarers and their forefathers who dared and still dare to voyage while I admire their dexterity from the shore. This perhaps is the end of my first voyage across the seven seas.

Transliteration

All italicised titles of literary texts and technical terms and geographical names in Bengali used in this volume have been transliterated according to the following system.

Vowels

Short	Long
a as in America	ā as in last
i as in pin	ī as in police
u as in put	ū as in rule
ṛ as in rill	

Diphthongs

e as in fete	ai as in aisle
o as in so	au as in house

Consonants

Guttural	k	kh	g	gh	ṅ
Palatal	c	ch	j	jh	ñ
Cerebral	ṭ	ṭh	ḍ	ḍh	ṇ
Dental	t	th	d	dh	n
Labial	p	ph	b	bh	m
Semi-vowels	y	r	l	v	
Sibilants	ś	ṣ	s		h

Special Consonants

Palatal 'r' pronounced with the tongue against the upper palate	ḍ	Palatal 'rh' pronounced with the tongue against the upper palate	ḍh
Plain 'h' as in house	h	Aspirated 'h'	ĥ
Anusvara, as in 'bang'	ṁ	Candrabindu, as in 'monsieur'	˜

The plural form of all technical terms has been shown with non-italicised 's'. The names of (urban) modern Bangladeshi authors and their works are presented as they themselves transliterate them. Where they have not done so, conventional usage has been followed for the names and the texts have been transliterated following the above system. Conventional usage has also been followed for Muslim names and all other names and terms from outside Bangladesh. All ancient and medieval geographical names have been transliterated, but conventional usage has been followed for the modern period.

Introduction

In a world racing towards a globalized village, it may be inconceivable, and is often overlooked, that among prehistoric groups, trade was a prime motive for intercultural contact. As Collin Renfrew (1969: 152) observes, "[a]lso obscured has been the fact that trade, as an agent of communication, and hence in establishing areas of cultural and material exchange, had a cultural significance which long preceded its economic one". Through the historic period, down to the beginning of European colonization, trade facilitated human communication and intellectual cross-fertilization, "which precipitated the flowering of many brilliant cultures" (McPherson 1998: 16).

The notion of 'trade' is most commonly explained as a voluntary act of exchange of goods, which may be accomplished by barter or cash. However, Colin Renfrew (1969) views the term in a wider perspective. "Trade", according to him, "is reciprocal traffic, exchange, or movement of materials or goods through peaceful human agency" (Renfrew 1969: 152). Admitting that the aspect of 'reciprocity' cannot always be demonstrated, he shows that 'trade' can be better comprehended by showing what it is not: it is not booty, gift, tribute or tax. The most crucial defining feature of trade is that "goods must change hands". The underlying implication of 'changing hands' is 'exchange' because any giving of goods involves receiving, excluding of course those "given under duress or as 'unsolicited gifts'". There may be numerous variants of 'changing hands' of goods, many of which may not be for monetary gain but for gratification of both the parties involved in the transaction. Further, the process of exchange "can be repeated several times for the same commodities" (*ibid.*) and thus involve more than two parties.

'Trade' is often distinguished from 'commerce'. The distinction is made in terms of scale of transaction and distance of movement of goods: the former (i.e., 'trade' is taken to involve buying and selling on a small scale and movement of goods over short distance while the latter (i.e., 'commerce') is taken to imply large scale transaction involving long distance movement of goods. However, for the purpose of the present study, 'trade' shall be taken to include the aspect of 'commerce' noted above.

"Trade became possible" as Michael (1985: 175) shows, "when man [sic.] had learned to exploit nature and to produce beyond his immediate needs. The surplus he thus created, he could exchange with other peoples, taking from them their surplus in return". The surplus gives rise to two kinds of trade: "of material commodities whose natural distribution is limited (e.g., salt, tin, amber, wine, opium, etc.), and of products which, through superior know-how or other economic factors, are most efficiently produced in a limited area (e.g., Hittite iron, slaves, Swiss cuckoo-clocks)" (Renfrew 1969: 154). From very early times humans have carried out trade, either exchanging their surplus commodities or selling them for a price. Often this activity had to be carried out with distant localities, which necessitated transportation overland or overseas. This study focuses on the latter, i.e., transportation overseas, which is often referred to as maritime trade.

The term 'maritime' denotes, as Naravane (1998: 5) explains, "something to do with shipping and sailing on the high seas, i.e., not in coastal waters, and includes both commercial and naval activities". McGrail (1984: 14) would extend Naravane's explanation because he includes within the ambit of 'maritime' questions related to landing places, harbours, nature of wood-working, sea-routes, cargo items and so on. Furthermore, it is important to note that 'maritime activity' is a broad concept, which includes all activities related to the sea. However, this study intends to focus on one aspect of maritime activities, which is trade. For the purpose of this study, 'coastal waters' will be excluded from Naravane's parameter and 'maritime trade' will be identified as that involving maritime vessels, regularly transporting commodities to and from various fixed nodal points (i.e., ports), *both* on the high seas as well as coastal waters.

As the title of this monograph *Excavating Waves and Winds of (Ex)change: A Study of Maritime Trade in Early Bengal* implies, the maritime trade of the geographical region that is examined in it is 'Bengal'. Undoubtedly, the region is an anomaly because it is politically non-existent today. What exists is an independent country called Bangladesh and a component state of the Union of India, known as West Bengal (Fig. 1). Bangladesh, which was the eastern wing of Pakistan, emerged as an independent country in 1971 after a bloody civil war. The eastern wing of Pakistan and West Bengal in India were politically divided during the partition of British India in 1947. Before the partition, 'Bengal' was a province of British India and its territorial limit extended from the foot of the Himalayas in the north to the Bay of Bengal in the south, and from the Brahmaputra in the east to the lower reaches of the Suvarṇarekhā in the west. Hence, any study of pre-1947 'Bengal' must include within its scope the entire area of West Bengal and Bangladesh. This is all the more imperative if one remembers that most of the area within the boundaries of West Bengal and Bangladesh has been considered a political unit since the Mughal period. Known as *Subāh Bāṅgālā* to the Mughals, the territorial extent of the

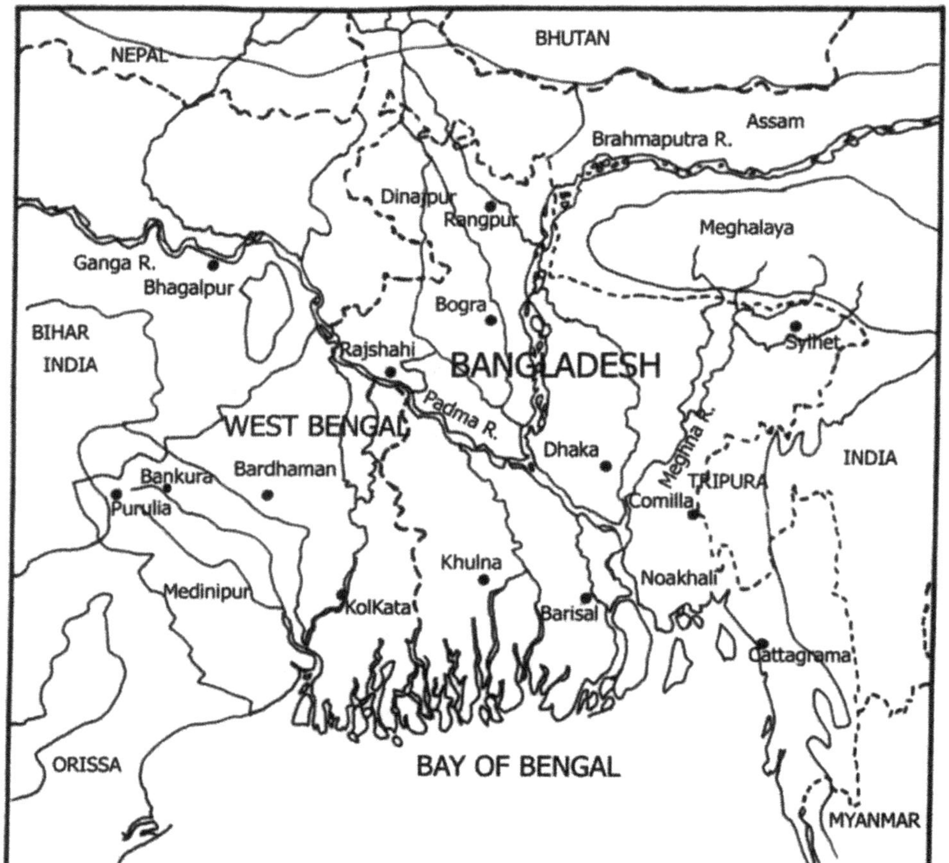

Fig. 1 Map of Bangladesh and West Bengal

unit included, besides British 'Bengal' also the *'Sarkārs'* of Sylhet and Pūrṇiyā, the 'Parganāh' of Āgmahal (Rajmahal) and the Teliagarhi Pass (S̃āotāl Parganās, Bihar). This area, though fragmented and varying during the pre-Mughal Muslim period, has nevertheless been a cultural unit, tied by the common thread of Bengali language.

Even when the language was at its nascent stage, during the reign of the Pālas, the Candras and the Senas (c. mid-8th to the 12th century AD), geographical and anthropological features had tied various ancient kingdoms into a unit that was often referred to as "the Eastern Country". Politically, the Eastern Country was composed of various provinces and kingdoms such as Puṇḍravardhana, Varendra, Gauḍa, Brahma or Uttara or North Rāḍha, Suhma or Dakṣiṇa or South Rāḍha, Vaṅga, Samataṭa and Harikela (Fig. 2). At the very east lay the kingdom of Samataṭa, which was bounded by the hills of Tripura in the east, the Meghnā in the west, and encompassed within its fold the Comilla-Noakhali region. The kingdom of Harikela lay immediately to the south of Samataṭa, roughly in what is now known as the Caṭṭagrāma (Chittagong) plains and may have included part of Sylhet region in later times. Further south lay the kingdom of Arakan, which included parts of southern Caṭṭagrāma in different periods. The core of Vaṅga territory lay within Vikrampura and Barisal regions but extended to the vast deltaic tract between Bhāgīrathī in the west, the Meghnā in the east and the Bay of Bengal in the south. The core of Puṇḍravardhana may have been the Barind or Varendra tract (substantial parts of Rajshahi, Dinajpur and Bogra regions) but extended to the foothills of the Himalayas in the north, Assam in the east and the Padmā in the south. The precise location of Gauḍa, although mentioned by Pāṇini, Kauṭīlya and Vātsāyan, is still uncertain. In the 7th century AD, its capital was Karṇasuvarṇa, about 20 kilometres south of Murshidabad and the kingdom may have included the northern part of West Bengal and the whole of north Bengal. From the end of the 8th century AD, Gauḍeśvara became the official title of the ruler of 'Bengal'. Rāḍha was often divided into Uttara or North Rāḍha and Dakṣiṇa or South Rāḍha. The former (i.e. Uttara-Rāḍha) lay between the Ajay and the Gaṅgā, sometimes even crossing beyond it to the north, while the latter (i.e., Dakṣiṇa-Rāḍha) lay between the Ajay and the Dāmodar rivers and its southern boundary crossed the Rūpnārāyaṇ.

Between the Pāla rule (which began in the mid-8th century AD), and the Gupta rule (which had ended by the mid-6th century AD) two distinct kingdoms had appeared in 'Bengal': Vaṅga ruled by Gopacandra, Dharmāditya and Samācāradeva from c. 525-575 AD and Gauḍa ruled by Śaśāṅka in the first half of the 7th century AD. During this era, also known as the post-Gupta era, Samataṭa had already emerged, Harikela was fast becoming known and the region of 'Bengal' was fast being Aryanized. But the 'process of Aryanization', as Ray (1994: 171) shows, had started earlier, not with infiltration of occasional religious preachers, traders or conquerors, but under the organised dominion of the Gupta Empire. During this era of Gupta rule, one hears of Puṇḍravardhana, Vaṅga, Samataṭa and Tāmralipti, the core of which lay in modern Medinīpur district.

The history of 'Bengal' before Gupta era is still vague. We do not know what relation the Śuṅgas (c. 180-68 BC) and the Kuṣāṇas (c. 1st century BC to 262 AD) bore with the various kingdoms of 'Bengal'. However, we do know that the Mauryas (c. 4th century BC to the 2nd century BC) had extended their sway over Puṇḍravardhana, Vaṅga, North Rāḍha and South

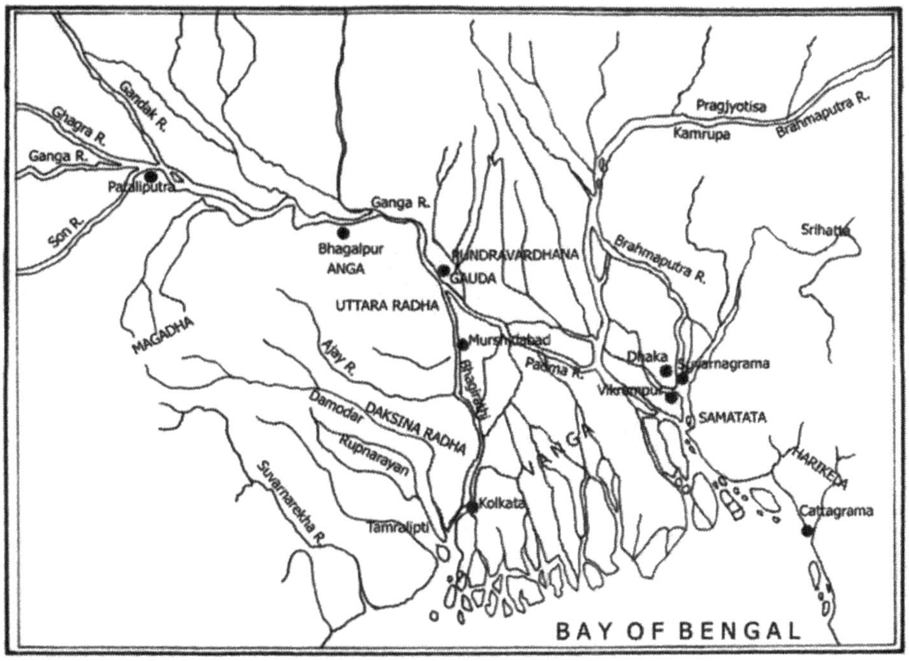

Fig. 2 Ancient political divisions of Bengal

Rāḍha. We also learn from Patañjali while commenting on *Mahābhāṣya* (IV.2.52) in the 2nd century BC that there existed 'eastern countries' comprising of Aṅga, Vaṅga, Suhma and Puṇḍra and from Pāṇini (*Ashṭādhyāyi*, VI.2.99) that Gauḍa and Vaṅga already existed by the 4th century BC. From around the same time, during Alexander's invasion (c. 327-325 BC), we hear of Gaṅgāridāi and Prasioi. Prasioi possibly lay to the west of the Gaṅgā-Bhāgirathī and included Tāmralipti and Gaṅgāridāi lay at the mouths of the Gaṅgā.

We have only scant information from various literary sources regarding 'Bengal' in the 5th century BC and beyond. The *Ācārāṅgasūtra*, a Jaina text from the 6th century BC, refers to the people of Vajjabhūmi and Subbhabhūmi (North and South Raḍha respectively) as rude barbarians. The *Aitareya Brāhmaṇa* refers to the Puṇḍras as 'dasyus' and the *Aitareya Araṇyaka* refers to the Vaṅgas as heathen and willful, and speakers of a language like that of the birds. Beyond this, we know very little about ancient 'Bengal'.

It is this 'Bengal' that the present volume examines. Because its boundaries have changed during various periods, it is not possible to demarcate the area of study with precision. Nevertheless, as the sketch of its history presented above shows, almost all of 'Bengal' lay within the geo-political entities currently known as Bangladesh and West Bengal. For the sake of convenience, these entities that lay between 20°50' and 27°09' N latitude and between 86°35' and 92°30' E longitude, will be referred to as 'Bengal'. In definitive terms, the area of 'Bengal' may be described thus: south of the southern foothills of the Himālayan range; the Brahmaputra River between Rangpur district of Bangladesh and the Indian state of Meghalaya; south of Gāro, Khāsiyā and Jaintiyā hills; west of the Barāk valley, the Tripura, the Lusāi, and the Ārākan hills; north of the Bay of Bengal; and east of Pūrṇiyā and Dvārabhāṅgā districts of Bihar, the low hill range in Rājmahal and Choṭanāgpur and the Suvarṇarekhā River in Orissa.

Maritime trade of this area, denoted with the convenient shorthand of 'Bengal', has been examined from earliest times to the first half of the 16th century AD. The downward limit of the study was determined by the arrival of the Portuguese in 'Bengal'. In 1518, only twenty years after Vasco da Gama crossed from Malindi on the east coast of Africa to Gujerat with the help of the famous Arab navigator Ahmad Ibn Mājid (Tibbetts 1981: 60), 'Bengal' was made directly aware of the Portuguese presence with the arrival of João Coelho in Caṭṭagrāma as a passenger on a Moorish boat, to be followed soon by Dom João de Silveira as the commander of the first Portuguese expedition. However, it was not till 1537, when Sultan Mahmud Shah permitted them to build factories at Sātgāon and Caṭṭagrāma and collect custom duties at the two ports, that they gained a foothold in 'Bengal'. In the very next year, the reign of Mahmud Shah ended and with him ended the Husain Shahi dynasty. The arrival of the Portuguese, as McPherson (1998: 138) observes, "does not mark the beginning of a new epoch in the commercial and political history of the area". Nevertheless, their arrival saw a change in the mood of the Indian Ocean Trade that heralded (if not actually effected) the end of the monopoly of the Arab, Persian, Gujarati and Coromandel merchants. It was also the first sign that a host of other European nations would soon follow, setting in motion the process of colonisation. Furthermore, with the end of the Husain Shahi dynasty, there began the Afghan era, when Sher Shah Sur, his successors, and the Karrani dynasty set in motion a distinctly different cultural and political mood. For convenience, the entire period of study has been broadly divided into five phases: the protohisoric period (from earliest times to 600 BC), early historic period (600 BC to 320 AD), the late historic period (320 to 750 AD), the early medieval period (c. 750 to 1200 AD) and the medieval period (c. 1200 to the end of the period of this study, i.e., the first half of the 16th century AD).

Excavating Waves and Winds of (Ex)change can rightfully claim the genealogy of scholastic research on the history of maritime activities of 'Bengal' that have been conducted since the late 19th century. Important among the scholarly forebears who produced fruitful work in the area are J. Kennedy (1898), R. K. Mookerji (1912), H. G. Rawlinson (1916), E. H. Warmington (1928), R. C. Majumdar (1927,

1937, 1938 and 1963), R. E. M. Wheeler (1955), A. L. Basham (1964), H. P. Chakraborti (1966), B. Srivastava (1968), P. C. Prasad (1977), Moti Chandra (1977), Bhaskar Chattopadhyay (1994), H. P. Ray (1998), Amitabha Mukherjee (1999) and Ranabir Chakravarti (1995, 1996, 1998 and 2001). However, the scope of their works permitted 'Bengal' to receive merely marginal treatment because their focus is not 'Bengal' but the entire South Asia. Consequently, 'Bengal' is only briefly touched upon as a part of South Asia and the role of 'Bengal' is shown as insignificant. Major players in these narratives of trade are shown as Greco-Roman, Arabian, Persian, Indian and Southeast Asian maritime entities. On the other hand, 'Bengal' does receive prime focus in the works of Tamonash Chandra Dasgupta (1935), Prabodh Chandra Bagchi (1944), Himanshu Bhusan Sarkar (1972), Ranabir Chakravarti (1992, 1992-93), Mamtazur Rahman Tarafdar (1995), Gautam Sengupta (1996) and Asok Datta (1999 and 2000). They emphasize the region in a manner that 'Bengal' appears to be the sole player, pushing all other regions into inconsequence. Moreover, they deal with specific aspects of maritime trade in their works.

Hence, if one begins to ask definite questions regarding maritime trade, most of the answers are obscure excepting a few oft-repeated names of ports and some commodities. Scarcity of data has restricted research to vague notions. Even today, very little is known about pre-Gupta 'Bengal'. In effect, much of the history of 'Bengal' begins from the early 4th century AD with large chunks of black holes till the Gupta era. Furthermore, one still does not have a complete chronological picture of maritime trade from earliest times to the first half of the 16th century AD because the period is riddled with various unresolved pieces of the jigsaw puzzle. The picture that emerges is extremely nebulous and the role of eastern Bengal (what today is Bangladesh) is marginal.

It is imperative therefore, to attempt to resolve these puzzles so that future work on social, economic or cultural dimensions can stand on firmer ground. It is for this reason the present volume attempts to portray a logically developed chronological overview of maritime trade focused on the entire region of 'Bengal' till the first half of the 16th century AD, with clear enumeration of all major aspects that any maritime trade entails. Which were the nodal points or ports engaged in that trade? What were the commodities of export or import of the region? What were the media of exchange? Which types of maritime vessels were employed for transporting the commodities and what were their construction processes? How were the ships navigated during coastal voyages or in the high seas? Which maritime routes connected the ports of 'Bengal'? Who were the traders and what was their operative milieu? In the pursuit of answer/s to the problem posed above, care has been taken not to get trapped into formulating a 'black box' narrative of chronological data, but rather attempt to unravel the 'why's and the 'how's. At the same time, this research takes into cognizance that it is necessary to articulate a reliable and empirical groundwork, which may lead to further analytical studies on maritime trade in 'Bengal'.

In order to arrive at the destination identified above, this research has adopted the following methodology: (1) extensive field-investigation of archaeological sites (including explorations and excavations) in West Bengal and Bangladesh from 1998 to 2006; (2) study of artifacts indicative of maritime trade that are preserved in museums and private collections in Bangladesh, India, Sri Lanka, Myanmar, Thailand, Singapore, Indonesia, Malaysia and the Philippines; (3) study of published literature and unpublished reports on epigraphic and numismatic findings as well as archaeological explorations and excavations conducted in Bangladesh and West Bengal; (4) ethnographic field-level investigation on traditional maritime practices of contemporary sea-faring communities in the coastal Bangladesh and West Bengal; (5) study of physiographic and geo-morphological features of Bangladesh and West Bengal through available maps, satellite images and published literature on geography and geomorphology; and (6) thorough survey of available literary evidences (Greek, Roman, Persian-Arabic, Chinese and South Asian) pertaining to maritime trade.

The evidences employed in this monograph need to be reckoned in view of quite a few constraints. Firstly, much of the field archaeological material from excavations and explorations that we have at hand in Bangladesh and West Bengal is prior to 600 AD. Secondly, of all the excavations and explorations that have been conducted so far, there is either very little published literature or it is almost impossible to access unpublished reports. Little that is available or accessible is imprecise and disorganized. The problem is aggravated by the fact that very few excavations have taken place in coastal West Bengal and Bangladesh. Furthermore, no marine archaeological discovery has yet been made within the area of study. Nevertheless, an attempt has been made to prioritize archaeological evidences (such as potteries, beads, seals and all the other relevant materials discovered either sporadically or in archaeological context), specially for the early historic period.

Absence of extensive archaeological data from 600 AD onwards, fortunately enough, is made up with a profusion of epigraphic evidences and as such, the late historic and the early medieval history of 'Bengal' is constructed primarily on these sources (although it is most regrettable that many of the copperplate land grants from ancient Samataṭa have not yet been deciphered). It is true that epigraphic sources rarely speak directly about maritime trade. But as Niharranjan Ray (1994: 100) correctly reminds us, "[w]hat is unmentioned is not necessarily non-existent". We need also to remember, as he further urges us, that "[i]nscriptions and literary accounts were not written to provide information about the basic products of a certain region or of its trade and commerce or of its social and economic condition" (*ibid.*: 101). Hence, careful evaluation of evidences that epigraphic sources offer us can often prove to be invaluable if we are prepared to make tangential inferences.

Two other important sources of evidences employed in this research are iconographic and numismatic in character. Although visual representation of maritime vessels of 'Bengal' is extremely rare, we are fortunate that a wealth of information may be accessed from neighbouring regions such as Orissa, Maharashtra and Andhra Pradesh in India and Java in Indonesia. As has been the case with this research, these evidences provided assistance to reach the destination *via negativa* – by discounting what was not. On the other hand, numismatic evidences profusely accessed in this research have been valuable in comprehending, in a very tactile manner, the complex world of the merchants and their operative milieu. This is particularly so, we need to remember, because long-distance itinerant traders and medium of trade were two factors intricately intertwined in shaping the intricate world of pre-modern trade.

Archaeological records, valuable as they are, become prominent in reconstructing prehistoric, protohistoric and early historic periods. However, in the historical period these become supplementary and secondary in character because of availability of written records. This consideration has made literary sources extremely helpful for this research. Indigenous creative literature, particularly the maṅgalakāvya corpus, offers a range of data on maritime culture of the Bengali people in the medieval period. Besides, South Asian theoretical treatises (such as Kauṭīlya's *Arthaśāstra*, the Smṛti texts and Bhojavarmanadeva's *Yukti Kalpataru*), creative literature (the *Mahāvaṁśa*, the *Rājavalliya*, the *Dīpavaṁśa*, the *Jātaka* tales, the *Mahābhārata*, Kālidāsa's *Raghuvaṁśa*) and historical accounts (the *Ain-i-Akbari* and *Riazu-s-Salatin*) have proved to be a plenteous field that has sustained our probing into some of the complex concepts and intriguing questions.

Among Greco-Roman accounts, Strabo's *Geography*, the *Periplus*, Pliny's *Natural History* and Ptolemy's *An Outline of Geography* remain indispensable in ascertaining the early historic period. Scholars are fully familiar with these oft-cited literary sources since they have attracted considerable attention for the last two centuries. Hence, a conscious attempt has been made to confine the investigation to re-evaluating existing opinions and making observations that appear to be particularly significant to elucidate archaeological evidences. The Chinese evidences are particularly helpful in counteracting Euro-centric overbalance and gaining valuable insight into maritime trade of 'Bengal'. Important information gleaned through close study of accounts and records provided by K'ang-T'ai, Fa-Hien, Hiuen-Tsiang, I-Tsing, Chau Ju-Kua, Ma-Huan and Fei Sin has indeed enriched this study.

The Arab-Persian merchants and seafarers, who dominated Indian Ocean trade circuits particularly in the early medieval period, have left behind valuable clues for our comprehension and reconstruction of the maritime trade scenario in 'Bengal'. Particularly important have been the accounts provided by Ibn Khurdādhbih and Ibn Battutā. Finally, no study of the medieval period can hope to be mature without taking into account the detailed information provided by European travellers, merchants and officials, such as Marco Polo, Duarte Barbosa, Tome Pires, Caesar Frederick, Ralph Fitch, Verthema, Jean Baptiste Tavernier and Thomas Bowrey. This study is indebted to the clarity and insight that these men from distant countries provide in their observations on medieval 'Bengal'. It is acknowledged that a few of the sources used in this research are from the second half of the 16th and the 17th centuries AD. Although they reach beyond the period of study, these are valuable indicators of conditions existing in the first half of the 16th century and earlier. Whenever accessed, their value and relevance in the analysis have been consciously taken into account.

Having listed the major literary sources accessed in this research, it is acknowledged that a constraint in employing these in critical evaluation arises from uncertainty as to whether the authors reported from first-hand experience or hearsay. Furthermore, some names and terms that non-natives have used create more confusion than clarity. The case of the City of Bengala may be cited as a glaring example. Hence, a conscious attempt has been made to evaluate these sources critically before they have been employed in filling the gaps in our knowledge.

The study of maritime trade is indispensably a multi-disciplinary subject. It entails knowledge of the environment and the nature of the coast as well as high seas. Hence, ethnographic, geographical and geological evidences have been utilized in some areas of investigation that consequently produced rich dividends. Because very little evidence on shipbuilding tradition and navigational techniques employed in 'Bengal' has survived, field-level ethnographic investigation undertaken for this research has helped immensely in filling the gaps in answers obtained from literary and other sources. In some other cases, such as identifying sites of maritime port, geographical (such as maps, satellite images etc.) and geological evidences (in the form of published reports) have proved to be invaluable.

Observations and deliberations of the investigation obtained from the sources mentioned above have been presented in seven chapters of *Excavating Waves and Winds of (Ex)change*. The first chapter locates the maritime ports that operated in the region of 'Bengal' from earliest times to the first half of the 16th century AD. The second chapter discusses the commodities that were exported and imported through the maritime ports of 'Bengal' during this period and attempts to delineate the complex port-hinterland relationship that arose because of these commodities. Chapter Three examines various media of exchange that circulated in 'Bengal'. The next chapter inquires into the types of vessels that were engaged in the maritime trade of 'Bengal', describes their process of construction, attempts to identify the indigenous tradition of maritime vessels and probes into the level of proficiency that Bengali shipwrights attained. Chapter Five examines various aspects of nautical science that evolved through this period and examines how maritime vessels were navigated during coastal voyages and in the high seas, and in what way the climate affected the sailing schedule. It also attempts to show the pattern of change in the navigational technology and its consequences in maritime voyages. Chapter Six identifies the trade routes which connected the ports of 'Bengal' with the Red Sea coast and the Persian Gulf in the west and Southeast Asia in the east. Instead of assimilating mere facts, the chapter also attempts to discern the pattern of change in the trade routes and comprehend why they changed. The last chapter, i.e. Chapter Seven, examines who the merchants were and what was their operative milieu.

Before engaging the reader in a voyage across two thousand years as delineated in these seven chapters – a voyage across the waves and winds of exchange that brings change – it is necessary that I state my subject position. I am a woman, an archaeologist by profession, a Muslim by birth and a citizen of Bangladesh. In my childhood, I learnt that there are seven seas somewhere across the Bay of Bengal. When my grandmother told me stories of Sindabad and Saiful Muluk sailing across the seven seas, or when Hemantakumar Mukhapadhyaya sang his famous song about the princess who lives beyond the seven seas and thirteen rivers, those waters held a mystery I could never fathom. This research has demystified the mystery of those seas and shown me that in the early medieval period, the Arab and Persian mariners and merchants referred to their maritime world of the Indian Ocean trade system as that of seven seas: from Siraf on the Persian Gulf via the Bay of Bengal to Khanfu (Canton) on the North China Sea.

The choice of the area of study of this monograph was generated out of a touch of postcolonial positioning. Laying aside romantic claims of a glorious past that usually motivates a nationalist stance, I wanted to 'discover' my past in a globalized world. I acknowledge that it is my construction. Nevertheless, it places Bangladesh not with its roots but routes out of which the roots may be constructed. Further, this construction is not framed in terms of vague issues of cultural traits but trade which, in pre-modern societies at least, was the most important agent for initiating change.

In other words, I have attempted to arrive at a construction that allows one to glimpse at Bengal (much of which is today Bangladesh) from earliest times to the first half of the 16th century AD in terms of its maritime trade, which in turn allows one to examine the routes that the people of this country chose to travel or were forced to travel because of trade. Hopefully, this will be a source of inspiration for the people of the country today, marginalized as they are in the globalized context of world trade and earn respect from the people of other nations. Hopefully, too, fruitful strategies may be devised so as the place Bangladesh in at least a more respectful and privileged position.

One
Ports

Port is a "place where vessels may discharge or receive cargo; it may be the entire harbor including its approaches and anchorages, or may be the commercial part of a harbour where the quays, wharves, facilities for transfer of cargo, docks, and repair shops are situated" (Snead 1982: 220). Against Snead's emphasis on physical aspects, Kidwai (1992: 10) gives a wider perspective when he says that a port is "the place of contact where goods and people as well as cultures are transferred between land and maritime space. It is a knot where ocean and inland transport lines meet and intervene". He goes on to point out, the concept of port is economic and is distinct from the physical concept of 'harbour'. The latter, i.e., a harbour, is "the sheltered area of deep water". Because the essential feature of one is economic while the other is physical, a busy port may not be a fine harbour. Snead (1982: 210) agrees when he notes that a harbour is a shelter and a place of security and comfort; it is a "portion of a water body where ships are protected, because the area is either in part landlocked or artificially sheltered". Not denying the importance of a 'harbour' as a physical concept, this study will place greater emphasis, as far as available materials permit to inquire on port as an economic concept "where ocean and inland transport lines meet and intervene" and as a place where goods, people and culture are transferred.

A particular type of port situated on long distance shipping routes and meets technical requirements of ocean-going vessels is known as an 'entrepôt', a "trans-shipment point where transfer of goods and/or passengers takes place from ship to ship" (Kidwai 1992: 10). Other ports may serve as 'collecting centres' and 'feeder points'. 'Collecting centres' may be identified as ports located near important ecozones, mineral-producing areas and regions with valuable forest products. Ports serving as 'feeder points' may be seen as supply centres where limited range of commodities are available. Located in the interior or near the coast, these ports feed the larger 'collecting centres' and entrepôts.

The physical and cultural factors that determine the origin, evolution and growth of a port are 'site', and 'situation'. "The site is the area of land and the associated waters on which the port and port town are actually developed. It includes local topography, drainage and soil/land stability as well as the depth, temperature and movement of waters within it" (Hoyle 1967: 8, n. 13). On the other hand, 'situation' brings together physical as well as cultural aspects. "It is the geographical position of a port in a broad sense; it incorporates the socio-economic and human environment of the hinterland on the one hand and the port's relationship to world sea lanes and other sea ports on the other" (*ibid.*: 7-8, n. 13). Security is another important aspect in the situation of a port. Economic and political factors also contribute immensely to shape the nature and life of a port. Sometimes, social forces, such as attitude of merchants and the state machinery, play crucial role in determining the fate of a port. This study will be able not only to identify the sites of various ports that operated in early 'Bengal', but also locate the situation of these ports.

Based on Bird's (1963: 24-34) hypothetical concept of a standard 'Anyport', Kidwai (1992: 11) has identified six stages in the evolution of a harbour in terms of the development of facilities it offers. Of these, the first three stages fall within the scope of this study. In the earliest stage, called the 'primitive', rudimentary storage and handling facilities are created and a jetty is designed to steepen the gradient between the land and the water. Next in the evolution is the 'marginal quay extension' stage, during which the primitive nucleus is extended lineally as greater demands were created by increasing number and size of vessels. The third stage is that of the 'marginal quay elaboration', during which "the construction of jetties extended into the water and of quays developed with the help of land excavations". Since Bird's concept of 'Anyport' draws upon the experience of the British ports, accepting his model for a study of ports in 'Bengal' may prove to be problematic. If we have fixed in our minds the historical 'mileposts' that Casson (1973: 367) draws our attention to, such as the earliest man-made installation at Delos in the 8th century BC, the introduction by the Romans of the use of concrete capable of setting under water, etc., and look for their parallels in 'Bengal', we may be led to treacherous grounds. As Himanshu Prabha Ray (1998: 185) implies through a question she poses, fair-weather sailing prevalent in Asia in the ancient period may never have necessitated coastal infrastructure in maritime trade. Vessels used in sea voyages along Indian coastline were hauled ashore for anchorage and repairs. Since they drew very little water, their entry into shallow estuaries was not hindered. Often, even down to the historical period, larger ships anchored at a distance from the coast and goods were ferried across to the shore in smaller crafts. "This practice was important", says Ray (*ibid.*), "because there are a few natural harbours along the vast coastline of India and hence the location of ports was determined not so much by geographical factors as by the resource of the hinterland".

Although, not all of Ray's observations may be applicable to 'Bengal', the essence is nevertheless important for reminding ourselves that it would be futile to look for ancient port sites with harbour installations as prime indicators. However, Ray appears to be unconsciously favouring the notion that all maritime ports, by the very nature of having to deal with maritime trade, have to be situated on the coast. Hence, a maritime port is necessarily a littoral port. This line of thought is fallacious – at least as far as 'Bengal' is concerned – because there was no littoral ports in the region of 'Bengal', all were estuarine ports. This was because the continental shelf along the coast of 'Bengal' slopes down very gently. Hence, the ships either had to anchor at a distance from the port (as the vessels over 9.14 m draught still have to do in Caṭṭagrāma) or anchor at ports situated on estuaries of large rivers. It is no coincidence that all existing ports in Bangladesh and West Bengal, which are capable of handling ocean-going vessels, are located not on the coast but in the estuaries or near the downstream end of large rivers. The Gaṅgā-Brahmaputra-Meghnā river system is one of the largest in the world. Most of the water of Bengal Basin flows through this system and discharge finally in the Bay of Bengal. The Huglī-Bhāgīrathī, the Gaṅgā-Padmā, the Brahmaputra-Jamunā and the Meghnā have a moderate gradient; the velocity of the current is not excessive and has wide bed of sufficient depth. Hence they meet all the conditions, necessary for favourable navigation. Nevertheless, as Deloche (1994: 43) points out, estuarine ports pose navigational hazards due to shallow depth and shifting sandbars. However, they also offer excellent shelter and facilitate easier connection as 'a knot where ocean and inland transport lines meet and intervene' through inland waterways or land routes. The picture is reversed along the East Coast of India and Sri Lanka where the slope of the continental shelf is very steep. Consequently, in this region, all the major maritime ports of ancient times were, and of contemporary times are, littoral.

EARLY HISTORIC PREAMBLE

Keeping in mind the above-mentioned considerations, we may begin our examination of the Sri Lankan Pāli chronicles, the *Mahāvaṁśa*, the *Rājavalliya* and the *Dīpavaṁśa*, believed to be the earliest literary reference to maritime activities in 'Bengal'. The chronicles, compiled from earlier sources and composed between the 4th century AD and the early part of the 5th century AD, do not make any allusion to ports in the story of Prince Vijaya landing in Sri Lanka in the 5th century BC. Chapter Six of the *Mahāvaṁśa* speaks of a country of the Vaṅgas and a nearby country of the Kaliṅgas, which were allied through matrimonial relationship. Siṁhavāhu, grandson of the king of the Vaṅgas founded a city called Sīhapura in the forested land of Lala (Lāḍha= Rāḍha). There, he had sons born unto him, the eldest of whom, Vijaya infuriated his subjects by his evil conduct. When the subjects demanded Vijaya's death, Siṁhavāhu must have been torn between duty of a king and love of a father, for, as the chronicles show, he put Vijaya not to death but condemned him to a journey, which meant death in any way.

> 43. Then did the king cause Vijaya and his followers, seven hundred men, to be shaven over half the head [shaving of head signified loss of freedom] and put them on a ship and sent them forth upon the sea, and their wives and children also. 44. The men, women, and children sent forth separately landed separately, each (company) upon an island, and they dwelt even there. 45. The island where the children landed was called Naggadīpa ['Island of children'] and the island where the women landed Mahilādīpaka ['Island of women']. 46. But Vijaya landed at the haven called Suppāraka but being there in danger by reason of the violence of his followers he embarked again. 47. The prince named Vijaya, the valiant, landed in Laṅka, in the region called Tambapaṇṇi on the day that the Tathāgata lay down between the two twinlike sāla-tree to pass into nibbāṇa (Geiger 1986: 51-54).

A closer examination of the passage cited above reveals "the haven called Suppāraka". A "haven" is a "sanctuary", even a port. In any case, the implication is clearly of a "safe anchorage". We need not argue about the historical existence of the port of Suppāraka or Sopara in the 5th century BC. What is important, concerned as we are, with maritime ports in 'Bengal', is that Suppāraka is mentioned as a haven, the point of departure of Vijaya and his men, women and children; the point of landing in Sri Lanka is not even mentioned. Hence, we may conclude that no such "haven" or "safe anchorage" existed in Rāḍha. That Vijaya and company were put on a ship and sent forth on the sea implies that seafaring activities were not unknown to these people of Rāḍha. Perhaps, in these very early times, the vessels were simply hauled ashore for anchorage. We are now speaking of unidentified and unidentifiable points on the Contai coast. As we shall see presently, another excerpt from the same text (Chapter XIX, verses 1-23), which describes transportation of the Bodhi-tree to Sri Lanka, Tāmralipti developed into a port not very far from these early launching points of seafaring activities.

There are two more descriptions of maritime voyages from 'Bengal' in the *Mahāvaṁśa*. One is about the journey of Vijaya's messenger carrying his letter to Sīhapura in Lala and Paṇḍuvāsudeva's journey to Sri Lanka (Chapter VIII, verses 1-12). With thirty-two sons of ministers, Paṇḍuvāsudeva is said to have "embarked" in the guise of monks and "landed at the mouth of Mahākandara river". It is clear that the island had already developed an estuarine-landing spot at the mouth of the Mahākandara river, which is now identified as the Mahaveligaṅgā (Perera 1951: 114). These, too, may not have been regular harbours, but the search for "safe anchorage" was obviously on. Noteworthy is the fact that Lala (or Rāḍha) was yet to develop similar estuarine landing spots. The second reference in the *Mahāvaṁśa* (Chapter VIII, Verses 18-24) recounts the flight of the beautiful daughter of Sakka Paṇḍu (a king who ruled from a city on the further side of the Gaṅgā, Morapura according to Mookerji 1957: 49).

Two points in the description are worth drawing attention to: (1) Sakka Paṇḍu "placed his daughter speedily upon a ship, together with thirty-two women-friends, and launched the ship upon the Ganges" and (2) they landed at "the haven called Goṇagāmaka". By this time, the launching point of ships has definitely moved from the coast to a safer point on the Gaṅgā, presumably a point on the estuary. It was not yet a regular harbour, for the king is described to have "launched the ship", as though from makeshift arrangements made on a dry bank where it had been earlier hauled for safety. Sri Lanka, on the other hand, had already developed a haven, i.e., a safe anchorage, at Goṇagāmaka, iden-tified as Trincomalee (Perera 1951: 114).

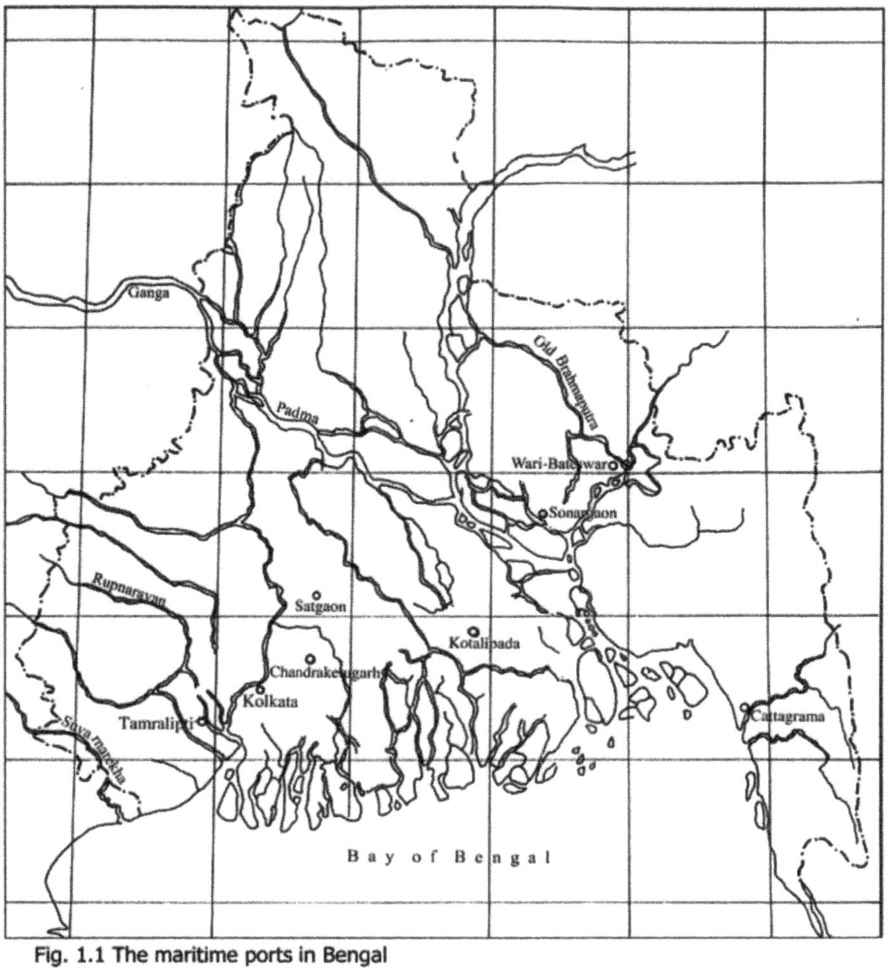

Fig. 1.1 The maritime ports in Bengal

Milindapañha (c. 1st century AD), the next important literary evidence from South Asia, indicates a dramatic growth in maritime contact with 'Bengal'.

> Just, O King, as a ship-owner who has become wealthy by constantly levying freight in some sea-port town, will be able to traverse the high seas, and go to Vanga, or Takkola, or China, or Sovira, or Surat, or Alexandria, or the Koromandel coast, or Farther India, or any other place where ships do congregate – just so, O King, it is he who in former births has undertaken and practised, followed and carried out, observed, framed his conduct according to, and fulfilled these thirteen vows, who acquires all the results of the life of a recluse, and all its ecstasy of peace and bliss becomes his very own (VI, 21, 360; Davids 1894: 269).

Even a cursory glance at the cited excerpt will reveal that the image of ships sailing from seaports had become widely known. Although no port is mentioned by name in Vaṅga and China and the Coromandel Coast, the narrator implies its existence by referring generally to "sea-port" at the beginning of the sentence.

We have traversed about five centuries to comprehend the early tentative beginnings on the coast, then moving to estuarine points and finally to ports with, what must have been, busy harbours. This journey is of anonymous port/s in Rāḍha and Vaṅga – unnamed and unnamable. However, a number of other literary evidences, as well as physiographic, geological and substantial archaeological evidences prove that from earliest times to the first half of the 16th century AD, one can name and identify sites of seven maritime ports in the region under study. These are Tāmralipti, Gaṅgābandar, Wārī-Baṭeśwar, Koṭālipāḍā (Candravarmakoṭa), Sātgāon, Sonārgāon and Caṭṭagrāma (Fig. 1.1). Below is the discussion of all these seven ports in detail.

TĀMRALIPTI

Considered to be one of the oldest maritime ports in entire South and Southeast Asia, Tāmralipti has a number of synonyms in South Asian literature (specially Pāli and Sanskrit). These are Tāmalittī, Tamalipti, Tamalika, Tamalipta, Tamraliptika, Velakula, Stambapu, Viṣṇugriha, Tamalini, and Gambhīra etc. It has also been cited as Dāmalipta in Daṇḍīn's *Daśakumāracarita* and in the *Abhidhānacintāmaṇi*, Tamalites by Ptolemy, To-mo-liti by Fa-Hien and Tan-mo-lih-ti by Hiuen-Tsiang.

Moti Chandra (1977: 130), attempting to prove the existence of Tāmralipti in the age of the *Mahābhārata* (which assumed its present form of compilation between the 4th century BC and the 4th century AD), has tried to show that the *Sabhāparva* of the *Mahābhārata* (ii, 27, 22-49) indicates knowledge of a sea-route between Tāmralipti and Bharukaccha (Barygaza/Bharuch) and also to Sumatra, Java and other places. Takakusu (1896: XXXIII-XXXIV) appears to be referring to Chandra and agreeing with him when he notes that the port "figures even in the sacred writings of the Hindus". As we shall see presently, these scholars are not far from the truth.

The Sri Lankan Pāli Chronicles speak of Tāmralipti for the first time in the *Mahāvaṁśa* (II) while recounting Siṁhalese King

Devānaṁpiya Tissa's exchanging of gifts with Emperor Aśoka. As recounted in *Mahāvaṁśa* (XIX, 1-8), Emperor Aśoka transported the Bodhi tree on a ship, which sailed down the Gaṅgā from his capital Pataliputra to Tāmalittī "in just one week". He travelled over land to Tāmalittī, well in time to receive the holy tree and worshipped it after having it "placed on the shore of the great ocean". Then he had the tree set on a ship (*Mahāvaṁśa*, XIX, 11). After due respects were paid, "[t]he ship, laden with the great Bodhi-tree, fared forth into the sea" (*Mahāvaṁśa*, XIX, 17). Finally, the ship arrived at Jabbukola (in Sri Lanka) (*Mahāvaṁśa*, XIX, 22-23). Although the harbour of Tāmalittī (Tāmralipti) is not clearly identified, the *Mahāvaṁśa* appears to imply its location at a point on or close to the Bay of Bengal coast ("the shore of the great ocean") and on or near the bank of the Gaṅgā (down which the Bodhi tree was transported from Pataliputra). Although Aśoka's journey by land-route, transportation of the Bodhi tree by riverine route and onward transportation of the tree on a maritime vessel all indicate that Tāmralipti had already developed into a "knot where ocean and inland transport lines meet and intervene", the transaction was more cultural in nature than economic. Lest we overlook, it is essential also to draw attention to an important indication of political nature: that the port was under the domain of the Mauryas.

Three *Jātaka*[1] tales, Mahājanaka Jātaka (Book XXII, No. 539; Cowell 1957, VI: 19-37), Śaṅkha Jātaka (Book X, No. 442; Cowell 1957, IV: 9-13) and Samudda-vāṇija Jātaka (Book XII, No. 466; *ibid.*: 98-104), make clear references to maritime activities in 'Bengal'. However, they certainly do not "mention of trade between Tāmralipti and Ceylon" as Niharranjan Ray (1994: 296) claims. In fact, there is no mention of Tāmralipti and Ceylon (Sri Lanka) in these tales. However, the three Jātaka stories, agree with one aspect of Aśoka's transportation of the Bodhi tree: all speak of ships sailing down the Gaṅgā. Instead of changing ships as in the case of transportation of the Bodhi tree, the Jātaka ships sail directly from the Gaṅgā to the sea. Thus, it appears that till at least the 4th century BC, the Gaṅgā played the role of an artery for inland connection. It may even have been navigable for maritime vessels up to a considerable extent. We need not interpret Benares (from where the carpenters and their families of Samudda-vāṇija Jātaka sail down in a ship) literally because the city features in the *Jātaka-mālā* more in a figurative and conventionalised manner than a historically authenticated urban centre. More important is the indication in all the Jātaka stories that Tāmralipti served a vast hinterland of lower and middle Gaṅgā valley. For this entire region, the river Gaṅgā and the port of Tāmralipti provided the sole outlet to the high sea. Furthermore, Mahājanaka Jātaka and Śaṅkha Jātaka bear indications that an unnamed harbour on the downstream end of the Gaṅgā or near its estuary had become a knot of economic nature since we hear of goods and people being transferred from inland lines of communication to the oceanic lines.

The next important reference to Tāmralipti as recounted in the Sri Lankan Chronicles is in the *Dāthā-dhātu-waṅso*. In it is recounted the legend of Dantakumāra who conveyed the tooth-relic in 371 AD, in a ship which plied regularly between Tāmralipti in 'Bengal' and the ports of Sri Lanka (Mookerji 1957: 50). Thus, by 371 AD, when the tooth relic was brought to Sri Lanka, Tāmralipti is definitely indicated as an entrepôt or a "trans-shipment point where transfer of goods and/or passengers takes place from ship to ship". The regularity of ships plying between Tāmralipti and Sri Lanka further implies maritime trade.

Later literary references give us further information regarding the site and situation of Tāmralipti. For example, Dāmalipta, as described in the story of Mitragupta in the Daṇḍīn's *Daśakumāracarita* (uchchhvāsa VI: 149-173) (c. 6th century AD), is a prosperous port-city of the Suhmas close to the sea and near the Gaṅgā. It is frequented by sea-going boats of different races, among whom feature prominently the Yavanas (Kale 1966: 320-339). Not only is the estuarine nature of the port confirmed, its economic aspect is also indicated in its prosperity. One may also deduce clear suggestions of a busy port where the Yavanas and people of other nations (and also the goods that they brought) were transferred. Not the least in importance is the reference of political significance: that the Suhmas controlled the port.

The situation of Tāmralipti is clearer in the *Kathā Sarit Sāgara*, a collection of popular stories composed by Somadeva between 1063 and 1082 AD, because isolated scenes of quite a few stories are set in the city of Tāmraliptī. In most of these stories, the name of the city is invariably bound with merchants, as in the case of the aged Dharmasena of the story titled "The Adventures of Pushkarāksha and Vinayavatī" (Penzer 1926: 17), the young, handsome and wealthy Samudradatta of "The Parrot's Story" (*ibid.*: 186-87), another merchant from Tāmraliptī, named Harṣagupta in the "Story of King Ratnādhipati and the White Elephant Śvetaraśmi" (Penzer 1925: 172-73) and a Brāhmin Vidūshaka who arrives at "the city of Tāmraliptī, not far from the sea" where he meets a merchant named Skandhadāsa in the "Story of Vidūshaka" (Penzer 1924: 68-73). However, in "The King who married his Dependent to a Nereid" one meets a king of Tāmraliptī, "a city on the shore of the eastern sea". The king, named Chaṇḍasiṃha, lives in a palace, which must have been spacious, and well planned for it is described to have had a pleasure with garden with tank attached to it (Penzer 1926: 209-216). Interestingly, the situation of Tāmralipti is not so much indicative of a maritime port as of a land of fabulous riches, like Baghdad of the *Arabian Nights*. Nevertheless, the substratum in both is clearly commercial. We may also note that only an estuary can meet the

[1] Although ascertaining definite period for these tales is difficult, for the purpose of this research Ghosh's (1323 BS: xi) conservative dating will be adopted, who placed the earlier forms of the tales to the 4th century BC or earlier.

conditions of Tāmralipti being located "not far from the sea" and "on the shore of the eastern sea".

Having examined South Asian literary evidences, let us now move on to Greco-Roman literary accounts of Megasthenēs (an ambassador of Seleukos to the court of Candragupta at Palimbothra, c. 302 to 288 BC), Strabo's *Geography* (60 BC-19 AD), the *Periplus of the Erythraean Sea* by anonymous author (60 AD), Pliny's *Natural History* (77 AD) and Ptolemy's *An Outline of Geography* (mid-2nd century AD). Of these five accounts, which refer or even slightly allude to maritime activities of 'Bengal', the *Periplus* is silent about Tāmralipti. Schoff (1995: 255), who translated the *Periplus*, believes that Tāmralipti and Gangê (Gaṅgābandar) were the same. Megasthenēs did not travel beyond Palimbothra. He wrote an account of India but the original form is now lost. McCrindle translated in English a collection and arrangement of detached fragments of Megasthenēs (which exist in the work of various classical historians) titled Megasthenēs Indica by Schwanbeck. He too is silent about Tāmralipti but his note on "the time taken to make voyages from the sea to Palibothra by the Ganges" (From Strabo, XV. i. ii, in McCrindle 1926: 48) appears to confirm the Jātaka stories cited earlier regarding navigability of the river by maritime vessels. Strabo, who makes similar observation in his account, possibly derived this information from Megasthenēs' account. Pliny is also entirely silent about Tāmralipti. However, he is aware of voyages from "the country of Prasii" to Ceylon (*Natural History*, VI, c. 22.24) and nard "which grows in the vicinity of the Ganges" (*Natural History*, XII, c. 26). He also knows about a people called Taluctae (*Natural History*, VI) who may be regarded as the inhabitants of Tāmralipti. He even writes that 'the final part' of the Gaṅgā flowed 'through the country of the Gaṅgārides' and its inhabitants, a people called Gaṅgārides-Caliṅgae (*Natural History*, IV, 22).

Ptolemy's town of Tamalites (which may be identified as Tāmralipti) is described to be in the territory of the Mandalai with its royal residence or capital at Palimbothra (i.e., Pataliputra or modern Patna). Tamalites, placed on the bank of the Gaṅgā, only half a degree south of Palimbothra, appear to be towns having administrative importance or with indeterminate position. Distinguishing Gangê (Gaṅgābandar) from Tamalites (Tāmralipti), Ptolemy makes it clear that he was not confusing one with the other, or Tāmralipti was not called by a different name (i.e., Gangê) by the Greco-Romans. Even if one takes into account the distortion in Ptolemy's map of South Asia, which makes the location of the town a matter of dispute, one cannot overlook the existence of two separate entities of Tāmralipti and Gaṅgābandar (Gangê). Despite Ptolemy's description of Tamalites, what is striking about all the Greco-Roman accounts is the complete silence about Tāmralipti as a maritime port. This striking aberration in Greco-Roman accounts deserves careful consideration, and that we will give while discussing the port of Gaṅgābandar.

The silence of the Greco-Roman accounts on Tāmralipti is well compensated by the Chinese. Two Chinese texts named *Shui-Ching-Chu* ("Commentary on the Water Classic") and *Fu-nan-chuan* appear to have been aware of its existence and importance since the 3rd century AD. *Shui-Ching-Chu* by K'ang-T'ai describes the voyage of an embassy from the king of Tan Mei (Tāmralipti) to the "Yellow Gate" (the Chinese Court) in the 3rd century AD. Petech (1950: 53) believes that the embassy was sent to the court of the southern Wu dynasty (222-280 AD) in Nanking since K'ang-T'ai was a subject of the same dynasty. On the other hand, *Fu-nan-chuan* not only shows that the Chinese were well acquainted with the exact location of Tāmralipti, but also the sea route to reach it. One does not also fail to notice the situation of Tāmralipti. It has been described as a kingdom and there is an indictation of political relationship between the Yellow Gate and Tāmralipti, verging on to political domination of the former. According to *Fu-nan-chuan*,

> ... coming out of the port of Chü-li [or T'ou-chüli, possibly on the western coast of Malay Peninsula, now in Thailand] one enters the great Bay. Travelling straight to the north-west for more than a year one reaches the mouth of the great river of India which is called the river Ganges. At the mouth of the river there is a kingdom called Tan-mei which belongs to Tien-chu. (Its rulers) sent letters to the Yellow Gate (the Chinese court), and was appointed by China king of Tan-mei (*ibid.*).

From the early 5th century AD we begin to get more information about Tāmralipti, possibly the most detailed and authentic accounts from three famous Chinese pilgrims. The earliest of the three was Fa-Hien who visited India in AD 399-414. He arrived at Tāmralipti by land route from Campa, resided in the city for two years and then sailed for Sri Lanka. In the excerpt quoted below, one does not fail to notice that Tāmralipti in the early 5th century AD is described as a kingdom with a considerable Buddhist population. The Buddhist institutions (saṅghārāmas) of the kingdom were definitely centres of great Buddhist learning to warrant Fa-Hien's residence there for two years.

> From there [Campa], continuing to go eastwards nearly fifty yōjanas, we arrive at the kingdom of Tāmralipti. Here it is the river empties itself into the sea. There are twenty-four saṅghārāmas in this country, all of them have resident priests, and the law of Buddha is generally respected. Fa-Hien remained here for two years, writing out copies of the sacred books (sūtras) and taking impressions of the figures (used in worship). He then shipped himself on board a great merchant vessel. ... Men of that country (Tāmralipti) say that the distance between the two is about 700 yōjanas (*Fo-kwō-ki*, XXXVII; Beal 1869: 147-48).

Both Legge's (1886: 100) and Giles' translation (1972: 65-67) describe Tāmralipti not as a "kingdom" but a "country" wherein was situated 22 monasteries and a sea-port. Although it is referred thus, we need not interpret Tāmralipti as an independent kingdom if we consider that Candra-varman of Puskarana in south-west 'Bengal' was the Candravarman of the Allahabad *prasasti* whom Samudra-gupta (c. 335-375 AD) had ousted before Fa-Hien's visit. It should be noted that our priest appears to have been too preoccupied with Buddhism; for he does not even allude to the commercial milieu of Tāmralipti as does the *Kathā Sarit Sāgar*. Let us also take into cognizance that Fa-Hien's account confirms Tāmralipti as a port and attests the possibility that a substantial number of people of Tāmralipti were adherents of Buddhism.

Over two and a quarter centuries after Fa-Hien, another celebrated Chinese pilgrim Hiuen-Tsiang, who travelled in South Asia from 629 to 645 AD, arrived in Tāmralipti by foot from Samataṭa. He too described it as a "country", with a capital by the same name (i.e., Tāmralipti) bordering the sea (Bay of Bengal). Hiuen-Tsiang's description implies that Tāmralipti was well connected by land as well as water, its economy was strong because of agricultural cultivation and natural products ("wonderful articles of value and gems"), and hence, the population was generally wealthy. However, Buddhism appears to have been on the wane because the number of monasteries decreased to ten from Fa-Hien's twenty-four. If Deva temples signify Brāhmaṇism, then there can be no doubt about its rise.

> From Samataṭa going west 900 *li* or so, we reach the country of Tan-mo-li-ti (Tāmralipti). This country is 1,400 or 1,500 *li* in circuit, the capital about 10 *li*. It borders on the sea. The ground is low and rich; it is regularly cultivated, and produces flowers and fruits in abundance. The temperature is hot. The manners of the people are quick and hasty. The men are hardy and brave. There are both heretics and believers. There are about ten saṅghārāmas, with about 1000 priests. The Deva temples are fifty in number, in which various sectaries dwell mixed together. The coast of this country is formed by (or in) a recess of the sea; the water and the land embracing each other. Wonderful articles of value and gems are collected in abundance, and therefore the people of the country are in general very rich. By the side of the city is a stūpa which was built by Aśōka-rāja; by the side of it are traces where the four past Buddhas sat and walked (*Si-Yu-Ki*, Book X; Beal 1906: 200-201).

The third celebrated Chinese monk I-Tsing, who departed from China in 671 AD and returned home in 695 AD, arrived in Tāmralipti in 673 AD and described it as "a port on the coast of Eastern India" (Takakusu 1896: 211).

> Tāmralipti is forty yoganas south from the eastern limit of India. There are five or six monasteries; the people are rich. It belongs to E. India and is about sixty yoganas from Mahābodhi and Srī-Nālanda. This is the place where we embark when returning to China (*ibid.*: xxxiii-xxxiv).

I-Tsing's Tāmralipti was also well connected by land as well as sea. After arriving at the port, the monk "with the teacher Teng, ... took the road straight to the west, and hundred merchants accompanied them to mid-India" (Lahiri 1986: 76-79). However, the land route was not very safe as he "met a band of robbers" on his return journey to the port. The port itself had become very important because not only I-Tsing but numerous other monks, at least four described in the Biographies of Eminent Monks (*Kao-seng chuan*), directly arrived here from China via Bhoga (Palembang) and Ka-cha. The condition of Buddhism must have further deteriorated at the end of the third quarter of the 7th century AD, because the number of monasteries had dwindled to five or six from Hiuen-Tsiang's ten. Nor did he remain in the port-city for Buddhist texts, as did Fa-Hien, but travelled to central India. Summing up the travel accounts of the three Chinese monks, we may note that Fa-Hien's departure from Tāmralipti and I-Tsing's arrival and departure clearly show that Tāmralipti served as a place of contact where people met and culture was exchanged between land and maritime space.

All the literary evidences discussed above amply prove the existence of the ancient port of Tāmralipti in 'Bengal'. However, when the question arises as to its geographical location, scholars are yet to reach firm agreement. Taylor (1847) and Fergusson (1971) have identified Tāmralipti at the modern Sonārgāon (23° 40′ N, 90° 36′ E.), the ancient Suvarṇagrāma. Disagreeing with them, Schoff (1995: 255) has identified it with Tamluk (22° 18′ N, 87° 56′ E). This view is supported by Śāstrī (1927: 167, 169-170), who, while discussing Ptolemy's Tamalites, has unhesitatingly identified Tāmralipti with the modern Tamluk, "a town lying in a low and damp situation on a broad reach or bay of the Rūpnārāyaṇ River, 12 miles above its junction with the Hughlī mouth of the Ganges". Most scholars of contemporary times, including Niharranjan Ray (1994: 244) have agreed with the above identification. However, in an earlier paper, Niharranjan Ray (1979) has suggested that "[f]or a proper identification of ancient Tāmralipta, we have to look further south of modern Tamluk". Asok Datta (2000: 136) agrees with Ray (1979) and believes that Tāmralipti lay further south of Tamluk. Because almost all literary sources locate Tāmralipti on the Gaṅgā and not Rūpnārāyaṇ, Datta argues that the original site of the ancient port must be looked for on the bank of the Gaṅgā. Accordingly, he has located Natsal, situated 10 km south of Tamluk, on the right bank of the Huglī. Citing archaeological materials found at Natsal, Datta concludes that Natsal was ancient Tāmralipti. In order to resolve the dispute and ascertain the exact location of the port, it is necessary to consider the physiographic features and geomorphological evidences pertaining to the site.

According to Ray (1994: 57), the ancient course of the Gaṅgā-Bhāgīrathī lay westward from Tribenī till it joined the Dāmodar from where it was renamed Saraswatī. Into the Saraswatī also flowed the Rūpnārāyaṇ, Ajay and other rivers from the hills of Chotanagpur and Manbhum. He goes on to say, "the Saraswatī later abandoned this course and flowed directly south, for sometime running along the course of the Rūpnārāyaṇ-Patraghāṭā. After the 8th century AD, the mouth of this older watercourse became that of the Saraswatī-Bhāgīrathī". Sometime between the 8th and the 14th centuries AD, the Saraswatī shifted eastward, to its contemporary course, through which the Gaṅgā-Bhāgīrathī also flowed for some time. From the 10th century onwards, the Gaṅgā-

Bhāgīrathī began to flow along its contemporary course till Kolkata-Betar, from where it continued south along the course of the Ādigaṅgā. Sometime in the 18th century, the river abandoned its Ādigaṅgā course and took up its present course along Bajbaj and Fāltā.

On the other hand, Rennell (1788) has identified a moribund channel of the Saraswatī, which flowed past Caṇḍītalā, Amta and joined the Rūpnārāyaṇ at Kolāghāṭ, was an ancient outlet of the Bhāgīrathī-Huglī. Rudra (1990: 248-250) picks up Rennell's argument to show that the Caṇḍītalā-Amta-Kolāghāṭ channel was the oldest course of the Bhāgīrathī-Huglī, which remained juvenile until 700 AD. Around that time, i.e., 700 AD, the river migrated eastward, to flow through the present Saraswatī channel till Sankrail, through the present Huglī channel from Sankrail to Geonkhālī and there to unite with the Rūpnārāyaṇ. The memory of the ancient Bhāgīrathī-Huglī uniting with the Rūpnārāyaṇ at Kolāghāṭ is still alive among the local inhabitants, who call the Rūpnārāyaṇ as the Gaṅgā from south of Kolāghāṭ. Early European cartographers, such as João de Barros (1550) (Fig. 1.2), Gastaldi (1561) and Blaev (1650) followed this popular tradition in identifying the Rūpnārāyaṇ estuary as the Gaṅgā in their maps. Comparing these two opinions, one finds a general agreement, of Saraswatī flowing through Dāmodar or Rūpnārāyaṇ and the eastward migration of its course. However, there are major differences; Ray (1994: 57) seems to be unclear about the role of the Rūpnārāyaṇ.

In order to arrive at a firm conclusion, two satellite images, which cover the 24-Parganas and Medinīpur districts of West Bengal, were examined for understanding the geomorphology of the region. These were Landsat-5, dated February 20, 1986, TM 234, path & raw 138-045 and scale 1: 250000 and Landsat-5, dated January 9, 1988, TM 234, path & raw 138-045 and scale 1: 250000. The result derived from the examination of the images is clearly in agreement with Rudra's (1990: 248-250) and Ghosh's (1998: 11) view. The image of the palaeo-channel clearly shows the changes of the course of the mighty river Gaṅgā from east to west. The images also show beach ridges running parallel to the present coastline. Visible in four different layers, these ridges show the progradation of the coastal plain (Jahan 2005b: 116). Thus, there can remain no doubt that the site of Tamluk (22°20′ N and 87°55′ E), during the early historic period, was closer to the seacoast. Because of the recession of the coastline, the present location of Tamluk is 50 km away from the sea. Therefore Tamluk, which lies on the ancient united course of the Bhāgīrathī-Huglī and Rūpnārāyaṇ, and which was much closer to the sea in ancient times, can rightfully claim to be on the bank of the ancient river Gaṅgā in accordance with literary tradition of Tāmralipti's location.

The conclusion drawn above does not negate Datta's (2000) claim over Natsal. We propose that Tamluk on the west bank

Fig. 1.2 Joao de Barros' map of Bengal (1550) after Majumdar 1943

of the Rūpnārāyaṇ, Natsal on the west bank of the Huglī, along with Harinārāyaṇpur and Deulpota on the east bank of the Huglī were all harbours of the ancient port of Tāmralipti (Fig. 1.3). If one recalls navigation practice in 'Bengal' (both riverine and marine), one will immediately remember that any large market town has a number of *ghāṭs* (quays). Sometimes these are built on important commercial or industrial points of the market-town, at other times according to available depth of water and necessary draught of vessels or even because passengers and goods require different facilities. Hence, if for example one asks any mariner plying on the coast of the Bay of Bengal to be transported to Caṭṭagrāma, he would immediately reply by wishing to know to which *ghāṭ* (pier) would the inquirer like to be transported. He is correct, for along the coast of Caṭṭagrāma lies Bārabkunda, Kumirā, Cāgtāi and Sadarghāṭ and "going to Caṭṭagrāma" could imply going to any of these *ghāṭs*. Following this simple logic, one could argue that Tāmralipti, which was a large port, possibly had a number of *ghāṭs*, which catered to different vessels according to their draught. Very much like the *ghāṭs* of Sadarghāṭ on the north bank of the Buḍigaṅgā and Jinjirā on its south bank, Harinārāyaṇpur and Deulpota may have served the eastern parts of the kingdom while Tamluk and Natsal may have served the western parts.

Having resolved the problem of the exact location of the ancient port of Tāmralipti, let us now examine archaeological evidences derived from the site to see if its claim as an ancient port is justifiable. K. N. Dikshit, who conducted the earliest archaeological survey of Tamluk in 1921-22, was rather disappointed by what he found in the famous port-site mentioned so frequently in early Buddhist and Classical literature.

> There are few high mounds now left to mark the position of the ancient city, but the mound on which the mission house is situated, another on which the temple of Bargabhima stands and the high land close to the river bed, from which a hoard of ancient coins was recovered some 40 years ago, must be considered to cover some of the ground occupied by ancient Tāmralipta (Dikshit 1921-22: 74).

Along with the hoard of ancient coins Dikshit refers to (which was a collection of about 350 coins, mostly of the rectangular cast types), terracotta objects from Śuṅga period were also recovered from the site in the late 19th century.

The first excavation at the site was conducted in a small scale by the Archaeological Survey of India under T. N. Ramachandran in 1940 (Ramachandran 1951: 226-239). Next, the Eastern Circle of the Archaeological Survey of India conducted two more small-scale excavations: first in 1954-55 and subsequently in 1973-74. The excavations revealed that the site had been occupied from the Neolithic to modern times with occasional breaks.

From then, a number of explorations in and around the principal site of Tamluk revealed a cluster of 28 sites of unspecified dimensions, mostly on banks of Rūpnārāyaṇ, Huglī and Haldi with a number of cultural materials from the Neolithic-Chalcolithic to the Pāla-Sena period. Some of the important sites, which stand near Tamluk, are Amritaberia, Natsal, Badur, Nandigram, Natpatia, Raghunathbari and Ratulia. Others, such as Tilda, Karnaji, Bahiri, Tikasi and Panna are situated farther away. The Table 1.1 contains the materials revealed from the explorations and excavations in and around the site of Tamluk till the post-Gupta era.

Apart from materials listed below in Table 1.1, stray pieces of sculpture belonging to Pāla and Sena periods and an inscribed seal with a seated Devi image of the early Pāla period have been obtained from surface collection (*Indian Archaeology – A Review* 1954-55: 20 and 1955-56: 62).

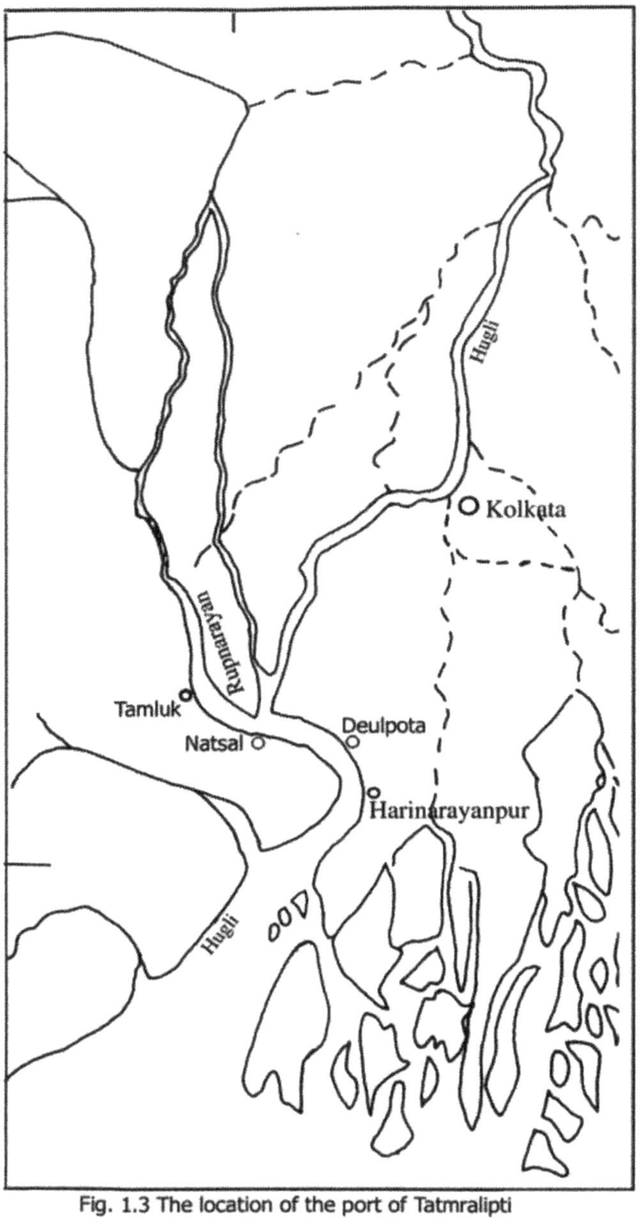

Fig. 1.3 The location of the port of Tatmralipti

Table 1.1:
Archaeological Findings from Explorations and Excavations in Tamluk and Its neighbourhood

Findings	**Neolithic-Chalcolithic**	**Maurya**	**Śuṅga**	**Kuṣāṇa**	**Gupta**	**Post-Gupta**
Pottery	Ill-fired and hand-made pottery, black & red ware, red ware, burnished black ware including a black ware sherd depicting a boat.	Northern Black Polished Ware (NBPW).	NBPW, red ware, black slipped ware.	NBPW, Rouletted Ware (RW), red polished ware, grey stamped ware, sprinkler, amphorae, earthen knobbed ware (Harinārāyaṇpur).	Moulded pottery.	Pottery with *Rāmāyaṇa* panel.

Terracotta		Human and animal figurines, sling balls.	Human and animal figurines, Plaques depicting Jātaka scenes, sling balls.	Human and animal figurines, Plaques depicting Jātaka scenes and other objects.	Human and animal figurines, plaques depicting urban scenes.	Plaques.
Beads		Terracotta and semi-precious stone.	Terracotta and semi-precious stone.	Terracotta, semi-precious stone including etched variety, bone, pearl and glass.	Terracotta and semi-precious stone.	
Other objects	Microliths, polished Neolithic celts (triangular & sub-triangular shapes), finished stone tools (hand axes), copper and bronze rings, bangles, bone tools (points, awls, harpoon with incised boat-motif, fish hooks, arrow-head).			Seals with Kharoshṭī-Brāhmī inscriptions, a terracotta votive tablet with Eurulon inscribed on it, a terracotta plaque depicting a soldier in Roman kilt, a terracotta double-headed deity, carnelian intaglios, amphora-like objects, terracotta votive carts, a terracotta tablet with alleged Greek inscription, sprinklers and a few terracotta figurines in non-Indian dress.	Sealing bearing the legend in late Gupta character.	Old Bengali inscriptions on clay tablets.
Coin		Silver & copper punch-marked, uninscribed & inscribed cast copper.	Silver & copper punch-marked and cast copper.	Cast copper and Puri-Kuṣāṇa.	Gupta gold (Kumāra-gupta and Viṣṇugupta).	
Structure		Remains of a burnt floor with a number of post-holes.		A brick-built stepped tank, a ring-well, a soak-pit and a series of hearths on a floor rammed with brick grits.		

Of all the materials discovered so far at Tamluk, Rouletted Wares (RW), Northern Black Polished Wares (NBPW), stamped wares, earthen knobbed vessel, terracotta and carnelian artifacts of Mediterranean influence, beads made of semi-precious stone (such as agate, carnelian, onyx, amethyst, jasper, quartz, amber and crystal), specially the etched variety and terracotta seals and sealing with Kharoshṭī-Brāhmī inscription deserve special attention. Because similar materials have been recovered from a number of sites in South Asia (Wārī-Baṭeśwar and Mahāsthāngarh in Bangladesh; Chandraketugarh, Śiśupālgarh, Arikamedu, Karaikadu and Alagankulam in India; Anuradhapura, Kantarodai, Mantai and Tissamaharama in Sri Lanka) and Southeast Asia (Beikthano in Myanmar; Bukit Tengku Lembu, Kalumpang Island, Kuala Selinsing and Tanjong Rawa in Malaysia; Kobak Kendal, Cibutak and Sembiran in Indonesia; Khuan Luk Pat, U Thong, Ban Don Ta Phet, Ban Chi Nam Lai and Prasat Muang Sing in Thailand; Trakieu and Oc-Eo in Vietnam; Palawan Island in the Philippines) and the Red Sea Coast (Berenike) (Jahan 2005b: 126-130).

Recovery of similar materials indicates contact between Tamluk and its neighbouring area with all the sites mentioned above. We may logically infer that the contact was of maritime nature since geographical location of all these sites (either on the coast or on river-banks with considerable depth) makes maritime transportation possible. Many of the cultural materials mentioned above bear (or bore) commercial value while others bear signs of commodities of commercial value. Hence we may further infer that maritime contact between Tamluk and its neighbouring area with all the other nodal points was trade-related since the materials (as commodities) appear to have changed hands by means of maritime vessels. While examining literary evidences, we found references to people being transferred from the Indonesian archipelagoes to Sri Lanka. We also found indications of goods being transferred but could not ascertain their exact nature. Archaeological evidences cited above clearly show which goods were transferred, or more specifically, traded. We will have occasion to examine further into the nature of commodities, mode of transportation and regularity of exchange in the following chapters.

A number of artifacts of Mediterranean origin and/or syncretic objects indicating Greco-Roman influence have been reported from Tamluk and its surroundings. One of these is clay sealing carrying three lines of an inscription in Greek. It was found at Tilda (district Medinīpur) and has been identified as a votive tablet. The word "Eurulon" has been read in the middle line and has been interpreted as "the East wind that comes with the dawn" (*ibid.:* 1955-56: 62). The sealing, dated to the 2nd century AD, is believed to have belonged to a Mediterranean sailor who had voyaged to the Gaṅgā delta. Other objects include a terracotta plaque depicting a soldier in Roman kilt, a terracotta double-headed deity (dated to the 1st century AD), carnelian intaglios with non-Indian motifs, some amphora-like objects, terracotta ram-shaped votive carts, some female figures possibly wearing Greek *chiton*, a terracotta tablet with alleged Greek inscription, sprinklers and a few terracotta figurines dressed in tunics, trouser like apparel, high boots, sandals, conical cap, diadem and tiara (*ibid.:* 1954-55: 20 and 1955-56: 62). The terracotta double-headed deity is believed to be Janus and is held by the Asutosh Museum of Indian Art, Kolkata (Fig. 1.4). One of the amphorae, measuring 66 cm and reportedly collected from Karnaji village, is held in a private collection at Dharas, in Medinīpur district (Sengupta 1996: 121). The sprinklers are believed to be Roman and have been dated to the 1st-2nd century AD (*Indian Archaeology – A Review* 1954-55: 20). Also worth noting are the seals with Kharoshṭī-Brāhmī inscriptions, quite a few of which have been found in and around Tamluk.

Discovery of the artifacts of Mediterranean origin in and around Tamluk, when all Greco-Roman accounts are silent regarding Tāmralipti, is curious, to say the least. It is all the more curious when we remind ourselves that there is no reference to direct contact between Rome (or Roman Egypt) and 'Bengal'. More importantly, not a single Roman coin has yet been discovered anywhere in 'Bengal' whereas these coins have been found in large number at all the major port-sites in the western coast of India, Sri Lanka and the south-eastern coast of India. It is well established that Roman trade and Roman coins went together. Hence, a straightforward conclusion that the artifacts mentioned above indicate maritime trade may be premature. We need to carefully weigh evidences regarding maritime routes and commodities traded before arriving at a firm conclusion. We also need to remember the historical existence of Greco-Bactrian kingdoms in and beyond the north-western frontiers of South Asia and need to consider whether these materials were syncretic objects indicating indirect Greco-Roman influence. Nevertheless, all these evidences of Mediterranean origin go to confirm the indications derived from the story of Mitragupta in the Daṇḍīn's *Daśakumāracarita*. There can thus be no doubt that Tāmralipti was frequented not only by the Chinese, but also people of other races. The Yavanas of the story of Mitragupta may well have been the Romans, the Greeks, Egyptians or Bactrians. The seals with Kharoshṭī-Brāhmī inscriptions also indicate the presence of Kharoshṭī-speaking people at Tāmralipti.

Tamluk has also yielded coins right from the Maurya period. These include silver and copper punch-marked coins, cast copper coins and a large number of uninscribed cast copper coins. Besides these, Puri-Kuṣāṇa coins and two gold coins of Kumāragupta and Viṣṇugupta respectively have also been reported from the site. Because metallic currency is of high value and low volume medium of exchange and hence easier to carry over a long distance, their existence implies trade, particularly long distance (including maritime) trade. Hence, discovery of coins at Tamluk may be accepted as an important indicator that the site functioned as an exchange centre.

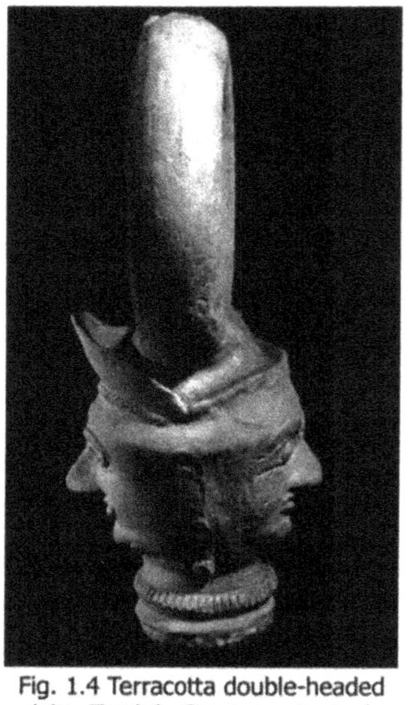

Fig. 1.4 Terracotta double-headed deity, Tamluk, Courtesy: Asutosh Museum of Indian Art, Kolkata

Having reviewed the archaeological findings at Tamluk and observed their distribution pattern, we are now in a position to ascertain the implication. Firstly, all the objects discussed above (except the coins) bear commercial value or sign of commercial value. Secondly, their distribu-tion patterns, as argued earlier, indicate transpor-tation by means of maritime mode of com-munication. Thirdly, pres-ence of coins implies existence of money-based economy at the site from the 3rd century BC to the Gupta period. Indication of money-based economy added with the presence of commodities bearing signs of commercial value and indication of maritime transportation can only lead to one conclusion: that Tamluk was a maritime port.

Since (i) South Asian and Chinese literary sources indicate that Tāmralipti was located near the seashore of 'Bengal', on the bank of the river Gaṅgā, (ii) physiographic conditions of Tamluk ideally suits its claim as the site of the ancient port and (iii) archaeological findings at the site justify the claim, we may conclude unhesitatingly that the maritime port of Tāmralipti was indeed located at Tamluk. The location of the archaeological sites on the bank of a mouth of the ancient Gaṅgā can only mean that Tāmralipti was an estuarine port.

Now, we may attempt to ascertain the physical aspects of the port. As argued earlier, the port of Tāmralipti was spread over a large area extending from Tamluk on the west bank of the Rūpnārāyaṇ, Natsal on the west bank of the Huglī, along with Harinārāyaṇpur and Deulpota on the east bank of the Huglī. We do not have enough data to ascertain exactly why this was so but surely Tamluk, Natsal, Harinārāyaṇpur and Deulpota all served as harbours.

Trial trenches dug in some of the high mounds Dikshit referred to and at a few other sites revealed no structural remains. Remains of a burnt floor with a number of post-holes from the Maurya age, a brick-built stepped tank, a ring-well, a soak-pit and a series of hearths on a floor rammed with brick grits from the Kuṣāṇa period are all the structural remains that have so far come to light (*Indian Archaeology – A Review* 1954-55: 20 and 1973-74: 33). Curiously, no structural remains have been unearthed from the Gupta age. Considering the reputation of the ports, these are scanty remains. The series of hearths may indicate a potter's kiln and hence may be taken to indicate the existence of production centres of earthenware. Considering the fact that sherds of Northern Black Polished Ware, Rouletted Ware, stamped ware, red polished ware and amphorae have been found, we may believe that some or all of these were produced at or near the port-site. The brick-built stepped tank, the ring-well and the soak-pit indicate daily-life public usage. The burnt floor with a number of post-holes possibly indicates some structure built on wooden posts. We are not certain if the structure was built for residential, commercial or administrative purpose. It could even have been used for storage. No sign of fortified area, signifying administrative centre, has been found. If there was an exchange centre at or near the port, remains of the shops have not come down to us. It appears that all structures built at the port for administrative, commercial and residential purposes were made of wood, mud and thatch. The image of the port thus derived, vague and sketchy though it is, does not agree with *Kathā Sarit Sāgara*, not even with the accounts provided by the three Chinese priests. We may consider *Kathā Sarit Sāgara* (composed in the 11th century AD) as a product of creative imagination coloured by glamorised fantasies of later times. But surely one could expect to find a mound indicating one of the monasteries that the Chinese accounts inform us about.

Till further material remains are unearthed through detailed horizontal excavations, we have to be satisfied with the image of Tāmralipti provided by archaeological evidences that have so far come down to us. And this image is of a typical temporary riverine landing site such as Nagarbāḍi on the bank of the Jamunā in Pabna (Bangladesh). Nagarbāḍi, till the Bangabandhu Bridge was inaugurated in 1998, was a riverine port for country boats transporting various commodities from and to north Bengal and a ferry point for transporting vehicles from Dhaka to north Bangladesh. It had virtually no administrative importance. However, it had a hive of restaurants serving the passengers who were ferried across and godowns owned by merchants for storing their commodities to be shipped in country boats. The landing site had to be shifted a number of times due to river erosion and each time the shops and the godowns also shifted. Importantly, when the port was shifted, it hardly left any mark on the old site because the shops and the godowns (constructed with temporary material such as corrugated iron sheets, bamboo and wooden posts) were shifted *en masse*.

We may suggest that Tāmralipti, a maritime port, was not an administrative centre but served mostly as a point for embarkation and disembarkation of passengers and loading and unloading of commodities. It was also a production centre for manufacturing pottery as the hearth unearthed testifies. Consequently, the structures constructed were meant for storing commodities, serving passengers and mariners and producing potteries. Most of these must have been constructed out of perishable materials such as mud, bamboo and wood posts and thatch roof. A few plinths may have been made of rammed brick grits and their signs still remain.

Literary, physiographic, geomorphological and archaeological evidences presented above definitely prove that Tamluk was the ancient port-site of Tāmralipti. Archaeological materials belonging to the Chalcolithic period, although not within our period of study, indicate that the site did not suddenly grow into prominence in the early historic times but had an earlier history. It may have been important for a sea-faring community, who may have abandoned it for some unexplained reason. It may not be too far fetched to suggest that the sea-faring community was akin to Vijaya. Material evidences listed in Table 1.1 clearly signify that the port rose into prosperity from the 3rd century BC to the 3rd century AD. Most of the artifacts that signify trade have been found during this span of time. Archaeological materials that have been found from the 4th century AD to the mid-8th century AD are mostly terracotta figurines. No materials, which can indicate trade as in the earlier levels, have been found in the later periods. Clearly, this is indicative of a significant decline in trade-related activities in Tāmralipti. This must be the reason why Fa-Hien, Hiuen-Tsiang and I-Tisng are silent about the port town and maritime trade. In the Dudhapani inscription of Hazaribagh, which records the name of Tāmralipti for the last time, is an important indicator of the state of the port in the 8th century AD (the assigned date of the inscription). As recorded in the inscription, "once upon a time three brothers – Udayamana, Sridhautamana, and Ajitamana – merchants, went on business from Adodhya to Tāmralipti", where they "made plenty of money" (verses 4-5, Kielhorn 1894: 344). Interestingly, the 8th century inscription remembers Tāmralipti not as a port of contemporary times but as a place of past glory (note "once upon a time") where north Indian traders could make "plenty of money". Hence, there can be little doubt that Tāmralipti must have ceased to exist as a port in the 8th century AD.

One of the major causes for the decline was the eastward migration of the Bhāgīrathī-Huglī. Because of the migration around 700 AD, the Rūpnārāyaṇ was reduced in water discharge from Kolāghāṭ to Geonkhālī. Tāmralipti, which lay between these two points, also lost navigability, leading to decay in the port. The break-up of the Roman Empire in 476 AD (and subsequent unsettled relationship between the Eastern Roman Empire and the Sassanids) resulted in the loss of the most important market for Tāmralipti. Political anarchy that engulfed Rāḍha, Puṇḍravardhana and Vaṅga during the period of *matsyanayaya* (c. 650 to 750 AD) and consequent absence of security, must also have contributed to the fall of Tāmralipti.

Findings presented above leave little doubt that Tāmralipti, cited in South Asian and Chinese accounts, was indeed located at Tamluk. It was an estuarine port with no permanent quays and wharves. The socio-economic environment of the port included production centres as well as commercial centres. It served mostly as a point for embarkation and disembarkation of passengers and loading and unloading of commodities. It was well connected with South Asian and Southeast Asian ports and functioned from the 3rd century BC to the mid-8th century AD.

GAṄGĀBANDAR

The ancient port of Gaṅgābandar is beset with a peculiar problem. Literary references on the port is provided only by overseas accounts: definitely by the Greco-Romans and possibly also by the Chinese. No extant South Asian records contain any reference about it. Of the Greco-Romans whose accounts have the slightest relation to the maritime activities of 'Bengal', Strabo's *Geography*, the *Periplus of the Erythraean Sea* and Ptolemy's *An Outline of Geography*, have all referred to Gangê, i.e., Gaṅgābandar. On the other hand, *Ch'ien Han-shu* (c. 1st century AD), a Chinese text compiled by Pan Ku, refers to a western country called Huang-chih, which some scholars have identified as Gaṅgābandar. These divergences have created confusion and disagreement among scholars. What needs to be settled, first of all, is if there was at all a port named Gaṅgābandar. It should be noted here that although the Romans called the port Gangê or Ganges, we have no way (as yet) of ascertaining what the local residents called it. Ray (1993: 303-304) added the suffix 'bandar' (lit. 'port') to 'Gaṅgā' (the river) and coined the name 'Gaṅgābandar' for the port. His naming of the port is acceptable (since the name denotes location of the port on the river Gaṅgā), as long as we must remember that the name is provisional and in no way indicates what the port may have actually been called by its local residents.

The earliest reference to the port of Gaṅgābandar is provided by Strabo (60 BC-19 AD), who cites a lost Greek work on geography by Artemidoros. According to the description of Strabo (or Artemidoros), Gangê (Gaṅgābandar) appears to be Prayāg (Allahabad), although McCrindle (1979: 77, fn. 2) believes it is Huglī.

> Ganges descends from the Emodoi Mountains towards the south, and on reaching the city of Gangê turns its course eastward to Palibothra and the mouth by which it enters the sea (*Geography*, Book XV, Section 72; *ibid.*: 77).

However, the *Periplus of the Erythraean Sea* (60 AD) appears to place Gaṅgābandar (or Ganges as it prefers to call it) on the seashore, next to the land inhabited by the Cirrhadae and other savage races. It is a market-town on the bank of the river Gaṅgā. The *Periplus* also locates an island in the ocean near the town, which is called Chryse.

> After these [Cirrhadae and other savage races], the course turns toward the east again, and sailing with the ocean to the right and the shore remaining beyond to the left, Ganges comes into view, and near it the very last land toward the east, Chryse. There is a river near it called the Ganges, and it rises and falls in the same way as the Nile. On its bank is a market-town which has the same name as the river, Ganges. ... And just opposite this river there is an island in the ocean, the last part of the inhabited world toward the east, under the rising sun itself; it is called Chryse; ... (§ 63; Schoff 1995: 47-48).

The description given above indicates that Ganges (Gaṅgābandar) was an estuarine port. As the *Periplus* indicates that the port was used for exporting "raw silk and silk yarn and silk cloth" from the western state of Ts'in of China to Damirica [Tamil lands] (§ 64; *ibid.*: 48), it is possible to believe that Gaṅgābandar was connected with T'sin through a land route via Lhasa and the Chumbi Vale to Sikkim (*ibid.*: 272-273). However, Chinese silk at the port of Gaṅgābandar was not easy to come by because "the land of this is not easy of access; few men come from there and seldom" (§ 64; *ibid.*: 48). Nevertheless, indications derived from the *Periplus* shows that Gaṅgābandar was a knot where ocean and inland transport lines (from T'sin) met and intervened.

Of all the accounts, that provided by Ptolemy (Klaudios Ptolemaios) in his *An Outline of Geography* (mid-2nd century AD) appears to locate Gangê (Gaṅgābandar) definitely by identifying it as the capital of a kingdom occupied by the people called Gaṅgāridai.

> All the country about the mouths of the Ganges is occupied by the Gaṅgāridai with this city: – Gangê, the Royal residence (146° longitude & 19° 15′ latitude) (Ptolemy's *Geography*, Book VII, Cap. 1, 81; Śāstrī 1927: 172).

Even if we ignore Ptolemy's latitude and longitude, what we cannot ignore is his identification of Tamalitēs (Tāmralipti), which was a town or administrative centre of a kingdom, whose capital was Palimbothra. Hence, as already mentioned in the earlier section of this chapter, Tāmralipti was not Gangê (Gaṅgābandar), at least according to the Roman accounts. Rather, it appears that Gangê was the capital of a kingdom named Gaṅgāridai.

Further information regarding the political situation of Gaṅgāridai may be obtained from Megasthenēs who says,

> [Ganges] flows from north to south, and empties its waters into the ocean forming the eastern boundary of the Gaṅgāridai, a nation which possesses a vast force of the largest-sized elephants. Owing to this, their country has never been conquered by any foreign king: for all other nations dread the overwhelming number and strength of these animals (From Diodorus II, 37 in McCrindle 1926: 32-33).

Megasthenēs further states that "The tribes which dwell by the Ganges are the Caliṅgae, nearest the sea, and higher up the Mandei, also the Malli, among whom is Mount Mallus, the boundary of all that region being the Ganges" (From Pliny *Natural History* VI. 21.9-22.1, in *ibid.*: 62). Pliny in his *Natural History* echoes the same view to state that the final part of the Gaṅgā flowed through the country of the Gaṅgārides. He also refers to a people called Gaṅgārides-Caliṅgae (Pliny, Book IV, 22). The people of Gaṅgāridai have also been mentioned by Virgil (*Geog.* III, 1. 27), Valerius Flaccus (*Argon.* Lib. VI, 1. 66) and Curtius (lib. IX, c. ii) who place them "along with the Pharrasii (Prasii) on the eastern bank of the Ganges" (Śāstrī 1927: 173).

According to Saint-Martin (cited by Śāstrī, *ibid.*: 174), Pliny's Gaṅgāridai represents the country of 'Bengal' in a general way. Their capital city, he believes, was Vardhana (contemporary Bardhamān in West Bengal). Śāstrī (*ibid.*: 174) mentions that,

> The name of the Gaṅgāridai has nothing in Sanskrit to correspond with it, nor can it be a word ... of purely Greek formation, for the people were mentioned under this name to Alexander by one of the princes in the North-west of India. The synonymous term which Sanskrit fails to supply is found among the aboriginal tribes belonging to the region occupied by the Gaṅgāridai, the name being preserved almost identically in that of the Goṅghrīs of S. Bahār, with whom were connected the Gaṅgayīs of North-western, and the Gaṅgrār of Eastern Bengal, these designations being but variations of the name which was originally common to them all.

Śāstrī (*ibid.*: 383) further believes "The Sanskrit synonym [of Gaṅgāridai] was either Gaṅgārāṣtra 'dominion of the (lower) Ganges', or Gaṅgā-Rāḍha – the territory of the Gaṅgā with Rāḍha (which is identical with Suhma)". Judging by all these accounts, it is only fair to say that the Gaṅgāridai (people or kingdom) cannot be a matter of fantasy or conjecture. They must have possessed considerable military might and their kingdom must have stretched beyond the mouth of the Gaṅgā.

Turning to the *Ch'ien Han-shu* (a Chinese text compiled by Pan Ku in the 1st century AD) one learns about a Chinese mission to a western country called Huang-chih, with the objective of obtaining lustrous pearls and living rhinoceroses. Although scholars are divided over the location of Huang-chih,[2] Amitabha Bhattacharyya (1977: 39-40) has followed Karlgren's system of pronunciation to show that Huang-chih should be *Gan-yi* or Gaṅgā. The mission sent by Wang Mang, then a regent of the boy-emperor who later founded his own Hsin Dynasty (9-23 AD), was not so much concerned with commerce as politics.

> During the Yüan-shih period of [the infant] Emperor P'ing [1-5 AD] Wang Mang was taking over the government and, desiring to display his majestic virtue, he sent costly gifts to the King of Huang-chih, requesting him to despatch an embassy with a live rhinoceros [or rhinoceroses] (Colless 1980: 164).

The excerpt quoted above makes an implied comment on the political situation of Huang-chih: the kingdom was independent. As for the voyage of the mission, Pan Ku sums up with the following words:

> Chief enterpreters [or the chief interpreter] attached to the Huang-men (the Yellow Gate, the Imperial Palace) who, together with volunteers, sail off [or sailed of] to purchase bright pearls, glassware [or beryl, Pi-liu-li], rare stones, and strange products, offering gold and various silks in exchange. In all the countries they visit they are provided with food and company, and they are taken to their destinations in the trading ships of barbarians, who also profit from this trade and engage in plunder and murder. Furthermore there are the hazards of tempests and death by drowning in the sea. If these are avoided it takes several years to make the outward and return voyages (*ibid.*).

Obviously Pan-ku does not speak specifically only of Huang-chih but of all the kingdoms visited by the mission. Nevertheless, the Chinese account reiterates that Huang-chih or Gaṅgābandar was indeed a "place of contact where goods and people as well as cultures [were] transferred between land and maritime space". Huang-chih being one of the countries visited must have been prosperous and the people were hospitable. It is even possible that Gaṅgāridai was a riverine country, in which maritime trade may have been well known (since the visitors are taken around in trading ships). However, judging by "plunder and murder", the country appears not to have been much civilised.

All these literary references prove beyond doubt that there did exist a port, separate from Tāmralipti, which was known to the Romans as Gangê. It was located on the seashore, on

---

[2] Pelliot (1912: 457-461) believes it is west coast of India, Hermann (1913: 553-561) shows it as Aghazi in Ethiopia, Ferrand (1919: 451-455) identifies it as Kāñcī in South India, Luce (1925: 92-99) doubts Kāñcī, Fujita Toyohachi (1943), Sastri (1938: 386) and Wheatley (1961: 8-13) believe it is Kāñcī, Hennig (1944: I, 323-330) believes it is Conjeveram or Sumatra, while Bagchi (1957: 772) and Colless (1980: 175) have shown it as Gaṅgā (Colless 1980: fn. 25).

the bank of the river Gaṅgā. It was possibly the same as Huang-chih of the Chinese accounts. However, there is no unanimous agreement among scholars about the location of the port-site and harbour of Gaṅgābandar. According to Heeren, the site was near the village of Duliapur, which is about 40 miles southeast of Kolkata on a branch of the Ichāmati River. Wilford, on the other hand, maintains that Gangê (Gaṅgābandar) was located at the confluence of the Gaṅgā and the Brahmaputra, where stood a town called Hastimalla in Sanskrit and Hāthimalla in the spoken dialect. Murray locates Gaṅgābandar at Caṭṭagrāma but Taylor in the neighbourhood of Sonārgāon (Suvarṇagrāma). Cunningham believes it was at Jessore. Others have placed it near Kolkata, or about 30 miles up the river Huglī, near a place called Chinsurā (Śāstrī 1927: 174-175). Another suggestion, has been made by Sircar (1971: 172-173), is that the port-site was at Gaṅgāsāgar (the name derived from conjunctive formation of the words Gaṅgā, i.e., the Huglī River and Sāgar, the Bay of Bengal). Schoff (1995: 255) has identified the market-town of Ganges as Tāmralipti, the modern Tamluk, which has been supported by many scholars. Kalyan Rudra and M. K. Mukherjee (1986) have suggested that Harinārāyaṇpur was Gangê (Gaṅgābandar). In this, literally, a wilderness of suggestions, Goswami (1966: 43) has proposed, "the site of Chandraketugarh seemingly represents the ancient market town of Gangê of the *Periplus*". Subsequently several scholars including Niharranjan Ray (1979) and Gautam Sengupta (1996: 121) have supported Goswami's proposition. An examination of physiographic, geological and archaeological evidences is necessary before arriving at a firm conclusion.

Chandraketugarh is actually the name of a gigantic rampart made of mud (Fig. 1.5), covering an area almost rectangular in shape, located at the village of Beracampa (Devālaya), which lies within the jurisdiction of Degaṅgā Police Station under North 24-Parganas District, West Bengal, India. It was built, so the local tradition goes, by a local ruler Chandraketu of the medieval period, as a defensive measure against militant incursion of a Muslim saint named Shah Syed Abbas Ali alias Goracand. Since the discovery of archaeological remains at and around Beracampa, located some 35 km north-east of Kolkata, the site has become known as Chandraketugarh (22° 41′ N & 88° 42′ E). Roughly, the site is spread over approximately two square miles in the villages called Beracampa (Devālaya), Ranakhola, Ghorapota, Dhanpota, Chuprijhara, Singer Ati, Shanpukur, Jhikra, Mathbaḍi, Hadipur and Gajitala. There are few more villages such as Ramnagar, Adampur, Piyara, Panditpol, Peelkhana, Haroa, Majer Ati, Atghara, Gazirhat, Bashabati, Khas Balanda, Uttar Ranigachi, Bhangore etc., which are all situated south of Beracampa and are associated with the site of Chandraketugarh because they yielded similar archaeological materials. The gigantic rampart of Chandraketugarh indicates that it was once a fortified city.

Fig. 1.5 A section of the rampart of Chandraketugarh

Physiographic aspects of Chandraketugarh and its neighbourhood demands particular attention for reconstruction of its past. Although North 24-Parganas district is situated in the mature segment of the Gaṅgā delta proper, the site itself rests on the Katwa surface, which is the oldest and highest surface formations in the region around Chandraketugarh, the average height of which is higher than the present flood level. Semi-perennial channels drain Chandraketugarh and its neighbourhood. Monsoon run-offs and tides sustain these channels. At one time a major distributary of the Bhāgīrathī which discharged its water in the Bay of Bengal through the Rāimaṅgal-Hariṇbhāṅga estuary but now nearly dead, the Bidyādharī flows from west to south about 10 km from the site. Rudra (1990: 250) reminds us, "[d]uring the 2nd century AD, Bidyādharī was one of the five important outlets of the Gaṅgā water and carried considerable discharge towards the sea. Hence Ptolemy named its estuary as Mega or great". From the north to the east, about 3 km from Chandraketugarh flows a tributary of the Ichāmati known as the Padmā. At present, both the rivers are disconnected from the Bhāgīrathī. The region is spotted with numerous marshes and *bils* (shallow lakes), which contain more water than the Bidyādharī and the Padmā. Backwaters and oxbow lakes of the two nearly dead rivers created the marshes and *bils*. Because a number of palaeo-channels appear to comb the area, it is possible that the rivers have undergone extensive lateral movement. Thus, the physiography of the site indicates the possibility of the existence of a maritime port at Chandraketugarh, on the bank of the Bidyādharī. Archaeological findings discussed below amply supports this claim.

Archaeological investigation of the site began in the early 20th century. In 1907, A. H. Longhurst of the Archaeological Survey of India visited Chandraketugarh. However, his report is disheartening. Having found only fairly large size bricks 38.1 cm long by 27.94 cm broad and moulded bricks and pottery assignable to an early period, he is of the opinion that the ruins were of little or no interest (*Annual Report of the Archaeological Survey of India, Eastern Circle* 1906-107: 12).

Two years later R. D. Bannerji visited the site with his team and recorded some antiquities, mostly of terracotta and a few metallic fragments. These are: fragment of a silver vessel, fragment of a copper jar badly eroded, terracotta plaque representing reeds tied with three bands, terracotta plaque bearing lower part of the legs of a women wearing anklets, steatite seal bearing the letter *mā* in Northern Brāhmī script of the 2nd or 3rd century BC, terracotta spire of roof, terracotta spindle-whorl and fragment of the fore-part of a terracotta figure of a lamb (Banerji 1911: 16-17). In 1911, Nagendra Nath Vasu collected six cast copper coins for the Museum of the Vaṅgīya Sāhitya Parishad, Kolkata (Haque 1996: 42). Growing interest in Chandraketugarh is reflected in the brief exploration report on Chandraketugarh published in 1922 by K. N. Dikshit (1922-23: 109-110). After a few more scattered explorations, Asutosh Museum of Indian Art, Kolkata carried out a thorough exploration of the site in 1955-56.

Archaeological investigation was intensified from 1956-57 to 1967-68 when the Asutosh Museum of Indian Art of the University of Calcutta carried out a series of regular excavations in five locations at Chandraketugarh. The locations are (i) Beracampa (west of Beracampa-Haroa Road), (ii) Khana-Mihirer-Dhipi, a fourteen-feet high mound north-east of Beracampa (north of Barasat-Bashirhat Road), (iii) Itakhola (west of the Beracampa-Haroa Road), (iv) Noongola (between Khana-Mihirer-Dhipi and Itakhola) and (v) Hadipur (a village outside the fortified area in the southern quarter of Chandraketugarh). The Table 1.2 gives a comprehensive picture of all the antiquities unearthed in the Asutosh Museum excavations (now held in the collection of the Asutosh Museum of Indian Art and the State Archaeological Museum, Kolkata) as well as other antiquities collected from surface findings by local inhabitants (now held in a number of private collections in North 24-Parganas).

Apart from the antiquities listed in Table 1.2, a few figurines of the Buddha (datable to the Pāla period) have also been reported from stray findings. These are now held in a private collection in Haroa.

Of all the materials discovered so far at Chandraketugarh, Rouletted Wares (RW), Northern Black Polished Wares (NBPW), stamped wares, terracotta and agate artifacts of Mediterranean influence, semi-precious stone (such as agate, carnelian, onyx, amethyst, jasper, quartz, chert and garnet) beads of specially etched variety, and terracotta seals and sealing with Kharoshṭī-Brāhmī inscription deserve special attention (as in the case of Tāmralipti). Footed wares and glass beads are additional materials found at Chandraketugarh, which were important for their commercial value. The distribution pattern of all these cultural materials connect Chandraketugarh with sites in South Asia (Wārī-Baṭeśwar, Tamluk, Śiśupālgarh, Arikamedu, Karaikadu, Alagankulam, Anuradhapura, Kantarodai, Mantai and Tissamaharama), Southeast Asia (Beikthano in Myanmar; Bukit Tengku Lembu, Kalumpang Island, Kuala Selinsing and Tanjong Rawa in Malaysia; Kobak Kendal, Cibutak and Sembiran in Indonesia; Khuan Luk Pat, U Thong, Ban Don Ta Phet, Ban Chi Nam Lai and Prasat Muang Sing in Thailand; Trakieu and Oc-Eo in Vietnam; Palawan Island in the Philippines) and the Red Sea Coast (Berenike) (Jahan 2004: 92-96). Like Tāmralipti, Chandraketugarh's contact with all the above-mentioned sites are trade-related and of maritime nature. Literary evidences cited earlier showed commodities (which included silk yarn) as well as people (the Chinese embassy) being transported to and/or from the port. Archaeological evidences add voluminously to the list of goods that were transported and traded.

Table 1.2:
Archaeological Findings from Explorations and Excavations at Chandraketugarh

Findings	**Pre-Maurya**	**Maurya**	**Śuṅga**	**Kuṣāṇa**	**Gupta**	**Post-Gupta**
Pottery	Red slip ware, painted grey coarse ware, red-and-buff ware, buff coarse ware.	NBPW, RW, stamped ware, fine grey ware, black slipped ware, black-and-red ware.	NBPW, RW, stamped ware, grey ware.	RW, NBPW, stamped ware, red slip ware, black-slipped spouted cups, red ware, black ware, grey ware including spouted cups, bottle-necked sprinkler, narrow-necked cylindrical vases.	Stamped ware, black ware, red ware, grey ware.	
Terracotta	Human and animal figurines.	Human and animal figurines.	Human and animal figurines, plaques.	Human and animal figurines, plaques, tablets on various themes.	Human and animal figurines, plaques, ear-studs.	Spindle-whorl.
Beads		Semiprecious stone, terracotta, ivory.	Semiprecious stone, bone.	Semiprecious stone, glass, bone.	Semiprecious stone, glass, terracotta.	Semiprecious stone, Bone, terracotta.

Bangles		Ivory.			Shell, ivory.	Conch-shell.
Other objects		Antimony rods of copper and ivory, bone objects, ivory objects, lime-stone animal figurine, steatite seal bearing the letter *mā*.	Awls and cosmetic sticks of bones and ivory, bone objects including one with Brāhmī script, a terracotta sealing with the legend *sadada* in Brāhmī, Steatite casket.	Antimony rods of copper, awls of ivory, copper and bones, copper bowls, wooden decorative pieces, a broken bowl of polished agate, seals and sealings with Kharoshṭī-Brāhmī inscriptions.	Awls and gaming dice of bone, ivory casket, an iron axe, earthen lamps, the lower part of a small sandstone Surya plaque, a stone inlaid silver and a plain copper ring, saddle-quern with pastle, a plano-convex sealing with Brāhmī script, a mutilated sealing with inscription *ye dharma hetu*, seals and sealing with Kharoshṭī-Brāhmī inscriptions.	A mutilated bust of Viṣṇu in sandstone, Black basalt *cakra* of Viṣṇu, a stone Viṣṇu plaque.
Coin	Silver & copper Punch-marked.	Silver, copper & billon punch-marked, uninscribed cast copper.	uninscribed cast copper.	Cast copper.	Cast copper, silver and gold.	

The following artifacts of Mediterranean origin and/or syncretic objects indicating Greco-Roman influence have been reported from Chandraketugarh. One of these is a broken bowl of polished agate from the Kuṣāṇa period. It may be mentioned that agate table-wares were fashionable in Roman world and were also found at Taxila (Chakraborty 2000: 406). The remaining artifacts are all of terracotta. These are a vase with elongated ovoid body and circular rim (Gupta 1997: 32), spouted cups and narrow necked cylindrical vases (*Indian Archaeology – A Review* 1963-64: 64), a terracotta male head and a terracotta head wearing a laurel leaf-wreath as crown (Chakrabarti 1996: 80), a terracotta plaque showing costumes and armour (Pamphlet on Exhibition on Roman Antiquities in India, Indian Museum, Calcutta, 1993), a terracotta seal depicting leaping bull, a terracotta head of a bearded warrior with ribbed headgear and a button-seal showing two formalised human figures leaping above a humped bull with outstretched arms on the obverse and a twin-tree with stylised leaves on the reverse. Of these, the ovoid vase shows Hellenistic influence, the terracotta plaque shows Greco-Roman influence and the two heads (including the one wearing a wreath of leaves), the spouted cups and cylindrical vases show Roman influence. The motif on the terracotta seal is believed to be a familiar motif in Minoan Crete. The terracotta head of a bearded warrior appears to indicate influence of the Eastern Mediterranean of the 7th-8th century BC while the button seal indicates influence of the Mediterranean area in general. Also worth noting are the seals and sealing with Kharoshṭī-Brāhmī inscriptions, quite a number of which have been found at and around Chandraketugarh.

Unlike Tāmralipti, the Greco-Roman accounts are not silent regarding Gaṅgābandar. Hence, finding the artifacts mentioned above is not surprising. However, we also need to bear in mind that no Roman coin has been discovered at or around Chandraketugarh. Nevertheless, all the artifacts bearing Mediterranean influence indicate that the port of Gaṅgābandar was frequented by people of Mediterranean origin (including the Romans and Greco-Bactrians). As in Tamluk, the seals with Kharoshṭī-Brāhmī inscriptions also indicate the presence of Kharoshṭī-speaking people at Gaṅgābandar.

Apart from all the objects discussed above, Chandraketugarh has also yielded a large number of coins. These include some silver punch-marked coins, few copper and billon punch-marked coins, cast copper coins and a large number of uninscribed cast copper coins (all dated to the Maurya period or c. 3rd-2nd century BC). The inscribed and uninscribed cast copper coins continued to circulate in the Śuṅga period. Although Imperial Kuṣāṇa coins have not been noticed at Chandraketugarh, locally minted cast copper coins have been found at the site. This type of coins, albeit few in number, have also been found from the early Gupta period. Besides these, a gold coin and a silver coin from the Gupta period have also been reported from the site. Discovery of coins at Chandraketugarh indicates that the site functioned as an exchange centre.

Some of the punch-marked copper coins reported from Chandraketugarh and now preserved in the State Archaeological Museum, West Bengal and Asutosh Museum of Indian Art, Kolkata show a hull of a ship (*Indian Archaeology – A Review* 1960-61: 70; 1961-62: 107; 1962-63: 46 and 1966-67: 48). One of them is a dolphin type found at Khana-Mihirer-Dhipi. Its aft section is shaped like a dolphin while the upper tip of the bow appears to be like a dolphin's snout. Furthermore, as Gourisankar De (2001: 147) points out, the ship motif also occurs on a type of billon coins. Six of these coins are preserved in the State Archaeological Museum, West Bengal. The copper punch-marked coins bearing ship motif further serve to strengthen Chandraketugarh's claim as a maritime port. It is worth further notice that some of the terracotta seals and sealing found at Chandraketugarh also bear ship motif. A detailed discussion of this will be taken up later in Chapter Four, which will substantiate the additional assertion made in favour of Chandraketugarh's claim as a maritime port.

Since (i) Roman literary sources indicate that Gangê was located near the seashore of 'Bengal', on the bank of the river Gaṅgā, (ii) physiographic conditions of Chandraketugarh ideally suits its claim as the site of the ancient port and (iii) archaeological findings at the site justify the claim, we may conclude unhesitatingly that the maritime port of Gangê/Gaṅgābandar was indeed located at Chandraketugarh.

The port was well connected, as all the archaeological objects discussed above show, with the ports of Sri Lanka, the eastern coast of India and Southeast Asia. As the *Periplus* indicates that the port was used for exporting "raw silk and silk yarn and silk cloth" from the western state of Ts'in of China to Damirica [Tamil lands] (§ 64; Schoff 1995: 48), it is possible to believe that the port was also connected with T'sin through a land route via Lhasa and the Chumbi Vale to Sikkim (*ibid.*: 272-273). However, Chinese silk at the port of Gangê/Ganges was not easy to come by because "the land of this is not easy of access; few men come from there and seldom" (§ 64; *ibid.*: 48).

The location of the archaeological site on the bank of a mouth of the ancient Gaṅgā and the description given in the *Periplus of the Erythraean Sea* (cited earlier) indicates that Ganges (Gaṅgābandar) was an estuarine port. The structural remains at Chandraketugarh from the Maurya to the Pāla-Sena period, summed up in Table 1.3 given below, may help us ascertain the physical condition of the port.

The physiographic features of the site discussed above indicate that the harbour of Gaṅgābandar was situated on the east bank of the Bidyādharī. Since Beracampa is nearest to the river, we may assume that the harbour was concentrated at this area. That no man-made installations indicating the existence of a harbour has been unearthed, we may believe that no jetties were constructed at the harbour. This is a typical feature of all estuarine ports of South Asia built during pre-Modern times. We may also believe that ships with shallow draught were anchored at riverbanks in a manner still seen in riverine ports of Bangladesh and West Bengal, where wooden planks are used to cross over to the shore. Larger ships may have anchored at a distance from the coast and goods may have been ferried across to the shore in smaller crafts.

Excavation report on the remains at Khana-Mihirer-Dhipi from the Maurya period informs us that structures were generally built with wooden posts and tiles. Śuṅga period remains show the use of bamboo in addition to the two mentioned above (*Indian Archaeology – A Review* 1962-63: 46). Kuṣāṇa remains from Beracampa add still another building material: mud used for making the plinth. The structures also seem to have been decorated with pottery finials. If we may add the evidences from Khana-Mihirer-Dhipi with those of Beracampa, we may believe that the structures at Chandraketugarh were possibly constructed with bamboo or wooden posts erected on mud plinth. The roof was made of tiles, further decorated with pottery finials (*ibid.:* 1956-57: 30; 1958-59: 56; 1959-60: 51). Another type of structural construction was the wattle-and-daub, as a trial excavation at Hadipur revealed. These structures were elaborate complexes "with tile roofs, mud floors, grain storage enclosures and ring-wells, forming a self contained unit possibly of a family" (*ibid.:* 1965-66: 60).

If contemporary practice in rural Bangladesh where habitational and commercial structures are still built on mud plinth with bamboo or wooden posts and tiled roof may be accepted as ethnographic evidence, we may assume that the wooden posts in Chandraketugarh were used in structures belonging to affluent families or business concerns while those of bamboo belonged to the less affluent section. Some of the structures belonging to the affluent section of the

Table 1.3:
Structural Remains at Chandraketugarh

Period	Location	Structure
Maurya	Beracampa	Tile fragments, decomposed wood and bamboos.
	Khana-Mihirer-Dhipi	House roofs were generally built of tiles with wooden posts.
	Itakhola	A pottery drain and an oblong area enclosed by vertical wooden planks. Signs of destruction of the dwelling houses.
Śuṅga	Beracampa	A drain of pottery-pipes fitted into each other.
	Khana-Mihirer-Dhipi	Tile fragments.
	Itakhola	The rampart, built of heaped-up earth. The basal layer of the rampart was composed of *surkhi*, brick-bats and potsherds. A massive wooden structure built of vertical logs set on horizontal planks and a soak-pit found below the rampart proper.
Kuṣāṇa	Hadipur	Elaborate house complexes of wattle-and-daub type with tile roofs, mud floors, grain storage enclosures and ring-wells.
	Beracampa	A ramp of rammed concrete and a rampart of earth erected on it. Signs of wooden or bamboo structures with tiled roofs, probably having pottery finials and earthen plinth. A massive brick structure built on wooden piles. A small square wooden enclosure, made of tightly-joined horizontal planks, reinforced by beams at the bottom and supported on wooden logs. A thick layer of paddy-husks was found on the horizontal planks.
Gupta	Beracampa	Kiln-burnt bricks.

	Khana-Mihirer-Dhipi	A massive square-shaped brick temple with miniature shrines on the sides and a *sarvato-bhadra* type polygonal brick temple.
	Noongola	Remnants of brick structures and a ring-well made of thick and large terracotta rings.
Post-Gupta	Khana-Mihirer-Dhipi	A small brick temple 5.94 m square. Circular brick basements, possibly the remains of votive *stupas*.
Pāla-Sena	Khana-Mihirer-Dhipi	Renovation of the upper part of the massive wall of the *sarvato-bhadra* temple. Remains of the plinth of a huge brick-built temple (15.75 m x 29.58 m) and a few other structures.

inhabitants were also provided with pottery drain pipes used as sewerage connection, as remains of such pipes have been found at Itakhola (Maurya period) and Beracampa (Śuṅga period) signify. The Itakhola pipes ended in a wooden reservoir (*ibid.:* 1959-60: 51-52, 1956-57: 30 and 1957-58: 51). Using the same ethnographic evidence, we may further postulate that the walls of the structures with wooden posts were made out of wooden planks while those of bamboo were made of interwoven bamboo mats. Some of the houses with bamboo mats may have used hay as roofing – the remains of which would have decayed beyond recognition. Destruction by fire, accidental or by arson we are not sure, may not have been uncommon because signs of "huge conflagrations which left their mark everywhere" have been found at Itakhola (*ibid.:* 1959-60: 51).

There can be no doubt that many of the structures at Chandraketugarh were used for residential purpose. The wattle-and-daub structures at Hadipur must have served such purpose. If we may assume that production of earthen wares was family-based, we may believe that many of the houses at Hadipur would have been used for producing Northern Black Polished Ware, Rouletted Ware, stamped ware etc. since a large number of potsherds with Kharoshṭī-Brāhmī inscriptions have been recovered from this area. Many of the bamboo-mat and wooden-plank type of structures at Khana-Mihirer-Dhipi, Itakhola and Beracampa may have been used for residential purpose. However, there must have been others which served a commercial purpose, as shops, offices of merchants and warehouses. We have observed earlier that literary sources have identified Gaṅgābandar as a market-town. We may point to one wooden structure unearthed at Beracampa that may have been used as a store by rice merchants. Report of *Indian Archaeology – A Review* (1963-64: 64) describes it thus: "a small square wooden enclosure, made of tightly-joined horizontal planks, reinforced by beams at the bottom and supported on wooden logs". A thick layer of paddy-husks found on the horizontal planks clearly indicates that the structure was used for storing paddy. There must also have been structures used for producing goods. Unfortunately, we cannot as yet identify them exactly. Nevertheless, recovery of lumps of agate and quartz together with some unfinished beads from the Śuṅga period at Khana-Mihirer-Dhipi (*ibid.:* 1961-62: 63) indicates that there must have been quite a few structures at the fore-mentioned area, which were used as factories for production of beads.

Gaṅgābandar was definitely an administrative centre as well, as the rampart quite forcefully testifies. Excavation in the rampart near the Itakhola area revealed that it was constructed in c. 1st century BC by piling up of earth on a basal layer composed of *surkhi*, brick-bats and potsherds. The moat around the rampart was created out of the digging and piling. Large number of coins found at the basal layer indicates the observance of some sort of ritual at the beginning of the construction. In the 1st century AD the rampart was reinforced. A massive wooden structure built of vertical logs set on horizontal planks and a soak-pit was found below the rampart proper. It is believed to be the foundation of some house complex built in c. 2nd century BC (*ibid.:* 1964-65: 52). We may tentatively propose that the house complex was the residence of the local ruler. The rampart may have been necessary as a measure of protection from external invasion. We are not sure of the nature of the residential construction after the rampart was erected in c. 1st century AD. Tile fragments, and decomposed wood and bamboo, which were found in the sections of the rampart near Beracampa when accidentally dug by the local people (*ibid.:* 1967-68: 50). These date from the Maurya period and hence could not be from the residential complex of the local ruler. Although we do not as yet have material evidence to reconstruct the interior of the rampart, one may justifiably believe that the nerve centre of Ptolemy's Gangê, the capital of a kingdom called Gaṅgāridai, lay within the high-rising earthen walls.

Based on cultural materials obtained from Chandraketugarh, we may firmly believe that the site was occupied continuously right from the pre-Maurya to the Pāla period without any break. However, as Table 1.3 shows, structural remains date from the Maurya period. From the Maurya to the Kuṣāṇa period, the structural remains indicate mundane, temporal and secular activities. From the Gupta period onward, the emphasis was clearly on temple building. Except for remnants of brick structures and a ring-well made of thick and large terracotta rings unearthed at Noongola and built during the Gupta period, the other structures of the same period are a *Sarvato-bhadra* type polygonal brick temple, a square-shaped brick temple with a flight of twenty-steps, two miniature brick shrines and basement of a votive *stupa* were unearthed at Khana-Mihirer-Dhipi. The two furnaces found near the temple appear to have been used for burning shells in order to produce lime that was used as mortar and for moulding decorative stucco panels of the temples.

The emphasis on religious structures continued in the post-Gupta period, as evinced from the excavated remains of a small brick temple (5.94 m square) and circular brick basements (possibly the remains of votive *stupas*) (*ibid.:* 1961-62: 63 and 1962-63: 47). The same is true of the Pāla-Sena period when another huge brick-built temple (15.75 m x 29.58 m) was built. It is possible that the earliest phase of its construction dates from the 7th-8th centuries AD. The rest of constructional work from this period includes a few unidentified structures and renovation work (*ibid.:* 1957-58: 51-53 and 1967-68: 50).

The analysis presented above clearly indicates that Chandraketugarh had turned into a religious centre during the Gupta period. Indications received from structural remains are further confirmed by coins unearthed from the site. Against continued circulation of a large number of coins from the Maurya to the Kuṣāṇa period, money economy during the Gupta period appears to have declined because only a silver, a gold and a few cast copper coins have come down to us. Decline in circulation of money is a clear indication of decline in trade. This is further confirmed by the antiquities. As shown in Table 1.2, antiquities recovered from the Maurya, Śuṅga and Kuṣāṇa periods are Northern Black Poished Ware, Rouletted Ware, stamped ware, semiprecious stone beads including etched variety, glass beads, and seals and sealing with Kharoshṭī-Brāhmī inscriptions. Antiquities from the Gupta period do not include Northern Black Poished Ware, Rouletted Ware and etched beads but we may discount these commodities because their use ceased after the Kuṣāṇa and hence they cease to function as indicators of trade for the Gupta period. What is striking is that stamped ware, semiprecious stone beads, glass beads, and seals and sealing with Kharoshṭī-Brāhmī inscriptions have not been found in contemporary South and Southeast Asian sites. This clearly shows that none of these commodities were exported from Chandraketugarh during the Gupta period. Hence, maritime trade at Gaṅgābandar had virtually ended with the beginning of Gupta period. Hence we may reasonably conclude that the period of operation of the port of Gaṅgābandar stretched from the 3rd century BC to the early 4th century AD.

Findings presented above leave little doubt that Gangê (Gaṅgābandar) cited in Roman accounts was indeed located at Chandraketugarh. It was an estuarine port with no permanent quays and wharves. The socio-economic environment of the port included production centres, commercial centres, residential quarters and an administrative centre.

WĀRĪ-BAṬEŚWAR

While Tāmralipti is profusely mentioned in South Asian and Chinese literary sources but is absent in Greco-Roman sources and whereas Gaṅgābandar is mentioned in Greco-Roman and Chinese sources but not in any South Asian literary source, Wārī-Baṭeśwar is completely absent in all literary sources. Nevertheless, archaeological and physiographic evidences clearly prove the existence of a maritime port at Wārī-Baṭeśwar in the early historic period.

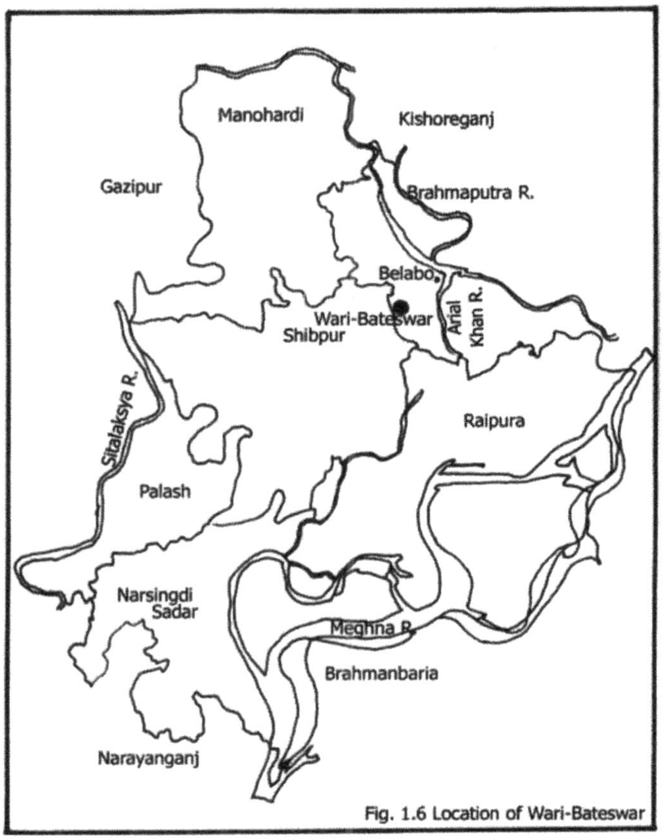

Fig. 1.6 Location of Wari-Bateswar

Physiography of Wārī-Baṭeśwar and its neighbourhood is particularly important for the reconstruction of its past. Wārī (24°05'46" N Lat. and 90°49'42" E Long.) and Baṭeśwar (24°05′34" N Lat. and 90°49′40" E Long.) are two adjacent villages in Amlabo Union under Belabo police station in Narsingdi district (central Bangladesh) located some four kilometers southwest of Belabo town (Fig. 1.6). It is situated on an isolated bit of the Pleistocene terrace at Manohardi-Śibpur, which is detached from the Madhupur tract by the Old Brahmaputra and the Lakṣyā rivers. As one approaches the villages from Narsingdi, one cannot fail to notice mounds and high land separated by irregular belts of marshlands. The soil of the entire area is red and pebble mixed. The villages of Wārī and Baṭeśwar stand on relatively flat ground, which is considerably higher than the surrounding area. The course of the Old Brahmaputra River is only four kilometers north-east, that of the Meghnā is a few kilometres south and that of the Āriyāl Khān River is about three kilometers east from the villages. The confluence of the Āriyāl Khān and the Brahmaputra rivers is four kilometers northeast of Wārī-Baṭeśwar. There exist marshland between the two villages and to their west, northwest and north. It is believed that the marshy lowlands were parts of an earlier course of the Brahmaputra. The emaciated and nearly dry channel of the river Koirā (Kaur) borders Wārī in the north. Śītalakṣyā, the other major river in the vicinity, flows some twenty kilometers west of Wārī-Baṭeśwar. Sonārgāon, another important town in the vicinity, lies about thirty-five kilometers south-west of the two villages. The environment described above immediately brings into relief three important physiographic features of the villages of Wārī and Baṭeśwar. They are: (i) the villages are situated on relative highland, which make them inaccessible to flood-water, (ii) low-lying marshland exist in the immediate vicinity of the two villages and (iii) the Brahmaputra-Āriyāl Khān confluence lies only four kilometers away.

Let us now remind ourselves that before the 17th century, the Brahmaputra used to flow through Sherpur and Jamalpur, by the Madhupur tract, intersect eastern part of greater Dhaka district, and flow into the Meghnā near Langal-bandh and Sonārgāon. After the 17th century, the river changed its course. Instead of flowing into the Meghnā at Langal-bandh and Sonārgāon, it began to flow into the Meghnā at Bhairab Bazar. This course is marked in Rennell's map of 1779. The Brahmaputra changed its course again in 1787 and began to flow through the Jamunā, which was till then a tributary. Consequently, Jamunā was transformed into the primary channel. On the other hand, the Brahmaputra was reduced to a subsidiary status and earned for itself the prefix "old", hence the name "Old Brahmaputra". If we allow ourselves the liberty of believing that in the beginning of the 1st millennium AD, the Brahmaputra possibly flowed along what today is known as the Āriyāl Khān, then it becomes clear that the marshland, which lies in the vicinity of Wārī-Baṭeśwar was probably a channel of ancient Brahmaputra (Jahan 1999: 210-212).

Furthermore, we need to remember that till 4000 Years BP, the funnel-shaped mouth of the Bay was possibly much wider than today and Dhaka and the surrounding regions were then at the head of the Bay. Because Matuail (in the flood plain east of Dhaka city) was under marine influence until about 2,400 Years BP (c. 350 BC), it can be reasonably assumed that the Bay was very close to the southern tip of Narayanganj district and the Brahmaputra would have fallen into the Bay at a point east of the tip. In such circumstances, the possibility of existence of a maritime port at Wārī-Baṭeśwar in the early historic period is not beyond belief. Archaeological findings discussed below adequately supports this claim.

Since the 40s of the last century, a large number of cultural materials of Wārī-Baṭeśwar have been reported from surface collections and chance excavations. The first extensive archaeological exploration at the site was carried out in 1998-99 season by the author. The findings of this aroused enough excitement and led to a number of excavations. In 2000, the International Centre for Study of Bengal Art carried out a small-scale trial excavation at the village of Wārī. Subsequent excavations at Wārī were conducted by the Department of Archaeology and Museums, Government of the People's Republic of Bangladesh in three seasons from 2003 to 2005. Besides, S.S.M. Rahman, Department of Archaeology, Jahangirnagar University also carried out small-scale excavations at Wārī in 2004 to 2005. The present authour carried out an extensive excavation with the Department of Archaeology and Museums, Government of Bangladesh in 2006. This time the excavation was conducted at three neigbouring villages of Narsingdi District. These are Wārī, Baṭeśwar under Amlabo Union in Belabo Police station and Sonārutalā (24°05'28" N and 90°49'18" E) under Kamrabo Union in Sibpur Police station.

Fig. 1.7 A section of the southern rampart of Asam Rajar Garh, Bateswar

The exploration carried out in 1998-99 revealed remnant of two fortified areas (henceforth referred to as outer and inner forts). Both the fortifications are gradually disappearing due to human and natural activities. The outer fort is located at Baṭeśwar and is locally known as Asam Rājār Garh (Fig. 1.7). At present it survives up to 4.87 m in height and the average breadth at the base is 35 m. According to the local inhabitants, an Assamese king and a Koch king took refuge here in the late 16th-early 17th century AD and built the rampart as a defensive measure against militant incursion of both the Mughals and the Pathans. The fort encloses a large area with the help of two earthen ramparts built on the south and the west. The northern and the eastern sides of the fort are bounded by the Koirā and the Āriyāl Khān, respectively. The southern rampart of the fort is 3.5 km long and ends at the River Āriyāl Khān. The Dāṅgir Bil (138 m in breadth) and the Baḍa Bāidyār Bil (42 m in breadth) intersect the rampart approximately 2 km and 3 km, respectively, from the southwest corner of the fort. The western rampart is about 1.7 km long and ends at the River Koirā. The Cārgāchiyā Bil (130 m in breadth) intersects the rampart at about 1 km from the southwest corner of the fort. The remaining portion of the rampart runs into Sonārutalā village.

The inner fort is bounded by four earthen ramparts and it encircles the entire village of Wārī. The northern and the southern ramparts measure 645 m and the eastern and the western ramparts measure 518 m. The average breadth at the base is 16.5 m. A canal, 30 m in breadth, surrounds the fort on its exterior like a moat. It dries up during the dry seasons but has running water during the wet seasons.

Fig. 1.8 Triangular-shaped iron tools, Wari-Bateswar

Artifacts obtained so far from chance excavations, archaeological explorations and excavations in and around the site of Wārī-Baṭeśwar are listed below: some stone implements, celts of fossil wood, a large number of triangular-shaped iron implements similar to prehistoric stone hand-axes (Fig. 1.8), iron arrowheads, iron spearheads (Fig. 1.9), iron nails, some lumps of iron ore, copper bangles, a quern with a pestle, a stone amulet, terracotta beads and balls, numerous potsherds of red ware (both course and fine), grey ware (both course and fine), red slipped ware, black slipped ware, Northern Black Polished ware, Rouletted ware, fragments of high-tin bronze knobbed vessels, glass beads (both translucent and opaque), finished as well as unfinished semi-precious stone beads. A close scrutiny of the beads revealed that they are mostly made of carnelian (including the etched variety), agate, quartz, amethyst, crystal, chalcedony, chert and jasper. Their shapes are divergent and include the following: globular, cylindrical, pentagonal, oval, trapezoid, rectangular, triangular, hexagonal, barrel, disc, spherical, crescent and diamond. Although most of these show one perforation, some show as many as four. The holes have been bored with remarkable skill, except in the cases of carnelian and agate, where the bores (made from both ends) fail to meet in a straight line. Along with these beads, a large quantity of core materials, flakes, chips (Fig. 1.10), beads without perforation and broken pieces of beads (Fig. 1.11) have also been discovered from the site.

Fig. 1.9 Iron spearheads, Wari-Bateswar

Fig. 1.10 Raw materials of semi-precious stone beads, Wari-Bateswar

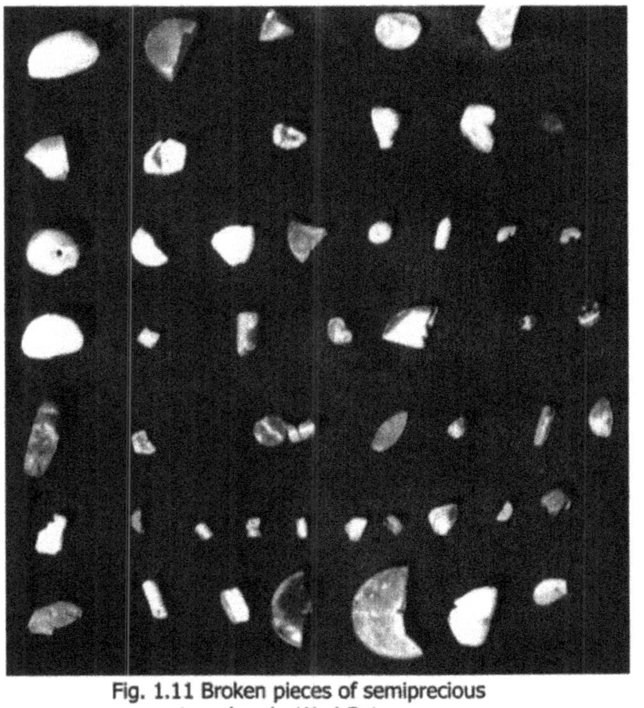

Fig. 1.11 Broken pieces of semiprecious stone beads, Wari-Bateswar

Apart from the cultural materials discussed above, the most enthralling finding from the Wārī-Baṭeśwar excavation 2006 conducted by the authour with the Department of Archaeology and Museums, Government of Bangladesh was a hoard (length: 125 cm, breadth: 58 cm and thickness: 53 cm) of 359 triangular iron objects (shaped like prehistoric stone hand-axes) from Baṭeśwar. The objects measure between 13.5 x 10 x 7 cm and 16.5 x 7.5 x 6 cm and their weight varies between 1.75 to 2.90 kg. Commenting on similar objects found earlier from chance excavations at the site, Chakrabarti (1992: 58) suggests that these are "iron blooms which were imported to the site as raw material". However, detailed first-hand examination of these objects obtained from the excavation of 2006 clearly showed that these are finished products with uniform shape and clearly marked working edge. All available indications suggest that these triangular objects were iron implements that were used as chisels for cutting and shaping wood and stone. Further, concentration of iron ore in Rājārbāg (a neighbouring village) and Baṭeśwar areas suggest that the raw material of these implements were obtained locally.

The excavation of 2006 also yielded remains of two overlying floors (both 10 cm in thickness) at Wārī. It appears that the floors occupied a large area of the south-eastern part of the inner fort. In the north-western segment of the same fort, laid bricks were found 8-9 cm below the surface covering an area 32 x 28.30 m in dimension. Though no alignment could be ascertained, it is not unlikely that the excavated brick strata formed the lowest level of what was once a brick-built structure, which is lost today because of pilferage by local inhabitants. The sizes of the bricks vary between 41 x 22 x 3 cm and 44 x 21 x 4 cm. Similar bricks have also been found in a reservoir (6.5 x 5 m) unearthed at Wārī from excavations conducted by the Department of Archaeology and Museums, Government of Bangladesh in three seasons from 2003 to 2005 (Alam *et al.* 2004). On the basis of their size, the bricks may tentatively be dated to the 7th-8th century AD. Some pieces of tiles have also been found during the excavation of 2006.

Based on cultural materials recovered so far from Wārī-Baṭeśwar, it appears that the site was occupied continuously from the early historic to modern times without any break. Of all the materials discussed above, Northern Black Polished Ware, Rouletted Ware, semi-precious stone beads (specially the etched variety) and glass beads deserve special attention (as in the case of Tāmralipti and Gaṅgābandar) for their commercial value. Knobbed vessels (so called because a conical knob, circumscribed by a series of concentric grooves or incisions, stand at the centre of the inner surface of the vessel's base) are additional materials found at Wārī-Baṭeśwar, which were also important for their commercial value. Knobbed vessels made of high-tin bronze (a copper-tin alloy, which contains more than 20% Sn) have been found only at Wārī-Baṭeśwar among all known sites in Bangladesh and West Bengal. Similar high-tin bronze (23-28% Sn) vessels of knobbed variety have been found at Ban Don Ta Phet in west-central Thailand (now preserved in the National Museum Bangkok). Another knobbed vessel, made of bronze, has been reported from Than Hoa Province of Vietnam (preserved in the Musee Guimet, Paris). Besides knobbed wares made of high-tin bronze, a sherd of coarse grey knobbed ware has been found at Wārī-Baṭeśwar (Haque *et al.* 2000: 297). Similar earthen variety of knobbed vessels has been discovered at quite a few sites in South Asia such as Harinārāyaṇpur (West Bengal, India), Sisupalgarh (Orissa, India) and Anuradhapura (Sri Lanka).

The distribution pattern of all these artifacts mentioned above connect Wārī-Baṭeśwar with sites in South Asia (Tamluk, Chandraketugarh, Śiśupālgarh, Arikamedu, Karaikadu, Alagankulam, Anuradhapura, Kantarodai, Mantai and Tissamaharama) and Southeast Asia (Beikthano in Myanmar; Bukit Tengku Lembu, Kalumpang Island, Kuala Selinsing and Tanjong Rawa in Malaysia; Kobak Kendal, Cibutak and Sembiran in Indonesia; Khuan Luk Pat, U Thong, Ban Don Ta Phet, Ban Chi Nam Lai and Prasat Muang Sing in Thailand; Trakieu and Oc-Eo in Vietnam; Palawan Island in the Philippines). This establishes that in the 3rd century BC Wārī-Baṭeśwar was already integrated in the Bay of Bengal littoral trade network. Thus archaeological evidences added with physiographic evidences clearly prove that Wārī-Baṭeśwar was indeed a maritime port.

A large number of silver punch-marked coins found at Wārī, Baṭeśwar and in neighbouring villages such as Kandua, Marjal, Joshor, Kundarpara, Jaimangal, Candipara, Patuli, Chula, Harisangan and Govasia serve as corroborative evidence to substantiate Wārī-Baṭeśwar's claim as a maritime port. The claim is all the more valid because the number is far greater than that obtained from other areas in Bangladesh which have also yielded similar coins (i.e., Bogra, Rajshahi and Mymensingh) (Karim 1399 BS: 5). It is also significant that most of these coins (found from 1933 to 1999) were discovered in earthen containers, at six spots at Wārī, all of which are located on the margins of marshlands. The coins are mostly circular, oval, rectangular and square in shape but a few are irregular. Various symbols such as boat, fish and lobster seen on some of these coins, cannot escape attention because they signify maritime connection. The presence of such a large number coins found in hoards on the margins of marshlands (which, as observed above, was a former channel of the Brahmaputra) further substantiate Wārī-Baṭeśwar as a port frequented by maritime merchants, because, as argued earlier, long-distance trade demands coins and/or bullion as media of exchange.

The location of Wārī-Baṭeśwar on the bank of an ancient course of the Brahmaputra can only mean that it was an estuarine port. The cultural materials indicative of maritime trade such as Northern Black Polished Ware, Rouletted Ware, semi-precious stone beads (specially the etched variety), glass beads, knobbed vessels (earthen and high-tin bronze) and punch-marked coins are roughly dated between c. 3rd century BC and the 3rd century AD. Hence, we may believe that the port's life span fell within the same period. The presence of silver punch-marked coins not only indicates that the inhabitants used money-based economy but also suggest that they possessed considerable purchasing capacity. Unlike Tāmralipti and Gaṅgābandar, we have no literary evidence to show that commodities and people were transported to and/or from the port. However, archaeological evidences cited above bear ample testimony as to which commodities were transported to and from Wārī-Baṭeśwar.

Like Tāmralipti, no man-made installations have been unearthed on the margins of the marshland and hence we may believe that no jetties were constructed at the harbour. The port site was possibly like Tāmralipti, made up of a few public utilities, warehouses and production centres for manufacturing semi-precious stone beads. The existence of the latter is indicated by the discovery of a large quantity of core and waste materials (such as semi-precious stone blocks, flakes, chips, unperforated and broken pieces of semi-precious stone beads) mentioned earlier. Discovery of the hoard of triangular-shaped iron implement and various iron tools such as arrowheads, spearheads and nails indicate the existence of production centres geared at manufacturing various types of iron implements as well. Innumerable potsherds seen scattered on the surface of the two villages and the discovery of various types of pottery may be taken to indicate the presence of production centres for manufacturing pottery. The remains of the brick structure from the 7th-8th century AD indicate early medieval habitation at Wārī-Baṭeśwar. Remains of mud ramparts at Wārī and Baṭeśwar indicate that the site was fortified. One may even suggest that the fortification is a sign that Warī-Baṭeśwar was an administrative center like Chandraketugarh.

No indication is available which may determine the cause of the decline of Wārī-Baṭeśwar as a port. One may nevertheless tentatively suggest that one of the reasons was the change of the course of the Brahmaputra. Because of the fall, some other site/s in the neighbourhood must have had taken up the role of Wārī-Baṭeśwar. In support of this argument we may remind ourselves that in c. 643 AD, Bhāskaravarman offered Hiuen-Tsiang official attendants to accompany him should he desire to return to China by the Southern Sea route (i.e., by way of Java or Sumatra) (*Life*, Book V; Beal 1973: 188; Baruah 1985: 75). The Nidhanpur copperplate inscription of Bhāskaravarman (Gupta 1967: 32-40) issued from Karṇasuvarṇa renewing an earlier grant of revenue-free land in Candrapura *viṣaya* (in the southern part of present Sylhet district as the Pascimabhaga copperplate land grant of Śrīcandra proves; *ibid.*: 116-117), clearly show that the entire tract of land from Murshidabad (where Karṇasuvarṇa was located) to Sylhet, including the entire downstream course of the Brahmaputra was within his domain. Hence, one may reasonably assume that Bhāskaravarman was referring to a port on the estuary of the Brahmaputra, which replaced Wārī-Baṭeśwar. The assumption is reasonable given the fact that the two copperplates of Devakhaḍga issued in c. 665 AD and found at Ashrafpur (a village under Shibpur police station; Laskar 1907: 85-91) indicate settlement at the area. A bronze votive stupa and remains of old bricks and fragmentary walls testifying the existence of a ruined Buddhist monastery at Ashrafpur (Zakariah 1984: 414) are further indications that a prosperous urban centre capable of patronising a Buddhist monastery flourished in this area. As we will see later in this chapter, Sonārgāon, hardly 35 kilometres to the southwest of Wārī-Baṭeśwar, served as a port from the mid-14th century AD and it was at this port that Ibn Battutā boarded a junk bound for Java. This strengthens the belief that in the intervening period between the fall of Wārī-Baṭeśwar and the rise of Sonārgāon there must have been one or more ports in the vicinity of these two sites.

KOṬĀLIPĀḌĀ (CANDRAVARMAKOṬA)

Like Wārī-Baṭeśwar, reference to Koṭālipāḍā is completely absent in all literary sources from the 4th century AD to the 7th century AD. This is not unexpected because Buddhist pilgrims provided almost the entire bulk of such evidence, and they visited only those places that were important as Buddhist pilgrimage sites or learning centres. Since these were absent in Koṭālipāḍā (the state appears to have been strongly inclined to Brāhmaṇism as the 'Seated Lakṣmī' device in the coins of Samācāradeva indicate), it is quite natural that they did not visit this part of 'Bengal'. However, Koṭālipāḍā has not remained entirely unnoticed to contemporary scholars. Bhattasali (1925-26: 86) has identified it as Candravarmakoṭa (lit. "Candravarman's fort") mentioned in Samācāradeva's Ghugrāhāṭi Copperplate (lines 18-20, *ibid.*: 79). He calls it "the biggest ancient earthwork known in Bengal", larger than even the fort at Mahāsthān, which is 1,000 yards by 1,500 yards. Raychaudhuri (1943: 30) notes the dominant but as-yet-unproven hypothesis that Candravarma, cited in the Susunia Rock Inscription and the Allahabad Praśasti (both 4th century AD), founded the fort. He also argues, "the marshy area called Koṭālipāḍā (...) was once a thriving seat of civilisation and possibly a centre of sea-borne trade and commerce" (*ibid.*: 7). Haroun er Rashid (1991: 130), offering a slightly deviant proposition, identifies Koṭālipāḍā or Gaurnadi (situated a little south of Koṭālipāḍā) as the probable site for Tilograma, the town that Ptolemy locates between the two mouths of Gaṅgā Kamberikhon and Pseudostomon. Nevertheless, no acceptable resolution of the puzzle has yet been found and the earthen ramparts of Koṭālipāḍā still stand as an unresolved puzzle in the history of 'Bengal'. In order to resolve the puzzle, epigraphic, numismatic and physiographic evidences will be mobilized to argue that it functioned as a maritime port from the end of the early historic period to the late historic period. Let us begin with a brief review of the topographical features of the site obtained from first-hand survey.

Koṭālipāḍā (approximately 23° N and 90° E) is a small town in southern Bangladesh, situated 24 km to the east of the present Gopalganj district headquarters. A distributary of the Madhumati, called the Ghāghar, runs one kilometre west of the town. Today, the area around Koṭālipāḍā is largely lowland, partly water-logged, from which linear strips of highland jut out. The eastern and the western strips of the highland are approximately 4 km long. At present the maximum height of these strips is 6 m and the spread at the base is 60 m. The western strip appears broken at the centre. On top of the southern part of the same (i.e., western) strip stands the infrastructure of the local administration. Outside the four strips, there still remain disjointed sections of canals (60 m wide and 2.2 m maximum deep), separated from each other by patches reclaimed by local inhabitants for rice cultivation. Nevertheless, the canals outside the northern and the western strips still stand out prominently. The area enclosed by the strips is lowland; particularly the northern portion where rice is cultivated, but the southern portion is comparatively higher and is dotted with signs of human habitation.

According to O'Malley's (1925: 16) report prepared three quarters of a century ago, the ruins of Koṭālipāḍā "was a great fort with mud-walls, ... which must have been one of the wonders of India when it was constructed". He further noted that the mud-walls were 15 to 30 feet (or 4.57 m to 9.14 m) high and enclosed an area about four square miles (or a little less than 10 sq km). On careful study of the present site of Koṭālipāḍā, one can still discern the highland area of the four strips forming four arms of a square. There can be little doubt that these arms were the earthen ramparts of a fort. The centre of the western arm, which appears broken today, was possibly the entrance to the ancient fort. The canals were once interconnected and formed the outer moat of the fort. There was another moat inside the rampart, traces of which can still be made out although it has almost dried up.

Bhattasali (1925-26: 85) observes, "brick constructions very often come up unexpectedly from low water-logged places". The author herself could locate very few indications of archaeological remains during her exploration at the site in 2000. Numerous human habitations sprawl all over the four ramparts of the ancient fort. At some places, in some homestead compounds, she has noticed brick structures immediately below the present soil level. However, those date to the British period. Since the entire area is waterlogged, the water level beneath the surface is quite high. Consequently, it may not be possible to excavate very deep. Thus, possibilities of future excavation also seem very dim. Nevertheless, as the physiographic features and geomorphological studies discussed below show, the location immediately outside the western rampart of the ancient fort at Koṭālipāḍā and on the eastern bank of the Ghāghar was very much a feasible site to host an estuarine port sometime near the end of the early historic period.

Koṭālipāḍā is situated on the south-eastern end of the Central Delta Basin, (also known as Faridpur Bil) which is an extensive area (1931 sq km) of swamps. These swamps lie to the north and south-east of Gopalganj town and to the east of Madhumati River. Its distance from Gopalganj is 29 kilometres by road, located south-south-east of the town. Further more, it is less than 25 kilometres east of the point where the Madhumati parts from the Khulna-Ātrāi. Because the river is intimately linked with the fate of Koṭālipāḍā, it is necessary to examine the entire course of the river.

The Madhumati originates as the Gaḍāi which issues from the Gaṅgā a few kilometers north of Kushtia town. Kālīgaṅgā branches off from it south of Kushtia town and joins the Kumār south of Shailakupa town in Jhenaidaha district. The mainstream of the Gaḍāi meanders through Rajbari district to join the Kumār in the northern border of Magura-Faridpur districts. From there it changes its name to Madhumati and flows in south-easterly direction through the bordering region of Faridpur-Magura districts and then in south-south-easterly direction through the bordering region of Faridpur-Narail districts. A branch of the Chitrā joins it when it reaches Gapalganj-Narail border. As it continues its journey in south-south-easterly direction, a stream called the Nabagaṅgā takes off from it in south-westerly direction to join the Chitrā. When the Madhumati reaches the northern-most tip of Bagerhat, the Āthārobākī takes off from it in the south-westerly direction, later to join the Chitrā. The Madhumati continues through the border of Bagerhat-Gopalganj districts in a south-south-westerly direction (where it is also called the Kālīgaṅgā) but changes to a southerly direction when it meanders through the border of Bagerhat and Pirojpur districts. Few kilometers south of Pirojpur town, the Kocha River joins it on its left bank and it changes its name to the Baleśwar. Further south, the Baleśwar is joined with the Ghāsiyākhālī River on its right bank. From the Bogi forest outpost of the Sundarbans, the river changes its name again to Hariṇghāṭā (the "Deer Ford"). Earlier, the Hariṇghāṭā was larger than the Marjāl and second only to the Meghnā, but diversion of the Gaḍāi through the Nabagaṅgā has reduced the stature of the Hariṇghāṭā.

When we compare the above course with Ptolemy's map of the Gaṅgā, even after acknowledging inaccuracies, we are able to come closer to reconstructing historical geography of the Koṭālipāḍā-adjacent area. Ptolemy's Gaṅgā, it is well known, empties in the Bay of Bengal through five mouths (Fig. 1.12). Three of these (the Kambyson, the Mega and the Kamberikhon) clearly issue from the Bhagirathi branch in the west. Its eastern branch, the Padma, has two mouths: the Pseudostomon and the Antibole. Comparing Ptolemy's map with the course of the Kumār-Madhumati-Hariṇghāṭā, one is left with little doubt, as Ray (1993: 82) suggests, that it is none other than Kamberikhon. Between the Kamberikhon and the Pseudostomon, Ptolemy shows an isthmus and at its head and on the seacoast, a town called Tilogramon.

The Madhumati is only 22 kilometres west of Koṭālipāḍā today. If we are prepared to accept that the Ghāghar was one of the distributaries of the Madhumati (the other distributary being the Kālīgaṅgā), then we may easily place Koṭālipāḍā on the bank of one of the major outlets of the eastern course of the Gaṅgā. It is even possible that the Ghāghar was an earlier channel of the Madhumati before changing course to the Kālīgaṅgā. In the 2nd century AD, Koṭālipāḍā lay not only on the bank of one of the major outlets of the Gaṅgā, it actually lay near the coast of the Bay of Bengal as the following study on coastline changes shows.

Reconstructing the shoreline of the Bengal Delta (from the Sundarban region to the Padmā-Meghnā course), Islam (2001: 138-139) shows that during the early mid-Holocene period (7,000 to 4,000 years BP), it lay further landward and since then, the Bay of Bengal has been moving uniformly in a southeast direction. The site of Khulna City was then under the Bay and possibly the coastline was very close to Jessore and Narail. The northern limit of the present day Sundarbans was established (with some local variation) at c. 3000 years BP and the Bay finally retreated from the Khulna region at about 1800 years BP (*ibid.*: 144). It follows quite logically that the Bay had retreated from the area around Koṭālipāḍā (which lies immediately to the east of Khulna region) around the same time, i.e., 200 AD.

Geomorphological studies indicate that the swamp we see today around Koṭālipāḍā was created sometime after 200 AD. According to F. H. Khan (1991: 18), the Central Delta Basin was formed "due to changing stream courses at short intervals and rapid building up of high levees by the streams". On the other hand, Morgan and McIntire (1959) have hypothesized that "part of the delta is subsiding as compensation to the elevation of the Tippera Surface and the Barind Tract". Rashid (1991: 30) supports the above hypothesis and adds that "absence of rapid deposition by the active distributaries (which flow towards its east)" gave rise to the basin. Strickland (1940) has proposed a third opinion. He shows that the rise of tidewater in once-active rivers (which reached a maximum height of 6 m) led to rapid deposition of silt on the southern side of the basin. The formation of this seaward ledge went along with compaction of the deposit, which led to depression of the area to its north. The ledge prevented inland deposition. The compound result of these factors gave rise to the basin. It is not within the scope of this study to ascertain which of the three opinions (i.e., changing stream courses, subsiding of the delta and action of tide water along with formation of this seaward ledge), is actually the cause of the formation of the swamps. However, what is clear is that the formation of the swamps is a later phenomenon.

Summing up our findings from physiographic features and geomorphological studies, we may state that in c. 2nd century AD, Koṭālipāḍā lay near the coast of the Bay of Bengal, on the bank of one of the major outlets of the Gaṅgā and that the marshes were created much later. These factors make Koṭālipāḍā a feasible site for an estuarine port, very much like all other maritime ports of 'Bengal'. Since the location of the site closely matches Ptolemy's Tilogramon, it is not unlikely that the port-town at Koṭālipāḍā was the same as the Roman geographer refers to. Epigraphic findings discussed below clearly show that in the 6th century AD, Koṭālipāḍā was not only a port but also an administrative centre.

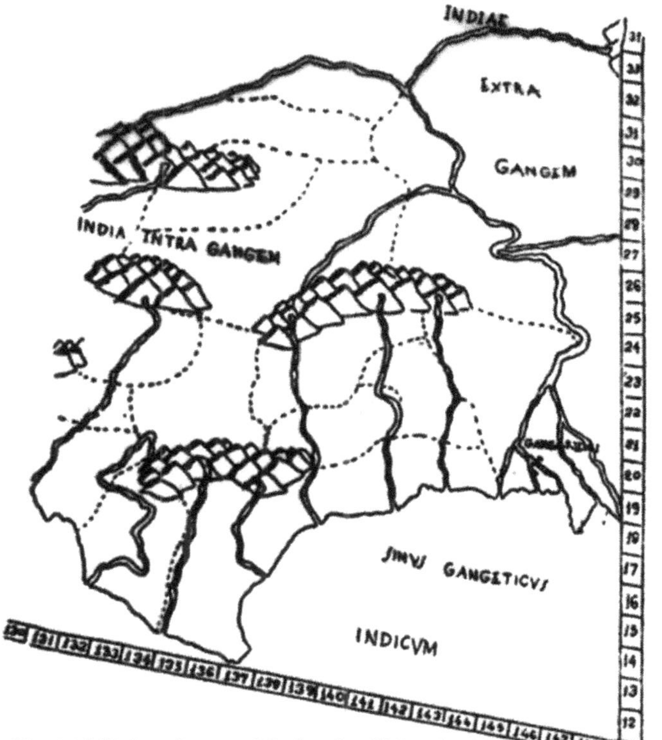

Fig. 1.12 Ptolemy's map of India after Majumdar 1943

Epigraphic evidence in the form of seven copperplates is valuable in ascertaining the function of Koṭālipāḍā in the 6th century AD. These copperplates were issued in the second and third quarters of the 6th century AD by three monarchs: Gopacandra (c. 525-540 AD), Dharmāditya (c. 540-560 AD) and Samācāradeva (c. 560 AD). The monarchs, whose relationship among them has not yet been ascertained, were contemporaries of the Imperial Guptas (who, during their reign, ruled over north Bengal). The copperplates are listed below:

1. Jayarāmapura Copperplate of the time of Gopacandra (Regnal Year 1); find-spot: Baleśwar in Orissa (Rajaguru 1963: 206).
2. Mallasarul Copperplate (of Vijayasena) of the time of Gopacandra (Regnal Year 3); find-spot: Burdwan District, West Bengal (Mukherji and Maity 1967: 87-95). Majumdar (1935-36: 158-159) has identified the places named in the copperplate which shows that the land granted lay along the north bank of the Damodar River, west of the city of Burdwan.

3. Faridpur Copperplate of the time of Gopacandra (Regnal Year 18); find-spot: greater Faridpur. The land that was granted belonged to the Vārakamaṇḍala *viśaya* (Mukherji and Maity 1967: 83-87).
4. Faridpur Copperplate of the time of Dharmāditya – Regnal Year 3; find-spot: greater Faridpur, Bangladesh. (It is cited henceforth as Faridpur Copperplate 1 of Dharmāditya.) The board of administration of Vārakamaṇḍala *viśaya* issued the seal. The land granted was also in the same *viśaya* (*ibid.*: 74-79).
5. Faridpur Copperplate of the time of Dharmāditya; find-spot: greater Faridpur, Bangladesh in 1892. (It is cited henceforth as Faridpur Copperplate 2 of Dharmāditya.) The land that was granted belonged to the Vārakamaṇḍala *viśaya* (*ibid.*: 79-83).
6. Kurpala Copperplate of the time of Samācāradeva (regnal year 7); find-spot: Kurupala village, situated in between Koṭālipāḍā and Ghugrāhāṭi village in greater Faridpur (Sen 1942: xvi). The inscription has not been deciphered as yet.
7. Ghugrāhāṭi Copperplate of the time of Samācāradeva (regnal year 14); find-spot: Ghugrāhāṭi, two or three miles from Koṭālipāḍā, in c. 1907. The land transferred in the copperplate lay on the east of a corner of Candravarman's fort (identified as the fort at Koṭālipāḍā) and the south of the village Gopendracoraka (identified with modern Govindapur village near Koṭālipāḍā) (Bhattasali 1925-26: 86).

In addition to the above, an undated seal from Nālandā issued during the rule of Samācāradeva, has also been discovered. The inscription on the seal has not been deciphered and details of the seal are not available (Shastri 1942: 31).

The find-spots of all the seven copperplates cited above indicate that the kingdom of Gopacandra, Dharmāditya and Samācāradeva extended over a vast territory from Baleśwar in Orissa, through southern part of West Bengal (Vardhamāna-bhukti) to southern part of Bangladesh (Navyāvakāśikā and Vārakamaṇḍala). Analysing the copperplates, Morrison (1980: 137, 146) shows that the form of government of the three monarchs was imperial. It was structured as "a graded territorial hierarchy under the authority of an emperor" and operated in four tiers: the central imperial government; the regional imperial government of units such as Navyāvakāśikā *bhukti*; the *viśaya* administration of units such as Vārakamaṇḍala and the local government formed by the *adhikarana* (council) and local notables (*mahattaras*).

The Faridpur Copperplate of Gopacandra, Faridpur Copperplates 1 and 2 of Dharmāditya and the Ghugrāhāṭi Copperplate of Samācāradeva were all issued from the district (*viśaya*) court of Vārakamaṇḍala, under Navyāvakāśika province (*bhukti*). The location of Navyāvakāśika *bhukti* cited in the copperplates may not be too difficult to surmise. If we remind ourselves (i) that the sea retreated from the Khulna region and the area around Koṭālipāḍā around the 2nd century AD and (ii) "*navyāvakāśika*" denotes "newly formed land" (Ray 1994: 272-273), then Navyāvakāśika *bhukti* must surely denote the entire Khulna and Faridpur region.

The exact location of Vārakamaṇḍala has not been mentioned in the copperplates. Nevertheless, as Morrison (1980: 34) argues, "the place of issue [of all the four plates mentioned above] was almost surely within close proximity of Kotwālipārā [Koṭālipāḍā] for the officers who are involved are spoken of as being local men, participating in local transaction". There actually is enough reason to believe that Vārakamaṇḍala was the district around Koṭālipāḍā and the latter (i.e., Koṭālipāḍā) was the headquarters of Vārakamaṇḍala. The reasons are as follows: (i) the land transferred in the Ghugrāhāṭi Copperplate lay within the jurisdiction of Vārakamaṇḍala *viśaya*; (ii) the land has been located as lying close to Govindapur village, which has been identified as Gopendracoraka village mentioned in the copperplate (Bhattasali 1925-26: 86); and (iii) the copperplate was found at Ghugrāhāṭi, two or three miles from Koṭālipāḍā. The Kurapālā Copperplate is yet to be deciphered. Nevertheless, the fact that it was found at Kurapālā (situated between Ghugrāhāṭi and Koṭālipāḍā) and that it was issued during the reign of Samācāradeva indicates that its content may be similar to the Ghugrāhāṭi Copperplate. The existence of a fort (Candravarmakoṭa) near the transferred land, as cited in the Ghugrāhāṭi Copperplate, can only mean that Koṭālipāḍā was important enough to be an administrative centre. As a corollary to the above, Bhattasali's identification of Koṭālipāḍā as Candravarmakoṭa is indeed acceptable.

As Sircar (1986: 363) argues, Vārakamaṇḍala *viśaya* must have included parts of Rajbari district as well because Dhruvilātī mentioned in the Faridpur Copperplate of Gopacandra and Faridpur Copperplate 1 of Dharmāditya has been identified with modern Dhulaṭ (near Pangsha, south of the Padma in the Rajbari district and about 28 miles to the north-west of the Faridpur town). The following excerpt from the Faridpur Copperplate 1 of Dharmāditya also indicates that Vārakamaṇḍala *viśaya* was a littoral region. "There is prevalent in this district [i.e., Vārakamaṇḍala *viśaya*] the rule of sale of lands at the rate of four Dīnāras for each Kulyavāpa, – a custom, established in the countries bordering the Eastern Sea" (Mukherji and Maity 1967: 77). There can be little doubt that the Eastern Sea or *prāk-samudra* cited in the copperplate could only have been the Bay of Bengal. This is further confirmed by Islam's study on coastline changes discussed earlier.

As following excerpt from the Dharmāditya's Faridpur Copperplate 1 reveals, Vārakamaṇḍala *viśaya* has more surprises to offer than being just a littoral region.

> The boundary indications [of the land granted] are stated as follows: On the east land, measuring a Pāṭaka, belonging to Himasena; On the south the village of Trighaṭṭikā and the land granted by the other copper-plate charter; On the west the locality of Śīlakunda, belonging to the village of Trighaṭṭikā, and on the north, the ship-building harbour *(nā-vatā-kṣeni)* and the Pāṭaka of land, belonging to Himasena (*ibid.*: 78).

The village of Trighaṭṭikā cited in the copperplate, as Sircar (1986: 366) observes, was possibly a locality having three *ghāṭs* (wharf or landing stages on a river). More interesting is the reference to *nā-vatā-kṣeni* or 'shipbuilding harbour', for it indeed establishes the existence of a shipbuilding technology in Vārakamaṇḍala *viśaya*.

These deductions, added to the fact that the district headquarter Candravarmakoṭa was situated near the sea, on the bank of a major outlet of the Gaṅgā, make it easy to believe that there existed a port at Candravarmakoṭa to facilitate connection with rest of the district as well as the kingdom. This appears to be almost a foregone conclusion given the fact that pre-modern communication in 'Bengal' was primarily riverine. We may further argue that the harbour at Candravarmakoṭa (which must have lain outside the fort, on the bank of the Ghāghar) was not only meant for inland communication but also served maritime activities because of its proximity to the sea. Otherwise, there would be no justification for a trade centre to develop so close to the sea, as the following examination reveals (Jahan 2003: 257).

If one carefully examines the epigraphic evidences it is not too difficult to find references to traders, administrative officers in charge of customs and monetised economy. The Faridpur Copperplate of Gopacandra mentions "principal traders" (*pradhāna-vyāpāriṇa*) (Mukherji and Maity 1967: 83-85) and the Ghugrāhāṭi Copperplate of Samācāradeva mentions "principal men of business" (*pradhāna-vyavahā(ri)ṇa)* (Pargiter 1911: 476, 485). These are strong indications that at the district headquarter of Vārakamaṇḍala, which we have identified with Candravarmakoṭa, there was a body of merchants who were influential and important enough to participate in local administration.

Faridpur Copperplate of Gopacandra names the viceroy Nāgadeva as simultaneously holding the post of the customs officer (*vyaparaṇda*) of Navyāvakāśikā (Mukherji and Maity 1967: 83-85). The Faridpur Copperplate 1 of Dharmāditya names the administrative officer Gopālasvamin as simultaneously in charge of customs (*viṣayadhiniyuktak vyaparakaraṇḍaya*) of Vārakamaṇḍala *viṣaya* under Navyāvakāśikā (*ibid.*: 79-81). That the state maintained the office of customs officer (*vyaparaṇda*), which high-ranking administrators held, implies that trade was of considerable importance to the state.

Numismatic and epigraphic evidences clearly show that the traders mentioned in the copperplates cited above used gold and silver coins as well as bullion (silver dust or *cūrṇī*) and cowries in their transactions. A detailed discussion of this will be taken up later in Chapter Three. For the purpose at hand, it may be sufficient to note that the Faridpur Copperplate of Dharmāditya, the Faridpur Copperplate of Gopacandra and the Mallasarul Copperplate of Vijayasena of the time of Gopacandra all refer to transaction of land with gold coins (*ibid.*: 77, 85, 93). From these indications, we may make two inferences: (1) that the economy at Vārakamaṇḍala was monetised and (2) that, as Kosambi (1970: 107) argues in a different context, "sale of land for cash ... implies rich trade in the neighbourhood". Gold coins of Candragupta II and Skandhagupta, which have been discovered in a field called Sonakanduri in the village of Guakhola (about three-quarters of a mile west of the south-west corner of the fort of Koṭālipāḍā; O'Malley 1925: 16), suggest that imperial Gupta gold and silver coins were in circulation in Dharmāditya and Gopacandra's kingdom. By the time of Samācāradeva, the state was issuing gold coins of its own because coins issued by the monarch have been recovered from a hoard in Muhammadpur in Jessore region (Bangladesh) (Mitra 1852: 401-402) and another from Hasnan in Huglī distict (West Bengal) (*Indian Archaeology – A Review* 1971-72: 72 & pl. LXVIII, nos. B-C). This may be accepted as an indication that by the time of Samācāradeva, the economy of his kingdom was stronger than before.

A large number of debased and crude imitations of Gupta gold coins have been found at Koṭālipāḍā, among which names of only two monarchs have been read with certainty. They are Prithuvira (Prithuva(ba)la) and Sudhanyāditya (Vāsuvarmana). Vāsuvarmana was possibly a ruler of of Sālastambha dynasty of Kāmrūpa. His coins have been found at Dhaka (including Savar), Bogra and Comilla (Mainamati, Salban Vihāra, Period III, cell 91) (Rashid 1975: 53). As for Prithuvira or Prithuva(ba)la, Mukherjee's (1993: 30) argument that he was a ruler of Samataṭa after Balabhaṭṭa is acceptable. Known find-spots of his coins (Koṭālipāḍā in Faridpur region and Pilak in South Tripura) and typological similarity with Balabhaṭṭa's coins justify his claim. Besides these imitation Gupta coins, those issued by Śaśāṅka (the ruler of Gauḍa from sometime before 606 AD till a little before 637-38) have been found on the bank of the river Arunkhali at Muhammadpur (now in Magura district, about 50 km northwest of Ghugrāhāṭi) (Mitra 1852: 402; Mukherjee 1993: 20).

All these post-Gupta and imitation-Gupta coins found in the kingdom of Gopacandra, Dharmāditya and Samācāradeva clearly indicate that the merchants of the kingdom conducted trade with neighbouring kingdoms. Discovery of Śaśāṅka's coins implies trade contact with Gauḍa in the first half of the 6th century AD, Vāsuvarmana's coins implies trade contact with Kāmrūpa in the second half of the 7th century AD while that of Prithuvira or Prithuva(ba)la's coins at the same place implies trade contact with Samataṭa in the early 8th century AD. It is noteworthy that a hoard containing coins of Candragupta II, Kumāragupta I, Skandhagupta, Śaśāṅka and Samācāradeva was found near Arunkhali River in Muhammadpur (Magura district). Another hoard containing coins of Samācāradeva was found at Hasnan in Huglī district. The Muhammadpur hoard definitely indicates the existence of a trade centre at the findspot since it was discovered near a river (which implies availability of riverine mode of communication) and since no coin in the hoard dated after Samācāradeva's coins (which implies that the hoard is from the time of Samācāradeva). Hence we may believe with enough justification that besides Koṭālipāḍā, there were other trade centres in the kingdom of Gopacandra and his successors.

We may sum up our findings by observing that the evidence of circulation of metallic currency, and the existence of traders and custom officials at Candravarmakoṭa clearly indicate that it functioned as an exchange centre in the 6th century AD. Furthermore, there is enough evidence to believe that there were more such trade centres in the kingdom of Gopacandra and his successors and that the traders of the kingdom maintained trade contact with neighbouring kingdoms of Gauḍa, Kāmrūpa and Samataṭa. These indications confirm our finding made earlier that Candravarmakoṭa was indeed a port. We may further believe that Gauḍa, Kāmrūpa and Samataṭa were part of the hinterland that the port of Candravarmakoṭa served.

The dominant but as-yet-unproven hypothesis that Candravarma (cited in the Susunia Rock Inscription and the Allahabad Praśasti) founded Candravarmakoṭa (the fort of Candravarma) is based on similarity of name. Actually it was Bhattasali (1925-26: 86) who initiated the hypothesis and argued, "the fortified settlement at Koṭālipāḍā may be approximately dated about 315 AD" by the same Candravarma of Susunia fame. Candravarma is identified in the Susunia Rock Inscription (4th century AD) as the "son of the illustrious Mahārājā Siṁhavarman, the lord of Puṣkaraṇā" (identified with Pokharaṇā on the bank of River Dāmodar in the district of Bankura, West Bengal) (Mukherji and Maity 1967: 41). Candravarma cited in the Allahabad Praśasti is one of a number of kings of Āryāvarta who were uprooted by Samudragupta (Raychaudhuri 1943: 30). At the present stage of our knowledge, we have no way to prove or disprove the hypothesis.

Nevertheless, because we have shown that there is all likelihood that Ptolemy's Tilogramon was indeed Koṭālipāḍā as Rashid (1991: 130) suggested, and then it follows that the port at Candravarmakoṭa must have existed in the 2nd century AD. There are at least two features that the port at Candravarmakoṭa has in common with the other two ports: (i) that it was an estuarine port and (ii) that a fort existed in its immediate vicinity. Having stated as much, we must concede nevertheless that these are tentative suggestions and we have to wait for results derived from excavations for an answer carrying greater certainty.

Clearly, the reason for the decline of Candravarmakoṭa is linked with the formation of swamps that lie in and around Koṭālipāḍā. Bhattasali (1925-26: 85) argued quite strongly that Candravarmakoṭa was abandoned as a "gubernatorial head-quarters ... about the 5th or the 6th year of the reign of Dharmāditya owing to an earthquake", but it continued to function as a district headquarters. He built his argument on the ground that the Ghugrāhāṭi plate granted almost the entire land in Vyaghracoraka, which is described in the copperplate as "full of pits and (..) infested with wild beasts" (*ibid.*: 79), to a Brāhmiṇ for no consideration. As the copperplate clearly shows, the land in Vyaghracoraka was bounded "on the west, [by] a corner of Chandravarman's fort" (*Ibid*). However, the numismatic evidences clearly show that mercantile activities must have continued at the site till the early 8th century AD. Hence we may tentatively propose, till further material evidence is discovered, that it fell into disuse shortly after, i.e., in the mid-8th century AD.

At the end of our deliberation, we must concede that the point that Bhattasali raised regarding Vyaghracoraka argues against the case that we have built: why at all should a flourishing commercial centre and a maritime port have a large tract of land quite near it which is of so little commercial value? To be quite honest, we have no answer to this question since we have so little information about habitation at the site.

It is also significant that the *Christian Topography* composed some years before the mid-6th century AD by Kosmas Indikopleustes, a much-travelled Alexandrian merchant who turned into a monk, lists the following as the most notable places of trade in South Asia during his time but in which there is no mention of Koṭālipāḍā (Candravarmakoṭa).

> Sindu, Orrhotha [a port possibly in Saurashtra], Calliana, Sibor [seaport, probably Chaul, 23 miles south of Bombay], and then the five marts of Male which export pepper: Parti, Mangarouth [Mangalor], Salopatana, Nalopatana, Poudopatana [the last three being situated somewhere between Mangalor and Calicut]. Then out in the ocean at the distance of about five days and nights from the continent, lies Sielediba, that is Taprobane [Ceylon]. And then again on the continent is Marallo, a mart exporting chank-shells, then Caber [Kaveripattam] which exports alabandēnum [unknown], and then farther away is the clove country, then Tzinista, which produces the silk (Book XI) (McCrindle 1897: 366-367).

Unless the clove country mentioned above is 'Bengal', which is extremely unlikely, Kosmas Indikopleustes testimony would imply that Koṭālipāḍā (Candravarmakoṭa) was possibly a port of lesser magnitude.

Notwithstanding Bhattasali's point regarding Vyaghracoraka "full of pits and (..) infested with wild beasts" and Kosmas Indikopleustes' silence regarding Candravarmakoṭa, we may still argue with equanimity that Candravarmakoṭa's claim to a maritime port stands its ground on the merit of numismatic, epigraphic and physiographic evidences. What is imperative now is to conduct an extensive exploration and a full-scale archaeological excavation at the site in order to eliminate the doubts regarding the existence of a port at Koṭālipāḍā.

SONĀRGĀON

Sonārgāon (23° 39' N and 90° 43' E) is today a small town situated about 27 kilometers to the southeast of Dhaka city, near the confluence of the Śītalakṣyā, the Dhaleśwarī, the Brahmaputra and the Meghnā. The name means "golden village". Numerous ruins spread over a vast stretch of land around the town clearly bear evidence that the site was the famed capital of medieval 'Bengal' known by the same name. The "very noble and plentiful" city of 'Cernomen' on the bank of the river 'Gangey' (Gaṅgā) that Nicolò de Conti (the Venetian nobleman who travelled and traded in southern Asia between 1419 and 1444 AD) speaks of may have been Sonārgāon as Mills believes (Mills in Ma-Huan 1970: 65). His travels as described by Ramusic in *Purchas His Pilgrims* is pitifully sketchy to draw a definite conclusion (Purchas 1906b: 396). Hence, for the earliest definitive evidence proving Sonārgāon as a maritime port we have to depend on the account of Ibn Battutā (1304-1368/69), which is based on his personal experience of his visit to eastern Bengal during the cold weather of 1346-47 (or, as Yule believes, during the cold weather of 1345-46) (Bhattasali 1922: 143-144). As Ibn Battutā describes,

> We travelled down the river [the Blue River or the Meghna] for fifteen days ... (Then) we reached the city of Sunurkāwān [Sonārgāon], where we found a junk on the point of sailing for the land of Jāwa (Sumatra), which is a journey of forty days from there, so we embarked on it (Gibb 1992: 271).

While there is no dispute about the administrative and maritime importance of Sonārgāon, what is unclear is the period during which the port was functional as well as its exact location. Unfortunately, no systematic archaeological excavation has been conducted at the site. Consequently, the state of current knowledge about Sonārgāon is dependent on literary, numismatic, epigraphic and architectural evidences. These, along with topographical features and drainage system of the site will be examined in order to arrive at a clear picture of the location and the period of operation of the port.

The stretch of land around the present town of Sonārgāon (henceforth mentioned as the Sonārgāon stretch) is bounded by the Meghnā in the east and the Śītalakṣyā in the west (Fig. 1.13). The Brahmaputra, flowing from the north to the south nearly parallel to the two rivers mentioned above, further bisects it near the middle. Thus, the stretch under review is divided into two unequal halves. A small rivulet called the Menikhālī issues from the Meghnā near Baidyer Bazar and flows in south-easterly direction to fall into the Brahmaputra near Kaikar Tek. A little south of this junction, a canal named Tribenī Khāl issues from the Brahmaputra and flows south-easterly direction to meet the Śītalakṣyā near the ruined Mughal fort of Sonākāndā. A little to the north of the

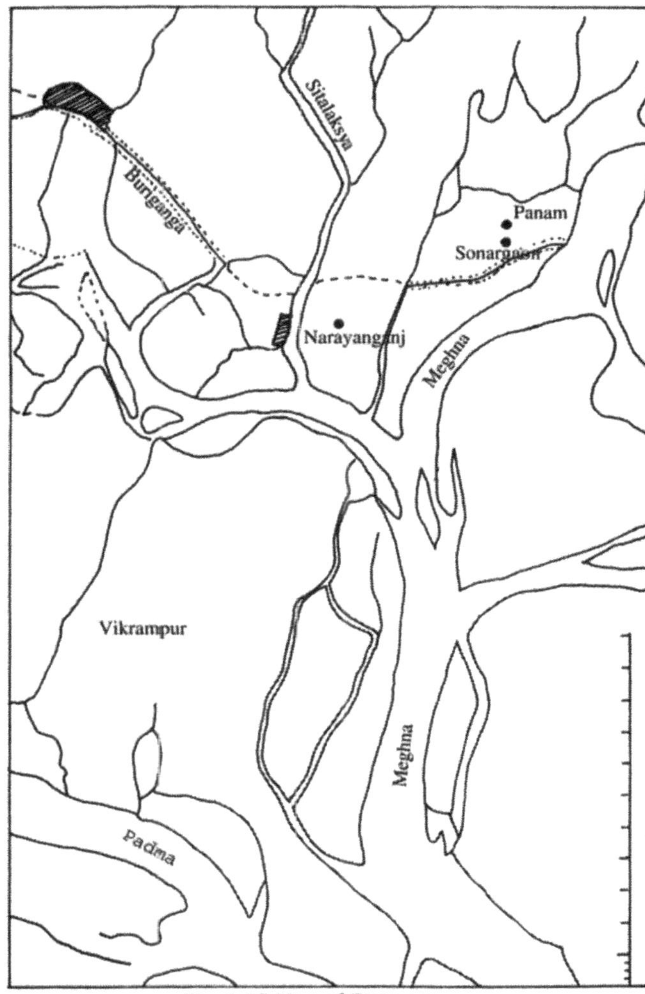

Fig. 1.13 Map of Sonargaon

Menikhālī Khāl is another rivulet, named Pankhirāj Khāl. It issues from the Meghnā River, flows first westward and then southwestward, to meet the Brahmaputra. The east-west rivulets, thus, divide the Sonārgāon stretch into five irregular quadrangles: two in the west of the Brahmaputra (which will be cited as the north-west and the south-west quadrangles) and three in the east of the same river (which will be cited as the north-east, the centre-east and the south-east quadrangles). The Śītalakṣyā and the Brahmaputra meet the Dhaleśwarī at the southern extremity of the stretch, and the latter (the Dhaleśwarī) flows into the Meghnā a little to the east. It becomes immediately apparent that the Sonārgāon stretch is extremely significant because of its location at the confluence of four major rivers of the Bengal delta. As will be seen later, the locational significance gave natural advantage to the site not only for trade but for administration as well.

Of the five quadrangles described above, the north-west, the south-west and the south-east quadrangles together form the Meghnā-Lakṣyā Doab. The north-east quadrangle is part of the Old Brahmaputra Floodplain. This part is low and marshy. It is inundated during the rainy season and is cultivated when the rainwater recedes in the winter. The centre-east quadrangle is highly concentrated with human habitation. It is one of the three isolated bits of the Pleistocene terrace of Madhupur Tract and hence is a much older formation. It may be recalled that the drainage pattern in this isolated bit is entrenched. Quite a few canals, which can still be seen traversing this quadrangle, may have arisen out of the natural drainage system.

The Menikhālī rivulet, which appears insignificant today, may not have been so in earlier times. James Wise (1874: 94) shows that the Menikhālī "was probably the course that [the Meghnā] took at some early date". If Wise's view is correct, then the Meghnā must have discharged into the Brahmaputra through this course of the Menikhālī. This, indeed, is confirmed by Alexander Cunningham (1969: 137), who, in his *Report of a Tour in Bihar and Bengal in 1879-80*, noted that the "old town of Sunārgaon is situated 2 miles to the north of an old branch of the Meghnā River, and three miles to the west of the present course of the stream. When the site was first selected, the Brahmaputra flowed three miles to the westward, between the Lakhia River and the present course of the Meghna". Cunningham's 'old branch of the Meghnā' must have been the Menikhālī because the land between it and the current course of the Meghnā (the south-east quadrangle) is part of the Meghnā-Lakṣyā Doab and hence a new formation that must have been created by aggradation and sedimentation of the Meghnā. Cunningham's observation further proves that the Brahmaputra bounded Sonārgāon on the west. This is a clear indication that the city of Sonārgāon was located in one of the three eastern quadrangles.

The physiographic features discussed above indicates that the site of the ancient city could not have been in the north-eastern quadrangle because it is a marsh land, nor in the south-eastern quadrangle because it is a new formation but in the centre-eastern quadrangle since it is an older formation and fit for human habitation (proved by high concentration of human habitation seen at present). This is further confirmed by the natives who resided at Sonārgāon in the second half of the 19th century. According to their verbal testimony, the village of Magrāpāḍā (in the centre-east quadrangle and on the northern bank of the Menikhālī) was the site of the ancient city (Wise 1874: 89). Hence it appears quite certain that the ancient city of Sonārgāon was situated on the northern bank of the Menikhālī (hence Ibn Battutā could arrive at the city by sailing down the Megh-nā) and was bounded on the west by the Brahmaputra. Indeed, architectural remains that still stand at the site confirm our deduc-tion.

Seven monuments that still stand in the Sonārgāon stretch date from the Sultanate period. These are (1) the Dewānbāgh Mosque (16th century AD) at Madanpur, (2) Bandar Shāhī Mosque (1482 AD) at Bandar, (3) Baba Salih's Mosque (1505 AD) at Bandar, (4) the Goyāldi Mosque (1519 AD) at Aminpur, (5) the tomb of Sultan Ghiyath al-Din A'zam Shah at Magrāpāḍā (early 15th century AD), (6) Fath Shah's Mosque (1484 AD) at Magrāpāḍā and (7) the Yusufganj Mosque (15th century AD) at Magrāpāḍā. Another monument, the Muāzzampur Shāhī Jami Mosque (1432/33-1435/36 AD) stands to the north of the stretch at the village of Mahjampur (the site of Muazzamābād, a mint-town of sultanate Bengal). Of the eight monuments mentioned above, four are situated in the centre-east quadrangle, thus marking it out as the area of greatest concentration of architectural remains from the sultanate period. The Khāshnagar Dīghi (large reservoir) at Panam, extending over an area of 9¾ acres, is also situated in this quadrangle. There can be little doubt that the large reservoir is the same that the *Ain-i-Akbari* noted as existing in the Sarkār of Sonārgāoṇ, in the township of *Kiyāra* (katārah) *Sundar*. The water of the reservoir had the ability to give "a

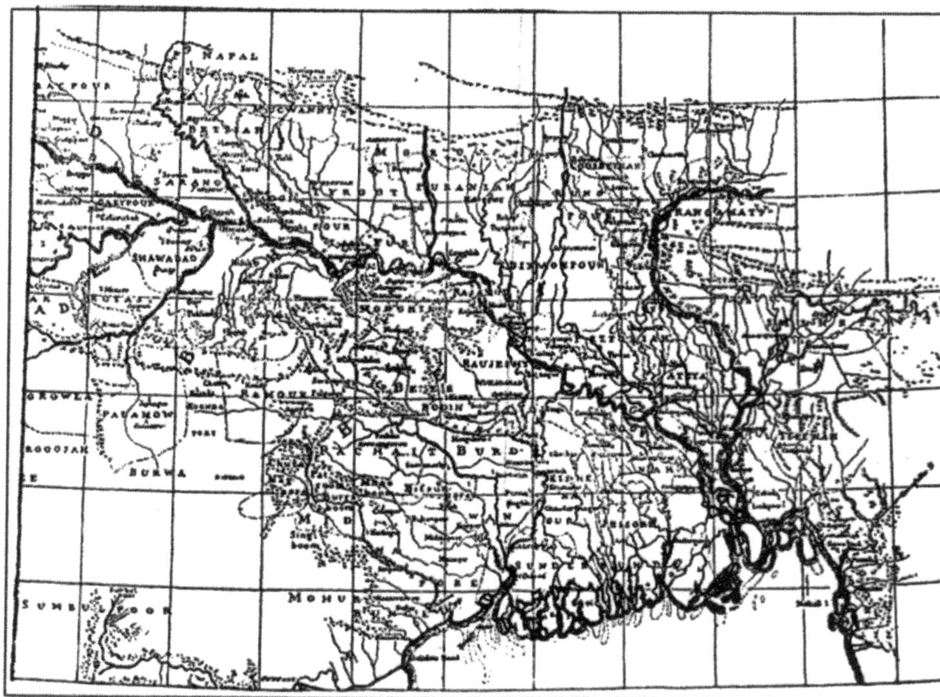

Fig. 1.14 Rennell's map of Bengal (1764-76) after Majumdar 1943

peculiar whiteness to the cloths that [were] washed in it" (Jarrett 1891: 124). The age of the Khāshnagar Dīghi is unknown. However, the fact that it is cited in the *Ain-i-Akbari* indicates that it existed in pre-Mughal times. Another important remain is the Damdama (i.e., fort or its bastion), situated on the bank of the Menikhālī rivulet. On physical inspection, it appears to be an elevated ground, circular in shape, surrounded by depressed land on three sides and the Menikhālī on the south. No trace of fortification exists today, although local residents claim that earthen ramparts enclosed the circular space. Cunningham (1969: 140) suggests that the *Damdama* was used as "a look-out tower". The period when the fort/tower was constructed is uncertain. However, one may believe that it dates from the Sultanate period because the architectural style of the Sonākāndā fort on the eastern bank of the Śītalakṣyā at Bandar (south-west quadrangle) that was reconstructed by Mughal governor Mir Jumla in the 17th century is significantly different.

According to Tarafdar (1999: 137), the harbour at Sonārgāon was situated in the south-west quadrangle, on the eastern bank of the Śītalakṣyā and was connected to the Meghnā by an artificial canal (the Tribenī Khāl). Aniruddha Ray (1999: 173) also locates the harbour near the same place, at Bandar. Although one may cite the existence of two monuments at Bandar (cited above) to confirm Ray and Tarafdar's view, it is more likely that the harbour was situated on the northern bank of the Menikhālī in the centre-east quadrangle. Ibn Battutā's testimony confirms our view for he appears to have arrived at Sonārgāon directly by the Meghnā and does not mention any artificial canal. Furthermore, the settlement pattern, physiographic features and concentration of sultanate monuments indicate that the centre-eastern quadrangle was the city. One would obviously expect that the harbour would be located at the same place as the city unless navigability of the river forced the harbour to be moved. It would also be logical to assume that the Brahmaputra was a deeper channel than the Śītalakṣyā since the Meghnā united with it and since the Śītalakṣyā was a distributary of the Brahmaputra. There can be no reason why ships would anchor at the bank of the Śītalakṣyā and the goods and the passengers would then be transported to the city through an artificial channel, unless the Brahmaputra ceased to be navigable by maritime ships.

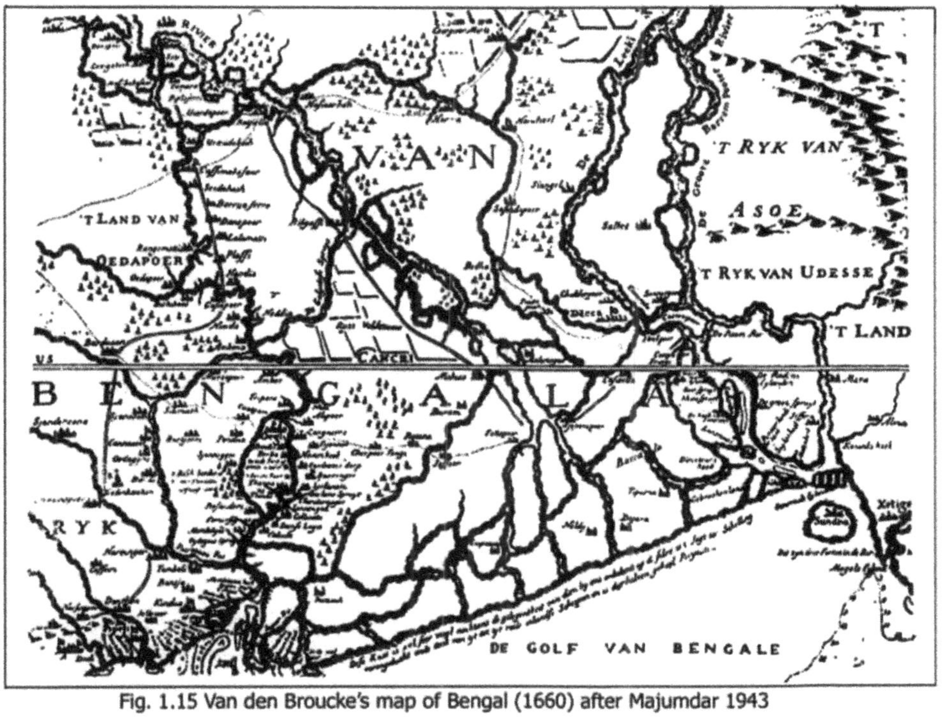

Fig. 1.15 Van den Broucke's map of Bengal (1660) after Majumdar 1943

The Brahmaputra ceased to be navigable when the river abandoned its course that flows past Sonārgāon and redirected its water along the course shown in Rennell's map of 1764-76 (Fig. 1.16), falling into the Meghnā near Bhairab Bazar. In Van den Broucke's map of 1660 (Fig. 1.17), we can see the Brahmaputra had already abandoned its old course that flowed to the west of Sonārgāon since it is shown uniting with the Meghnā (and still retaining the name of Brahmaputra). The Śītalakṣyā, shown in the map as the River Lecki, is marked out as a wide channel. The Menikhālī channel is shown connecting the Śītalakṣyā and the Brahmaputra (actually the Meghnā) and Sonārgāon is marked out on the northern bank of the Menikhālī. Still a century earlier, in the map of João de Barros of 1550, the Śītalakṣyā is not shown at all. Here too, the Brahmaputra is shown to have united with the Meghnā and the combined stream is shown to have united with the Gaṅgā (the Buḍigaṅgā stream that once flowed past Dhaka city). At the point of confluence is marked out Bander (literally, the "harbour"). Barros' Bander cannot be contemporary Bandar because it is marked to the west of the Brahmaputra-Meghnā, whereas the contemporary Bandar stands on the east bank of the Śītalakṣyā. The Bander in de Barros' map can only be the harbour of Sonārgāon. The Menikhālī is absent in this map. We have no map to show the courses of the rivers in earlier centuries but can only refer back to the topographical features discussed earlier to believe that prior to 1550, the Brahmaputra flowed past the western end of Sonārgāon and was joined by the Meghnā through the Menikhālī.

It appears quite certain that the Brahmaputra had already changed its course by the mid-15th century AD. When Fei Sin visited the sultanate of 'Bengal' in the early 15th century AD (1411-1414), he speaks of only one port at Ch'a-ti-kiang (Caṭṭagrāma) (Bagchi 1945: 120). We hear of Sonārgāon also from Ma-Huan, whose account, as narrated in *Ying-yai sheng-lan* (1451) is based on first hand information that he gathered during his visit to Pang-ko-la (Vaṅgala, or sultanate Bengal). He was attached as an official translator to the fourth, the sixth and the seventh Chinese naval expeditions carried out under the command of Grand Eunuch Cheng Ho. In the seventh expedition carried out in 1431-33, Ma-Huan sailed in a detached fleet to 'Bengal'. On this occasion, he reached 'Bengal' in the first half of 1432 (Mills in Ma-Huan 1970: 35). Ma-Huan (*ibid.*: 159-160) clearly says that one had to change to a small ship at Caṭṭagrāma to reach Sonārgāon. He disembarked from the small ship at Sonārgāon and then journeyed to the capital. The draught of the junks by which Ma-Huan and the Chinese delegation arrived at Caṭṭagrāma was at least twenty feet (Mills in *ibid.*: 31). It must have been much too large for the combined stream of the Gaṅgā and the Brahmaputra that discharged into the Bay of Bengal and hence they had to re-embark on a smaller vessel. Thus it appears that by the mid-15th century AD, only smaller ships used to ply to Sonārgāon. In 1586, Ralph Fitch also appears to have had sailed for Pegu in a small ship or foist, not from Sonārgāon but from Serrepore (Śrīpur near Rājābāḍi), situated six leagues from Sonārgāon, at the confluence of the Meghnā and the Padmā (Foster 1968: 28). Wise (1874: 87) is more specific about the location of Śrīpur for he says it was "nearly fifteen miles south-west of Sonārgāon". Furthermore, Fitch describes Sonārgāon not as a port but an important mart. Even Tome Pires, the Writer and Accountant of the Portuguese factory in Malacca who completed writing his *Suma Oriental* between 1512-1515 AD, does not mention Sonārgāon. These references indicate that Sonārgāon completely ceased to be a maritime port sometime between the mid-15th and early 16th century AD. We may tentatively fix the date to the second half of the 15th century AD.

Having thus ascertained the date of Sonārgāon's demise, we may now investigate into its rise. Raychaudhuri (1943a: 33) believes it was in or after the 13th century AD when one comes across the name of Sonārgāon for the first time in *Tarikh-i-Firozshāhī* by Zia-ud-Din Barnī. While describing Sultan Ghiyath al-Din Balban's military expedition in 'Bengal' to punish his rebellious governor Mughisuddin Tughral (1268-1281 AD) who had declared independence, Barnī describes Balban entering into an agreement with Rai Danuj of Sunārganw (Sonārgāon). In c. 1280 AD, "Balban marched with all speed, and in a few days arrived at Sunārganw. The Rāī of that place, by name Danūj Rāī, met the Sultān, and an agreement was made with him that he should guard against the escape of Tughril by water" (Barnī 1871: 116). It is generally accepted that Rai Danuj cited above was Daśarathadeva (Arirāja Danujmādhava), a powerful monarch whose kingdom extended over eastern Bengal. From five copperplate landgrants issued by Daśarathadeva and his father Dāmodaradeva, Sircar (1982: 141-142) has shown that they belong to the Deva dynasty, originally feudatory rulers under the Senas in south-eastern Bengal. Daśarathadeva (c. 1255-1290) appears to have inherited his father's kingdom in Comilla, Noakhali and Caṭṭagrāma and assumed the title of a sovereign monarch. From the Ādāvāḍī copperplate that he issued from Vikrampura in 1283 AD (Majumdar 1929: 181-82) it becomes clear that he had swept the Senas from power since Vikrampura is known to have been the Sena capital after Bakhtiyar Khalji's conquest of north Bengal. Although Raychaudhuri (1943a: 33) inferred from Barani's reference to the meeting of Danuj Ray and Balban that Daśarathadeva had transferred his capital from Vikrampura to Suvarṇagrāma (Sonārgāon) sometime before 1280 AD, Qanungo (1948b: 64) has rightly pointed out that the meeting took place at the frontier of Sonārgāon and not in Sonārgāon. The Ādāvāḍī copperplate clearly shows Vikrampura was very much in existence in 1283. We have no other evidence to show why, if at all, the capital was shifted to Sonārgāon. Be that as it may, it seems highly unlikely that a maritime port would have existed at Sonārgāon simply because one does not come across any indicator substantiating maritime trade.

It is uncertain as to when exactly the Muslims conquered Sonārgāon. Nevertheless, we can easily see the dramatic rise in the fortune of the city from the early 14th century AD. In 1301, Shams al-Din Firuz Shah (1301-1322) established his independent dynasty and issued coins from Sonārgāon, the earliest of which dates from 1305. This may be taken as a clear indicator that the city was becoming economically and commercially significant. Shams al-Din Firuz Shah's son Ghiyath al-Din Bahadur Shah minted gold and silver coins from Sonārgāon. In one such coin minted in 1328, the city is styled Hazrat Sonārgāon, which indicates further rise of its importance. During the reign of Fakhr al-Din Mubarak Shah and his dynasty (1338-1352), the status of Sonārgāon was further elevated because it became the capital of an independent sultanate in eastern Bengal. Hence, there can be no doubt regarding administrative importance of the city in the 1330s. It was a little after this time that Ibn Battutā visited Sonārgāon. The impression that one derives from his account (Gibb 1992: 267; Bhattasali 1922: 135-136) is that its exchange centre offered a variety of commodities, specially rice and cotton cloth, at a very competitive price and that silver as well as gold coins were in circulation. Since Sonārgāon was already a maritime port in 1340s when Ibn Battutā visited, and since coins began to be issued from here from 1305, one may confidently suggest that the city established contact with international maritime trade network in the early 14th century AD.

As already established, the location of the harbour on the north bank of the Menikhālī (Meghnā) clearly shows Sonārgāon was an estuarine port. Ibn Battutā's testimony appears to indicate that in the 14th century AD, large ships with considerable draught could anchor on the bank of the Menikhālī (Meghnā). As Fei Sin and Ma-Huan's testimonies indicate, the port could handle only ships with shallow draught from the early 15th century AD. Ibn Battutā's testimony establishes that the port facilitated transportation of passengers. Although Nicolò de Conti's testimony is sketchy, it too suggests transportation of passengers and connection with the port of Caṭṭagrāma. Silver and gold coins minted at the city indicate the trade was monetary based. The port must have fetched considerable revenue for the state exchequer because even in the late 16th century AD, when the port had significantly declined, it fetched 82,632 *dām* (copper coin) (Jarrett 1891: 138).

The Khāshnagar Dīghi indicates that there was a production centre of cotton textiles in Sonārgāon. As noted above, Ibn Battutā's testimony indicates the city was also a significant exchange centre. In the early 15th century AD, Fei Sin found bazars "which carries on a business in all kinds of goods" (Bagchi 1945: 121). The same is confirmed by two other Chinese literary sources, *Si yang ch'ao kung tien lu* by Huang Sing-ts'eng (1520) and *Shu yu chou tseu lu* (1574) (*ibid.*: 123, 130). Ralph Fitch's account adds a few more details.

> The houses here, as they be in the most part of India, are very little, and covered with strawe, and have a fewe mats round the walls, and the doors to keepe out the tygers and the foxes. Many of the people are very rich (Foster 1968: 28).

Of course Fitch's testimony is well beyond our time frame. Nevertheless, if we are prepared to see that he is speaking of a time when the glory of Sonārgāon was already a matter of the past and make due consideration for the time of its glory, we may add quite a few brick-built structures and paved streets to the picture. The architectural monuments that still stand on the site will surely vouchsafe in favour of our conjecture. Till detailed excavation is carried out at the site, we have to remain satisfied with this conjectural image of the port of Sonārgāon.

SĀTGĀON

About four miles to the north-west of the town of Huglī, on the left bank of the Saraswatī is situated the village of Sātgāon (22° 58′ 20″ latitude and 88° 25′ 10″ longitude). The Portuguese called it *Porto Pequeno* (literally, the "Small Port"), in contradistinction to Caṭṭagrāma, which they called *Porto Grande* (the "Great Port") (Campos 1919: 21). Wilford 1799: 278) describes it as 'Ganges Regia', while Maulavi Abdus Salam, the translator of *Riyazu-s-Salātīn* (1786-88), as the site of "the ancient royal port ... of Bengal" (Salim 1904: 29n). Although Abdus Salam locates the site of the port "at the point of junction of the Hūghlī and the holy Saraswātī" (*ibid.*) and Campos (1919: 21-22), "on the river Saraswatī, which branches off from the Hooghly below Tribeni", Niharranjan Ray (1994: 247) is more correct in locating it "beside the Saraswatī, two miles from Tribenī and very close to the confluence with the Bhāgīrathī". This location is clearly marked out in João de Barros' map of 1550, which shows 'Satigam' on the north bank of the Saraswatī, a little to the west of its confluence with the Bhāgīrathī and the Yamunā. The port was also known as Saptagrāma, the name having derived from seven villages which were consecrated to seven sages (Hunter 1876a: 309). Testimonies provided by Tome Pires (early 16th century AD), Cesare Federici (1567 AD), Ralph Fitch (1586 AD) and quite a few literary works from the end of the 15th century AD leave no doubt or disagreement that the village of Sātgāon and its vicinity was indeed the site of the famous medieval port. What need to be confirmed, though, are the time of the rise and the fall of the port and an assessment of the physical and socio-economic environment of the port-site.

The early history of Saptagrāma is uncertain. Nevertheless, there have been a few attempts to prove that it functioned as a maritime port since the early historic period. "From ancient times", said Campos (1919: 21), "the chief port and emporium of trade on the Western side of Bengal, was Sātgāon, ...". Echoing similar views, Rev. James Long states that "Sātgāon [was] the royal emporium of Bengal from the time of Pliny down to the arrival of the Portuguese" (Hunter 1876a: 309). Citing Pliny and Ptolemy, he attempts to show that "Tribeni was formerly noted for its trade" (*ibid.*: 311). Unfortunately Pliny makes no mention either of Saptagrāma or Tribenī. Ptolemy mentions Tribenī, but only as a sacred place from where three rivers part in three directions (Śāstrī 1927: 99, 101). Early medieval accounts of Persian and Arab travellers, geographers and merchants are also silent regarding Sātgāon/Saptagrāma. Although Long's argument does not appear to stand ground, there may be a grain of truth in his assertion.

A small-scale excavation conducted at Saptagrāma on the bank of the river Saraswatī revealed punch-marked and cast copper coins, few sherds of the Northern Black Polished Ware, terracottas, Rouletted ware, black ware, medieval pottery and architectural members detached from Brāhmaṇical shrines (*Indian Archaeology – A Review* 1961-62: 59; Ray 1998: 30). Remains of ships have reportedly been found on the southern bank of the Saraswatī near Ādi Saptagrāma (old Triś-bighā) railway station (Ray 1999: 156). Unfortunately, no detail on ship-fragments is available. Nevertheless, the remaining archaeological materials prove beyond doubt human settlement existed here in the early historic period. Since it was situated on the bank of a major outlet of the Gaṅgā, one may logically assume that in the early historic period, Saptagrāma was a riverine port. The architectural members detached from Brāhmaṇical shrines and numerous stone images from the Pāla-Sena period reportedly found at Sātgāon (*ibid.*: 153) are indicators that the site was a religious centre in the early medieval period. The same is true of neighbouring Tribenī, as vouchsafed by "clear traces of mutilated Hindu idols" seen on the walls of the mosque of Zafar Khan at Tribenī (Blochmann 1870: 282). However, all these material evidences dating from pre-Muslim conquest attests that Saptagrāma and Tribenī's primary importance in the early medieval period was more in religious matters than in trade and commerce. Sātgāon may have been "Saptagrama that figures so prominently in the ancient Puranas" (Campos 1919: 22), but the maritime port of Sātgāon emerged after Muslim conquest as architectural remains, numismatic and literary evidences amply testify.

Sātgāon came under Muslim rule for the first time in 1298 AD when Zafar Khan conquered it. However, it was not until 1313, during the reign of Sultan Firuz Shah (1301-22 AD), that the Muslims succeeded in conquering the entire region around Sātgāon (Rahim *et al.* 1981: 208). During the reign of Ghiyath al-Din Tughlaq (1320-1325 AD), 'Bengal' was divided into three administrative units and Sātgāon was made the centre of one of these (the other two being Sonārgāon and Lakhnauti) (*ibid.*: 212). Sātgāon is mentioned for the first time in Muslim historical accounts in the *Tārikh-i-Fīroz Shāhī* of Ziāu-d dīn Barnī (mid-14th century AD) who notes that "Sultan Muhammad bin Tughlik (sic.) Shāh (1325-1350 AD) ascended the throne at Tughlikābād in the year 725 H (1325 AD) [and] "brought the people of many countries under his rule in Hindustān" including Sat-gānw, Lakhnauti and Sunār-gānw (Barnī 1871: 235-236). Barnī's note clearly indicates that by 1325, Sātgāon had become as important as Lakhnauti and Sonārgāon.

It is believed that Sātgāon began to serve as a mint-town from the period of Sultan Ghiyath al-Din Tughlaq's reign, although no coin issued by him has yet been found. The earliest existing specimen minted at this town is dated 1329 and the last in 1552 (Ray 1999: 153). The earliest gold coin minted from Sātgāon was in 734 AH (1333-34 AD) when Muhammad bin Tughlaq struck one in his name. "*'Arṣah* Sātgāon" inscribed on his coins (Tarafdar 1999: 121) indicate that the administrative unit of Sātgāon was known as an *'arṣah* (equivalent to *zilla* or district of later times as Karim 1987: 413 shows). These are clear signs that the city was becoming economically and commercially significant in the 1320s and the 1330s. In the early 16th century AD, Tome Pires (1967: 91) describes Sātgāon as "a good port" with a "good entrance". Since deterioration in navigability due to siltation may have occured in later times, we can confidently believe that the Saraswatī was navigable by maritime vessels in the 15th century AD and earlier.

Since (1) archaeological evidences suggest that Sātgāon has been serving as a riverine port from the early historic period, (2) the drainage system of the site was favourable for navigation by maritime vessels in the 15th century AD and earlier, (3) it became an important administrative centre in 1324 AD and (4) coins began to be issued from here from 1329 AD, one may confidently suggest that the city established contact with international maritime trade networks in the second quarter of the 14th century AD. Our conclusion pushes Niharranjan Ray's opinion forward by about half a century. Without explaining the reasons, Ray (1994: 247) concluded that Sātgāon grew up as a large port-city "[s]omewhere in the second half of the thirteenth century". Clearly, this is erroneous because of our argument cited above.

The most prosperous period for Sātgāon as a port may have been between the mid-15th and early 16th century AD. One of the reasons, as Ray (1999: 154-155) argues, was the struggle over the port of Caṭṭagrāma between the sultanate of 'Bengal', the kingdom of Tripura and the kingdom of Arakan. The demise of Sātgāon began in the latter part of the 16th century AD, because of silting of the River Saraswatī. "The great stream of the Ganges, which formerly flowed southwards from Sātgāon by way of the Saraswatī, gradually deserted this channel and diverted its water into the Huglī, then a comparatively small river" (Hunter 1876a: 308). While there is unanimity among scholars that the decay of the port was primarily due to silting of the Saraswatī (Ray 1999: 157; Salim 1904: 29; Tarafdar 1999: 137), there exists disagreement as to when it ceased to function completely.

The port was still functioning in 1567 when the Venetian merchant Caesar Frederick arrived at Sātgāon. However, it was already declining for he describes a place called Buttor, where one had to change to a smaller ship.

> A good Tide's rowing before you come to Satagan [Sātgāon], you shall have a place which is called Buttor, and from thence upwards the Ships doe not goe, because that upwards the River is very Shallow, and little water. ... The small Ships goe to Satagan and there they lade (Purchas 1905b: 113-114).

That the river was choking Sātgāon is further confirmed by João de Barros, who writes in the mid-16th century AD "Sātgāon is a great and noble city, though less frequented than Caṭṭagrāma, on account of the port not being so convenient for the entrance and departure of ships". (Hunter 1876a: 309)

Ralph Fitch, who arrived in Sātgāon (Satagam) in 1586, refers to it not as a port but "a faire citie for a citie of the Moores, and very plentiful of all things" (Foster 1968: 26). By that time Huglī was already on the rise as a port for, according to Fitch's description, it had become the Porto Piqueno of the Portuguese and "the place where the Portugals keep in the country of Bengala" (*ibid.*: 25). On the other hand, the English trader Peter Mundy, writing from

Patna sometime between 1628 and 1634, names six "Ports on the Sea Coast neerest unto Puttana as [he] was informed of by Merchants, etts. in Puttana ..." (Temple 1914: 152). Three of these were in Orissa while the remaining three (Sātgāon, Śrīpur and Caṭṭagrāma) were in 'Bengal'. What he says of Sātgāon clearly shows that ships were being anchored at three harbours, viz. "Hooglee [Huglī], Heegeele [Hijilī in Medinīpur district] and Sategame [Sātgāon]". While Mundy's account affirms the existence of the port between 1628 and 1634, it also indicates gradual shifting towards Huglī had already begun. When Manucci arrived in 'Bengal' in 1663, he visited Huglī, resided there for two months, nearly got married, but made no mention of Sātgāon (Manucci 1907, II: 89-95). Evidently, the port had passed into oblivion by then.

Evidently, Sātgāon was overtaken by Huglī. Or rather, on the ashes of the former, arose the latter. In order to ascertain the exact year when Sātgāon was abandoned, it may be helpful to turn to Charles Joseph, who describes the following in a paper written in 1841.

> Hooghly owed its celebrity to the Portuguese, before whose time it was probably an inconsiderable village. They are stated to have established a factory and built a fort there in 1599; ... The Portuguese settlement appears to have risen rapidly to great magnificence. In 1631, it was besieged by the whole of the Mogul army of Bengal, ... It appears that at the time [when it fell in 1632], there were no fewer than sixty-four large vessels, fifty-seven grabs, and two hundred sloops anchored off the town ... (Joseph 1881: 792).

Hunter (1876a: 310) adds that Huglī was made a royal port of the Mughals in the same year (i.e., 1632); concurrently, they withdrew all public officers from Sātgāon. Thus, with Huglī enjoying royal patronage, Sātgāon must have lost significance as a port immediately or shortly after 1632.

Having ascertained the rise and the fall of Sātgāon, let us now attempt an assessment of the physical and socio-economic environment of the port-site. A total of seven stone inscriptions have been found at Sātgāon, dating from the reign of Rukn al-Din Barbak Shah (1459-1474 AD) to Ala al-Din Husain Shah (1493-1519 AD). These indicate that brick-built structures began appearing at the site from the mid-15th century AD. One of the stone inscriptions dated 1505 AD shows that Sultan Ala al-Din Husain Shah had constructed a bridge to facilitate communication between Sātgāon and Tribenī (Ray 1999: 155). We may thus surmise that the peak of prosperity of the port-city was reached between the mid-15th and the first quarter of the 16th century AD. In the second half of the 19th century, Blochmann (1870: 280) found only a ruined brick-built mosque (constructed sometime before 1529-30 AD) with a few tombs near it as the only remnant of the medieval port and administrative centre. He also noted that the ground between the village (Sātgāon), the highway adjacent it (the Grand Trunk Road) and the Saraswatī to be "very uneven, and looks as if it had been the site of an extensive settlement. At one place, not far from the road, the capital of a large pillar emerges from the ground" (*ibid.*: 281). In the 1870s, "foundations of a fort built by the Musalmāns [were] still visible near the Sātgāon bridge" (Hunter 1876a: 310). These architectural remains clearly indicate that the port city was spread over a large area and was connected with Tribenī. Although the function of all the structures remains unclear, we can definitely say that there were quite a few of them including a mosque, a fort and a bridge. The image thus obtained is affirmed by *Riyazu-s-Salātīn,* because it says "Sātgāon was a large city, thickly populated, and was the seat of a Governor" (Salim 1904: 29).

European accounts, beginning with Varthema in the early 16th century AD, are nearly silent about the physical aspects of the port. Nevertheless, the map of João de Barros clearly shows that Sātgāon was an estuarine port and the harbour was located on the south bank of the Saraswatī. What possibly existed was a typical temporary landing site similar to the other ports discussed above. Caesar Frederick's testimony indicates that the port could handle only ships with shallow draught from around the mid-16th century AD. However, Tome Pires' testimony shows that even in the early 16th century AD, it was very much capable of handling ships with considerable draught. As Campos (1919: 22) observed, "[t]he main current of the Hooghly till the middle of the sixteenth century streamed through the Saraswati; hence the importance of Sātgāon which was more accessible to larger ships".

We may believe that storage facilities at the port was similar to what Manrique (1927: 27) describes as existing at Huglī "at the time that the Emperor Acabar was at the head of the Mogol Monarchy", i.e., 1556-1605 AD.

> Portuguese traders who came from various parts of India with their vessels laden not only to sell the goods they brought, but also to buy and ship the products of that country. With this object they loaded their merchandise and had large golās or store-houses erected, which were divided into chambers by screens made of a kind of strong cane, ... called by the natives bambus. In these, which they thatched with straw, they kept their goods and wintered [i.e., weathered the rainy season] five or six months, until the return of the season favourable for the homeward voyage (*ibid.*).

The evidence cited is well beyond the time frame of this research. However, we may very well argue that the Portuguese merchants of the second half of the 16th century AD did not introduce a new practice. Rather, it is possible that they actually followed local practice since what Manrique describes is clearly reminiscent of Caesar Frederick's description of the temporary exchange centre at Buttor with "Houses and Shops made of straw" (Purchas 1905b: 113-114).

Silver and gold coins minted at Sātgāon indicate the trade was monetary based. Caesar Frederick's account of the port shows that it handled "thirtie or five and thirtie ships great and small" each year. If this is what the port handled at a time of its decline, we may presume a higher number when the port was at the peak of its glory in the mid-15th century. Frederick's account also shows that the port facilitated transportation of pasengers as well as goods. The port must have fetched considerable revenue for the state exchequer because even in the late 16th century AD, as testified by Abu'l-fazl 'Allami's *Ā'īn-i Akbarī* (1595-96), it fetched 12,00,000 *dāms* or 30,000 Rupees as revenue (Jarrett 1891: 141). Considering that the port was past its prime during the reign of Emperor Akbar, one can safely assume that it must have fetched substantial sum of money for the state when Sātgāon was at its prime – and hence it must have had dealt in considerable volume of merchandise.

None of the travel accounts or Bengali literary works indicate that there was any major production centre at Sātgāon that produced exportable commodities. We only hear of the production centre from *Riyazu-s-Salātīn,* which speaks of "factories of the Christian Portuguese, and other traders" (Salim 1904: 29). However, this testimony must be taken to indicate the condition after 1536 when the sultan of 'Bengal', Ghiyath al-Din Mahmud Shah (1532-38), granted permission to the Portuguese to build factories in Sātgāon and Caṭṭagrāma and also to collect excise duties from ships visiting these ports. As Campos (1919: 113) observed, "Sātgāon was the emporium of Portuguese trade since 1537. It was then the chief mart where all the merchants of Northern India flocked with their merchandise". But that part of the story of Sātgāon is beyond the time frame of this research.

Quite a few literary works composed by Bengali poets indicate that Sātgāon was a major exchange centre where affluent merchants resided. Important among these is the maṅgalakāvya, the generic name for verse narratives eulogising various deities (such as Manasā, Caṇḍī, Dharma, Śitalā etc.) composed by numerous poets of 'Bengal' (such as Bijaygupta, Baṁśīdāsa, Nārāyaṇa Deva, Bipradās, Ketakadāsa, Kṣemānanda and Kavikañkaṇa Mukunda) from the 13th to the 18th centuries AD. Some of these are still performed in rural areas of Bangladesh and West Bengal. The maṅgalakāvyas, which are of interest for this study, are the *Manasāmaṅgala* (written in praise of goddess Manasā, also known as the *Padma Purāṇa* and the *Manasā Vijaya*) and the *Caṇḍīmaṅgala* (written in praise of goddess Caṇḍī), parts of which describe sea-voyages by merchants C̃ād (in *Manasāmaṅgala*), Dhanapati and Śrīmanta (in *Caṇḍī-maṅgala).* However, while examining these narratives, it is important to remember that the descriptions are coloured by fanciful exaggerations. "It is highly probable that these literary works actually contain the animated descriptions of the commercial and maritime activities of Bengali people of the pre-Muslim period", however, and this is more important, "the poets dealing with the subjects belonged to a later age" (Dasgupta 1935: 13-40). Hence information derived from these narratives needs considerable screening.

In the *Caṇḍīmaṅgala* by Kavikañkaṇa Mukunda (composed in 1555-56 AD) describes two trading voyages – one by merchant Dhanapati Datta and the other by his son Śrīmanta. During their voyages, both Dhanapati and Śrīmanta halt at Saptagrāma for two days and trade (Mukunda 1986: 201, 238). Commenting on the port, the poet says, merchants from Kaliṅga, Telaṅga, Aṅga, Baṅga, Karnāṭa, Magadha, Mahārashṭra, Gujarāt, Bārendra Port, Vindhya, Piñgala, Utkala, Drāviḍa, Rāḍhā, Vijayānagara, Mathurā, Dvārikā, Kāñcīpura, Prarāga, Godāvarī, Gayā, K̃oca, Śrīhaṭṭa, Laṅka, Malayā country, Baṭeśwar and many other towns and kingdoms gathered for trading, in their junks (*jaṅga diṅgā*) laden with goods. The merchants of Saptagrāma, as a result, do not have to go anywhere and could live luxuriously at home (*ibid.*: 237-38).

Vipradāsa Pipilāi in his *Manasā Vijaya* (composed in 1494 AD) describes rows of houses displaying flags. These appear to be abodes of Hindus because images of various deities are enshrined in these and sounds associated with Hindu rituals are described to be issuing from these. The poet also speaks of numerous Muslims – Mughal, Pathans and others (Sen 1953: 143). Since some of the passages in the *Manasā Vijaya* describing Saptagrāma are later interpolations (reference to the Mughals, for example), we may turn to Bāsudev Ghosa, a contemporary of Caitanya (1486-1533), for greater accuracy.

In his *Kaḍcā*, the poet describes people of almost all occupational groups including *kavirāj*, weaver, barber, *byāpārī* (a small-scale trader or a peddler), *byābasāyī* (a trader) and *baṇik* (a merchant). Among the merchants, the poet describes the *gandhavaṇik* or the spice merchants, the *śaṅkhavaṇik* or the dealers in conch-shells and the *suvarṇavaṇik* or the gold merchants (Ray 1999: 156). Bṛndābana Dāsa's *Śrīśrīcaitanya Bhāgabata* (Antya, Chapter 5; 440: 380-381), composed in c. 1537-38, does not refer to Saptagrāma as a port but his description gives the impression of a mercantile centre inhabited by numerous Hindu merchants (*baṇik*) and even a few Muslims (*yavanas*). Vipradāsa Pipilāi in his *Manasā Vijaya* indicates that Saptagrāma was a port and was inhabited by very affluent people. However, he does not refer to them specifically as merchants (Sen 1953: 142-143). Jayānanda's *Caitanya-maṅgala* (1971: 231), composed in c. 1550-1560 AD, makes a brief reference to Saptagrāma but indicates that the merchants (*baṇik*) were Hindus and were very affluent.

The essential aspects of the image of Sātgāon thus evoked by the Bengali poets are confirmed by European accounts. In the early 16th century AD, we find Tome Pires (1967: 91) describing Sātgāon as "a very good city and rich, where there are many merchants". Le Bleau, who visited Sātgāon in 1575, must have been struck by its temples and markets with inexpensive goods because he hardly speaks of anything else (Ray 1999: 156). However, with all its temples, we must not forget the merchants and their maritime trade because it must have been their wealth that supported all these temples.

CAṬṬAGRĀMA

Among all the ports discussed in this study, Caṭṭagrāma (22° 20' N and 91° 50' E) is the only one that still survives ravages of time. It is situated on the north bank of the river Karṇafulī, about 17 kilometres upstream from the mouth of the river. There is very little disagreement that the current site of the port is the same referred by Ibn Battutā, Ibn Mājid, Ma-Huan, Fei Sin, Caesar Frederick, Ralph Fitch, Niccolao Manucci, Francois Bernier, Sebastien Manrique and others. The Arab-Persian traders and travelers have called the port Samandar, Sudkawan and Shātījām, the Europeans have called it Chatigan (and Chatganw), the Chinese, Che-ti-chiang (or Ch'a-ti-kiang), while the local Muslim rulers named it Islāmābād (and Fatehābād). In 1550, João de Barros clearly marked the port as Chatigam (Caṭṭagrāma) on his map and in 1660 van den Broucke marked it as Xetiga.

Although the history of the port can be traced back from the time of Ibn Battutā, what seems to be uncertain is when the port was established. No systematic archaeological excavation has been conducted at Caṭṭagrāma, which functions today as the prime maritime gateway for Bangladesh. Another problem is that Caṭṭagrāma is not mentioned by any of its known names in classical Sanskrit literature of early period. Hence we have to depend on all the travellers, traders, diplomats and missionaries cited above, along with few more, who have left literary accounts of the port. These, together with epigraphic and numismatic evidences and information derived from ancient and medieval geographical treatises may be pieced together to ascertain when the port of Caṭṭagrāma was established.

One may begin with Ptolemy's Pentapolis (150° & 18°) (*Geography*, Book VII, Caption 2: 2), because it is the earliest location of the port so far attempted by scholars such as Wilford (1822: 444-45) and Śāstrī (1927: 195). Pentapolis lay in Airrhadoi, which was the entire stretch of land "from the mouth of the Brahmaputra to that of Nāf or even lower to Arakan River" (Gerini 1909: 28). The argument put forward in favour of the identification was that 'Pentapolis' denotes an aggregate of five cities while 'Caṭṭagrāma' in Bengali is believed to be a derivative of the Sanskrit 'Caturgrāma', which denotes an aggregate of four villages. Hence it is argued that Caṭṭagrāma was known as Caturgrāma in the 2nd century AD and Ptolemy must have translated it as Pentapolis.

The position Gerini (*ibid.*: 35) obtained for Pentapolis by calculation "falls a short distance below the Caṭṭagrāma inlet". But after allowing corrections for minor inaccuracies on Ptolemy's part, he locates the city "a little further up above the Caṭṭagrāma inlet, either on the coast or on some of the islands at the embouchure of Old Brahmaputra". Gerini dismisses the identification of Caṭṭagrāma with Pentapolis on the ground that 'Caṭṭagrāma' as 'the aggregate of four villages' is too far removed etymologically and phonetically from 'Pentapolis' as 'the aggregate of five cities'. Nevertheless, it is very probable, as Gerini shows, that there existed a sea port or mart known as Pentapolis to Ptolemy and his contemporaries, somewhere on the coast stretching from the Karṇafulī estuary (Caṭṭagrāma inlet) to the Meghnā estuary (embouchure of Old Brahmaputra) or on islands near this coast.

In the 7th century AD, Chinese pilgrims have identified a port named Harikela. According to I-Tsing, two Chinese monks named Wu-hsing and Chih-hung arrived at Harikela (*O-li-ki-lo* or *A-li-ki-lo*) by ship from Sri Lanka. He locates the port to the north-east of Sri Lanka, and "on the east of Eastern India", at a distance of about a month's sail (Lahiri 1986: 95). We may remind ourselves that Śrīcandra's Rāmpāl copperplate (10th century AD) describes King Trailokyacandra (c. 900-929 AD) of the Candra dynasty as "the support of the royal majesty smiling in the royal umbrella of the king of Harikela" (Basak 1913-14a: 141). Hence, the port of Harikela must have been located in the kingdom of Harikela. Furthermore, a large number of coins bearing the legend "Harikela" and issued between the 7th to the mid-11th centuries AD have been discovered in Caṭṭagrāma (near the Caṭṭagrāma University Campus), Sylhet, Comilla (Mainamati) and Tripura (Belonia and Pilak Pathar). (For further detail, see Chapter Three.) These coins clearly indicate that the kingdom of Harikela may have extended from Sylhet in the north to the Karṇafulī in the south. Since Comilla region is definitely known to have been part of Samataṭa (testified by I-Tsing's account of Seng-che Ch'an-shih living in the Rāja-vihāra in San-mo-tan-t'e or Samataṭa ruled by the Khaḍga monarch Rājabhaṭa, Lahiri 1986: 86-87) we may believe that Harikela was Caṭṭagrāma region that lay between the rivers Choto Phenī and Karṇafulī. The Harikela coins were found in Tripura, Sylhet and Comilla regions because all these regions together constituted one kingdom. For a more precise location of Harikela we may cite Kantideva's copperplate (9th century AD) (Majumdar 1941-42: 316), which records granting of land at Harikela-maṇḍala. Since the copperplate was discovered at Bara-akhra temple in Caṭṭagrāma city, we may logically believe that the granted land was in or near the city. All these evidences indicate that northern Caṭṭagrāma region was known as Harikela. Hence, it is most likely that the port of Harikela was situated on the coast of northern Caṭṭagrāma region.

Harikela (or its phonetic derivatives) features in Arab-Perisan geographic treatises as well. In 1120 AD, an Arab author named Sharaf al-Zaman Tahir Marvazi mentions Hd.kira (possibly a phonetic variation of Harikela) as a town "which adjoins the coast of the Sea of Aghbab [i.e., the Bay of Bengal]. This (i.e., the Sea of Aghbab) is an unpleasant sea but on its coast lie many vast towns". Further, he locates the town of Hd.kira in the kingdom of Dhm or Dahum (Chakravarti 1998: 258). If Dahum was indeed Dharmapāla (c. 775-810), then it must be obvious that Marvazi's information was long outdated since the Pāla monarch was long dead when our scholar was composing his text. Nevertheless, Marvazi indicates that Harikela was within the Pāla kingdom of 'Bengal'. Another phonetic derivative of Harikela is mentioned in *Ḥudūd al-'Ālam,* a Persian work on geography by an anonymous author that was composed in 982 AD. It notes "five large towns situated on the seacoast, .. the royal power [over which] belongs to Dahum". These are N.myās, Harkand, Ūrshīn, S.m.nd.r and Andrās (Minorsky 1937: 87). If Harkand is identified with Harikel, then we must recognise that besides Harikela there was another large town situated on the seacoast named S.m.nd.r or Samandar.

Samandar features prominently as a port in the works of a number of Arab and Persian geographers, traders and travellers from the 9th to the 14th centuries AD. Mukherjee (1992b: 99), Karim (1987: 62) and Chakravarti (1998: 258) are unanimous in their identification of the port with Caṭṭagrāma. Among the Arab-Persian sources, the earliest to mention Samandar is Ibn Khurdādhbih (b. c. 820, d. c. 912 AD) whose work on world geography is titled *Kitāb al-Masālik wa'l-Mamālik* (the Book of Roads and Kingdoms). Although the original version of the work prepared in c. 846-7 AD is lost, what survives by the same title is an abridged version prepared not later than 885-6 AD. Ibn Khurdādhbih notes that Samandar was a port where ships would arrive after a journey of around three days from Kalyakān (Calingapatam), al-Lawā and Kanja (two other ports on the eastern coast of India). The port (of Samandar) was located at a distance of fifteen to twenty days' journey by means of a river from Kāmrūn (Kāmrūpa in Assam). Two more ports which the merchants would touch after Samandar were Urnshīn, located at a distance of four days' journey and Abīna, located some four more days' journey away (Ahmad 1989: 5, 22-25). We may infer from Ibn Khurdādhbih's account that Samandar was reachable by a river from Kāmrūpa that possibly fell in the Bay of Bengal (since our author appears to be describing a route of maritime ships along the western, northern and the eastern coast of the Bay).

Al-Idrīsī wrote his book on geography titled *Nuzhatu-l Mushtak* sometime in the mid-12th century AD, gathering information from various authors and travellers. According to him, Samandar (or Samundar as he prefers to call it) was some thirty miles from the port of Kanja. He describes Samandar as

> a large town, commercial, and rich, where there are good profits to be made. It is a port dependent upon Kanauj [Kāmrūpa?], king of this country. It stands upon a river which comes from the country of Kashmir (Al-Idrīsī 1867: 90).

Al-Idrīsī (*ibid.*) also confirms that merchandise from Kāmrūpa (Assam) were brought down to the port of Samandar by a river coming from the country of Kashmir. If the country of Kashmir may be taken to imply Tibet, then there is only one river, which fits the description, and it is Brahmaputra. This claim is further justified when one is reminded that Minhāju-d-din's *Tabaqāt-i-Nāsirī* (1260 AD), while narrating the history of Muhammad Bakhtiyar's ill-fated expedition to Tibet, describes an "exceedingly large" river in front of a town in Kāmrūd or Kāmrūpa. In Minhāju-d-din's own words, "It is called Bangamati [i.e., the Brahmaputra]. When it enters the country of Hindustan it receives in the Hindi language the name of Samandar" (*Minhāju-s Sirāj* 1869: 310). One needs to remember that the Brahmaputra changed its course quite a few times. Hence al-Idrīsī's location of Samandar on "a river which comes from Kashmir" can only mean the Brahmaputra flowing in one of its earlier courses. Hence, Al-Idrīsī's account may be taken to indicate that the river from Kāmrūpa, on the mouth of which was situated Samandar, must have been the Brahmaputra.

Samandar as a port features even in a 14th-century Arab account, titled *Subh ul Asha* by al-Qalqashandi (c. 1353-1418). The author was a judge in Cairo, who never visited 'Bengal', but drew his material on topographical description of India from the works of various authors such as Abul Fida, al-Biruni, Ibn Khurdādhbih and others (Zaki 1981: 21, 58). In the Chapter Six of *Subh ul Asha,* where he describes the routes leading to the Countries of Sindh and India, he clearly indicates that Samandar was on the coast of Bay of Bengal.

> One who follows the coastline: from Bullīn to Bās, 2 days; then to Sinjilī and Kabshakān, 2 days; then to the mouth of the Kūdāfarīd, 3 farsakhs; then to Kaylākār, 2 days; from there to Samandar and from Samandar to Ūsīr, 12 farsakhs; then to Abīna, 4 days (*ibid.*: 94).

Examination of accounts drawn from Ibn Khurdādhbih, *Hudūd al-'Ālam,* Marvazi, Al-Idrīsī and al-Qalqashandi make it clear that Samandar was definitely in Eastern Bengal, somewhere on the coast and reachable by the river Brahmaputra. If we examine João de Barros' map, one cannot but notice the wide estuary of the Gaṅgā and the Brahmaputra partly blocked by a few islands including Sandwīp. Caṭṭagrāma (Chatigam) is shown on the bank of the Karṇafulī but not far from the coast. More importantly, the mouth of the Karṇafulī appears to be at the southern extremity of the Gaṅgā-Brahmaputra estuary. We may logically believe that the estuary in the mid-9th century AD (when Ibn Khurdādhbih prepared his original manuscript) must have been wider with fewer islands compared to that of the mid-16th century AD (as shown in de Barros' map), if we make possible allowances for additional land formation that must have been taken place in the intervening seven centuries. This is also indicated, if one needs to be reminded, by Islam's study of coastline changes, which shows that the funnel shaped mouth of the Bay was possibly much wider than today. Hence, the possible location of Samandar that would fit all Arab-Persian accounts is the Caṭṭagrāma coast (from the Karṇafulī estuary to the Choto Phenī estuary) and the Noakhali coast. However, we must not forget the *Ḥudūd*, which indicates that Harikela and Samandar were two different ports.

Although Lama Tāranāth, in his *History of Buddhism in India* (1608 AD), speaks of "a monastery called the Piṇḍa-vihāra in the city of Caṭighābo in Bhaṃgala" (Chimpa and Chattopadhyaya 1970: 255), there is no mention of its maritime activities in his reference. Since Tāranātha speaks of Caṭighābo in the chapter titled "Account of the Period of King Gobicandra and Others", it is logical to assume that the city of Caṭighābo existed during the reign of the king Govindacandra (c. 1020-1050 AD) of the Candra dynasty although the Tibetan scholar appears to place the king in the last quarter of the 7th century AD. The Venetian Marco Polo is entirely silent regarding the ports of 'Bengal'. It is most unlikely, as Olchiski (1960: 38, n. 73) rightly believes, that the Italian adventurer ventured to 'Bengal', let alone visit Caṭṭagrāma as Sharif (1375: 175-176) and Chowdhury (1994: 19) believe. *Chu-fan-chi* composed in the mid-13th century AD by Chau Ju-kua (Hirth and Rockhill 1965) is also silent about the ports in 'Bengal'. Hence, let us turn to Ibn Battutā (1304-1368/69), whose account is based on personal experience of his visit to eastern Bengal in the cold weather of 1346-47 (or 1345-46).

Ibn Battutā sailed from Cālicūt to the Maldives (Kannalūs Island) and after a brief sojourn, sailed for 'Bengal'. He arrived at Sudkāwān after 43 nights. In his own words,

> The first city in Bengal that we entered was Sudkāwān, a large town on the coast of the great sea. Close by it the river Ganges, to which the Hindus go on pilgrimage, and the river Jun unite and discharge together into the sea (Gibb 1992: 267).

Although some attempts have been made to identify Sudkāwān as Sātgāon, we can reject these as Bhattacharyya (1977: 25) does, because Ibn Battutā situated his port on the "coast of the great sea", which does not agree with the location of Sātgāon in the present Huglī District. According to Gibb, Jun "is Ibn Battutā's transcription for Jumna, here obviously represents the Brahmaputra", Kāmrū is Kāmrūpa, the Blue river is the Meghnā and Habnaq was a town near Habiganj or perhaps Habiganj itself because a low mound called Habang still stands a little south of Habiganj (Gibb 1992: 366, fn. 7, 9 and 10). Thus there can be no doubt that Sudkāwān was Caṭṭagrāma and by the mid-14th century AD, it was already a well-established port. It is curious that Ibn Battutā had already visited Sudkāwān by the time al-Qalqashandi wrote his work. However, the former makes no mention of Samandar while the latter is completely oblivious about Sudkāwān. Since Ibn Battutā's account is based on first hand experience, and hence more reliable, it is possible to conclude that al-Qalqashandi's information was outdated, for it was based on Ibn Khurdādhbih. More importantly, Ibn Battutā provides the earliest definitive evidence regarding the existence of Caṭṭagrāma as a maritime port.

From the first half of the 15th century AD, we have four travel accounts, three of which are Chinese and one, European. The Chinese sources are Ma-Huan's *Ying-yai sheng-lan* (1451), Fei Sin's *Sing ch'a sheng lan* (1436) and Kung Chen's *Hsi-yang fan-kuo chih* (1434). The European account is by Nicolò de Conti who, as stated earlier, sailed from Cernomen (possibly Sonārgāon) and left 'Bengal' by way of Buffetanya. Scholars agree that Conti's Buffetanya was Caṭṭagrāma (Mills in Ma-Huan 1970: 65). However, there is hardly any information regarding the port of Caṭṭagrāma. Kung Chen's work (*Hsi-yang fan-kuo chih*) is mostly "a word-for-word reproduction of the *Ying-yai sheng-lan*" (*ibid.*: 57). Hence, we may concentrate on Ma-Huan's and Fei Sin's accounts.

Ma-Huan, who reached 'Bengal' in the first half of 1432, has precious little to say about the port of Chen-ti-chiang.

> Setting sail from the country of Su-men-ta-la [Semudera, on the north coast of Sumatra], you make Mao mountain [Poulo Weh, island off the north coast of Sumatra] and Ts'uilan islands [the Nicobar and Andaman islands]; [then] you proceed on a north-westerly course, and, after travelling with a fair wind for twenty days [representing a voyage of 61 miles a day], you come first to Che-ti-chiang, where the ship is moored (*ibid.*: 159 and n. 4-7).

As discussed earlier, from Che-ti-chiang, Ma-Huan travelled in a small ship to enter an estuary and after 500 *li* or 175 miles, he arrived at So-na-erh-chiang or Sonārgāon (*ibid.*: 159-160, n.1). The course of journey that Ma-Huan provides makes it clear that Che-ti-chiang is but a phonetic derivative of Caṭṭagrāma.

The port in 'Bengal' that Fei Sin writes about is Ch'a-ti-kiang, which is at slight phoenetic variance from Ma-Huan's Che-ti-chiang. However, there can be little doubt that both the words used by the Chinese are but derivatives of 'Chittagong/Caṭṭagrāma'. From Fei Sin one gets an impression that Caṭṭagrāma was a port of relatively high importance and had a custom station.

> The country has a sea-port on a bay called Ch'a-ti-kiang. Here certain duties are collected. When the king heard that our ships had arrived there, he sent high officers to offer robes and other presents, and over a thousand men and horses also came to the port (Bagchi 1945: 120-121).

Towards the end of the 15th and early 16th century AD, we encounter the name of a port called 'Shātījām' in the works composed by two Arab navigators. These are Ibn-Mājid's *Kitāb al-Fawā'id fī uṣūl al-baḥr wa'l-qawā'id* (c. 1489-90), and Sulaimān al-Mahrī's *'Umdat al-Mahriya fī dabt al-'ilm al-bahriya* (1511), *Minhaj al-fakhir fī 'ilm al-bahr al-zakhir* and *Tuhfat al-fuhil fī tamhid al-usul* (c. first half of the 16th century). Ibn-Mājid speaks of Shātījām in a brief *qasida* on the ending of sailing season.

> Every late traveller enters Shātījām
> When he comes from India and Maldives, so be silent
> (Tibbetts 1981: 241).

In the *Minhaj*, the bearings Sulaimān al-Mahrī provides for Shātījām from Lakīfār (possibly a cape near Rabnabad Islands in Barisal region) using Sundib (Sandwīp) as an intermediary point, leaves no doubt that the port in question is Caṭṭagrāma (*ibid.*: 357).

Summing up on geographical treatises and travel accounts cited above, it becomes clear that these sources refer to four ports on the coast stretching from the Meghnā estuary to the Karṇafulī estuary. These were (1) Pentapolis (2nd century AD), (2) Harikela (7th, 10th and 12th centuries AD), (3) Samandar (9th, 10th, 12th and 14th centuries AD) and (4) Sudkāwān/ Shātījām/ Buffetanya/ Che-ti-chiang/ Ch'a-ti-kiang (14th to the first half of the 16th centuries AD).

In order to locate all these port-sites (considering the possibility that they were separate), an examination of the travels of Sebastien Manrique may be helpful. During his missionary and diplomatic activities in the Caṭṭagrāma coast and the Arakanese capital from 1630 to 1635, the ports that Manrique touched were Caṭṭagrāma, Dianga, Rāmū, Angarcale (Angerkel) and the town of Arakan (i.e., Mrohaung the Arakanese capital). He clearly states that Dianga was situated on the southern bank of the Karṇafulī, south of Caṭṭagrāma port (Manrique 1927: 284-285). Hosten (1925: 76) has produced a Dutch print with which he reasonably claims that Dianga was indeed situated on the southern bank. It may be noted that van den Broucke locates Dianga halfway between Caṭṭagrāma and Rāmū, at the Dak'hindāṅgā or Brāhmaṇdāṅgā, both on the Sāṅgu River (Blochmann 1968: 25). Manrique (1927: 277) locates Angarcale (Angerkel) "three leagues from Dianga". E. Luard and H. Hosten, the translators of *Travels of Fray Sebastien Manrique,* further pinpoint Angarcale on the bank of Sangā (Sāṅgu) River, where now stands a village called Hāṅgarkhālī (*ibid.*: 86, fn. 12). Rāmū is situated further south, on the bank of the Rāmū or Bākkhālī River. Francis Buchanan, who visited this place in 1789, describes the river as deeper than the Mamoree (the Mātāmuhurī River) at Chakoriya and the tidal current in it went upstream to a considerable distance (Schendel 1992: 59). Mrohaung (Mrauk-U), the capital of Arakan from 1433 to 1785, was in Akyab district on the bank of Lemru River.

It is important to note that (1) all the four ports mentioned above were situated not on but a little away from the coast, on the bank of a river and (2) all of them were located south of the Karṇafulī estuary. It should be noted that 'Bengal', Arakan, Tripura and the Portuguese fought bitterly over control of Caṭṭagrāma but none of the parties attempted to build another port north of the Karṇafulī estuary when their adversary had the port under their possession. Physical features of the coast clearly explain why they did not. As discussed earlier, the slope of the continental shelf along the eastern coast of the Bay of Bengal is gentle (2°-8°). Hence, no littoral port is possible in this region. Furthermore, there is no estuary on the coast between the mouth of the Karṇafulī and the mouth of the Choto Phenī since no river falls into the bay from this part of the coast. This can only mean that on the entire coast of Caṭṭagrāma, no port could ever have existed at any time between the Karṇafulī estuary and the Choto Phenī estuary. If we have to look for port-sites on the Caṭṭagrāma coast (including Akyab), they must be the five that Manrique has described: Caṭṭagrāma, Dianga, Angerkel, Rāmū, and Mrohaung.

As for the Noakhali coast, one possible site is the Choto Phenī estuary. However, even today mariners sailing indigenous vessels are hesitant to anchor on the river because, as they say, it is extremely unsafe. Because the channel of the river flows south without any meandering curves, tidal current is strong along the entire navigable stretch. Another possible site, as it was argued by the author elsewhere (Jahan 2000), is Mandari (4 km north of the medieval city of Bhulua) on the Bārunī Channel of the Meghnā now extinct. However, Mandari is untenable as Samandar because almost the entire Noakhali and south-western part of Comilla regions is absent in João de Barros' map of 1550. As argued earlier, the estuary in the mid-9th century AD (when Ibn Khurdādhbih prepared his original manuscript) must have been still wider with fewer islands compared to that of the mid-16th century AD (as shown in de Barros' map). One would logically expect it so because the Middle Meghnā Floodplain, the low floodplain of the Tippera Surface and the Meghnā Estuarine Floodplain of the Active Delta, being land formations created by sedimentation and accretion, would not have been built in the mid-9th century AD. Hence, Pentapolis, Harikela and Samandar could not have been situated on the Noakhali coast.

If our argument placed above is tenable, we must believe that Pentapolis, Harikela and Samandar could only have been situated on the Caṭṭagrāma coast. Following Gerini's argument, Pentapolis could only be located somewhere on the coast stretching from the Karṇafulī estuary to the Meghnā estuary (on Noakhali coast). The Karṇafulī estuary is the only place that can offer safe anchorage. Hence, not going into the etymology of Caturgrāma, we must trust our knowledge of Caṭṭagrāma coast's environment to believe in our deductions made above. The same argument applies for Samandar if the possible location of the port that would fit all Arab-Persian accounts is the Caṭṭagrāma coast (from Karṇafulī estuary to the Choto Phenī estuary) and the Noakhali coast. If we follow the *Ḥudūd,* which indicates that Harikela and Samandar were two different locations, we could eliminate Rāmū and Mrohaung from the list of the four that we obtained from Manrique since they are too far south and are linked culturally and historically more with Arakan than 'Bengal'. Hence we may believe that Harikela could have been Angerkel on the Sāṅgu River. However, as argued above, numismatic and epigraphic evidences appear to indicate that Harikela was in northern Caṭṭagrāma. If this is tenable, we must believe that the port of Harikela was situated on the coast between the Karṇafulī estuary and the Choto Phenī estuary. Once again, because the Karṇafulī estuary is the only possible site for a maritime port, Harikela must have been on the Karṇafulī estuary. This line of argument may be further substantiated by reminding ourselves that the find-spot of Kantideva's copperplate is Caṭṭagrāma. If our deliberations are acceptable, we must believe that the *Ḥudūd* was misinformed that Harikela and Samandar were two different locations.

Hence we may believe that the port of Caṭṭagrāma was already established in the 2nd century AD, when it was known as Pentapolis to the Greco-Romans. From the 9th to the 14th centuries AD, it was known as Samandar to the Arab-Persian seafarers and geographers and from the 14th to the first half of the 16th centuries AD, it was known variously as Sudkāwān, Shātījām, Catigabho, Buffetanya and Che-ti-chiang (Ch'a-ti-kiang). The local people knew it as Harikela from the 7th to the 10th centuries AD and from the 10th century onwards, as Cittagong. The name Cittagong may have arisen in 953 AD, if we may accept the testimony of the Arakanese chronicle *Ra-dza-weng*. According to the chronicles, a Buddhist sovereign of the Arakanese Candra dynasty, named Tsu-la-taing Tsan-daya (951-957), "went on an expedition to Bengal (called Thu-ra-Tan) and set up a stone pillar as a trophy at the place since called Tset-ta-goung, or as commonly written, Chittagong" (Phayre 1844: 36). 'Tset-ta-goung' denotes 'there will be no war'. Citing the Arakanese chronicle Phayre (*ibid.*) explains, the pillar was so called because the king remarked that to make war was improper and he abandoned his conquest at the request of his nobles. If 'Cittagong' may be taken to be the phonetic derivation of 'Tset-ta-goung', then this may indeed be the earliest reference to the port by its current name. Caṭṭagrāma, Cāṭḡā, Cāṭigābho, Che-ti-chiang and Ch'a-ti-kiang are all phoenetic derivatives of Cittagong.

Now that we have established the rise of Caṭṭagrāma, let us investigate another moot point regarding the port that has been raised by travel accounts of Ludovico di Varthema, Duarte Barbosa and Tome Pires. These along with few other travel accounts refer to a port called Bengala (or Banghella), which scholars have been variously identified as Gauḍa, Caṭṭagrāma, Sātgāon, Sonārgāon, Śrīpur and Dianga. Blaev's map (1650), and Vignorla's map (1683) place it on the southern bank of the Karṇafulī. It is not within the scope of this research to resolve the issue. However, it is necessary to establish what Varthema, Barbosa and Tome Pires indicated by the port of Bengala since their accounts fall within the time frame of this research and have important bearings on it.

The Italian traveller Ludovico di Varthema, who arrived at Banghella in c. 1508, locates the port at a distance of 700 miles (or 11 days' sail) from Tenasserim, which is an acceptable approximation of the actual distance between these two points (Varthema 1928: 79). Although this helps us to identify definitely the city of Banghella as Caṭṭagrāma, we must concede that when Varthema (*ibid.*: 80) locates Pego (Pegu) at a distance of about a thousand miles from Banghella, we are at a loss because the actual distance between these points is only a little over 650 miles as calculated from *The Mercantile Marine Atlas* (Goodal 1952: Plate 22). At the same time, Sātgāon too fails to qualify as the city of Banghella because the atlas cited above logs the distance between Kolkata and Rangoon as 737 miles (*ibid.*) and therefore the distance between Sātgāon and Pegu must have been much less than 800 miles. Hence, we may overlook the thousand miles of Banghella-Pego distance as a slip on Varthema's part and trust his accurate estimation of Banghella-Tenasserim as a definite indicator that the port in question was indeed Caṭṭagrāma.

Duarte Barbosa lived in Portuguese India from 1500 to 1516 or 1517. In his account written in 1518, the Portuguese traveller describes the location of Bengala thus:

> Further on, leaving this River Ganges and following the coast in a northerly direction, comes the kingdom of Bengala wherein are many towns, as well inland as on the coast ... [T]his sea is a Gulf which runneth in between two lands and going well into it there is to the north a right great city of the Moors, which they call Bengala, a very excellent sea-haven ... (Barbosa 1921: 135-136).

If we remember that the Bay of Bengal converged into a funnel at the mouth of the Meghna – a funnel that was much greater five centuries ago than that seen today – then it is possible to see that one would indeed have to follow "the coast in a northerly direction" to arrive at the heartland of the kingdom of Bengala. Hence the port of Bengala was definitely in eastern Bengal and so one cannot argue that Sātgāon was the City of Bengala. There can hardly be any doubt that when Barbosa says, the "sea is a Gulf which runneth in between two lands", he is describing the Bay of Bengal as it is situated between the east coast of south India and Caṭṭagrāma-Arakan-Tenasserim coast. Then he says, "going well into it [the Bay of Bengal] there is to the north a right great city of the Moors, which they call Bengala". This part of the description is accurate because the port of Caṭṭagrāma does indeed lie to the north of the bay. Hence, Barbossa's City of Bengala cannot but be Caṭṭagrāma.

It is not possible that Barbosa mixed up Gauḍa and Caṭṭagrāma as one city. Actually, he does not mention the capital city of Bengala even once. As Campos (1919: 21) explains, Caṭṭagrāma was the gateway to Gauḍa.

> When the Portuguese came to Bengal, Chittagong was its chief port, and the main gateway to the royal capital Gaur. ... Situated as it is at the mouth of the Meghna, this port was most convenient for navigation. The Meghna was the principal route to Gaur ...

Hence, there can be no room for mixing up the capital with the port city. It is unwise to pick up excerpts from Barbosa's account and attempt to fit those into one's pet theory as Cortesao (1945: 11) did. He believed that Barbosa referred to Gauḍa by the name City of Bengala because Caṭṭagrāma, at his time, was not a city of Moors (as Barbosa said) but of heathens (since the port was not within the domain of Bengal sultanate). Obviously Cortesao assumed that with the change of reigning monarch, the entire population also changed their faith. It is indeed possible that Caṭṭagrāma, prior to the arrival of the Portuguese, was always inhabited by a large number of Muslim merchants (Cortesao's Moors).

Tome Pires (1967: 90-91) did not travel to the City of Bengal but says it was the principal port, "whence the kingdom derive[d] its name. It [took] two days to go from the mouth of the river [Ganges] up to the city ...". Clearly, Pires had Gauḍa in mind when he was writing about the City of Bengal in the early 16th century AD. Cortesao, the translator of Pires' *Suma Oriental*, confirms this impression and states that "[t]he 'City of Bengal', was the ancient capital of 'Bengal', the great historic city of Gaur or Gour" (*ibid.*: 90, fn 2). However, Pires mixed Caṭṭagrāma with Gauḍa, for the latter was not a port. Hence, we must accept his testimony regarding the principal port to imply Caṭṭagrāma and the remaining description to imply Gauḍa.

Having now sorted out major questions regarding Caṭṭagrāma, let us now attempt an assessment of the physical and socio-economic environment of the port-site. As mentioned earlier, no systematic archaeological excavation has yet been carried out. From scattered references to the port prior to the inception of Muslim rule from the reign of Sultan Fakhr al-Din Mubarak Shah (1338-49 AD), such as Lama Tāranāth's Piṇḍa-vihāra, we may infer that the city was prosperous enough to support famous Buddhist monasteries. The prosperity is vouchsafed by the discovery of Harikela coins and copperplate land grants. However, we have hardly any information regarding the physical environment of the port-site.

Information is relatively more plentiful from c. mid-14th century AD. According to a Persian account by Shihabuddin Talish (MS Bodleian 589), after his conquest, Fakhr al-Din Mubarak Shah had built an embankment *(āl)* from Chandpur, opposite the outpost of Sripur, to Caṭṭagrāma (Sarkar 1907b: 421). He also built quite a few mosques and mausoleums (Karim 1987: 167). Fei Sin's testimony from the early 15th century AD, that the king "sent high officers to offer robes and other presents" to the visiting Chinese delegation and that "over a thousand men and horses came to the port" (Bagchi 1945: 120-121), indicates that the administrative centre at Caṭṭagrāma was no insignificant frontier outpost. It must have been well managed and administered by high officials. Indeed, a silver coin issued by Sultan Jalal al-Din Muhammad Shah in 818 AH (1415-16 AD) that bears the imprint of *'Arṣah Chātgāwn* as the issuing mint (Karim 1960: 81), clearly demonstrates that the administrative unit of Caṭṭagrāma had attained the status of an *'arṣah* (equivalent to a *zilla* or an administrative district of later times). It may be recalled that Sātgāon was also an *'arṣah,* while Muazzamabad near Sonārgāon was an *iqlim* (equivalent to an administrative division of later times). Only one architectural monument, a mosque at Jobrā village in Hāṭ-hāzārī Police Station, bears testimony to the earliest stamp of the inception of Muslim rule. Inscription still stands on a wall of the mosque declaring in Persian that Rasti Khan built it in 1460 AD (Alam 1965: 14).

Except for a brief period from 1416 to 1420 AD, when Danuj Mardana Deva and his successor Mahendra Deva briefly ruled over Caṭṭagrāma, the port was under the control of the 'Bengal' sultanate till the mid-15th century AD. From around the mid-15th to the end of the 15th century, it was held by the Arakanese (although the northern part of the Caṭṭagrāma district, beyond the port, may have been under the domain of the 'Bengal' sultanate, as the mosque of Rasti Khan indicates). At the end of the continuous tripartite war between Arakan, 'Bengal' and Tripura, the Sultanate of 'Bengal' wrested control of Caṭṭagrāma in c. 1517 (Tarafdar 1999: 60). A new administrative headquarters was established at Fatehābād, eight miles to the north of the present location of Caṭṭagrāma city. According the *'Ahādis ul-Khawānin* (or *'Tārīkh i Hamīdī*) by Maulawi Hamidullah Khan Bahadur (1871 AD), Nusrat Shah built a mosque of coloured enameled bricks, a palace and a tank at Fatehābād (Blochmann 1872: 337). About four miles to the north of Fatehābād, at Hāṭhāzārī, a ruined mosque built by Sultan Shams al-Dīn Yusuf Shah (1474-1481 AD) still stands (Karim 1967: 322-325). Daulat Uzir Bahram Khan, in his *Laili-Majnu* (a narrative in verse composed in the 16th century AD), describes Fatehābād as a heavenly city with a fort situated near the seashore and on the bank of the river Karṇafulī (Khan 1958: 87). Only the two mosques of Rasti Khan and Sultan Shams al-Dīn Yusuf Shah still stand to confirm these assertions. It is possible that most of the structures that were erected at or around Caṭṭagrāma during the sultanate period were timber-built – a tradition that was common even in the mid-20th century. This may be the reason why so few remains have come down to us.

Nevertheless, remains of two other mosques have been found but both of these are located away from medieval Fatehābād. One of these is the mosque at Parāgalpur village in Mīr Sarāi Police Station, which was constructed on the ruins of an earlier brick-built mosque errected by Chuti Khan (a general of Sultan Nusrat Shah and a governor of Caṭṭagrāma) sometime after 1515 AD. Even though no stone inscription has been found, the existence of Chuti Khan's mosque is testified by fragmentary remains inscribed with Arabic alphabets that reportedly lie scattered in the courtyard of the present mosque (Alam 1965: 14). The second mosque still stands at Masjidda village, near Kumira. It is believed that Hamid Khan built the mosque during the reign of Sultan Ghiyath al-Din Mahmud Shah (1533-1538 AD) (Karim 1967: 325-329).

When the Portuguese were granted permission to build factories and collect excise duties in Caṭṭagrāma, they built their fort and custom house in the city (Campos 1919: 39) but their church and commercial house were at Dianga (Karim 1987: 13). These references indicate that the administrative centre at Caṭṭagrāma must have gained in prominence, specially after Nusrat Shah's conquest.

In the early 15th century AD Caṭṭagrāma had emerged as a mint-town, as testified by the silver coin issued by Sultan Jalal al-Din Muhammad Shah (1415-1432 AD) cited above. Danuj Mardana Deva and his successor Mahendra Deva also minted coins from Caṭṭagrāma in 1339 and 1340 Saka, corresponding to April 1416 to April 1418 AD. Coins struck by Jalal al-Din Muhammad Shah in 1420 and Nasiruuddin Mahmud Shah in 1438-39 (both sultans of 'Bengal') and the Arakanese king Basawpyu in 1460 (Ray 1999: 362) clearly show the mint was significant enough to be used by 'Bengal' as well as Arakan. The commemorative gold coin issued by King Dhanyamānikya of Tripura on his conquest of the port-town in 1513 may have also been minted at Caṭṭagrāma. We may thus believe that the port assumed tremendous importance in the economy of 'Bengal', Tripura and Arakan by the early 15th century AD. Because silver coins were minted in the city, there can hardly be any doubt that trade was monetary based.

Numerous tombs and cenotaphs in Caṭṭagrāma testify to the proselytyzing activities of Muslim saints even before the advent of Muslim rule. One of the most famous of these is a group of twelve graves, popularly known as the tomb of Bara Aulia, that lie at a village called by the same name, near Kumirā. "According to tradition, a Muslim King named Shahaji came to these parts accompanied by twelve saints ..." (Ali 1964: 7). Another tomb believed to be of Mohsen Aulia who died in 1397, lies at Baṭṭalī village, Ānwārā Police Station (Alam 1965: 12-13). However, the most famous is the 'tomb' (actually a cenotaph) of Bayazid Bistami at Nasirabad, near Caṭṭagrāma city. The 'tomb' complex consists of a cenotaph (a simple square structure that stands on a mound), a richly decorated 18th-century mosque that stands near the base of the mound and a large tank. It is popularly believed that Bayazid Bistami (777-874 AD), a renowned saint who was born in Bistam (in Persia), arrived in Caṭṭagrāma in the 9th century AD and resided there for three years. Although he is said to have travelled extensively, his biography makes no mention of his supposed stay in Caṭṭagrāma. As Ali (1964: 11-12) says, "it is difficult to believe that Sultan Bayazid Bistami ever came to Chittagong".

If one is prepared to peel through layers of religious legends, and lay aside supernatural fabrications of the devotees, it is possible to link these saints with Muslim merchants who began visiting Samandar from the 9th century AD or even earlier. Although we have no conclusive evidence from the history of 'Bengal', the Arakanese chronicles provides with an important clue. Citing the chronicles, Phayre (1844: 36) has shown that during the reign of the king Ma-ha-toing Tsan-da-ya or Mahā Taing Chāndra (r. 788-810), "several *Ku-la*, or foreign ships, were wrecked upon the Island of Ran-byi, and the people in them said to be Mussalmans, were sent to Arakan proper, where they were settled in villages". Khurdādhbih's *Kitāb al-Masālik wa'l-Mamālik,* the original version of which must have been prepared c. 840 AD, shows that Arab-Persian scholars were informed about maritime route to 'Bengal' by the mid-9th century AD. Hence, the actual journey by Arab-Persian mariners must have begun earlier, i.e., the end of the 8th century AD as indicated by the Arakanese chronicle and many of the much-revered Muslims saints might have been Muslim merchants from the Middle East.

The current location of the harbour of Caṭṭagrāma port on the bank of the Karṇafulī indicates that it was always an estuarine port. We may assume, given the pattern discerned in physical facilities offered by other ports, that there were no jetties at the harbour during the time frame of this research. Temporary landing arrangements may have been made for embarkation and disembarkation of passengers and goods from ships that anchored at the harbour. As mentioned above, the draught of the junks by which Ma-Huan and the Chinese delegation arrived at Caṭṭagrāma was at least twenty feet (Mills in Ma-Huan 1970: 31). Hence Ma-Huan's (*ibid.*: 159) testimony, that their ships were "moored" at Che-ti-chiang, appears to indicate that large ships with draught of twenty feet or more could anchor at Caṭṭagrāma in the first half of the 15th century AD. Even in the early 16th century AD, Barbosa (1921: 136) vouchsafes that the port of Caṭṭagrāma was "a very excellent sea-haven".

We have no information as to what facilities the port provided. Because Fei Sin's account shows that at Ch'a-ti-kiang "certain duties are collected" (Bagchi 1945: 120) we may believe that there was a customhouse at the port. The Chinese accounts clearly indicate that the port handled passengers. From Maulana Muzaffar Shams Balkhi's letter to Ghiyath al-Din Azam Shah (1389-1410 AD) requesting the sultan to issue a farman "to the officials (Kārkuns) of Chātgāon, directing them to accommodate in the first ship the band of Darwesh pilgrims for Mecca" (Askari 1956: 190), we may logically believe that Hajj pilgrims had begun to sail for Mecca from Caṭṭagrāma by the late 14th century AD.

However, the fact that the Maulana had to write to the sultan with a note of urgency also hints that such voyages of the pilgrims had not become very common and that the transit facilities for passengers in the late 14th or early 15th century AD may not have been very comfortable.

Caṭṭagrāma must have become a commercial centre of high repute in the 16th century AD. This is testified by Varthema (1928: 79) who praises the city of Banghella (Caṭṭagrāma) as "the best that [he] had hitherto seen" and found there "the richest merchants [he] ever met with". In 1532, De Barros confirms Varthema by observing the following: "Chittagong is the most famous and wealthy city of the kingdom of Bengal, on account of its port, at which meets the traffic of all that eastern region" (Campos 1919: 113). Caṭṭagrāma (the City of Bengala) must have been a well-known production centre of cotton textiles, sugar, and "ginger conserve, also of oranges, lemons and other fruits which grow in this land" (Barbosa 1921: 145-147). Varthema (1928: 79) confirms Barbosa's observation on cotton textiles and adds silk textiles to the list. He also observes that fifty ships laden with cotton and silk textiles sailed each year from Caṭṭagrāma. The fact that in 1569 Caesar Frederick travelled from Pegu to Caṭṭagrāma in a ship laden with "Silver and Gold ... and no other kind of Merchandize" indicates that the port was the most important centre in 'Bengal' for importing bullion (Purchas 1905b: 136). The account of Vincent la Bleau, the French merchant and traveller who arrived in Caṭṭagrāma (Castigan or Shatigan) in 1575, confirms Caesar Frederick's information that Caṭṭagrāma was a centre for bullion trade because he (la Bleau) writes of making profit by trading in gold and silver (Ray 1999: 364). Of course Frederick and la Bleau's testimonies are well beyond our time frame. Nevertheless, because sultanate Bengal continuously minted silver coins and intermittently gold coins as well (discussed in detail in Chapter Three), we may believe that the testimonies cited above may be taken to indicate condition of earlier centuries as well.

****

Thus far we can sum up the findings by stating that a total of seven maritime ports operated in early 'Bengal', all of which served as feeder ports. These were Tāmralipti (c. 3rd century BC to the mid-8th century AD), Gaṅgābandar/Chandraketugarh (c. 3rd century BC to the 5th century AD), Wārī-Baṭeśwar (c. 3rd century BC to the 3rd century AD), Koṭālipāḍā/Candravarmakoṭa (c. 2nd century AD to the early 8th century AD), Sonārgāon (early 14th to the second half of the 15th century AD), Sātgāon (early 14th century to 1632 AD) and Caṭṭagrāma (prior to the 2nd century AD to the present). Hence, Niharranjan Ray's (1994: 127) opinion after the demise of Tāmralipti, "from the 8th to the 13th century AD, no other commercial centre developed anywhere in Bengal" that needs to be revised. It is also highly significant that four of the seven ports were located in Bangladesh, where, from the 3rd century BC onwards ports have functioned one after the other in contrast to a gap perceived from the 8th to the early 14th century AD in West Bengal. It is also important to note that all the ports mentioned above were located in estuaries. Since no man-made installations have been unearthed at any of the port sites, we may believe that no jetties were constructed at any of the harbours. We may also believe that ships with shallow draught were anchored at riverbanks in a manner still seen in riverine ports of Bangladesh and West Bengal, where wooden planks are used to cross over to the shore. Larger ships may have anchored at a distance from the coast and goods may have been ferried across to the shore in smaller crafts.

Two

Commodities and Hinterland

The seven ports studied in the previous chapter will remain skeletal till one identifies the commodities – central concern in any trading activity – which were imported or exported from there. In attempting to identify the commodities of trade, it is useful to remember that

> [p]re-modern trade was primarily a function of three factors. Some areas or communities had a technological advantage which could not be diffused or copied elsewhere. Goods produced under such conditions were of course subject to the rationale of price considerations. Secondly, the geographical determinants of production were absolute in many cases, and certain commodities had unique sources of supply. Lastly, consumer tastes and social conventions played an important role in shaping the demand for high-valued luxury articles, though changes in socially determined demand were often a function of incomes and comparative prices (Chaudhuri 1985: 16).

While Chaudhuri's observations are important, there is nevertheless an underlying assumption that pre-modern trade was primarily for elite consumption. If one attempts to identify commodities only with these three factors in mind, one may come up with muslin, malabathrum and beads. Even archaeological remains often appear to confirm that pre-modern trade was predominantly of luxury goods because these artefacts such as etched beads, Northern Black Polished Ware and Rouletted Ware are easier to identify and are non-perishable in nature. Consequently, as Ray (1998: 41) observes, "the importance of trade in subsistence goods has often been underplayed in archaeological literature and it has often been argued that except for the large urban centres other areas were generally self-sufficient; the ordinary peasant could not afford what was not grown locally, thus inhibiting any large-scale movement of staple goods". Hence, we will attempt to avoid falling into the trap of looking only for luxury goods and attempt to identify indicators pertaining to staple goods as well.

Because perishable materials leave no trace, abundant production and surplus for a sufficiently long period of time as indicative of export, may be accepted as a dependable indicator to determine whether certain items may have been exported from a region. Following this logic, Chaudhuri (1985: 182) observes that "[t]he most important consideration [for long distance trade of the Indian Ocean before 1850 or 1800] was the ability of a local economy to create a surplus over and above the subsistence demand and to maintain this level of productivity over a sufficiently long period of time". Rice is often cited as a case to prove this point. However, we will make use of archaeological, literary, epigraphic and numismatic evidences to arrive at a strong and reliable empirical base instead of looking only at abundant production and surplus.

Finally, Chaudhuri's (*ibid.:* 184) observation, "[p]re-modern trade was not altogether a matter of chance; but it was characterized by a high degree of fluctuation from year to year" is another important consideration, which needs to be taken into account in any analysis on trade commodities. However, paucity of data may restrict one's earnest attempts to move according to this direction.

Apart from commodities that were imported and exported, mention must also be made of ballast that sailing ships carried for their stability. This was necessary when a particular port of call could not offer enough cargo and the vessel concerned was in the danger of missing its sailing schedule because of monsoon winds. Ships sailing out from the Indian Ocean littoral usually carried roughly hewn stones, ingots of iron and other heavy metals and water jars as ballast. On the other hand, ships sailing from the Middle East to South Asia often carried dates as ballast commodity.

Not all the commodities exported through the ports located in the region of 'Bengal' were local products. It will be seen that many were products of neighbouring regions, which used the ports on the 'Bengal' coast for transhipment. Hence, important to a port is its 'hinterland', loosely defined as "the area which a port serves" (Sargent 1938: 16, n. 4). More specifically, it may be described as "organized and developed land spaces which are connected with a port by means of transport lines and which receive or ship goods through that port" (Weigend 1958: 192-193, n. 3). As McDowell and Gibbs (1954: 76) observe, the safe anchorage that a port may offer, "is, however, second to the all-important hinterland. Lacking that hinterland, harbors possessing great natural advantages such as Port Mahon on Minorca, Ireland Island in the Bermudas, and Lyttleton, New Zealand, can possess only strategic value".

The complexity of port-hinterland relationship is manifest in economic and geographical factors such as transport facilities, market organisation, shipping services and port facilities. One also needs to take into consideration the matter of prevailing political conditions. Prevailing political relationship between two regions, one land-locked and the other littoral, may considerably influence the use of a port in the littoral region by the land-locked region. Another aspect of the relationship, which often escapes notice, is that a port does not have exclusive claim to any part of its hinterland and an inland area may be the hinterland of several ports.

These are the areas of inquiry that this chapter intends to take up. It has been organised so to ascertain (i) the commodities that were exported through the ports of

'Bengal', (ii) those, which were, imported through the ports of 'Bengal', and finally (iii) the hinterland from and to which these commodities moved.

EXPORTED COMMODITIES

Commodities exported from the ports of 'Bengal', as discussed in this section, have been grouped under three categories: raw materials, manufactured goods and faunal merchandise.

Raw Materials: Agricultural, Forest And Mineral Products

RICE

Favoured by climatic and soil conditions, rice (*Oryza sativa*) is currently the principal agricultural product of Bangladesh and West Bengal. Paddy (*dhānya*) was cultivated from remote antiquity as the staple food-crop of the people in ancient 'Bengal'. We need to ascertain if this staple food-crop was ever exported from 'Bengal'.

We may begin by briefly reminding ourselves regarding the settlement pattern and spread of agriculture in 'Bengal', which followed the course of the great river systems. The Indo-Aryan settlers in the middle Gaṅgā plains, who were familiar with the technique of transplanting paddy since the 5th century BC (Sharma 1983: 96), may have significantly contributed to the spread of agriculture by introducing the technique in their early settlements in 'Bengal'. An important indicator of the diffusion of Indo-Aryan culture is the Northern Black Polished Ware (henceforth referred to as NBPW), which appears in Bāngarh, Chandraketugarh and Tamluk in West Bengal and Mahāsthāngarh and Wārī-Baṭeśwar in Bangladesh. Dilip Chakrabarti (1992: 178) has ascertained that the chronology of NBPW in the eastern parts of South Asia is between c. 300 BC and 100 AD. Hence it is possible to believe that by the 1st century AD, Indo-Aryan agrarian settlements were well established along the Bhāgīrathī-Huglī in Rāḍha and Vaṅga, and along the Karatoyā and the Ātrāi in Puṇḍravardhana. If our argument placed above is acceptable, we may rightly believe that wet-rice cultivation from the 1st century onwards must have led to abundant production leading to surplus of rice. By the 3rd century AD, one could reasonably expect conditions mature enough for export. Five archaeological artifacts from the 3rd century AD confirm this cultural-ecological indication.

The first is a seal-impression of personal character and/or religious significance. It was found at Chandraketugarh and is now preserved at Balanda Museum, Haroa in the district of 24-Parganas (North). It displays three stalks of paddy issuing out of a base and two auspicious symbols (svastika and conch). The second is a partly broken seal, which was possibly used as a charm. It was discovered at Hadipur near Chandraketugarh and is now preserved in the private collection of G. S. De, Habra, 24-Parganas (North). It shows a lady dressed in a chiton and wearing a head-dress and earrings holding a stalk of grain with her right hand. An inscription in Kharoshṭī-Brāhmī has been translated by Mukherjee (1990: 59) as follows: "let the paddy-winning {goddess} be connected [with the devotee]". He suggests that the lady possibly represents a deity presiding over paddy. She was propitiated for a rich harvest. These two terracotta objects clearly establish that rice cultivation was well-known in the western part of Vaṅga and possibly in the entire lower Gaṅgā valley.

The third terracotta object was found at Chandraketugarh and is now held by the Balanda Museum, Haroa. An inscription in Kharoshṭī-Brāhmī on one side of the object speaks of one Karachhugmā or Karaphagmā "who has a crore of plough-men" [working under him] (*ibid.*: 46). A stalk of grain is seen immediately before the first letter of the inscription. Although the inscription does not mention rice as such, one may logically infer, given the current pattern of agricultural production in the region, that Karachhugmā or Karaphagmā was a farmer who produced rice. It must be quite obvious that the farmer in question must have been very affluent, even if we make due consideration for obvious exaggeration in the expression "a crore of plough-men". Seen in relation to the first two terracotta objects mentioned above, there can be little doubt that the region around Gaṅgābandar and possibly the entire lower Gaṅgā valley was producing abundant rice in the 3rd century AD.

The fourth terracotta object is the 'Grain and Taurine' seal-impression found at Chandraketugarh and held by the Directorate of Archaeology, West Bengal. It shows a stalk of grain on the right side of a ship. The Kharoshṭī-Brāhmī inscription on the seal-impression reads "*jitatradhana yaśo-dasya tridesayātrā*" which has been translated as "the journey to (or in) three directions of Yasoda, who has earned food-wealth" (i.e. "whose wealth is earned by selling food") (*ibid.*: 45). Jana (1998: 247) reads the inscription and the pictorial symbols to signify that the seal "belonged to a merchant who engaged in overseas trade in food grains in three directions (or three countries)". The fifth seal-impression, also from Chandraketugarh and held by the Indian Museum, Kolkata, displays a plant in a basket placed on board a ship with a mast flying a banner. A marginal legend in Kharoshṭī-Brāhmī inscription has been read by Mukherjee (1990: 47) as "*suriddhayasa Dvijammasya jaladhiśakrah*" meaning "the ship called '*jaladhiśakra*' (i.e. Indra of the ocean)[1] belongs to Dvijanma who is famous as very wealthy". As Jana (1998: 247) correctly shows, the seal indicates that it belonged to a merchant who was an overseas food grain trader. This is corroborated by the pictorial symbol of the ship carrying a basket with a stalk of

[1] "Jaladhisakra" should posibly be tranlsted as "Sakra of the ocean" as the suffix "sakra" indicates.

grain. We may further infer that the food-grains consisted mostly of rice as indicated by the first two terracotta objects mentioned above and the current pattern of agricultural production in the region.

Considering the signification of all the five terracotta objects discussed above, and the fact that they were found at or near Chandraketugarh, we believe that Gaṅgābandar was a rice-exporting port in the 3rd century AD. We may include Tāmralipti as well if we are prepared to acknowledge that the terracotta objects speak of abundant rice production in the entire lower Gaṅgā valley.

The indication of food grains contained in the Mahāsthān fragmentary stone plaque inscription (now held by the Indian Museum Kolkata and palaeographically datable to the first half of the 2nd century BC, Dani 1963: 57) is linked with famine. Hence one can hardly expect export from Puṇḍravardhana in the 2nd century BC. However, this situation appears to have been completely transformed in the 3rd century AD, from which time we have at hand a seal-impression. It was found at Bāngarh and is now held by the Asutosh Museum of Indian Art, Kolkata (Accession no. 1035). The seal-impression shows stalks of grain standing prominently on a double-prowed vessel without any mast (Fig. 2.1). The Kharoshṭī-Brāhmī inscription on the margin reads "*sasadhi* (or *dhe*) *dhi* (or *dhe*) *ṭha ḍhālī*," which B. N. Mukherjee (1990: 15-16) sanskritises as *sasyadi-dhṛtasthālī* (literally, "a vessel containing grain, etc."). We may infer that the seal-impression was attached to consignments of grains sent from Bāngarh in Puṇḍravardhana by boat and hence we may believe that it indicates surplus production in Puṇḍravardhana. Of course the seal-impression does not mention rice, but given the current pattern of agricultural production in the region of north 'Bengal', we may logically believe that rice was one, if not all of the grains. Since Vaṅga was quite definitely exporting rice in the 3rd century AD, and since the entire lower Gaṅgā valley appears to have been producing abundant rice, we may tentatively suggest that the consignments from Bāngarh in Puṇḍravardhana was not meant for the lower Gaṅgā valley but for export from Gaṅgābandar or Tāmralipti.

Fig. 2.1 A seal from Bangarh
Courtesy: Asutosh Museum of Indian Art, Kolkata

Since the 6th century BC, the middle Gaṅgā valley has been noted for its agricultural prosperity. One of the most fertile tracts in South Asia, the valley enjoys profuse rainfall and alluvium deposit from the Gaṅgā, the Yamunā and other Himalayan streams. As mentioned earlier, agrarian communities of the valley was familiar with the technique of transplanting paddy since the 5th century BC and hence must have enjoyed the benefit of increased production since that time. Archaeological evidences from early historic sites of the middle Gaṅgā valley clearly indicate greater use of agricultural iron tools such as axes, adzes, knives, razors, nails, sickles etc. Particularly noteworthy are iron plough-shares found in Kausambi and Vaisali dated between 300 BC-100 BC. Awareness of and eagerness for irrigation, as reflected in the Kuṇāla Jātaka (Book XXI, No. 536; Cowell 1957, V: 219), indicate a highly advanced system of agricultural practice among the agrarian community of the valley. That the tribes of the Sākiya and Koliya, as described in the Kuṇāla Jātaka, had a dam constructed on the river Rohiṇī flowing between the cities of Kapilavatthu and Koliya and drew its water by means of canals for cultivation of their crops, clearly indicate that the agrarian community of the middle Gaṅgā valley had a highly advanced system of cultivation during the early historic period. When all these conditions are taken into consideration, one may justifiably expect a flourishing agrarian economy in the valley with surplus rice production. Since rice was being exported from Gaṅgābandar, and since quite a few Jātakas (discussed in Chapter One) indicate movement of commodities from the middle Gaṅgā valley to Tāmralipti, we may believe that rice from the middle Gaṅgā valley may have been exported from Gaṅgābandar and Tāmralipti.

Rice export from Vaṅga in the late historic period is indicated by two seal-impressions dated to the 4th century AD. One of them, found at Chandraketugarh and held by the Asutosh Museum of Indian Art, Kolkata shows a yupa-like device and traces of Brāhmī legend that reads, in translation, "[g]rains (of the value of 90) kārshapaṇas" (Mukherjee 1990: 49). The second seal-impression was found at Gajitala near Chandraketugarh and is now preserved in the Indian Museum, Kolkata. It displays three stalks of grain. These seal-impressions do not speak of rice. However, the indication that the merchants in Gaṅgābandar were engaged in rice export in the previous period and that the present cultivation pattern in the region shows predominance of rice, may be added together to place a strong case that the grains spoken of in the seal-impressions must have been rice.

Kālidāsa's *Raghuvaṁśa* (5th century AD) indeed serves as corroborating evidence. In the excerpt quoted below, we may believe that the poet had in mind a simile that would immediately evoke the image of Vaṅga and its submission.

> They, who lowly bowed down to his lotus-like feet and who (therefore) were reinstated after having been ousted, honoured Raghu by presenting him with their wealth like Kalama plants which are bent down to their roots and which present fruit (corn) when they are transplanted after having been first uprooted (Canto 4: verse 37; Nandargikar 1982: 105).

Kalamā, it may be noted, was a transplanted variety of rice: "plants of rice grown thickly in a burnt piece of land early in the wet season and then transplanted to another soil, of a softer nature, and full of water, about July and August" (*ibid.*: 674). We may rightly believe that the association of Kalamā plants with Vaṅga was so strong that the first was almost connotative of the second. Hence, by inference, we may argue that rice from high-yielding transplanted paddy was not only the most familiar grain in Vaṅga in the late historic period but also the most extensively cultivated. Indications of abundant production and surplus derived from archaeological and literary sources are reliable enough to believe that rice was exported from Gaṅgābandar.

We have no material evidence to show that rice was also exported from Tāmralipti and Koṭālipāḍā (Candravarmakoṭa) during the late historic period. Nevertheless, we may justifiably argue in favour of export from these ports as well simply because Gaṅgābandar does not appear to have enjoyed any unique advantage to claim sole dealings in export of rice. The case of Koṭālipāḍā (Candravarmakoṭa) is stronger. The abundance of rice in Vaṅga that *Raghuvaṁśa* indicates could easily have led the port, located on the south of newly-accretated land (Navyāvakāśikā) that must have been very fertile, to become a major rice exporting centre. We may recall that in the late 19th and the early 20th centuries, Barisal (south of Koṭālipāḍā was known as the granary of 'Bengal'. Koṭālipāḍā (Candravarmakoṭa) appears to have been ideally placed for shipping out the surplus of rice that the eastern Vaṅga must have produced in the late historic period.

In the first half of the 7th century AD, Hiuen-Tsiang had noticed abundant grain-produce in the kingdom of Pun-na-fa-tan-na or Puṇḍravardhana and rich crops in the country of San-mo-ta-cha or Samataṭa (*Si-Yu-Ki*, Book X; Beal 1906: 194, 199). There can be little doubt that major portion of these crops and grain-produce were rice because, as Ray (1994: 105) argues, it was indeed "the staple sustenance of the country, and to speak of crops was to speak of rice". Sandhyākara Nandī's *Rāmacarita* (Canto III, verse 17b), which praises "paddy plants of various kinds" grown in Varendrī, bears evidence that abundant rice was produced in 'Bengal' in the 11th century AD (Sandhyākara Nandī 1910: 66). Two land grants from the 12th century AD, the Anulia copperplate of Lakṣmaṇasena (verse 10) and the Edilpur copperplate of Keśavasena (verse 24), speak of land growing excellent and extensive paddy in Puṇḍravardhana (Majumdar 1929: 89-90, 129). The fifty varieties of paddy that the *Śūnya Purāṇa* (composed by various Dharma Cult poets from Rāḍha between the 10th to the 16th centuries AD or even later) mentions were cultivated in 'Bengal' (Dasgupta 1935: 249-250) are but another testimony of abundant production of the grain. Although we have no evidence that speaks of production of rice in Vaṅga, given the indications of the previous period, there is no reason to expect otherwise.

Convincing proof that rice was produced and exported from Samataṭa in the early medieval period is available in the form of literary evidence. Khurdādhbih from the 9th century AD testifies that it was available at Caṭṭagrāma (Samandar) (Ahmad 1989: 5). Because we have indications of abundant production of rice during the early medieval period, it would be logical to believe that the commodity was exported from Caṭṭagrāma throughout the period. However, it must be conceded that we have no material evidence to prove it.

In the mid-14th century AD, Ibn Battutā's 'Bengal' was not only "a vast country, abounding in rice" but also selling it at inexpensive price (Gibb 1992: 267). That rice was exported from 'Bengal' in the mid-14th century AD is definitely confirmed by the visiting Chinese merchant Wang Ta-yüan in his account from 1349-50. It was exported to the Maldive Islands in exchange of cowries (Tarafdar 1995: 61, n. 16). This is further confirmed by Ma-Huan and Fei Sin's descriptions of commodities available in 'Bengal'. We need to remember that the mammoth maritime expeditions sent by the Ming dynasty in the first half of the 15th century AD (in which both Ma-Huan and Fei Sin participated) was actually state-sponsored trading missions. As Mills observes, "both Ma-Huan and Fei Hsin specify the articles which the Chinese used as 'trade goods' at different ports" (Mills in Ma-Huan 1970: 4-5). Ma-Huan's testimony from the 1430s speaks not only abundant production of rice, grown twice a year, but also of "husked and unhusked rice [that] is slender and long" and "small red rice" (Ma-Huan 1970: 161). Fei Sin does not mention rice as such, nor does he list it among the "natural products" of 'Bengal'. Nevertheless, he does say "[t]he soil is fertile and produces in abundance, for they have two crops every year" (Bagchi 1945: 123). There can be little doubt, given the pattern of crop production in Bangladesh and West Bengal today, and the testimonies of Ibn Battutā and Ma-Huan, that Fei Sin had rice in mind. Hence, it is not surprising that all these evidences testifying surplus of rice in Sultanate Bengal should have led to export in the mid-14th and the 1430s as Wang Ta-yüan and Ma-Huan's testimonies clearly prove.

We have quite a few references to rice export from the 16th century AD. From Tome Pires (1967: 17) we learn that rice from 'Bengal' was exported to Aden in the early 16th century AD. Caesar Frederick, the Venetian merchant who arrived in 'Bengal' in 1567, says rice was exported from Sātgāon (Purchas 1905b: 114). Ralph Fitch, who travelled through the region of eastern 'Bengal' in 1586, writes, "much rice" was sent from Sonārgāon, "wherewith they serve all India, Ceylon, Pegu, Malacca, Sumatra, and many other places" (Foster 1968: 28). Manrique (1927: 56) reports from the 1630s "a hundred vessels are yearly loaded up in the ports of Bengala with only rice, sugar, fats, oils, wax, and other similar articles". William Methwold, from the same period, confirms by observing that "once a yeere there ariveth at Musulipatnam a fleet of small vessels" loaded with rice and other commodities (Moreland 1931: 40).

The literary evidences cited above clearly establish rice export from 'Bengal' from the mid-14th to the early 17th centuries AD. We have no definite evidence to show which ports were used for the export of rice. Nevertheless, if we are prepared to accept Fitch and Frederick's testimonies as indicative of prevailing conditions in the early 16th century AD, we may surmise that Sātgāon was one of the ports. Fitch's testimony is curious since he appears to be indicating that rice was exported directly from Sonārgāon. As already discussed in Chapter One, Sonārgāon ceased functioning as a maritime port by the early 16th century AD. We must, therefore, maintain that the goods sent from Sonārgāon were off-loaded either in Sātgāon or Caṭṭagrāma, from whence they were carried by maritime vessels.

SILK

In the 1st century AD, Chinese raw silk, silk yarn and silk cloth were brought to 'Bengal' as transit items, which were then shipped from Gaṅgābandar. The *Periplus of the Erythraean Sea* (§ 64) testifies, from "a very great inland city called Thinae" in "a land called This" [western state of Ts'in in China], "raw silk and silk yarn and silk cloth are brought on foot through Bactria to Barygaza [Broach], and are also exported to Damirica [Tamil lands] by way of the river Ganges" (Schoff 1995: 48). However, Chinese silk at the ports in the region of 'Bengal' must have been a rare commodity for the *Periplus* (§ 64) also cautions that "the land of This is not easy of access; few men come from there and seldom" (*ibid.*: 48).

Silk was definitely available in Kāmrūpa in the first half of the 7th century AD because we hear from Bānabhaṭṭa that, Bhāskaravarman (king of Kāmrūpa from 594-650 AD) sent Harṣavardhana "silken towels, pure as the autumn moon's light" and black aloes-wood "contained in sacks of woven silk" as gifts (Bānabhaṭṭa 1897: 214). However, it is possible that Bhāskaravarman's silk was not locally produced in Kāmrūpa because production of raw silk was unknown in 'Bengal' till the Sultanate period when it was introduced, in all probability, from China.

'Bengal' appears to have been producing raw silk and limited amount of silk goods in the early 15th century AD. As Ma-Huan (1970: 163) observed in the 1430s, "[m]ulberry trees, wild mulberry-trees, silk-worms, and cocoons – all these they have; [but] can make only fine silks, embroidered silk kerchiefs, and coarse silks; they do not understand how to make silk-floss". This observation indicates that in the first half of the 15th century AD, the silk production in 'Bengal' was still elementary since the local producers did not know the technique of making silk-floss, a 100% pure dyed filament silk that lays flat when wrapped on the hook. Silk production must have developed tremendously within the next three-quarters of a century because we hear Varthema, observing that "[f]ifty ships are laden every year ... with cotton and silk stuffs" from the city of Banghella (established in Chapter One as Caṭṭagrāma where Varthema arrived in 1508) (Varthema 1928: 79). Later in the 16th century AD, Ralph Fitch had also observed "much ... cloth of silk" in Bacola (Foster 1968: 28). As *Ain-i-Akbari* (late 16th century) testifies, Ghoraghat was another silk producing centre (Jarrett 1891: 122). Peter Mundy (who visited South Asia sometime between 1628 and 1632) further testifies, Sherpur (near Bogra) was a renowned production centre for silk textile called Ambar or Jettalees ("a thinn silke coloured Tiffany" i.e., taffeta) (Temple 1914: 155). Export of raw silk and *moga* (*mūga*, a wild silk, the produce of *Antheroea assama*, found in Assam) to Musulipatnam in the 1630s is confirmed by Methwold (Moreland 1931: 40).

These literary references should be seen in the larger context of silk production and trade in medieval 'Bengal'. Silk became an important cash crop in the 16th century AD and remained so till the 18th century AD. The phenomenal rise in silk production before the arrival of the Europeans placed 'Bengal' as one of the three important raw silk-exporting regions of Asia – the other two being China and Persia. Even after the Europeans arrived on the scene, 'Bengal' continued to enjoy benefits from substantial international trade in raw silk. Based on the observations made by the French traveller Jean Baptiste Tavernier (1889, II: 2) in the 17th century AD regarding the production of silk yarn at Kasim-bazar (Malda district, West Bengal), as well as Peter Mundy and Ralph Fitch cited above, we may believe that Malda, Murshidabad, Rajshahi, Bogra and Baccola (Barisal) were important silk producing and manufacturing regions. The silk products were definitely exported through Caṭṭagrāma, as indicated by Varthema. Silk-yarn produced in Murshidabad and Malda could easily have been exported through Sātgāon because the port provided easy access through the Bhāgīrathī-Huglī.

Besides 'Bengal', silk was also produced and manufactured in the neighbouring Coach kingdom. According to Tome Pires (1967: 89), the Coach kingdom (Kāmrūpa-Kāmta or Cooch Behar) produced plentiful silk. In the fourth quarter of the 16th century AD, Ralph Fitch had also observed "much silke" in the country of Couche (Foster 1968: 25). It may therefore be reasonable to suppose that silk products from Cooch Behar were exported through 'Bengal'. Since the Brahmaputra-Meghnā provided the easiest access to the kingdom, it may be assumed that Caṭṭagrāma was the port through which the export was made.

MALABATHRUM

Malabathrum (Cinnamomum) is a common evergreen tree of the Himalayas that grows at heights between 3,000 and 7,000 feet, from the Masuri eastwards to Sylhet, Assam, Rangpur, the Khasia and Jaintia Hills and Burma. Its leaves are aromatic and are used as a condiment all over South Asia. The greatest supply of malabathrum comes from the Eastern Himalayas, where one of the local varieties is known as *Cinnamomum albiflorum,* designated *tejpātā* in Bengali. The word 'malabathrum' was possibly derived from a compound of *tamala* (the Sanskrit name of *Cinnamomum albiflorum*) and *patra*, 'a leaf' (Śāstri 1927: 219-220).

The Romans considered malabathrum to be one of the most treasured ingredients for ointments and perfumes. The *Periplus of the Erythraean Sea* testifies that it was obtainable at a market town located on the river Gaṅgā (§ 63; Schoff 1995: 47). The demand of the Roman consumers for malabathrum and its unique source of supply at the fore-mentioned market town clearly indicate that the commodity was exported from Gaṅgābandar.

Regarding the place of origin of the best quality of commodity, Ptolemy in his *Geography* (Book VII, Cap. 2.16) points to Kirrhadia. Although the *Periplus* (§ 62; Schoff 1995: 47) identifies the Kirrhadia (or Cirrhadae) as "a barbarous tribe" who lived near the sea between Orissa and the mouth of the Gaṅgā, Schoff (*ibid.*: 253) disregards this location and proposes that the Kirrhadia was "a Bhota tribe, whose descendants, still known as Kirata, live in the Morung, west of Sikkim". This identification appears plausible since malabathrum, as stated above, grows in Himalayan foothills. However, habitation of the Kirata people may not have been confined only to Morung but over much of Assam, for the *Mahābhārata* locates them in the vicinity of the Lauhitya (Brahmaputra). Lessen too believes that the Kirātas were a people living in the neighbourhood of the Brahmaputra (Śāstri 1927: 191-95). Because malabathrum is still grown in the same region, it would be reasonable to conclude that in the early historic period, malabathrum obtained from the mouth of the Gaṅgā originated in the foothills of Eastern Himalayas, mainly the region around the Brahmaputra in Assam.

SPIKENARD

Gangetic spikenard (*Nardostachys jatamansi*, order *Valerianaceae*) is a herb found in the Himalayas from Garhwal eastward to Sikkim, and ascends to 17000 feet. As the *Periplus of the Erythraean Sea* testifies, it was exported to Rome from Gaṅgābandar (§ 63; Schoff 1995: 47). There, the oil extracted from the Gangetic spikenard was considered a valuable ingredient of medicinal ointments and perfumes. If Pliny's observation is considered as authentic, and there is no reason that it should be otherwise, Gangetic spikenard was the most valuable ointment in Rome in the 1st century AD.

The Gangetic spikenard exported to Rome possibly came from the eastern Himalayan region because geographical proximity and easier access through riverine routes indicate this. From the region today known as Nepal, it could have been transported overland to any of the numerous tributaries of the Gaṅgā (such as the Kosī), and then down the Gaṅgā and the Bhāgīrathī-Huglī to Gaṅgābandar. The easiest means of transporting the commodity from the region today known as Sikkim would have been down the Tistā, the Tāṅgon, the Mahānandā and the Bhāgīrathī-Huglī to Gaṅgābandar.

Trade in spikenard was prevalent even in the late 13th century AD. As Marco Polo (II, LV) reports in his account of Bangala, "They grow cotton, in which they drive a great trade, and also spices such as spikenard, galingale [roots which resemble ginger], ginger, sugar, and many other sorts" (Yule 1903, II: 115). Since it is likely that Marco polo would have heard about Caṭṭagrāma (because of its geographical proximity to Pagan) from those participating in the Mongol military campaign against Pagan and because it was the only functioning port in the late 13th century AD, we may believe that the spikenard Marco Polo mentions was exported from Caṭṭagrāma. The source of the spikenard must have been the same as it was in the early historic period, i.e., eastern Himalayan region, where various Nepalese principalities and the Sikkimese theocracy had emerged in the medieval period. However, Tome Pires does not mention Gangetic spikenard. He mentions Delhi and Mandu in his list of places where the commodity was available. It appears from his report that the Sultanate of Delhi had the Himalayan region under its control and because of its unfriendly relations with Bengal, spikenard was exported from Cambay (Pires 1967: 514).

ALOES-WOOD

Aloe leaf is a valuable ingredient for *ayurvedic* medicine and a kind of incense (*tailaparnika*) is extracted from the wood. Going by the authority of Kauṭīlya's *Arthaśāstra* (2.11.57-58), it is possible to ascertain that in Joṅga and Doṅga, two localities in Kāmrūpa (Assam) were famous for aloes-wood (*agaru*). "Aloe from Joṅga is black, black-variegated or variegated with round spots. That from Doṅga is dark" (Kangle 1963: 116). As Bānabhaṭṭa (1897: 214) testifies, Bhāskaravarman (king of Kāmrupa from c. 594-650) sent to Harṣavardhana black aloes-wood and black aloes oil as gift. Assam must have continued producing abundant aloes-wood in the 10th century AD because *Ḥudūd al-'Ālam* observes, "In no place of Hindūstān are fresh aloes ('ūd-i tar) found but in the (possessions) of the king of Qāmarūn and of Dahum (Dharmapāla)" (Chapter 10: 7; Minorsky 1937: 87). Even in the 16th century AD, Abu-l-Fazl in his *Ain-i-Akbari,* makes a special mention of the *sarkār* of Sylhet (located immediately south of Assam) as an area with abundant aloes-wood (Jarrett 1891: 125). These evidences establishing abundant availability and surplus of aloes-wood over a reasonably long period of time clearly indicate that the commodity may have been exported from Kāmrūpa.

There can be little doubt that aloes-wood was exported from Samandar in the 9th century AD because Ibn Khurdādhbih's account is unequivocal regarding the matter. "It [i.e., Samundar] has rice, and aloes-wood is brought here from a distance of fifteen to twenty days' journey by means of a river from Kāmrūn (Kāmrūpa) and other places" (Ahmad 1989: 5). The merchandise must have been exported even in the 12th century AD because Al-Idrīsī observes:

> The aloes-wood is brought here [i.e., Samundar] from the country of Kāmarūt [Kāmrūpa] from a distance of fifteen days' journey, (floated down) in sweet water (by river?). In that region, there are places where aloes-wood of fine quality and sweet odour grows (or: of fine qualities grows in its seas), and it is brought there from the Qāmarūn Mountains (Al-Idrīsī's *Kitāb*

Nuzhat al-Mushtāk fi'Khtirāq al-Āflāq, 8th section of the 2nd clime, 41-45; Ahmad 1960: 64).

In all probability, the fame of aloes-wood exported from Samandar gave rise to the variety called Samandarūk which al-Bīrūnī (937-1048 AD) called the choicest of all aloes-wood (*ibid.*: 101).

The *Si yang ch'ao kung tien lu* by Huang Sing-ts'eng (1520) and the *Shu yu chou tseu lu* (1574) both list aloes wood as one of a number of gifts that the sultans of 'Bengal' sent to the Chinese emperors (Bagchi 1945: 127, 133). Obviously the aloes wood was obtained from Assam. Although the gift from the sultan of 'Bengal' may not indicate trade between China and 'Bengal', these references nevertheless show that there existed a demand for this highly valued luxury article among the elite in 'Bengal' and China. The Chinese sources further prove that Assamese aloes wood was available in 'Bengal' in the early 15th century AD. Export of aloes from Kāmrupa through 'Bengal' may have been difficult in the medieval period because in his list of places where it was available, Tome Pires (1967: 514) does not mention it; rather he says that the aloes-wood from Sumatra were the "most esteemed". We do not hear of export of aloes-wood from 'Bengal' from any other source. However, one hears of the commodity being available in Patna in the 17th century AD. These vicissitudes in trade must have been the result of political conditions rather than fluctuation in production of aloes wood. During the sultanate period, there was an acrimonious relation between these two neighbours. Other than occasional raids and unsuccessful campaigns, none of the sultans of 'Bengal' (including Ala-ud-din Hossain Shah and Nusrat Shah) ever managed to extend their sway over medieval Assam. The situation was reversed in 1663 when the Mughal general Mir Jumla succeeded in enforcing a humiliating treaty on the Assamese, forcing them to cede territories on the west bank of the Bharali and Kalang rivers (Baruah 1985: 231-233, 263-264). Hence, the aloes-wood available in Patna in the 17th century AD was possibly from Assam but it may not have been exported.

EBONY

Diospyros *Linn.* Order, Ebenaceae is a fairly important genus that embraces about 59 species of South Asian forest trees. They occur chiefly in South India, Ceylon, Burma and Eastern 'Bengal'. All the species yield useful timbers, of which the best are the various forms of ebony (Diospyros Ebenum and Diospyros melanoxylon). Diospyros Ebenum is a large tree not very common in India, where it is found in the Deccan and Karnatak. This species is perhaps the best ebony-yielding tree and the only one that gives black heartwood without streaks or markings. Diospyros melanoxylon is a medium-sized tree found in South India. However, Diospyros tomentosa extends its area to the deciduous forests of central India, Chotanagpur, Bihar and the Western Peninsula. Diospyros tomentosa is the tree that gives the ebony most largely used in North India. It is probably this variety that was found also in East 'Bengal' especially in Sylhet, Tipperah, the Khasia Hills and North 'Bengal'.

We hear of the availability of ebony in 'Bengal' for the first time from Strabo who cites Megasthenes (4th centuries BC) and notes that the timber grew in the land of the Prasioi (McCrindle 1979: 46). We hear of ebony again from (popularly known as Si'di' Capudān), captain of the fleet of Ottoman Sultān Suleimān, who observes in his *Mohi't* (composed in 1554) "Bengal is abundant in ivory and ebony" (Hammer 1836: 467). Clearly, al-Chelebi's observation implies that ebony was exported from 'Bengal'. Since the *Mohi't* was composed in Ahmedabad in Gujarat and is based on earlier Arabic-Persian works, one may reasonably assume that al-Chelebi's source of information was from the market network in the Arabian Sea littoral or the Ottoman Empire. Hence, it is possible that ebony from 'Bengal' had its market in the above-mentioned region. Ebony must have been exported from Shātijām (Caṭṭagrāma) since al-Chelebi has given detailed note for navigation to the port in the *Mohi't* (Chapter Nine, Section 3, Twenty-eighth Voyage), and mentions none other in 'Bengal'.

EMERY

Emery is an impure variety of corundum (derived mostly from magma) adulterated with spinel, garnet etc. It is a mineral substance used chiefly as an abrasive agent because of its great hardness. Of late, artificial products such as carborundum, alundum, etc. have challenged its use. India possesses large resources of corundum in Mysore, Madras, Singhbhum, Rewah (Pipra), parts of Bihar, the Zanskar range in Kashmir and the Khasi Hills in Assam.

The *Ḥudūd al-'Ālam*, composed in 982 AD, testifies that "[f]rom it (Kāmrūpa) come(s) emery (*sunbādha*)" (§ 10, Minorsky 1937: 86). The testimony is acceptable because existing sources of emery in the Khasi Hills in Assam suports its claim. Hence we may believe that emery from Kāmrūpa was exported through Samandar (Caṭṭagrāma) in the early medieval period.

BETEL-NUT AND COCONUT

The second Āśrāfpur copperplate of Devakhaḍga (Laskar 1907: 89), which records granting "[a]t Talapataka, half a *pataka* [of land] including the two areca-gardens", clearly indicates that betel-nut was definitely produced in eastern Puṇḍravardhana in the 8th century AD. It must also have been known in Assam a century earlier because Bhāskaravarman sent to Harṣavardhana "luscious milky betel nut fruit, hanging from its spray and green as young *hārita* doves" as gift (Bānabhaṭṭa 1897: 214). By the 11th century AD, betel-nut as well as coconut must have become well-known because Śrīcandra's Rāmpāl copperplate (lines 17, 23-26; Majumdar 1929: 8) records granting of land with both the agricultural products in a village under Pauṇḍrabhukti. This is further attested by the *Rāmacarita* (Canto III, verse 19b) which bears evidence that Varendrī was famous for both the fruits (Sandhyākara Nandī 1910: 67).

By the next (12th) century, six copperplate land grants indicate abundant production of these two commodities in Pauṇḍrabhukti (Varendrī) and Vardhamāna-Bhukti (Uttara-Rāḍha Maṇḍala and Khaḍi-maṇḍala). These are Bhoja-varman's Belāva, Vallālasena's Naihāṭī, Lakṣmaṇasena's Anulia, Tarpandīghi, Govindapur and Sundarban copperplates (Majumdar 1929: 24, 90; Mukherji and Maity 1967: 269, 276, 293, 300). We have three land grants from the 13th century AD containing information regarding coconut and betel-nut in Puṇḍravardhana-Bhukti (Vikramapura, Navyakhanda in Vaṅga, Vikramapura and Candradvipa). These are Keśavasena's Edilpur, Viśvarūpasena's Calcutta Sāhitya-Pariṣat and Madanapāḍā copperplates (Majumdar 1929: 130, 138, 140). Hence, there can be no doubt that Puṇḍravardhana (including Vikramapura and Varendra), coastal regions of Vaṅga (Candradvipa and Khaḍi-maṇḍala) and Rāḍha became regions producing abundant – we may even say surplus – betel-nut and coconut by the end of the 12th century AD.

There is little doubt that these agricultural products were consumed locally. However, as to their export to Sri Lanka, as almost all versions of the *Manasāmaṅgala* claim, one needs to proceed with caution. In Bijayagupta's *Padmāpurāṇa* composed in 1494-95, C̃ād Saodāgar barters coconut for conch shells and betel-leaf and betel-nut for precious stone (1962: 259-267, 269, 275). In Narayana Deva's *Padmā-purāṇa* composed in the 16th century AD, the same merchant barters betel-nut, betel leaf and coconut for precious stones (1942: 212, 215). In Srīrāy Binod's *Padmā-purāṇa* composed in the 16th century AD, C̃ād Saodāgar barters coconut for conch shells and betel-nut and betel-leaves for precious stones (1993: 216, 217). In Baṁśīdāsa's *Manasāmaṅgala* (16th century AD), the Bengali merchant exchanges betel-nut for ten gems. He even claims that Bengali merchants introduced coconut to some foreign countries (Dasgupta 1935: 26-27). Only in the *Caṇḍīmaṅgala* by Kavikañkaṇa Mukunda does one notice a reverse of the trend noted above for Dhanapati nor Śrīmanta carry betel-nut to Sri Lanka but wish to obtain it from there in exchange of myrobalan (Mukunda 1986: 209, 254).

In his typical style of making sweeping generalisations, Niharranjan Ray (1994: 118-119) claims "betel and coconut were also exported into neighbouring regions". The source he substantiates his claim with is the medieval maṅgalakāvya corpus cited above. Tamonash Chandra Dasgupta is more cautious in his analysis. Commenting on Baṁśīdāsa's *Manasāmaṅgala* and Kavikañkaṇa Mukundarāma's *Caṇḍī-maṅgala* in particular and the maṅgalakāvya corpus in general, Dasgupta (1935: 26) acknowledges that "the prices are ludicrously exaggerated, for during the time when these were written, sea-voyage was reduced to a vague tradition in which facts and fiction were hopelessly blended together". Although he has no doubt that the maṅgalakāvya corpus "contain some elements of truth", it is extremely doubtful if those elements of truth pertained to coconut.

The reasons are not hard to find. We have definite information that the Portuguese were importing coconut products to 'Bengal' in the 17th century AD. Therefore, if coconut was ever exported from 'Bengal', it must have been between the 11th century AD (when the fruit is mentioned for the first time in Śrīcandra's Rāmpāl copperplate) and the 16th century AD (after which the Portuguese began to import coconut products to 'Bengal'). However, Sri Lanka abounds in coconut and the inhabitants must have been familiar with the fruit since the 6th century AD, if not earlier. According to the Durava community of Sri Lanka, they owned coconut plantation from Devundara to Unavatuna planted by King Agbo I (575 - 608 AD) (Hussein 2006). Hence we may safely discount the claim made in the maṅgalakāvya corpus as fictitious.

Even if we assume that Sri Lanka needed to import the commodity for some reason, Malabar and the Maldives (enjoying geographical proximity) could easily have been more viable sources than the further off 'Bengal'. Malabar exported copra (dried kernel of coconut), ripe coconut and coconut products (coconut oil and coir) in the early 16th century AD (Pires 1967: 82). The Maldives exported coconut and its products in the mid-14th century AD (Gibb 1986: 241) and in the early 17th century AD (de Laval's account in Purchas 1905a: 560). These are definite indicators showing that neither geographical determinants of production nor unique source of supply can place coconut as an indispensable commodity for Sri Lanka to import form 'Bengal'. Hence, we can safely lay coconut aside as an exported commodity.

As for betel-nut, we may begin again with Niharranjan Ray (1994: 118-119) for he substantiates his claim that the product was exported from 'Bengal' with Baṁśīdāsa's *Manasāmaṅgala* and Kavikañkaṇa Mukunda's *Caṇḍīmaṅgala*. (Actually, as observed earlier, Kavikañkaṇa Mukunda does not indicate export but import of betel-nut.) He goes on to argue, "[i]n ancient times, betel was exported to Persia and the Arab lands whose merchants loaded their ships with it at the west Indian port of Suparaka or Supparaka or Sopara ..." (*ibid.*: 119). The name *śupārī* for betel, prevalent all over South Asia, was derived from the name of the port where the commodity was available. Finally, he seals his argument with the claim, without pointing out his source, that "[t]here is evidence of 'Bengal' gaining much revenue from this extensive trade in betel right up to the time of the English East India Company, under whose rule betel was a monopoly trade in 'Bengal'" (*ibid.*: 119).

Even if we accept the argument that there was extensive maritime export-trade in betel from the mid-18th to the mid-19th century AD when the English East India Company ruled 'Bengal', Ray's claim regarding betel trade from the 8th century AD (when the commodity is first reported in the Āśrāfpur copperplate of Devakhaḍga) to the mid-17th century AD (when Company rule commenced in 'Bengal') is questionable. First of all, none of the Arab-Persian accounts mention betel as a commodity exported from Samandar/Caṭṭagrāma or Sātgāon. If the betel-nuts they obtained from Soppara were originally from 'Bengal', the Arab-Persian merchants could have easily collected the commodity from the two above-mentioned ports. Even Chau Ju-kua's work on Chinese and Arab trade in the 12th and the 13th centuries AD does not mention India or 'Bengal' as sources of betel-nut but points to the island of Hainan (China), Kiau-chi (Tongking) and Ma-i (the Philippines) (Hirth and Rockhill 1965: 213-214).

In the early 16th century AD, Tome Pires (1967: 86) observed that Sri Lanka "has a great deal of areca ... It is eaten with betel. It is a food-stuff and very cheap". He also included areca and betel among the merchandise of Malabar and Deccan (*ibid.*: 52, 82). From the same source we learn that "[t]he best betel [available at Malacca] is from the kingdom of Goa. From Chaul to Cambodia, and in all the islands, even beyond the Moluccas, it is found in abundance" (*ibid.*: 516). These evidences show that neither geographical determinant of production nor unique source of supply can place areca as an indispensable commodity for Sri Lanka to import from 'Bengal'.

Furthermore, there is contradictory information in the original source, the maṅgalakāvya corpus, upon which much of the argument for betel trade is based. Most of the texts belonging to the corpus show the merchant hero (be it Cā̃d Saodāgar or Dhanapati) bartered betel-nuts for precious stones. However, neither Dhanapati nor Śrīmanta carry betel-nut to Sri Lanka but wish to obtain it from there in exchange of myrobalan. Prakash (1985: 54) supports Kavikaṅkaṇa Mukunda's testimony by pointing out that 'Bengal' imported betel-nut from Sri Lanka in the 17th century AD. Hence it is unreasonable to seriously doubt that betel-nut was ever exported from 'Bengal' to Sri Lanka or Gujarat through maritime routes.

SPICES

Long pepper (*Piper longum*, Linn., order *Piperaceae*), grows abundantly from Nepal eastward to Assam, the Khasia hills and 'Bengal'. The major production areas for long pepper in Bangladesh are Faridpur, Noakhali, Barisal, Mymansingh, Bogra, Rangpur, Comilla and Caṭṭagrāma, while that for ginger in Bangladesh today are Rangpur, Dinajpur, Rajshahi, Kushtia and Jessore. Galangal (an aromatic root) is hardly known in Bangladesh today. In the medieval period, these commodities were valued for their use in medicines and cookery.

According to Marco Polo's (Polo N.D.: 204) report from the end of the 13th century AD, merchants from various parts of India came to 'Bengal' to purchase galangal, ginger and many sorts of drugs. In the first half of the 15th century AD, the only condiment and/or herbal-medicinal ingredient that Ma-Huan (1970: 161) mentions is ginger. Verthema's testimony from the early 16th century AD confirms Ma-Huan's impression for the only commodity of the above-mentioned category he found abundantly available in 'Bengal' was ginger (Varthema 1928: 79). Barbosa (1921: 145) adds long pepper to ginger and says both of these were cultivated in 'Bengal'. In 1567, Caesar Frederick had found only long pepper (and not ginger) being exported from Sātgāon (Purchas 1905b: 114).

In the early 16th century AD, Tome Pires (1967: 89) observed that pepper (Piper nigrum) was available abundantly in Cooch Behar. In the *Riazu-s-Salatin* (composed at the end of the 18th century AD) Ghulam Husain Salim (1904: 11) confirms that black pepper was grown in Cooch Behar. However, in the fourth quarter of the 16th century AD, Ralph Fitch reported that the kingdom imported pepper from Couchin China (Foster 1968: 25). Obviously Fitch was mistaken, as Ray (1988: 134) believes. Since he mentions Couchin China, it is more probable that the kingdom *exported* pepper to Couchin China instead of *importing* it.

Reviewing the observations on the availability and export trend of spices, condiments and/or herbal-medicinal ingredients made above, it may be concluded that ginger and long pepper were exported from 'Bengal' and black pepper was exported from Cooch Behar. Since Rangpur was under Cooch Behar in the Medieval Period, it is possible that ginger was also exported from the kingdom. We hear only of Sātgāon as the port that handled long pepper. However, Marco Polo, Varthema and Ma-Huan's testimonies imply that the commodity was exported through Caṭṭagrāma. It is also possible, as geographical proximity and easy access through riverine routes indicate, that ginger grown in Kushtia and Jessore was also exported from Sātgāon while long pepper grown in Barisal, Mymansingh, Bogra, Rangpur, Comilla and Caṭṭagrāma were exported through the port of Caṭṭagrāma. Easy access down the Brahmaputra and the Meghnā indicates that black pepper from Cooch Behar was exported through Caṭṭagrāma.

GUM-LAC AND INDIGO

The resin that a parasitic insect (Coccus lacca) produces on various trees is known as gum-lac or simply lac. In Bangladesh today, lac is cultivated on Baḍai (*Zizyphus jujuba*) trees, only in the western part of greater Rajshahi, in Shibganj and Nawabganj upazilas. In West Bengal, it is produced in Malda district. In 'Bengal', lac was used for extracting scarlet colour, which was used for dyeing cotton textiles. After extracting the colour, the residue was used for embellishing toys and making seal-wax. Of the 15 species of indigo found growing in the region of 'Bengal', *Indigofera tinctoria* was cultivated for indigo dye (a form of glucoside soluble in water). It also has medicinal value and is praised in the ancient medicinal treatise *Caḍak Saṁhitā*. In the 19th century, indigo was widely cultivated in Nadia, Jessore, Bogra, Rangpur and Dhaka (Ahmed 2003: 251). Horrendous tales of coercion and torture by the English planters is still recounted all over 'Bengal'.

Lac was a major exportable commodity during the sultanate period. In support of this claim, we may cite Ma-Huan (1970: 163) who reported in the first half of the 15th century AD that lacquered articles were one of the commodities that 'Bengal' offered for sale. In his description of Aden and its trade, Barbosa observes,

> ... many ships come also from Bengala, Çamatra [Sumatra] and Malaca, which bring as well abundance of spices, drugs, silk, benzoin [incense], lac, sanders-wood [sandalwood], aloes-wood, rhubarb in plenty, musk, thin Bengala cloths, and sugar (great store); ... (Barbosa 1918: 56).

The lac imported to Aden in the early 16th century AD must have been from 'Bengal' because in 1567, Caesar Frederick had observed that the commodity was being exported from Sātgāon (Purchas 1905b: 114). In 1666, Tavernier (1889, II: 21-22) reported that the European traders used to obtain the commodity mostly from Pegu and 'Bengal'. Lac produced in 'Bengal' was cleaner and hence more expensive than that from Pegu. The Dutch traders used to export lac to Persia, where it was also used for dying textiles. Since the elite would have used dyed cotton textiles, the Dutch export of lac to Persia possibly served the ruling elite of the Safavid (1502-1736) dynasty. In the absence of chemical dye, it is possible that demand for lac in the Persian market would have existed even during the reign of Ilkhani (1206-1353) and Taimuri (1369-1500) dynasties. Based on these premises, it may be tentatively suggested that lac was exported from Sultanate Bengal. Easy access down the Gaṅgā, the Jalaṅgi and the Bhāgīrathī-Huglī indicates that lac produced in Rajshahi and Malda regions was transported to Sātgāon for export. It may have been handled by Arab-Persian traders before the Dutch, who marketed this commodity in Persia to serve the demand for dyed cotton textiles in flourishing urban centres such as Tabriz, Herat and Shiraz in Persia.

Moreland (1920: 197) observed that some dyes such as indigo were exported from South Asia in the second half of the 16th century AD. Although there is voluminous material on indigo cultivation during the colonial era, we have very little material evidence to prove that it was exported from 'Bengal' during the period under review. Nevertheless, the phenomenal rise in the cotton industry in the medieval period suggests increased demand, and hence production, of indigo at home. Given the fact that chemical dye was not available, we may concede that some amount of indigo may have been exported in the early 16th century AD. We may expect that shipment of indigo from Nadia and Jessore was sent to Sātgāon by some of the east-west channels connecting Kapotākṣa, Ichāmati and the Bhāgīrathī-Huglī and that from Bogra, Rangpur and Dhaka was sent to Caṭṭagrāma by the Ghāghaṭ, the Karatoyā, the Dhaleśwarī, the Padmā and the Meghnā.

Manufactured Goods

RAW COTTON AND COTTON TEXTILE

Locally produced cotton in Bangladesh, known as American Cotton *(Gossypium hirsutum)* in Kushtia and Chuadanga districts and Comilla Cotton *(Gossypium arboreum)* in the hilly region of Caṭṭagrāma and Caṭṭagrāma Hill Tracts, hardly meets the country's demand for cotton yarn and textiles. However, there can be little doubt that cotton textile was one of the major items of export from 'Bengal', especially during the medieval period. The best quality of cotton in 'Bengal' was grown in the region of Sonārgāon, Kapasia and Jaṅgalbaḍi (in Narayanganj, Gazipur and Kishorganj districts, respectively) and on "[a] tract of land extending from Ferringybazar [...] 12 miles east of Dacca along the bank of Megna to Idelpore, 20 miles north of the sea" (Mitra 1978: 155-156).

Among all cotton textiles produced in the region, undoubtedly muslin was the most famous. The fame of muslin is well summed up by Tavernier's anecdote of Muhammad Ali Beg, a Persian ambassador to India, who returned home to his sovereign Shah Safavi II (1629-42) with the gift of "a cocoa-nut of the size of an ostrich's egg, enriched with precious stones; and when it was opened a turban was drawn from it 60 cubits in length, and of a muslin so fine that you would scarcely know what it was that you had in your hand" (Tavernier 1889, II: 7). Although it is not certain whether the muslin in Tavernier's anecdote was definitely from 'Bengal', since varieties of fine muslin were also produced in north-western India, we can be certain about the quality of Bengal's muslin from Sebastien Manrique's testimony made in the first half of the 17th century AD. According to the missionary, merchants used to pack a length of the textile inside "hollow bambus, about two spans long" and carried the commodity to distant lands such as "Corazane (Khurasan), Persia, Turkey and many other countries" (Manrique 1927: 57). Because references to cotton textiles, specially muslin, repeatedly recur in numerous literary sources from the early historic period, we may as well make a chronological study, beginning from its earliest known reference and identify the periods when it was exported.

While discussing precious commodities available in 'Bengal', Kauṭīlya (4th century BC) notes the existence of four varieties of textiles. In the *Arthaśāstra* (2.11.29: 102-105) he observes,

> The dukūla from the Vaṅgas is white and smooth. That from the Puṇḍras is dark and smooth like a gem. That from Suvarṇakuḍya is of the colour of the sun, with gem-smooth water-weave, with a uniform weave and with a mixed weave (Kangle 1963: 119-120).

Sarkar (1973: 179) informs us that Suvarṇakuḍya probably was Assam. He also believes that the *dukūla* variety of cotton textile from Vaṅgas that the *Arthaśāstra* speaks of was possibly muslin. However, there is no definite indication to prove it as such.

Export of *dukūla* textiles from the region of 'Bengal' may have begun as early as the 3rd century BC. As recorded in the *Mahāvaṁsa* (XI: 19, 28-33), King Devānaṁpiya Tissa of Siṁhala sent gifts for Emperor Aśoka through the port of Tāmralipti in the middle of the 3rd century BC. In return, Aśoka sent as gifts "all that was needful for consecrating a king, marvellous in splendour" (Geiger 1986: 78-80). Although an exchange of gifts between royalties cannot be considered a transaction of trade, nevertheless, the list of gifts exchanged by Devānaṁpiya Tissa and Aśoka is a valuable document of commodities that we may believe were considered important and luxurious in the kingdoms of the two monarchs. Hence, these commodities may have had considerable demand in their respective foreign market (i.e., Aśoka's commodities in Sri Lanka and vice versa). It may therefore be reasonable to accept the list as an important indicator of trade between Sri Lanka and the Maurya Empire subsequent to, if not before, the royal consecration.

Sarkar (1973: 179-180) shows that two items on the list of articles sent by Aśoka, i.e., "a parasol and a set of garments that had no need of cleansing" (*Mahāvaṁsa* XI: 28-33, Geiger 1986: 79-80) possibly were made out of the *dukūla* variety of textile noted in the *Arthaśāstra*. Justifying his claim, Sarkar shows that the *Bṛhatsaṁhita* of Varāhamihira, composed in the 6th century AD, makes it mandatory that "the traditional royal parasol/umbrella shall be covered with new *dukūla*-fabric of white colour". As for the "set of garments that had no need of cleansing", Sarkar argues that Aśoka must have sent only precious materials available in his kingdom for the occasion was the royal consecration of Devānaṁpiya Tissa. Because Kauṭīlya identifies *dukūla* textile as a precious commodity, it is not unlikely that Aśoka's gift was indeed made from the same material. Hence, by way of circuitous reasoning we may accept Sarkar's argument that the white *dukūla* variety of textile from Vaṅga may have been exported from Tāmralipti in the 3rd century BC.

There exists archaeological evidence to indicate that Sarkar's proposition may not be far from the truth. Evidences of cotton fragments and thread have been found recently at the burial site at Ban Don Ta Phet in central Thailand. Fragmentary remains of textile have been also found at Ban Chiang in south-eastern Thailand. Specialists from the National Museum in Bangkok have examined the Ban Don Ta Phet fragments and have dated it to the 4th century BC. They have also identified the fibre as *cannabis sativa* that might have derived its origin from the cotton plant (*Gossypium* species) found in South Asia (Glover 1990: 175). The discovery is significant because it indicates textile export from South Asia to Southeast Asia. Since Kauṭīlya's testimony shows that Vaṅga, produced white *dukūla* in the 4th century BC and since it is expected that a burial site would contain ritually pure articles (a quality that *Bṛhatsaṁhita* of Varāhamihira lays on the same textile) it may not be unreasonable to believe that the Ban Don Ta Phet textile was the white *dukūla* from Vaṅga.

The *Periplus of the Erythraean Sea* unquestionably substantiates that muslin was a quality export commodity in the 1st century AD. This is the earliest definitive reference to muslin. Section 63 of the text states that "muslins of the finest sorts, which are called Gangetic" were shipped from "a market-town which has the same name as the river, Ganges" (Schoff 1995: 47). Hence, there can be no doubt that "Gangetic muslin" was exported to the Roman Empire from Gaṅgābandar. Schoff (*ibid.*: 256-258) believes that these were varieties of muslin of the Dhaka region, which the Romans called *Ventus textilis*, or *nebula*. Because Wārī-Baṭeśwar was situated in the region where the best quality of cotton was grown (i.e., Sonārgāon, Kapasia and Jaṅgalbaḍi) we may tentatively suggest that "Gangetic muslin" was also exported from this port.

After a long silence, we hear of cotton textiles again from the Arab-Persian accounts. As recorded in *Kitāb al-Masālik wa'l-Mamālik* by Ibn Khurdādhbih (mid-9th century AD), the country of Rahmi (identified as Pāla kingdom) produced cotton textiles (Ibn Khurdādba 1867: 14). The account of the Arab traveller and merchant Sulaiman al-Tajir (who made several voyages to South Asia and China) proves that fine quality cotton textile was maufactured in Ruhmi (identified with the Pāla Empire) in the 9th century AD. He says, "[t]here is a stuff made in his country which is not to be found elsewhere; so fine and delicate is this material that a dress made of it may be passed through a signet-ring. It is made of cotton, and we have seen a piece of it" (Sulaiman 1867: 5). Sulaiman's textile must have been muslin because his description of the textile bears close similarity with that of muslin by Tavernier. *Ḥudūd al-'Ālam* (composed in 982 AD) does not speak of production of cotton textile but raw cotton. It records that the kingdoms of Qāmarūn and Dahum "produce in large quantities good cotton which (grows) on trees yielding their produce (*bar dihadh*) during many years" (10.7; V. Minorsky 1937: 87).

Although none of the above accounts speak explicitly of export of cotton textiles, we may believe that muslin was definitely exported because its source of supply was unique. Since the *Ḥudūd* indicates abundant supply and surplus of cotton and Ibn Khurdādhbih's account indicates abundant supply of cotton textiles, we may add them together to argue in favour of availability of cotton textiles over a reasonably long period of time. Hence, it is possible that besides muslin, other varieties of cotton textiles were also exported from Kāmrūpa and the Pāla kingdom. Since Caṭṭagrāma was the only port in 'Bengal' in the 9th and the 10th centuries AD and since the Arab-Persian merchants frequented it, we may firmly believe that cotton textiles mentioned in the Arab-Persian accounts were exported from this port.

One learns from Chau ju-kua's *Chu-fan-chi*, a record on Chinese and Arab trade in the 12th and 13th centuries AD, that native products of P'ōng-kié-lo (i.e., Vaṅgāla or Vaṅga) included "cotton stuffs (*tóu-lo*) and common cotton cloth" (Hirth and Rockhill 1965: 97). Although Chau ju-kua does not explicitly mention export of cotton textiles, Marco Polo's testimony from the last quarter of the 13th century AD indicates export of raw cotton. He says, "[t]hey grow cotton, in which they drive a great trade ..." (Yule 1903, II: 115). Given the long history of cotton textile in 'Bengal', it may not be too far fetched to imagine that Chau ju-kua's testimony implies export of the commodity. It is likely that the port through which the commodities were exported was Caṭṭagrāma since Marco Polo could have heard about it from reports reaching the Chinese capital after the first Mongol invasion of Pagan (1277 AD).

We hear of *dukūla* again in the 14th century AD. Citing the authority of the *Nāgarakṛtāgama* (65. 3/2), Sarkar (1973: 179-180) points out that *dukūla* was in great demand in Indonesia in 1365 AD. We also hear from Ibn Battutā that "a single piece of cotton cloth is sold in their country [i.e., China] for the price of many pieces of silk" (Gibb 1986: 284). Digby (1982c: 142) suggests, "a large portion of the cottons which reached China came from the three main coastal areas of production which had been exporting overseas since the classical times, Gujarat, Coromandel and Bengal". This is credible because in the early 15th century AD, Fei Sin shows interest in "cotton stuffs" and "veils of sundry colours to veil the face" by showing them prominently in his list of "natural products" available in 'Bengal' (Bagchi 1945: 123). Ma-Huan (1970: 162-163) shows even more interest and provides elaborate information. He says, five or six varieties of fine cotton textiles were manufactured in 'Bengal'. These were as follows.

1. The *pi* cloth (also called *pei-po*), "as fine as starched paper", made in pieces which were over 36.7 inches wide and 57 feet 1 inch long.
2. The ginger-black (alternate reading, ginger-yellow) cloth (also called *man-che-t'i* and possibly *bejutapauts*), "closely-woven and strong", made in pieces about 48.9 inches broad and over 51 feet long.
3. Cotton crepe (also called *sha-na-pa-fu* or *shanbaff*), "quite like a raw plain crepe", made in pieces 61.2 inches broad and 30 feet 7 inches long.
4. Cotton gauze used "to bind round the head" (also called *hsin-pai-ch'in-ta-li*), "the stitches [of which] are fine and equal", made in pieces 36.7 inches and 61 feet 2 inches.
5. *Sha-t'a-erh* (possibly *chautahi*, 'fourfold', a cloth used in Punjab for counterpanes), made in pieces 30.6 inches broad and 40 feet 9 inches long.
6. *Mo-hei-mo-le* (possibly *malmal* or cotton velvet) with raised flossy surface about half inch thick on both sides, made in pieces 48.9" broad and 20 feet 4 inches long.

Three of the varieties mentioned by Ma-Huan, i.e., the *man-che-t'i*, the *sha-na-pa-fu* and the *sha-t'a-erh* were possibly *beatihas, sinabafos* and *chautares* respectively that Tome Pires (discussed below) also mentions. Irfan Habib (1982b: 79) has identified these varieties as muslin. Thus we can definitely conclude that three varieties of muslin as well as other varieties of cotton textiles were exported in the 15th century AD. Because Fei Sin and Ma-Huan disembarked in Caṭṭagrāma, Sonārgāon and Paṇḍua/Gauḍa, the textiles that they identify may have been available in exchange centres at these cities. Since the Chinese appear to have journeyed up the Gaṅgā-Meghnā channel, it would be reasonable to expect that the textiles from the exchange centres at Pandua/Gauḍa were transported through the same channel and exported from Caṭṭagrāma and Sonārgāon.

'Bengal' had well-established export markets for various types of cotton textiles before the Portuguese arrived in the early 16th century AD. In 1498 AD, Vasco da Gama carried back to Portugal the information that 'Bengal' could be very lucrative for trade in "very valuable cotton goods" because "[c]loths which sell on the spot for twenty-two shillings and six pence fetch ninety shillings in Calicut" (Campos 1919: 25). Varthema's report adds further detail to the volume of export. He says, "[f]ifty ships are laden every year ... with cotton and silk stuffs" from the city of Banghella (Varthema 1928: 79). Some of the varieties that he names are *bairam, namone, lizati, ciantar, doazar*, and *sinabaff*. These were exported to Turkey, Syria, Persia, Arabia, Ethiopia and all over India. Duarte Barbosa, writing a few years later, confirms Varthema because he specifically mentions that cotton textile was exported from the prosperous city of "Bengala" (Caṭṭagrāma).

> [I]n it [i.e., the City of Bengala] are woven many kinds of very fine and coloured clothes for their own attire and other white sorts for sale in various countries. They are very precious also some which they call *estravantes*, a certain sort, a very thin kind of cloth much esteemed among us for ladies' head-dresses, and by the Moors, Arabs and Persian for turbans. Of these great store is woven so much so that many ships take cargoes thereof for abroad; others they make called *mamonas*, others *duguazas*, others *chautares*, others *sinabafas*, which latter are the best of all, and the Moors hold them the best for shirts. All these sorts of cloth are in pieces, each one whereof contains about three-and-twenty or four-and-twenty Portuguese yards. Here they are sold good cheap ... (Barbosa 1921: 145-146).

In his description of Aden and its trade cited earlier, Barbosa was seen to have observed that "thin Bengala cloths" were imported to the port. There can be little doubt that the commodity was muslin.

Tome Pires (1967: 92) also notes the great demand of 'Bengal' textiles "all over the East", specially Burma, Borneo, Java and the Liu Kiu Islands. In the *Suma Oriental* (1512-1515), he says merchants from 'Bengal' brought to Malacca twenty varieties of "fine white cloths", including "seven kinds of *sinabafos,* three kinds of *chautares, beatilhas, beirames*" (*ibid.*: 92). As mentioned earlier, Irfan Habib (1982b: 79) has identified these varieties as muslin. It is also important to note that according to Tome Pires (1967: 90), "Tripura [had] an infinite amount of cotton". Hence, Caṭṭagrāma served not only 'Bengal' but Tripura as well. Si'di' al-Chelebi observes in the *Mohi't* that "Bengal is abundant in ... the finest muslin turbans, the very best *jutār [cautār],* and most precious Indian stuffs come from thence; the finest muslin sashees are called *malmal*, and most precious of them *malmali-shāhī* ..." (Hammer 1836: 467). Observing Bengal's extensive trade in muslin in the 1730s, Manrique praises its quality with the following words:

> Most of the cloth is made of cotton and manufactured with a delicacy and propriety not met with elsewhere. The finest and richest muslins [*cassas*] are produced in this country, from fifty to sixty yards long and seven to eight handbreadths wide, with borders of gold and silver or coloured silks (Manrique 1927: 56).

When compared to all centuries prior to the 16th, one becomes immediately aware of voluminous rise in export of cotton textiles in the early 16th century AD. One of the factors that contributed to the phenomenal growth of cotton textile was the introduction of the spinning wheel and the bow-string (*kaman* and *resta*) possibly in the 15th century AD (Tarafdar 1995: 71-72). The wheel must have become quite common in the early 16th century AD because one hears Barbosa (1921: 146) observing that cotton textiles "are spun on wheels by men and woven by them".

We specifically hear of Sātgāon from Caesar Frederick, who observed in 1567 that "Cloth of Bombast of divers sorts" were exported from Sātgāon (Purchas 1905b: 114). Ralph Fitch, who toured 'Bengal' in 1586, observed that in Sonārgāon was available the "best and finest cloth made of cotton that is in all India. ... Great store of cotton cloth goeth (goes) from here, and much rice, wherewith they serve all India, Ceylon, Pegu, Malacca, Sumatra, and many other places" (Foster 1968: 28). He also notes, "clothe made of cotton" in the country of Couche (Cooch Behar) (*ibid.*: 25). Towards the end of the 16th century AD, the *Ain-i-Akbari* by Abul Fazl Allami also noted that "[t]he Sarkar of Sonārgāon produces a species of muslin very fine and in great quantity" (Jarrett 1891: 124).

All these references are well beyond the time frame of this research. Nevertheless, Abul Fazl's note is important because it confirms Sonārgāon as a production centre of fine quality muslin in great quantity. Frederick's observation is important because it shows some amount of cotton textiles must have been exported from Sātgāon as well. However, other indicators cited above show that most of cotton and cotton textiles were exported from Caṭṭagrāma. On the other hand, Ralph Fitch's observation confirms that Sonārgāon was a major exchange centre for cotton textiles. Hence, till the early 16th century AD when the maritime port was functioning at Sonārgāon, cotton textiles must have been exported from there as well. His observations on Cooch Behar (to the north of 'Bengal' extending from the Karatoyā in the west and the Barnadi in the east) indicate that the kingdom may have exported cotton textiles. Since it was a land-locked kingdom, cotton textile from the kingdom may have been transported down the Brahmaputra and the Meghnā and then exported from the port of Caṭṭagrāma.

Paṭṭa-bastra

Paṭṭa-bastra is mentioned profusely in various medieval texts such as *Varṇaratnākar* compiled by Pandit Jyotirishvar composed in the 14th century AD, Narayana Deva's *Padmā-purāṇa*, Bijayagupta's *Padmāpurāṇa*, Srīrāy Binod's *Padmā-purāṇa*, Kavikaṅkaṇa Mukunda's *Caṇḍīmaṅgala,* Kṛttivās's *Rāmāyaṇa, Māṇikcandra Rājar Gān,* Muhammad Kabir's *Manohar-Madhumālatī* etc. However, it is not to be confused with jute sari. As Surendranath Sen has shown, *paṭṭa bastra* was actually a type of coarse textile that was often used by the poor and the mendicants (Ray 1997: 27). Hence, all reference to maritime trade in *paṭṭa-bastra* should be seen as trade in coarse variety of cotton textile. Although there is no specific mention as such, we may expect this variety was also exported since Varthema uses "cotton stuffs" and Frederick uses "divers sorts" to include a wide variety.

HOME FURNISHINGS

According to *Suma Oriental* (1512-15), "very rich bed-canopies, with cut-cloth work in all colours and very beautiful" and "wall hangings like tapestry" were exported from 'Bengal' to Malacca (Pires 1967: 92). Pires is not alone in this curious observation. Even in the 1730s, Methwold found that each year a fleet of small ships arrived at Musulipatnam from 'Bengal' carrying, along with numerous other articles, "very curious quilts and carpets stitched with .. moga" (Moreland 1931: 40). Unfortunately, we have very little information regarding production centres of these articles to even hazard a guess. Nevertheless, there is no reason to doubt that those home furnishings as luxury commodities were exported in the early 16th century AD. We have no indication for identifying the ports from which home furnishings were exported but there appears to be no reason why we should not expect it to have been made both from Sātgāon and Caṭṭagrāma.

SUGAR

Sugar-cane (Saccharum officinarum, *Linn.*) was another food-crop, which was widely cultivated in 'Bengal' till the second half of the 19th century when it was overtaken by jute cultivation. Today, it is cultivated extensively in Rajshahi, Dinajpur and Kushtia regions of Bangladesh and West Dinajpur and Malda in West Bengal.

Both Dioskorides (McCrindle 1979: 45, fn. 2) and Pliny (The *Natural History,* Book XII, C 17; *ibid.*: 122) inform us that sugar was available in early historic India. Evidence proving cultivation of sugarcane in early historic 'Bengal' can easily be obtained from Aelian (Claudius Aelianus), the Roman rhetorician of the 2nd century AD. In his work on zoology titled *History of Animals* he mentions a kind of honey extracted from reeds, which he says, grew in Prasii. According to Lucan, the inhabitants of the region near the mouth of the Gaṅgā consumed "sweet juices from tender reeds" (*ibid.*: 122, f.n. 3). Among South Asian authors, Suśruta (I, 45, 149; Acharya 1860: 208; 4th-5th century AD) informs us about a type of sugar-cane called *pauṇḍraka*, which, according to most commentators of Sanskrit lexicons, was named after the place of its origin, i.e., the Pauṇḍra country (North 'Bengal'). We come across two references to the fame of sugar-cane cultivation in Puṇḍra at the end of the 10th century AD in Rājaśekhara's *Kāvyamimāṅsā* XII (Cakravartī 1960: 105) and in Varendrī in the 11th century AD in Sandhyākara Nandī's *Rāmacarita* (III, 17b; Sandhyākara Nandī 1910: 66). This line of argument does help one to substantiate Aelian's claim but leads us no further to production of sugar in 'Bengal' before the medieval period. However, because the *Aṅguttaranikāya*, Dioskorides and Pliny show that molasses and sugar were known in India, and because sugar-cane was produced in the early historic Puṇḍra, we may infer that sugar and molasses may have been produced in the latter region (Puṇḍra) as well. Nevertheless, we must concede that available indicators do not suggest abundant and surplus production of sugar over a long enough period of time to warrant its export. Nor is there any other evidence to prove its export. Hence we must reject Ray's (1994: 115) suggestion "that a great influx of money came into the country on account of sugar, much of which was produced from cane of Puṇḍra".

We have conclusive proof that 'Bengal' began to export sugar during the medieval period since Marco Polo actually reports sugar among a list of other agricultural commodities as "productions of the soil; to purchase which merchants from various parts of India resort thither" (Polo N.D.: 204). In the early 15th century AD, Fei Sin noted that sugar was one of Bengal's "natural products" (Bagchi 1945: 123). Ma-Huan, who visited 'Bengal' in 1432 is more elaborate in his *Ying-yai sheng-lan*, for he says the people of the country of Pang-ko-la (i.e., 'Bengal'), "have such things as granulated sugar, white sugar, crystallized sugar" among a host of other commodities (Ma-Huan 1970: 162). These evidences clearly prove that sugar was exported from 'Bengal' in the late 13th and the first half of the 15th centuries. *Si yang ch'ao kung tien lu* by Huang Sing-ts'eng (1520) and *Shu yu chou tseu lu* (1574) both list crystallised sugar as one of a number of gifts that the sultans of 'Bengal' sent to the Chinese emperors (Bagchi 1945: 127, 132). Although these evidences do not indicate export, they certainly imply that sugar was a valuable commodity in 'Bengal' and China (hence it was presented as an item of gift).

In the early 16th century AD, when Varthema visited 'Bengal', he too had noted that "[T]his country abounds ... in great quantity of sugar ..." (Varthema 1928: 79). Barbosa's account, written in 1518, speaks explicitly of sugar as a major export commodity of 'Bengal'.

> Much good white *sugar* is also made here from canes; but they know not how to compress it and make it into loaves; so they wrap it as a powder in parcels of untanned leather, well-sewn. Great store of this is taken in cargoes and carried for sale to many lands for it is a principle article for trade (Barbosa 1921: 146-147).

The passage on Aden cited earlier, where Barbosa refers to goods imported to the port includes sugar and it must have been from 'Bengal'. In 1567, Caesar Frederick had noticed ships in Sātgāon being loaded with "great abundance of Sugar" (Purchas 1905b: 114). Manrique (1927: 56) and Methwold (Moreland 1931: 40) confirm large-scale sugar export from 'Bengal' in the 1730s. Even if one lays aside Frederick's, Manrique's and Methwold's observations because they fall outside the time frame of this research, the accounts of Varthema and Barbosa can leave no doubt regarding export of sugar from 'Bengal' in the early 16th century AD.

Since Rajshahi, Dinajpur and Kushtia in Bangladesh and Malda and West Dinajpur in West Bengal, India are regions where sugar is mostly produced at present, and since Puṇḍra was noted for production of sugar-cane in the late historic and the early medieval periods, it would be reasonable to assume that the same region, i.e., northern 'Bengal' was the origin of most of sugar produced in medieval 'Bengal'. Available literary references suggest that the commodity was exported from both Sātgāon and Caṭṭagrāma.

SALT

Salt is obtainable from three sources: (1) seawater, (2) brine-springs, wells and lakes, and (3) rock-salt deposits. In Bangladesh today, salt is manufactured almost entirely from seawater, mainly around Cox's Bazar. The same technique is also applied in the coastal region of Medinīpur district of West Bengal, where people contain seawater in pits during high tide, which later evaporates in the sun.

As recorded in the Rāmpāl copperplate (lines 17, 23-26), the land that Śrīcandra granted in the 11th century AD in Nānya-maṇḍala of Pauṇḍrabhukti produced salt (Majumdar 1929: 8). Similarly, the land that Bhojavarman granted in the 12th century AD in the Adhahpattana-maṇḍala of the Pauṇḍrabhukti also produced salt (Belāva copperplate, lines 27-29 and 37-41; *ibid.*: 24). In all probability, salt in the above-mentioned grants was produced from brine-wells. The salt mines mentioned in the Irda copperplate of Nayapāladeva (Majumdar 1933-34: 158) were definitely rock salt deposits. The saline rocks mentioned in the Dhulla edict of Śrīcandra (Sircar 1959a: 140), must also have been rock-salt deposits. Hence there can remain little doubt that 'Bengal' has been familiar with salt production techniques for a thousand years. Rahim (1963: 393) believes that salt manufacture, both from seawater and sub-soil brine, grew to be one of the principal industries during the Muslim rule. Rahim has not explained the reasons behind his opinion but it is possible that he was referring to Mughal and not Sultanate Bengal.

We receive contradictory information from the 16th century AD regarding export of salt. In Kavikañkaṇa Mukunda's *Caṇḍīmaṅgala* (mid-16th century AD), both Dhanapati Datta and his son Śrīmanta wish to obtain salt (*labaṇa*, possibly sea-salt) from Sri Lanka in exchange of rock-salt (*saindhaba*) (Mukunda 1986: 210, 254).

Kavikañkaṇa Mukunda's poetic fancy is substantiated by Caesar Frederick who had observed in 1569 that shipment of two hundred shiploads of salt (that must have been produced from seawater) was sent each year from Sandwīp (Taylor 1840, I: 70-71). On the other hand, in the late 16th century AD, Abu'l Fazl lists salt as an imported item (Jarrett 1891: 122). Since Sandwīp developed as a port only after the arrival of the Portuguese and since there is no reference to salt export prior to the 16th century AD, it is extremely doubtful if salt was exported from 'Bengal' through maritime mode of transport during the time frame of this research.

FRUITS AND VEGETABLES

In the *Suma Oriental*, Tome Pires (1967: 92) has observed that "sugar preserves of various kinds in great plenty" and "all the myrobalans in conserve, ginger, oranges, cucumbers, carrots, rapes, lemons, quinces, figs, pumpkins, Indian gourds and many other fruits" were exported from 'Bengal' to Malacca. Some of these fruits were preserved in vinegar. As mentioned earlier in Chapter One, Duarte Barbosa's account from the early 16th century AD testifies that "ginger conserve, also of oranges, lemons and other fruits which grow in this land" were manufactured in the city of Bengala (Caṭṭagrāma) (Barbosa 1921: 147). In 1567 Caesar Frederick had observed, "Myrabolans dried and preserved" being exported from the port (Purchas 1905b: 114). Preserved fruits and pickle continued to be produced even in the late 17th century AD, as Thomas Bowrey's account vouchsafes. He informs us that the Portuguese settlers living at Huglī prepared "vizt. Mangoe [astringent dried fruits of several species], Orange, Lemon, Ginger, Mirabolins, Rinco Roots, etc." and "several sorts of achar, as Mangoe, Bamboo, Lemon etc." for sailors of maritime vessels (Bowrey 1905: 192-193).

Besides preserves and pickles, 'Bengal' also exported a variety of vegetables, as Pires' observed. Some of these, such as gourds, all kind of beans and vegetables were abundantly produced in the 1530s, as Ma-Huan (1970: 161) had noted. Fei Sin had also observed availability of vegetables in 'Bengal' (Bagchi 1945: 123). These evidences clearly indicate export of vegetables from 'Bengal' from the first half of the 15th to the early 16th century AD.

We have no way of ascertaining in which regions of 'Bengal' the exported fruits and vegetables were grown. However, if the current pattern of production may be accepted as an indicator, we may note the following regions renowned for particular products. Rose apple, star apple, rozelle, myrobalan and cucumber are widely grown nearly everywhere in Bangladesh today. Pumpkins are grown extensively along the old Brahmaputra and the Madhumati, and the sandy Padmā levee of the Southern districts, Indian gourd between Toṅgī and Pubāil, mango in north 'Bengal' and carrot in Dhaka and Caṭṭagrāma. Citrus fruits are abundant in Rajshahi, Khulna, Jessore, Bakerganj, Dhaka, Comilla and Caṭṭagrāma. Quince is cultivated in plenty in the Madhupur Tract and in the northern region while Cape gooseberry, mostly in Dhaka. The best sapodillas come from Faridpur. Melon and watermelon are grown extensively along the banks of the Gaṅgā, Padmā, Gaḍāi-Madhumati, Old Brahmaputra, Karṇafulī, Sāṅgu, Mātāmuharī and other rivers.

Assuming that a similar pattern was prevalent in the medieval period, it would be logical to believe that the fruits and fruit preserves could have been exported from both Sātgāon and Caṭṭagrāma. Sātgāon can stand a good chance in claiming a definite role in exporting fruit preserves because of Caesar Frederick and Thomas Bowrey's observations. On the other hand, Caṭṭagrāma's claim in exporting these products can be substantiated from Barbosa's account. The case of oranges deserves separate attention. Because the fruit grows abundantly in Assam and Bhutan, it is possible that the exported commodity Pires refers to, originate in the above-mentioned countries.

PEARLS, PRECIOUS AND SEMI-PRECIOUS STONES AND OPAQUE GLASS

Chien Han-shu (Ch.28 B, p. 32 a-b), the Chinese text from the 1st century AD, informs that envoys were sent overseas by the Chinese emperor Wu-ti (140-87 BC), to buy "lustrous pearls, glass, rare stones and strange products in exchange for gold and various silks". They sailed as far as Huang Chih (identified as the Gaṅgā delta). As Sarkar (1973: 183) argues, the articles purchased by the Chinese delegation must have been procured from the Gaṅgā delta (and not Southeast Asia, the other option that they had), because by that time 'Bengal' had developed "a material culture and contained a port of international stature capable of matching the shopping list of the Chinese emissaries". Besides *Chien Han-shu,* a few other Chinese records of earlier times have also noted that commodities such as lustrous pearls, glass, rare stones etc. were imported to China. Hence, there is no doubt that China imported these commodities but from 'Bengal'.

Pearls

There can be little doubt that pearls were exported from Gaṅgābandar in the 1st century AD because the *Periplus* (§ 63) clearly says that Gangetic pearls were brought from a market-town on the bank of the Gaṅgā (Schoff 1995: 47). Schoff (*ibid.*: 256) explains that these must have been of inferior variety, "being small, often irregular, and usually reddish", that are obtainable from the River Gaṅgā. One of the regions producing pearls could have been Dhaka since it is still renowned for the pink variety. Pearl features again among the natural products of 'Bengal' that Fei Sin lists in the early 15th century AD (Bagchi 1945: 123). These too must have been river pearls obtained from the Gaṅgā.

These evidences conclusively prove the export of pearls from 'Bengal' in the early historic and the medieval period. While Gaṅgābandar was definitely the port from which pearls were exported in the early historic period, Sonārgāon and Sātgāon could have been the ports in the medieval period since river pearls obtained from the Gaṅgā would have been available in the immediate hinterland of these ports. As will be seen later, pearls were also imported to 'Bengal' in the medieval period.

Precious and Semi-precious Stones
And Semi-precious Stone Beads

According to the *Ratnaparikṣā*, the *Bṛhatsaṁhita*, the *Navaratnaparikṣā*, and the *Ratnasaṁgraha*, Puṇḍra was once famous for diamonds. Furthermore, if *Agastimata* can be credited, then it must be believed that some diamonds were also found in Vaṅga (Ray 1994: 112). However, we must concede that the above-mentioned literary sources are vague and imprecise in meeting our criterion of export: abundant supply and surplus of a commodity over a reasonable long period of time. Nor do they indicate that 'Bengal' was a unique source of precious stones. There can be no doubt that in the late 16th century AD 'Bengal' imported diamonds, emeralds, pearls, carnelians and agates as Abu'l Fazl clearly shows (Jarrett 1891: 122). On the other hand, judging by showers of praise and considerable space that Pliny (*Natural History,* XXXI, c. 7; XXXII, c. 2; XXXIII c. 4; XXXV c. 6; XXXVII, c. 1, 2, 4-10, 13; McCrindle 1979: 128-135) heaps on precious stones available in India, it appears that the last-mentioned country met the criteria of export in the early historic period. As the current pattern of production in India suggests, most of the precious stones in the early historic period must have been produced in south India. Hence we may reject any suggestion that precious stones were produced or exported from any of the ports of 'Bengal'. However, we have archaeological evidence at hand to prove conclusively that 'Bengal' was indeed engaged in a flourishing maritime trade in semi-precious stone beads.

As discussed in Chapter One, beads of semi-precious stones such as agate, carnelian, onyx, amethyst, jasper, quartz, amber and crystal have been found in and around Tamluk. These have been dated to the 1st and 2nd century AD. At Chandraketugarh, agate, carnelian, onyx, amethyst, jasper, quartz, chert and garnet have been found and these are dated to c. 300 BC to 50 AD and c. 300 AD to 500 AD. A large number of beads of semi-precious stone such as carnelian, agate, quartz, amethyst, crystal, chalcedony, chert and jasper have also been found at Wārī-Baṭeśwar (Fig. 2.2). Beads found at Mahāsthāngarh are made of agate, carnelian, chert, chalcedony, crystal, garnet, jasper, marble, onyx etc. Since the findspots of these beads were port sites or in the immediate vicinity of such sites, there can remain little doubt that semi-precious stone beads were exported from Tāmralipti, Gaṅgābandar and Wārī-Baṭeśwar from the 3rd century BC to the 5th century AD. Bone-beads from the Gupta age, found in Chandraketugarh, indicate that the commodity must have been added to the existing list of stone beads in the late historic period.

Fig. 2.2 Semi-precious stone beads, Wari-Bateswar

Of all the semi-precious stone beads, etched beads, a special type of agate and carnelian beads with a white design etched on its polished surface, are an important indicator of trade between South and Southeast Asia during the early historic period and hence they deserve special consideration in the present research. The etching was produced by applying a paste of natural soda and crushed shoots of *kirar* (*cappari aphylla*) on the stone and baking it on fire. The technique was known only in South Asia since the Harappan Civilisation (3rd-2nd millennium BC). However, it fell into disuse, and was revived again in the Gaṅgā valley between 600 BC and 200 AD.

As already pointed out in Chapter One, etched beads conclusively prove maritime trade because they have been found in Bangladesh (Wārī-Baṭeśwar and Mahāsthāngarh), West Bengal (Tamluk, Bāngarh, Chandraketugarh, Hari nārāyaṇpur and Deulpota), Myanmar (Beikthano and Halin, Aung Thaw 1968: 66), Thailand (Ban Chiang, Ban Tung Ketchet, Kok Samrong, U Thong, Krabi, Khao Sam Kao, Ban Kao and Ban Don Ta Phet), Malaysia (at Tanjong Rawa

Kalumpang island, Kuala Selinsing), Indonesia (at Leang Buidane cave in Salebabu island), Philippines (in Palawan Island) and China (Yunnan province, one in Tomb 13 at Shi Zhai Shan and another in Tomb 24 at Lijiashan). Etched beads found in China confirm the evidence provided by *Chien Han-shu*. Going by the evidence of the lone etched bead found at Mahāsthāngarh, it is possible to believe that these beads were also marketed locally.

No evidence exists that the stone-beads were manufactured from core material quarried at find spots or their vicinity. In India today, the largest supply of agate is comes from Ratanpur in Rajpipla zone in Gujarat. Madhya Pradesh and the Deccan Trap areas provide varieties of agate, carnelian, jasper, opal and onyx. Quartz is found in most of the states in India but mostly in Andhra, Bihar and Rajsthan. Crystal comes from the Deccan Trap. Rajmahal traps in Bihar still produce agate, carnelian and quartz in abundance. Garnets are quarried most abundantly from the metamorphosed rocks in Rajsthan. It is also found in Andhra Pradesh, Tamil Nadu and Karnataka. Amber, a mineral resin (i.e., fossilised gum of extinct coniferous trees), is found in the Hukawng valley of North Burma and was required for artistic handicrafts (Moreland 1920: 197). The largest reserve of good quality marble is found in Rajasthan. It is also available in Madhya Pradesh, Bihar, Uttar Pradesh, West Bengal, Hariyana and Gujarat.

The nearest source for agate, carnelian and quartz for the early historic 'Bengal' could have been Rajmahal traps in Bihar. Remaining stones could have come from Gujarat, Madhya Pradesh, Rajasthan, south India and Burma. Hence, it is possible that the raw materials for the beads were imported by land route, from the above-mentioned regions of India. As discussed in Chapter One, Wārī-Baṭeśwar, Bāngarh, Chandraketugarh, Harinārāyaṇpur and Deulpota were production centres where the beads were manufactured. They were then exported from Wārī-Baṭeśwar, Gaṅgābandar and Tāmralipti.

Glass

Quality glass is manufactured from pure quartz-sand of uniform grain and texture, containing no iron impurities. Such sand can be obtained from the crushing of pure quartoze Vindhyan sandstone (found at several localities in Uttar Pradesh), Cretaceous and Archaean sandstone and Gondwana sandstone (found in Rajmahal Hills) and other pure quartzites of some parts of Madras and Bombay. Sand-deposits of the necessary purity appropriate for glass manufacture are found in Hoshiarpur district, Punjab, at Sawai Madhupur in Jaipur state, Madh in Bikaner and near Zawar in Udaypur district in India.

Although proximity of Rajmahal Hills indicates feasibility of glass manufacture in 'Bengal', there is no material evidence to confirm its manufacture during the early historic period. However, Pliny (*Nat. Hist.*, XXXVI, lxvi) confirms "in India glass is made also of broken rock-crystal and that for this reason no glass can compare with that of India" (Pliny 1962: 153). Since Kopia near Maidaval in the Basti district, Uttar Pradesh, Nevasa and Kolhapur in Maharashtra and Arikamedu in Tamil Nadu (Dikshit 1969: 39; Chaudhuri 1990: 217-225) were well-known glass manufacturing centres in the early historic South Asia, one may suggest that glass was imported to 'Bengal' by land route from the above-mentioned areas for local use and may have been exported as well. Of these, Kopia stands a better chance because the easiest route for exporting glass manufactured there would have been down the Gaṅgā to Tāmralipti.

It is possible that glass was manufactured and exported in the medieval 'Bengal' because Kavikañkaṇa Mukunda, in his *Caṇḍīmaṅgala* (mid-16th century AD), lists it as one of the commodities that the Bengali merchant Dhanapati and his son Śrīmanta wish to exchange for sapphire in Sri Lanka (Mukunda 1986: 209, 254). In support of Mukunda's claim, we may cite *Shu yu chou tseu lu* (1574) which lists vases of opaque glass as one of a number of gifts that the sultans of 'Bengal' sent to the Chinese emperors. The same source also lists opaque glass as one of the commodities available in 'Bengal' (Bagchi 1945: 132). Since Kavikañkaṇa Mukunda, in his *Caṇḍīmaṅgala*, shows that both Dhanapati and Srimanta halt at Saptagrāma and trade at its exchange centre, it is likely that glass was exported from Sātgāon.

Glass beads

As already discussed in Chapter One, oblate and spherical black glass beads inlaid with white stripes belonging to the North Indian (Ahichchatra-Kausambi) tradition have been found at Chandraketugarh and Harinārāyaṇpur in West Bengal. This type has also been found at Mahāsthāngarh in Bangladesh, Kodumanal in Tamil Nadu, India, Prasat Muang Sing and Ban Chi Nam Lai in Thailand. Because the beads belong to the North Indian tradition, it can be concluded without hesitation that the beads found at Chandraketugarh, Harinārāyaṇpur and Mahāsthāngarh were produced at Ahichchatra and Kausambi. The distribution pattern of find-spots indicates that glass beads belonging to the North Indian tradition were exported from Gaṅgābandar and Tāmralipti (since Harinārāyaṇpur was one of the harbours of the latter port) to Prasat Muang Sing and Ban Chi Nam Lai in Thailand. From the presence of these beads at Mahāsthāngarh (an urban centre of political importance during the early historic period), it is possible to surmise that they must have been traded internally in 'Bengal' and may have been used by the elite.

POTTERY

Rouletted Ware

Rouletted Ware is so called because a variety of forms including triangles, diamonds, parallelograms, wedges, and dots are 'rouletted' on a particular type of pottery. It is usually wheel-thrown and slipped, with an unusually smooth surface. Its usual colour is grey and has a ring, which sounds almost metallic. Rouletted Ware was a luxury item and was possibly meant for the use of the elite class. This type of ware has been reported from Chandraketugarh, Deulpota, Atghara, Harinārāyaṇpur and Hadipur (24-Parganas), Tamluk, Tilda, Bahiri, Boral and Natshal (Medinīpur), Maṅgalkoṭa (Bardhamān), Saptagrāma (Huglī) in West Bengal and Mahāsthāngarh and Wārī-Baṭeśwar (Fig. 2.3) in Bangladesh.

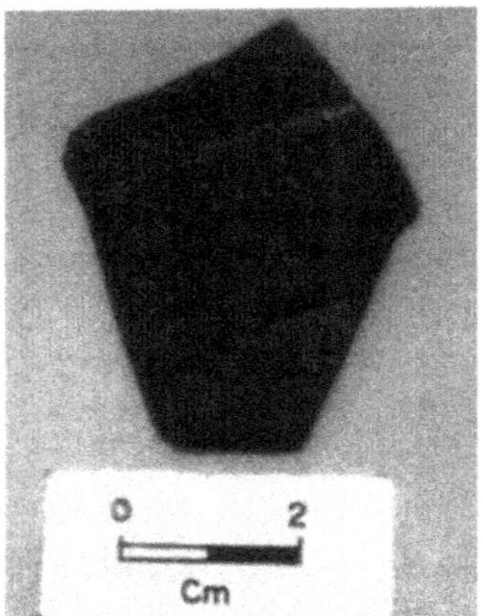

Fig. 2.3 A sherd of Rouletted Ware, Wari-Bateswar

Besides Bangladesh and West Bengal, Rouletted Ware has also been reported from a number of sites in Pakistan, India and Sri Lanka. The sites in India are Śiśupālgarh, Manikpatna and Radhanagar (in Orissa); Junnar, Paithan, Nasik, Nevasa, Ter (in Maharashtra); Kondapur, Salihundam, Vamulapadu and Satanikota (in Andhra Pradesh) Maski, Brahmagiri and Chandravalli (in Karnataka), Kanchipuram, Karaikadu, Arikamedu, Kaveripattinam, Karur, Manigramam, Uraiyur, Alagankulam and Sengamedu (in Tamil Nadu), Ayodhya (in Uttar Pradesh) and Rajghat (in Bihar). Sites, which yielded Rouletted Ware in Sri Lanka, are Kantarodai, Mantai, Tissamaharama, Ambalantota and Anuradhapura-Gedige (Fig. 2.4). In Pakistan, the ware has been reported from Taxila. Rouletted Ware has also been found in a number of sites in Southeast Asia. These are Beikthano (in Myanmar), Bukit Tengku Lembu (Malaysia), Kobak Kendal and Cibutak (in Java, Indonesia) and Sembiran (in Bali, Indonesia), Tra Kieu (in Vietnam) and Berenike (on the Red Sea coast).

Fig. 2.4 Sherds of Rouletted Ware, Anuradhapura, Sri Lanka

Archaeological excavations have yielded very little evidence in terms of dates with the help of which dispersion and spread of Rouletted Ware can be identified. The little evidence that is available shows that the earliest Rouletted Ware in South Asia is from Anuradhapura. Since Deraniyagala's (1990: 274) radiocarbon dating has ascertained its manufacture in 250 BC, the same can be accepted as the commencement date for Rouletted Ware in South Asia. On the other hand, the terminal date can be accepted as the 3rd century AD, since, as Ghosh (1986: 79) has logically argued, the ware has not been found at Nagarjunakonda (Andhra Pradesh). On the basis of above arguments, it is possible to place South Asian Rouletted Ware in the broader time bracket of the 3rd century BC to the 3rd century AD.

Although Rouletted Ware from West Bengal and Bangladesh has not been dated, a relative chronology can nevertheless be worked out. In order to do that, one needs to remember that in most cases, Rouletted Ware in West Bengal and Bangladesh has been found with NBPW. As Dilip Chakrabarti (1992: 178) has ascertained, the earliest occurrence of NBPW in the eastern parts of South Asia is c. 300 BC. Accepting a similar date for West Bengal and Bangladesh, which falls within this region, it is possible to benchmark c. 300 BC for the earliest occurrence of 'Bengal' Rouletted Ware.

What is most significant about all the findings of Rouletted Ware noted above is that they are all comparable in form, texture, colour of the slip and general appearance to the earliest examples of the same found at Arikamedu during the 1945 excavation. Since 1945, scholars have tried to solve the problem of origin of the distinctive rouletted decoration, which was believed to have been made with roulette. Since the decoration was identified as distinctly non-Indian and since it bore similarity with imported Arretine ware found at Arikamedu, Wheeler concluded that the designs as well as finer quality Rouletted Ware found at the site were imported from the Mediterranean region, while the cruder variety was locally made. The imitations of Rouletted Ware made locally were believed to be distinct because of the softer fabric and coarse rouletted design (Wheeler *et al.* 1946: 46; Wheeler 1947-1948: 200; 1976: 50). However, as Begley (1983: 469, 478 and 1988: 439) has pointed out, Rouletted Ware at Arikamedu predates Arretine imports. Therefore, Arretine ware could not have been the source of inspiration for Rouletted Ware. She is of the opinion that the Rouletted Ware of Arikamedu was probably produced locally, possibly made at Arikamedu, or in the vicinity of the settlement. Because the technique of rouletting was not known to the cultures of south India at that time, Begley too believes that it was possibly introduced from the Mediterranean region, where it was practiced from the 4th century BC.

Having examined the opinions of Wheeler and Begley, it is necessary now to look into the scientific analysis of Rouletted Ware in order to investigate its alternative production centres. In a recent Neutron Activation Analysis (NAA) for 20 rare elements performed on nine sherds of Rouletted Ware (two from Anuradhapura, two from Arikamedu, one from

Karaikadu, three from Sembiran and a single sherd from Pacung), it was found that all of them are close in composition. Hence, Ardika & Bellwood (1991: 224) conclude, "a single manufacturing source for all the samples listed, both Indian and Balinese, is a definite possibility".

Two X-ray diffraction (XRD) analyses have so far been performed on Rouletted Ware. One of these, performed by Ardika & Bellwood on eight sherds (one from Sembiran, four from Anuradhapura and three from Arikamedu), has revealed that all contain essentially the same minerals, which are mainly quartz with traces of mica, muscovite, potassium feldspar and plagioclase feldspar. The basic composition of slip and sherd interior was also found to be similar, except for one sample from Anuradhapura. Traces of hematite were also found in its slip. What is most significant is that the composition of the rouletted sherd from Sembiran is not identical with the soil samples from the find spot and local sherds.

Another XRD analysis was performed by Vishwas D. Gogte (1997: 69-85 and 2001: 197-202), on Rouletted Ware and clay from Mahāsthāngarh in Bangladesh, Tamluk and Chandraketugarh (West Bengal), Śiśupālgarh and Manikpatna (Orissa), Nasik (Maharashtra), Kottapatnam (Andhra Pradesh), Hampi/Annegondi (Karnataka), Arikamedu, Alagankulam, Adichanallur (Tamil Nadu) in India, Tissamaharama in Sri Lanka and Tra Kieu in Vietnam. The analysis showed that the Rouletted Ware from all the sites mentioned above is mineralogically identical with the Rouletted Ware and the clay from Chandraketugarh. Furthermore, the XRD pattern of the Nasik sample matched closely with the clay from Tamluk and to a lesser extent, with that of Chandraketugarh. From these results, Gogte (1997: 83) concludes "Rouletted Ware was produced at multiple production centres in the lower Gaṅgā plain with the epicentre in the Chandraketugarh-Tamluk region of Bengal".

All the three tests discussed above point to a single conclusion. The "single manufacturing source" indicated by the NAA and similar mineral content indicated by Ardika & Bellwood XRD analysis is further supported by Gogte XRD analysis, which shows that the "single sources" is none other than lower Gaṅgā plain in general, and Chandraketugarh-Tamluk region in particular.

Gogte (2001: 198) conducted another XRD analysis on NBPW and Rouletted Ware from Mahāsthāngarh in Bangladesh and found that

> the clays used in the production of all varieties of Northern Black Polished Ware having surface colours of black, red, brown, golden yellow and silver have been found to be exactly identical with those of the Rouletted Ware found at the site. It has been shown that in the production of Northern Black Polished Ware and Rouletted Ware not only the same technology was employed but also that they were produced from the same type of clays of the Gaṅgā Plain. It was also suggested that the lustrous Rouletted Ware might simply be treated as yet another variety of Northern Black Polished Ware with an indented circular decoration.

Hence it can be concluded that NBPW and Rouletted Ware were both produced in the lower Gaṅgā plain. However, because it has not been possible to identify kilns, which may have produced this type of ware, it is not possible to state with certainty where the production centres may have been located. Nevertheless, find-spots of the ware indicate that they were produced at or around Tamluk, Chandraketugarh and Wārī-Baṭeśwar. Since Rouletted Ware has also been found in Orissa (India), south India, Sri Lanka, Myanmar, Malaysia, Bali (Indonesia), Vietnam and Berenike (on the Red Sea coast), one can definitely conclude that these were exported from Tāmralipti, Gaṅgābandar and Wārī-Baṭeśwar.

Northern Black Polished Ware

Northern Black Polished Ware (NBPW) is usually made of superfine clay of the Gaṅgā Plain. It is well fired, thin

Fig. 2.5 Northern Black Polished Ware, Wari-Bateswar

sectioned, and has a strikingly lustrous surface. It was a precious deluxe ware and was used by the elite class of the society (royalty and Buddhist monks) as a luxury item. NBPW usually were bowls, dishes with carinated handles and spouted jars. The chronology of NBPW in the Middle Gaṅgā Plain ranges from c. 700 to 100 BC (Lal 1984: 94), whereas in the eastern parts of South Asia the chronology ranges from 300 BC to 100 BC (Chakrabarti 1992: 178).

The distribution of NBPW in South Asia is indeed widespread. In Bangladesh, the ware has been found at Wārī-Baṭeśwar (Narsingdi district; Fig. 2.5) and Mahāsthāngarh (Bogra district). In India, it has been found in West Bengal at Bāngarh, Chandraketugarh and Tamluk; in Orissa at Kalahandi and Śiśupālgarh; in Maharashtra at Nasik, Ter and Brahmapuri; in Andhra Pradesh at Amaravati-Dharanikota, Amaravati-Vaddamanu and Chebrolu; in Tamil Nadu at Arikamedu, Alagankulam and Korkai; in Madhya Pradesh at

Rajgir, Eran and Ujjain; in Uttar Pradesh at Hastinapur, Ahichchatra, Sravasti, Kausambi and Sarnath and in Bihar at Vaishali, Chirand, Rajghat and Pataliputra. In Pakistan, it has been found at Udegram, Charsada and Taxila, in Nepal at Tilaurakot, and in Sri Lanka at Mantai, Anuradhapura-Gedige (Fig. 2.6) and Tissamaharama. All of these NBPW are from the period of 300 BC to 100 BC.As discussed above, this type

Fig. 2.6 Northern Black Polished Ware
Anuradhapura, Sri Lanka

of ware was locally produced. The Indo-Aryan settlers in the middle Gaṅgā plains may have introduced this type of ware as their settlements gradually spread in Rāḍha and Puṇḍravardhana during Maurya rule. Consequently, a number of production sites may have developed in the lower Gaṅgā Valley, along the banks of the Bhāgīrathī-Huglī. However, because it has not been possible to identify NBPW-producing kilns, it is not possible to identify the production centres of the wares with certainty. Nevertheless, since the wares have been found at Tamluk, Chandraketugarh and Wārī-Baṭeśwar, it would not be unreasonable to assume that some of the production centres were located in or around the find-spots. The chronology and distribution pattern of NBPW clearly indicates that these were exported to southeast Indian coastal sites and Sri Lanka from the ports of Tāmralipti, Gaṅgābandar and Wārī-Baṭeśwar.

Stamped Ware

Stamped ware is so called because motifs of birds, fish and stylised palmettes are stamped below the rim of bowls or cups with wide mouth, tapering sides and flat base. The earliest specimen of the ware was found at Taxila where the excavator identified it as Hellenistic in origin (Marshall 1951: 434). This view is confirmed by the stamped designs on the ware. From Taxila the ware seems to have spread down the Gaṅgā valley to Sanghol (Gupta 1987: 100), Hastinapur (Lal 1954-55: 63) and Sonkh near Mathura, where stamped wares with figural designs have been found. At each of these sites, as Ray (1998: 59) has shown, stamped wares were locally produced.

From the Gaṅgā valley, the characteristic motifs of stamped wares appear to have spread to the mouth of the Gaṅgā since quite a few stamped potsherds have been found at and around Chandraketugarh. One of these from Chandraketugarh (now held by the State Museum, West Bengal and bearing accession no T 549) is a terracotta potsherd measuring 13x4 cm. It has been dated to the 1st century AD. Stamped near the rim are a lotus and a Kharoshṭī-Brāhmī legend "Salatheotha or Sanas(r)as(r)a" (Mukherjee 1990: 52). Mukherjee (*ibid.*: 52) believes that the legend possibly refers to the potter or owner's name. Another stamped potsherd measuring 8.5 cm in length (now held by the Indian Museum, Kolkata and bearing accession no 89/47) was found at Hadipur and has been dated to the 1st century AD. Interestingly, the potsherd in question is a fragment of Rouletted Ware of whitish colour. On it is stamped the motif of a lotus inside a circle and a Kharoshṭī-Brāhmī inscription which in translation reads "of Yasa, the Yaksa of grain" (*ibid.*: 54). The same site (i.e., Hadipur) has yielded yet another terracotta object (currently held at the Indian Museum, Kolkata and bears accession no. 90/151). It is an amphora-like vessel (18.3 cm high). On it is stamped a Kharoshṭī inscription that has been read as "Dajadaṁḍadapa" ((*ibid.*: 57). Mukherjee (*ibid.*) believes that the inscription is possibly the name of the potter or the owner of the vessel. Grey ware potsherd with stamped leaf design, another with rosette design, and a third with stamped wheel and rosette design, all dating from the Gupta age, have been found in Khana-Mihirer-Dhipi in Chandraketugarh. Chandraketugarh has also yielded NBPW sherds with stamped rosette designs. The most distinctive stamped ware fragment found at the site is a black-and-red ware sherd. The decoration on it is seen on the interior just below the rim and is quite similar to Wheeler's Type 10 at Arikamedu. It consists of a row of stamped medallions with a bird motif engraved within a square panel (*Indian Archaeology – A Review* 1957-58: 52).

There can be little doubt that the stamped ware sherds found at Tamluk and Chandraketugarh are from stamped ware manufactured at Chandraketugarh. This is amply demonstrated by NBPW sherds bearing stamped rosette designs and a Rouletted Ware sherd that have been found at Chandraketugarh. Since it has already been established that NBPW and Rouletted Wares were produced locally at Chandraketugarh, it would be reasonable to believe that the NBPW sherd with stamped design was also manufactured locally. The fact that Hadipur was a production centre and that similar production centres also existed at or near Tamluk (shown in Chapter One) indicate the presence of infrastructural conditions necessary for producing stamped ware at Tamluk and Chandraketugarh. Kharoshṭī and Kharoshṭī-Brāhmī inscriptions stamped on a few sherds is yet another indicator that stamped wares were locally produced because most of the artefacts bearing similar inscriptions have been found at Tamluk and Chandraketugarh and its neighbourhood.

From Chandraketugarh, stamped ware appears to have spread along the western coast of the Bay of Bengal to Sri

Lanka. This is indicated by stamped ware sherds that have been found at Manikpatna and Radhanagar in Orissa (Pradhan *et al.* 2000: 484), Satanikota in Andhra Pradesh, Arikamedu, Kottapatnam and Alagankulam in Tamil Nadu. Another stamped bowl has been reported from Gedige at Anuradhapura (Deraniyagala 1986: 45). Further specimens of stamped wares in Sri Lanka are several fragments found at Kantarodai.

Stamped ware sailed to Indonesia as well, as testified by a rim sherd found at Sembiran on the north coast of Bali. The rim sherd is direct and everted with an un-thickened lip. It is glossy black in colour and bears close similarity with Wheeler's Arikamedu type 10. On the inner side of the rim can be seen a stamped panel with a bird (possibly a peacock) motif. Since the stamped motif of birds is non-indigenous in origin, it is believed that the ware, of which the sherd was a part, was not locally produced (Ardika & Bellwood 1991: 224).

Since no scientific analyses have been conducted so far, we have no way of showing with absolute certainty that the stamped ware produced at Gaṅgābandar (Chandraketugarh) and Tāmralipti (Tamluk) were exported to maritime ports in Orissa, Andhra, Tamil Nadu, Sri Lanka and Sembiran. Indeed, one may very well argue that stamped ware from Arikamedu travelled to Sembiran and the motif travelled also from Arikamedu to Chandraketugarh and Tamluk. However, argument in favour of Chandraketugarh and Tamluk as a possible source of stamped ware found on the eastern coast of south India, Sri Lanka and Bali may be presented with greater weight. The earliest specimen of the ware was found at Taxila and later in the upper Gaṅgā valley imply that the motif spread down the Gaṅgā to Tāmralipti and Gaṅgābandar. Absence of the ware on the West Coast of south India confirms that it did not arrive at Tāmralipti and Gaṅgābandar via Sri Lanka or Arikamedu. Consider also the fact that the stamped motifs have been identified as Hellenistic and not Roman. There can be little doubt that the motifs of the ware found at Taxila were actually Bactrian Greek in origin. It may be recalled that at the end of the 2nd century BC, the Bactrian Greek king named Demetrios crossed the Hindukush and conquered a vast portion of Punjab and West India. According to the *Gargi Samhita,* he is believed to have conquered as far as Pataliputra (Bhattacharjee 1979: 227). The Bactrian Greek kingdom extended into the north-western region of South Asia from the end of the 2nd century BC to the second half of the 1st century BC and that Taxila was the headquarters of a Bactrian Greek king named Antialcidas. Because Arikamedu was a Roman emporium, stamped motifs could not have originated there. Consider further the fact that potsherds of Rouletted Ware (Ardika & Bellwood 1991: 224) and a potsherd inscribed with Kharoshṭī legend (Mukherjee 1990: 73) have been found at Sembiran. As already established the Rouletted Ware fragment could have been manufactured only at Tamluk/Chandraketugarh region. Since most of the artefacts bearing Kharoshṭī and Kharoshṭī-Brāhmī inscriptions have been found at Tamluk, Chandraketugarh and its neighbourhood, the potsherd inscribed with Kharoshṭī legend must also have originated at Tamluk/Chandraketugarh region. Thus, it is possible that the stamped ware variety of pottery found on the sites-near-to-coast on both sides of the Bay was exported from Tāmralipti and/or Gaṅgābandar during the early historic period.

Footed Ware

Footed Ware is a type of pottery found in the shape of small dish with flaring out-turned rim and a base or foot shaped as a ring, containing decoration below the rim on the inner surface and on the base. The scheme of decoration of this type of ware invariably consists of a ring of stamped ribbed leaves and a grooved circle or spirals at the centre. Footed ware has been found at Chandraketugarh in West Bengal and at Arikamedu and Karaikadu in Tamil Nadu, India. They have also been found at Shaikhan Dheri near Charsada in Pakistan. All these are from a century before and after the Christian era (i.e., 100 BC to 100 AD). Comfort (1991) and Slane (1991) have shown that footed wares are not indigenous to South Asia and bear close similarity with ware found in the Mediterranean world. It is possible that they were manufactured at Shaikhan Dheri in the Bactrian Greek kingdom in the north-western region of South Asia. Begley (1991: 183) believes "the route of contact between Shaikhan Dheri and Chandraketugarh would have been inland through the Gaṅgā plains and coastal between Chandraketugarh/Tamluk and locations on the Coromandel Coast". Based on these observations, it is possible to believe that footed ware type of potteries were imported from Shaikhan Dheri in the Bactrian Greek kingdom to Gaṅgābandar and Tāmralipti in 'Bengal' by land routes for local use among the elite and were exported from there by sea routes to the Coromandel Coast.

Amphora

Amphorae were elongated jars with tapered bottom and handles attached to the sides. These were used in ancient times for transporting edible materials, both liquid and solid, to and from the Mediterranean world. The edible materials transported in amphorae include wine, oil, vinegar, honey, olives, fruit, fish (preserved with salt or in oil), etc.

Amphora fragments have been found in 26 sites in India. These include two sites in West Bengal (Tamluk and Chandraketugarh) and two in Tamil Nadu (Arikamedu and Karaikadu). Amphora sherds found in India belong to imported as well as local varieties. These fragments are not uniform in terms of fabric and belong to a wide time period in terms of manufacture. The imported amphorae were, almost exclusively, manufactured in the Mediterranean world. Studies on Arikamedu amphorae have shown that many of these are Rhodian and Greek in origin, from the 1st century BC (Will 1991: 153). However, most of the amphora sherds found at Chandraketugarh (Fig. 2.7) and Tamluk in West Bengal have been identified as locally made, which were imitated from imported versions of the same ware. Furthermore, three amphora-like vessels stamped with Kharoshṭī-Brāhmī inscriptions have been found at Hadipur. One of these (preserved at the Indian Museum, Kolkata, accession no. 90/151) has already been cited earlier while discussing stamped ware. The second is a piece of 18 cm long and has been dated to the 4th century AD. Incised near its neck are Kharoshṭī and Kharoshṭī-Brāhmī legends that have been translated as "Jarama, samtvasya, Napuvra and Solasha" (Mukherjee 1990: 56). Mukherjee (*ibid.*) believes that they could be names of the owner of the potter. The third piece (preserved at the Indian Museum, Kolkata, accession no. 90/160) is 15 cm long and has been dated to the 3rd century AD. Inscribed on it is a Kharoshṭī legend which has been read as Vaja and a Kharoshṭī-Brāhmī legend which has been read as Vala (*ibid.*: 57). These vessels leave no doubt that amphorae were locally produced. Against all these evidences of local manufacture, only one intact amphora of Roman origin (Dressel 28 type) has so far been discovered near Tamluk at Karnaji village in Medinīpur (Sengupta 1996: 128, Pl. I). It could easily have come as a memento or could even have been shipped from Arikamedu. Thus, amphorae as an indicator of Indo-Roman trade operated directly from Tāmralipti stand little ground.

Fig. 2.7 An amphora, Chandraketugarh

We may therefore conclude that a large number of amphorae were locally manufactured and may have been used for exporting edible items and was not an exportable commodity by itself. There may have been a non-commercial use for the amphorae as well. Since water jars are known to have been used in pre-modern maritime vessels as non-commercial ballast, it may not be too far-fetched to claim that amphorae produced at Arikamedu were filled with water and were used as such for ships from the port. The sherds found at Chandraketugarh and Tamluk may simply have been from amphorae abandoned at Tāmralipti and Gaṅgābandar.

Miscellaneous Varieties of Pottery

There are quite a few references to export of pottery in the medieval period. In Baṁśīdāsa's *Manasāmaṅgala* (16th century AD), C̃ād Saodāgar exchanges earthenware for bell-metal utensils in Sri Lanka (Dasgupta 1935: 27). The second reference is from Ma-Huan (1970: 163), who mentions basins and bowls among other commodities that Bangala had "for sale". The third reference is from Tome Pires (1967: 92), who in his *Suma Oriental* (1512-1515) had observed that merchants from 'Bengal' used to "bring an abundance of strongly scented vases in dark clay". These were "highly esteemed" and "very cheap" in Malacca. In the second half of the 17th century AD, Niccolao Manucci (1907, II: 426) had found at Patna plentiful of pottery "which emits a pleasant odour, and is so fine that it is no thicker than paper". It is possible that this type of pottery was the same that Pires refers to. Hence, one may conclude that the pottery exported to Malacca (as per Pires' information) and Sri Lanka (as per Baṁśīdāsa's indication) may have been exported from the port of Sātgāon in the early 16th century AD.

RELIGIOUS OBJECTS OF WORSHIP

According to Burmese chronicles, Buddhist images from Benares were imported to Pegu in the mid-11th century AD. The relevant passage from *Shwemawdaw Thamaing* that records such a shipment is quoted below because it shows, besides trade, archaeological vandalism as well.

> In Benares land there was an ancient pagoda on the top of the river Ganges' bank. When the bank washed away, men picked up the relics and holy images that had been enshrined there, and gave them to their children to play, for there was no longer anyone to worship them. Now Nga Dula a ship's captain saw this, and he thought "The folk of the east country deem these images divine and worship them. I shall get gain if I sell them to the folk of the east country". So he bought them for a fitting price and came with them to the landing stage of Pegu. ... Men told king Tissa [1043-57] ... and he rewarded Nga Dula richly and ennobled him (Harvey 1967: 11).

Harvey (*ibid.*) believes that there possibly "was a regular manufacture of such images for the Burma market long after Buddhism had died in Upper India". However, the cited passage does not indicate regular manufacture or regular intercourse. Nevertheless, given its long tradition of sculptural excellence in the middle Gaṅgā valley, we may believe that images produced there (even in the 11th century AD) could not be copied elsewhere. Moreover, because of consumer taste and social conventions in Burma, market demand for Buddhist images is a definite possibility in the 11th century AD. Both these indicators make it possible to believe that occasional shipment of Buddhist images may have been made from the middle Gaṅgā Valley to Burma. Since the only active port in 'Bengal' during this time was Samandar, it may be suggested that the shipments were made form this port.

STEEL PRODUCTS

In West Bengal, low-grade iron ore is available in Birbhum, Bankura, Bardhamān, Medinīpur and its surrounding area. However, the richest area for iron ore in India is the Singhbhum iron belt in Bihar and adjoining Mayurbhanj region in Orissa. The Singhbhum iron belt was a major source of iron for 'Bengal' since the early historic period. Furthermore, native mode of smelting was known for a long time in Birbhum district (Hunter IV 1877: 318-319). The Santhal and other aboriginal tribes inhabiting Bankura district extracted iron from ferruginous laterite for their own want even in the second half of the 19th century (*ibid.*: 211). Even in the early 20th century local iron smelters (called Kols) in the Santhal Parganas (Bihar) extracted the metal from iron ores found in basaltic trap and trappean beds and also in old sandstones and laterite (O'Malley 1910: 15). These indications show that in the past, iron was worked on an extensive scale in 'Bengal'.

Steel manufacturing processes must have been known in 'Bengal' since the early medieval period because literary sources speak of Vaṅga and Aṅga (Monghyr and Bhagalpur) as regions famous for locally produced swords of unique quality (*Agni Purāṇa*, CCXLV: 22-27; Dutt 1904: 886). *Agni Purāṇa*'s claim may not be an empty boast because Tamil Nadu has been producing Wootz steel (an ultra-high carbon steel with 1-2% carbon) since the 2nd century BC and exported it to Europe, China, the Arab world in the 11th and the 12th centuries AD (Srinivasan and Ranganathan 2003). It is not inconceivable that the technology was diffused from south India to 'Bengal' in the early medieval period. The Singhbhum iron belt may easily have provided the raw material needed for the production of steel.

Hence, it is not surprising that Chau ju-kua's *Chu-fan-chi*, a record on Chinese and Arab trade in the 12th and the 13th centuries AD, mentions "fine swords" (Hirth and Rockhill 1965: 97) as one of the native products of P'ōng-kié-lo (i.e., Vaṅgāla or Vaṅga). The tradition of producing steel and its products must have been prevalent even in the 1530s because Ma-Huan (1970: 163) had observed that "steel, spears, knives, scissors and other such articles, all these they [i.e., the people of Bengal] have for sale". A definite indicator of steel export is provided by the *Suma Oriental*, which records that merchant from 'Bengal' shipped steel to Malacca but is silent about steel products (Pires 1967: 92).

Arguments placed above leave no doubt that steel, and possibly steel products as well, were exported from 'Bengal' during the medieval epriod. Since Ma-Huan halted at Caṭṭagrāma, Sonārgāon and Gauḍa during his visits to 'Bengal', it may be reasonably assumed that the products he noted were available at exchange centres in the three cities. Hence we may reasonably assume that these products were exported from Sonārgāon, Caṭṭagrāma and Sātgāon.

Faunal and Human Merchandise

RHINOCEROS AND RHINOCEROS HORNS

Rhinoceroses (the Malayan and the Sumatran variety) were plentiful in 'Bengal' and Assam till the beginning of the 20th century. Today, they have become extinct in Bangladesh. However, they are still found in Assam. The animal is represented in a class of Gupta gold coins issued by Kumāragupta I (c. 415/16-455/556 AD), in which the monarch is shown killing a rhinoceros (Gupta 1996: 72). We may reasonably assume that the above is an acceptable indicator of the availability of the animal in 'Bengal' during the Gupta period. Hiuen-Tsiang had observed the existence of rhinoceros in Campā (modern Bihar) in the 7th century AD (*Life*, Book IV: Beal 1973: 128). The animal was to be seen in the jungles of southern 'Bengal' even in the 1630s, as Manrique (1927: 394) testifies.

Chien-Han-Shu, the Chinese text compiled by Pan Ku in the 1st century AD, records dispatching an imperial embassy to Huang-chih (Gaṅgābandar) for obtaining a living rhinoceros.

> During the Yüan-shih period of Emperor P'ing (AD 1-5), Wang Mang, [in his capacity] as counsellor, and desirous of manifesting the brilliance of his majestic virtue, sent rich gifts to the king of Huang-chih, at the same time commanding him to dispatch an embassy to present a live rhinoceros [as tribute] ... (Wheatley 1961: 11).

The envoys must have been successful in obtaining more than one rhinoceros because elsewhere Pan Ku noted the existence of the animal in the imperial park. "In the interior of the imperial park are unicorns from Chiu-chen (Vietnam), horses from Ta-yüan (Ferghana), rhinoceroses from Huang-chi, birds from T'iao-chih (Mesopotamia; probably ostriches)" (Colless 1980: 161). Thus, *Chien-Han-Shu* appears to show quite clearly that live rhinoceroses were shipped from 'Bengal' in the 1st century AD.

Demand for rhinoceros in China is a classic example of consumer taste and social convention. According to the Asian Civilizations Museum in Singapore,

> The ancient Chinese believed that poisoned wine could be detected and neutralised if poured into a rhinoceros horn cup. The Taoists also used rhinoceros horn for temple worship as early as the Han dynasty (text accompanying display of rhinoceros horn cups, Asian Civilizations Museum in Singapore).

However, the horn found other uses as well. Exhibits in the Shosoin Repository in Japan, which hosts the earliest datable rhinoceros horn objects (from the 8th century AD, Tang China), show that rhinoceros horn was also used for making girdles, amulets in the shape of fish pendants, measuring sticks and even Buddhist scriptures. Nevertheless, the Chinese carved most of the horns they imported into cups. Once a native to China, the rhinoceros must have been persistently hunted because of its demand, for it disappeared entirely from the country by the time of the Song dynasty. When it started becoming rare, the Chinese began to import rhinoceros horns from South Asia, Java and Sumatra. Later, they began to import it even from Africa. (From a text accompanying a display of rhinoceros horn cups, Asian Civilizations Museum in Singapore.) Hence, all export of rhinoceros or its horns from 'Bengal' must have been meant for China.

Arab-Persian authorities definitely show that rhinoceros horns were shipped from 'Bengal' in the 9th and the 10th centuries AD, if not earlier. One may cite Masudi from the 9th century AD, who confirms, "in his time there was a great trade in rhinoceros horns with China and Rahma [Rāhma, i.e., the Pāla Empire] ..." (*Prairies d'or* I, 385, cited in Hirth and Rockhill 1965: 233 fn.). *Ḥudūd al-'Ālam,* a Persian geography composed in 982 AD by an anonymous author, further shows that the horns were obtained from Qāmarūn (Kāmrūpa), "a kingdom in the eastern part of Hindūstān. Rhinoceroses and gold-mines are numerous there" (Minorsky 1937: 87). One hears of export of rhinoceros horns again from Si'di' al-Chelebi in the mid-16th century AD. However, he observes that "their horns are but two palms long" while those from Abyssinia were much longer (Hammer 1836: 467).

The export of rhinoceros horns from 'Bengal' and Assam in the early medieval period must have been made from Samandar since it was the sole maritime port of 'Bengal' in the 9th and the 10th centuries and since, as discussed in Chapter One, merchandise from Kāmrūpa (Assam) were brought down to the port of Samandar (Caṭṭagrāma) by the River Brahmaputra. In the medieval period, the same port (Shātijām or Caṭṭagrāma) exported the commodity since al-Chelebi has given detailed note for navigation to the port in the *Mohi't* (Chapter Nine, Section 3, Twenty-eighth Voyage) and mentions none other in 'Bengal'.

IVORY

From Si'di' al-Chelebi's *Mohi't* one learns of export of ivory from medieval 'Bengal' (Hammer 1836: 467). This is curious since 'Bengal' had to import elephants in the medieval period (discussed later in this chapter). Since elephants were available in the hill tracts of 'Bengal' and Assam, we may believe that the hinterland for ivory may have been both these kingdoms. The port of export must have been Caṭṭagrāma because, as mentioned above, this is the only port in 'Bengal' that al-Chelebi mentions.

HORSES

We learn about horse-trade from B. N. Mukherjee (1990: 47) who has read a terracotta seal-impression (2 cm diam) from Chandraketugarh that is believed to be a trader's identification ticket. Inside a decorated circular border, the impression shows a horse in profile with its head facing a ship with a single mast flying a banner. The horse, clearly showing its mouth, eye, ear, hind leg and tail, stands prominently in the composition. The seal-impression has been dated to the 3rd century AD because of its paleographic features and is now preserved at the Department of Archaeology, West Bengal. It bears a two-lined Kharoshṭī-Brāhmī inscription on the obverse and the reverse bears indistinct impression of an oval seal.

The seal-impression bearing a ship and a horse may not by itself be a convincing proof of horse-trade if we do not have further evidence to substantiate the claim. That evidence is a piece of information that K'ang T'ai (an envoy of a Wu emperor of China) collected during his mission as an envoy to Fu-nan in c. 245-250 AD, which is now recorded in the Chinese text *Tai-P'ing Yu-lan*. K'ang T'ai states that "the Yüeh-chih merchants are continually importing them (horses) to the Ko-ying country by sea (on ship)" (Petech 1950: 53). Reducing the choice for the position of Ko-ying either somewhere on southern Malay Peninsula or on the south-east coast of Sumatra, Wolters (1967: 57) argues in favour of the latter position. Yüeh-chih merchants were traders from the Kuṣāṇa kingdom. That they had settlements in Southeast Asia is proved by the discovery of a seal with Kharoshṭī-Brāhmī inscription at U-Thong in Thailand and a seal matrix in tin also with Kharoshṭī-Brāhmī inscription at Oc-eo. These evidences conclusively prove that around the 3rd century AD, horses were shipped from ports in 'Bengal' by Yüeh-chih merchants from the Kuṣāṇa kingdom. As testified by the continued presence of Kharoshṭī-Brāhmī inscriptions at Chandraketugarh till the 5th century AD, the trade in horse from Gaṅgābandar possibly continued till that time.

KING-FISHER'S FEATHERS

In the early 15th century AD, Fei Sin observed that king-fisher's feathers were among natural products of 'Bengal' – implying thereby that these were exportable commodities (Bagchi 1945: 123). The commodity was (and still is) considered a luxury item in China where it was (and still is) used for making ornaments for the head. Chau Ju-Kua notes that the feathers were mostly imported to China from Chon-la (Kamboja), although it was a forbidden item (having been banned by the Chinese Emperor in 1107 AD because "depriving of living creatures of their life, in order to get their plumage for a perfectly frivolous purpose" was deemed unworthy) (Hirth and Rockhill 1965: 235-236). Because one does not hear of king-fisher's feathers from 'Bengal' any more and because the major supplier for the commodity was Kamboja, it is unlikely that it was a regular export item from 'Bengal'.

CĀMARA (YAK-TAIL)

As Sulaimān al-Tajir (1867: 5) testifies, "the staff called *samara*" (cāmara or chowrie) was available in Ruhmi (identified with the Pāla Empire) in the 9th century AD. Al-Mas'udi (10th century AD) confirms Sulaimān by observing that "[t]hey export from this country the hair called *Samara,* from which fly-whisks are made, with handles of ivory and silver. These are held over the heads of princes when they give audience" (*ibid.*: 5, fn 2). Testimonies of Sulaimān and Al-Mas'udi can leave no doubt that the bushy tail of yak, known as cāmara even today in Bangladesh, was exported from 'Bengal' in the 9th and the 10th centuries.

Climatic conditions would not permit yak to live in 'Bengal' and hence it is not possible that yak-tails exported from 'Bengal' originated from this country. It is more probable that the tails came from Bhutan, since Ralph Fitch had observed in the second half of the 16th century AD that the people of Bottanter (Bhutan) "cut the tailes of their kine, and sell them very deere, for they bee in great request, and much esteemed in those parts. ... They buie and sell by scores upon the ground". Then he adds, "they bee much used in Pegu, and China" (Foster 1968: 27).

CONCH

As *Ḥudūd al-'Ālam* (10.7; Minorsky 1937: 87) testifies, white conch, "which is blown like a trumpet (*būk*) and is called *shank*", was a product of Dahum (Dharmapāla, here implying his kingdom, i.e., the Pāla kingdom). *Ḥudūd*'s testimony is indeed striking because, as mentioned earlier, in both Bijayagupta's and Srīrāy Binod's *Padmā-purāṇa*, C̃ād Saodāgar barters coconut for conch shells. If we are to credit all the three texts as authentic records of trade, we must believe that conch shells were available in the Pāla kingdom in the 10th century AD (hence the reference of availability in the *Ḥudūd*) but the commodity became rare in the late 15th and the 16th centuries (hence C̃ād Saodāgar procures it in Sri Lanka). However, we do not hear of abundant supply and surplus of conch shells in 'Bengal' from any other sources. The nearest source of abundant supply of conch shells is Orissa, which was under the domain of Devapāla (c. 810-847 AD). Hence, either the *Ḥudūd* was misinformed, as it was in the case of Samandar and Harikela, or Dahum must be taken to imply Devapāla's kingdom, part of which was Orissa. In either case, we may omit conch shells from the list of commodities exported from 'Bengal'.

EUNUCHS AND SLAVES

Marco Polo (II, LV) provides the earliest account of trade about slaves and eunuchs in 'Bengal'. He writes:

> There are numbers of eunuchs there, insomuch that all the Barons who keep them get them from that province. .... And the people of India also come thither in search of the eunuchs that I mentioned, and of slaves, male and female, of which there are great numbers, taken from other provinces with which those of the country are at war; and these eunuchs and slaves are sold to the Indian and other merchants who carry them thence for sale about the world (Yule 1903, II: 115).

In the early 16th century AD, maintaining eunuchs must have been a widespread practice among the affluent section of the society in 'Bengal'. As Tome Pires observed, "[t]hey [i.e., the Bengalees] are more in the habit of having eunuchs in Bengal than in any other part of the world. A great many of them are eunuchs" (Pires 1967: 88). If we may trust Barbosa's account, it is possible to believe that the eunuchs were procured locally. He says:

> The Moorish merchants of this city [of Bengala] ofttimes travel up country to buy Heathen boys from their parents or from other persons who steal them and castrate them so that they are left quite flat. Many die from this; those who live they train well and sell them. They value them much as guardian of their women and estates and for other low objects. These eunuchs they hold in high esteem as men of upright character and some of them become their lords' factors, and some Governours and Captains of the Moorish Kings, so that they become very rich and have great estates (Barbosa 1921: 147).

As for slaves, there can also be no doubt that they were sold in local markets. Consider, for example Ibn Battutā's firsthand account.

> A beautiful young girl fit to serve as a concubine, was sold in my presence for one gold *dinar*, which is equal to 2½ *dinars* of gold of Maghrib. I bought at nearly the same price, a young slave woman named Ashurah who was endowed with exquisite beauty. One of my comrades bought a pretty little slave called Lulu, – pearl – for two gold *dinars* (Bhattasali 1922: 136).

Slave trade is further confirmed by a report that Dom Jão do Leyma sent to the Portuguese king in 1518, where he mentions that a male slave could be obtained in 'Bengal' for six *tanga* and a young woman for double the price (Ray 1988: 124). As the Persian account of Shihabuddin Talish shows (Sarkar 1907b: 422) and Arasaratnam (1994: 155) argues, slave trade continued till the 17th century.

Discounting Talish and Arasaratnam (because their evidence is from a period beyond the scope of the present research), we are left with no confirmation of Marco Polo's assertion that eunuchs and slaves were exported from 'Bengal'. Hence, it would be unwise to include them in the list of maritime merchandise exported from 'Bengal'.

IMPORTED COMMODITIES

Commodities imported through the ports of 'Bengal', either for home consumption or for neighbouring kingdoms, have been grouped in this section under three categories: edible, mineral and forest products, manufactured goods and faunal merchandise.

Edible, Mineral and Forest Products

SPICES

In the gastronomic traditions developed by the Muslims in South Asia (including 'Bengal'), Persia, and the Arab world, the three spices that acquired great value were clove, nutmeg, and mace. These came from the eastern part of the Indonesian archipelago, popularly known as the Spice Islands. Of these, Amboina provided the most cloves, while the other islands were the source of nutmeg and its derivative, mace. Cinnamon, which came from Sri Lanka, began to acquire an important place from the 17th century AD. Even if we leave aside cinnamon since its import is not encompassed within the time frame of this research, there can be little doubt that clove, nutmeg, and mace were imported by maritime means of transportation during the Sultanate period.

The above is indeed confirmed by Tome Pires (1967: 93) who shows that in the early 16th century AD, pepper, cloves, mace, nutmeg were imported to 'Bengal' from Malacca by Bengali traders. Black pepper was obtained mostly from the interior of Sumatra and the hinterland of Patani on the Malay Peninsula. Import of black pepper is indeed intriguing because Pires also noted that abundant pepper was grown in Cooch Behar.

Ray (1998: 116) believes, cinnamon, cassia and cloves must have been used in South Asia for medicinal purposes from much earlier times because they are mentioned in the works of Caraka (2nd century AD) and Suśruta (4th-5th century AD). The same argument could be used for mace and nutmeg, which are still used in *Ayurvedic* medicine in 'Bengal'. However, 'Bengal' may not have imported all these spices by maritime means of transportation because clove and nutmeg were available in Assam. We hear from Bānabhaṭṭa that in the first half of the 7th century AD, Bhāskaravarman sent to Harṣavardhana "clove flower bunches, and nutmeg clusters, all bristling with masses of ripe fruit" as gift (Bānabhaṭṭa 1897: 214). Since clove flowers are mentioned and nutmegs are described to be in clusters, one may logically surmise that both the spices were locally produced in Assam and not imported. We also hear of "vast fields for growing fine *elā* (cardamom) plants" in the 11th-century AD Varendrī in Sandhyākara Nandī's *Rāmacarita* (Canto III, verse 18b; Sandhyākara Nandī 1910: 67). Hence, we may conclude that 'Bengal' possibly imported some herbal products such as cinnamon, cassia and mace for medicinal use from the 2nd century AD onwards.

We have no indication regarding the ports that dealt with the import of spices. Since the commodity must have been in demand all over 'Bengal', we may logically expect it to have been imported through all the ports. It would be reasonable to believe that the middle Gaṅgā plain also imported spices from the Southeast Asia through Tāmralipti and Gaṅgābandar because these two ports served as the gateway to the region.

OPIUM

Opium, an intoxicant and medicinal ingredient which is extracted from poppies, had four production areas in the early 16th century AD. These were Thebes in the kingdom of Cairo, Aden, Cambay and Cous (Cooch Behar) (Pires 1967: 513). During the same period, Bengali merchants brought back with them from Malacca "opium from Aden and some little from Bengal" (*ibid*.: 93). This bit of information is indeed curious because, unless it was an oversight on Pires' part, there should be no reason for Bengali merchants to import opium produced in 'Bengal' from Malacca. Furthermore, the same source notes that the kingdom of Cooch Behar, which lay immediately to the north of 'Bengal', produced abundant opium (*ibid*.: 89), which was considered to be "a good merchandise, consumed in great quantity, and very valuable" (*ibid*.: 513). He further testifies that the kingdom was a major exporter of opium to Malacca.

A possible explanation for overlooking a nearer source (from Couch Behar) and going for a distant one (from Aden) could be hostile relationship between the two kingdoms. The opium from 'Bengal' that the Bengali traders carried back with them could have been from Cooch Behar. If that were the case, then it is unlikely that opium would always be imported from Malacca. It is more probable that Tome Pires was writing at a time when stressful conditions existed between the two kingdoms and hence, opium would normally be imported by 'Bengal' from Cooch Behar by land and/or river routes. Interestingly, Ralph Fitch makes no mention of opium in the kingdom when he visited it in the last quarter of the 16th century AD. The implication may be that Cooch Behar had ceased producing quality opium by that time.

SANDALWOOD

Sandalwood (Santalum album, *Linn*.) is known in 'Bengal'i and Indian vernaculars as *candan*. It is obtained from a small evergreen tree seen in the dry regions of South India (Mysore, Coorg, South Maratha, Hyderabad, Karnatak, the Western Ghats, Nilgiri hills, Coimbatore) and in North India chiefly as a cultivated plant. Sandalwood is not produced in Bangladesh or West Bengal. Kauṭīlya's *Arthaśāstra* (4th century BC), while discussing the precious commodities available in contemporary South Asia, informs that in ancient times, the major sources of the wood were Jāpa, Joṅga and Turūpa localities situated in Kāmrūpa. Sandalwood from Jāpa was red and had the fragrance of a lotus, while those from Joṅga and Turūpa were red or red-black and smooth (2.11.47-48; Kangle 1963: 116). It must have been these varieties of sandalwood that the Mlechchha kings of Lauhitya paid as tribute to Bhima when the latter, as described in the *Mahābhārata*, subjugated various kings of 'Bengal' and its adjoining regions (Sabhā Parva, Section XXIX; Ganguli 1990, II: 61-62).

In the first half of the 7th century AD, Bhāskaravarman sent to Harṣavardhana *gosisra* sandal as gift (Bānabhaṭṭa 1897: 214). Even Chau Ju-Kua notes that India (T'ien-chu) produced sandalwood (Hirth and Rockhill 1965: 111). These references may make it possible to believe that 'Bengal' met its requirement for sandalwood from Assam. What is striking is that it features as a commodity of maritime trade for the first time in the medieval period. Going by information provided by Tome Pires (1967: 93), one learns that Bengali merchants brought sandalwood from Malacca on their return voyage. The source of the commodity was Timor (Prakash 1985: 54). Unless sandalwood disappeared entirely from Kāmrūpa or the sandalwood from Malacca was of a different variety, import of the commodity indicates that in the early 16th century AD, Kāmrūpa had strained its relation with 'Bengal'.

CAMPHOR

Camphor is obtained by distillation of the wood of *Cinnamomum camphora* and is found mostly in Malay Peninsula, Sumatra and Borneo. It is used for medicinal purpose and protecting garments from insects. It has also been used in *Ayurvedic* medicine in South Asia for a long time. We hear from Bāṇabhaṭṭa that, Bhāskaravarman sent to Harṣavardhana "camphor cool, pure, and white as bits of ice", in the first half of the 7th century AD (Bāṇabhaṭṭa 1897: 214), but there is no way of knowing whether these were imported from Assam or locally produced. We can definitely say that camphor was imported to 'Bengal' in the early 16th century AD when Tome Pires (1967: 93) noted that Bengali merchants from Malacca brought the commodity back with them on their return voyage.

MERCURY (QUICKSILVER)

Mercury, a rare element as the earth's crust and a liquid metal at ordinary temperature, is mostly obtained by reduction from the mineral cinnabar (a dense red mineral). Mercury was known in ancient China and South Asia and was found in Egyptian tombs that date from 1500 BC. Because it forms an amalgam with gold very easily, it was used in pre-Modern times mostly for gold recovery from ores. The ancient Greeks used the metal in ointments; the Romans used it in cosmetics and South Asian as a medicinal ingredient. Approximately 50% of the global supply of mercury comes from Spain and Italy with much of the rest comes from Yugoslavia, Russia, and North America. Cinnabar is found in all localities, which yield quicksilver, such as Spain, New California, Slovenia, Tuscany, Serbia, Peru, and the province of Kweichow in China.

Mercury features in the list of imported items in 'Bengal' for the first time in the Medieval Period. In the early 15th century AD, Fei Sin mentions the name of the commodity (quick silver) as one of those the Chinese brought with them in 'Bengal' for trade (Bagchi 1945: 123). Judging by the list of places where mercury is obtainable, there can be little doubt that Fei Sin's mercury was a Chinese product. In the early 16th century AD, Tome Pires (1967: 93) observed that the Bengali merchants imported mercury to 'Bengal' on their return voyage from Malacca. Thus, there can be little doubt that Baṁśīdāsa's *Manasāmaṅgala* (16th century AD) reflects a bit of historical fact when it notes that Cānd Saodāgar exchanged oil and clarified butter for quick-silver (Dasgupta 1935: 27).

Because our source of information on import of opium, sandalwood, camphor and mercury is Tome Pires and because he mentions the names of Bengala (Caṭṭagrāma) and Sātgāon as the two ports of 'Bengal' (Pires 1967: 90-91), we may believe that all these four items were imported through both these ports. This expectation is logical because these items would have been used all over 'Bengal'.

VERMILION

Vermilion is the standard name in English given to artists' red pigment produced from artificially made mercuric sulphide, while cinnabar is the name given to the natural mineral. In earlier times, it was known as Chinese red. Although it was well known to the Romans and widely used in China since the 3rd millennium BC, its use is not found in ancient Egyptian or early Mesopotamian objects. That the Chinese merchants introduced the commodity to South Asia is amply testified by the phonetic similarity between *sindūra* in Sanskrit and *ts'in-t'ung* (or "China lead") in Chinese. In Sanskrit, vermilion is also called *nāgarakta* or "dragon's blood" – a name that may have arisen from China and carried to South Asia by Chinese merchants (Bagchi 1981: 76).

As Fei Sin testifies, Chinese merchants accompanying his mission to 'Bengal' sold the commodity in the early 15th century AD (Bagchi 1945: 123). His testimony would have been a stray account had not Thomas Bowrey (1905: 232-233) reported in the 1670s that the English imported vermilion to Patna and that the product had a ready market there. Hence it may be assumed with a fair amount of certainty that the commodity had a market in 'Bengal' during Fei Sin's visit as well. One may even suggest, citing phonetic similarity of *sindūra* in Sanskrit and *ts'in-t'ung* (or "China lead") in Chinese, that the entire South Asia met its demand for *sindūra* for ritual use since the late historic period by importing it from China since geographical determinant of production was absolute in this case and the commodity had a unique source of supply in pre-modern times.

All pre-modern use of vermilion must have been based on cinnabar because artificially made mercuric sulphide may not have been known then. Since China was the only major source of cinnabar in Asia, vermilion imported to 'Bengal' in the medieval period must have originated in China but may have been procured by merchants in 'Bengal' from Malacca. Because the commodity would have been used all over 'Bengal', we may believe that it was imported through all the three functioning ports, i.e., Sonārgāon, Caṭṭagrāma and Sātgāon.

GOLD

In pre-modern times, gold was primarily required as a media of exchange (which included gold coins and bullion) and making ornaments. The gold coin called *caltis* referred to in the *Periplus of the Erithraean Sea* (Schoff 1995: 48) is possibly the earliest reference to locally minted gold coins. It may have been sustained by, as the *Periplus* observes, gold mines near the port of Gaṅgābandar. The post-Gupta gold coins issued by Samācāradeva, Śaśāṅka, Jayanāga, Pṛthuvīra (Prithuva(ba)la) and Sudhanyāditya (Vasuvarmana), which were regular currency in the 6th and the 7th centuries AD (De 1970: 144), were mostly debased. Although these coins indicate that the financial structures of the issuing authorities had some gold to sustain these currencies, the debased nature of the coins do not speak of affluent economies. After their absence during the Pāla-Sena period, gold coins re-surfaced during the Sultanate period. In spite of the fact that the gold content in these coins is very high, they may not have been minted in large numbers. Hence, it may appear that gold did not have much use as a medium of exchange during the entire period under study. However, we must remember that gold coin was not the sole medium of exchange in which gold was used because bullion and gold dust may also have been used as a medium of exchange during some periods. Moreover, gold ornaments also had widespread use in 'Bengal'. If these considerations are borne in mind, then it is conceivable that the demand for gold in 'Bengal' could not have been insignificant.

One source of the inflow of gold must have been gold coins of foreign origin that came in by way of trade. Although gold coins were not commodities of trade but currencies which were accepted by local merchants with balance of trade in their favour, the intrinsic value of the precious metal converted it into a commodity once it was extracted from the currency system that issued it. Kuṣāṇa, Gupta and Abbasid gold coins found in 'Bengal' (discussed in detail in Chapter Three) entered by means of trade. Surprisingly, no Roman gold coin has yet been found anywhere in Bangladesh and West Bengal. Of the three issuing authorities mentioned above, only those of the Abbasids is relevant for this study on maritime research since the Kuṣāṇa coins must have entered 'Bengal' through land routes and the Gupta coins must have circulated in internal trade (since most of 'Bengal' was part of the Gupta Empire). The number of Abbasid gold coins is negligible (only 13 have so far been noticed) and hence it implies negligible inflow of gold as minted currency. At the same time it is unthinkable that no gold coins entered 'Bengal' during the prosperous days of the early medieval period, since balance of trade prior to pre-modern period, was always in favour of 'Bengal'. Till further material evidence comes to light, we are left with no alternative but to believe that the gold must have been imported as bullion. In order to ascertain its inflow; let us first determine local and neighbouring sources of gold.

No significant deposit of gold, either vein or river-washed, is known to have existed in Bangladesh. In West Bengal, gold is obtained at Medinīpur, Baghmundi Thana of Purulia district and Bankura (West Bengal). In pre-modern times, rivers were the major source of gold in the region that is today known as West Bengal. The rivers flowing through Singhbhum, which lies 75 to 150 miles west of the mouth of Gaṅgā in West Bengal, are known for a long time to have produced alluvial gold through gold panning. One of these rivers is the Suvarṇarekhā whose name was derived from words denoting gold (Krishnaswamy 1972: 177). It is possible that the *Periplus* refers to this source when it notes the existence of gold mines near the Gaṅgā (§ 63; Schoff 1995: 48). Because one does not hear of gold mines near the Gaṅgā at a later period, it may be assumed that the above source of gold gradually became insignificant. Moreover, as Deyell (1990: 249) argues, "at no period could the amount of gold recovered annually have been significant in terms of the mass of gold consumed by a mint in its gold coin production". The reasons he cites are (1) only 10 mg of gold have been found per cubic metre of gravel in Singhbhum region; (2) the ratio of productivity between Singhbhum and Kolar (in south India) was 1 to 1500; and (3) gold panning was highly labour intensive and it is unlikely that anything like the Assamese scale of activity (discussed below) was possible in this region. It is doubtful if the entire 'Bengal' could meet its requirement of gold bullion from the sources discussed above. Hence, we need to examine if gold bullion could have been imported from neighbouring kingdoms.

Ancient Assam was renowned for its gold washing industry. The precious metal was washed from many rivers; the most productive of which was the Subarnasiri. Availability of gold in ancient Assam is worth noting because Thakur (1972: 88) believes that Samudragupta might have obtained his gold from Assam and other local mines within his empire. The fame of Assamese gold must have reached even the Arabs and Persians in the 10th century AD because the *Ḥudūd al-'Ālam* informs us that "gold-mines are numerous" in Qāmarūn (Kāmrūpa) "a kingdom in the eastern part of Hindūstān" (Minorsky 1937: 87). The *Ḥudūd* must have been composed from distant hearsay because Assamese gold was obtained by gold-washing and not mining. During the reign of the Ahom kings in the medieval period, thousands of labourers called *sonwals* were employed by the state employed for gold washing. As Tavernier (1889, II: 283-284) testifies, Kāmrūpa was producing gold even in the second half of the 17th century AD. The authenticity of these sources of information is attested by the fact that even in modern times, "alluvial gold has been recovered in Subarnasiri River, the Lohit-Brahmaputra and other rivers in Lakhimpur, Darrang and Sibsagar districts" (Krishnaswami 1972: 177). Although all the sources mentioned above indicate abundant supply and surplus of gold in Assam over a long period of time, 'Bengal' did not import gold from the above kingdom (at least in the medieval period) because Tavernier (1889, II: 283-284) reports that gold in Kāmrūpa was not exported or made into coins but was used in local trade.

Tavernier further informs us that there was a gold mine in Tripura in the second half of the 17th century AD, which yielded "gold of very low standard". The gold, along with locally produced coarse silver, was sold to China in exchange of silver (Tavernier 1889, II: 275). Tavernier may have been misinformed because gold that was obtainable in Tripura was mostly from river-washings of Assam and northern Burma. Be that as it may, it is quite certain that 'Bengal' did not import gold bullion from Tripura because available source indicates its export to China.

River-washed gold may have been available in India as well. The name of the River Son (which met the Gaṅgā near the site of the ancient capital Pataliputra) has been derived from a local expression denoting gold. Greco-Roman authors refer to the Son as *Erannoboas,* a name they must have derived from *Hiranya-vahā* in Sanskrit which denotes "carrying gold" (McCrindle 1979: 43). That the name literally implies what it denotes is attested by the fact that in modern times, alluvial gold has been obtained from the river by washing the stream gravel (Krishnaswamy 1972: 177). A second source of gold in India is vein-gold (associated with quartz-veins or reefs) extracted from mines at Kolar district in Karnataka. In ancient times, gold must have been available at a number of mines in Peninsular India as indicated by signs of gold working in diggings, heaps of crushed quartz and stone mortars found in Kolar and Hutti in Karnataka, Anantpur in Andhra Pradesh and a number of other places (Wadia 1961: 475). The gold from Karnataka was possibly exhausted by the Sultanate period (Ray 1997: 26). Vein gold, in Archaean quartzites and phyllites belonging to the iron ore stage, is also found in the southern portion of Singhbhum district, near Lowa in Bihar. Interestingly, as Krishnaswamy (1972: 177) reports, three old workings can be noticed in the area. Known as Tama Pahar, Bhaluk Khad East and Bhaluk Khad West, the thickness of the lode at the three spots varies from 1.22 metres to 4.6 metres. Unfortunately, it is not certain how old exactly these workings are. Even if 'Bengal' imported gold from anywhere in India, only that from south India could be transported by maritime route and hence would be within the purview of the present research. However, there is very little indication that gold bullion was imported from south India.

River-washed gold was also available in Burma (Myanmar). According to a geological survey report made in the late 19th century, gold "is found in the form of fine grains and leaflets in the recent deposits of the Irrawaddi valley and of all its tributaries". According to the same report, "the surface sands along the bank contain probably not less than 30 grains of gold per ton of drift, which would be good enough to pay working on a large scale" (Griesbach 1892: 129-130). Another report from the same period indicates that gold was also available, but in small scale, in the Tenasserim River, at the old town of Tenasserim (Bose 1893: 163). As the following report suggests, medieval Tenasserim had its own source of gold.

> On the right bank of the Great Tenasserim River a good show of gold was brought to light, but this again is situated below a pagoda. There is a tale told that the last queen of ancient Tenasserim held the monopoly for the manufacture of gold ornaments ... (Hughes 1893: 48).

It is possible that Burma and Tenasserim provided 'Bengal' with considerable gold in the medieval period because the ship in which Caesar Frederick travelled from Pegu to Caṭṭagrāma in 1569 "had not any thing in her save victual and ballast, Silver and Gold, which from Pegu they carrie to Bengala" (Purchas 1905b: 136). His manner of description appears to imply a standard practice and not an exceptional event. Although Frederick's testimony is a little removed from the limit of our time frame, Irrawadi and Tenasserim gold by way of Pegu meets our criterion of abundant supply and surplus over a reasonably long period of time and geographical determinant of production.

We have two sources to confirm gold import through maritime trade during the medieval period. One of these is Fei Sin's account (early 15th century AD) where it is stated that the goods used by the Chinese in trading in 'Bengal' included gold (Bagchi 1945: 123). Because we cannot accept Fei Sin's testimony as an evidence of regular trade, we may move on to Tome Pires, our second source. He observed in the early 16th century AD that "[g]old is worth a sixth part more in Bengal than in Malacca" (Pires: 1967: 93). Thus, we may conclude that in the medieval period, sources of gold bullion imported to 'Bengal' were Pegu, Tenasserim and Malacca through the ports of Sonārgāon, Sātgāon and Caṭṭagrāma. Since there is no definite indicator regarding import of gold through maritime trade during the earlier periods, we may tentatively suggest that most of it must have come in by land routes.

SILVER

In pre-modern times, silver was primarily used for minting coins. Available evidences suggest that silver coins were in regular circulation in 'Bengal' from the Maurya period till the early 16th century AD. Nevertheless, three periods can be easily identified when silver coins dominated existing currency systems. There are (1) from the 3rd century BC to the 3rd century AD when silver punch-marked coins that were in circulation in Vaṅga, Rāḍha, Suhma and Puṇḍra, (2) from the 8th to the mid-11th centuries AD during most of which time Harikela silver coins were in circulation in Harikela and Samataṭa, and (3) the Sultanate period when silver *taṅkās* were in circulation in the entire sultanate Bengal. These coins indicate that the financial structures of the issuing authorities had abundant silver to sustain these currencies. Furthermore, because they have been found in large numbers (to be discussed in greater detail in Chapter Three), we may believe that the economies of the respective issuing authorities were affluent. We must also take into consideration the possibility that besides silver coins, bullion and silver dust may also have been used as a medium of exchange during some periods. Hence, it is conceivable that the demand for silver in

'Bengal' was considerable, particularly during the three periods mentioned above.

There is no silver mine either in Bangladesh or West Bengal. As a matter of fact, there is no source of pure silver ores anywhere in South Asia. Hindu Kush, now in Afghanistan, was the major source of coinage silver for South Asia till the early 13th century AD when the Mongols conquered the region (Deyell 1990: 251). The metal is locally produced in India from argentiferous galena, an ore of lead in which silver occurs as an impurity. Two important sources for galena in India are Metri in Bellary district (UP) and Zawar in Udaypur district (Rajasthan). Some amount of silver is also collected from argentiferous galena found in Orissa and at Beheraki and Lakṣmīpur under Santhal Parganas in Bihar. Mines in these sites have been worked since the early historic period. The most important source of silver in the immediate vicinity of 'Bengal' is the Bawdwin mines of Myanmar where silver is extracted from argentiferous lead-zinc ores.

The only known source of silver in the early historic 'Bengal' was Gauḍa, as the *Arthaśāstra* (2. 13.10) speaks of a class of silver known as Gauḍika (Kangle 1963: 127). Since it is inconceivable that the above source could have met the total demand for silver used in punch-marked coins that were issued from the 3rd century BC to the 3rd century AD, one is led to believe that silver must have been imported. The nearest region that had and still has abundant supply and surplus over a long period of time is Bawdwin in Myanmar. As recorded in Father Sangermano's documents compiled during the last two decades of the 18th century AD, the Burmese produced abundant silver that was exported in great quantities despite severe laws forbidding its export. He further testifies that the silver was drawn from Bawdwin, which was located "to the east of Canton [Kaungton near Bhamo], towards the Chinese province of Juana [Yunnan], the country of Sciam [Shan]" (Sangermano 1969: 215).

Bawdwin produced around 2 million ounces of silver in 1918 (Harvey 1967: 310). If we remember that prior to the Spanish conquest of Central America in the 16th century AD, when voluminous quantity of silver poured into the world market, production of silver in the world was substantially less, it will become immediately apparent that Bawdwin was the most important regional source of silver. John Deyell (1983: 207-224) has shown that silver from Bawdwin was transported by land and river routes to the Brahmaputra valley and the Arakan coast. From the Brahmaputra valley, the metal was transported again by river and land routes to 'Bengal' and from the Arakan coast, silver was transported to 'Bengal' by maritime route. Hence, it is possible that Tavernier (1889, II: 283-284) was misinformed when he wrote that Kāmrūpa had its own source of silver in the second half of the 17th century AD. In all probability, Kāmrūpa also depended on Bawdwin for its silver.

Pires' testimony, that "some silver" was available in Arakan (Pires 1967: 96), confirms Deyell's thesis. The geographical proximity of Harikela and Arakan also indicate that the source of Harikela silver coins must have been Arakan. However, it appears that in the medieval period, Bawdwin silver was imported to 'Bengal' from Pegu in Burma because Tome Pires testifies to that effect. "A great deal of silver", says Pires (*ibid.*: 100), "is taken from Pegu to Bengal, where it is worth somewhat more". Caesar Frederick's testimony cited earlier, that silver and gold were usually shipped from Pegu to 'Bengal', confirms Tome Pires. Acrimonious political relation between Assam and 'Bengal' could have been a reason for dependence on maritime mode of transportation. Tarafdar (1995: 61) is of the opinion that in the early 16th century AD, Bengali merchants imported from Malacca as well. However, this is unlikely because, as Tome Pires (1967: 93) informs us, compared to the price of silver in Malacca, it was a fifth to a quarter cheaper in 'Bengal'. Although Fei Sin lists silver as one of the commodities that the Chinese merchants used for trading in 'Bengal' (Bagchi 1945: 123), we must discount this bit of evidence because it is not indicative of regular trade. Thus we may conclude that in the medieval period, silver was imported from Pegu and Arakan. Because silver would have been in demand in all urban centres, we may logically expect it to have been imported through all the three medieval ports, i.e., Sonārgāon, Sātgāon and Caṭṭagrāma.

There can be little doubt that in the early medieval period, Arakanese silver imported for Harikela coins was transported by maritime means through the port of Harikela (Caṭṭagrāma) simply because it would have been more convenient. However, the silver for the punch-marked coins may have been transported by land and river routes via the Brahmaputra Valley.

COPPER

Copper was important in the early historic period producing various articles, wares and commodities in bronze (an alloy of copper and tin) and brass (an alloy of copper and zinc). Copper was also necessary for making gold ornaments and to strengthen silver alloys. However, its most significant use was in minting coins. Copper punch-marked coins from the Maurya period (3rd-2nd centuries BC) were in circulation in Rāḍha, Sumha, Gauḍa, Varendra, Puṇḍravardhana and Vaṅga. Cast copper coins from Maurya and Kuṣāṇa period were in circulation till the Gupta period in Rāḍha, Suhma and in the south-westernmost areas of Vaṅga. Die-struck copper coins, though not in great number, were issued by Gupta emperors Samudragupta, Candragupta II, Kumāragupta I during their reign from the mid-4th century AD to the mid-5th century AD (Gupta 1996: 74). (Detailed discussion on coinage system will be presented later in Chapter Three.)

There is no copper mine in Bangladesh. In India, the three major areas for mining copper are the Khetri belt in

Rajasthan, the Singhbhum belt in Bihar and the Guntur belt in Andhra Pradesh. In the early historic period, considerable quantities of copper were smelted in these regions and also at various parts of the Himalayas (Kullu, Garhwal, Nepal, Sikkim and Bhutan). Copper was mined in Rajasthan even during the reign of the Delhi Sultans and the Mughals (Ray 1997: 26). Some amount of copper was available in the northern part of the Medinīpur, Bankura and Purulia districts of West Bengal and in Deogarh subdivision under Santhal Parganas in Bihar. As Sengupta (1996: 123) points out, ancient copper mines are known to have existed at Tamkum in Bankura district and Chhedapathar in Medinīpur district. Although these sources may have provided some amount of copper in the early historic period, the copper belt of Singhbhum-Hazaribagh in Chotanagpur plateau in Bihar was the primary source of the metal.

Copper could have been procured from the mines of the copper belt of Singhbhum-Hazaribagh in Chotanagpur plateau, specially from the mines in the Rakha hill area, because these bear indications of working in ancient times. Because this area was situated near an over-land route running from Magadha in south Bihar to Tāmralipti through the areas of Hazaribagh, Ranchi, Singhbhum, Purulia and Bankura (in the Medinīpur district). Maity (1975: 161) believes that the signs of ancient working in the Chotanagpur area date from the Kuṣāṇa times. These plentiful sources of supply indicate that there would have been little necessity to import copper through maritime routes in the early historic 'Bengal'.

In the early medieval period, the use of copper came to be restricted to different varieties of wares, religious objects and ornaments. One would naturally expect that the copper belt of Singhbhum-Hazaribagh would provide for home consumption. However, such was not the case because in the early 15th century AD, as Fei Sin testifies, the Chinese traders accompanying him in 'Bengal' had copper in their basket of commodities (Bagchi 1945: 123). Even in the early 16th century AD, Tome Pires (1967: 93) notes that Bengali merchants imported copper from Malacca to 'Bengal'. This is indeed striking because during the same period, a Gujarati ship arrived each year to the ports of Martaban and Dagon in the kingdom of Pegu with copper (*ibid.*: 101), which indicates that copper was available in Rajasthan and was being exported from Gujarati ports. Since Bihar, Rajasthan and Andhra (the three major sources of copper in South Asia) did not lie within the sultanate of 'Bengal', it is possible that strained political relations forced 'Bengal' to import copper from Malacca.

IRON

The sources of iron ore noted in the previous section indicate that various kingdoms in the early historic and the late historic 'Bengal' could easily have used locally available iron ore or imported the commodity through land routes. These ores must have been used in manufacturing steel, which were exported from the ports of 'Bengal' to Malacca in the early 16th century AD. However, one stumbles with surprise when one learns from Fei Sin that in the early 15th century AD, the goods used by the Chinese in trading in 'Bengal' included iron (Bagchi 1945: 123). On the other hand, the Chinese account named *Shu yu chou tseu lu* (compiled in 1574 by Yen Ts'ong-kien) lists iron as one of the commodities available in 'Bengal' (*ibid.*: 132). Although the testimony provided by *Shu yu chou tseu lu* falls outside the time frame of this research, it may be taken to indicate varying market conditions or that a different quality of iron was imported in the early 15th century AD.

Copper and iron would have been required in urban centres all over 'Bengal' and hence we may logically expect it to have been imported through all the three medieval ports, i.e., Sonārgāon, Sātgāon and Caṭṭagrāma.

TIN AND LEAD

In pre-modern times, tin and lead were used mostly for minting coins. A small portion of tin was mixed with lead for minting lead coins of the Kura kings and the Maharathis of western Deccan, the Satavahanas (Ray 1998: 78) and the Guptas (Gupta 1996: 75). The use of these two metals must have been limited in 'Bengal' since lead coins were never minted here. Tin was used in 'Bengal' mostly for producing various kinds of bronze artefacts, utensils and religious icons. Tin and lead (along with a few other metals) were also used as a hardening alloy for minting silver coins. They may also have been used for manufacturing mirrors since a thin sheet of lead mixed with a little tin served as a reflecting surface.

Bangladesh and West Bengal do not produce any tin or lead. A small quantity of lead is produced in India from lead ores (principally argentiferous galena) at a number of places in southern Bihar, Orissa, Madhya Pradesh, Rajasthan, Tamil Nadu, the Himalayas and Andhra Pradesh. These sources may have served in pre-modern periods as well. India has no significant source of indigenous tin. However, it is believed that tin was formerly produced in South Asia in a large scale, as large mounds of slag that were found in parts of Bihar, Mewar and Jaipur indicate. A small quantity of tin may have existed in the Chotanagpur plateau (Bihar) where cassiterite was reported to have been found. Another deposit of tin was located close to Giridih in south Bihar. Because it is normally found in riverbeds along with alluvial gold, it is possible that tin was available in the riverbeds of the Subarnasiri, the Lohit-Brahmaputra, the Suvarnarekhā and the Son. Both lead and tin may have been locally available in South Asia even in the 12th and the 13th centuries AD because Chau Ju-Kua, testifies so in his work titled *Chu-fan-chi* (Hirth and Rockhill: 1965: 111).

The indications cited above leads one to believe that 'Bengal' may have imported the little tin and lead that it required over-land and river routes from India. This impression is confirmed by Ralph Fitch who travelled from Agra "down the river Jemena" to Satagam in 1586, "in the companie of one hundred and fourscore boates" laden with quite a few commodities including lead (Foster 1968: 18). 'Bengal' may have imported lead from Burma as well, which supplied British India with the metal till 1940, because a prosperous lead industry based on deposits of argentiferous galena is known to have existed in Bawdwin in the Shan States of Upper Burma (Wadia 1961: 478) and because the same source supplied 'Bengal' with silver. Burmese lead may have arrived by overland route via the Brahmaputra Valley and by maritime route via Arakan and Pegu, the same way as silver. Once again, Tavernier (1889, II: 283-284), in the second half of the 17th century AD, appears to have been misinformed when he reported that lead was locally produced in Kāmrūpa. Like silver, lead in Kāmrūpa must also have been imported from Burma.

Another source for the import of lead to 'Bengal', as Tome Pires (1967: 93) informs us, was Malacca. In the early 16th century AD, this entrepot appears to have turned out also to be a supplier of tin for 'Bengal' because we learn from Pires (*ibid.*: 93) once again that Bengali merchants brought back the metal from Malacca. The origin of the tin must have been Thailand, Malaysia and the "Tin Islands" of Indonesia, where tin deposit, mostly in the form of cassiterite ($SnO2$) and tin bearing granite rocks, is found extensively (Hoskins 1969).

RUBY

We may believe that ruby was imported from Pegu in Burma in the early 16th century AD. Tome Pires (1967: 96) provides the following description of how the semi-precious stone was transported from its source to Pegu.

> [A] not very civilised people" who inhabit "the great mountain range which is called Capelanguam" [i.e., Capelang, the Ruby country north of Ava, according to Yule, Pires 1967: 96, f.n. 2] "bring the ... rubies to the great city of Ava ... and from there they go to Pegu, and from Pegu they are distributed to Bengal, Narsinga and to Pase and Malacca".

Tin, lead and ruby must have been imported through Caṭṭagrāma and Sātgāon because these were the two ports functioning in the early 16th century AD.

Manufactured Goods

PORCELAIN

As Rougeulle (1996: 160) observes, an interesting change appeared in the Chinese trade scenario in the 8th century AD. During this century, the famous porcelain and stone ware of China began to be exported in quantity while silk lost its pre-eminent position. Chinese porcelain, which has long been associated with elite Muslim culture in 'Bengal', began to be imported in the early 13th century AD. We hear of porcelain import for the first time in the early 15th century AD from Fei Sin who noted that porcelain was one of the commodities that the Chinese merchants offered for trade in 'Bengal' (Bagchi 1945: 123). Demand for the commodity must have increased significantly in the early 16th century AD for we hear Tome Pires (1967: 93) saying that Bengali merchants, on their return voyage from Malacca, carried back with them "white porcelain in plenty" and "large green porcelain ware from the Liu Kiu Islands." A large number of fragments of porcelain ware that have been found at Gauda (the capital of Sultanate Bengal from 1432) serve as important archaeological evidence corroborating the literary sources cited above (Ray 1997: 35). As a luxury item, porcelain must have been in demand in all the urban centres of the Sultanate Bengal. Hence we may expect that all the three ports of the medieval period handled its import.

HIGH-TIN BRONZE KNOBBED VESSELS

High-tin bronze is a copper-tin alloy, which contains 20-30% tin and is easy to cast because its melting point is relatively low (about 900°c) (Bennett and Glover 1992: 198). Knobbed vessels are so called because a conical knob, circumscribed by a series of concentric grooves or incisions, stand at the centre of the inner surface of the vessel's base. Fragments of two high-tin bronze knobbed vessels have been found during chance excavation at Wārī-Baṭeśwar in Bangladesh (Fig. 2.8). No other finds of high-tin bronze vessels have been reported from any other sites in Bangladesh and West Bengal in India.

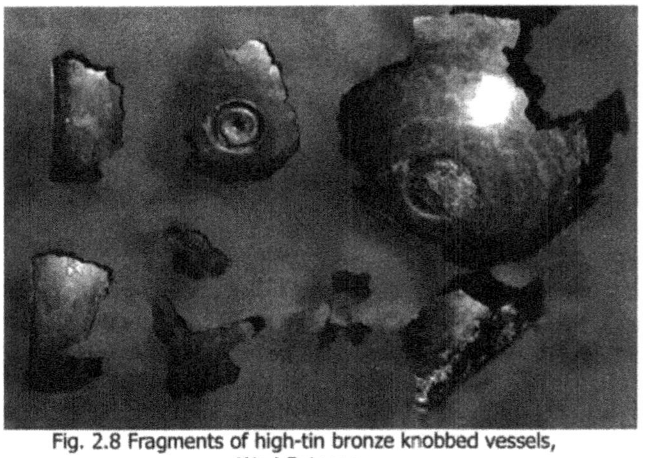

Fig. 2.8 Fragments of high-tin bronze knobbed vessels, Wari-Bateswar

Fig. 2.9 High-tin bronze knobbed vessel, Ban Don Ta Phet, Thailand
Courtesy: National Museum, Bangkok

As noted in Chapter One, similar high-tin bronze knobbed vessels have been found at Ban Don Ta Phet in west-central Thailand (Fig. 2.9) and a bronze knobbed bowl has been reported from Than Hoa Province of Vietnam. The Ban Don Ta Phet discovery is significant because at the site, 300 bronze wares were discovered in 90 funerary deposits, most of which are made of high-tin bronze (23-28% Sn). Among these, the number of high-tin bronze knobbed vessels is over 20 (Glover 1996a: 140, 142). The Thai wares, so far unique to Thailand, is believed to have been imported to the country from Vietnam because it "most closely resembles some objects in bronze and pottery from the contemporary Dongson Culture of North Vietnam" (Glover 1996b: 84, fn. 17). There are few more knobbed wares have been reported from South Asia. Some of these were discovered in India at Nilgiri Hills, where a number of other kinds of high-tin bronze wares have also been found. Two others were found in Pakistan at and near Taxila. The knobbed ware found at Taxila is of silver and the other found near Taxila is of granite (Fig. 2.10).

Fig. 2.10 A granite reliquary from Taxila
Courtesy: British Museum, London

The function of knobbed vessels has intrigued scholars. Knox believes that "the Nilgiri bowls almost certainly come from megalithic graves" (Knox 1985: 525), while the granite bowl from Taxila "was almost certainly a foundation deposit for a stupa" (Glover 1996b: 79). Although scholars are not unanimous in their opinion, it is clear that the wares were not meant for secular or utilitarian purposes such as cooking or serving food. Rather, as Glover rightly surmises, they possibly "served some special purpose for ritual and funerary use only". He interprets the motif of the base knob and concentric circles as a maṇḍala, "a schematic cosmological symbol representing perhaps Mount Meru and the surrounding oceans". He further points out that the vessels "are witness to the adoption in Thailand, by some groups of Indian moral, philosophical and political concepts" (Glover 1996b: 79).

In order to ascertain the origin of high-tin bronze knobbed vessels, one needs to remember that the use of the alloy was known in South Asia because vessels made of the alloy have been found in sites such as the Bhir mound at Taxila in Pakistan, Adichchanallur in Tinnevelly District, Tamil Nadu, and Coimbatore in the Nilgiri Hills. Strabo's *Geography* (XV, 67) indicates that the use of the alloy may have been known in South Asia as early as the 4th century BC. When travelling through this region with the Macedonian army, writes Strabo, Nearchos had observed that the local people used "copper which has been fused but not wrought" with the strange result that "if vessels of this material fall to the ground they break like earthenware" (McCrindle 1979: 73). The metal that Nearchos refers to, Glover (1996a: 140-142) believes, was actually a high-tin bronze alloy.

Sharada Srinivasan's (2005) study shows that the manufacture of high-tin bronzes is both ancient and widespread in India. Hence, it is possible to believe that archaeological evidences of high-tin bronze wares offered by Taxila, Adichanallur and Coimbatore was manufactured locally. On the other hand, high-tin bronze wares have been reported from a large number of sites such as Kok Khon in Sakorn Nakorn Province, Ban Chiang and Ban Nadi in north-east Thailand, Huai Pan near Chombung, Pak Beung and Khao Kwark Cave in Ratchaburi Province, Ban Don Ta Phet Ongbah Cave in Kanchanaburi Province in Thailand. These indicate that the use of high-tin bronze may have been known in Southeast Asia as well. Availability of the raw material in Thailand and Malaysia further substantiate the above view.

The high-tin bronze knobbed vessels found at Wārī-Baṭeśwar are unique in the entire South Asia and match closely with those found in Thailand. Hence, the Wārī-Baṭeśwar vessels must have been imported from Thailand. The Thais, in their turn, may have imported them from Vietnam. At the same time we must concede that because the knobbed ware was meant for ritual and funerary use only, there is likelihood that those found at Wārī-Baṭeśwar were gift items.

TEXTILES

Although cotton textiles featured prominently among export items of 'Bengal', non-cotton luxury textiles, mostly of Chinese origin, featured in its list of imported items. One hears of imported Chinese silk and satin – not for re-export as in the early historic period but for local use – for the first time in the early 15th century AD. The source is Fei Sin, who observed that silk and satin were in the basket of commodities that the Chinese merchants offered for trade in 'Bengal' (Bagchi 1945: 123). A definite indication of import of these luxury commodities is obtainable from the *Suma Oriental*, where Tome Pires (1967: 93) observes that the Bengali traders brought back from Malacca "silk, ... white and green damask [and] *enrolados* [possibly a sort of woollen cloth] from China".

MATS, CARPETS AND CAPS

A curious item that the Chinese merchants used for trading in 'Bengal' in the early 15th century AD, according to Fei Sin (Bagchi 1945: 123), was grass-mat. These could be mats called *yé-sin-tién* by Chau Ju-kua in his work on Chinese and Arab trade in the 12th and the 13th centuries AD. These mats were manufactured in the islands of Tan-jung-wu-lo (dependency of Sho-p'o or Java) and P'u-li-lu (in the Philippines). The same source gives the following description of the mats:

> They are made from a plant resembling the rattan in shape and more than ten feet in length with a longitudinally striped and smooth surface without knots, which is called ye-sin-ts'au. The women in these foreign parts gather (this vine), peel it and weave it into mats. They are sometimes dyed with red and black checkered patterns, when they are called "figured mats" or hua-tien. They are warm in the winter and cool in the summer, and are very convenient to carry about (Hirth and Rockhill 1965: 220).

However, it is rather surprising that 'Bengal' would import the commodity considering the fame of locally produced mats which Abu'l Faẓl Allami qualifies as "woven silk" (Jarrett 1891: 122). In *Caṇḍīmaṅgala* by Kavikaṅkaṇa Mukunda (1986: 196, 231), both Dhanapati and Śrīmanta expect to obtain woollen clothes and decorated blanket in exchange of *pāṭi* (mats). Hence, mats can be taken to be an export commodity of 'Bengal' rather than an imported item. It is possible that Fei Sin's mats were fancied as a luxury item and did not feature in the list of regualr imports.

In the early 16th century AD, two new luxury items cropped up. These were carpets and caps of scarlet-in-grain. According to Tome Pires (1967: 93), Bengali merchants on their return trip from Malacca transported these items back home. No information is available regarding the country of origin of these commodities. However, the scarlet colour of the caps reminds one of the famous Fez caps that the affluent Muslims in South Asia sported even in the early 20th century. Given the fact that the ruling elite in 'Bengal' were mostly Muslims and that Malacca, as an emporium, offered commodities from Persia and the Ottoman Empire, it may be tentatively suggested that the carpets may have been Persian in origin and the caps of scarlet-in-grain may have been from Fez in Turkey.

We may logically expect that all the three ports of the medieval period imported textiles, mats, carpets and caps because, as luxury items, these must have been in demand in all the urban centres of Sultanate Bengal.

SWORDS

As Tome Pires (1967: 93) notes, Javanese krises and swords were among other commodities that Bengali merchants carried back with them from Malacca in the early 16th century AD. It is possible that these items had a demand among the nobles of 'Bengal'. Because it has been already pointed out that 'Bengal' exported steel, it can be reasonably assumed that swords were also manufactured at home. Hence, krises and swords from Java may have been fashionable as luxury items, which were in demand mostly for their exotic value. We may expect that these were imported through Sātgāon and Caṭṭagrāma, the two functioning ports in the early 16th century AD.

Faunal and Human Merchandise

ELEPHANTS

Elephants (*Elephas maximus*) were plentiful in 'Bengal' till the beginning of the 20th century. Traditionally, they used to be caught in *kheddas* or stockades, which Strabo describes in detail (*Geography*, Book XV, 42). Today, they are still seen in Caṭṭagrāma, Caṭṭagrāma Hills and Sylhet regions of Bangladesh.

In ancient 'Bengal', elephants were valued mostly for their use in warfare. As Aelian notes, these animals (as well as horses) were "held in the highest esteem by the Indians" (*On the Peculiarities of Animals*, C. XXV; McCrindle 1979: 142). Going by Diodorus Siculus, the Roman historian from the days of Julius Caesar and Emperor Augustus, "Alexander did not undertake an expedition" against Gaṅgāridai, the greatest of all Indian nations, for he was "deterred by the multitude of their elephants" (*Bibliothéké,* XVIII, 6; *ibid.*: 201). In another passage, he notes that Gaṅgāridai possessed "four thousand elephants well trained and equipped for war" (Diodorus, II, 37 in McCrindle 1926: 32-33). Hence, there can be little doubt that the armies of ancient kingdoms in the region of 'Bengal' were well equipped with elephants. It is quite likely that these elephants were either available in 'Bengal' or were imported from neighbouring kingdoms because even in the 7th century AD, Hiuen-Tsiang had observed "many hundred wild elephants" in Campā (modern Bihar) (*Life*, Book IV: Beal 1973: 128) and Kumāra-rāja (Bhāskaravarman, the king of Kāmrūpa) possessed an army of 20,000 elephants (*Life*, Book V; *ibid.*: 172). Both Mas'ūdī (1867: 25) and *Ḥudūd al-'Ālam* (10.7; Minorsky 1937: 87) speaks of numerous elephants being available in Rahma (identified as the Pāla kingdom). Hence, 'Bengal' did not need to import elephants at least till the 10th century AD and there could possibly have been no maritime trade in elephants till that period.

However, the situation was different in the second half of the 17th century AD. As Bowrey (1905: 179-181) observes,

> The nabob and Some Merchants here [in Dhaka] and in Ballasore and Pipli have about 20 Saile of Ships, of considerable burthen that annually trade to Sea, Some to Ceylon, Some to Tennassaree. These fetch Elephants ... The Elephants of Ceylon are best Esteemed of here and all Hindostan over ... They are brought from the Dutch ... in Gala, or Colomba or Japhnapatam ...

The growing demand for elephants in the Mughal army must have made trade in elephants profitable in the 17th century AD.

We have no conclusive evidence of maritime trade of elephants from the 13th century AD to the early 16th century AD. However, given the fact that the Muslim rulers of 'Bengal' were constantly waging wars against Assam, Cooch Behar, Tripura, Arakan and Burma, it is unlikely that their supply of war elephants came from their enemies. Supply from local sources of elephants must have been marginal because most of the hills in Caṭṭagrāma, Caṭṭagrāma Hills and Sylhet regions lay beyond their authority. It is more likely that 'Bengal' under Muslim rulers, from the 13th century onwards, was often forced to import elephants from Sri Lanka and Tennassarim like the Mughal viceroys and the Nawabs of 'Bengal'.

HORSES

A significant reason behind the decline in horse trade by the Yüeh-chih merchants from the Kuṣāṇa kingdom was the rise of the nomadic Huns in Central Asia in the 5th century AD and consequent decline in security in over-land trade routes from the region. For this reason, Chakravarti (2001: 90-91) argues, war horses began to be imported to South Asia from Arabia, Fers (Persia) and Sham (Syria) by sea-route after 600 AD. It is more probable that 'Bengal' had an alternative source for horses. However, it is more likely as R. C. Majumdar and Radhagovinda Basak (1943: 279) argue that during the Pāla rule, "horses were imported from Kamboja". He substantiates his argument by citing Devapāla's Monghyr copperplate inscription ("the young steeds gazed for long at the mates, who had their pleasing notes mixed up with (shrill) sounds of (horses) in the land of Kamboja", Mukherji and Maity 1967: 123). Although Majumdar (1943c: 126) takes Kamboja to be north-western region of South Asia, it is more convincing that the land indicated is Tibet because Kamboja was a South Asian name for Tibet and because the early medieval kingdom of the Kambojas was founded by Tibetan migrants (Sircar 1982: 111). It is thus unlikely that horses were imported to 'Bengal' by maritime route in the early historic period. We may therefore suggest that Tibetan horses had supplanted horses from Central Asia.

It is quite certain that by the early 13th century AD, 'Bengal' was also importing horses from Central Asia because, it may be recalled, Muhammad-i-Bakhtiyar, the Turkish adventurer who made Lakṣmana Sena flee from Nadiya, was mistaken for "a merchant who had brought horses for sale" (Minhaj-ud-Din 1869: 309). This reference, however, speaks of import by land route. Actually, most of the horses of the Sultanate period may have been imported by land route from Delhi, where existed a large horse market (Ray 1997: 33). It is also known that Persian horses were sent from Hormuz and Kais to the south India kingdom of Pandya and each of these horses cost 220 gold *dinārs*. Syrian, Yemeni and Iraqi horses were also exported to South Asia from ports such as Bahrain, Zofar, Kulhat, and Aden (Digby 1982b: 148-149). When we recall that in the mid-16th century Kavikaṅkaṇa Mukunda (1986: 210, 254) in his *Caṇḍīmaṅgala* shows both Dhanapati and Śrīmanta offering sheep in Sri Lanka, hoping to receive horses in return, it strikes one as a possibility that some of those horses from the Middle East were also imported to sultanate Bengal by maritime route.

Elephants and horses must have been imported through all the three ports that functioned in the medieval period. We may justify our claim by pointing out that the final destination of these items would have been military and administrative centres, all of which could have been reached by Caṭṭagrāma, Sonārgāon and Sātgāon.

MUSK

As Fei Sin informs us, musk was one of the items that the Chinese merchants offered for trading in 'Bengal' (Bagchi 1945: 123). In the early 16th century AD, it was imported from Pegu. As Pires (1967: 96) reports, the musk came from animals such as goats. A "not very civilised people" who inhabited the Capelanguam mountain range bordering Arakan used to procure the musk and carry it to Ava from where they were transported to Pegu for shipment to 'Bengal', Narsinga, Pase and Malacca. The latter evidence leave no doubt that musk was a luxury item which was imported for elite consumption. Like textiles and other luxury items, there can be little doubt that musk too must have been imported through Sonārgāon, Sātgāon and Caṭṭagrāma.

COWRIES

In addition to metallic pieces, cowries were also used as a medium of exchange in 'Bengal' since the early historic period (Fig. 2.11). Evidence in support of the use of cowries in the 2nd century BC may be found in the fragmentary stone inscription from Mahāsthāngarh. The inscription in Brāhmī

Fig. 2.11 Cowries from Chandraketugarh

records "*gaṃda ... (y)ikehi*" (lines 5-6; Barua 1934: 58). "As *gaṇḍaka* was not the name of any class of specie or any other medium of exchange", Mukherjee (1991c: 299) argues, "the concerned term should be indicated by the expression ...

yekehi. The only word which may fit here is *kākaṇiyikehi* (*kākaṇiyakaih*), meaning by *kākaṇyakas* or *kākaṇikas*, also known as *kākaṇis*". Hence, the passage should be read as "*gaṇḍakākaṇiyikehi*". Mukherjee further shows that the *Arthaśāstra* of Kauṭīlya (3.20.8-10; Kangle 1963: 124, 291) uses the term *kākaṇī* to indicate kapardaka or cowry and *gaṇḍa* in rural 'Bengal' denotes the number 'four'. Hence, he argues, "the epigraph in question seems to allude to the filling up of a treasury by cowries counted in terms of *gaṇḍakas*". Hence it is possible to believe that cowries were in circulation as a medium of exchange in Rāḍha, Suhma, Vaṅga, Gauḍa, Puṇḍravardhana and Varendra (i.e., the regions of 'Bengal' where the authority of the Mauryas was acknowledged), in the 2nd century BC.

During the Pāla-Sen period, the base of currency in Vaṅga, Rāḍha, Suhma, Puṇḍravardhana and Samataṭa was mainly formed by cowries imported from outside. This is confirmed by Sulayman al-Tajir in his *Akhbār al-Sīn wa'l-Hind* (An account of China and India), a collection of several reports prepared between 800 and 851 AD, Sandhyākara Nandī's "historical *kāvya*" *Rāmacarita* (IV, 36b; Sandhyākara Nandī 1910: 92) and archaeological evidence from Pāhāḍpur (Qadir 1980: 20). We will have ample space to discuss the matter in further detail in Chapter Three.

Both Ma-Huan (1970: 161) and Fei Sin (Bagchi 1945: 123) confirm that cowries were used as a medium of exchange in 'Bengal' in the first half of the 15th century AD. In the early 16th century AD, the practice continued because we hear Tome Pires observing that in 'Bengal' cowry (locally called *cury*) was used as a medium of exchange. He further points out that "[t]he Bengal cowries are larger with a yellow stripe in the middle; they are valid throughout Bengal and they accept them for a larger number of commodities as they would gold" (Pires: 1967: 93-95).

Cowires were also the basic currency of Kāmrūpa in the early medieval period. As the *Harṣacarita* by Bānabhaṭṭa (1897: 214) testifies, Bhāskaravarman sent to Harṣavardhana "heaps of black and white chowries (sic.)" as present. The Tezpur Rock inscription of Harjaravarman (r. 815-835) further demonstrates the use of cowries in Kāmrūpa (Baruah 1985: 165). As records of British administration show, cowries were in circulation as currency in Laur (a principality in Sylhet region that lay to the north of the Surmā) till 1765 (Gait 1926: 278).

The source of these cowries was Maldives, as the following excerpt from Ma-Huan's observation from the Maldives Islands show.

> As to their cowries: the people there collect them and pile them into heaps like mountains; they catch them in nets and let the flesh rot; and [then] they transport them for sale in Hsien Lo [Thailand], Pang-ko-la [Bengal], and other such countries, where they are used as currency (Ma-Huan 1970: 150).

It must be added here that J. U. G. Mills, the translator of the above text, adds that Ma-Huan did not say "Pang-ko-la" ('Bengal'). It was added later by Feng Ch'eng Chün on the strength of a statement made by Huang Sing-ts'eng in his *Sí yang ch'ao kung tien lu* (1520) (*ibid.*: 150, fn. 6). If there is any doubt regarding Ma-Huan's testimony, one can turn to Ibn Battutā who affirms that the people of the Maldives sell cowries "in exchange of rice to the people of Bengal". These could be purchased at a rate varying between four hundred thousand to twelve hundred thousand shells for a gold *dinar* (Gibb 1986: 243). Tome Pires (1967: 93-95) also declares with authority that "[t]hese selected [cowries] come from the Maldive (Diua) Islands in large quantities". Barbosa also confirms that cowries used to come from Maldive Islands (Barbosa 1921: 105). It is possible, as Mukherjee (1992b: 59) shows, that cowries for Kāmrūpa were also imported from Maldives Islands.

Cowries were used as a medium of exchange from the 2nd century BC to the early 16th century AD as we will attempt to demonstrate in Chapter Three. They were always imported from the Maldive Islands. As Chaudhuri (1985: 18) shows, because "the Maldive variety could be exchanged for the necessities of life – rice and cotton textiles – [it] gave rise to an ancient and continuous trade between the islands and India". We may accept Chaudhuri's observation as applicable to 'Bengal' as well because of the following reasons. Firstly, the Maldives had an abundant supply and surplus in the medieval period as Ma-Huan's testimony cited above clearly shows. Hence we may believe that the same was applicable for earlier periods as well since there appears to have been no significant change in geo-physical conditions. Secondly, the cowries used in 'Bengal' (large, with a yellow stripe in the middle as Pires shows) had a unique source of supply, i.e., the Maldives.

We have very little indication regarding the ports that dealt with the import of cowries. Since the commodity must have been in demand all over 'Bengal', we may logically expect it to be imported through all the ports. It would be reasonable to believe that Kāmrūpa also imported cowries from the Maldives Islands through Caṭṭagrāma in the early medieval period since it has already been established that the kingdom exported aloes-wood through the same port in the same period. Laur, which lay to its south, must have used the same port to meet its demand for cowries.

PEARLS

In the early 16th century AD, large quantities of seed-pearls were brought back by Bengali traders from Malacca on their return journey (Pires 1967: 93). In his translator's note, Cortesao points out that by seed-pearls, Pires "really means proper pearls" (Cortesao in *ibid.*: 517). Pires (*ibid.*: 517) further observes that pearls available in Malacca came from Dahlak (an island in Red Sea, subject to Abyssinia), Bahrein (close to Arabia), Ceylon and Hainan (an island between the kingdom of Cochin China and China). The Chinese pearls were the whitest, the Ceylonese, the best and the Bahreinian, the roundest. Pearls were imported to 'Bengal' even in the late 16th century AD since we have Abu'l Fazl's *Ain I Akbari* to testify to that (Jarrett 1891: 122). Because Sātgāon and Caṭṭagrāma were the two functioning ports in the early 16th century AD, we may reasonably believe that pearls were imported through both these ports.

SLAVES

There appears to be quite a long history of importing slaves in South Asia from Abyssinia, Zanzibar and the eastern coast of Africa. In the 15th century AD, they began to participate in the administration in the sultanates of Delhi, Gujarat and 'Bengal' (Ray 1997: 48). As Tome Pires (1967: 88) had observed in the early 16th century AD, Abyssinian slaves came to be "kings and great lords in the kingdom [of Bengal]". Although Pires's details are inaccurate, we may turn to *Tarikh-i Firishta* for learning what actually transpired. In the 1460s and the 1470s, there arose in 'Bengal' the institution of military slavery, under which black *(habashi)* slaves from Abyssinia began to be recruited for military and civil service (Briggs 1910: 340-343). Ironically, they ended in doing just the opposite of what they had been recruited for. In 1486, one of them named Barbak Shah-zadah seized power and established the rule of the Abyssinian monarchs (1486-1493). He is also believed to have recruited 8,000 Abyssinian slaves as palace guards and soldiers. When 'Ala al-Din Hussain Shah established the Hussain Shahi dynasty in 1493, he is said to have banished most of the slaves from 'Bengal' and they departed for Gujarat and Deccan (South India) (*ibid.*: 350).

The legacy of Abyssinian slaves and monarchs clearly shows that in the second half of the 15th century AD, if not earlier, slaves were imported to 'Bengal'. However, there is no definite indication that they were transported through martime routes. It may be helpful to remember that during the Sultanate period, Delhi was a flourishing centre for slave trade from where slaves were transported by land-route even to Khorasan (Ray 1997: 33). Hence, it is not unlikely that the Abyssinian slaves were also procured from this market by land route.

****

From deliberations made in this chapter, we may sum up the relationship between the ports and their hinterlands in table 2.1.

Table 2.1:
Hinterlands Served by the Seven Ports of Bengal

Port	Hinterland
Tāmralipti	Rāḍha, Puṇḍravardhana, the Middle Gaṅgā valley, and eastern Himalayas, Bactrian Greek kingdom.
Gaṅgābandar	Vaṅga (western), Puṇḍravardhana, the Middle Gaṅgā valley, eastern Himalayas, Kāmrūpa, China, Bactrian Greek kingdom.
Wārī-Baṭeśwar	Vaṅga (eastern), Puṇḍravardhana.
Candravarmakoṭa	Vaṅga (eastern).
Sātgāon	Vaṅga (western), the Middle Gaṅgā valley, eastern Himalayas.
Sonārgāon	Sultanate Bengal, Cooch Behar, Tripura.
Caṭṭagrāma	Samataṭa, Vaṅga (eastern), Puṇḍravardhana, Sultanate Bengal, Bhutan, Cooch Behar, Kāmrūpa, Tripura.

Period-wise breakdown of the hinterlands of the seven ports is summed up in the following table.

Table 2.2:
Period-wise Breakdown of the Hinterlands

Period	Hinterland
Early Historic	Puṇḍravardhana, Rāḍha, Vaṅga, Middle Gaṅgā valley, China, Eastern Himalayas, Kāmrūpa, Bactrian Greek kingdom, Central Asia.
Late Historic	Puṇḍravardhana, Rāḍha, Gauḍa, Middle Gaṅgā valley, Vaṅga, Central Asia.
Early Medieval	Puṇḍravardhana, Varendra, Vaṅga, Samataṭa, Middle Gaṅgā valley, Kāmrūpa, Bhutan, Laur.
Medieval	Sultanate Bengal, Cooch Behar, Tripura, Eastern Himalayas, Assam and Bhutan.

It is clear from our analysis that most of the ports listed above served not only 'Bengal' but also the land-locked kingdoms to its northwest, north and northeast. Among all the seven ports, Gaṅgābandar had the largest hinterland, spread from Central Asia and Bactrian Greek kingdom in the northwest to China in the northeast. The hinterland for Tāmralipti was also large, spread from the Bactrian-Greek kingdom in the northwest to the eastern Himalayas in the north. In contrast, the hinterlands for the medieval ports appear to have shrunk considerably. These were important for land-locked kingdoms such as Tripura, Assam, Cooch Behar and Bhutan. Interestingly, Kāmrūpa extensively used the ports of 'Bengal' in the early historic and the early medieval periods but decreased their dependence in the medieval period. Acrimonious political relationship with the Sultanate Bengal must have had forced Kāmrūpa (Assam) in the medieval period to conduct most of its maritime trade through land routes across Burma.

As for the commodities imported and exported through these seven ports, we may sum up our findings in the four tables given below.

Table 2.3:
Period-wise Breakdown of the Exported Commodities
In Relation to the Ports and Their Hinterlands

Commodities	Port	Period	Hinterland
Rice	Tāmralipti	Early Historic	Puṇḍravardhana, Rāḍha, Middle Gaṅgā valley

		Late Historic	Puṇḍravardhana, Rāḍha, Middle Gaṅgā valley
	Gaṅgābandar	Early Historic	Puṇḍravardhana, Vaṅga, Middle Gaṅgā valley
		Late Historic	Puṇḍravardhana, Vaṅga, Middle Gaṅgā Valley
	Candravarmakoṭa	Late Historic	Vaṅga
	Sonārgāon	Medieval	Sultanate Bengal
	Sātgāon	Medieval	Sultanate Bengal
	Caṭṭagrāma	Early Medieval	Puṇḍravardhana, Varendra, Samataṭa
		Medieval	Sultanate Bengal
Silk	Gaṅgābandar	Early Historic	China
	Sātgāon	Medieval	Sultanate Bengal
	Caṭṭagrāma	Medieval	Sultanate Bengal, Cooch Behar, Tripura
Malabathrum	Gaṅgābandar	Early Historic	Eastern Himalayas, Kāmrūpa
Spikenard	Gaṅgābandar	Early Historic	Eastern Himalayas
	Caṭṭagrāma	Medieval	Eastern Himalayas
Aloes-wood	Caṭṭagrāma	Early Medieval	Kāmrūpa
Ebony	Caṭṭagrāma	Medieval	Sultanate Bengal
Emery	Caṭṭagrāma	Early Medieval	Kāmrūpa
Spices	Sātgāon	Medieval	Sultanate Bengal
	Caṭṭagrāma	Medieval	Sultanate Bengal and Cooch Behar
Lac and indigo	Sātgāon	Medieval	Sultanate Bengal
	Caṭṭagrāma	Medieval	Sultanate Bengal
Raw cotton and cotton textiles	Tāmralipti	Early Historic	Vaṅga
	Gaṅgābandar	Early Historic	Vaṅga
	Sonārgāon	Medieval	Sultanate Bengal
	Sātgāon	Medieval	Sultanate Bengal
	Caṭṭagrāma	Early Medieval	Vaṅga, Kāmrūpa
		Medieval	Sultanate Bengal, Tripura
Home furnishings	Sātgāon	Medieval	Sultanate Bengal
	Caṭṭagrāma	Medieval	Sultanate Bengal
Sugar	Sātgāon	Medieval	Sultanate Bengal
	Caṭṭagrāma	Medieval	Sultanate Bengal
Fruits and fruit preserves	Sātgāon	Medieval	Sultanate Bengal
	Caṭṭagrāma	Medieval	Sultanate Bengal, Assam and Bhutan
Pearls	Gaṅgābandar	Early Historic	Vaṅga
	Sonārgāon	Medieval	Sultanate Bengal
	Sātgāon	Medieval	Sultanate Bengal
Semi-precious stone beads	Tāmralipti	Early Historic	Rāḍha
	Gaṅgābandar	Early Historic	Vaṅga
	Wārī-Baṭeśwar	Early Historic	Vaṅga
Glass	Tāmralipti	Early Historic	Middle Gaṅgā valley
	Sātgāon	Medieval	Sultanate Bengal
Glass beads	Tāmralipti	Early Historic	Middle Gaṅgā valley
	Gaṅgābandar	Early Historic	Middle Gaṅgā valley
Rouletted ware	Tāmralipti	Early Historic	Rāḍha
	Gaṅgābandar	Early Historic	Vaṅga
NBPW	Tāmralipti	Early Historic	Rāḍha
	Gaṅgābandar	Early Historic	Vaṅga
	Wārī-Baṭeśwar	Early Historic	Vaṅga
Stamped ware	Tāmralipti	Early Historic	Rāḍha
	Gaṅgābandar	Early Historic	Vaṅga
Footed ware	Tāmralipti	Early Historic	Bactrian Greek kingdom
	Gaṅgābandar	Early Historic	Bactrian Greek kingdom
Buddhist images	Caṭṭagrāma	Early Medieval	Middle Gaṅgā valley
Steel and steel products	Sonārgāon	Medieval	Sultanate Bengal
	Sātgāon	Medieval	Sultanate Bengal
	Caṭṭagrāma	Medieval	Sultanate Bengal
Rhinoceros and rhinoceros horns	Gaṅgābandar	Early Historic	Vaṅga
	Caṭṭagrāma	Early Medieval	Vaṅga, Kāmrūpa
	Caṭṭagrāma	Medieval	Sultanate Bengal and Assam
Horses	Gaṅgābandar	Early Historic	Central Asia
	Gaṅgābandar	Late Historic	Central Asia
Ivory	Caṭṭagrāma	Medieval	Sultanate Bengal, Assam
Cāmara (yak-tails)	Caṭṭagrāma	Early Medieval	Bhutan

Table 2.4 clearly shows two peak periods of maritime trade in terms of commodities exported. These were the early historic and the medieval periods. In contrast, a noticeable slump may be easily discerned in the late historic period. Four manufactured items that stand prominently in the medieval period are cotton textiles, silk yarn and textiles, sugar and

steel products. On the other hand, manufactured items of the early historic period were of completely different character because these include luxury earthenwares (NBPW, Rouletted Ware and stamped ware) and semi-precious stone beads. Most of the remaining export-items were non-manufactured commodities belonging to agricultural, forest and faunal categories. This trend in export may now be compared with the trend in import that may be discerned in the tables given below.

Table 2.4:
Period-wise Breakdown of the Exported Commodities

Period	Commodities
Early Historic	Rice, silk, malabathrum, spikenard, raw cotton and cotton textiles, pearls, semi-precious stone beads, glass, glass beads, Rouletted Ware, NBPW, stamped ware, footed ware, rhinoceros and rhinoceros horns, horses.
Late Historic	Rice, horses.
Early Medieval	Rice, aloes-wood, raw cotton and cotton textiles, Buddhist images, rhinoceros and rhinoceros horns, yak-tails.
Medieval	Rice, silk, spikenard, ebony, ginger, long pepper, black pepper, lac, indigo, raw cotton and cotton textiles, home furnishings, sugar, fruits and fruit preserves, pearls, glass, steel and steel products, rhinoceros and rhinoceros horns.

Table 2.5:
Period-wise Breakdown of the Imported Commodities
In Relation to the Ports and Their Hinterlands

Commodities	Port	Period	Hinterland
Spices	Tāmralipti	Early Historic	Puṇḍravardhana Rāḍha, Middle Gaṅgā valley
		Late Historic	Puṇḍravardhana, Rāḍha, Middle Gaṅgā valley
	Gaṅgābandar	Early Historic	Puṇḍravardhana, Vaṅga (western), Middle Gaṅgā valley
		Late Historic	Puṇḍravardhana, Vaṅga (western), Middle Gaṅgā valley
	Wārī-Baṭeśwar	Early Historic	Puṇḍravardhana (eastern), Vaṅga (eastern)
	Candravarmakoṭa	Late Historic	Vaṅga (eastern)
	Sonārgāon	Medieval	Sultanate Bengal
	Sātgāon	Medieval	Sultanate Bengal
	Caṭṭagrāma	Early Medieval	Samataṭa, Vaṅga (eastern)
		Medieval	Sultanate Bengal
Opium, sandalwood, camphor and mercury	Sātgāon	Medieval	Sultanate Bengal
	Caṭṭagrāma	Medieval	Sultanate Bengal
Vermilion	Sonārgāon	Medieval	Sultanate Bengal
	Sātgāon	Medieval	Sultanate Bengal
	Caṭṭagrāma	Medieval	Sultanate Bengal
Gold	Sonārgāon	Medieval	Sultanate Bengal
	Sātgāon	Medieval	Sultanate Bengal
	Caṭṭagrāma	Medieval	Sultanate Bengal
Silver	Sonārgāon	Medieval	Sultanate Bengal
	Sātgāon	Medieval	Sultanate Bengal
	Caṭṭagrāma	Early Medieval	Harikela and Samataṭa
		Medieval	Sultanate Bengal
Copper and iron	Sonārgāon	Medieval	Sultanate Bengal
	Sātgāon	Medieval	Sultanate Bengal
	Caṭṭagrāma	Medieval	Sultanate Bengal
Tin and lead	Sātgāon	Medieval	Sultanate Bengal
	Caṭṭagrāma	Medieval	Sultanate Bengal
Ruby	Sātgāon	Medieval	Sultanate Bengal
	Caṭṭagrāma	Medieval	Sultanate Bengal
Porcelain	Sonārgāon	Medieval	Sultanate Bengal
	Sātgāon	Medieval	Sultanate Bengal
	Caṭṭagrāma	Medieval	Sultanate Bengal
High-tin bronze vessels	Wārī-Baṭeśwar	Early Historic	Vaṅga
Textiles, carpets, caps and musk	Sonārgāon	Medieval	Sultanate Bengal
	Sātgāon	Medieval	Sultanate Bengal
	Caṭṭagrāma	Medieval	Sultanate Bengal
Swords	Sātgāon	Medieval	Sultanate Bengal
	Caṭṭagrāma	Medieval	Sultanate Bengal
Elephants and horses	Sonārgāon	Medieval	Sultanate Bengal
	Sātgāon	Medieval	Sultanate Bengal
	Caṭṭagrāma	Medieval	Sultanate Bengal
Cowries	Tāmralipti	Early Historic	Puṇḍravardhana, Rāḍha,
		Late Historic	Rāḍha, Gauḍa, Puṇḍravardhana and Varendra
	Gaṅgābandar	Early Historic	Puṇḍravardhana, Vaṅga (western)
		Late Historic	Puṇḍravardhana, Vaṅga (western)

	Wārī-Baṭeśwar	Early Historic	Puṇḍravardhana (eastern), Vaṅga (eastern)
	Candravarmakoṭa	Late Historic	Vaṅga (eastern)
	Sonārgāon	Medieval	Sultanate Bengal
	Sātgāon	Medieval	Sultanate Bengal
	Caṭṭagrāma	Early Medieval	Samataṭa, Vaṅga (eastern), Kāmrūpa, Laur
		Medieval	Sultanate Bengal
Pearls	Sātgāon	Medieval	Sultanate Bengal
	Caṭṭagrāma	Medieval	Sultanate Bengal

Table 2.6:
Period-wise Breakdown of the Imported Commodities

Period	**Commodities**
Early Historic	Spices, high-tin bronze vessels, cowries.
Late Historic	Spices, cowries.
Early Medieval	Spices, silver, cowries.
Medieval	Spices, opium, sandalwood, camphor, mercury, vermilion, gold, silver, copper, iron, tin, lead, ruby, porcelain, textiles, carpets, caps, musk, swords, elephants, horses, cowries, pearls.

There can remain little doubt that Table 2.6 given below clearly highlights the medieval period as the time when Bengal's import reached its peak. Most of the items imported during this period were luxury commodities, meant for elite use in urban areas. One may thus infer a high rise in urbanisation and diversification of consumer taste. In contrast, there hardly appears to be any luxury item in the list of imported commodities from the previous three periods. Two items that run constantly throughout the time frame of this research were spices and cowries.

Although there can hardly be any doubt regarding the trend summed up above, one nevertheless harbours a nagging suspicion that the tables of exported and imported items possibly do not reveal the complete picture. We must remember that we have two sources with plentiful information for the medieval period (i.e., Fei Sin and Tome Pires) but none for the earlier three periods. This is particularly true for the medieval period.

Three
Media of Exchange

Having identified the port sites and commodities for export and import, it is now necessary to investigate the medium of exchange for commercial transaction that existed in 'Bengal' during the period under review. A mode of transaction in exchange centres may be direct – of commodity for commodity. The difficulty in this process, commonly called barter (or *badal-bāṇijja* as in the maṅgalakāvya corpus), is not only in identifying "two persons whose disposable possessions mutually suit each other's wants" but also arriving at an agreement at the rate at which the exchange is to be made (Walker 1886: 4). Hence the importance of medium of exchange, which may be defined as "some commodity which every one shall freely receive in exchange for what he has but does not desire personally to consume, in the confident assurance that, with it, s/he can, at any time, and of kinds and in quantities to suit his/her immediate wants, obtain from others what they have but do not desire to use" (*ibid.*: 2). Thus, certain commodities such as rice, salt or wheat may be used as standard medium of exchange (henceforth termed as 'commodity money').

In order to attain greater portability and homogeneity in exchange-related transaction, precious metals such as gold, silver and copper, either in bar or in dust began to be used as medium of exchange. As a device of ensuring quality and standard, various stamps were impressed on metal pieces of standard weight by responsible authorities. Punch-marked coins, the earliest of such metallic currencies, could even be accepted outside the zone of influence of the issuing authority as bullion pieces. In later times, technological development led to the introduction of cast and die-struck coins. Deliberation on metallic currency is extremely relevant and important in this investigation because, as high-value and low-volume medium of exchange, they are easier to transport over a long distance. Hence, existence of metallic currency is an important indicator of the existence of long distance (including maritime) trade. Furthermore, existence of currency implies existence of authority-structure – be it a merchant or financial guild operating at a micro level or a state operating at a macro level.

It is usually assumed that barter is a primitive form of exchange while minted metal coins indicate sophisticated commerce. However, as Humphrey (1985: 48-72) has shown, barter is not necessarily an earlier phase in the evolution of mode of transaction; it may very well co-exist with money-based economy. What need to be taken into consideration in the context of this investigation is, "the more primitive and sophisticated types of exchange need not be treated as merely having evolutionary and mutually exclusive and oppositional features" (Chakravarti 2001: 24). Keeping these factors in mind, we will now proceed to investigate the medium of exchange used in 'Bengal' for commercial transaction from earliest times to the first half of the 16th century AD.

EARLY HISTORIC PERIOD

The Pre-Maurya Era (c. 600 BC to 325 BC)

The *Mahābhārata*, narrating Bhima's conquest of kingdoms and tribes of the Eastern Regions, lists sandalwood, aloes, clothes, gems, pearls, valuable corals, blankets, gold and silver as articles that were offered to him as tribute (Sabhā Parva, Section XXIX; Ganguli 1990: 61-62). Although there is no reference to the use of the above-mentioned precious commodities as media of exchange, one may speculate that at least gold was used as such because the contemporary middle Gaṅgā plain knew the use of metallic currency known as *niṣka*. The *Mahābhārata* makes two references to the term. The Anuśāsana Parva (13.43) refers to people with a hundred and a thousand *niṣkas*, and the Droṇa Parva (67.10) refers to 108 *niṣkas* of gold. Similarly, Pāṇini also refers to gold *niṣkas* (Thakur 1970: 25). As Maity (1970: 16) explains, the term '*niṣka*' originally denoted gold ornament worn on the neck, but it later came to be used as an isolated gold piece of fixed weight and standard.

The Maurya Era (c. 324 to 187 BC)

The Maurya era has not only yielded numerous coins, but also various types and denominations, which need to be examined in some detail in order to comprehend their significance. As discussed earlier in Chapter Two, cowries were used as a medium of exchange in Rāḍha, Suhma, Vaṅga, Puṇḍravardhana and Varendra (i.e., the regions of 'Bengal' where the authority of the Mauryas was acknowledged). As Mukherjee (1992a: 42) suggests, these were useful as a medium of exchange because "their intrinsic value was incorruptible and their supply did not essentially depend on the will of political authorities". In addition to cowries, punch-marked coins found in different parts of West Bengal and Bangladesh conclusively prove that this form of metallic currency was in extensive circulation in Puṇḍravardhana, Rāḍha, Suhma and in the south-westernmost area of Vaṅga. In terms of their metallic content, the punch-marked coins found in 'Bengal' belong to three categories: silver, copper and billon. The billon coins, as a recent analysis shows, contain 50% silver and 50% copper (personal communication Pranab K. Chattapadhaya, Centre for Archaeological Study and Training, Eastern India, Kolkata).

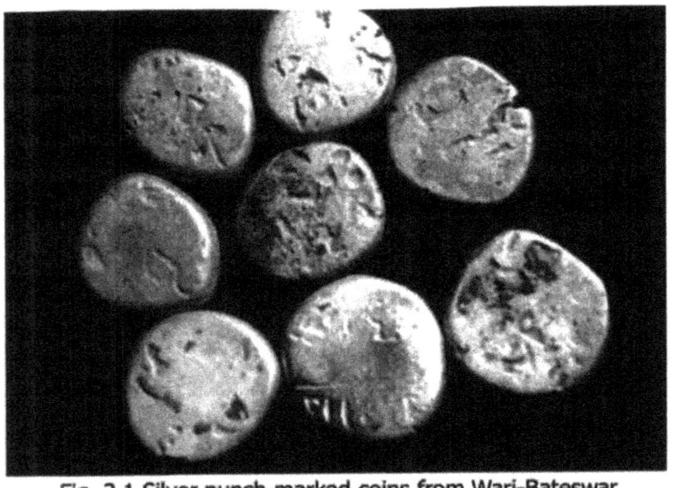

Fig. 3.1 Silver punch-marked coins from Wari-Bateswar

Fig. 3.2 Silver punch-marked coins from Wari-Bateswar

Fig. 3.3 Punch-marked coins from Chandraketugarh
Courtesy: Asutosh Museum of Indian Art, Kolkata

Silver punch-marked coins have been found at Fetgram and Baigachha (Rajshahi district), Mahāsthāngarh (Bogra district), Bhairab Bazar (Kishoreganj district) and Wārī-Baṭeśwar (Fig. 3.1 and 3.2) and neighbouring villages (Narsingdi district) in Bangladesh and Chandraketugarh (Fig. 3.3), Tamluk and Maṅgalkoṭa in West Bengal. These have been reported also from Medinīpur, Bankura, Birbhum, Bardhamān, Murshidabad and Dinajpur districts in West Bengal. Most of these coins are round, oval, square, rectangular and oblong in shape, weighing between 3 and 3.45 gm (i.e. about 47 to 54 grains) (Sarmadhikari 1984: 39). They were minted in accordance with early South Asian silver *kārshāpaṇa* or *purāṇa* or *dharaṇa* standard of 32 *krishṇalas* or *ratis* (i.e. c. 3.732 gm or about 57.6 grains). These coins are possibly referred in the *Arthaśāstra* as *paṇa* and *kārshāpaṇa*; in other texts they are referred as *dharaṇa* and *purāṇa*. Some coins found to measure half in weight (i.e., from c. 1.7 gm upward) possibly denoted *ardha-paṇa* (half *paṇa*) or half *kārshāpaṇa* (Mukherjee 1991c: 283). A total of 172 obverse symbols (such as "sun with rays", "a six-armed figure", "elephant", "bull", "rhinoceros", "boat", "four or two fishes in a tank") have so far been noticed on these coins (*ibid.*). Many of these symbols are also seen in punch-marked coins of different series found in other parts of South Asia.

Copper punch-marked coins have been found at Mahāsthāngarh (Bogra district) in Bangladesh and Chandraketugarh and Deulpota (24-Parganas district), Tamluk (Medinīpur district), Maṅgalkoṭa (Bardhamān district), and Dihar (Bankura district) in West Bengal. Hence, the area of circulation of these coins appears to have been Rāḍha, Suhma, Vaṅga (south-westernmost area) and Puṇḍravardhana. These coins appear in square and rectangular shapes. Their sizes vary from 13 mm x 11 mm, 14 mm x 7 mm to 15 mm x 14 mm or 16 mm x 17 mm while their weight vary from 1.45 (about 22 grains) to 3.62 gm (about 56 grains). They too appear to have been minted following the silver *kārshāpaṇa* standard of 32 *ratis* (i.e. about 57.6 grains) and appear in half unit pieces as well. So far Sarmadhikari (1984: 39-40) has identified thirteen symbols (such as "a boat", "two thatched cottages attached to each other", "bow and arrow" etc.) on the obverse side of the copper punch-marked coins.

In addition to copper and silver, a small number of punch-marked billon coins have also been reported from, what appears to have been, a limited area of circulation: Bāngarh in Dinajpur, Harinārāyaṇpur in South 24-Parganas and Chandraketugarh in North 24-Parganas. They are square or circular in shape, bear three symbols (seen on copper punch-marked coins) on the obverse side and weigh from 11 to 51.75 grains. It is believed that these coins were also struck on the weight standard of 57.6 grains and hence those weighing 11 to 13 grains are believed to have been quarter unit pieces (Mukherjee 1991c: 286).

When compared in terms of number, billon coins appear to have been least in circulation, followed by copper coins that prevailed to a greater degree. However, they cannot compare with silver coins, which had predominant circulation. As De (2001: 146-147) observes, billon punch-marked coins were struck with the purpose of making fractional transactions possible. They also indicate petty transactions at the hands of 'common' people.

Obverse symbols, distribution pattern and weight standard all indicate that the punch-marked coins were the currency of the Maurya Empire and hence almost attained the significance of a pan-South Asian currency. In the initial stage, they were possibly introduced in the northern and southwestern territories of 'Bengal' by the Maurya administration. However, as Vanaja (1983: 4) shows, some symbols (specially those punched on the reverse) indicate that issuing coins may not have remained a state privilege; local authorities such as government representatives and/or trade guilds may have minted these coins later on to facilitate trade. Examination of a number of these coins shows admixture of alloy at a greater rate than required. This actually is in line with recommendations made in the *Arthaśāstra* (2.12.24; Kangle 1963: 124). Nevertheless, as Mukherjee (1991c: 298) observes, the fact that they were accepted by the people indicate not only regular use but also that the issuing authorities were trusted by the people.

Cast copper coins (inscribed as well as uninscribed) have also been found at Tamluk (from Period II, 3rd-2nd century BC) and at Chandraketugarh (from Period I, 4th-3rd century or 3rd-2nd century BC). At Chandraketugarh, cast copper coins have been found along with punch-marked coins, which signify concurrent use of both types. Issuing authority of the cast copper coins is uncertain. However, it is not impossible that these were issued by merchants' guilds, very much like the punch-marked coins and circulated in Suhma and Vaṅga.

Neither the *Arthaśāstra* mentions any gold coin (Kangle 1965: 181), nor has any been found in archaeological excavations or explorations. Following the *Arthaśāstra*, Kangle (*ibid:* 181) suggests that two kinds of currency (*paṇayātrā*) may have been used during this era – one for trade (*vyāvahārikī*) and the other for receipt in treasury (*kośapraveśyā*) (2.12.25; Kangle 1963: 124). He assumes that *kośapraveśyā* had a slightly higher content of the principal metal. Not only does Kangle's suggestion lack substantiation by material evidence, it is also illogical because such a system would only give rise to senseless complications in everyday life.

The Post-Maurya Era (C. 186 BC to 320 AD)

We have only cast copper coins from the post-Maurya era. For convenience, these will be discussed under three categories: (1) pre-Kuṣāṇa, (2) non-Kuṣāṇa and Kuṣāṇa and (3) imitation-Kuṣāṇa, Kuṣāṇo-Rāḍha and Kuṣāṇo-Vaṅga.

PRE-KUṢĀṆA CAST COPPER COINS

Pre-Kuṣāṇa cast copper coins were all locally struck, either by regional kingdoms or by local authorities and guilds. The main age of their circulation was possibly from the 2nd century BC to c. 1st century BC. However, in certain regions, these coins appear to have been used in c. 2nd-3rd century AD and even during the Gupta era. No pre-Kuṣāṇa gold coins have yet been reported.

Pre-Kuṣāṇa cast copper coins have been discovered mostly in the districts of North and South 24-Parganas, Medinīpur, Bardhamān, Howrah and Nadia (all in West Bengal, India). The sites in these districts are Deulpota, Chandraketugarh, Atghara, Pakurtala, Tamluk, Ichapur, Dihar, Pokharna, Maṅgalkoṭa, and Harinārāyaṇpur. The distribution pattern of the coins discovered so far clearly indicate that their main circulation areas were Rāḍha, Suhma and south-westernmost area of Vaṅga. Puṇḍravardhana was possibly the secondary circulation area of pre-Kuṣāṇa cast copper coins since they have also been discovered, in relatively lesser number, from Murshidabad, North Dinajpur (West Bengal, India) and Bogra (in Bangladesh). In these areas, the greatest concentration of these coins has been at Bāngarh and Mahāsthāngarh.

It is likely that the authorities minting these cast copper coins followed the tradition of Maurya punch-marked coins because the symbols and weight standard of the pre-Kuṣāṇa coins are strikingly reminiscent of the punch-marked coins. An exception is a copper coin bearing Greek legends both on the obverse and the reverse. The legend on the obverse reads "ONEP[OY]" which denotes "of Thner" (Mukherjee 1991c: 288); that on the reverse is not legible. Mukherjee (*ibid.*: 289) believes that the coin may have been a memento and was not used as a medium of exchange. In addition to the above, Vanaja (1983: 6) reports the discovery of uninscribed cast copper coins at Chandraketugarh, which he believes, were in circulation from a little later in the mid-2nd century BC to the beginning of the Christian era. These coins display various symbols.

It is possible that the cast copper coins were prevalent in Rāḍha, Suhma and Vaṅga during the Maurya era (possibly issued by merchants' guilds) continued to circulate in the post-Maurya era. Because Puṇḍravardhana appears to have been a secondary area of circulation of pre-Kuṣāṇa cast copper coins, and since neither Śuṅga nor any other form of coins appear to have been prevalent in these areas, it is likely that Puṇḍravardhana maintained close trade links with Rāḍha, Suhma and the south-westernmost areas of Vaṅga.

NON-KUṢĀṆA AND KUṢĀṆA COINS

With the rise of the Kuṣāṇas in the 1st century BC, coins of foreign origin began to appear in the region of 'Bengal', none of which, strikingly enough, is Roman in origin. Except three, which are non-Kuṣāṇa coins from c. 1st to the 3rd century AD, all the rest are Kuṣāṇa in origin. Of these non-Kuṣāṇa coins, one is a Scytho-Parthian copper piece issued by Azes I (seated king: standing Hermes). The coin was reportedly discovered at Harinārāyaṇpur (*Indian Archaeology – A Review* 1957-58: 73) and is now preserved at the Indian Museum, Kolkata (accession no. 7358/C3816). The second is a debased gold piece of unknown origin (king at alter: enthroned Ardokhsho of the Gadakhara family) that is reported to have been found at Mahāsthāngarh and is now held at the Indian Museum, Kolkata (accession no. c 18777). The third is an Indo-Greek silver coin issued by King Menander. It was acquired from a collector in the Bardhamān district and is now preserved at the Bardhamān University. Mukherjee (1991c: 290) justifiably suggests that the first and the second could have arrived either by way of trade or as a memento while the third may not actually have been found in the region of 'Bengal'.

Compared to the non-Kuṣāṇa coins discussed above, the number of Kuṣāṇa coins in copper and gold is fairly large. As a matter of fact, the Kuṣāṇas are credited with introducing gold coins for the first time in South Asia. Influenced by the Roman Empire, Kadphises II struck a gold coin equivalent to the Roman *aurei* possibly to facilitate, as Warmington (1974: 296-299) suggests, the voluminous Indo-Roman trade and the silk traffic transported down the Indus. His source of gold, though, was not the Roman Empire. It came mostly from Mesene and Characene in the Near East (since the Kuṣāṇas conducted trade through the Persian Gulf) and to some extent also from South Asia (especially the Gaṅgā and the Indus).

Kuṣāṇa gold coins found in 'Bengal' have been reported from the following places: two at Mahāsthāngarh in Bangladesh, and one each at Malda, Farakka (Murshidabad district), Pandu Rajar Dhibi (Bardhamān district), Tamluk (Medinīpur district), Dewanati (North 24-Parganas district), Mahanad (Huglī district) (Banerji 1951: 107; Mukherjee 1991c: 291; Vanaja 1983: 14). The coins from Pandu Rajar Dhibi and Tamluk have been attributed to Kaniṣka I. The Dewanati coin has been attributed to Huvishka. Some of these coins display the Brāhmaṇical god Śiva (four-armed and two-armed) and the Persian god Ardokhsho (Mukherjee 1991c: 291). One of the Mahāsthāngarh coins (preserved at the Varendra Research Museum, Rajshahi) is of Vāsudeva. The other (acquired by the Indian Museum, Kolkata) has been attributed to Kaniṣka I but it is suspected of being an imitation because of corrupt legend. Majumdar (1932: 127-129) dates the coin to the 3rd century AD and believes "it is not impossible that it was issued from some part of Eastern India". The Malda coin (held in the private collection of Mr. Stapleton) is a coin of Vāsudeva.

A large number of copper coins bearing Kuṣāṇa devices have also been reported from West Bengal. The earliest of these, a coin with diademed bust on the obverse and king on horse back on the reverse, is ascribed to V'ima Kadphises (*Soter Megas*). It was found at Kankandighi in 24-Parganas South (and is now held in the collection of Sri Bimal Kumar Datta of Jaynagar-Majilpur in the same district) (Mukherjee 1988: 49-54). Numerous copper issues of V'ima, Huvishka and Vasudeva I have also been reported from 24-Parganas, Bardhamān, Medinīpur and Huglī and other districts in West Bengal (Chattopadhyay 1967: 238). Only one issue of Kaniṣka has come to our knowledge. Originally reported as an Indo-Scythian coin of *Kanerki*, it was found at Tamluk in Medinīpur district (Hoernle 1882: 113). In Bangladesh, Kuṣāṇa copper coins have been found only at Mahāsthāngarh (Vanaja 1983: 14). Numerous deities of Persian origin, such as Ardokhsho, Athsho, Oesho, Oado, Mao and possibly Nana are represented on these coins.

Distribution pattern of the copper issues shows the concentration in areas lying on both sides of the Huglī. This added to their numerous presence in the same area makes it possible to believe that Kuṣāṇa copper coins arrived by means of trade and were used as a regular currency in trade-related activities in Rāḍha and Vaṅga. They also imply continuance of trade noted in the earlier century and that external trade was conducted with Kuṣāṇa Empire since it is established that these regions lay outside the empire. The trade-related activities were limited to the urban centre of Puṇḍranagara (since some Kuṣāṇa copper coins have been found at Mahāsthāngarh).

Discoveries of Kuṣāṇa gold coins are much less than the copper coins. The distribution pattern of the gold coins highlights their sparse presence in Puṇḍravardhana, Varendra, Rāḍha, Suhma and Vaṅga. Only eight gold coins can be counted in the list given above. A few of these are not even genuine but imitation. These facts appear to convince Mukherjee (1991c: 291) that the Kuṣāṇa gold coins were never in regular circulation in the above-mentioned territories but were brought here possibly as mementos. However, one suspects that Mukherjee may not be entirely correct. If the copper coins are believed to have had arrived in Suhma, Rāḍha and Vaṅga by means of trade, it would be logical to suppose that gold coins could also have arrived by the same means. It is not unlikely that lesser number of gold coins has been discovered not because they never existed but because when discovered, people simply melted them for the intrinsic value of the precious metal. Moreover, as the *Periplus* (§ 63, Schoff 1995: 47) testifies, prevalence of *caltis* at Gange proves that gold coins were in circulation in the 1st century AD. One may agree with Mukherjee (1991c: 301) that *caltis* were "pieces of gold money called Kalita" because (i) no gold coin with the name *caltis* has as yet been discovered in Bangladesh and West Bengal and (ii) the term *kalita* in

Sanskrit denotes 'numbered' (Sircar 1971: 142 fn. 4). If that were the case then we may believe that gold money as well as Kuṣāṇa gold coins were used in regular circulation in Vaṅga, Suhma and Rāḍha. Their secondary area of circulation may have been Puṇḍravardhana and Varendra.

IMITATION-KUṢĀṆA, KUṢĀṆO-RĀḌHA AND KUṢĀṆO-VAṄGA COINS

Soon after Kuṣāṇa copper coins began to appear in Rāḍha and Vaṅga by way of trade and began to gain acceptability as local currency, there also appeared local imitations of those coins. This happened, believes Mukherjee (1991c: 293), "some time in or after the period of Kaniṣka I (c. 78-100 AD)". The imitation coins (henceforth cited as imitation-Kuṣāṇa) have been found in a large number in North and South 24-Parganas, Bardhamān, Medinīpur and Bankura (and possibly Huglī as well). The devices in the imitation-Kuṣāṇa coins have been derived from coins struck by Kaniṣka I (obverse: 'King standing and sacrificing at an altar'; reverse: 'Oado' or 'four-armed Śiva', or 'Mao', etc.), Huvishka (obverse: 'King riding on an elephant; reverse: 'Mao') and Vasudeva I (obverse: 'King standing and sacrificing at an altar'; reverse: 'seated Ardokhsho' or 'Śiva with bull') (*ibid.*: 291). Minting of indigenous currency can only mean existence of local authority structure/s, either in the form of mercantile guilds or state/s.

Mukherjee (*ibid.*: 292-293) has shown by means of metrological analysis that the imitation-Kuṣāṇa coins can be divided in seven groups. Interestingly, while coins of groups 1, 2 and 3 are related to copper coins issued by Kaniṣka I, Vasudeva I and most of Huvishka, respectively; those of groups 4 to 7 do not conform to any known weight type of Kuṣāṇa currency. This finding leads him to conclude, quite logically, that imitation-Kuṣāṇa type of coins fall into two categories. The first category consists of copper coins struck in close imitation of Kuṣāṇa weight system and the second category, of coins with a different weight system. Since the coins of the second category have been found mostly in Rāḍha and Vaṅga, Mukherjee names them 'Kuṣāṇo-Rāḍha' and 'Kuṣāṇo-Vaṅga' respectively. These coins began to appear about the 2nd century AD in denominations of tetra-*kārṣāpaṇa*, tri-*kārṣāpaṇa*, double *kārṣāpaṇa*, and half *kārṣāpaṇa* and are circular in shape (or at least were intended to be as such). They were struck by some form of authority-structure/s, which may have been mercantile guilds or state/s. They continued to imitate well-known Kuṣāṇa devices but in weight system they followed that of indigenous uninscribed cast copper coins. It is possible that their use continued in the same area even in the Gupta age.

A second series of Kuṣāṇo-Rāḍha and Kuṣāṇo-Vaṅga coins, that are distinct from the first because of their relative crudeness, have recently been identified (Mukherjee 1991a: 49). These coins appear in double *kārṣāpaṇa*, one-and-half *kārṣāpaṇa*, three-fourth *kārṣāpaṇa*, half *kārṣāpaṇa*, one-fourth *kārṣāpaṇa*, and one-eighth *kārṣāpaṇa*. Hence, their denominations are also different from the first series. The second series has been found in the districts of 24-Parganas (South), Bardhamān, Medinīpur, Bankura and Purulia. Interestingly, the second series of Kuṣāṇo-Rāḍha or Kuṣāṇo-Vaṅga are comparable with Puri-Kuṣāṇa coins (so called because one of their earliest discoveries was made in Puri district in 1893). Puri-Kuṣāṇa coins have been reported from a number of coastal (Ganjam, Puri, Cuttack and Balasore) and interior (Mayurbhanj and Keonjhar) districts of Orissa, a coastal district (Srikakulam) in Andhra, a few districts (the Rakha copper mines area of Singhbhum and Dhanbad) in Bihar bordering Orissa and West Bengal.

LATE HISTORIC PERIOD

The Gupta Era (c. 320 AD to the mid-6th century AD)

It is well known that the Gupta dynasty produced a wealth of gold, silver, copper and lead coins, although 'Bengal' was familiar only with the two most precious varieties – gold and silver. Indeed, one of Ray's (1994: 302) primary evidences for proving Bengal's "pinnacle of commercial prosperity" is the Gupta gold and silver coins. In his fabulous 'Bengal', "currency of gold and silver was almost universal" and "even ordinary householders used gold and silver coins in land transactions". Before affirming or rejecting such claims, it is necessary to take stock and so, the "black-box" of data produced below may be forgiven for its cumbersome appearance.

Table 3.1:
Gupta Gold Coins Found in Bengal

Type	Monarch	Find-spots
King & Queen	Candragupta I	24-Parganas (North), Bardhamān.
Standard	Samudragupta	Bardhamān, Huglī, 24-Parganas (North), Medinīpur, unspecified site in Bangladesh.
Archer	Samudragupta	24-Parganas (North).
Aśvamedha	Samudragupta	Comilla.
Archer	Candragupta II	Kalighat (Kolkata), Huglī, Bardhamān, 24-Parganas (North), Murshidabad (?), Faridpur, Bogra, Jessore, Comilla.
Umbrella	Candragupta II	Huglī.
Archer	Kumāragupta I	Huglī.
Elephant-rider	Kumāragupta I	Huglī.
Horseman	Kumāragupta I	Medinīpur, Huglī.
Lion-slayer	Kumāragupta I	Huglī, Bardhamān, Bogra.

Kārttikeya	Kumāragupta I	Bardhamān.
King & Lakṣmī or Queen	Skandagupta	Medinīpur.
Archer (light)	Skandagupta	Huglī, Bardhamān, Bogra.
Archer (heavy)	Skandagupta	Huglī, Faridpur.
Archer	Kumāragupta II	Kalighat, 24-Parganas (North & South), Medinīpur.
Archer	Vainyagupta	Kalighat, Huglī.
Archer	Narasiṁhagupta	Kalighat, Huglī, Murshidabad, Birbhum, Nadiya (Ranaghat).
Archer	Kumāragupta III	Huglī, Bardhamān.
Archer	Viṣṇugupta	Kalighat, Huglī, North 24-Parganas, Tilda (Medinīpur).

Gupta gold coins were referred to as *dīnāras* (possibly named after Roman *denarius aureus*). These were struck in varied standards. Coins issued by Candragupta I and Samudragupta weigh c. 120-121 grains. There was a trend of increasing the weight during the reign of Candragupta II, Kumāragupta I and Skandagupta. The latter monarch struck coins first in 130-132 grains and then raised the weight to 144 grains. Some coins of later monarchs weigh even more than 144 grains. The lighter (130-132 grains) and heavier (144+ grains) varieties of gold coins were distinguished as *dīnāras* and *suvarṇas*, respectively (Mukherjee 1992a: 52). However, the gold content of the heavier variety of coins decreased to about 70 grains only (Cunningham 1967: 15-16). Decrease in gold content was possibly the result of the weakened economy of the Gupta Empire, shaken as it was by Huna invasions. If gold coins are necessitated by international trade (maritime and overland) in luxury items, decline in gold content may be seen as depreciation of the home economy in the international market.

Gupta silver coins, referred to as *rupakas* and weighing between c. 27 to 34 grains, have been reported from only two sites: Muhammadpur (near Jessore) and Chandraketugarh. The discovery at Chandraketugarh was of only one coin. Nearly rectangular in shape and weighing 1.83 grams, the coin is preserved at the Asutosh Museum of Indian Art, Kolkata. On the other hand, a detail of the content of the earthen pot in which the Muhammadpur hoard was discovered in 1852 is not available; nor do we know where they are now. What we know is simply that "specimens of the silver coinage of Chandra Gupta, Kumāra Gupta and Skanda Gupta" were discovered near the Arunkhālī River at Muhammadpur (Mitra 1852: 401-402).

Although it is generally believed that 16 *rupakas* were equal to one *dīnāra* (De 1970: 143), Mukherjee (1992a: 55-56) argues that the ratio of value between *dīnāra* and *rupaka* was 1:15. He builds his argument on land-measurement and price as given in two copperplates of the time of Kumāragupta I (Dāmodarpur and Baigram, 448 AD). His argument is mathematically accurate and is more acceptable than De's (1970: 143) argument because the latter's computations are based on two copperplates (Dāmodarpur 448 AD and Pāhāḍpur c. 479 AD) whose issue dates are separated by 31 years between them. Mukherjee's revised ratio of value complicates further the exchange value of gold and silver during the reign of the Guptas, which Chakravarti (1943: 665) had drawn attention to. Whereas Chakravarti worked out the exchange value of gold to silver to be 1:4.6, Mukherjee's computation (at 127 grains/*dīnāra* during the reign of Kumāragupta I) is 1:3.8. This still remains extremely perplexing, especially because the relative value of gold and silver in western part of South Asia in the 2nd century AD was 1:10.

As already noted earlier, no Gupta copper coins have been found in 'Bengal', although Samudragupta, Candragupta II and Kumāragupta I are known to have minted them. However, cast copper coins from earlier eras (such as Kuṣāṇo-Rāḍha and Kuṣāṇo-Vaṅga) were in circulation during the Gupta rule. This has been established by excavations conducted at Maṅgalkoṭa (Bardhamān district, West Bengal), where pre-Gupta cast copper coins were found at the Gupta level. Candragupta II, Kumāragupta I and Skandagupta also minted lead coins but none of these have been found in 'Bengal'. As Sharma (1966: 86) observes, "the comparative scarcity of Gupta copper coins suggests that money economy was becoming weaker at this time".

Based on Fa-Hien's testimony (*Fo-kuo-chi* XVI), that "[i]n buying and selling commodities they [in the Middle Country] use cowries" (Legge 1886: 45), it is generally accepted that the same was valid for the currency system in Gupta Bengal. "In fact", says Mukherjee (1992a: 58), *kapardakas* or *cowries* could have formed the primary currency for ordinary transaction in daily life". Because Kuṣāṇo-Rāḍha and Kuṣāṇo-Vaṅga cast copper coins appear to have been used in lower West Bengal during the Gupta rule, it is possible that these were in circulation along with the cowries and were used for smaller transactions. Sharma (1966: 88) believes barter too may have been in use. Gold coins were used only for larger transactions such as buying and selling of land. Discovery of Gupta gold and silver coins proves beyond doubt that these were in circulation in 'Bengal'. However, even a cursory glance will reveal that most of the find-spots are in the southern part of West Bengal, along the course of the Bhāgīrathī-Huglī.

Data given in the Table 3.2 does not include several coins of Narasiṁhagupta held in the Nahar Collection and Vaṅgīya Sāhitya Parishad collection in Kolkata. Most of the remaining coins have been found in seven hoards. The find-spots of these hoards are Kalighat (in Kolkata) in 1783, Muhammadpur near Jessore in 1852, Madhavpur near Huglī in 1883, Hasnan in Huglī district in 1976 and Bainchigram also in Huglī district in 1981. The coins from Comilla were found in an excavation at Salban Vihāra, Mainamati, in two hoards, both of which belong to Phase III dated to the 8th century AD. Among these hoards, we have some information about the contents of Kalighat hoard. The hoard was found by a Nab-Kishen, who, in a fit of colonial subservience, handed them over to Warren Hastings, the then governor of Bengal. In his turn, the governor sent 172 of the coins to the Court of Directors of the English East India Company, believing that he was making the most munificent present to his masters. However, the Court melted these down in a mercenary fit. The remaining coins were preserved at the British Museum (possibly 24), the Ashmolean (later Bodleian) Museum at Oxford, the Hunterian collection, the Public Library at Cambridge, the Banks, Cracherode and Payne-Knight collections. From available information, it appears certain that the hoard contained coins of Candragupta II, Narasiṁhagupta, Kumāragupta II and Viṣṇugupta (Allan 1975: cxxiv-cxxvi). The Hasnan hoard contained a gold coin of Samācāradeva (*Indian Archaeology – A Review* 1971-72: 72 & pl. LXVIII, nos. B-C). Three post-Gupta gold coins were found in the Muhammadpur hoard (Bhattasali 1925-26: 79-80). Hence we may logically assume that Kalighat, Hasnan, Muhammadpur and Mainamati hoards were collected any time after the Gupta era and may not provide reliable information regarding trade in the Gupta age.

Discounting the content of the two collections and the two unknown hoards, an ascending curve can be traced in Table 3.2. Beginning from Candragupta I (0), the curve reaches a peak in Candragupta II (18) and then descends from Kumāragupta I (11), to Skandagupta (8) and crashes to Kumāragupta II (1). A second ascending curve may be traced from Budhagupta (0), through Vainyagupta (4) to a smaller peak in Narasiṁhagupta (7) and then a sudden collapsed plateau in Kumāragupta III (1) and Viṣṇugupta (1). The first curve reflects the rise and fall of the Imperial Guptas during the 4th and the 5th centuries AD and may be taken to indicate the economic condition in 'Bengal'. The second curve reflects the pseudo imperial glory during the 6th century AD. As Mukherjee (1992a: 28) shows, the content of the precious metal in Gupta gold coins began to decline from the time of Skandagupta. His coins, along with those issued by Kumāragupta II, Budhagupta and Vainyagupta contain over 70% gold.

However, a sharp decline in gold content can be seen in the coins issued by Narasiṁhagupta. While some of his coins contain over 70% gold, others have slightly over 50%. The latter percentage continued throughout the end of the Gupta rulers. Studied together, the two curves may be taken to indicate the comparative state of foreign trade. Greater gold content and peak in the first curve indicate that the reign of Candragupta II saw the most prosperous condition in foreign trade. Low content of gold in the second curve reflects a drastic fall in the foreign trade during the 5th century AD. Furthermore, scarcity of silver coins indicates that trade was predominantly in costlier luxuries and articles for the affluent elite. The lower strata of the society had to depend on cowries or even barter. Hence it is questionable as to how much of the affluence attained during the reign of Candragupta II trickled down to the peasants and the common artisans.

The distribution pattern of the coins shows that the heaviest concentration is in Kolkata (Kalighat, unknown number in the hoard of 200 coins) and Huglī (32 from 3 find-spots). Low concentration can be noted in Bardhamān (2), 24-Parganas (North and South, 3), Medinīpur (2), Faridpur (Koṭālipāḍā, 4), Bogra (1), Jessore (unknown number in a small hoard), southern Bengal (unspecified locality, 3), Nadiya (1), Comilla (2) and Murshidabad (2). Region-wise analysis shows that no coin was found in the central part of eastern Bengal while only four coins have been found in north Bengal. The greatest concentration is in the lower part of West Bengal. North Bengal's share is specially striking, given the fact that Gupta dominion was longest in the north. The distribution pattern of the Gupta coins may have resulted from their use in commerce during subsequent ages. Nevertheless, the "universality" claimed by Ray does becomes strongly susceptible to doubt.

Table 3.2:
Gupta Coins in Bengal: Findspots (all gold, unless specified)

Findspots	Candra I	Samudra	Candra II	Kumāra I	Skanda	Later Monarchs	Total
Bardhamān		1	1				2
24-Parganas (North & South)		1	1		1 silver	Kumāra II (1)	3+1 silver
Huglī		1	12	10	2	Narasiṁha (4) Kumāra III (1), Viṣṇu (1), Vainya (1)	32
Kolkata	A hoard of around 200 coins at Kalighat which contained coins of Candra II, Kumāra II, Vainya, Narasiṁha, Viṣṇu.						200±
Medinīpur				1	1		2
Faridpur (Koṭālipāḍā)			1		3		4
Bogra					1		1

Jessore	Unknown number in a small hoard. Silver coins of Candra II, Kumāra I and Skanda						?
Southern Bengal (?)						Vainya 3	3
Comilla, Mainamati		1	3				4
Nadiya						Narasiṁha (1)	1
Murshidabad						Narasiṁha (2)	2
Total	0	4	18	11	8	14	254± 1 silver

It is striking that only eight Gupta coins have been found in three port sites and their vicinity: 1 gold coin in Tamluk (Kumāragupta I) and 1 gold coin in Tilda (Viṣṇugupta), 4 gold coins in Koṭālipāḍā (Candragupta II and Skandagupta), and 1 gold coin (Candragupta I) and 1 silver coin (Skandagupta) in Candraketugarh. Given the total number of approximately 250 or more Gupta coins found in 'Bengal', eight coins in maritime port sites do not indicate a great deal of maritime trade. Hence, one increasingly begins to suspect that whatever was the contribution of foreign trade to the affluence of 'Bengal' during the Gupta reign; it was much more from over-land than maritime trade.

The Post-Gupta Era (c. 525 to 750 AD)

Media of exchange during this era was more varied than even the Gupta era. Not only were gold and silver coins in circulation (as chance discoveries and archaeological excavations prove) but also bullion (silver dust or *cūrṇī*) and cowries (as epigraphical records show). Let us begin our discussion on the medium of exchange as indicated by epigraphic sources.

The use of *dināra* for sale transaction of land during the reign of Dharmāditya is recorded in the Faridpur copperplate of Dharmāditya (regnal year 3) (Mukherji and maity 1967: 77). Similarly, the Faridpur copperplate of Gopacandra (regnal year 18) and the Mallasarul copperplate of Vijayasena of the time of Gopacandra (regnal year 3) (*ibid.*: 85, 93) also bear testimony to the use of *dināra*. The Faridpur copperplate of Dharmāditya (undated) refers to silver coins and *gaṇḍakas* in addition to *dināras*. Mukherjee (1993: 6) amends the relevant passage to makes it intelligible and renders it as "six *purāṇas*, filled up with *gaṇḍakas*" instead of "three silver coins and six *gaṇḍakas*" as given in Mukherji and Maity (1967: 82). He then goes on to argue that payment of *purāṇas* or unit of *purāṇas* was made in *gaṇḍakas* (denoting 'four') of *kapardakas* (cowries). Thus he concludes that in the post-Gupta era in Vaṅga gold *dināras*, silver coins and cowries were used as a medium of exchange. Mukherjee's argument is acceptable because the passage as rendered by Mukherji and Maity is quite meaningless since *gaṇḍakas* denote 'four'. Hence it must be read to imply "six *gaṇḍakas* (of *kapardakas*)". One may thus accept the epigraphical evidences as testifying the use of *dināras*, silver currency and cowries in Vaṅga during the reign of Gopacandra and Dharmāditya in the 6th century AD.

Since no minted coin bearing the names of Dharmāditya and Gopacandra have come down so far, it may be reasonable to assume that during the reign of the above-mentioned rulers, imperial Gupta gold and silver coins were in circulation in Vaṅga. This proposition is all the more acceptable if we remember that during Dharmāditya and Gopacandra's reign, the Guptas were ruling over north Bengal and that gold coins of Candragupta II and Skandagupta were found in a field close to Koṭālipāḍā (vide O'Malley 1925: 16), which we have already established in the Chapter One as a port and administrative centre of Gopacandra and his successors.

Besides gold *dināras*, silver coins and cowries, the kingdom of Gpacandra and his successors also knew the use of dust money. In the Jayrampur Copperplate of the time of Gopacandra regnal year 1, we come across a curious term '*cūrṇikās*', when it announces that the annual tax to be paid for the land granted was to be a lump sum *(arya-piṇḍaka)* of 100 *cūrṇikās* (Sircar 1986: 531). Sircar (1951-52: 45) explains this curious use of the terms by citing Oriya lexicons where *cūrṇī* and *purāṇa* are used as synonyms of *kāhāṇa* or Sanskrit *kārṣāpaṇa*. Based on the conversion rate given in a commentary of Varahamihira's *Brihatsamhita* by Utpala in the 10th century AD, where one *purāṇa* (also called *kārṣāpaṇa*) was shown equivalent to 1280 cowrie-shells (*svetika*) (Dvivedi 1897: 987), we may further note that *cūrṇī*, *purāṇa* and *kārṣāpaṇa* were all equal to 1280 cowrie-shells. If the word *cūrṇī* can be taken to be a derivative from the stem *cūrṇnin*, meaning "made or mixed up with anything powdered or pounded", then it is possible to accept Mukherjee's (1982: 70) interpretation that the term *cūrṇī* denoted "dust money".

Mukherjee's interpretation may not be very far fetched since we learn from the account of the Arab traveller and merchant Sulaiman al-Tajir that in the 9th century AD, "(e)xchanges are carried on in his states [i.e., Gurjara Pratihara Empire] with silver (and gold) in dust ..." (Sulaiman 1867: 4). The possibility of "dust money" being a medium of exchange in the Pala kingdom proper (i.e., 'Bengal') may be justified with the information provided by Sulaiman (*ibid.*: 5) and Ibn Khurdadba (1867: 14) that plenty of gold and silver were available in the Pāla kingdom (Ruhmi). As a proof of actual use of "dust money", one may cite a Tibetan account, according to which one Nag-tcho was dispatched from Tibet to Vikramasila monastery in 'Bengal' in the second quarter of the 11th century AD to facilitate Atisa Dipaṁkara's visit to Tibet. For his expenses he was given 35 ounces of gold. At Vikramsila when Nag-tsho met Atisa, he presented to him a bar of gold and gold dust in a small bag (Das 1965: 60, 65).

Since we have established *cūrṇī* as a synonym of silver *kārṣāpaṇa* (the standard weight of which was 32 ratis), we may conclude our investigation on *cūrṇī* on a firm note by agreeing with Mukherjee (1982: 70) that it signified "a unit of silver in dust weighing 32 ratis ... equal in value to 1280 cowries". Hence, the Jayarampur inscription of Gopacandra clearly indicates that besides Gupta gold and silver coins and cowries, silver dust (*cūrṇī*) was also used as a medium of exchange in the region of Daṇḍabhukti (in Medinīpur district) during the reign of Gopacandra.

During Śaśāṅka's era, we learn that a term called *paṇa* was used while referring to the medium of exchange. The Egra copperplate of the time of fore-mentioned monarch informs us that one droṇavāpa of land was sold in Ektākaśa *viṣaya* (possibly Medinīpur district) for 4 *paṇas* (Sircar 1983: 727). Since the *Arthaśāstra* uses the *paṇas* to refer to a silver piece of 32 *ratis*, *Manusmṛti* uses it refer to a copper coin of 80 ratis and some later texts use it to denote a unit of calculation consisting of 80 cowries, we may argue that any of the three uses could apply in the Egra copperplate. However, if *paṇas* denoted a copper coin of 80 *ratis* or a unit of calculation consisting of 80 cowries, the price of land would have been unbelievably low (compared, for example, to Gopacandra's era in Vaṅga where one *kulyavapa* of fallow land was sold for 4 *dināras*). Hence, it is logical to assume that in the Egra copperplate, *paṇas* denoted a silver coin of 32 *ratis*. Since no such coin has come down to us, Mukherjee (1993: 14) proposes that the term may have been another name of *cūrṇī* and was used to denote a unit of silver dust of 32 *ratis*.

Having ascertained the medium of exchange as indicated by the epigraphic sources, we may now continue our examination with the help of numismatic evidences. We may begin with coins that are typologically close to or follow the tradition of the Gupta coins (consequently they have often been cited as "imitation Gupta" coins). These post-Gupta coins may be divided into two groups for convenience: the earlier series (consisting of coins issued by Samācāradeva, Śaśāṅka and Jayanāga) and the later series (consisting of those issued by a host of rulers including the Rātas and the Khaḍgas). Although the post-Gupta coins were mostly minted in gold, Rashid (1975: 44) has reported that a few copper and silver coins were recovered from Mainamati. A silver coin of Śaśāṅka has also been reported in Sundarganj, 24-Parganas, West Bengal (Lahiri 1981-82: 74). Expressing his doubt about silver coins of Śaśāṅka, Mukherjee (1993: 11) argues that five silver coins of the monarch, as reported by M. Harunur Rashid and P. K. Bhattacharyya, are possibly unofficial imitations in debased gold. Since we lack sufficient information regarding post-Gupta coins in silver and copper, the following examination will be restricted to gold coins only.

POST-GUPTA GOLD COINS: EARLY SERIES

Post-Gupta gold coins of the early series that have so far been discovered were issued by five monarchs: Samācāradeva, Śaśāṅka, Jayanāga, Virasena Kramaditya and 'Maya'. Three of them, i.e., Samācāradeva, Śaśāṅka and Jayanāga, have used the device of the 'Seated Goddess' on the reverse, which may be seen in Gupta gold coins as well. However, their distinct devices are on the obverse: Śaśāṅka's 'Bull and Śiva', and Samācāradeva and Jayanāga's 'Rājalila' (enthroned king with female attendants) and the 'King-and-Elephant'. Samācāradeva's devices of the 'Archer-King' and the 'Seated Lakṣmī' bear greatest resemblance to coins issued by the Guptas, particularly those of Narasiṁhagupta. Jayanāga, who also issued coins with the 'Archer-King' device, deviate further away stylistically and the workmanship also deteriorates slightly. Śaśāṅka, who never used the 'Archer King' device, sought rather his distinct mark by using devices such as 'Śiva and his Bull' or the 'Bull' alone. The workmanship of his coins deteriorates a little more than the coins of Jayanāga.

Samācāradeva's debased gold issues bearing his own name, is the earliest known evidence of post-Gupta coins. These have been recovered from a hoard in Muhammadpur in Jessore region (Bangladesh) (Mitra 1852: 401-402) and another from Hasnan in Huglī distict (West Bengal) (*Indian Archaeology – A Review* 1971-72: 72 & pl. LXVIII, nos. B-C). Samācāradeva's coins can be divided into two classes: the Archer type (148.2 grains, 50.5% gold content) and Seated-king type (149 grains, 39.02% gold content).

At least 19 gold coins have so far been found which appear to have been issued by Śaśāṅka. Known find-spots of these are Mahananda (Huglī district), Muhammadpur (Jessore region), Mainamati (Comilla region) and Kachua (near Chandpur in Comilla region). Śaśāṅka's coins may be divided into two classes. Class I bear the device of 'Śiva on bull' on the obverse and 'goddess Lakṣmī seated on lotus' on the reverse. Struck on a weight standard of 144 grains, percentage of gold in total metal content of the coins belonging to Class I is 49-52% (group 1), 32-36% (group 2) and 16.34%-21.23% (group 3). Coins belonging to Class II show variations of the devices of Class I and are struck on a weight standard of 90 grains. Percentage of gold in total metal content of these coins is 74.66%. Mukherjee (1993: 11-12) believes that Class I coins were meant for circulation in Gauḍa, Vaṅga and possibly some other regions of his kingdom while Class II were meant for circulation in Samataṭa. Mukherjee's argument is persuasive because Śaśāṅka's Class II coins follow weight standard of Maya's coins and because these have been found in the region that once was a part of Samataṭa (south-east Bangladesh).

At least four gold coins (currently held by the British Museum) have been identified as issues of Jayanāga. Struck in the weight standard of 144 grains, the coins bear the device of standing king holding a bow and arrow and the legend 'Jaya' on the obverse. The device on the reverse is 'goddess Lakṣmī seated on a lotus being consecrated by two elephants'. Coins issued by Jayanāga contain only 20% of gold.

Besides those discussed above, four more post-Gupta coins have been discovered so far. Three of these are gold coins bearing the name of Virasena Kramaditya. Devices featured in these coins are 'standing bull', 'a post and a couchant calf' on the obverse and 'seated Lakṣmī holding a lotus and a fillet' on the reverse. The legend on the obverse reads Śrī-Vira(se)na while that on the reverse reads Kramaditya. Lahiri (1981-82: 74) believes that the issuer of the coin may have ruled in eastern Bengal as a successor of Samācāradeva. However, stylistic and typological dissimilarities of Virasena's coins with those of Samācāradeva make Lahiri's suggestion unacceptable. It is more probable, as Mukherjee (1993: 22) suggests that Virasena came sometime before Śaśāṅka. Two of his coins are now held by the British Museum (believed to have been found near Varanasi) and one by the Indian Museum, Kolkata. The coins have been struck in weight standard varying between 161.7-162.5 grains. Gold content of the coin held by the Indian Museum is 95.71%. The region in which Virasena's coins circulated is unknown.

An Archer type of gold coin bearing the name 'Maya' on the obverse and a two-armed standing goddess on the reverse (presently in the collection of S. Sethia, Kolkata) has been found in southeastern Bangladesh. Its gold content is very high (95.57%) and has been struck on a weight standard of 90 grains. Because it bears a four-pronged symbol, which is a legacy of Gupta coins, and since the feature is absent in the specie of Śaśāṅka, Mukherjee (*ibid.*) has placed the coin at a time earlier than Śaśāṅka. Because the coin was found in southeastern Bengal, we may believe that Maya's coin(s) circulated in Samataṭa.

POST-GUPTA GOLD COINS: LATE SERIES

Quite a few post-Gupta gold coins of the late series have so far been discovered. Based on deterioration in quality of the devices and fall in the quantity of gold in the coins, the issuing monarchs can be identified in the following chronological order:

1. Devavarmana and Vāsuvarmana (wrongly considered so far as Sudhanyāditya)
2. Śrīkumāra
3. Jivadhāraṇarāta and Śrīdhāraṇarāta of the Rāta dynasty
4. Devakhaḍga, Rājabhaṭa and Balabhaṭṭa (of the Khaḍga dynasty) and Prithuvira, or Prithutala or Prithubala (Mukherjee 1992a: 38).

Coins isued by all these monarchs continued to follow a weight standard of approximately 90 grains but adopted new devices (i.e., 'a royal figure holding a bow and an arrow' on the obverse and 'a multi-armed standing goddess' on the reverse). Another characteristic feature of these coins is a border of thick dots, as seen in Śaśāṅka's gold coins Characteristic features of these coins are gradual deterioration of the quality of minting, crude execution of the devices and fall in the quantity of gold. These coins were in circulation in Vaṅga and Samataṭa in the second half of the 7th century AD and their circulation ended by the end of the 7th or early 8th century AD. Most of the coins have been found in the regions of Faridpur (including Koṭālipāḍā), Dhaka (including Savar), Bogra, Jessore (including Muhammadpur), Comilla (including Mainamati) in Bangladesh and the state of Tripura in India.

A gold coin held by the Indian Museum, Kolkata with inscribed legend on the obverse that has been doubtfully read as *De[va]* and marginal legend on be reverse deciphered as *De(va) va(r)m(ā)* has been identified by Mukherjee (1993: 24) as an issue of Devavarman. He was probably a successor of Bhāskaravarman of Kāmrūpa and ruled over a portion of 'Bengal' annexed by the latter. It is possible, as Mukherjee (*ibid.*) proposes, that the Devavarma of the coin may have been the Devavarma (T'i-p'o-po-mo) whom I-Tsing mentions in his preface to the *Biography of Eminent Monks* (*Kao-Seng chuan*) (Lahiri 1986: 50-51). The coin shows on the obverse a royal male figure in a *tribhanga* posture, a staff planted inside a pot *(khumbha)* and topped by (what appears to be) a vertically placed conch-shell. On the reverse, the coin displays an eight-armed female deity (Sarvani) in *tribhanga* posture holding the child Ganeśa and a garland of flowers on her two sides. The gold content of the coin is 68.70% of the total metal content and its weight standard is 90 grains.

A few gold coins bearing quite similar devices as those of Devavarmana (except a few minor variations such as the position of the conch-shell) but of inferior execution have inscribed on them a legend on the reverse which has been read by Mukherjee (1993: 43) as Śrī-*Vāsuva (or dha?)(r)m(ā)*. Arguing against earlier readings of "Sudhanyā(ditya)", Mukherjee shows that the correct reading should be "Vāsuvarmana", who was possibly a successor of Devavarmana. Weight standard and gold content of Vāsuvarmana's coins are the same as that of Devavarmana. Accepting Mukherjee's reading of Vāsuvarmana instead of Sudhanyā(ditya), we may note that at least five of his coins have been found in the regions of Dhaka (including Savar), Faridpur (Koṭālipāḍā), Bogra and Comilla (Mainamati, Salban Vihāra, Period III, cell 91; Rashid 1975: 53). Three more similar coins of unknown provenance are now held by the British Museum.

Mukherjee (1993: 25) draws attention to a few more gold coins issued by an anonymous ruler. The device on the obverse is the same as that of Devavarmana's coins (except the position of the conch-shell and the presence of an additional figure of a standing horse) and the device on the reverse is similar to the coins issued by Vāsuvarmana. One of the coins has been recovered from Salban Vihāra (cell no 79) in Mainamati (Comilla). Similar coins have been reported from different parts of 'Bengal'. The British Museum and the Indian Museum each holds a specimen of this class of coins. The weight-standard of these coins is half satamana (90 grains) and the gold content of a specimen held by the Indian Museum, Kolkata is 62.44%. If the style of execution is acceptable as a reliable indicator, it is possible to believe that the issuer was the successor of Vāsuvarman.

A class of gold coins bearing the legend "Śrīkumāra" on the obverse was wrongly read by N. K. Bhattasali as "Śrī Krama(ditya)". The weight-standard of these coins is half satamana (87 grains). The percentage of gold content is not known but according to Mukherjee (*ibid.*: 26), the gold content is possibly around 50%. Quite a few coins of Śrīkumāra have been found so far. Two of these were found in Savar, another two were recovered from Mainamati (including one from Salban Vihāra Cell no. 13; Rashid 1975: 52) and some from a hoard at Paglatek in the Goalpara district, Assam (now held at the State Museum, Guahati). The find-spot of two coins held by the Indian Museum is unknown. Stylistically, these coins bear close resemblance with those issued by Devavarman. However, on the obverse of Śrīkumāra's coins the royal figure holds an arrow pointing downward and the conch-shell is crudely depicted. The goddess on the reverse appears to be six-armed and the object held by her (Ganeśa in Devavarmana's coins) is crude to the point of being unrecognisable. Because some of the Śrīkumāra's coins appear to be quality-wise inferior to other, Mukherjee (1993: 26) suspects those to be imitations or belonging to a second series.

Gold coins issued by Jīvadhāraṇarāta, displaying the legend "Jiva" (or "Jima") on the obverse, bear close resemblance with those issued by Śrīkumāra. However, one cannot but notice deterioration in the style of execution, so much so that the arrow held by the king on the obverse appears to be a strange object and the pot on which the standard is implanted appears to be an arrow-head. The facial expression of the goddess on the reverse is quite repulsive and the object held by her resembles more a sickle than Ganeśa. The weight-standard of these coins is half-satamana (90 grains) (*ibid.*: 44-45). The percentage of gold content of Jīvadhāraṇarāta's coins has not been ascerained. However, following Mukherjee (*ibid.*), we may assume that it was possibly around 50%. The find-spot of two of Jīvadhāraṇarāta's coins is known. They were recovered from excavations at Salban Vihāra, Period III, cell 2 and 91 (Rashid 1975: 53-54). Another coin from an unknown find-spot is held in a private collection in Kolkata.

A good number of gold coins bearing the legend "Śrī" on the obverse have been identified by Mukherjee as issues of Śrīdhāraṇarāta. As a matter of fact, of all the coins issued by the known monarch of Samataṭa, Śrīdhāraṇarāta's are most numerous. Some of these have been recovered from a hoard of Samataṭa pieces in Paglatek (Goalpara, Assam), some other (along with Śaśāṅka's coins) from a hoard in Dar Hasnabad (24-Parganas, West Bengal), and a few more from excavations at Mainamati (Comilla, Bangladesh). The devices used in Śrīdhāraṇarāta's coins are similar to those of Jīvadhāraṇarāta except that the pot in which the standard is implanted on the obverse appears like an arrow-head in some, a circle in others and a vessel with two leaves in still others. The goddess on the reverse is six-armed in some and eight-armed in others while the object held by her now appears to be a sickle with a long handle. The weight-standard of Śrīdhāraṇarāta's coins is half satamana (varies from c. 75 grains to little above 88 grains) and the gold-content of two coins held by the Indian Museum, Kolkata are 57.37% and 54% (Mukherjee 1993: 45).

A gold coin bearing the legend "Khaḍga deva" on the obverse has been recovered from an excavation at Salban Vihāra, Period III, cell 98 in Mainamati (Rashid 1975: 57). We may believe that Devakhaḍga issued the coin. Devices used in the coin are quite similar to those of Śrīdhāraṇarāta but a couchant bull is represented on top of the standard on the obverse and the six-armed goddess on the reverse appears to be holding a stick (Mukherjee 1993: 45-46). The weight-standard of the coin is half satamana. Although the gold content of Devakhaḍga's coin is not available, one may assume, following Mukherjee (*ibid.*) that the presence of the precious metal was around 50%.

Gold coins bearing the legend of "Rāja bhaṭa" display devices similar to those of Devakhaḍga, but the style of execution appears to be less refined. Four coins of this ruler are held by the Assam State Museum, Guahati and one by the Los Angeles Country Museum. The weight-standard of these is half-satamana (varying from about 73 grains to little above 86 grains) and the gold content is moderately to heavily debased. Two of the coins are so heavily debased that they look almost like silver coins (*ibid.*: 28 and 46).

Two gold coins and one heavily alloyed coin of Balabhaṭṭa have been recovered from excavations at Salban Vihāra in Mainamati (Comilla). His coins have also been found in South Tripura, which are now held in the private collection of S. K. Bose in Shillong (Meghalaya, India). Balabhaṭṭa's coins may be grouped in two classes. A coin belonging to Class I (now held in a private collection in Kolkata) has been struck in half-satamana weight-standard, the legend "Va(Ba)la bhaṭa" is inscribed in two lines on the obverse and its gold content is quite low. Although it is stylistically quite close to Devakhaḍga's coin, the execution of the devices is much cruder (*ibid.*: 46-47). A coin belonging to Class II (now held by the Indian Museum, Kolkata) has been struck in suvarṇa standard (144 grains) and the percentage of gold in the total metal content of the coin is 97.6 (*ibid.*: 29). The obverse of the coin displays a fully dressed male figure in *tribhanga* posture, holding a bow in his left hand and a downward-pointing arrow in the right hand. The legend "Vaṅgaśrī" is inscribed vertically and "Bala bhaṭa" in two lines. The reverse shows goddess Lakṣmī sitting on a lotus, holding a fillet in her right hand and a casket in the left (*ibid.*: 47).

Some heavily debased gold coins, struck in the half-satamana weight-standard bear the legend 'Prithuvira' or 'Prithuva(ba)la'. Known find-spots of these coins are Koṭālipāḍā (Majumdar 1943c: 53-54) and Pilak area in South Tripura (now held in the collection of S. K. Bose, Shillong) (Mukherjee 1993: Plate VIII.3). The obverse displays a crudely represented royal figure holding a bow and an arrow and a standard implanted in a pot. The reverse shows another crudely represented figure, this time that of a goddess, holding some object. Mukherjee (*ibid.*: 30) believes that Prithuvira or Prithuvala may be a ruler of Samataṭa after Balabhaṭṭa.

The gold content in all the post-Gupta coins discussed above, including both the early and the late series, may be summed up in the following table.

Table 3.3:
Gold-content of the Post-Gupta Coins

Samācāradeva	50.50%	39.02%
Virasena Kramaditya	95.71%	
Maya	95.57%	
Śaśāṅka	74.66%	52%-16.34%
Jayanāga	20%	
Devavarmana	68.70%	
Vāsuvarmana	68.70%	
Anonymous	62.44%	
Śrīkumāra	50% (?)	
Jīvadhāraṇarāta	50% (?)	
Śrīdhāraṇarāta	57.37%	54%
Devakhaḍga	50% (?)	
Rājabhaṭa	Low	
Balabhaṭṭa	97.60%	Low
Prithuvira	Low	

Of all these rulers, Virasena Kramaditya, Maya and Balabhaṭṭa issued coins with gold content exceeding 95%. They are followed by the following five rulers who issued coins with gold content ranging from 75% to 50%: Śaśāṅka (Series II, 74.66%), Devavarmana (68.70%), anonymous ruler following Vāsuvarmana (62.44%), Śrīdhāraṇarāta (57.37%) and Samācāradeva (50.50%). The lowest gold content is to be found in coins issued by Jayanāga, Rājabhaṭa and Prithuvira. Interestingly, the table does not show a gradual debasement from the time of Samācāradeva to Prithuvira but speaks of three curves. The first curve begins with Samācāradeva one of whose issues register 50.50% gold, climbs to over 95% in the issues of Virasena Kramaditya and Maya and the falls to 74.66% in Series II of Śaśāṅka and dips to 20% in Jayanāga. The second curve is more of a plateau with Devavarmana, the anonymous ruler following Vāsuvarmana and Śrīdhāraṇarāta, all three of whose coins range between 69% and 57% while Vāsuvarmana may have been close to Devavarmana, and Śrīkumāra and Jivadhāraṇarāta may have been close to Śrīdhāraṇarāta. The last curve is dramatic. It begins with low in Rājabhaṭa, climbs to a sharp peak at 97.60% in Balabhaṭṭa (the highest gold content among all the rulers) and then suddenly falls to an abysmal depth in Prithuvira. Actually, except for the high gold-content issues of Balabhaṭṭa, all three rulers of the last curve may be considered to form a low plateau.

HARIKELA COINS

Whereas the coins discussed above bear the influence of or follow the tradition of the Gupta coins, there appeared a completely different series of coins in the 7th century AD which cast aside most of hitherto-used stylistical, typological and metrological features. Known as Harikela coins, this series appears to have been influenced or inspired by the coins issued by the monarchs of the Arakanese Candra dynasty (mid-4th to mid-10th century AD, with a break in the 7th century AD; Mukherjee 1981-82: 60; Aung 1997: 3-5). Typically, the Harikela coins are thin in fabric and bear devices of a recumbent bull on the obverse and a tripartite symbol on the reverse. The tripartite symbol resembles a trident and is decorated with garlands on both sides and symbols of the sun and the moon on top. Devices of both the reverse and the obverse are enclosed within an inner circle and an outer border of dots. A legend in Brāhmī on the obverse reads "Harikela" or "Harikelā". Circular in shape (or more accurately, intended shape), the size of these coins generally varies from 2.6 cm to 3.07 cm in diameter and weight varies from 5 to 7.5 gm (Mukherjee 1981-82: 59). Although a few coins are executed in a crude style, most of them are quite remarkably produced.

While most of the Harikela coins were minted in silver, a few pieces in gold and copper (bearing a couchant bull on the obverse and a tripartite symbol on the reverse) have also been recovered. Two gold pieces were found in cell no. 62 of the Salban Vihāra (Period III). Rashid reports that a couple of copper pieces were also found. Unfortunately, they are not currently traceable and hence very little is known about these coins (Rashid 1975: 57-58). The gold pieces are debased, thin in fabric and were struck on an 8 gm weight-standard. These features make it possible to believe that the pieces were minted sometime in the late 7th or early 8th century AD or, in Mukherjee's (1975-76: 24) words, during "the early stage of this area's familiarity with thin silver pieces" when post-Gupta types had not become extinct.

Harikela coins were used as a regular currency of Samataṭa from the 7th century AD onward. Based on typological features, Mukherjee (1981-82) has divided the coins in Series I (7th century AD) and Series II ($8/9^{th}$ to $12^{th}/13^{th}$ centuries

AD). Coins belonging to Series I, which fall within the purview of the era under study, have been reported from Tripura, the village of Zobra, near the Chittagong University Campus, Sylhet region and Mainamati in Comilla region. Coins found at Zobra were in a hoard that contained 36 Harikela coins in two denominations and a gold earring. Those found in the Sylhet region were also in a hoard of between 30 and 40 coins. One coin, possibly from this region, is now held in the cabinet of the Assam State Museum, Gauhati (*ibid.*: 62-63).

Recovery of Harikela coins belonging to Series I from the Sandoway district of Arakan (*ibid.*: 63) clearly proves that these were used in trade with Arakan. Similarly, some of the silver coins found in one of the hoards at Salban Vihāra bearing the 'Bull' and the 'Tripartite' devices and the legend *Dharmavijaya* (Khan 1963: 25) may also have come by way of trade if we believe that they were issued by the Arakanese king Dharmavijaya (665-701 AD) (Aung 1997: plate 6). These evidences clearly indicate close trade contact between Samataṭa and Arakan.

A curious feature of Harikela (Series I) coins is the absence of the name of the ruling monarch as the issuing authority. This indicates that a local guild or local authority struck this type of coins. It is more likely that the coins were issued by a local guild since we do not hear of a powerful local authority in any of the copperplates or from any other sources. In that case we may even tentatively suggest that the guild was of Arakanese merchants because Harikela was under Arakan before the Khaḍga annexation.

EARLY MEDIEVAL PERIOD

Our deliberation on the early medieval period deals with the ruling dynasties of the Pālas, the Candras, the Devas, the Varmans and the Senas.

The Pālas, the Varmans and the Senas

The medium of exchange in the Pāla, Varman and Sena kingdoms have perplexed scholars for a long period and a note of hesitation can still be discerned in their discourse on the subject. There can be little doubt that one of the medium of exchange in the Pāla kingdom was cowry. This is amply testified by *Akhbār al-Sīn wa'l-Hind* (lit. An account of China and India), a collection of several reports prepared between AD 800 and AD 851 by Sulaiman al-Tajir and others. It is the earliest and the most authentic account of South Asia and China in Arabic literature. According to *Akhbār al-Sīn wa'l-Hind*:

> In his [i.e., the Pāla rulers of Bengal, Dharmapāla and/or Devapāla] country cowry-shell is used which is the money of this land, that is to say, his wealth. ... All this is purchased in the kingdom of Dharma with cowry which is the money of the kingdom (Ahmad 1989: 44).

It should be noted, the *Akhbār al-Sīn wa'l-Hind* is at pains to point out twice that cowry-shells, and not gold or silver coins are the currency of the kingdom (the goods are "purchased .. with cowry"), although, as Sulaiman reports, gold and silver are available in the country and that the king considered these cowries as "his wealth". Further evidence of the use of cowries in the Pāla Empire in the 12th-century AD is provided by the Sandhyākara Nandī's 'historical *kāvya' Rāmacarita* (IV, 36b), according to which Madanapāla maintained a grand army (mahāvāhinī) "by cowries (as wages) and daily bread" (Sandhyākara Nandī 1910: 92).

Chau Ju-kua also testifies that in the 12th and the 13th centuries AD, the people of P'ong-k'ie-lo "use[d] (pieces of) white conch shells ground into shape as money" (Hirth and Rockhill 1965: 97). Chau Ju-kua based his report on hearsay and hence instead of cowries, we hear of "conch shells ground into shape as money". These literary evidences are further substantiated by the discovery of a jar containing over 3 kilograms of cowries from the level of the Pāla period in the archaeological excavations conducted at the circumambulating passage of the central block (western wing) in the ruined monastery at Pāhāḍpur (Qadir 1980: 20). Similar hoard of cowries has also been found at a Pāla site in Colgong in Bhagalpur region (Dikshit 1938: 33 and 34). The problem with cowry as a medium of exchange, as repeatedly observed by scholars, is that it would not have facilitated long-distance itinerant traders, whether over-land or maritime.

A few scholars have attempted to prove that minted coins, in addition to cowries, were in circulation in the Pāla kingdom. One of them is Chakrabarti (1992: 79), who "believe[s] that there is no justification to claim that minted coins were not in circulation during the Pāla period. The inscriptions which are the most important source of the Pāla period are clear on this point". The evidence often cited to prove the above-mentioned view is the Mahābodhi inscription of the time of Dharmapāla, which records the excavation of "a deep lake (...) at a cost of three thousand *dramma*" (Mukherji and Maity 1967: 113). Another oft-cited reference is the Bhaturiya inscription of the time of Rājyapāla, which records concessional tax (*nikara*) on a village "at one hundred *purāṇas* apparently per annum" (Sircar 1959b: 152-153). Still another is the Gayā inscription of Govindapāla (Sircar 1963-64: 237-238). It records the granting of a donation of 50 *kārṣāpaṇas*, which would annually yield an interest of 16 *kārṣāpaṇas*. A marginal note inscribed in the left margin of the Gayā inscription of Govindapāla stipulates that the payment of "these *kapardakas*" were to be made with the image of the deity and two humans as witnesses. The quoted words "these *kapardakas*" may denote, as Sircar (*ibid.*: 233) believes, the annual interest of 16 *kārṣāpaṇas* on the original grant of 50 *kārṣāpaṇas*, or as Mukherjee (1982: 79, fn. 66) believes, "the value of the endowment." In both cases it appears that *kārṣāpaṇas* could be converted to *kapardakas* or cowries. These evidences appear to show that three types of minted currency, *dramma, purāṇa* and *kārṣāpaṇa* were in circulation in the Pāla domain.

Sircar (1968: 280) cites Manu (VIII.136), Yājñavalkya (I.364) and *Amarakoṣa* to show that *kārṣāpaṇa* was originally a silver coin weighing one *kārṣā* (80 *ratis* or 146.4 grains) but was later made 32 ratis (58.56 grains). It was also known as *purāṇa* or *dharaṇa.* The same authority also cites *Līlāvatī* composed by the great astronomer Bhāskar-ācārya around the end of the 13th century AD to show that one *dramma* was equivalent to one *kāhaṇa* (i.e., *kārṣāpaṇa)* and was equivalent to 1280 cowries (*ibid.*: 281). Hence we may assume that *dramma, purāṇa* and *kārṣāpaṇa* cited in the Pāla records were equivalent denominations and signified 1280 cowries.

Scholars in favour of believing in the possibility that minted coins were in circulation in the Pāla kingdom offer two numismatic evidences to justify their claim. The first evidence is a gold coin bearing the legend of *Devapāla* that shows stylistic similarities with the archer type of Gupta coins. Also cited are five copper coins unearthed at Pāhāḍpur, bearing a coarse device of a recumbent bull with the legend "Śrī Vigraha" on the obverse and three fishes on the reverse (Ahmed 1975: 29). A few debased silver coins bearing the legends *Vigra* and *Śrīvigra* were also found in Bihar (including Ghosrawa, Buxar, Hajipur and an unnamed site in Purniya district). All these *Vigra* and *Śrīvigra* coins are believed to have been issues of Vigrahapāla.

Unfortunately, none of the evidences stand ground on close scrutiny. The gold coin bearing the legend of *Devapāla*, as Chakrabarti (1992: 79) observes, "may [..] be a commemorative medallion issued on a particular occasion". The bull: three fishes coins have been attributed to the Pandya kingdom of south India (Chattopadhyaya 1977: 63 and 266). As for the debased silver coins from Bihar bearing the legends *Vigra* and *Śrīvigra*, Mukherjee (1982: 69) shows that these are basically related to the "bust" and "altar with attendants" type of Sassanian or Indo-Sassanian coins that were minted in regions much to the west of Bihar. The reverse of these coins also shows some stylistic similarity with the Adivaraha coins introduced by the Pratihara king Bhoja I. It also needs to be noted, as Mukherjee (*ibid.*) points out, that a large number of coins bearing "Śrī-Vigra" legend have been unearthed from different parts of U.P. He also draws attention to an inscription recovered from Siyadoni (Lalitpur district, U. P.), which refers to the rule of the Pratiharas and mentions "Vigraha-dramma", "Vigrahapāla-dramma", "Vigrahatungiya-dramma" and "Vigrahapāliya-dramma".

Hence, it is extremely doubtful, to say the least, that any of the *Vigra* and *Śrīvigra* coins were issued by Pāla monarchs. Rather, it appears that the *drammas* of the Mahābodhi inscription were coins of the Pratiharas, which must have continued to circulate for some time in north Indian territories that Dharmapāla annexed from the Partihara monarch Vatsarāja. Similarly, *Vigra* and *Śrīvigra* coins may have continued to circulate for some time in the territories annexed by Devapāla from Bhoja I. Some of these coins may also have entered the Pāla kingdom by way of trade. However, Mukherjee (*ibid.*) cautions us, it would be a mistake to assume that the Pāla kingdom was a regular area of Śrī-Vigra *dramma* coins since only a few of these coins have been found in the region of 'Bengal'. Moreover, low silver content (about 48.15) of these coins would also make them unacceptable for long as *drammas* or *purāṇas* of high intrinsic value (i.e., 58.56 grains of silver). Hence, those coins, which entered the Pāla domain by way of trade or were found to be there after the Pāla conquest must have been ultimately converted as devalued pieces equivalent to their inherent worth in silver content, i.e., less than half their face value.

Because the arguments in favour of the hypothetical existence of Pāla coins crumble when examined with rigours, we are forced to arrive, *via negetiva*, at one possible conclusion: *drammas, purāṇas* and *kārṣāpaṇa* were not coins issued by Pāla monarchs. Since they are mentioned in Pāla records, they either entered the Pāla domain by way of trade and were existent as remnants of Pratihara rule over newly-acquired Pāla territories (as in the case of *dramma*) or were denominations of theoretical value (as in the case of *purāṇa* and *kārṣāpaṇa).* We have already established the former; the latter we will attempt to establish after reviewing the media of exchange prevalent in the Sena domain.

As regards the media of exchange of Varmana kingdom, no archaeological evidence has as yet been cited to prove the circulation of minted coins. The matter is further complicated by epigraphic evidences, which are completely silent on the subject. The Belava copperplate of Bhojavarman (Basak 1913-14b: 37-43), the Samantasar copperplate of Harivaraman and the Vajrayogini copperplate of Samalavarman (Bhattasali 1954: 255-263) make no mention either of cowries or of minted coins.

As for the Sena kingdom, one may reasonably believe that cowries were widely used since Minhāju-d-din's *Tabaqāt-i-Nāsirī* (1260 AD) offers definite evidence. "In that country [of Rai Lakhmaniya] the current money [was] *kaudas* (*kauris*) instead of *chitals* [silver], and the smallest present he [Rai Lakhmaniya] made was a lac of *kaudas*" (Minhāju-s Sirāj 1869: 308). Verse 6 of the Deopārā inscription of Viijayasena (Majumdar 1929: 51) which compares pearls with cowries, authenticates Minhāju-d-din's testimony at least to the extent that the Senas were accustomed to cowries. As discussed below, epigraphic evidences also testify that cowries (*kapardakas*) were a medium of exchange in the Sena kingdom.

However, Minhāju-d-din's testimony is contradicted by Ānandabhaṭṭa's *Vallāla-carita*, a semi-historical and controversial work possibly composed in early 1510 AD which is nevertheless credited to "contain a core of social historical truth" (Ray 1994: 163). A legend contained in the *Vallāla-carita* recounts how Vallabhānanda, a rich merchant of *suvarnavaṇik jāti* (an occupationally differentiated endogamous group of gold merchants) in the Sena kingdom, had made an advance of 10 million *niṣka* to Vallālasena when requested by the latter for his military campaign against the king of Udantapuri. Being repeatedly unsuccessful, Vallālasena resolved to try for the last time and requested for an additional loan of 15 million suvarṇa. Vallabhānanda agreed but demanded the revenue of Harikela in return. Enraged by his audacity, Vallālasena confiscated treasures of many merchants and vented 7his wrath on them (Ray 1993: 212). We will return to the legend at a later point but for the moment it may suffice to note that if *Vallāla-carita's* testimony is to be credited, we must believe that the media of exchange of the Sena domain included *niṣka* and *suvarṇa.* The legend recounted above does not explain *niṣka* and *suvarṇa* but according to Manu, a *niṣka* was a gold coin equal to four *suvarṇa* i.e., 560 grains or 320 *ratis* (Thakur 1970: 28). Hence a *suvarṇa* must have also been a gold coin but weighing 140 grains or 80 ratis.

The currency units that recurrently occur in Sena copperplate land grants are *purāṇa, kapardaka, kapardaka-purāṇa,* and *cūrṇi.* The Govindapur and the Sundarban copperplates of Lakṣmaṇasena mentions *purāṇa* ("... yielding annually 900 *purāṇas* ..." in the Govindapur plate, Majumdar 1929: 97 and "... yielding an annual income of fifty *purāṇas* ..." in the Sundarban plate, Mukherji and Maity 1967: 293). Verse 13 of the Madhainagar copperplate of the same monarch mentions *purāṇas* and *kapardakas* separately (*kapardakāṣtha ṣasthi purāṇadhik śatamulyatpattik,* "... yielding an annual income of 1 hundred *purāṇas* and sixty-eight *kapardakas* ..." Majumdar 1929: 114). These two units (i.e., *purāṇas* and *kapardakas*) are used in conjunction as what appears to be a separate unit called *kapardaka-purāṇa* in the Naihati grant of Vallālasena (Banerji 1917a: 161; Majumdar 1929: 78), the Barrackpur grant of Vijayasena (Banerji 1919-20: 286; Majumdar 1929: 66), the Anulia and the Tarpanadighi copperplates of Lakṣmaṇasena (Majumdar 1929: 90, 104; Mukherji and Maity 1967: 300, 310-311).

In attempting to decipher the meaning of the term *kapardaka-purāṇa,* Bhandarkar (1921: 139, 176) logically argues that it cannot "denote a *purāṇa* which is equal to one Kapardaka or cowrie in value" since a *purāṇa* was a silver coin weighing 32 ratis (58.56 grains). However, the explanation he offers, that it is "a *purāṇa* .. shaped like a Kapardaka or cowrie" is equally absurd because not a single coin of such a shape has been discovered anywhere in South Asia. Chakravortty (1932: 599) offers a more reasonable view by showing that *kapardaka-purāṇa*" refers to a silver coin which, however, was paid in cowries, i.e., *purāṇa* was merely a theoretical currency and was linked up with the real currency of the country, the cowries which changed hands in exchange transactions". He further argues, "the monetary condition under the Senas seems to be that the silver coin *purāṇa* was the standard coin of the realm but not in general use, and was equated to and paid for in cowries ..." One could follow this line of argument and believe that *rūpyaṇi* ("silver coin") cited in verse 23 of the Deopārā inscription of Vijaysena (Majumdar 1929: 54) actually refers to the silver *purāṇa.*

We come across the unit "*cūrṇi*" in the Madanpāḍā and the Calcutta Sāhitya-Parishad copperplates of Visvarupasena. The grant states the yield of one piece of land to be "hundred *cūrṇis* together with thirty-two *purāṇas* – 132" ("*samdvatrimsat-puran-ottara-cūrṇṇi-śat-aika* 132") and of another piece to be "six hundred cūrṇis together with twenty-seven *purāṇas*" ("*saptavimśati-purāṇ-ādhika-sām-curṇṇī-ṣaṭ-śatik-otpattika*") (Sircar 1960: 325; Sircar 1977: 50). The Calcutta Sāhitya-Parishad copperplate records the annual yield of the granted land to be five hundred *cūrṇās* ("...*cūrṇā pañcaśatik bhūmi* ..." Majumdar 1929: 147). As established in the previous section, *cūrṇi, purāṇa* and *kārṣāpaṇa* were equivalent and *cūrṇi* was a unit of silver dust (or ingot) which was equivalent to the weight of a silver *kārṣāpaṇa* (i.e., 57.6 grains or 32 ratis) or 1280 *kapardakas* or cowries. The use of the term *cūrṇi* in the two grants mentioned above implies that the medium of exchange was current during Sena rule.

As the Tibetan account related to Atisa Dipaṁkara cited in the previous section shows, it was not only silver but also gold that was used as a medium of exchange during the period under study. That the same medium of exchange was used as a unit of revenue accounting is explicitly proven by the Monghyr copperplate of Devapāla which includes gold among other kinds of revenues payable to the king ("... the customary taxes, payable as gold and like and all other kinds of revenue ..." Mukherji and Maity 1967: 126). Similarly, the Bhagalpur copperplate of Narayaṇapāladeva also indicates that "taxes and gold" (*kar* and *hiraṇya*) and "rents and gold" (*ibid.*: 176), along with other revenues and dues, were payable to the king by the subjects. The same may be noted in the Nalanda copperplate of Dharmapāla ("... samuchita-dēya-bhā[ga-bhōga]-kara-hiraṇya-adi ...", Bhattacharyya 1935-36: 292) and the Nalanda copperplate of Devapāla (Shastri 1924: 318).

That similar custom of revenue accounting was prevalent in the Varman and Sena kingdoms is amply testified by the Belava copperplate of Bhojavarman ("... with all rājabhoga, kara and hiraṇya tributes", Basak 1913-14b: 43) and the Barrackpur copperplate of Vijayasena ("... all sorts of dues and along with taxes and tributes of gold enjoyed by the king, ...", Majumdar 1929: 66). De (1970: 144-145) has interpreted these references to prove the existence of gold coins. However, because no such coin from the period under review has as yet been discovered and because the copperplates mention only *hiraṇya* or "gold" and not "gold coins", it is logical to agree that *hiraṇya* or "gold" in all these copperplates refer "to a medium of exchange, but not to gold coins".

It is in this light that one needs to read the Silimpur stone inscription. As stated in verse 22 of the inscription, King Jayapāladeva of Kāmrūpa (c. 12th century AD) wanted to present to the Brāhmaṇ named Prahāsa "nine hundred *hemas*" (*hemam nava satani*) (Basak 1915-16: 292). Although Basak (*ibid.*: 295) translated the relevant passage as "nine hundred gold coins", it is logical to accept Mukherjee (1982: 71) who interprets each *hema* (literally, "gold") "to denote a piece of gold metal weighing 80 ratis, which was the standard weight of suvarṇa (gold) coins". It is in the same light that we must interpret the legend of Vallālasena and Vallabhānanda: that *niṣka* was a piece of gold metal equal to 320 *ratis* and *suvarṇa* was the same weighing 80 *ratis*. It is thus possible that *kañcaṇa* (Majumdar 1929: 48) cited in the Deopārā inscription of Vijayasena refers not merely to "gold" as Majumdar (*ibid.*: 54) translates it but actually to gold pieces of the same weight standard as mentioned above. This line of argument makes sense as to why the Pāla, Sena and Varman copperplates refer to *hiraṇya* and *kañcaṇa*. This also explains why the *purāṇas* and the *kārṣāpaṇas* cited in the Pāla inscriptions and the *purāṇa* of the Sena inscriptions were never unearthed: like *kapardaka-purāṇa*, these too were theoretical currencies. However, unlike *kapardaka-purāṇa* that was linked up with cowries, *purāṇa* and *kārṣāpaṇa* were linked with silver. This goes to confirm our observation made earlier that *rūpyaṇi* ("silver coin") cited in the Deopārā inscription of Vijaysena (*ibid.*) referred to silver *purāṇa*.

We may now conclude our examination of Pāla and Sena kingdoms by noting that the media of exchange that was prevalent in these kingdoms were cowries (*kapardaka),* silver and gold. Silver and gold were used both in the forms of dust and bar. That gold was also a medium of exchange in the Varman kingdom is testified by the Belava copperplate of Bhojavarman cited earlier. Since the Varmans maintained close contact with the Pālas and since by the time of their rise the dynasty of the Candras had been extinguished, it is possible to believe that the media of exchange prevalent in their kingdom was similar to that of the Pālas. This view is further substantiated by the fact that the media of exchange of the Senas, who supplanted the Varmans, was not too dissimilar from the Pālas.

For the sceptics one may cite the case of the kingdom of Pagan. Although the Pyus are known to have introduced gold and silver coins for the first time in Southeast Asia – even the silver coins of Arakan issued by its Candra dynasty in the 4th century AD are believed to have been modelled on them – the Pyu practice was not retained by the Paganese kings when they came to power in the mid-11th century AD (Aung 1967: 55, 57). Besides copper, gold and precious stones, the most common medium of exchange was silver. In some cases, even actual barter was resorted to. As Aung (*ibid.*: 57) informs us 1 Kyat of gold was worth 10 Kyat of silver and 1 Kyat of silver was worth 0.5 Kyat of copper – where Kyat was not a unit of value but of weight, being 1/100th part of a viss (approximately 3.6 pounds, *avoirdupois*). It may be important to see this practice of using precious metal as a medium of exchange in the context of increased volume of Pagan's trade from previous centuries and the economic basis of Pagan's power as having been both agriculture and trade (*ibid.*: 55, 57). It may be of interest for the sceptics to note further that even during the French Revolution, Father Sangermano (1969: 214) writes from Burma that the local population used "no coined money, but in their commercial transactions they made use of gold and silver bullion", although there was coinage in Arakan and Tenasserim. Hence, the Burmese were obliged to employ scales in all payments. The use of scales in all commercial transactions should give us a valuable bit of insight into a similar, albeit hypothetical, use of the device in early medieval 'Bengal'.

The Devas and the Candras

Having come to a reasonable conclusion regarding the media of exchange that was prevalent in the Pāla, the Varman and the Sena kingdoms, let us now turn our attention to the kingdoms of the Devas and the Candras. Compared to poor numismatic finds of the former three kingdoms, we are now confronted with abundant evidence of a similar nature from the latter two. The question now is not whether minted currency was at all in circulation in these kingdoms but what information regarding trade we may infer from them.

Numerous silver coins of the 'Bull: Tripartite' type and bearing the Brāhmī legend *Paṭṭikeḍā* inscribed on the obverse were unearthed during excavations at Mainamati (in Comilla district of Bangladesh). Following the arguments placed by Khan (1963: 25), there can remain little doubt that these silver pieces, commonly known as the Paṭṭikeḍā coins, were in circulation during the reign of the Devas. All archaeological and palaeographical indications speak in favour of Khan's argument. So called because the legend *Paṭṭikeḍā* is inscribed on them, these coins are all very thin in appearance and were possibly die-struck. On the obverse, they display a seated and humped bull framed within an inner circle and an outer border of beads, and on the reverse, a tripartite symbol (described as "Tri-ratna" in Khan 1963: 25 and "Triglyph" in Rashid 1975: 47) with two wreaths dangling from the peak of the symbol's two outer projections. Two symbols of what appear to denote the sun and the moon may be seen on top of the tripartite symbol. As on the obverse, the devices on the reverse are also placed within an inner circle and an outer border of beads (Mukherjee 1975-76: 19-20). Peculiarly, no name of issuing monarch is inscribed on them.

Most of the *Paṭṭikeḍā* coins were found in three hoards. One of these, found at Ānandarājā's palace (mound no. 5), contained 63 coins (Ramachandran 1946: 217). The second and the third hoards, recovered from monastery cells at Salban Vihāra (belonging to the Period III, dated to the 8th century AD), contained 52 and 172 coins respectively. The second hoard was made up of coins in three denominations while the third was made up of only coins in the largest denomination (Khan 1963: 25). The coins closely resemble the Arakanese silver coins of the Candras (Aung 1997: Pl. 3-6) and the Harikela (Series I) silver coins in terms of fabric, types and style of execution. It is even possible, as Mukherjee (1981-82: 63) believes, that the Paṭṭikeḍā coins were inspired by the Harikela (Series I) coins.

The earliest literary reference to *Paṭṭikeḍā* may be found in a copy of the *Aṣṭasahasrika Prajñāpāramitā* made in 1015 AD (Cambridge University Library manuscript no. Add. 1643), which contains a miniature painting of Cuṇḍa (the sixteen-armed Buddhist goddess) labelled "*Pattikere Cuṇḍavarabhavane Cuṇḍa*" (Mitra 1971: 244). The name surfaces again in the Mainamati copperplate of the time of Harikāldeva (1220 AD) which records granting of land in favour of a Buddhist monastery built in the city of Paṭṭikerā (Bhattacharyya 1933: 282-287). The name Pateikkaya (obviously a derivative of Paṭṭikeḍā) is to be found in an inscription dated to the Pagan period (1044-1287 AD) which places the kingdom to the west of Pagan (Harvey 1967: 326). Burmese chronicles also recount the story of a princess of Pateikkaya being married to King Alaungsithu (1112-67 AD) (Harvey 1967: 49). As Dinesh Chandra Bhattacharyya (1933: 284) observes, the modern *parganā* of Pāiṭkārā or Pāṭikārā was named after the city of Paṭṭikerā, although the hills are under the jurisdiction of a separate *parganā* named Meherakula. In documents from the 18th century, the *parganā* is referred to either as 'Pātikerā' or 'Patikerā'. All these references do not leave any doubt about the existence of a kingdom called Paṭṭikeḍā from the 11th to the 13th centuries AD. However, as Mukherjee (1975-76: 28) argues, the stratigraphic evidence of the Paṭṭikeḍā coins show that "the name concerned or one of its variants came into existence by the 8th century AD". Since these coins were in circulation in the kingdom of the Devas, we may reasonably assume that the kingdom of the Devas was known as Paṭṭikeḍā (or one of its variants) in the 8th century AD.

The Devas are known to have issued pure gold coins bearing the 'Archer' and the 'Seated Goddess' devices. The only specimen of this type, recovered from a level dated to Period III of Salban Vihāra (cell 13), carries on the obverse the legend Śrī Bhaṅgāla-(mṛ)gā(ṅka) (Rashid 1975: 49-50). Since the appellation *Śrī-Bhaṅg(ā)la-mṛgāṅka* has also been read on the royal seal affixed to the Mainamati copperplate of Ānandadeva and the Devaparvata copperplate of Bhavadeva (Gupta 1979: 145 and Sircar 1951: 83), both Mukherjee (1975-76: 25) and Rashid (1975: 50) have convincingly shown that the Salban Vihāra gold coin was issued by the early Devas. The Devas also issued debased gold coins in thin fabric, bearing the 'Bull' and 'Tripartite' devices. Two specimens of the type (Antiquity nos. 1392 and 1393 of 1964) have been recovered from cell no. 62 of the Salban Vihāra (Period III) (*ibid.*: 57).

The coin bearing the 'Archer' and the 'Seated Goddess' devices indicate that this type was issued when the tradition of minting coins in imitation of the imperial Gupta species had not completely died out in trans-Meghnā region (as in later times when the 'Bull: Tripartite' type of silver coins became prevalent). On the other hand, the device and the fabric of the 'Bull: Tripartite' type of debased gold coins indicate that they were prevalent immediately before the introduction of the 'Bull: Tripartite' type of silver coins but later than the 'Archer: Seated Goddess' type of gold coins. Hence, the gold coins (the 'Archer: Seated Goddess' type and the 'Bull: Tripartite' type) are possibly representatives of the currency system of the kingdom of the Devas prior to the introduction of the silver 'Bull: Tripartite' type of coins. The question is why was it necessary to switch from traditional devices of the imperial Guptas to the devices of the Harikela coins and those of the Arakanese Candras? We will seek to answer this question later in this section.

The 'Bull' and the 'Tripartite' devices can also be seen in a series of silver coins bearing legends such as Lalitākara, Ramyākara, Pradyumnākara, Antākara or Annākara. R. D. Banerji (1920: 85) was the first to draw attention to four coins of this new type held in a private collection in Kolkata and he attributed them to Arakan because of "the recumbent humped bull and the trident-like ornaments" they exhibit. Their subsequent discovery in a large number from Salban Vihāra led Dani (1962: 141-2) to propose that they were issued by the Candra dynasty of East Bengal. Rejecting Dani's and Banerji's propositions, Rashid (1975: 45) has argued that the coins should be ascribed to a hitherto-unknown dynasty of the Akaras in eastern Bengal (8th-9th centuries AD).

Rashid is well justified in his argument since the coins were recovered from the 8th-9th centuries AD levels of the Mainamati excavations. Supporting his claim Mukherjee (1975-76: 23) shows that similarity of the devices seen in the Akara and the Paṭṭikeḍā coins and their recovery from the same site argue well in favour of the reign of the Akara dynasty. He also shows that the palaeographic features of the legend on the Akara coins are more developed than those of the Paṭṭikeḍā coins. The stylistic traits of the devices on the Akara coins also exhibit greater degree of degeneration than the Paṭṭikeḍā coins. Nevertheless, Mukherjee is hesitant in accepting these coins as conclusive proof of the reign of the Akara dynasty and leaves the issue open by proposing that they may have been drifts. Chakrabarti (1992: 82), betraying a literary mind-set, echoes a similar hesitation.

Mukherjee and Chakrabarti need not have been hesitant because had the Akara coins been drifts, they could only have been from Harikela or Arakan (the only regions known to have issued coins with comparable devices). However, none of these regions are known to have been ruled by any Akara dynasty. Hence, we may accept Rashid's proposition as sound. We may tentatively suggest that the Akara dynasty ruled the trans-Meghnā region of Paṭṭikeḍā/Samataṭa in the 9th century AD, sometime after Kāntideva (c. 800-825 AD) when the reign of the Devas ended and before Trailokyacandra (c. 900-929 AD) when the reign of the Candra dynasty of 'Bengal' began. We may also add that the name of the dynasty concerned should perhaps be "Kara" and not "Ākara" as the names Lalitākara (Lalita + Kara), Ramyākara (Ramya + Kara), Pradyumnākara (Pradyumna + Kara) and A(nnā or ntā)kara (A<nnā or ntā> + Kara) indicate.

The currency that circulated during the reign of the Candras is generally known as Harikela silver coins (Series II). These coins have been found mostly in the Belonia subdivision of the South Tripura district of Tripura. A hoard was also found at Sagar Dheba (South Jolaibari) in the Pilak Pathar area of Tripura (Mukherjee 1981-82: 62). Significantly, none of the Harikela (Series II) coins were found in the Mainamati ruins.

Compared to the Harikela coins of the 7th century AD (series I), the coins of Series II are lighter in weight and their flan is thinner and larger. In most cases, the coins of the Series II are struck only with obverse device and the reverse is blank (Mukherjee 1982: 71). The devices and the legend of Series II coins are adopted from the coins of the first series. In most cases, the adopted device is that of the obverse of Series I (the recumbent bull); in some cases, the reverse device of Series I (the tripartite symbol) has also been adopted. The size of most of these coins varies from 4.8 to 5.35 cm in diameter and their weight ranges from 2.3800 gm to about 2.3660 gm. (*ibid.*: 72). These were possibly coins of higher denominations because coins of smaller size and lesser weight have also been found. Identifying the latter as coins of lower denomination Mukherjee (1981-82: 61) shows that their size varies from 2 to 2.9 cm in diameter and their weight generally ranges between 0.8392 gm to 1.9912 gm. These Harikela (Series II) coins may have followed the *purāṇa* weight-standard (i.e., 57.6 grains or 32 ratis) (Mukherjee 1982: 72).

Besides the Harikela coins belonging to Series I and II, Mukherjee (1981-82: 61-62) has also identified an intermediate series of coin (he calls it series IA), which betrays features of transition from Series I to Series II. Most interestingly, coins of Series IA display devices in both obverse and reverse although the fabric is thinner than that of Series I. Mukherjee (*ibid.*) has identified three groups of these coins and has found the minimum size and weight of coins belonging to each group to be 2.7 cm and 3.2611 gm (group 2), 3.1 cm and 5.425 gm (group 1), and 4 cm and 3.5044 gm (group 3). Thier time of minting is uncertain. Since they appeared prior to the Harikela Series II coins, one may assume that these coins were in circulation in the 9th century AD, after the Devas but before the Candras.

The legend of the Harikela coins (Series IA and II) indicates that their area of circulation and regular use must have been Harikela (i.e., approximately the region of Caṭṭagrāma). The palaeographic features of the legend *Harikela* inscribed on these coins are generally more developed than the coins of Series I. For this reason, Mukherjee (1982: 72) suggests that the Harikela (Series II) coins may have continued to circulate at least in parts of Harikela even after the fall of the Candras till the 12th or 13th century AD.

Another type of silver coins has been identified by Mukherjee (1981-82: 67-68) as the Harikela Associated series. These coins show typological, stylistic and metrological similarities with the Harikela coins. Interestingly, they have been found only with the Harikela Series II coins. A few of these bear the 'Bull' and the 'Tripartite' devices and have inscribed on them the legend *(Lā)lagiri*. Some other coins display only the 'Bull' and betray affinity with the Harikela Series II coins. Instead of the legend *Harikela,* these bear various legends such as *Veraka* (along with variants such as *Vereka, Vareka, Vareke* and *Verake), Viraka, Piraka, Virita, Sivagiri, Jayagiri* etc. Still others betray an affinity with the Harikela Series II (lower denomination) coins and display legends such as *Vareka* (or *Vareke*), *Va*(or *Ra*)*r*(i)*ta* and *Api* (?).

It is possible that as the legend *Harikela* refers not to a reigning monarch but a geographical unit, all the legends of the Harikela Associated series also refer to localities and territories. Thus, *Veraka* (along with variants such as *Vereka, Vareka, Vareke* and *Verake)* may actually refer to Vārakamaṇḍala, Varākamaṇḍala and/or Varukamaṇḍala cited in the three Faridpur copperplates of Dharmāditya and Gopacandra or the River Barak in Sylhet region (Bangladesh). Similarly, *Piraka* may be a variant of Peranatana-*viṣaya* mentioned in the Mainamati copperplate of Ānanadadeva (Gupta 1979: 146). *Sivagiri* and *Jayagiri* may have been some hilly tract in the neighbourhood of Caṭṭagrāma, Tripura or Sylhet (as the suffix 'giri' suggests) similar to Rohitagiri cited in the Dhullā copperplate land-grant of Śrīcandra (Sircar 1959a: 135) and *(Lā)lagiri* may have been adjacent to the Lalambi forest in Pascimbhag copperplate of Śrīcandra (Gupta 1967: 102). Hence, we may suggest that the legends inscribed on the coins under review refer to localities where the coins were minted and circulated. The fact that the coins of the Harikela Associated series have been found only with the Harikela coins (Series II) and that the coins of these two series display palaeographical affinity, indicate that the localities where the coins of the Harikela Associated series were minted were all in Harikela. Further, they must have been minted at a time when the Harikela coins (Series II) were in circulation (Mukherjee 1981-82: 68).

Harikela (Series II) coins could have been influenced by external source. The outward appearance of the flan of quite a few coins of the fore-mentioned type resemble thin and large gold coins of the Abbasid Caliph Abu Ahmed Abdallah al-Must'asim Billah (AD 1242-1258), one of which has been recovered from the area of the main *stupa* at Kutila Mura (upper level of Period III, comparable to Period IV of Salban Vihāra). Lalmai-Mainamati has also yielded a broken silver piece belonging to the early Abbasid period, Pāhāḍpur has yielded a thin silver coin of the Abbasid Caliph Harun-ar-Rashid (AD 788) and a set of 12 Abbasid gold coins from a jeweller's shop at Chandpur in greater Comilla region. These findings indicate that 'Bengal' was quite familiar with the Abbasid coinage system. Hence, it is not impossible that the fabric, shape and size of the Harikela (Series II) coins were influenced by the Abbasid coins.

When compared with the numismatic evidences from the Deva and Candra kingdoms, their epigraphic evidences create a completely different impression. This is mostly because there is no reference to medium of exchange in any of them. Unless the medium of exchange was completely separate from revenue accounting, one is confronted with a perplexing situation as to why the records of land-grants should make no direct reference to the complex monetary system that the extensive number of coins discussed above indicate to have existed in the Deva and Candra kingdoms. Let us begin with the Devas. Of their five copperplates so far discovered, only the Devaparvata copperplate of Bhavadeva has been read by Sircar (1983: 744-750) but no English translation of the plate has yet been published. Gupta (1979: 141-148) has produced a tentative reading of the Mainamati copperplate of Ānandadeva. The remaining three copperplates are yet to be deciphered and published. The two publications cited above are silent regarding the medium of exchange of the Deva kingdom.

Of the ten Candra copperplates discovered so far, the abstract and part-translation of the Idilpur copperplate of Śrīcandra has been published (Bhattasali 1923-24a: 189-190; Majumdar 1929: 166-167). Two of Ladahacandra's and one of Govindacandra's copperplates have only been briefly reviewed (Zakariah 1997: 222-225). None of these contain any information regarding monetary system. The incomplete Kedarpur copperplate of Śrīcandra (Bhattasali 1923-24a: 188-192) and the Madanpur plate of the same monarch (Basak 1949-50: 51-58; Sircar 1949-50: 337-339) are also silent about its monetary system. The same is true of Kalyāncandra's copperplate (Dani 1966: 22-45). The only reference to the monetary system in the remaining three copperplates of Śrīcandra, i.e., the Pascimbhag (Chowdhury 1966: 180), the Rāmpāl (Basak 1913-14a: 139) and the Dhullā (Sircar 1959a: 140), is the following stock phrase: "*samasta-rāja-bhōga-kara-hiraṇya-pratyāya-sahitā*" ("with all the income such as taxes and tributes of gold enjoyed by the king", Chowdhury 1966: 187-188). The stock expression of the Candras is reminiscent of the similar stock expression of the Pālas, the Varmans and the Senas. This indicates continued use of gold as a unit of revenue accounting and as a medium of exchange during the reign of the Candras.

A possible answer to the perplexing question as to why the Candra and Deva documents should make no direct reference to the complex monetary system is that the Paṭṭikeḍā, the Harikela (Series IA and II) and the Harikela Associate series coins were not issued by these ruling dynasties. This indication is indeed confirmed by the absence of royal names in the legend of the types of coin mentioned above. As Mukherjee (1982: 73) suggests, "these could have been struck by local guilds, if not by local authorities". If they were indeed minted by local guilds, perhaps the coins may be taken as an indication that formation of indigenous commercial capital was taking place in Harikela.

MEDIEVAL PERIOD

A curious testimony that the maṅgalakāvya corpus provides is the prevalence of *badal bānijya* (barter) in maritime trade during the medieval period. Consider, for example, Kavikaṅkaṇa Mukunda's *Caṇḍīmaṅgala*. Both Dhanapati and his son Śrīpati clearly enumerate the commodities that they carry from 'Bengal' and those that they expect to barter in return from Sri Lanka (Mukunda 1986: 195-196, 231). There is even an elaborate scene describing barter taking place between the Bengali merchant and the Sri Lankan king in Śrīrāy Binod's *Padmā-purāṇa* (Binod 1993: 215-219), Nārāyaṇa Deva's *Padmā-purāṇa* (Deva 1942: 212-218), Bijayagupta's *Padmāpurāṇa* (Bijayagupta 1962: 266-275), Vipradāsa Pipilai's *Manasāvijaya* (Sen 1953: 149) and Tantrabibhūti's *Manasāpurāṇa* (1980: 171-174).

Besides the curious references to barter, literary evidences amply testify that gold and silver coins as well as cowires were used as the medium of exchange in Sultanate Bengal. According to *Tabakāt-i Nāsirī* by Minhāju-s Sirāj, after Ikhtiyār-uddīn Muhammad Bakhtiyār Khaljī overran Nadiīyā in 1204, he "established the seat of his government at Lakhnauti" ... "and struck on the coins" (Minhāju-s Sirāj 1869: 309). A gold coin that has been discovered bearing the name of Muhammad bin Sam (Muhammad Ghuri) is believed to have been one of the coins struck by Muhammad Bakhtiyār Khaljī in 1205 AD. Hence, it is clear that coins began to be struck by Muslim rulers right from the inception of their reign. However, as Tarafdar (1995: 31) observes, it was a commemorative issue and hence had little bearing on the contemporary monetary system.

One learns from *Chu-fan-chī*, composed in the mid-13th century AD by Chau Ju-kua, the people of P'ŏng-k'ié-lo ('Bengal') "use (pieces of) white conch shells ground into shape as money" (Hirth and Rockhill 1965: 97). About a century later, when Ibn Battutā visited eastern Bengal, he noted the rates of local commodities in terms of *dirhāms*, silver *dinārs* and gold *dinārs*. For example, 25 *ratl* of rice (a *ratl* being equal to 14 seers or 28.8 lb. *avoirdupois*) cost 1 silver *dinār*, a *ratl* of *ghee* or sugar cost 4 *dirhāms* while a slave girl cost 1 gold *dinār* (Husain 1953: 234-235). Ibn Battutā used currency denominations of the Islamic world in general to refer to gold and silver currency denominations of the contemporary Bengal Sultanate. As Tarafdar (1995: 38) observes, Ibn Battutā's coins "were obviously identical with the silver and gold coins which were in circulation at the time of Ibn Battutā's visit to Bengal". According to Husain (1953: 234 fn. 3 and 4), "[a] silver *dinār* may be taken as another term for a silver *ṭaṅka*". Similarly, a gold *dinār* may be taken to imply a gold *ṭaṅka*. A gold *ṭaṅka* was equivalent to 10 silver *ṭaṅka* (Yule 1866: 440). Husain (1953: xlix-l) also shows that the "*[d]irhām* was an Egyptian and Syrian coin, not an Indian one". It was equivalent of a *hastkānī* or ⅛ *ṭaṅka*. It must be noted that Ibn Battutā also categorically mentions the use of cowries as a medium of exchange (Gibb 1992: 243 and 267).

Ma-Huan, who visited Pang-ko-la (Vaṅgala or Sultanate Bengal) in 1432 AD, confirms the use of cowries and silver coins called *t'ang-ch'ieh* (*ṭaṅka*).

> The king of the country uses silver to cast a coin named *t'ang-ch'ieh* [the *tanka* according to Giles]; each coin weighs three *ch'ien* [172.68 grains] on our official steelyard; the diameter, [in terms of] our official *ts'un*, is one *ts'un* two *fen* [1.4 inches]; it has lines [or characters] on the reverse; [and] in every purchase and sale they all use this coin for calculating prices in petty transactions. The cowries go by the foreign name of *k'ao-li*; [and] in trading they calculate in units [of this article] (Ma-Huan 1970: 161).

Mills adds in a footnote that in two other manuscripts of Ma-Huan's text, the reading is "they also calculate"; and then he gives alternate reading of the passage as "that is in addition to the *tanka*" (*ibid.*: 161, fn. 8). Fei Sin, who visited 'Bengal' between 1411-14 AD, denies that coins were used as a medium of exchange in trade. "In their very extensive trade", he says, "they use cowrie shells instead of coin". However, he also appears to imply the existence of silver coins because he recorded that the sultan of 'Bengal' gave away "silver money" as gift to the soldiers accompanying the Chinese embassy. The existence of gold coins may also be inferred from his observation on the value of business of the local merchants, which he estimates to be "ten thousand pieces of gold" (Bagchi 1945: 122).

Two more Chinese records contain information on the medium of exchange in 'Bengal'. One of these is *Si yang ch'ao kung tien lu* compiled by Huang Sing-ts'eng in 1520. According to *Si yang ch'ao kung tien lu,* both silver coins called *tangka* (*ṭaṅka*) and cowries were used as a medium of exchange in trade. The official weight of the silver coins was 3/10 of a *tael* (approximately 3.6 drams) and the diameter was 1.2 inches (slightly over 3 centimetres) (*ibid.*: 125). According to the other record called *Shu yu chou tseu lu* (compiled in 1574 by Yen Ts'ong-kien), the prevalent silver coin of the country was *tangka (ṭaṅka),* each of which weighed 2.8 Chinese ounces. However, in markets people use cowries instead of coins (*ibid.*: 131-132).

Tome Pires (early 16th century AD) confirms the use of both silver coins and cowries.

> The silver coinage is called *tanqat.* It weighs half a tael, which is nearly six drams. The coin is worth twenty *calains* [sic. *calaim*?] in Malacca, and seven *cahon* in Bengal. Each *cahon* is worth sixteen *porr*, each pon is worth eighty cowries *(buzeos);* so that a *cahon* is worth one thousand two hundred and eighty cowries, and a *tancat* is worth eight thousand nine hundred and sixty cowries, [at the rate of cowries] four hundred and forty eight to the *calaim* [tin coin] ... In Bengal the cowries are called *cury* (Pires 1967: 93-94).

Pires (*ibid.*: 95) further describes the 'Bengal' cowries as "large, with a yellow stripe in the middle". He noted with an air of confidence that "[c]owries are current coinage ... in all the kingdom of Bengal" (*ibid.*: 94) and "they are valid throughout Bengal and they accept them for a large number of commodities as they would gold" (*ibid.*: 95). A Portuguese official named Dom João de Leyma, who visited 'Bengal' in a trading mission in 1517, records the price of various commodities and slaves in *ṭañgās* (20 chicken cost one *ṭaṅkā* and a male slave, six *ṭaṅkās*) but writes that the coin of the country was sea shells (possibly cowries) (Ray 1988: 124).

Among the indigenous sources, we learn from *Caṇḍīmaṅgala* by Kavikañkaṇa Mukunda that cowries were used for procuring articles of daily necessity such as food. The poet narrates the marketing of a maid-slave named Dubalā, who goes to the market with 50 *kāhaṇs* of cowries and buys a long gourd pumpkin *(lāu),* green pumpkin gourds *(kumḍā),* hundreds of mangoes, oil and numerous other articles (Mukunda 1986: 157-158).

The majority of evidences cited above clearly indicate that cowries as well as silver coins (*ṭaṅkā*, *ṭaṅka*, *tancat* or *ṭañgās*) were used as medium of exchange in Sultanate Bengal. Although Ibn Battutā's testimony appears to indicate the prevalence of gold as well as silver coins as medium of exchange, from Fei Sin we receive the impression that the metallic currencies may have been for ceremonial distribution but not as a currency of trade. We will take up this question again after discussing numismatic evidences.

Going by the evidence offered by Tome Pires, we may believe that the cowries were counted thus: 16 *paṇas* = a *kāhaṇ* = 80 cowries. Although the exact rate of cowries must have varied, generally, a *ṭaṅkā* would fetch eight thousand nine hundred and sixty cowries. Kavikañkaṇa Mukunda's testimony indicates that the cowries were commonly used as a medium of exchange for low-value commodities that the majority of the population would use in daily life.

The testimonies offered by Chau Ju-kua, Ibn Battutā, Ma-Huan, Fei Sin, Huang Sing-ts'eng, Yen Ts'ong-kien, Tome

Pires and Kavikañkaṇa Mukunda may now be examined against the available silver and gold coins that were issued by various sultans of Delhi, their governors, the independent sultans of 'Bengal' and two Hindu kings during the period under review. All these coins listed below in tables 3.4 and 3.5 added together stand at 35 gold, 2248 silver, 11 copper and 1 billon. All these, except about 30 coins of the Deva monarchs, were issued by the sultans of Delhi, their governors and the independent sultans of 'Bengal'. The sheer number far surpasses those of any other period so far discussed. These coins are also significant because they testify to the existence of 22 mint towns from which they were issued, which in turn bear testimony to urbanisation during the period under study.

Among all the coins listed above, only those of Muhammad bin Sam and Nasir al-Din Mahmud declare them as *tankah.* The coins of Jalalal al-Din Radiyah and Ghiyath al-Din Balban bear the legend *al-fiḍḍah* (a term used for referring to silver) while the others bear no legend declaring their denomination (Karim 1960: 5-8). Sultan Mahmud of Ghazni (998-1030 AD) is believed to be the first monarch to have issued a coin bearing the legend *ṭañka* in Sanskrit. The term *ṭañka* denotes "silver of a particular weight". Its Persian derivative is *tankah* and Bengali derivative, currently the name of the currency in 'Bengal', is *ṭākā*.

While Mahmud's *ṭañka* followed the Central Asian weight standard of 140-150 grains, Shams al-Din Iltutmish reformed the existing currency system in Sultanate Delhi by issuing silver coins named *ṭañka* or *tankah* weighing 96 ratis or 172.8 grains (Habibullah 1991: 433-34). The average weight of silver issues prevalent before the Khalji dynasty (1290-1320 AD) is between 170 to 175 grains. Muhammad bin Tughlaq, "the Prince of Moneyers", is known to have issued silver *ṭañka* of 172.8 grains and 175 grains, silver *adlī* of 140 grains and copper *fāls* of 72 grains weight. He also issued billon coins and token currency incopper and brass (Ali 1989: 198, 203, 209-214). Except his gold issues, which have been discussed separately, details of Muhammad bin Tughlaq's silver and copper issues minted in 'Bengal' are not available.

Table 3.4:
Bengal Coins of Delhi Sultans

Sultan	Date	Metal	Find-spot	Mint
Muhammad bin Sam (Muhammad Ghuri)	1205	Gold (2 or more)	Unknown	Gauḍa (?)
Shams al-Din Iltutmish (r. 1210-1236), issued by Governor Daulat Shah	1229	1 (metal unknown)	?	?
Jalalal al-Din Radiyah (r. 1236-1240)	1236-37	Silver (5 or over)	Gauhati hoard, others unknown.	Lakhnauti
Nasir al-Din Mahmud (r. 1246-1266)	1247, 1257, 125(?)	Silver (3 or over)	Gauhati hoard, others unknown	Lakhnauti
Nasir al-Din Mahmud (issued by Governor Ikhtyar al-Din Yuzbak)	1255	Silver (?)	?	?
Ghiyath al-Din Balban (r. 1266-1286)	1266-1274	Silver (5 or over)	Munghyr, Sultanpur, others unknown	Lakhnauti
Ghiyath al-Din Tughlaq (r. 1320-1325), issued by Governor Nasir al-Din Ibrahim)	Undated (before 1325)	Silver (3 or over)	Sonapat hoard, others unknown	?
Muhammad bin Tughlaq (r. 1325-1351)	1326-1334	Gold (4), silver (34), copper (4)	Murshidabad, Mymensingh, Enayetpur, Kalna (1st and 2nd hoards); others unknown	Lakhnauti, Sātgāon, Sonārgāon
Total = Gold: 6 (or more). Silver: 50 (or over). Copper: 4				

Table 3.5:
Coins Issued by the Independent Rulers of Bengal

Dynasty	Sultan	Date	Metal	Find-spot	Mint
	Ali Mardan Khalji	Disappeared	Gold (1)	Unknown	Disappeared
	Ghiyath al-Din Iwad Khalji	616, 617, 619-621 AH	Silver (27 or more)	Unknown	None mentioned
	Mughith al-Din Yuzbak	653 AH	Silver (5 or more)	Unknown	Lakhnauti
Balbani	Rukn al-Din Kaika'us	690-91, 693-98 AH	Silver (16 or more)	Sylhet, Dhaka, other spots unknown	Lakhnauti
Firuz Shahi	Shams al-Din Firuz Shah	701-716, 717-720, 722 AH	Gold (1) silver (67 or more)	Sylhet, Nowgong, Kalighat, Dhaka (Purinda), Mymensingh (Enayetpur), Kalna (hoard), other spots unknown	Lakhnauti, Sonārgāon, Bang (?)
	Jalal al-Din Mahmud	704, 707 or 709 AH	Silver (2)	Dhaka (Purinda), other spots unknown	Lakhnauti
	Shihab al-Din Bughdah Shah	717, 718 AH	Silver (11 or more)	Murshidabad, Nowgong (Rupaibari), other spots unknown	Lakhnauti
	Ghiyath al-Din Bahadur	710, 711, 713, 717, 720-23, 728 AH	Gold (3), silver (73 or more), billon (1)	Mymensingh (Enayetpur), Dhaka, Sylhet (Kastabir Mahalla), Nowgong (Rupaibari), Kalna (2nd hoard), other spots unknown	Lakhnauti, Sonārgāon, Ghiyathpur (near Enayetpur in Mymansingh)

	Fakhr al-Din Mubarak Shah	1338-1349	Gold (1), silver (25 or more)	Sylhet, Dhaka, Khulna, Sylhet (Kastabir Mahalla), Dhaka (Rupganj), other spots unknown	Sonārgāon
	Ikhtyar al-Din Ghazi Shah	1349, 1350, 1352	Silver (?) (4 or more)	Sylhet, Cooch Behar (hoard), other spots unknown	Sonārgāon
	Ala al-Din Ali Shah	741-746 (?) AH	Silver (9 or more)	Murshidabad, Kalna (1st and 2nd hoards), other spots unknown.	Firūzābād (Pāṇḍua)
Ilyas Shahi	Shamas al-Din Ilyas Shah	740 (?), 743, 744, 746, 758, 759-60 (?)	Gold (1), silver (301 or more).	Khulna, Sylhet, Nadiīyā, Bhagalpur, Sylhet (Kastabir Mahalla), Dhaka (Ketun), Khulna, Rupganj hoard, Kalna (1st and 2nd hoards), other spots unknown	Firūzābād, Sonārgāon, Sātgāon, Shahr-i-Naw (Pāṇḍua)
	Sikandar Shah	750-745, 756-792 AH	Gold (3), silver 288 or more)	24-Parganas, Khulna, Dhaka, Sylhet (Kastabir Mahalla), Rupganj, Kalna (1st and 2nd hoards), other spots unknown	Firūzābād, Sātgāon, Shahr-i-Naw, Sonārgāon, Mu'azzamābād (near Sonārgāon), Awwalistān (Kāmrūpa)
	Ghiyath al-Din Azam Shah	788, 790, 795-801, 803, 805, 807, 810-813 AH	Silver (248 or more)	Dhaka, Khulna, Sibsagar, Kāmrūpa, Rupganj, other spots unknown	Firūzābād, Sātgāon, Jannatābād (Lakhnauti), Mu'azzamābād
	Saif al-Din Hamzah Shah	813, 814 AH	Silver (32 or more)	Dhaka, Khulna, Rupganj (hoard), other spots unknown	Firūzābād, Sātgāon, Mu'azzamābād
	Shahid al-Din Bayazid Shah	814-817 AH	Silver (78 or more)	Dhaka, Khulna, Kalna, Rupganj, other spots unknown	Firūzābād, Sātgāon, Mu'azzamābād
	Ala' al-Din Firuz Shah	817 AH	Silver (8 or more)	Rupganj, Dhaka, other spots unknown	Sātgāon, Mu'azzamābād
Rājā Ganeśa	Jalal al-Din Muhammad Shah	818-19, 821-25, 827-28, 834-35 AH	Gold (2), silver (251 or more)	Dhaka, Rupganj, other spots unknown	Firūzābād, Sātgāon, Mu'azzamābād, Fatehābād, Chātgāon (Caṭṭagrāma), Rohtaspūr (Rohtasgarh?), Sonārgāon
	Shamas al-Din Ahmad Shah	836 AH	Silver (4 or more)	Unknown	Not legible
Deva	Danuja Mardana Deva	1339, 1340 śaka	Silver (possibly 24)	Pāṇḍua, Basudevpur (Khulna), Nimgachi (Pabna), Rupganj (hoard), others unknown	Pāṇḍunagara (Pāṇḍua or Firūzābād), Suvarṇagrāma (Sonārgāon) Cātigrām (Caṭṭagrāma)
	Mahendra Deva	1340, 1341 (?) śaka	Silver (possibly 6)	Rupganj (hoard), others unknown	Pāṇḍunagara, Cātigrām
Restored Ilyas Shahi	Nasir al-Din Mahmud Shah	841, 846-848, 851-854, 858-860, 862-864 AH	Gold (2), silver (71 or more)	Unknown	Fatehābād (Faridpur), Mahmūdābād, Khazānah (treasury), Dār al-darb (mint)
	Rukn al-Din Barbak Shah	864, 867, 868, 870, 873, 875, 877, 878 AH	Silver (113 or more), copper (1)	Murshidabad, Sylhet (Bashail), Mahāsthāngarh, other spots unknown	Bārbakābād (Mahisantosh), Muzaffarābād (near Pāṇḍua), Firūzābād, Sātgāon, Jannatābād, Khazānah (treasury), Dār al-ḍarb (mint)
	Shams al-Din Yusuf Shah	880-884 AH	Silver (26 or more)	Mahāsthāngarh, Sylhet (Kankaribag and Bashail), other spots unknown	Khazānah (treasury), Dār al-darb (mint), Sonārgāon (?).
	Jalal al-Din Fath Shah	886-890 AH	Gold (3), silver (17 or more)	Sylhet (Kankaribag), other spots unknown	Khazānah (treasury), Dār al-darb (mint), Fatehābād (Faridpur), Muhammadābād
Abyssinians	Saif al-Din Firuz Shah	892, 893, 895 AH	Silver (10 or more)	Šāotāl Pargana, Sylhet (Rautkhai), other spots unknown	Khazānah, Dār al-darb, Fatehābād, Muhammadābād
	Shams al-Din Muzaffar Shah	896 AH	Gold (4), silver (10 or more)	Unknown	Khazānah (treasury), Fatehābād, Bārbakābād
Husain Shahi	Ala al-Din Husain Shah	899-901, 903-907, 909-910, 912-915, 917, 919, 921-922, 924 AD	Gold (6), silver (223 or more)	Murshidabad, Hill Tippera, Šāotāl Pargana, Mymensingh, Dhaka, Birbhum, Sylhet (Kakaribag), Malda, Rautkhai, Raipura (hoard), other spots unknown	Khazānah (treasury), Dār al-darb (mint), Husaynābād, Chanrābād, Fatehābād, Mu'azzamābād, Muhammadābād

	Nasir al-Din Nusrat Shah	918, 922-928, 930, 934 AH	Gold (1), silver (180 or more), copper (5)	Dhaka, Pabna, Hazaribag, Birbhum, Paighatta, S̃āotāl Pargana, Mymensingh, Pāhāḍpur, Kankaribag, Sonakhira, Raipara (hoard), other spots unknown	Khazānah (treasury), Dār al-darb (mint), Husaynābād, Nusratābād (near Ghoraghat), Khalifatābād (Bagerhat), Fatehābād, Mahmūdābād, Muhammadābād, Bārbakābād
	Ala' al-Din Firuz Shah	938, 939 AH	Silver coins (38 or more)	Dhaka, Birbhum, Raipara (hoard), other spots unknown	Khazānah (treasury), Husaynābād, Fatehābād, Nusratābād
	Ghiyath al-Din Mahmud Shah	933-35, 938-41, 943-44, 945 (?) AH	Gold (2), silver (135 or more), copper (1)	Birbhum, Dhaka, Mymensingh, Sonakhira, Raipara (hoard), other spots unknown	Husaynābād, Nusratābād, Khalifatābād, Fatehābād, Muhammadābād, Khalifatābād (Badarpūr)
Total = Gold: 30. Silver: 2198 (or more). Copper: 7. Billon: 1					

Among all the coins listed in the Table 3.5, only one coin issued by the restored Ilyas Shahi sultan Jalal al-Din Fath Shah (r. 1481-86 AD) and held by the Bangladesh National Museum, bears the legend *sikkah tankah* (Karim 1960: 101). Thus we are left only with the silver coins of Nasir al-Din Mahmud (Delhi sultanate) and Jalal al-Din Fath Shah (Bengal sultanate) to confirm Ma-Huan and Tome Pires regarding the name of the prevalent currency of the Bengal sultanate. This currency in silver called *ṭaṅkā, tankah* or other phonetic variations, "supported by denomination of cowries, not copper – remained as a coinage of commercial transaction in Bengal down to the (...) middle of the 16th century" (Digby 1982a: 99).

The copper and billon issues shown in Table 3.5, unlike the coins of the Delhi sultanate, never became regular denominations in the coinage system of the Bengal Sultanate. Billon coins were issued only by the Firuz Shahi sultan Ghiyath al-Din Bahadur (r. 1322-25), immediately before Muhammad bin Tughlaq's conquest. Faced with Tughlaq's invasion and consequently under financial constraint, Ghiyath al-Din may have been forced to issue the coin as a measure of exigency. Among all the independent sultans of 'Bengal', Rukn al-Din Barbak Shah (restored Ilyas Shahi dynasty, 1459-74 AD) appears to have been the first monarch to issue copper coins (Ahmed 1936: 111-112). They are seen again during the reign of the Husain Shahi dynasty, when two sultans, Nasir al-Din Nusrat Shah (1519-31 AD) and Ghiyath al-Din Mahmud Shah (1532-38 AD), issued coins in copper. Besides copper and billon coins, some half-unit silver coins were issued by the Ilyas Shahi sultan Sikandar Shah and two Husain Shahi sultans, Nasir al-Din Nusrat Shah and Ala' al-Din Firuz Shah. The number of these fractional issues that have been found is extremely small: two half-units of Shah Sikandar, three half-units and four quarter-units of Nasir al-Din Nusrat Shah and one half-unit of Ala' al-Din Firuz Shah. Since the copper and fractional silver coins are more numerous during the Husain Shahi dynasty and since these obviously signify lower denominations, we may justifiably believe that there was an attempt to circulate these coins in order to facilitate transactions of lower value. However, their relatively insignificant presence (only ten fractional silver and 7 copper coins) compared to over 2158 full-unit silver coins (plus the 30 coins of the Deva dynasty) indicates that lower denomination coins were never important in the monetary system of Sultanate Bengal. Not only does it signify that transactions of higher value were carried out almost exclusively with full-unit silver coins, but also confirms almost all the literary sources mentioned earlier that cowry was used for transactions in daily life. Kavikaṅkaṇa Mukunda may be outside the time frame of the present research, but his description may well contain more than a grain of truth as far as transactions of everyday life were concerned.

The gold coins deserve special consideration. According to Habibullah (1948b: 143), these coins were intended for proclamation of sovereignty and ceremonial distribution but not as a currency of trade. For example, both Fakhr al-Din Mubarak Shah and Shams al-Din Muzaffar Shah issued gold coins to commemorate the first year of their reigns. In addition to similar commemorative pieces struck to mark the first year of reign, both Jalal al-Din Fath Shah and Ala al-Din Husain Shah issued gold coins to celebrate the institution of a *Qadam Rasul* (stone slab believed to bear the foot-print of the Prophet) and the victory over Kāmrūpa, Kamta, Jajnagar and Orissa. As already indicated, the gold coin of Muhammad bin Sam was issued to commemorate the Muslim conquest of Gauḍa. Ali Mardan Khalji also issued a gold coin to commemorate his declaration of independence (Tarafdar 1995: 54-55, fn. 41-42).

Tarafdar (*ibid.*: 37-38) has challenged the above-mentioned view by arguing that except for gold coins issued by Ali Mardan Khalji and Muhammad bin Tughlaq, all others fall within the range of 158 to 170 grains and hence may be taken to be following a recurring weight pattern (Table 3.6).

The same recurring pattern may also be noted, to a considerable extent, if their size, design and legends are taken into consideration. Furthermore, Ibn Battutā clearly mentioned the price of various commodities and slaves in terms of gold and silver coins. Hence, Tarafdar (*ibid.*: 37) rightly concludes, "[h]ad each of these [gold] pieces possessed a unique nature represented by its size, weight, design and legends, one would safely argue that they were issues on certain ceremonial occasions so that they only had some commemorative significance". Since such is not the case, but since some of the coins do declare commemorative intention, Tarafdar (*ibid.*: 38) is inclined to believe that "they served the double purpose of exchange at the international commercial level and of signifying memorable events of the times when they were struck". The very fact that gold content of coins issued in the Sultanate Bengal was extremely high (as Table 3.7 shows) is a further indication that these served as a medium of exchange in the international commerce.

Nevertheless, the overwhelming majority of silver coins so far discovered in 'Bengal' must be taken to indicate that it (and not the gold coins) was the dominant coinage in high-value commercial transactions and international trade in Sultanate Bengal.

From Ma-Huan's testimony cited above we learn that "each coin weighs three *ch'ien*" (i.e., 172.68 grains). Hence we may deduce that the silver coinage adhered to the 172.8 grains or 96 *rati* standard in the first half of the 15th century AD. In the early 16th century AD, Tome Pires (cited above) found a silver *tanqat* to have weighed half a tael or nearly six drams. Since 437.5 grains equal 1 ounce or 16 drams, Pires' *tanqat*, weighed 27.34375 grains x 6 = 164.0625 grains. However, the general standard of silver issues is 166 grains although a few weigh 160 grains (Ali 1989: 248). Exceptions to the above were the fractional denominations of half-unit and quarter-unit silver coins. The weight of Ilyas Shah's half-unit silver pieces is 83-84 grains and the average weight of the Husain Shahi half-unit pieces is 80 grains. Nasir al-Din Nusrat Shah even issued quarter unit silver coins with average weight of 40 grains (Tarafdar 1999: 160). Except for gold coins issued by Ali Mardan Khalji and Muhammad bin Tughlaq, all other issues in gold fall within the range of 158 to 170 grains (see Table 3.6).

An important question that needs to be resolved is whether the coins issued during the Muslim rule in 'Bengal' were directly related to trade or to the plundering of Hindu kingdoms. Let us begin with Tarafdar's (1995: 31) observations on the coins issued in the 13th century AD:

> As trade routes, urban centres and centres of industrial production were yet to be properly organised or activised though the linking up of Bengal with the international trade system controlled by the Arab merchants, these coins [of the 13th century] could hardly be expected to serve as a medium of exchange at the commercial level.

This implies that the coins were minted with gold and silver plundered from local rulers and Hindu temples largely as an insignia of royalty. As Eaton (1997: 96) points out,

> ... the sequence of local conquests and bulges in the money supply suggests that Indo-Turkish rulers were driven into Bengal's hinterland, at least in part, by their thirst for uncoined silver. Each new conquest on Bengal's southern, eastern, or northern frontiers was followed by an expansion in the volume of silver coinage in circulation, the victors minting *tankas* from the accumulated silver stocks of defeated Hindu kingdoms.

Table 3.6:
Gold Coins of Sultanate Bengal

Sl. No.	Sultan	Date	Weight	Size
1	Muhammad bin Sam (Muhammad Ghuri)	1205	172.40 gr.	0.91 inch
2	Ali Mardan Khalji	Disappeared	35.00 gr.	0.67 inch
3	Shams al-Din Firuz	Disappeared	170.00 gr.	0.95 inch
4	Ghiyas al-Din Bahadur	728 AH/1327-28 AD	165.00 gr.	No record
5		728 AH	165.00 gr.	0.90 inch
6		728 AH	165.00 gr.	0.90 inch
7	Muhammad bin Tughlaq	734 AH/1333-34 AD	172.00 gr.	No record
8		734 AH	198.30 gr.	0.65 inch
9		734 AH	198.60 gr.	0.70 inch
10		735 AH/1334-35 AD	198.30 gr.	0.65 inch
11	Fakhr al-Din Mubarak Shah	739 AH/1338-39	168.82 gr.	0.875 inch
12	Shams al-Din Ilyas Shah	Disappeared	166.00 gr.	0.94 inch
13	Sikandar Shah	Obliterated	158.00 gr.	0.70 inch
14		Obliterated	No record	No record
15		Disappeared	167.00 gr.	No record
16	Jalal al-Din Muhammad Shah	?	168.00 gr.	1.40 inches
17		Illegible	160.00 gr.	0.95 inch
18	Nasir al-Din Mahmud Shah	Disappeared	166.00 gr.	0.85 inch
19		849 AH/1445-46 AD	159.00 gr.	0.70 inch
20	Jalal al-Din Fath Shah	886 AH/1481-82	163.32 gr.	0.851 inch
21		887 AH/1482-83	160.00 gr.	0.82 inch
22		890 AH/1485-86	No record	No record
23	Shams al-Din Muzaffar Shah	896 AH/1490-91 AD	No record	No record
24		896 AH	No record	No record
25		896 AH	162.50 gr.	1.04 inches
26		896 AH	No record	No record
27	Ala al-Din Husain Shah	899 AH/1493-94	176.4 gr.	1.05 inches
28		899 AH	163.50 gr.	0.97 inch
29		905 AH/1499-1500 AD	162.00 gr.	No record
30		907 AH/1501-02 AD	164.33 gr.	No record
31		907 AH1501-02 AD	164.50 gr.	0.85 inch
32		919 AH/1503-04 AD	159.00 gr.	0.85 inch

33	Nasir al-Din Nusrat Shah	922 AH/1516-17 AD	163.40 gr.	0.601 inch
34	Ghiyas al-Din Mahmud Shah	Disappeared	No record	No record
35		Disappeared	No record	No record

Table: 3.7:
Sample Gold-content of Coins of Sultanate Bengal
Held by the Bangladesh National Museum

Sl. No.	Sultan	Date	Mint	Weight	Gold content
1	Fakhr al-Din Mubarak	737 AH	Sonārgāon?	168.82 gr.	96.58% - 97.49%
2	Jalal al-Din Fath	886 AH	Fatehābād	163.32 gr.	100%
3	Shams al-Din Muzaffar	896 AH	Khazānah	162.50 gr.	100%
4	Nasir al-Din Nusrat	922 AH	Disappeared	163.40 gr.	100%
5	Ghiyath al-Din Mahmud	Disappeared	Disappeared	165.07 gr.	100%

Table: 3.8:
Silver Coins of the Sultans of Bengal

Dynasty	Sultan	Reign	Years	Coins	Coins/Year
	Ghiyath al-Din Iwad Khalji	1213-1227	14	27	1.9
	Mughith al-Din Yuzbak	1255-1257	2	5	2.5
Balbani	Rukn al-Din Kaika'us	1291-1300	9	16	1.78
Firuz Shahi	Shams al-Din Firuz Shah	1301-1322	21	67	3.12
	Jalal al-Din Mahmud	c. 1304-1309	5	2	0.4
	Shihab al-Din Bughdah Shah	1317-1318	1	11	11
	Ghiyath al-Din Bahadur	1310-1312; 1322-1325	6	73	12.17
(Sonārgāon)	Fakhr al-Din Mubarak Shah	1338-1349	11	25	
	Ikhtyar al-Din Ghazi Shah	1339-1352	13	(?) 4	
(Lakhnauti)	'Ala al-Din 'Ali Shah	1341-1342	1	9	
Ilyas Shahi	Shams al-Din Ilyas Shah	1342-1357	15	301	20.07
	Sikandar Shah	1357-1389	32	288	9
	Ghiyath al-Din Azam Shah	1389-1410	21	248	11.80
	Saif al-Din Hamzah Shah	1410-1411	1	32	32
	Shahid al-Din Bayazid Shah	1411-1414	3	78	26
	'Ala al-Din Firuz Shah	1414	<1	8	
Rājā Ganeśa	Jalal al-Din Muhammad Shah	1415-1432	17	251	14.76
	Shams al-Din Ahmad Shah	1432-1433	1	4	
Restored Ilyas Shahi	Nasir al-Din Mahmud Shah	1433-1459	26	71	2.73
	Rukn al-Din Barbak Shah	1459-1474	15	113	7.53
	Shams al-Din Yusuf Shah	1474-1481	7	26	3.71
	Jalal al-Din Fath Shah	1481-1486	5	17	3.4
Abyssinians	Saif al-Din Firuz Shah	1486-1490	4	10	2.5
	Shams al-Din Muzaffar Shah	1490-1493	3	10	3.33
Husain Shahi	Ala al-Din Husain Shah	1493-1519	26	223	8.57
	Nasir al-Din Nusrat Shah	1519-1532	13	180	13.84
	Ala' al-Din Firuz Shah	1532	<1	38	
	Ghiyath al-Din Mahmud Shah	1532-1538	6	135	22.5

The "bulges" that Eaton refers to may be illustrated with the help of Table 3.8 given above.

In support of Eaton's observations, one may easily point to the re-conquest of Lakhnor in Birbhum from Viṣṇu of Jajnagar by Ghiyath al-Din Iwad Khalji (1213-1227 AD) and extension of his territory up to the bank of the Dāmodar. Consequently, says Minhāj, "elephants and much treasures fell into his hands" (Qanungo 1948a: 22). The rulers of Bang, Kāmrūpa and Tirhut are also believed to have paid him tributes. Even Sultan Kaikaus's issues minted towards the end of the 13th century AD may be credited to the conquest of southeastern Bengal, which led to a substantial inflow of bullion.

The relation between plundering Hindu kingdoms and issuing coins with bullion inflow appears to have continued even in the 14th century AD, when Sultan Fakhr al-Din Mubarak Shah (1338-49 AD) conquered Sonārgāon. The voluminous production of Shamas al-Din Ilyas Shah (1342-1357 AD), who minted over 300, coins must also have been connected with his conquest of Tirhut and Kāmrūpa and raids to Kathmandu and Orissa (Roy 1948: 103-110). Similar relations must have existed between Sultan Sikandar's re-conquest of Kāmrūpa in 1358 AD and minting over 288 coins; Jalal al-Din Muhammad's re-conquest of eastern Bengal in 1420 AD and minting of over 251 coins; and Sultan Ala al-Din Husain Shah's re-conquest of Kāmrūpa in 1494 AD and minting of over 223 coins.

However, looting was not the only source of gold and silver for minting the coins. Consider for example the inscription on the margin of a coin issued by Sultan Rukn al-Din Kaikaus which specifically declares "[t]his silver (coin was) struck at (Hazrat) Lakhnauti from (?) the land-tax of Banga in the year 690" (Karim 1960: 25). A similar inscription declaring the minting of coins from land-tax may also be seen in a coin issued by Sultan Jalal al-Din Mahmud in 709 or 707 AH (Karim 1960: 30). Consider also that Ghiyath al-Din Azam Shah (1389-1410 AD), who, during his 21 years of reign, issued over 248 silver coins but is not known to have engaged in any significant act of plundering. Similarly, Rukn al-Din Barbak Shah, who issued over 113 coins, annexed Bakerganj, and re-conquered the cis-Karatoyā region from the king of Kāmrūpa, does not appear to have had his coffers filled with loot. Nasir al-Din Nusrat Shah, who issued over 180 coins and annexed Tirhut; was more preoccupied with Babur's military engagements against the Afghans. Ghiyath al-Din Mahmud Shah, who issued over 135 coins, lost territories instead of looting others in his struggle against the wily Sher Khan.

Not denying the impact of local conquests on 'bulges' in the money supply in Sultanate Bengal, we must also remember that such an equation was no exception for pre-modern societies. And if indeed any territorial conquest is linked with looting, then no king on this earth, including the 'much-venerated' Guptas, can be absolved for such atrocities. Kingship tacitly recognises war and war tacitly recognises looting; even today in Iraq when kingships are supposedly institutions of the past. What is significant is that the sultans of 'Bengal', instead of hoarding the looted gold, as the Senas, the Varmans and the Pālas, circulated it as currency. It certainly helped in paying for the sultan's army and buying the luxury commodities for the nobles, but it also benefited trade and commerce. That the 'Bengal' sultans committed themselves to "dethesaurization" or releasing of treasure from hoards into monetary circulation and that the coinage closely adhere to the 172.8 grains or 96 *rati* standard, imply the existence of a well-organised monetary system linked to international trade. As Eaton (1997: 96) himself acknowledges, "substantial quantities of treasure were imported in exchange for goods locally manufactured for export". Fei Sin's testimony should leave no lingering doubt regarding the matter.

****

We may now sum up our findings in this chapter by making the following observations. Among all the media of exchange that prevailed in 'Bengal' during the time frame of this research, cowries appear to have persisted right from the Maurya era when it was introduced in 'Bengal' for the first time. Commodity money may have prevailed only in the pre-Maurya era. We hear of, or may surmise the prevalence of barter in the early historic period and the medieval period. It is not unlikely that barter persisted, albeit in varying degree of puissance, during the entire period of this research.

We may tentatively suggest that bullion money of fixed weight and standard such as the gold *niṣka* may have been introduced for the first time in the second half of the 4th century BC. We have conclusive evidence of the use of similar medium of exchange (bullion money) in the Kuṣāṇa era, when gold money (*caltis*) was used as a regular currency in trade-related activities in Suhma or southern Rāḍha and Vaṅga. Bullion money reappeared in the 6th century AD, during the reign of Gopacandra, when silver dust (*cūrṇī*) was used as a medium of exchange in at least some parts of Vaṅga. From then, bullion money must have persisted till the end of the early medieval period since we have conclusive proof of the use of silver dust in some parts of the kingdom of Gauḍa during Śaśāṅka's reign (7th century AD) and the use of silver and gold both as dust and bar in the Pāla, Sena, Varman and Candra kingdoms.

Coins appear to have been introduced for the first time in 'Bengal' during the Maurya era as punch-marked issues. Although silver punch-marked coins were most widely used, copper and billon issues were prevalent as well. The primary areas of circulation of the punch-marked coins were Puṇḍravardhana, Rāḍha, Suhma, and south-westernmost part of Vaṅga. Cast copper coins were known during the Maurya and the post-Maurya era. In the latter era, gold and copper coins issued by the Kuṣāṇa Empire (that entered by way of trade) as well as those issued by the Kharoshṭī-using rulers circulated in Suhma or southern Rāḍha and Vaṅga. The use of gold coins continued through the late historic and medieval periods. Among these, the gold content of the post-Gupta coins varied considerably. The prevalence of minted silver coins was seen in 'Bengal' under the Guptas, Sultanate Bengal and Samataṭa (almost continuously from the 7th to the 11th centuries AD).

All the coins discussed above were issued by ruling authorities except in two particular instances when guilds of merchants issued them. These were during the reign of the Mauryas and the reign of the Khaḍgas, the Devas and the Candra.

Four
Ships and Shipbuilding

Having ascertained the ports, the commodities and the medium of exchange, it is now necessary to enquire into the sea-going means of transportation that would be indispensable for maritime trade to function. It is often overlooked that "[i]n any pre-industrial society, from the upper Palaeolithic to the nineteenth century AD, a boat or a ship was the largest and most complex machine produced" (Muckelroy 1978: 3). Used since prehistoric times – and it continues to be used today – ships evolved from a simple form using a pole, oar or paddle, to more advanced form using sails and engines. What types of vessels were engaged in the maritime trade of early 'Bengal'? Which of these were indigenous crafts? What level of proficiency did Bengali shipwrights attain? These questions are of importance for this study because types of ships, their sailing capabilities and source of their energy required for motion would determine the feasibility of voyages, which would in turn influence maritime trade. Furthermore, as Ray (1998: 162-163) reminds us, "[a]n analysis of shipbuilding technology .. provides an understanding of the basic framework within which maritime trade network operated ...". We also need to bear in mind that the level of development of shipbuilding technology could influence to a considerable extent a community's or a nation's level of participation in the international trade.

Before these questions are examined, it is important to set the parameters of this study regarding ships and shipbuilding. If, as the Oxford English Dictionary insists, a ship is the generic name for "any large sea-going vessel", it follows that 'shipbuilding' is the process of construction of a ship. It may be added that contrary to the feminist pronoun which stands for the term, a ship was indeed macho for it sported a masculine pronoun prior to the 16th century AD. A distinction is often made with a related term, 'boat', which usually denotes a small vessel. However, as Greenhill reminds us, the use of the term ship or boat "depends so much on what people thought at the place and time" (Greenhill and Morrison 1995: 9). He adds with a bit of humour "[a] ship is what in a particular group at a particular time people called a ship. A boat is what they called a boat" (*ibid.*). For the purpose of this study, however, we shall limit ourselves to ships that sailed on seas and estuarine rivers where the ports were situated, and used non-mechanical (i.e., manual or natural) energy for their motion.

Material evidence of shipwreck from the period under review is extremely scanty. Recent underwater explorations conducted at Dwarka, Bet Dwarka and Somnath by the National Institute of Oceanography (Goa, India) have yielded a large number of stone anchors. These anchors may not be from a time "earlier than the historical period but not later than the 14th century AD" (Gaur *et al.* 2005: 165) and indicate "that different type and origin of boats visited Dwarka in the past" (*ibid.*: 175). The institute has also located a wreckage of a 17th century Portuguese ship in Goa waters. However, "not a single piece of wood could be traced" from this wreck (*ibid.*: 170). Another partially exposed wreckage, found at Poompuhar near the cost of Tamil Nadu, is of an 18th century British ship (*ibid.*). Unfortunately, none of these evidences are directly relevant for this study.

The dismal condition for research, accentuated by sparse evidence obtainable from marine archaeology, can nevertheless be overcome if we accept literary evidence as one of our primary sources and enhance these with epigraphic, numismatic and iconographic evidences (paintings, drawings, terracotta and stone reliefs etc.) wherever available. In our attempt to identify the types of indigenous vessels that were engaged in the maritime trade of early 'Bengal', we will depend primarily on ethnographic evidence of indigenous sea-going vessels, which are still in use in contemporary Bangladesh and West Bengal, India and match these with literary evidence. The use of ethnographic evidence can be well justified on the ground that "each boat was made for a utilitarian purpose and the nature of the environment in which they worked has not changed appreciably in the last five thousand years" (Greenhill and Morrison 1995: 17). In attempting to identify indigenous crafts, we will follow the suggestion made by Greenhill and Morrison (*ibid.*: 20) that development of boats is "conditioned by the geography of the local waters, climate, purposes for which the boat was needed, availability of materials for their construction, tradition of craftsmanship which grew up among the boat-builders and the general state and nature of the culture of the people building them".

Avoiding all attempts to arrive at the "origin" of shipbuilding tradition, we will simply follow the utilitarian principle that "[b]oats were developed when there was a need for them, and were almost invariably built for basic utilitarian requirements: they were either necessary, beneficial, essential or important to help people live" (*ibid.*: 15). At the end of the chapter, we will attempt to reach a definite conclusion regarding the types of vessels that were engaged in maritime trade and the tradition of shipbuilding in 'Bengal' during the period under study. (All information on contemporary sea-going vessels discussed below, unless otherwise indicated, has been obtained from field level investigation conducted by the author at Lakṣmīpur, Caṭṭagrāma, Cox's Bazar, Maheśkhālī and Sandwīp in Bangladesh in 2000 and 2001, and Bālāgarh and Dighā in West Bengal, in 2002.)

PROTOHISTORIC PREAMBLE

In a riverine delta like 'Bengal', utilitarian requirement of boats is almost an unquestioned corollary of living. Hence, one would expect boats even in early human settlements. This is proved by the discovery of three terracotta objects from Black and Red Ware deposit at the protohistoric site of Pāṇḍurājārdhibi in Bardhamān. Dated to the 2nd millennium BC, the terracotta objects (two black and one red) have been identified by Asok Datta (1995: 223) as the earliest models of boats in the eastern part of South Asia. One of the black models is broken and the other measures 5 x 2.5 cm. The red model, which is also broken at the centre, measures 6.3 x 5.2 cm. The black models are flat-bottomed and rectangular in shape (with corners rounded). This type of boats is still used in various parts of Medinīpur, specially in Contai sub-division for ferrying passengers across rivulets and canals. The red model is also flat-bottomed but the outer part of the distant end is convex like the prow of riverine crafts. The hull-shape indicates that this too was a riverine craft. As riverine crafts, these models say little regarding our query on maritime crafts but are nevertheless important because they prove that by the 2nd millennium BC boat-building technique had certainly developed in Rāḍha and possibly in the whole of 'Bengal'.

Since boats were being built in Rāḍha in the 2nd millennium BC, we may safely assume that the people of the seacoast would also have developed boats but their geographical condition would necessarily impel them to make sea-going vessels. The purpose for which their boats were built could almost certainly have been related to fishing and trading. Seven Neolithic-Chalcolithic sites discovered in coastal West Bengal near Tamluk (along the lower course of the Rūpnārāyaṇ) that have revealed bone tools, specially the harpoon and fish hooks (see Table 1.1 in Chapter One), testify to our assertion regarding the existence of seafaring communities in coastal 'Bengal'.

There should be little reason to suspect the capabilities of the people living in coastal 'Bengal' since archaeological records suggest that even before 40,000 BC, the proto-Australoid people had sailed from Southeast Asia to Australia (Mulvaney 1975). This achievement is significant in our research because Ray (1994: 32-36) has shown through linguistic analysis that the Austric-speaking proto-Australoids were one of the earliest settlers in 'Bengal' and their descendants, the Muṇḍās and the Sāõtāls, still live in pockets of Bangladesh and West Bengal. Ray further argues through anthropological and linguistic study, that the Austric-speaking peoples of the coastal regions and islands had maritime contact with the peoples of Melanesia, Polynesia and elsewhere.

> [F]or the purposes of trade and commerce a kind of long canoe (*ḍoṅgā* – also an Austric word) and big boats were constructed, together with the arrangement of long pieces of tree trunks in the form of rafts. It is still customary for small boats and other vessels constructed from tree trunks to ply the waterways in great numbers in lower, east and south Bengal, and in such crafts the Austric-speaking people plied the waterways of river and sea, developing their wide maritime trade (*ibid.*: 40).

The *ḍoṅgā* that Ray refers to is still seen in Bangladesh, used by farmers to transport themselves across flooded areas (Fig. 4.1). It is a flat-sheered and bulb-shaped dugout made out of palmyra palm, the trunk end of which is sealed with mud or the palm's soft interior. In Noakhali and Caṭṭagrāma regions of Bangladesh, dugouts or logboats made not out of palmyra but of sturdier trees sailed across the open sea to interior villages even in the mid-20th century (Greenhill 1971: 111-113). As Greenhill and Morrison (1995: 102) assure us, "[a] well-made logboat from a small log can be efficient, light and sea-worthy".

Fig. 4.1 A donga from Kushtia

Availability of suitable trees necessary for construction of boats in deltaic 'Bengal' and its neighbourhood obviously posit the logboat as one of the earliest prototypes in the history of traditional boat-building. "The logboat is made by hollowing out a log and thus producing a basic boat structure, that is, a watertight and more or less boat shape which increases its power to carry burdens by an amount equal to the weight of wood cut out" (*ibid.*: 75). Greenhill and Morrison (*ibid.*) also point out, with primitive tools, it was much easier to hollow out a log than to join them together in order to construct a watertight plank-built boat. It was only with the availability of improved tools and skills that planks were added to widen and deepen logboats, and thus evolved the *saraṁgā*.

The *saraṁgā*, sometimes is as long as 18-21 m, is a sea-going vessel from Barisal and Khulna region that is used for cargo-carrying and fishing. It is fitted with a light mast stepped at the bow and a square sail. A *saraṁgā* is made by scooping out a single tree with fire and adzes till the shell was only about 2.5 to 3.75 cm thick. The ends are left solid but are rounded and tapered. It is then expanded by softening the sides with fire and forcing them apart. Consequently, the dugout acquires a gently curved sheer and the ends rise to form low overhangs. After expansion, the shell is fitted with solid floor timbers so as to help retain its shape. The sides are then extended with tiers of plank (usually one, sometimes two or more on each side). The seam between the planks and the dugout is carefully caulked with old rope and then sealed with grey mud, over-laid successively with strips of palm leaves, tightly bunched coarse grass and split bamboo strips. The planks, with caulking in place, are then lashed with split bamboo, which passes through holes drilled in the gunwale and the planks. Finally, the holes are plugged and the bamboo stitching jammed with old rope.

We do not know when the *saraṁgā* evolved – nor is it our purpose to determine the date of its origin. What interests us at this point is that the stone tools found at the Neolithic-Chalcolithic sites of the coastal regions of West Bengal include polished Neolithic celts of triangular and sub-triangular shapes and axes. These may be considered as improved tools and may be taken to be indicative of the availability of improved skills which would have been necessary for planks to be added to logboats for construction of the *saraṁgā* type of boat. Hence, we believe that plank-extended dugouts like *saraṁgā* plied along the coast of 'Bengal' during the Neolithic-Chalcolithic period.

With these definite historical benchmarks as our points of reference, we may now venture to identify Vijaya's ship, which, as we observed in Chapter One, is the earliest literary reference to maritime activities in 'Bengal'.

EARLY HISTORIC PERIOD

If the account of Bhima's subjugation of the eastern kingdoms as narrated in the Mahābhārata (Sabhā Parva, Section XXIX; Ganguli 1990: 61-62) is any reliable indication of the people living in 'Bengal' in the early historic period, we may safely believe that the subjects of "the kings that dwelt on the sea-shore" (possibly south of Suhma) and "the Mlechchha kings dwelling in the marshy regions on the seacoast" (possibly south of Vaṅga) were seafaring people because geographical conditions would require them to be so. Proximity to the sea suggests that maritime activities were not only necessary but also essential for life.

From the time of Bhima's subjugation of the eastern kingdoms to that of Asoka's sending of the Bodhi Tree to Sri Lanka, shipbuilding technology in 'Bengal' appears to have had developed considerably. As the transportation of the Bodhi-tree to Sri Lanka indicates, by the 3rd century BC sea-going ships were sailing from Tāmrlipti (*Mahāvaṁśa,* XIX, 1-8, Geiger 1986: 128-129). Even the *Ch'ien Han-shu* (1st century AD), notwithstanding its tone of condescending civility a typical of a race that considers itself 'civilized', notes that members of the Chinese mission were "taken to their destinations in the trading ships of barbarians" (Colless 1980: 164). Despite the fact that "the trading ships of barbarians" do not necessarily indicate only those of Huang-chih (Gaṅgābandar) but all the countries that the Chinese mission visited, one may nevertheless read the implied indication that trading ships were definitely being operated in Gaṅgābandar. Unfortunately, we have neither material evidence nor detailed descriptions in literary sources to arrive at a definitive image of the maritime vessels referred to in the *Mahāvaṁśa* and the *Ch'ien Han-shu.*

This, however, is not to claim that visual representation of water-borne vessels is completely absent. We encounter quite a few representations of these in the Maurya punch-marked copper coins reported from Chandraketugarh and now held at the State Archaeological Museum, West Bengal and Asutosh Museum of Indian Art, Kolkata (*Indian Archaeology – A Review* 1960-61: 70; 1961-62: 107; 1962-63: 46 and 1966-67: 48). One of the coins shows a vessel, the aft section of which is molded like a dolphin and the upper tip of the bow resembles a dolphin's snout. Furthermore, as Gourisankar De (2001: 147) points out, single-decked water-borne vessels may be seen on a type of punch-marked billon coins (2nd century BC-1st century AD) found at Chandraketugarh. Further examples of water-borne vessels on punch-marked silver coins, all dating from the 2nd century BC to the 1st century AD, are provided by two specimens found at Kotasur, in Birbhum district, West Bengal (*Indian Archaeology – A Review* 1987-88: 111) and more than ten specimens found at Wārī-Baṭeśwar (Fig. 4.2). However, all these representations of water-borne vessels, judging by the hull shape and absence of masts and steering oar, cannot be considered anything more than small riverine crafts. Leaving these aside, we may investigate into other sources that will, hopefully, lead us to a clear perception of maritime vessels that sailed to and from the ports of 'Bengal'.

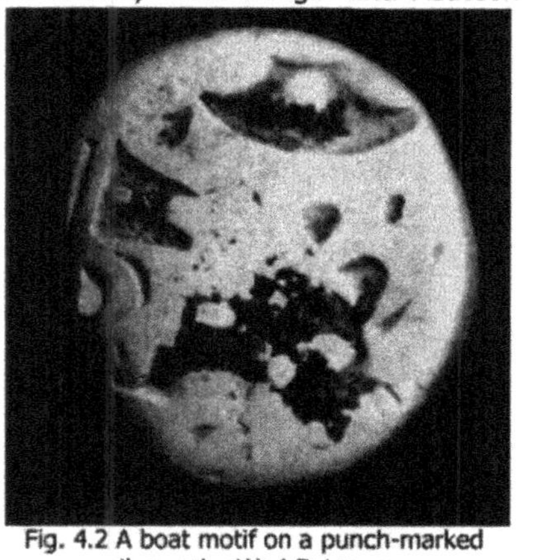

Fig. 4.2 A boat motif on a punch-marked silver coin, Wari-Bateswar

Plank-extended Dugout

According to the *Mahāvaṁśa,* cited earlier in Chapter One, King Siṁhavāhu had Vijaya's head shaven, along with his followers, and "put them on a ship and sent them forth upon the sea" (Chapter VI 42-43; Geiger 1986: 51-54). The narrative goes on to describe that the wives and children of the condemned men were put aboard two separate ships. If the account has any credence, then it has to be acknowledged that approximately in the 5th century BC, the people of Ladha (=Rāḍha) or its immediate vicinity were capable of constructing and voyaging in ships large enough to accommodate seven hundred men. Fa-Hien adds a few more details. King Siṁhavāhu, he says, "prepared two large ships (boats) in which he stored much provision (cured rice or other grain)" (Beal 1906: 238). Significantly, the text gives no impression that this was a maiden maritime voyage but more significantly, the condemned men were put on a voyage which, to King Siṁhavāhu and his subjects, was as good as being put to death. Although Schlingloff (1988: 197) believes that stereotyped numbers such as 500 or 700 often encountered in South Asian narratives are "definitely within the realm of possibility", we may safely discount them as fanciful imagination but read the underlying implication that Siṁhavāhu's vessels were indeed large crafts, capable of carrying considerable numbers of passengers.

Another sea voyage recorded in the *Mahāvaṁśa* (and referred to in Chapter One), is that of Bhaddakaccānā (daughter of Sakka Paṇḍu) with thirty-two women-friends. Sakka Paṇḍu "launched the ship upon the Ganges, saying: 'Whosoever can, let him take my daughter'. And they could not overtake her, but the ship fared swiftly thence" (Chapter VIII, Verses 18-24; Geiger 1986: 63-64). This incident, which took place after Vijaya's landing and was completed within two days, is overlaid with obvious miraculous embellishment. Discounting the miracles, or better still, leaving them aside for the devotees, points to be noted are that the number of passengers is only thirty-three and the ship is said to have fared swiftly. Although the *Mahāvaṁśa* describes a few more maritime voyages, it is silent about the shape, class or any detail of the vessels except hinting at their size by informing us that they carried a large number of passengers. All these references help us to deduce that in the 5th century BC, there existed large ships in Rāḍha capable of making long-distance maritime voyages.

A wall painting in Ajanta cave XVII (6th century AD) was formerly identified with the landing and coronation of Vijaya in Ceylon by several authors of the 19th century such as Fergusson and Burgess (1880) and Griffiths (1896: 38). Later, some scholars such as Mookerji (1957: 29-31), Schlingloff (1988: 197) and others followed Griffiths and echoed his view. The representation shows three vessels. All these vessels, carrying horse-and elephant-riders, show a *makara*-shaped stem. Two of them are shown with two oars each, one of which is a rowing-oar and the other is a steering-oar. Even ribs can be discerned in two vessels. The plank lines on the hull have not been produced, because – as Schlingloff (*ibid.*) believes – the vessels were painted. A decorated border is seen running along the rim. None of the vessels shows any mast. Even if one is prepared to discount the horses and the elephants as heroic exaggerations are usually added to tales of glory and adventure, and also that Vijaya was supposed to have landed in one and not three vessels, one cannot overlook the bowl shape of the vessels. More significantly, thwarts, beams and deck-planking are absent; neither the stern nor the stem is raised, even the gunwale is not curved, as one would expect from a sea-going vessel and as another Ajantā painting shows (Cave II, dated 525-650 AD).

After a careful examination of the narrative description of the *Mahāvaṁśa* and Siṁhala Avadāna with the painting of Ajanta, there is no doubt left that the Ajanta artist had in view the Siṁhala Avadāna only. Therefore it is pointless to look for Vijaya's vessel in the fore-mentioned Ajanta painting. On the other hand, ethnographic and archaeological evidences lead us to believe that Vijaya and Bhaddakaccānā's ships were indeed extended logboats or dugouts such as the *saraṁgā*. Their sea-worthiness has been proved. Further, an 18.29-21.34 m long *saraṁgā* could be described as a large boat and could carry over 50 people.

Reed Boat

Ichapur, one of the seven Neolithic-Chalcolithic sites referred to earlier, has revealed a burnished black ware sherd incised with a boat (now held at the Tāmralipta Museum and Research Centre, Tamluk). This has aroused considerable interest. According to Dasgupta (1975: 4-5), the boat was made of reeds and the mast, of a tree trunk. Dasgupta's identification is acceptable if one goes by the hull-shape which may be taken to be made out of bundles of papyrus stalks, reeds or even bamboos held together by firm vertical ties (hence the vertical lines on the drawing of the boat).

At its face value, Dasgupta's claim is not insignificant because we learn from Pliny (23-79 AD) that reed boats used to ply from Prasii to the island of Sri Lanka. He reports in his *Natural History* (VI. 24. 82), that

> The island in former days, when the voyage to it was made with vessels constructed of papyrus and rigged after the manner of the vessels of the Nile, was thought to be twenty days' sail from the country of Prasii, ... (McCrindle 1979: 103).

Pliny's 'vessels of the Nile', Hornell (1970: 229, 49) informs us, were bipod-masted reed canoes constructed of bundles of papyrus stalks and were possibly used in the early dynastic times in Egypt for fetching timber from Phoenicia. The *Natural History* was composed in 77 AD but because Pliny appears to have acquired his information from a source dated to the 3rd century BC (i.e., Eratosthenes, the President of the Alexandrian Library from 240 to 196 BC), it may be assumed that vessels made of reed, which used rigging similar to that used on the Nile, plied between Sri Lanka and 'Bengal' in the 3rd century BC. Hence, the boat incised on the Ichapur sherd may actually represent one of these vessels.

However, Dasgupta's identification of the Ichapur boat is questionable on technical grounds. As Hornell (*ibid.*: 49) points out, because thwarts and deck beams were absent in reed boats, we must assume that the mast must have been secured to reed bundles at the sides. Hence, the mast of a reed boat "must be made of two units, either in the form of a straddle-legged sheer mast or of two lateral and vertical poles extending a rectangular sail, as used by canoes on Chilka

Lake in India" (*ibid.*). Neither of these is seen in the drawing. Furthermore, during field-level investigation conducted by the author along the Dighā coast and the Caṭṭagrāma-Cox's Bazar coast and offshore islands, it was found that reed boats are not used in the entire belt; nor has any mariner or shipwright even heard of such boats being used anywhere along the coast of Bangladesh and West Bengal. Furthermore, as Paris (1951: 296) informs us, "there is no trace today along the coasts of India, Ceylon or Sumatra of papyrus boats rigged like those of the Nile".

Even if the boat on the Ichapur sherd were not made of reeds, it would appear, following Pliny that reed boats did ply from Prasii to Sri Lanka in the early historic period. As Hornell (1970: 229) shows, reed boats could sometimes attain large size and carrying capacity. They could easily make coastwise voyages of short duration.

> Reed canoes under sail, with favourable conditions of wind and weather, would make ideal despatch vessels in an emergency when speed was the essential factor, for their lightness and extremely shallow draught would ensure a rapid passage if the wind were suitable; their great spread of sail carried on a lofty straddle mast and their light draft would ensure a good turn of speed (*ibid.*).

Nevertheless, it is extremely doubtful if one could sail along the east coast of peninsular India in reed boats (as Pliny claims) because, as Hornell (1923: 289) cautions us, "travel [along the coast] by sea is out of the question as no landing can be made on this surf-beaten coast except by catamaran". It is more likely that Pliny wrote on hearsay and like Paris (1951: 296), we must dismiss Pliny's reference to reed boats as a piece of confused information. It is likely that Pliny misinterpreted extended logboats (in which the side planks were stitched) as bundles of papyrus stalks tied together as in reed boats. If our argument is acceptable, we may believe that in the early historic period, extended logboats from Prasii sailed to Sri Lanka in 20 days.

Hence, it is unlikely that the Ichapur representation from the Neolithic-Chalcolithic period is a reed boat. It is also likely that Pliny wrote on hearsay and like Paris (1951: 296), we must dismiss Pliny's reference to reed boats as a piece of confused information. It is likely that Pliny misinterpreted plank-extended logboats or dugouts (in which the side planks were stitched) as bundles of papyrus stalks tied together as in reed boats.

Single-masted Ship

We encounter an interesting type of ship on a terracotta seal-impression from Chandraketugarh (henceforth cited as the Trapyaka seal-impression; Fig. 4.3). The seal-impression (2 cm diam) is now held at the Department of Archaeology, West Bengal and has been dated to the 3rd century AD because of its paleographic features. Mukherjee (1990: 47) has identified it as a trader's identification ticket. The seal-impression shows a ship with a single mast inside a decorated circular border. The mast is placed amidships and two parallel ropes are shown reaching out to the end of stem- and sternposts. The ropes at the top end terminate in a bundle that may be the rolled up sail and the top may be a masthead cap. On the right edge of the ship stands a figure of a horse in profile, with its head facing the mast. The impression also bears a two-lined Kharoshṭī-Brāhmī inscription. The first line has been read as "Tasvodajana Hovaji(no)ṇa T(r)apya" and the second line as "Gasa". Mukherjee (*ibid.*) has translated these lines as follows: "ship of the class of *Trapyaka*, belonging to (i.e., owned by) the powerful Tasvodaja family". The reverse side of the seal-impression bears an indistinct imprint of an oval seal.

Fig. 4.3 The Trapyaka seal-impression, Chandraketugarh. Courtesy: B.N. Mukherjee

Four more seal and seal-impressions, all in terracotta and bearing ship motif, have been discovered from the same site. The first of these, a seal-impression 3.2 cm in diameter and dull red in colour, is now held at the Department of Archaeology, West Bengal (henceforth referred to as the Grain and Taurine seal-impression; Fig. 4.4). It shows a ship with a single mast sporting a flying banner inside a decorated circular border. On the right of the ship is depicted a stalk of grain and on its left, a taurine symbol. The mast has a tripod base. Near the top of the mast the sail is rolled up with rings; from it, a pair of parallel ropes descends on each side of the mast. Jana (1998: 248-49) may be quite correct in assuming that the ropes are part of the rigging arrangement. The steering device can be seen near the stern of the ship, which is a quarter-paddle. This impression, too, is a trader's identification ticket for it bears a groove on the reverse side and has been dated to c. 3rd century AD.

Fig. 4.4 The Grain and Taurine seal-impression, Chandraketugarh. Courtesy: B.N. Mukherjee

The second terracotta seal-impression (henceforth referred to as the Indra seal-impression; Fig. 4.5) is also a trader's identification ticket from c. 3rd century AD. It is pink and nearly round (3.5 cm diam), and is now held at the Indian Museum, Kolkata. Depicted on it is a ship with a single mast that is fitted on the foredeck and displays a flying banner and has a plant placed in a basket on its board. An up-turned conch is shown on the upper right corner. The seal-impression also shows a horizontal bar attached to the sternpost, which appears to indicate a tiller. The inscription, in mixed Kharoshṭī-Brāhmī, reads *'Soridhajasā'* and *'Dijammasa Jaladhisakla'*. Mukherjee (1990: 47) has translated the inscription as "[the ship called] 'jaladhiśakra' (*i.e.* 'Indra of the Ocean') belongs to Dvijanma who is famous as very wealthy".

Fig. 4.5 The Indra seal-impression, Chandraketugarh. Courtesy: B.N. Mukherjee

The third, too, is a terracotta impression of round seal, which is now held at G. S. De collection in Habra, West Bengal. Within a circular border, it too shows a ship with a single mast sporting flying banner. Like the Indra seal-impression, it also bears an upturned conch symbol placed at the upper right hand corner (Fig. 4.6). However, palaeographic features indicate that it belongs to an earlier date, possibly the 2nd century AD. An inscription in the seal-impression reads *Jemdhaś jujusya,* which Mukherjee (*ibid.*: 48) has translated as "of Juju, the conquering king". According to Mukherjee (*ibid.*), the inscription and the ship motif in the seal-impression (henceforth referred to as the Juju seal-impression) may be taken to indicate that a king named 'Juju' had a strong fleet of his own for maritime trade or military expedition.

Fig. 4.6 The Juju seal-impression, Chandraketugarh. Courtesy: B.N. Mukherjee

The fourth is a round terracotta seal with a hemispherical back. The diameter of the impression it makes is 3.8 cm. Discovered at Beracampa in a slightly damaged condition, the seal is currently held in the G. S. De collection, in Habra, West Bengal. The seal shows a ship with one mast, at the top of which flies a banner within a border of dots. Above the ship is a round object that may represent the sun (*ibid.*: 57). Based on palaeographic features, the seal (henceforth referred to as the Sun seal) has been dated to c. 2nd century AD. An unbaked clay sealing of Chandraketugarh (currently preserved in the Asutosh Museum of Indian Art) displays yet another ship with single mast inside a decorated circular border. The mast is placed amidships and it sports a flying banner. A quarter paddle may be identified near the sternpost (Fig. 4.7).

Fig. 4.7 An unbaked clay sealing, Chandraketugarh. Courtesy: Asutosh Museum of Indian Art, Kolkata

In all the six seal and seal-impressions discussed above, the depiction of the ships show some common features but also a few dissimilarities. All of them are ships with a single mast. However, the Indra seal-impression and the Sun seal show the mast in the fore deck but all others (the Juju, the Grain and Taurine, the Trapyaka seal-impressions and the unbaked clay sealing) show it amidships. The mast of the Grain and Taurine seal-impression has a tripod base. Quarter paddle as steering device can be seen in the Sun seal, the unbaked clay sealing, the Grain and Taurine seal-impression and the Juju seal-impression. On the other hand, the Indra seal-impression possibly shows a tiller-fitted steering device. The sternpost of all the ships except the damaged Trapyaka seal-impression and stemposts of all the five are raked. Although sails are absent, Hornell (1920: 221) rightly believes that the vertical masts "carrying yards triced to the mast-heads", as shown in two of the seal-impressions, indicate that the ships "carried a large square sail on each mast".

Summing up the common characteristics, we may note that the ships depicted in the Chandraketugarh seal and seal-impressions show single-masted ships with raked stem and sternposts and quarter paddle as steering device. Within this general pattern, we may further identify the following three types. (1) The ships on the Juju and the Trapyaka seal-impressions appear to be quite similar because both show the mast amidships. Since one of these has been identified as a *trapyaka,* we may identify both as belonging to the *trapyaka* type. (2) Ships with tripod-based mast placed amidships as in the Grain & Taurine seal-impression; we may identify this type as CKG 1. (3) Ships with its mast placed in the fore deck as in the Indra seal-impression and the Sun seal; we may identify this type as CKG 2.

Among the single-masted ships the *trapyaka* is extremely significant because the *Periplus* mentions the *trappaga* as a type of ships that plied along the Gujarat coast. It says:

> Native fishermen in the King's service, stationed at the very entrance in well-manned large boats called trappaga and

cotymba, go up the coast as far as Syrastrene, from which they pilot vessels to Barygaza (§ 44; Schoff 1995: 40).

We find further reference of the *trappaga* type of vessels in the *Aṅgavijja,* a Jaina text dating back to the 4th century AD (but which contains earlier materials). The text devotes an entire section to ships, which it classifies by tonnage capacity: small, medium and large. The *trappaga* (or the *tappaka* as the *Aṅgavijja* calls it) has been classified as a medium sized ship.

Scholars seeking to identify the *trappaga* type of ships with greater detail have come up with divergent views. Huntingford (1980: 162) simply identifies *trappagas* as "fairly large ships". McPherson (1998: 34) suggests that the *trappaga* of the *Periplus* was similar to the modern *kotia*. However, as Hornell (1920: 142) shows, "Kotia is two-masted (main and mizzen masts), with poop, carved square stern and quarters and with a rudder trunk and with Arab Lateen sails". He further observes that *kotias* bear distinct Portuguese influence, "for their high poops and squared sterns derive these characteristic features directly from the early caravels" (*ibid*.: 143). Hence we may reject McPherson's suggestion. On the other hand, Schoff (1995: 182) cites Lassen to argue that *trappaga* has been derived from *trapâka,* "a type of fishing boat mentioned by other travellers in this region". Lassen's identification may be closer to the truth not only because of phonetic similarity but also because the *Periplus* associates *trappaga* with "native fishermen".

Adding together the evidences drawn from Chandraketugarh seal-impressions, the *Periplus* and the *Aṅgavijja* we may believe that the *trapyaka* was a medium sized ship with a single mast, raked stem and sternposts. The mast of these ships was placed amidships. These ships appear to have been used in the Gujarat coast for fishing and pilotage. As the seal-impressions from Chandraketugarh imply, they were used in the 'Bengal' coast for maritime trade as well.

Double-masted Ship

The ship motifs depicted on the obverse of the Satavahana coins from Andhra Pradesh are often cited as evidence of double-masted sea-going vessels, which plied on the eastern coast of India in the 2nd century AD. All the ships on these coins are two-masted with clearly raked stem and sternposts and carry "yards triced to the mastheads in such a way that it is clear they carried a large square sail on each mast" (Hornell 1920: 216). Despite Hornell's firm assertion that all the ships were steered with the help of two quarter paddles, one on each side, the visual representations show otherwise. Even the shapes of the ships are significantly different. Hence, we need not quite lump them all as belonging to a uniform class. In a recent research, Bhandare (1999) has correctly argued that the representation of the ships display variations in shape, number of mast-heads, buoys, signaling devices like flags, etc.

The Satavahana ships possibly mark an important point in the history of maritime ships of the Bay of Bengal rim because of the introduction of the second mast fitted to increase the speed of the ship. They were introduced at a time when, as Ptolemy testifies in his *An Outline of Geography* (Cap. 13, § 7-8; Śāstri 1927: 24), transoceanic voyages became possible from Paloura (Jelasur near the mouth of the Subarṇarekhā in Orissa) to Sada (on the eastern side of the Bay of Bengal, between Pegu and 'Bengal'). Indeed Hornell (1920: 216) may not have been far from truth for believing that the earliest South Asian colonists set sail in these ships for the Malay Archipelago.

It is important to note that one class of the Satavahana double-masted ships bears a strong resemblance with a ship seen on an oval-shaped (1.1 x 2.5 cm) seal-impression that has been found in the district of south 24-Parganas (and is now held at the State Museum in Kolkata). The seal-impression (henceforth referred to as the 24-Parganas seal-impression) has been dated to the 2nd century AD (Mukherjee 1990: 61). Although the steering device of the ship is indistinct in the seal-impression, it clearly displays two long masts and raked stem and sternposts, very much like the Satavahana ship. Hence, there can be little doubt that some of the Satavahana double-masted ships called on the maritime ports of 'Bengal'.

It is most exciting that the double-masted class of ships can also be identified in a Rouletted Ware sherd, dated to the 1st-2nd century AD that has been unearthed from Alagankulam in Tamil Nadu (Kasinathan 1997: 19-20). The sherd bears the figure of a ship with raked sternpost, two quarter paddles as steering device and a mast. The rigging arrangement as shown in the figure makes it evident that the ship was fitted with a second mast, which is not visible because the sherd is fragmented. The ship's stempost is also not visible because of the fragmentation. However, from what remains of the figure it is clear that the ship depicted on the Alagankulam Rouletted Ware sherd was also a double-masted Satavahana vessel. Following Gogte's (1997: 69-85 and 2001: 197-202) argument, discussed earlier in Chapter Two, we may believe that the Rouletted Ware sherd of Alagankulam originally came from Chandraketugarh. Hence there is a strong likelihood that the Alagankulam representation of the double-masted Satavahana vessel was actually made by artisans at Chandraketugarh. This may be taken to confirm the indications derived from the 24-Parganas seal-impression that the double-masted Satavahana ships called on early historic ports of 'Bengal'.

Multiple-masted Sewn-plank Ship

The *Periplus of the Erythraean Sea* (60 AD) gives us the clearest textual clue to a type of vessel which called on ports in early historic 'Bengal'. However, the reference is brief: "those which make the voyage [from Coromandel Coast] to

Chryse [Myanmar] and to the Ganges are called *colandia*, and are very large" (§ 60; Schoff 1995: 46). In order to ascertain the identity of the ship, we need to sift through a considerable amount of tortuous scholarly discourse and evidence drawn from various sources.

The name of the ship as given in the original version of the *Periplus* is κολανδιοΦώντα *(kolandiophonta)*, which Schoff (*ibid.*: 246) assures us, is corrupt. He believes that the original name was *colandia* and it was the name of a ship of Malay origin, which translates simply as "ship". These, he says quite confidently, "must have been similar to the Chinese junks or the Burmese *laung-zát*". But according to Rajendralala Mitra (1961: 182), the word has been derived from Sanskrit *kolantarapota,* which means "ships for going to foreign shores". This, in effect would imply that the ship was South Asian in origin.

Hornell (1920: 215) is of the view that *kolandiophonta or kolandia* "must almost certainly have been two-masted vessels with pointed ends and probably equipped with a stout outrigger, counterparts of the present-day Sinhalese *yathra-oruwa* (*yathra-dhoni* in Tamil), but unlike them, steered by quarter oars, the rudder not being then invented". His conclusion is based on two reasons: (1) phonetic similarity of the suffix "kolan" in *kolandiaphonta* with the word *kūllan* or *kūlla*, the Tamil term both for a large outrigger fishing canoe and for the outrigger frame alone and (2) Pliny's account of ships "built with prows at each end" that plied "[t]he sea between the island [of Taprobane, i.e., Sri Lanka] and India", as described in the *Natural History* (VI. 24. 82) (McCrindle 1979: 103). Hornell (1920: 216) further shows that the *kolandia* "probably had also a fairly close kinship with the two-masted Javanese outrigger ships of the Borobudur sculptures". His argument is based on the fact that the *Periplus* shows the *kolandia* trading in Chryse in which region Hornell includes the islands of Sumatra and Java. Following Hornell closely, McPherson (1998: 34) argues that the descendant of the ancient *kolandiophonta* were the Sri Lankan sewn-plank *yathra dhoni,* now obsolete, which sailed to south India and the Maldives carrying rice, salted fish, cloth and coir products.

Projecting another dissenting view, Christie (1957: 345-353) has shown that *kolandiophonta* is a corrupted Greek form of Southeast Asian ships known as *k'un-lun-po*, which actually denoted 'ships (*po*) of various littoral peoples of South East Asia (*k'un-lun*)'. Christie cites quite a few Chinese sources in order to prove that the term 'po' actually signified 'ships'. One of these is Wan Chen, who, in his account of the South during the Wu dynasty (AD 222-77), says "foreigners [i.e. natives of S. E. Asia] call ships *po*". The largest of these resembled covered galleries from above and were about 170 feet in length. These could carry six to seven hundred people and a large amount of cargo. According to K'ang T'ai, another source from the same Wu period, Indo-Scythian traders transported horses in ships known as *po* (*ibid.*: 347). As we may recall, the Indo-Scythians were the Kharoshṭī speaking traders in Gaṅgābandar.

Based on another 3rd century Chinese literary source (*Nan Chou I Wu Chih,* "Strange Things of the South"), Manguin (1996: 189-190) adds that the *kunlun bo* were ships of Southeast Asian origin that could carry some 600 tons of load. These were rigged with multiple masts and sails.

We have yet another Chinese source, Hui-Lin, whose *I Ch'ieh Ching Yin I* ("Dictionary of Sounds and meanings of words in the Vinaya", c. 8th century AD) shows that 'po' signifies 'the great ships of the sea' or simply, 'a sea-going ship'. Hui-Lin describes the *kun-lun* ships of sewn-plank construction and gives a clear description:

> (These ships) lie 6 or 7 ft. deep in the water. They are fast and can transport more than 1,000 men, apart from cargo. They are also called 'Khun-Lun' ships. Many of those who form the crews and technicians of these ships are Ku-Lun people. ... (The ships) are several (200 feet?) long, and divided fore and aft into three sections. Sails are hoisted to make use of the wind, and (indeed, these ships) cannot be propelled by the strength of men (alone) (Needham 1971: 459).

Thus, all the Chinese sources appear to indicate that *k'un-lun-po* were large merchantmen manned mostly by k'un-lun people.

Opinion thus far obtained is divided between South Asian origin (Hornell, McPherson, Rajendralala Mitra) and Southeast Asian origin (Schoff, Christie and Manguin). In the absence of archaeological evidence, most of the scholars have been forced to base their argument on phonetic origin of *'colandia'*, which can be *kun-lun po*, *kūllan* or *kolantarapota.* Of all the opinions discussed above, Hornell's attempt seems to be illogical because he tries to bring the accounts of Pliny and *Periplus* together and says *colandia* is the only vessel that matches with Pliny's description. However, he seems to have overlooked the fact that Pliny was speaking of ships that plied "[t]he sea between the island [of Taprobane, i.e., Sri Lanka] and India" (McCrindle 1979: 103) while the *Periplus* speaks of "those which make the voyage [from Coromandel Coast] to Chryse [Myanmar] and to the Ganges" (§ 60; Schoff 1995: 46). Moreover, no outrigger ships sailed to and from the coast of 'Bengal' and the Borobudur ships were restricted to the Indian Ocean from Sri Lanka to the Indonesian islands. Hence, Sinhalese *yathra-oruwa* could not have been the much illusive *'colandia'* that we are trying to identify. On the other hand, Mitra has forwarded no convincing argument besides phonetic similarity. He does not cite his source nor discuss in detail how the ship is described in his Sanskrit source.

Discounting these arguments, it appears that the Chinese descriptions are closer to *colandia* or *kolandiophonta.* Hence, the ship that *Periplus* refers to was possibly the *k'un-lun-po*, a large vessel (of over 60 m in length) of Southeast Asian origin. It plied between the Coromandel Coast, Chryse and the Ganges in 'Bengal' in the early historic period. The ship used to be rigged with multiple masts and sails and could carry over 600 to 1,000 passengers besides cargo. Since Southeast Asia was unknown to the *Periplus* (the farthest port east it refers to is Chryse, i.e., Burma, beyond which it knows only China), it described *colandia* or *kolandiophonta* as making voyages to Chryse. Given the physiographic condition of 'Bengal' waters, we must believe that the *colandia* would have made offshore anchorage for handling commodities from maritime ports of 'Bengal'.

With this identity of the *colandia* in mind, we need to read the Śaṅkha Jātaka where is recounted the story of a rich Brāhmiṇ named Śaṅkha from Benares (then called Molinī). He set out on foot from home to an unnamed harbour and sailed on a ship for Gold Country ("Golden Chersonese"). However, the ship was wrecked in the high sea. After seven days of swimming, a deity named Maṇi-mekhalā was pleased with his faith and "caused a ship to appear, made of seven things of price; in length it was eight hundred cubits, in width six hundred cubits, twenty fathoms in depth; it had three masts made of sapphire, cordage of gold, silver sails, and of gold were also the oars and rudders". Then, setting the Brāhmiṇ on board, the deity guided the ship to Molinī (Book X, No. 442; Cowell 1957, IV: 9-13).

If we peel through the layers of imaginative fantasy meant to succor the devotees, we may arrive at the implied existence of a type of maritime vessel that was wide bodied (4:3 ratio), fitted with three masts, oars and rudder. Because sternpost rudders were adopted from the Chinese only in the 12th century (Deloche 1996: 212), it is quite possible that the Śaṅkha Jātaka ship was fitted with a quarter paddle. Nothing further can be deduced with certainty. These characteristics fit well with the *colandia*. It is therefore proposed that the triple-masted ship described in the Śaṅkha Jātaka was a *colandia*.

LATE HISTORIC PERIOD

We have very few evidences from the late historic period to ascertain the type of ships that sailed to and from the ports in 'Bengal'. Kālidāsa's *Raghuvaṁśa*, Canto IV, verse 36 does refer to the people of the Vaṅgas as *nau-sadhanodyatan* (thereby implying that the people were skilled in the use of boats), but says nothing about the ships they sailed in. The *nā-vatā-kṣeni* or "shipbuilding harbour" inscribed in the Faridpur Copperplate (6th century AD, discussed earlier in Chapter One) does indicate that ships were constructed in 'Bengal' but again is silent about the types that were constructed here. The Kailan copperplate of King Śrīdhāraṇa Rāta of Samataṭa describes the Kṣīrodā river, which encircled the provincial headquarter Devaparvata, as adorned by clusters of boats (Sircar 1947: 225). However, there is no indication regarding their constructional types or use.

Of the Chinese sources, Fa-Hien's *Fo-kwō-ki* (5th century AD) has very little to say about the type of ships that sailed to and from 'Bengal', except that he voyaged from Tāmralipti to Sri Lanka in fourteen days and that the ship was "a great merchant vessel, which carried about two hundred men"(Beal 1869: 166). In the first half of the 7th century AD, Hiuen-Tsiang informs us that Kumāra-rāja (Bhāskaravarman, the king of Kāmarūpa) possessed 30,000 ships (*Life*, Book V; Beal 1973: 172). Although it is likely that most of these were meant for riverine rather than maritime use, we have little information regarding the constructional features of these vessels. Similarly I-Tsing, who writes about boarding a Persian ship (with single mast and two sails) at Canton in 671 AD (Lahiri 1986: 76-79) is entirely silent about the type of vessel that he sailed from Ka-cha (Kedah) to Tāmralipti.

Nevertheless, the epigraphic and literary references cited above create an impression of proliferation of shipbuilding technology in 'Bengal' during the late historic period. We have just one reference, cited below, to transform the impression to more of a definite picture. As recounted in the *Dāthā-dhātu-waṅso*, Dantakumāra and his wife boarded at Tāmralipti "a vessel bound for Ceylon, firmly constructed with planks sewed together with ropes, having a well-rigged, lofty mast, with a spacious sail, and commanded by a skilful navigator, on the point of departure" (Mookerji 1957: 21). The description of the ship indicates that in the 4th century AD when the Tooth Relic was transported to Sri Lanka, sewn-planked ships with single mast and spacious sail plied between Tāmralipti and Sri Lanka. However, we have no way of identifying with certainty the type of ship that Dantakumāra sailed to Sri Lanka. Nevertheless, given the fact that we have at hand quite a few archaeological remains indicating the presence of ships with single mast in the early historic period, we may suspect that Dantakumāra sailed in a *trapyaka*, CKG 1 or CKG 2 type of ship.

Rummaging South Asian sources for further information, one may cite the illustration of the famous sea-going vessel at Ajanta Cave II (dated 525-650 AD) that is shown with three oblong sails and an oar. Interesting though it is for its appropriation of characteristic features of different types of ships, it is pertinent evidence for maritime vessels calling on ports situated on the west coast of India and can be of little interest for our research.

EARLY MEDIEVAL PERIOD

The ruined Buddhist temple of Borobudur in Central Java, built sometime in the beginning of the 8th century AD during the Golden Age of the Śailendra Dynasty, is decorated with about 1300 panels in bas-relief. Nine maritime vessels with outriggers (henceforth referred to as the Borobudur ships; Figs. 4.8-4.11) and two riverine vessels are seen on ten of these panels. These vessels have often served as a point of reference in scholarly deliberations on pre-modern maritime

Fig. 4.8 A ship depicted on a panel, Borobudur Temple, Java

culture of South and Southeast Asia, and are even cited as important visual evidence of Bengal's maritime trade. For example, Schoff (1995: 243) has identified the vessels as "the Gujarati ships of Boroboedor". Mookerji (1957: 31-34) and Rao (1988) have echoed similar opinion and have argued that they are ships of Indian origin. Sarkar (1937: 595) has gone to the extent of claiming that these ships are of Bengali origin and testify a "brisk commercial intercourse between Java and Bengal". The author of this book has discussed the Borobudur ships elsewhere in detail (see Jahan forthc). For the purpose at hand, the argument given below should suffice.

Fig. 4.9 A ship depicted on a panel, Borobudur Temple, Java

Five of the Borobudur ships are shown with two masts and four with one mast. Some of the masts are clearly represented as bi-pod or tri-pod in form with elongated canted square-sails, which, as Needham (1971: 458) points out, is a "characteristic Indonesian type". Hornell (1920: 220-221) further observes that bi-pod and tri-pod designs have never been used in South Asia. "Compound masts are essentially Mongoloid in origin, being seen today only among the Burmese, the Indonesians and the southern Chinese" (*ibid.:* 220-221). The outriggers of the Borobudur ships are very complex, fitted with a compound float and are held in position by three or four sturdy booms. It was possible for the crew to position themselves on these devices when necessary in order to stabilize the vessels. According to Hornell (1920: 219) "[n]o Indian or Sinhalese outrigger boats have more than one float supported by two booms". Moreover, the Borobudur ships used "two separate rudders precisely as the large Malay praus ... seen in Macassar harbour" (Hornell 1920: 219). Hence, there is ample reason to dismiss Schoff (1995), Mookerji (1957: 31-34), Rao (1988) and Sarkar (1937), and believe that the Borobudur ships were "local Javanese vessels, with lineal descendants of similar size still surviving in the coasting trade of East Java" (Hornell 1920: 216, fn. 3). Further, outrigger ships never developed in the northern Bay littoral precisely because the environmental condition is not suitable for its operation. Hence, it is inconceivable that the Borobudur ships ever visited the ports of 'Bengal'.

Fig. 4.10 A ship depicted on a panel, Borobudur Temple, Java

Having dealt with an intriguing question, we may now concentrate on the early medieval epigraphic, iconographic and literary sources. All the vessels mentioned in the Pāla epigraphic records (the Nālandā copperplate of Dharmapāla, Bhattacharyya 1935-36: 290; the Bāngarh copperplate of Mahipāla I, Banerji 1917b: 327; and the Kamauli copperplate of Vaidyadeva, Venis 1894: 355) appear to have been riverine crafts used in military expeditions. The same is true of Sena records as exemplified in the Deopāḍā inscription of Vijayasena (11th c. AD):

> As his fleet in his sport of conquest of the Western Dominions advanced along the course of the Ganges, his boat shone like the digit of the moon in the water of the river on Śiva's head, –

Fig. 4.11 A ship depicted on a panel, Borobudur Temple, Java

first stuck in the mud of ashes and then released (Mukherji and Maity 1967: 255).

A visual impression of these riverine crafts may be received from a Pāhāḍpur plaque that shows a boat with a steering paddle and two men on board. There can be no disagreement with Husain (1963: 11) who observes that the fishermen of Bangladesh use similar boats even to this day. Another visual representation of a riverine boat can be seen on a red sandstone sculpture piece (15.9 x 10 cm) from the 9th century AD. It was found at Mahāsthāngarh in Bogra and is now held at the Varendra Research Museum, Rajshahi (Acc. VRM 2681). The piece shows a headless boatman holding an oar and four females, presumably goddesses, seated in a row (Rahman 1978: 341).

Turning to literary references, one finds that the *Caryāpada* (9th-12th centuries AD) refers only to riverine vessels. The same is true of most of the court-sponsored literature produced during the period. For example, the Pāla poet Sandhyākara Nandī's *Rāmacarita* (Canto II, verses 7b and 10 b) speaks of King Rāmapāla's "tumultuous army" that included "a fleet of riverine boats" (Sandhyākara Nandī 1910: 38, 40). However, this dismal silence on indigenous maritime vessels is occasionally punctuated by a sudden reference that appears like a revelation. Consider, for example, the qualifications used in the eulogy of Dharmapāla again in the *Rāmacarita*: "[his] fleet of stone-boats appeared splendid, when it crossed the sea (floating) like bitter gourds, (and) whose pure fame also became resplendent after having crossed the sea" (Canto I, verse 4b, Sandhyākara Nandī 1910: 3). Clearly, this is a proud proclamation of a kingdom that could boast of considerable maritime experience.

This view appears to be further confirmed by the *Yukti Kalpataru* by Bhoja Narapati – a South Asian treatise on the art of shipbuilding that was composed in c. 11th century AD. However, we must proceed cautiously with the text. Notwithstanding the fact that the manuscript was found in the Calcutta Sanskrit College Library, the identity of the author of the *Yukti Kalpataru* is uncertain. It is unlikely that he was King Bhojavarmanadeva of the Varman dynasty of Eastern Bengal (Vaṅga and Samataṭa) or the Pratihara King Bhojadeva I. Rather, it is more likely that he was the Paramāra king of Malwa (Chattopadhyay 1994: xiii). Nevertheless, the text may be accepted as a repository of indigenous knowledge on shipbuilding in South Asia during the early medieval period. Hence, one may arguably believe that it had some bearing on 'Bengal'.

The *Yukti Kalpataru* categorises vessels into two broad classes: (1) *sāmānya* or ordinary and (2) *viśeṣa* or special. *Viśeṣa* vessels are further categorised into two sub-classes: (2a) *dīrghā* (long) and (2b) *unnatā* (high). The following tables illustrate dimensions of vessels belonging to these classes and sub-classes. (Dimensions in the table given below are drawn from Bag 1988: 8-9; most of the English equivalents and the analysis of measurements has been worked out by the author.)

Table 4.1: *Sāmānya* (Ordinary) Vessels
[a = 8 cubits; ratio L:B:H::2:1:1]

Sl. No.	Names of vessels	English equivalents	Length (cubits)	Breadth (cubits)	Height (cubits)
1	*Kṣudra*	Diminutive	16 = 8x2 = 2a	4 = 8x1/2 = 1/2a	4 = 4x1 = 1/2a
2	*Madhyamā*	Medial	24 = 8x3 = 3a	12 = 8x3/2 = 3/2a	8 = 8x1 = a
3	*Bhīmā*	Overpowering	40 = 8x5 = 5a	20 = 8x5/2 = 5/2a	20 = 8x5/2 = 5/2a
4	*Capalā*	Flippant	48 = 8x6 = 6a	24 = 8x3 = 3a	24 = 8x3 = 3a
5	*Paṭalā*	Tapering at both ends	64 = 8x8 = 8a	32 = 8x4 = 4a	32 = 8x4 = 4a
6	*Abhayā*	Fearless	72 = 8x9 = 9a	36 = 8x9/2 = 9/2a	36 = 8x9/2 = 9/2a
7	*Dīrgha*	Elongated	88 = 8x11 = 11a	44 = 8x11/2 = 11/2a	44 = 8x11/2 = 11/2a
8	*Patraputā*	Shaped like a cup made of tree leaves	96 = 8x12 = 12a	48 = 8x6 = 6a	48 = 8x6 = 6a
9	*Garbharā*	Hollowed	112 = 8x14 = 14a	56 = 8x7 = 7a	56 = 8x7 = 7a
10	*Mantharā*	Slothful	120 = 8x15 = 15a	60 = 8x15/2 = 15/2a	60 = 8x15/2 = 15/2a

Table 4.2: *Viśeṣa Dīrghā* (Special and Long) Vessels
[a=8 cubits; ratio L:B::8:1]

Sl. No.	Names of vessels	English equivalents	Length (cubits)	Breadth (cubits)	Height (cubits)
1	*Dīrghikā*	Large and deep	32 = 8x4 = 4a	4 = 8x1/2 = 4/8a	3 = 8x3/8 = 3/8a (H = B - 1)
2	*Taraṇi*	Means of crossing	48 = 8x6 = 6a	6 = 8x3/4 = 6/8a	4 = 8x1/2 = 4/8a (H = B - 2)
3	*Lolā*	Restless	64 = 8x8 = 8a	8 = 8x1 = 8/8a	6 = 8x3/4 = 6/8a (H = B - 2)
4	*Gatvarā*	Fast-moving	80 = 8x10 = 10a	10 = 8x10/8 = 10/8a	8 = 8x1 = 8/8a (H = B - 2)
5	*Gāminī*	Mobile	96 = 8x12 = 12a	12 = 8x6/4 = 12/8a	9 = 8x9/8 = 9/8a (H = B - 3)
6	*Tarī*	Swift-moving	112 = 8x14 = 14a	14 = 8x14/8 = 14/8a	11 = 8x11/8 = 11/8a (H = B - 3)
7	*Jaṅghāla*	Speedy	128 = 8x16 = 16a	16 = 16x1 = a	12 = 8x6/4 = 12/8a (H = B - 4)
8	*Plāvinī*	Drenching	144 = 8x18 = 18a	18 = 8x18/8 = 18/8a	14 = 8x14/8 = 14/8a (H = B - 4)
9	*Dhāriṇī*	Carrying	160 = 8x20 = 20a	20 = 8x20/8 = 20/8a	16 = 8x2 = 16/8a (H = B - 4)
10	*Veginī*	Swift	176 = 8x222 = 22a	22 = 8x22/8 = 22/8a	17 = 8x17/8 = 17/8a (H = B - 5)

Table 4.3: *Viśeṣa Unnatā* (Special and High) Vessels
[a = 8 cubits; ratio L:B:H::2:1:1]

Sl. No.	Names of vessels	English equivalents	Length (Cubits)	Breadth (cubits)	Height (cubits)
1	*Ūrddhvā*	Lofty	32 = 8x4 = 4a	16 = 8x2 = 2a	16 = 8x2 = 2a
2	*Anūrddhvā*	Lowly	48 = 8x6 = 6a	24 = 8x3 = 3a	24 = 8x3 = 3a
3	*Svarṇamukhī*	Sennapod	64 = 8x8 = 8a	32 = 8x4 = 4a	32 = 8x4 = 4a
4	*Garviṇī*	Proud	80 = 8x10 = 10a	40 = 8x5 = 5a	40 = 8x5 = 5a
5	*Mantharā*	Slothful	96 = 6x12 = 12a	48 = 8x6 = 6a	48 = 8x6 = 6a

According to Mookerji (1957: 15-16), *sāmānya* classes of vessels were riverine and *viśeṣa* classes of vessels were maritime crafts. However, Bag (1988: 8) cites the *Yukti Kalpataru* (verse 95) to show that all *sāmānya* type vessels except *mantharā* are *ambudhagati* (sea going). He argues that the categorisation was based on usage. The *sāmānya* types were cargo vessels and hence were shorn of decoration. On the other hand, "[t]he *Viśeṣa* types were specially decorated and foils of iron, copper, gold, load stone etc. were used in construction and decoration" (*ibid.*).

As the tables show, the *Yukti Kalpataru* clearly used dimension of vessels for categorisation. Interestingly, all dimensions given are multiples of 8. *Viśeṣa Unnatā* vessels were constructed in the following ratio:- Length: Breadth: Height :: 2:1:1. *Sāmānya* vessels (except *Kṣudra* and *Madhyamā* classes) were constructed in the same ratio. The only difference of the *Sāmānya* and the *Viśeṣa Unnatā* vessels lie in the manner of progression in dimension. Whereas the dimension of *Viśeṣa Unnatā* vessels progress as multiples of even number, that of the *Sāmānya* vessels progress as multiples of odd as well as even numbers, (except that the multiples of 4, 7, 10 and 13 are missing). Obviously, some of the *Sāmānya* class of vessels, the dimension of which are multiples of even numbers, are of similar size as the *Viśeṣa Unnatā* vessels. Thus, the *Capalā* type of *Sāmānya* vessel has the same dimension as the *Anūrddhvā* type of *Viśeṣa Unnatā* vessel. It is also important to note that the *Paṭalā* and the *Patrapuṭā* types of *Sāmānya* vessel indicate shape. In other words, the *Paṭalā* type must have indicated double-ended vessels while the *Patrapuṭā* type must have indicated wide-bodied vessels whose maximum width at gunwale level was equal to its height.

The *Viśeṣa Dīrghā* vessels follow a completely different principle. The dimensional ratio of vessels belonging to this sub-class, is Length : Breadth :: 8:1. In order to give the vessel a semblance of length, the height is reduced to the extent that the vessels of this sub-class are shorter in height than their breadth. Moreover, the longer the vessel, the greater is the reduction in height. Thus, the initial equation is as follows: Height = Breadth - 1 cubit. However, the equation gradually progresses to Height = Breadth - 5 cubits. There can be little doubt that reduction in height was meant for swift transportation and maneuvering as necessary in naval warfare, ferrying across rivers etc.

Evaluating Bag's and Mookerji's argument, and our analysis given above, we may conclude that both the *Sāmānya* and the *Viśeṣa Unnatā* vessels, except the *Mantharā* type, could have been used for maritime transportation. However, because the *Yukti Kalpataru* (ver. 188) states that the ships whose height is more than 35 cubits bring prosperity and those more than 50 cubits bring joy or two-thirds of that (50 cubits) cause misfortune (*ibid.*: 9), we may infer that the larger vessels were considered more suitable for maritime voyages. The difference between the *Sāmānya* and the *Viśeṣa Unnatā* vessels lay in decoration and added comfort. Hence, the *Sāmānya* class of vessels were specifically meant for transportation of cargoes while the *Viśeṣa Unnatā* sub-class of vessels could accommodate passengers as well and may have been meant for use by royalty. Since the *Yukti Kalpataru* also indicates that the ships could be fitted with cabins extending from one end to the other *(sarvamandirā)* or at the middle *(madhyamandirā)*, we may assume that such arrangements were made in the *Viśeṣa Unnatā* sub-class of vessels. The *Sāmānya* class and *Viśeṣa Dīrghā* sub-class of vessels may have had their cabins fitted on the fore deck *(agramandirā)*.

As for masts, the *Yukti Kalpataru* notes the use of one to four, obviously depending on the size of the vessels. Unfortunately, there is no indication of the position of masts. However, the text recommends painting of the masts in white, red, yellow and blue. Once again, there is no indication regarding symbolic use of colour. It is recommended that the sails be made of *avājñāsika* cloth, which remains unidentified. The text also speaks of shaping the prows like lions, buffaloes, serpents, elephants, tigers, birds, frogs and even humans (*ibid.*: 10).

Citing an earlier text titled the *Vṛiksh-Āyurveda* (1st century AD), in which four classes of timber is distinguished, the *Yukti Kalpataru* advises that the Ksatriya class (characterized by lightness and hardness) be used for construction of ships. It also advises against the use of iron for joining the planks of ships together since magnetic field in oceanic depth supposedly cause such ships to capsize. Instead, it recommends the use of mortised joints with non-ferrous material (Mookerji 1957: 13-14).

Having examined the theoretical discourse of the *Yukti Kalpataru*, we need to examine actual practice to see how much of the suggestions made in the text were actually followed by the shipwrights of early medieval 'Bengal'. With this objective, we may take up the *bālām* for close scrutiny, whose existence in the early medieval period may be determined by iconographic, ethnographic and literary evidences.

The Bālām

The earliest literary reference to the *bālām* that we have is from a Persian manuscript named *The Fathiyah i 'Ibriyah* (also called Tarikh Fath i Āshām), or History of the conquest of Āssām. It was written by Ibn Muhammad Wali, or Shihabuddin Talish, between 1662 and 1663 AD. It records that in 1662 Meer Jumla, the Mughal viceroy of 'Bengal', sent to Assam a powerful armada, which included two of these vessels (Blochmann 1872: 73). If we discount this reference as riverine, and hence not of interest to this study, then another reference from a copy of *The Fathiyah i 'Ibriyah* preserved at the Bodleian Library (MS. Bod. 589, Sachau and Ethe's Catalogue, No. 240) leaves no doubt that these vessels were used for maritime activities as well. According to it, 135 Arakanese ships were captured when the Mughal fleet conquered Caṭṭagrāma in 1666. Of these, 22 were *bālāms* (Sarkar 1907a: 414). These must have regularly sailed from Arakanese ports to Caṭṭagrāma. These references, we acknowledge, are way beyond the time frame of this research. However, we have reasons to believe that the history of *bālāms* may be traced further back to the early medieval period. In order to justify our claim, we need to begin with an ethnographic study of the *bālām*.

Basil Greenhill, who undertook fieldwork in Bangladesh between 1950 and 1959, has observed that the *bālāms* were sewn-planked vessels fastened with fine splicing of bamboo and "quite without iron in their whole structure" (1971: 114). Today, as revealed in field-level investigation carried out by the author in Caṭṭagrāma coast, the class of vessels has become totally extinct, although its memory is very much alive among the older shipwrights of Sandwīp. They still remember the sewn-planked vessels, which appeared wide-bodied because their width was proportionately greater than the other classes of vessels. However, they remember more of the metal fastened *bālāms* because sewn-planked vessels were fast becoming obsolete during their youth.

As the shipwrights of Sandwīp remember, the larger *bālāms* were sea-going vessels, some of which were over 18 metres long, over 2 metres deep and 3.5 to 4.25 metres wide. Their carrying capacity varied between 600 *maunds* (over 20 tons) to 1,200 *maunds* (a little under 45 tons). They were operated with vertical and semi-balanced rudders on the quarter. Most of these vessels were fitted with two masts (placed in the fore and aft deck). The primary mast was placed in the fore-deck, in a tabernacle made out of heavy log. A square sail was set on this mast. The second mast, placed in the aft deck, was short and was used to set a lateen sail. These masts and sails used numerous stays and hence the rigging system of the vessel was quite complex. "*Bālāms* so rigged" notes Greenhill (1971: 115) had "a distinctly medieval appearance under sail". Aged sailors claim, *bālāms* also used topsails, which were set during suitable sailing conditions. When necessary, the crew of 16 or less would row the boat standing. Preferred timbers for construction of these vessels were *segun* (teak), *pitraj*, *suruj*, *gamari*, *garjan*. There were no fixed decks or cabins. According to Chakravarti and Dasa (1330: 19), who published a history of Sandwīp over seventy-five years ago, the people of the island (of Sandwīp) used to make coastal voyages to Myanmar in sewn-planked *bālāms*.

As Greenhill (1971: 114-115) points out, the *bālāms* were originally plank-extended dugouts. The greatest number of planks that he had observed was five on each side. "The heavy floor which keep the expanded dugout base in shape [were], in *balams* built in the classic tradition, secured with treenails". As in plank-extended dugouts, the bow and stern of many big *bālāms* were shaped as "a tall tapering board which occupie[d] the space between the plank ends above the flat top of the *goloi*-like end of the dugout". However, others did not have the board; instead, they had stem and sternposts of heavy timber lashed into place. Another type of stitched-plank vessels called *murinas*, was double-ended. The aged shipwrights of Sandwīp do not remember the dugout base of the *bālāms*. Describing the construction process, they say, the entire centre-board of the boat, from the bow to the stern, was shaped from a single piece of log. The log was hollowed out to a point where the thickness of the sides equaled the thickness of the planks with which the hull was built. The shipwrights' testimony actually supports Greenhill's observation because the hollowed centre-board was a vestige of the dugout base.

The very mode of construction of the *bālāms* indicates that they pre-date the arrival of the Portuguese. As observed earlier, the *bālāms* were originally sewn-planked vessels "quite without iron in their whole structure". Mathew (1999: 98) has shown that "[t]he use of iron nails in shipbuilding in India became more and more common since the beginning of the 16th century AD. This practice started by the Portuguese in India was accepted by the Indian shipwrights in the 16th and 17th centuries AD and was transmitted to their successors". Hence, stitched planked *bālāms* must have originated in the 15th century AD or earlier. In order to determine how far earlier, we may make a brief study of the *vallams* of Kerala.

The *bālāms* of 'Bengal' bore strong affinity not only in name but also in the construction of *vallams* of Kerala. As Hornell (1920: 155) points out, on the Tinnevelly coast in Kerala, there are fishing boat canoes called *ballams* or *vallams*. The Kerala *vallams* are similar to ordinary Malabar dugout because they are keel-less and have "retained the original rounded bottom of the dugout". The essential difference "is that the original dugout has been spread and its sides raised so that considerable stability is acquired". The Kerala *vallams* are designed mostly for sailing although paddles are also used. They are fitted with a medium-sized mast nearly amidships and use a single short and wide lug, not too dissimilar from the square sail. Because the operational draught is high and the thwarts are low, the vessels are very stable but difficult to row. They are double ended as well as flat-sterned and are fitted with a powerful rudder that is fixed with gudgeon and pintle. There is a wide variety of *vallams* in Kerala. These are *kettu*, *kolli*, *cundan*, *komban*, *orrakkori*, *muri*, *emaka*, *valiya*, and *katattu*. All these are stitched plank-extended dugouts (Greeshmalatha and Rajamanickam 1993: 39).

The point of similarity between the *bālāms* of 'Bengal' and the *vallams* of Kerala is that both are sewn-planked extended dugouts. This is not to suggest that the Kerala *vallams* travelled to 'Bengal' or the other way round. Two different peoples may very well arrive at the same solution for sailing, as indicated earlier, not so much because of some universal structural pattern but because of similar geographical conditions, availability of materials, tradition of craftsmanship and the general state and nature of the culture of the people building them. It must have been this similar solution arrived at by the peoples of 'Bengal' and Kerala that struck the Arab-Persians who began to venture in the shores of both the region by the 9th century AD, because, as Hornell (1920: 155) points out, "almost the same term [i.e., *ballam* or *vallam*] is used by Mesopotamian Arabs for all dugout canoes and for all boats of canoe form – long, narrow and keelless". We may therefore believe that the plank-extended dugouts that the Arab-Persians saw in 'Bengal' in the 9th century AD were named *ballam* by them. Hence, we may logically believe that the early forms of *bālāms* had already developed in 'Bengal' in the early medieval period. At this point we may remind ourselves that plank-extended dugouts have a long history in 'Bengal'. Indeed, it may not stretch one's imagination too far to see that the *bālāms* belonged to the same tradition as the plank-extended dugouts of the historic period such as the *saraṁgā*.

From the early historic period, the plank-extended dugouts must have undergone considerable evolution as the *Chittagong Gazetteer* indicates. In the mid-20th century, the *Gazetteer* had noted the existence of four types of *bālāms*: the *ad bālām* with one plank each side, the *bālām* proper with two planks on each side, the *gadu*, with three planks on each side, and the *jalyanao* with four planks on each side (Greenhill 1971: 114). We may believe that the early historic plank-extended dugouts had one plank each side. By the early medieval period, these boats had developed with two planks a side and these the *Chittagong Gazetteer* terms as the *bālām* proper. It must have been these boats that the Arab-Persians saw when they arrived in Caṭṭagrāma coast in the 9th century AD or earlier. We may further believe that these early historic *bālāms* were double-ended vessels with stem and sternposts of heavy timber lashed into place because Deloche (1996: 209) has shown with enough reason that double-ended vessel with "longitudinal curve of the hull and a sharp, raked stern" was possibly the standard in South Asian maritime tradition till the 14th and 15th centuries AD. As Needham (1971: 391) shows, the hull of the classical type of junks is like "the half of a cylinder or parallelepiped, bent upwards towards each end, and there terminated by final partitions". These partitions were rectangular transom stern and bow. The *bālāms* with tall tapering board in the bow and stern, though not rectangular, appear to have borrowed the stern and bow from Chinese junks. Following this line of argument, we may believe that these *bālāms* (with tall tapering board in the bow and stern) evolved after the 13th century AD since when (as we shall show in the following section) the junks began to venture into 'Bengal'.

The *bālām*, as discussed above, does not match the classes of vessels mentioned in the *Yukti Kalpataru*. Whereas the length: width ratio given in the text is 2:1 and 8:1, the same ratio in the *bālām* is approximately 5:1. Ignored also is the suggestion that the prows should be shaped like animals or birds. However, the *bālām* does abide by the suggestion that iron should not be used and masts should be limited to four or under. We may even believe that the preferred timber species for shipbuilding, specially *segun* (teak) and *gamari* belonged to the Ksatriya class. These indications may justifiably make us suspect that the *Yukti Kalpataru* had little bearing on the indigenous shipbuilding tradition of 'Bengal'. However, we will suspend our evaluation till we have examined the maṅgalakāvya corpus in the medieval period.

The quasi-vacuum created by the *Yukti Kalpataru* need not hinder our investigation because we have already succeeded in tracing the *bālām* to the early historic period. We may continue our investigation with the help of Arab-Persian literary sources, because, as already established in Chapter One, Arab-Persian merchants began trading in Caṭṭagrāma from the 9th century AD. Since these merchants sailed from the Persian Gulf region, we may reasonably assume that they used ships commonly known as the *dhow*.

The Dhow

The *dhow* is a generic term used by the Europeans to describe ships of Arab and Persian origin. Inclusive in the term is a wide range of forms and sizes. Mostly built by sewn plank technique, the *dhows* were the dominant vessels in the Arabian Sea and western Indian Ocean from the 6th century AD till the arrival of the Portuguese. Judging by Muqaddasī's *Ahsanu 't-Taqāsīm fī Ma'rifati 'l-Aqālīm* (985 AD), which gives the following list of thirty-six types of boats, it becomes clear that there were various types of *dhows* that sailed during the period of our study.

> Safīnah, jāsūs, zawraq, raqqīyah(?), talawwa, 'irdās, ṭayyār, zabzab, kārawānīyah, muthallathah, Wāsiṭīyah, malqūṭah, shankūlīyah, burākīwah, khaiṭīyah, shamūṭ, musabbaḥīyah,

jabalīyah, Makkīyah, zīrbādīyah, barkah, sūqīyah, ma'bar, walajīyah, ṭairah, bar'ānī, shabū, markab, shadhā, burmah, qārib, dūnīj, ḥamāmah, shīnī, shalandī, bīrajah (Has'an 1928: 131).

All these types are difficult to trace today because their names must have changed. Hence we can only surmise after McPherson (1998: 32-33) that "[o]n some routes, large deep-sea *dhows* were necessary to cope with the strong monsoon winds across the Arabian Sea, while smaller shallow-draught vessels were better suited to coastal routes and in shallow seas".

For further information on *dhows*, we may examine Marco Polo, who provides a detailed account of similar ships that he saw at Ormuz towards the end of the 13th century AD and hence deserves to be quoted in full.

> The vessels built at Ormus are of the worst kind, and dangerous for navigation, exposing the merchants and others who make use of them to great hazards. Their defects proceed from the circumstance of nails not being employed in the construction; the wood being of too hard a quality, and liable to split or to crack like earthenware. When an attempt is made to drive a nail, it rebounds, and is frequently broken. The planks are bored, as carefully as possible, with an iron auger, near the extremities; and wooden pins or treenails being driven into them, they are in this manner fastened (to the stem and stern). After this they are bound, or rather sewed together, with a kind of rope-yarn stripped from the husk of the Indian (cocoa) nuts, which are of a large size, and covered with a fibrous stuff like horsehair. This being steeped in water until the softer parts putrefy, the threads or strings remain clean, and of these they make twine for sewing the planks, which lasts a long time under water. Pitch is not used for preserving the bottoms of vessels, but they are smeared with an oil made from the fat of fish, and then caulked with oakum. The vessel has no more than one mast, one helm, and one deck. When she has taken in her lading it is covered over with hides, and upon these hides they place the horses which they carry to India. They have no iron anchors, but in their stead employ another kind of ground-tackle; the consequence of which is, that in bad weather, (and these seas are very tempestuous), they are frequently driven on shore and lost (Polo N. D.: 43-44).

Hornell (1920: 217) informs us that the ships that Marco Polo describes "were much more like the Laccadive Island boats than the Arab carrying craft of the present day as represented in the baggalas, dhangis and gunjos of the Persian Gulf and West Coast of India", which are mostly two-masted and joined with iron bolts. Marco Polo's poor opinion of the Arab *dhows* is not surprising since he was well acquainted with Chinese junks. Nevertheless, as Ibn Battutā observes, sewn-plank ships had a definite advantage: "when they happen to strike against a rock, the thread will yield a little, but will not soon break, contrary to what happens when put together with iron nails" (Lee 1829: 178).

The method of caulking that Marco Polo refers to is quite similar to that reported by Abu Zayd in the 10th century AD. He says, the "oil mixed with other materials [dammar and lime are those employed today] is used to pay the bottoms of sea-going ships to close the holes drilled for the sewing twine and for the caulking of the seams" (Hornell 1970: 234). The oil referred to in both the sources may have been whale oil. Citing Reinaud, Schoff (1995: 155) notes that "[t]he old Arab voyagers of the 9th century AD describes the fishermen of Siraf in the Gulf as cutting up the Whale-blubber and drawing oil from it, which was mixed with other stuffs, and used to rub the joints of ships' planking".

In his *Kitāb Nuzhatu-l Mushtāk fi Ikhtirāku-l Āflāq,* Al-Idrīsī (12th century AD) must have had the *dhows* in mind when he made the following note regarding construction of ships:

> All travelling boats of the sea of India and China, whether big or small, are constructed out of well-hewn wood. These (planks) are put edge to edge and trimmed, and then sewn with fibre. Then they are caulked with the small intestines and the oil of *al-baba. Al-baba* is a huge animal found in the Sea of India and China. Some of them are as large as a hundred cubits and twenty cubits wide (10th section of the 1st clime, 3-4; Ahmad 1960: 35).

Citing the ship painted in the *Maqāmāt* of al-Ḥarīrī in c. 1225-1235 AD, Tibbetts (1981: 49) convincingly argues that "[t]he hulls must have been two ended which was the original form of the Arabian Sea ship and as they possessed a rudder, this was probably attached to the sternpost ...". It may be further noted that the Ḥarīrī ship is a single-masted vessel fitted with a steeply raked sternpost. The mast is placed amidships and the cabin on the foredeck.

The *dhows* were fitted with a main mast and a mizzenmast, rigged with lateen (more accurately, settee) sails set in fore and aft configuration which made it possible for the ships to sail into the wind. Although the origin of such sails is unknown, it is possible that they made their first appearance in the Mediterranean in the 4th and 5th centuries AD (Angelucci 1970: 28) and was probably borrowed from the Arabs (Chitnis 1999: 21). The following observation by Bowen provides us with a clear picture of the maneuvering flexibility that the lateen sails afforded the *dhows*. "These boats were rigged with large lateen sails which could be trimmed into the wind closely so that the boats pointed a good 4 points off the wind, but they were shallow draught and slipped to leeward about 2½ points, so that the best actual course was 6½ points off the wind" (Bowen 1960: 130).

As John Edye (1834: 11) observes, the *dhows* were of about 150 to 250 tons' burthen. These vessels were fitted with a forward-raked mast and measured about 85 feet in length from stempost to stern, a little over 25 feet in breadth and nearly 12 feet in depth. A large *dhow* could carry 70 war-horses, 50 soldiers and 50 rowers as well as passengers and various cargo (Gibb 1986: 229). These were laden heavily and travelling in these ships was not quite pleasant. 'Abd al-Razzāq, the Timurid envoy to Calicut, who had to travel in a *dhow* in the mid-15th century AD, became, in his own words, "in some manner unconscious" because of the stench that emitted from the ship (Razzāq cited by Digby 1982c: 129). These ships were engaged in trade between the West Coast of India and southern Arabia even in the first half of the 19th century. In 'Bengal', the *dhows* featured prominently in the trade of rice and cowries between 'Bengal' and the Maldives.

Having thus obtained a workable impression of the *dhows*, we may now turn to Arab-Persian accounts for further information regarding the types which may have plied to 'Bengal'. As Ibn Khurdādhbih's *Kitāb* (c. 846-7 AD) indicates, Arab-Persian ships made coastal voyages through the Palk Straight and round the shores of Bay of Bengal. Although he does not mention any type of ship, it is clear that the ships that reached 'Bengal' were smaller shallow-draught vessels. These must have been similar to the ships from the Gulf of Persia and Arabia that Edye (1834: 12) refers to as "Country Traders". Even in the first half of the 19th century, these ships carried all the trade between 'Bengal' and the Gulf of Persia. Other possible identities of the medieval Arab-Persian ships which sailed to 'Bengal' are *zaruk* which is seen today mostly in the coastal region of the Red Sea, the Gulf of Aden and the Persian Sea and the *jalbas* from the Red Sea region – if these names may be accepted as phonetic derivatives of Muqaddasī's *zawraq* and *jabalīyah* referred to earlier.

There are many variations of the *zaruk*. The most distinctive feature of the vessel is that "both the stem and stern run to a sharp point, with a very gentle sheer on the gunwale line, but with a long slope upwards from the keel at both ends" (Hornell 1970: 239). It "has a fin-like rudder attached to the gudgeons and pintles or else slung from coir lashing from the stern-post. The control may be direct, by a tiller fitted to the rudder head, or indirect by a complicated system of tackles" (*ibid.*: 241). The vessels are swift-running and because they are light of draught, they can easily navigate through sandbanks and coral reefs. Since Khurdādhbih's ships made a coastal voyage to reach 'Bengal', it is possible that these were sewn-plank ships like the *zaruk* but with a simpler rudder system than that described by Hornell. Although *zaruks* may appear to be a far shot, we have definite evidence for the *jalbas*. We will take this up in the next section because the evidence indicates of their use in the medieval period.

MEDIEVAL PERIOD

Aniruddha Ray (1997: 39) finds it difficult to accept that ships were still being built in 'Bengal' in the 14th and 15th centuries AD. He further observes that the description of shipbuilding in (medieval) 'Bengal' has not come down to us. Ray appears to disregard Ma-Huan's testimony given in the first half of the 15th century AD in which the Chinese diplomat clearly states, "[w]ealthy individuals who build ships and go to various foreign countries to trade are quite numerous; ..." (Ma-Huan 1970: 160). The implication is clear: the wealthy individuals must have built ships locally. Man-Huan's testimony is corroborated by the maṅgalakāvya corpus, as our following examination will reveal. This is not to imply that the corpus leaves us a graphic account of medieval shipbuilding practices. However, if we are prepared to peel away grossly exaggerated poetic fancy, we may arrive at a core, which may well leave us with some indications of what we seek.

Let us begin by culling out all information given in the maṅgalakāvya corpus. In Bijayagupta's version, composed in 1494-95 AD, the merchant's fleet consists of fourteen ships. These are (1) the *Maṅgalā* (a wide-bodied vessel), (2) the *Candrapāṭ*, (3) the *Sindūrkaṭuyā* (a ship housing dancers), (4) the *Hāsamaḍā* (a ship carrying 700 horses), (5) the *Magar* (which served ritual purposes), (6) the *Dhuturār Phul* (a beautifully decorated vessel), (7) the *Gaurāṅgo* (a ship housing guards), (8) the *Samudra Uthāl* (a large vessel heavy of draught), (9) the *Sumantabahāl* (another large vessel heavy of draught), (10) the *Śaṅkhacūḍa* (a ship with great width carrying precious materials), (11) the *Garuḍa Mahārathī* (a speedy vessel), (12) the *Siṁghamukha* (another vessel for ritual purposes), (13) the *Candrarekhā* (carrying miscellaneous articles) and (14) the *Madhukar* (the flagship of C̃ād). Although the text cites another vessel named the *Gaṅgār Caraṇ*, this name may be a spurious addition (Bijayagupta 1962: 241-244). Only two of these vessels are anywhere near the suggestions made in the *Yukti Kalpataru* by Bhoja: (1) the *Maṅgalā*, described as a wide-bodied vessel that appears to be reminiscent of the *Sāmānya* class of vessel known as the *Patrapuṭā* and (11) the *Garuḍa Mahārathī*, a speedy vessel that appears to be reminiscent of the *Viśeṣa Dīrghā* class of vessel known as the *Veginī*.

Nārāyaṇa Deva, who composed his version in the early 16th century AD, also describes fourteen ships, but his names are different. The *Madhukar* (which served ritual purposes), the *Āgal-pāgal* (carrying goats), the *Candanapāṭ* (a lofty vessel from which distant shores could be visible), the *Ṭiñāṭhuṭī*, the *Jātrābar* (carrying areca-nut and betel-leaf), the *Sutārekhi* (another lofty vessel), the *Māṇikyameḍuyā* (rowed by 1600 oarsmen), the *Hiṅgulabāḍi*, the *Kājalarekhi* (still another lofty vessel), the *Śaṅkhacuḍa* (a cargo-carrier of conch-shells and vermilion powder), the *Ratnamālā* (a vessel carrying turmeric), the *Udayatārā* (carrying Cāndo's treasury), the *Durgābar* (vessel carrying gourd and coconut) and the *Kharasān* (Deva 1942: 187-188). Of these vessels, only four are anywhere near the suggestions made in the *Yukti Kalpataru* by Bhoja: the *Āgal-pāgal*, where the name appears reminiscent of the *Sāmānya* class of vessel known as the *Capalā;* the remaining three, i.e., the *Candanapāṭ*, the *Sutārekhi* and the *Kājalarekhi*, may be taken to indicate the *Viśeṣa Unnatā* class of vessels known as the *Ūrddhvā*.

Baṁśīdāsa's text (composed in the second half of the 16th century AD) describes another set of fourteen ships (such as the *Gaṅgāprasād*, the *Sāgarafenā*, the *Haṁsarava*, the *Rājavallabha*), details of which are not much different from Bijaygupta's version. The deck of his *Madhukar* is a veritable town complete with markets, a fresh-water tank (on which grow aquatic plants and fish), vegetable and flower gardens (Dasgupta 1935: 22).

Srīrāy Binod's version (composed in the 16th century AD) also has the typical set of fourteen ships, but the poet is more imaginative with names. Beginning with the *Madhukar* (the flagship of Cāndo), he continues with the *Durgābar*, the *Teladhār*, the *Sonāmukhī*, the *C̃āpāḍāla*, the *Rañgiyācāmar*, the *Monasukh*, the *Hākinī-ŝākhinī*, the *Kājol-koṭhā*, the *Baḍodhum*, the *Choṭadhum*, the *Halabalaṅkā*, the *Śaṅkhacuḍa*, and ends with the *Cuyāṭhuṭī* or the "mouse-lipped". He further describes these ships being rowed in the sea by oarsmen singing *sari* songs (Binod 1993: 195). Only one of these vessels are anywhere near the suggestions made in the *Yukti Kalpataru* by Bhoja: the *Sonāmukhī*, which is literally a colloquial equivalent of the *Viśeṣa Unnatā* class of vessels known as the *Svarṇamukhī*. Interestingly, the name is similar to one of the boats shown in the etchings of country boats made by G. A. Prinsep in 1830 is titled "*Sona Mookhee*". It was a state pleasure boat (*bajarā*) with cabins extending to three-quarters of the deck, leaving only the fore-deck open for guests to sit. In 1794, we find that a report of the East India Company notes the decision to sell another *bajarā* named the "*Sonamukhee*" (Yule and Burnell 1903: 120).

Kavikañkaṇa Mukunda, who is slightly less flamboyant in his fanciful imagination, assigns seven ships to Dhanapati's fleet (but actually names six). As described in his *Caṇḍīmaṅgala* (mid-16th century AD), the merchant's flagship too is the *Madhukara* (the Bee) fitted with cabins of gold. The other ships are the *Durgābara*, the *Guyārekhi*, the *Śaṅkhacuḍa*, the *Madhupāla* and the *Chotamuṭhuṭi*. Dhanapati's son Śrīmanta builds seven ships which are named the *Madhukar* (the flagship fitted with Śrīmanta's cabin), the *Siṁhamukhī* (its prow resembling the head of lion), the *Guyārekhi*, the *Raṇajayā* (the Victorious in War), the *Raṇabhīmā* (the Mighty in War), the *Sarbadharā* (the All-container) and the *Nāṭaśālā* (the Amusement Hall). These ships are a hundred yards in length and twenty yards in breadth and the prows are surmounted with figureheads of the *makara,* the elephant and the lion (Mukunda 1986: 195, 230). Among these only the *Raṇabhīmā* appears to be phonetically reminiscent of the *Sāmānya* class of vessel known as the *Bhīmā* in the *Yukti Kalpataru* by Bhoja. However, the dimension of the ships given by the poet, i.e., a hundred yards (200 cubits) in length and twenty yards (40 cubits) in breadth, or 5:1 is nowhere near the *Yukti Kalpataru*'s suggestions.

On close examination, it becomes clear that all the names of ships cited above actually do not signify types of vessels; they are simply ships named as such. Consider for example the following citation from Bijayagupta's text:

> At the head sails the ship named *Maṅgalā* ...
> Following it sailed the ship named *Candrapāṭ* ...
> Following it sailed the ship named *Sindūrkaṭuyā* ...
> Following it sailed the ship named *Hāsamaḍā* ...
> (Bijayagupta 1962: 241-242)

This manner of description of the merchant's fleet is typical of the *Manasāmaṅgala.* Hence, there can be little doubt that the description of ships thus culled together is given in the most general of terms. Except a few resemblances in shaping of the prow and a few vague reminiscences in ship-types, the descriptions of the ships do not match the *Yukti Kalpataru.* This can either mean that the *Yukti Kalpataru* was never followed in 'Bengal' or that it was a long forgotten text.

Another aspect that stands out on close examination is that the merchant fleet of C̃ād and Dhanapati are vaguely reminiscent of the fleet of travelling boats which accompanied dignitaries and high officials in 'Bengal' when river boats were the sole means of communication. Hornell (1924: 186), possibly referring to early 19th century 'Bengal', says in the old days the British Governor General used to travel in houseboats of considerable magnitude. Known as *bajarā* (or 'budgerow'), the hull of these boats belonging to the affluent class were fully decked and on this was built substantial wooden walled cabin, with Venetian windows and flat-roof. The cabin, extending up to three-quarters of the deck and leaving about a quarter of the forward end free, was divided into a number of rooms and was luxuriously fitted, "providing all the comforts and conveniences of a bungalow ashore" (*ibid.*). The Governor General's *bajarā* would be followed by a fleet of smaller boats. It included a kitchen boat, accounted perhaps the most important by the master, and others that served to accommodate guests, aides-de-camps, clerks, the military escorts and a veritable host of servants. *Bajarā* were also used by territorial river lords and wealthy merchants as ceremonial barges. As Hornell (*ibid.*: 246-247) describes, these were "gay with paint and gaudy trappings, the prow surmounted with figurehead of a horse or bird, and the high towering stern ending with some other fanciful figure". Prinsep's "*Sona Mookhee*" confirms that Srīrāy Binod's *Sonāmukhī* was actually a type of *bajarā.*

If we re-examine the fleet of C̃ād and Dhanapati, identifying the *Madhukara* as a fine *bajra*, accompanied by few smaller *bajras* housing the entertainers, priests, servants and soldiers and a number of other cargo vessels, we derive quite an acceptable picture of a merchant's fleet of ancient times as recorded in the maṅgalakāvya. Even the presence of the soldiers agree with medieval sailing practice, because, as Digby (1982c: 152-153) shows, almost all the Chinese and South Asian merchant ships that sailed along the western and eastern coast of India in the medieval period, carried armed soldiers to protect themselves from pirates. Thus it appears that the maṅgalakāvya poets derived their merchants' ships form convoy of *bajarās* used in the medieval pleasure trip of the royalty and convoy of mercantile ships. Śrīmanta's ships and even some of C̃ād's ships (such as the *Tiñāṭhuṭī* or the Parrot-beaked), appear to have been like the ceremonial barges of wealthy merchants, with prows of the ships displaying figurehead of birds or other animals.

The maṅgalakāvya corpus gives a clearer impression of the shipbuilding process. However, we may begin by noting that the earliest of these, Vipradāsa Pipilāi's *Manasā Vijaya* (composed in 1494 AD) does not describe shipbuilding. Instead, we find C̃ādo (i.e., C̃ād) surfacing his submerged ships with the help of divers (Sen 1953: 139). The practice is still seen in rural areas where boats are submerged in water during the dry season when not expected to be used for a prolonged period of time. Clearly, Vipradāsa Pipilāi implies that the merchant has not been sailing for quite some time.

In Baṁśīdāsa's *Padmapurāṇa*, the merchant Candradhar surfaces thirteen ships that his father used for trading voyages and has one built of *manapaban* timber by master carpenter Giribar. The carpenter with his sixteen hundred men turns heaven and the earth but cannot locate the fabled tree. Finally, they learn that it can be obtained only with the grace of Śiva, who can be appeased only with the sacrifice of a hundred thousand goats, sheep and buffaloes. Our merchant readily complies, Śiva is appeased and a branch of the tree is felled in the Himalayan region, from where it is floated down a river. The actual construction of the vessel is preceded by the ritual known as *sonār-jal* ("gold-nailing"), in which the merchant pierces a golden nail on the keel. Then the dimension of the vessel is determined: a thousand yards in length and six and half cubits from the keel to the central deck (clearly an absurd proportion). Next, a bamboo pole is carefully marked for measuring the depth of water. What follows next is a clear indication of construction in shell sequence. First, the hull is constructed by laying the planks edge to edge. These are joined with iron nails struck from both outside and inside. Baṁśīdāsa describes the process of chaulking as "soldering" the planks at their edges (*rāṅgajhāl*) and this is done after completing the hull. Next, the sternpost (*māñjākāṭha*) is fitted and to it is attached the helm (*hāl*) decorated with gold and silver. Then the deck, made of wooden planks laid edge to edge, is fitted. Next follows the fitting of the mast (*mālum kāṭha*). When these are complete, a decorated pavilion is constructed on the ship. Lastly, the oculi is attached to the prow (Baṁśīdāsa: 1357: 92-94).

In the *Manasāmaṅgala* by Jagajjīvana, the merchant C̃ād orders the master craftsman Kundāi to construct fourteen vessels immediately. He sets off to the forest with his apprentices and fells various trees. These include *sāral, piyāl, pipli, khajur, śāl, piyali, simli, c̃āpā, nageśvar, bakul, kāṭhāl, nim, nārikel, jalpāi* and *tāl*. Soon he has three or four hundred thousand planks ready. These he joins with iron nails (*lohār gojāl*) and constructs the ships (Jagajjīban 1984: 121). In Srīrāy Binod's *Padmā-purāṇa*, the merchant Candradhar fetches seven hundred carpenters and orders them to construct vessels from *manpaban* timber. The carpenters comply and saw the timber in the required size. Before commencing the actual construction of the vessel, the merchant offers homage to Biśvakarmā who promises to construct the vessels unseen by others. After offering salutations to Biśvakarmā and worshipping Hara and Gauri in preliminary rituals, the merchant inaugurates the building of his vessel by striking the prow. The keel is laid first and to it is added the stern and stemposts at the two ends. The measurement is then checked and the keel is trimmed. Planks were then joined to give shape to the hull. When it was done, the ribs and deck beams were fitted (Binod 1993: 188-189).

In Kavikaṅkaṇa Mukunda's *Caṇḍīmaṅgala,* Śrīmanta's seven ships are built by the gods: divine craftsman Biśvakarmā, his son Dārubrahmā and Hanumāna. With his nails, Hanumāna saws timber of teak, *gāmbhārī, tamāl, piyāl, k̃āṭhāl* and *tāl* species as Dārubrahmā makes large pegs *(gajāl).* Then sharpening his instrument, Dārubrahmā shaves numerous planks. Next, the father and son peg the planks and constructs beautiful vessels. First was fitted a vessel 100 yards in length and twenty in breadth with a prow shaped with ivory and decorated with a *makara* head and oculi. Thus was built the vessel named Madhukar with the mast on top and the seat for the helmsman at one side. It also contained cabins *(rai-ghar)* in the middle and two rows of seats for the oars-men *(pāiṭ).* Construction of the remaining vessels then followed one after another (Mukunda 1986: 230).

In the *Padmapurāṇa* by Nārāyaṇa Deba and Jānakī Nātha, the merchant commands all the carpenters to go to the mountains specifically urging them to fetch none other than *manpaban* timber. When the timber is fetched, the carpenters invoke Biśvakarmā and the god saws the timber overnight. Then the carpenters shave the plane of the planks. When informed thus, the merchant performs rituals on a suitable day and lays the keel, to which the carpenters smear vermilion dots as signs of well-being. *Manpaban* planks are then joined to the two sides of the keel and the hull is constructed without any crack or leak. The mast is fitted next and gold and silver moulds are attached. Finally, two-and three-parted ribs are constructed and fitted in a row (Deba and Nātha 1382: 139, 141-142).

The mode of construction indicated in the above texts implies that shipbuilding in medieval 'Bengal' generally followed the principles of shell-sequence. The ships were mostly double-ended (Srīrāy Binod's *Padmā-purāṇa*) and single-masted. The seat for the helmsman at one side (in Kavikaṅkaṇa Mukunda's *Caṇḍīmaṅgala*) indicates that the vessel was steered by a quarter paddle. Although joining of wood is not specified, we do learn that the preferred timber species for shipbuilding were teak, *gāmbhārī, tamāl, piāl, k̃āṭhāl* and the fabled *manpaban*. These may be thought to belong to the Ksatriya class of wood as recommended by Bhoja in the *Yukti Kalpataru.* A noteworthy feature in two texts cited above (Baṁśīdāsa's *Padmapurāṇa* composed in the second half of the 16th century and Jagajjīban's *Manasāmaṅgala,* 17th century AD) is that iron nails are described as being used in the construction. Tantrabibhūti's *Manasāpurana,* another text composed in the 17th century, speaks of rows of *lohāIr gajāl* (iron nails or pegs) being used in the construction of Cāndo's (i.e., C̃ād Saodagar's) ships (Tantrabibhūti 1980: 132). Curiously, Bhoja in the *Yukti Kalpataru* forbids the use of nails. On the other hand, Kavikañkaṇa Mukunda's *Caṇḍī-maṅgala* mentions merely "*gajāl*", which does not necessarily denote only iron nails but also treenails or any type of peg. Dasgupta (1935: 16) appears to have missed the point in his translation of "*gajāl*" in Kavikañkaṇa Mukunda's *Caṇḍī-maṅgala* simply as "nails", thus implying iron nails.

At this stage it is necessary to compare our findings on the medieval shipbuilding practice as given in the maṅgalakāvya corpus with current practice followed by shipwrights in Bangladesh and West Bengal. This may lead us to a position from where we may evaluate both the maṅgalakāvya corpus and the *Yukti Kalpataru.*

According to the shipwrights in the Caṭṭagrāma coast and offshore islands, the first step in shipbuilding, after acquiring the timber, is seasoning. For this purpose, the timber is submerged in salt-water, in the canals or river where the yard is located, for a minimum of 15 days to maximum of 6 months (on rare occasions even for a year). However, it is also not unusual for vessels to be constructed without seasoning of the timber. If asked what difference it makes in seasoning, the shipwrights laugh slyly and say, those vessels become our constant customers – for they need repairing off and on.

When the timber has been seasoned, the carpentry phase of boat-building begins. The shipwrights of Bangladesh and West Bengal do not follow any śāstric text to guide their construction but largely depend upon their experience and visual estimation. One aged shipwright in Caṭṭagrāma recalled, though, a master craftsman under whom he had apprenticed, who actually drew upon a large floor mat the vessel to be built in actual size. Nevertheless, such practice is extremely rare.

The first part of the carpentry phase involves laying of the keel, which is a seamless length of timber, rectangular in cross-section. The keel is laid on a narrow and low wooden bench of level height (Fig. 4.12). The stem and sternposts, which are also rectangular in cross-section and seamless, are joined to the keel with large iron nails (*gajāl perek*, 15 to 20 cm long). A scaffolding of bamboo and timber is built to hold the posts in position. When the keel and posts are securely in position, the carpenters begin the next part, which is planking. The first strake (preferably seamless, otherwise splice joined) is nailed at an angle, on both sides of the keel. The angle at which the strakes are joined contributes to the hull shape. Next, six or seven strakes (depending on the vessel size) are laid edge-to-edge and joined with nails struck from the outside. These strakes are widest near the centre of the vessel (15 cm wide) and gradually narrow down towards the stem and sternposts (12 to 7.5 cm wide). Having secured seven or eight strakes above the keel, U-shaped ribs are inserted one after another (beginning with the centre and gradually extended to the sides) and are held in position by temporary wooden support (Fig. 4.13). The ribs are made of three pieces, splice joined above the bend of the 'U'. With the ribs in position, the carpenters proceed to lay planks on the exterior of the ribs; edge to edge, joining them with iron nails about 15 cm apart, till the sheer strake is laid. When the planking is finished, thwarts are nailed to the gunwale. The planks of the deck are laid above the thwarts. The cabins are constructed next and then the mast/s are fitted. The

Fig. 4.12 The laying of the keel, stem and sternposts of a ship, Sandwip

Fig. 4.13 A skeleton-built boat under construction, Cox's Bazar

Fig. 1.14 A Kalpat Mistri preparing cotton thread in Sandwip

Fig. 4.15 A Kalpat Mistri inserting cotton thread for chaulking a ship, Sandwip

remaining accessories, such as oar/paddle, rudder, anchor and sails are made next. The shipwright has the rudder and the anchor made by iron-smiths, who are not part of the carpentry construction team.

At the end of the carpentry stage, the carpenters leave the boatyard, handing over the next phase of the job to the caulkers and painters, who are known as *kālapāt Mistri.* Their first step is to make cotton thread (Fig. 4.14) and then insert the thread between seams of adjacent planks, from outside the hull (Fig. 4.15). Sometimes cotton is applied directly instead of the thread. Next they apply putty (made of juice extract from *garjan* trees) on both sides of the cotton thread. Next, tar is applied on the lower section of the hull which will remain submerged. A coat of crude oil *(māitya tel)* is applied on the upper part of the hull, till the sheer strake and in the interior of the vessel. Above the sheer strake, the boat is decorated where desired with synthetic enamel paint. When old boats are renovated or repaired, the old coat of tar is taken off by applying fire to the bottom of the hull and then scraping off the burnt residue.

The skeleton sequence of boat-building described above, according to the shipwrights, has become widely prevalent since only the last few years. They acquired this method from the boat builders of Dhaka and adjoining areas. Earlier, they say, the shell-sequence was the dominant process. Following this process, the keel was joined to the stern and stem posts and the strakes were flush laid and joined edge to edge. The first strake was laid on both sides of the keel and the rest of the strakes followed from the bottom to the top. When the shell was complete, they proceeded to insert the ribs (Fig. 4.16). The rest of the process was similar to that described above.

Fig. 4.16 A shell-built boat under construction at Digha

The three sources discussed above, i.e., the maṅgalakāvya corpus, the *Yukti Kalpataru* and contemporary practice of shipwrights, are widely divergent on a few areas. For example, neither the maṅgalakāvya corpus nor the *Yukti Kalpataru* mentions seasoning of timber and caulking of vessels that the shipwrights of Bangladesh and West Bengal undertake. The maṅgalakāvya corpus describes shell sequence in shipbuilding process that appears to have been prevalent among the shipwrights of Bangladesh and West Bengal till recent times. Hence, we may accept with enough certitude that the maṅgalakāvya corpus reflects shipbuilding practice of the medieval period. As for the *Yukti Kalpataru*, we have so far found very few points of similarity, either with actual practice of with the maṅgalakāvya corpus. Hence, we may conclude that the text was either not known or followed in 'Bengal', or had become unknown by the 15th century AD when the earliest text of the maṅgalakāvya corpus was composed. Having derived this conclusion, we may now look for types of ships that may have plied to and from the ports of 'Bengal' in the medieval period.

The Paṭiyā

The earliest literary reference that we have of the *paṭiyā* is from Caesar Frederic, who, in 1567, describes his journey along the coast from the Port of Orisa (Orissa) to the harbour Piqueno (Satagan or Sātgāon). "They goe as it were rowing alongst the coast fiftie and four miles, and then we enter into the river Ganges: from the mouth of this River, to a City called Satagan, where the Merchants gather themselves together with their trade, are an hundred miles, which they rowe in eighteene houres ...". The vessels (Barkes,[1] as Frederic calls them) that plied between Sātgāon and the Port of Orissa were "light and armed with Cares, like to Foistes".[2] He adds that the locals "call these Barkes, Bazaras and Patuas: they rowe as well as a Galliot, or as well as ever I have seene any" (Purchas 1905b: 113). The Port of Orissa that Frederic refers to must have been Pipli, "at one time a very famous port, and the most important harbour on the Orissa coast, on the Suvarṇarekhā River, about 16 miles from its mouth ..." (translator's footnote, Bernier 1968: 443). There can be little doubt that Frederic's Patuas were actually

[1] Bark or BARQUE was a class of sailing ship with three or more masts, the rear (mizzenmast) being rigged for a fore-and-aft rather than a square sail. Until fore-and-aft rigs were applied to large ships to reduce crew sizes, the term was often used for any small sailing vessel. Hence, the passage cited above should be read to imply "a small sailing vessel".

[2] Light vessels of the galley type, propelled by oars as well as sails.

paṭiyās, a vessel of Orissan origin, with largest concentration of which is currently seen at Talesri on the mouth of the Suvarṇarekhā. The "seven-oared scallop" that Bernier voyaged in, from Pipli to Huglī nearly a century after Frederic (*ibid.*), must also have been a *paṭiyā*. The same is true about the *petooa* that F. B. Solvyns depicted in the late 18th century. As the field-level investigation carried out by the author at Dighā revealed, *paṭiyās* are still used in fishing in the Contai and northern Orissa coast, venturing as much as 20 km deep into the Bay (Fig. 4.17).

Fig. 4.17 A patiya at Digha

We may reasonably assume that the *paṭiyās* Caesar Frederic saw plying from Pipli to Huglī in 1567 were active in the early 16th century. Actually, its history may very well stretch back much earlier because the *paṭiyās* are reverse-clinker type of vessels and similar vessels have been identified in a 12th-century stone relief in the Jagamohana of the temple of Jagannath at Puri in Orissa and a sculptural boat model from eastern India (Fig. 4.18) that is believed to be from the 11th-12th centuries AD (Guy 1997: 770-771) and is now held by the Victoria and Albert Museum in London. Although the exact provenance of the sculptural boat model is unknown, it has "elements which relate to the Orissan boat tradition" (*ibid.*: 769) and is strikingly similar to the stone relief in the temple of Jagannath at Puri. This is not to claim that the *paṭiyā* is an exact replica of the stone relief and the sculptural boat model. Nevertheless, the very fact that reverse-clinker type of vessels was being built in Orissa in the 11th-12th centuries AD indicates that the *paṭiyā* was not a 16th-century innovation.

Fig. 4.18 A sculptural boat model, Victoria and Albert Museum, London. Courtesy: Gerd J.R. Mevissen

Reverse-clinker types of vessels are so called because of the manner of their planking. As McGrail *et al.* (1999: 121) explain, "each succeeding strake of planking overlaps *in*board the upper edge of the strake below, rather than overlaps *out*board, as is generally found in European clinker-built boats". In the vessels planked in the reverse-clinker technique, the first strake beside the keel runs uninterrupted along the full curved length of the vessel, from the stempost to the stern, rising well above the waterline. The number of strakes that follow are shorter in length and do not approach the posts. These strakes are planked in reverse-clinker technique. Above these lower posts are fitted more strakes that run the full length of the vessel. These may be planked flushed, in reverse-clinker or even in clinker technique. In Bangladesh, reverse-clinker technique is known as *digkata* and boats built in such technique have been identified at Sylhet, Mymansingh and Khulna. Reverse-clinker vessels are important because they disprove the earlier belief that sewn-planking was the "universal" technique of indigenous boat-building tradition in South Asia.

The building of the *paṭiyā* follows shell-sequence with planks secured by iron hooked-nails. More importantly, the planking technique followed is a combination of reversed clinker and clinker.

> From keel to the 8th strake, the planks overlap in a reverse manner i.e. the inside upper-edge of the lower strake overlaps the outside of the lower edge of the upper strake. The ninth to the sheer strake (11th strake) are broad straight timbers laid in ordinary clinker style. The ninth strake is laid on the strake below it at almost right angle, thus forming a chine. This change in planking gives the boat its particular shape and combined attributes of both clinker techniques (Mishra 2000: 624).

The *paṭiyās* are narrow and deep vessels with sharp bow and stern. As Mishra (*ibid.*: 626) has pointed out, its keel is T-shaped in cross-section. Known as hogged-keel, it may be shaped out of a single member or by joining a horizontal beam (hog). Preferred timber species for building the *paṭiyā* are Orissa *sal* (*Shorea robusta*) and *arjun*.

Although today the *paṭiyās* are fastened with iron hooked-nails, it is not impossible that at an earlier stage, the fastening was done with pins of split bamboo as reported in the case of *khil nauka* type of clinker-built boats seen in Noakhali in the 1920s. These pins were charred to soften their outer surface and were then driven into holes slightly smaller in diameter than the pins themselves (Greenhill 1971: 107).

Three varieties of the *paṭiyā* may be seen today plying in the northern Orissa coast and adjoining West Bengal. These are the motorised *paṭiyā*, the sailing *paṭiyā* and the oared *paṭiyā*. The oared *paṭiyās* measure between 7.74 m to 8.52 m in length, 1.72 m to 1.82 m across and 1.03 m to 1.17 m in depth. These vessels are built with 14 to 15 strakes on each side. Usually eight oarsmen row the oared *paṭiyā*. On the foremost crossbeam sits the bow oarsman and rows to starboard. The oarsman behind him rows to portside. The remaining six are double-banked and they sit on the three following crossbeams. The sailing *paṭiyās* are usually about 7 m in length, 1.5 m across and 0.7 m in depth. They are built with 11 strakes on one side. There is only one sail, rigged to a bamboo mast that stands directly on the keel, near amidships. The sail is best described as a type of lug but is handled like a lateen. The motorised *paṭiyās* are often 8.5 m to 10.5 m in length and are built with 14 to 16 strakes on each side (Kentley *et al.* 1999: 153-155; Blue *et al.* 1997: 197-203).

Since Caesar Frederic refers to the *paṭiyās* as "light and armed with Oares" and the sailors rowed these vessels and that Bernier refers to these as seven-oared vessels, we may safely assume that they had the oared variety in mind. However, it is very likely that the sailing *paṭiyās* were also used for maritime commerce. We may even conjecture a combination of sailing and oared *paṭiyās* traversing the coastal route connecting Sātgāon and Pipli.

The Bajarā

The earliest literary reference to Bazaras (anglicized corruption of *bajarā*) that we have is from Caesar Frederic cited above, who, in 1567, wrote of vessels of this class plying between Pipli and Sātgāon. We come across it again nearly a century in the 17th-century Persian manuscript *The Fathiyah i 'Ibriyah*, which records that in 1662, Meer Jumla, the Mughal viceroy of 'Bengal', had embarked on a campaign against Assam with 323 ships, 4 of which were Bajrahs (*bajarās*) (Blochmann 1872: 73). T. A. Bowrey (1905: 228, 277) also shows the *budgaroo* (*bajarā*) in one of his drawings of the five boats of Eastern India that he made in 1670. The Antwerp artist F. B. Solvyns (1799) also published drawings of about thirty typical Bengali vessels, one of which is a *bajarā*. The etchings of "country boats" of the Gaṅgā delta made by Prinsep in 1830 provide us further visual evidence in the form of four *bajarās*.

Although Hornell (1924: 186) describes quite a few varieties of *bajarās*, we need to consider the largest variety that he calls *bajarā* proper because the others appear to be more favourable for riverine conditions. The *bajarā* proper served the double purpose of carrying passengers and goods. It was 30 to 50 feet long, 8 to 16 feet broad and 4 to 6 feet deep. Three-quarter length of the deck was taken up by flat-roofed cabins, leaving about 8 to 12 feet in the fore-deck open to sky. When necessary, two to four oarsmen positioned on each side of the fore-deck would be engaged in rowing the vessel. Their oars were bamboo poles to which were attached long wooden blades.

> The vessel [was] steered by a long and powerful sweep hung from the stern, having a very large oval blade. The fixed single mast [was] stepped amidships; a slender removable upper mast [was] usually added connected by wooden pegs or iron bolts. The mainsail (*gachh badam*) [was] square with a bamboo-yard along the upper margin; in fine weather a square topsail (*dogibadam*) [was] hoisted above the main sail (*ibid.*).

As the *Hobson-Jobson* adds, the *bajarā* (or the Budgerow) was "[a] lumbering keelless barge, formerly much used by Europeans travelling on the Gangetic rivers. Two-thirds of the length of it was occupied by cabins with Venetian windows" (Yule and Burnell 1903: 120). A visual representation of these vessels may be seen in Prinsep's etching. However, as a letter written by the Christian missionary Claudius A. Barbier during his visit to 'Bengal' in the early 18th century says, sometimes cabins *in the bajarās* were limited to one or two on the stern. Further, size of *bajarās* determined the number of oarsmen who could vary from six to forty. These vessels plied not only to and from the Huglī but also between Dhaka and Caṭṭagrāma (*Bengal Past & Present* 1910: 203, 207, 211).

Caesar Frederic's reference to the *bajarā* is a clear indication that vessels of this class were being used in the medieval period, along the Contai and northern Orissa coast. However, the vessel has become completely extinct, at least in Contai and Caṭṭagrāma coast. During her field visits to Caṭṭagrāma, Bālāgarh and Dighā, when the author asked local shipwrights and mariners about the *bajarā*, none of them appeared to have heard about it.

We do not know anything about the construction process of the *bajarās*, as the information is not available. Form the general process followed in the construction of the round-hulled and smooth-skinned (*binekata*) vessels described by Greenhill (1971: 86-91), it may be assumed that the *bajarās* were round-bottomed and double-ended vessels without keels, although the central plank was thicker than the rest of the boat. The two ends of these vessels rose above the water to terminate in *golois* (solid blocks of timber). The building of the *bajarās* followed shell-sequence with the strakes joined edge to edge. The lower strakes were joined to the central plank that was so laid as to attain the shape of a leaf. These were then surmounted by a series of horizontal strakes to form the topside of the vessel. Greenhill shows that the planks of the *binekata* vessels are stapled with iron nails. However, as the name *binekata* (literally, "nail-less") suggests, the *bajarās* must have been sewn-planked at an earlier stage. The lower shape of the hull also suggests that the *bajarās* may have been *Patrapuṭā* class of *sāmānya* (cargo-carrying) vessels described in the *Yukti Kalpataru*.

The Jāliyā

Friar Nicholas Pimenta, a Jesuit missionary in 'Bengal' had observed in a letter dated 8 September 1602 that the ships "most in use are called Jaleas, which consist of a single tree trunk, and have thirty oars" (Hosten 1925: 55). We hear of a similar vessel, this time spelt as *jalia,* from a Portuguese report on their forts and settlements in India (dated 1644). It recounts the adventure of a Sebastian Gonçalves Tibau, a native of Portugal of humble origin. The enterprising Portuguese arrived in 'Bengal' in 1605. After setting himself up in the salt trade "he bought a jalia, a kind of vessel that is there used for fighting and trading at once" (*Bocarro* 1615, cited in Yule and Burnell 1903: 362). It appears that both the Portuguese and the Arakanese used this type of vessel in their fleets when they fought over each other to possess Caṭṭagrāma and Sandwīp in 1602 (Campos 1919: 68-71). This seems very possible when we remind ourselves that Sandwīp grew to be a renowned shipbuilding centre by the second half of the 16th century AD, so much so that Caesar Frederick observed that "the Sultan of Constantinople found it cheaper to have his vessels built here, then at Alexandria" (Taylor I, 1840: 70-71). The vessels built at Sandwīp, as Rizvi (1970: 225) believes, were none other than the *jāliyās*.

The Portuguese missionary Sebastien Manrique, who sailed extensively on the Caṭṭagrāma and Arakan coast from 1629-35, describes quite extensively a class of vessel he refers to as Geliās. However, we must remember that he is describes only those used for naval warfare. According to Manrique,

> [T]he Magh kings [of Arakan] decided to always retain Portuguese in their service, ... on the understanding that they maintained a certain force of their countrymen and also Geliās. Geliās are very swift vessels which are used on the Ganges for fighting. They are usually propelled by thirty-eight rowers ... [The Portuguese were authorized to take their vessels into the principality of Bengala ... Here they would sack and destroy all the villages and settlements on the banks of the Ganges ... This raiding was pronounced by the Provincial Council at Goa to be just ... (Manrique 1927: 285).

Luard and Hosten, the translators of Manrique's *Travels* adds that some Geliās were "so long that they have up to fifty oars on each side, but there were not more than two men to each oar" (*ibid.*: 33, fn. 24).

The Portuguese Geliās voyaged from Dianga even to the port of Pipli in Orissa. A missionary named Baltwar de St Ursula had arrived at Pipli in one of these vessels and on its way back, the Portuguese crew had captured a Moorish ship (*ibid.*: 441-442). The Mughals also maintained Geliās. That the Arakanese maintained Geliās in their navy is confirmed by Manrique who reports that in 1630 the Arakanese king had ordered his Captain-General of sea and land forces to prepare five hundred of these vessels and forty Galleys and to sail to Dianga where they were to suppress the Portuguese (*ibid.*: 90). Manrique informs us that the Nawab of Dhaka "deputed a Mirzā" [a nobleman] to fetch two Portuguese merchants from Sātgāon and he himself travelled by "the swiftest of boats called Geliās" (*ibid.*: 32).

Manrique himself travelled on a Portuguese Geliā in 1629 from Huglī "down the Ganges" to reach Dianga in fourteen days (*ibid.*: 83). Again, on 2nd July 1630, he "embarked on a Geliā manned by powerful rowers" that carried him "along a narrow, boiling river, across the mouths of several streams and arms of the sea, all dangerous to navigate" because it was the rainy season (*ibid.*: 94-95). So tempestuous was his voyage along the coast that he had to disembark at Ramu, where the local governor persuaded him to travel to the Arakanese capital by land. In 1635, he travelled again on a Geliā from Mrauk-U to Dianga. Soon after he departed from Dianga, boarding another Geliā from Patanga (on the mouth of the Karṇafulī) and rowing past Sandwīp, Dakṣiṇa Śāhbājpur and Hātiyā, through the estuary of the Meghnā and then through "one of the branches of the mighty and ancient Ganges" which had jungles on both banks (*ibid.*: 394). Unfortunately, he was captured by the Mughals on one of the channels of the Huglī River before he could reach his destination.

Some years after Manrique, in 1663, a Venetian tourist named Niccolao Manucci visited 'Bengal' and recorded the name of vessel called *julia*. While travelling through the Sundarbans, he learnt about a ferocious Portuguese from Chatigaõ (Chātgaṇw) who reportedly killed a Royal Bengal Tiger single-handed. "His boat was the *Julia*, and his own name was Manoel Coelho" (Manucci 1907, II: 87).

In the Arakanese court of the 17th century AD, a number of Muslim poets such as Ālāul, Māgan Thākur and Kāzī Daulat, composed verse narratives in Bengali based on indigenous and Perso-Arabic tales which have become treasures of Bengali literature. Some of these, such as *Candrābatī* (1652-59) by Māgan Thākur and *Padmābatī* (1651) by Ālāul refer to a few types of ships, which are important to note. *Candrābatī*, for example, mentions the names of the *gorāb* and the *jāliyā* (Sharif 1977: 296). On the other hand, *Padmābatī* mentions the names of the *sulup, the macuyā,* the *gorāb,*[3] *the jāliyā*, the *kāṣdā*, the *p̃āti* (*ibid.*: 299).

Today, a type of vessels known as the *jāli* is seen plying in Caṭṭagrāma coast. The most distinguished feature of these vessels is their flat stern and sharply raked stempost, which projects diagonally away from the keel. These are carvel-built vessels where the planks are assembled edge to edge on pre-fabricated frames. The carrying capacity of these vessels usually varies between 2,000 *maunds* (over 72 tons) to 6,000 *maunds* (over 218 tons). The length varies between 25 m to 12 m from bow to stern, The 6,000-*maund jālis* are about 18.5 m long from bow to stern, 4.5 m wide from starboard to

[3] Husain (1953: 176, fn. 2) shows that 'ghurāb' means a crow. The term was used to indicate "a long-pointed and low warship".

port side, and 3 m deep from the sheer strake to the bottom of the hull. Most of these vessels are equipped with six oars and two masts. The masts are placed in the fore and aft deck and use lateen sails. They also carry topsails, which are set during suitable sailing conditions. The crew of a *jāli*, besides the serang (*sāreṅ*), consist of 8 to 9 *khālāsīs* (sailors). Sometimes a *bhāndārī* (cook) is also taken as a member of the crew, while at other times, one of the *khālāsīs* performs the duties of a cook.

As reported by mariners of Caṭṭagrāma coast, smaller *jālīs* were known as *sulluks*. These vessels have become extinct today. Their carrying capacity ranged from 2,000 *maunds* (over 72 tons) to 4000 *maunds* (over 145 tons). These vessels were fitted with two masts. These also carried lateen sails and used topsails when conditions were favourable. *Sulluks* were operated with ten crews: a serang and 9 *khālāsīs*.

Because the *'sulup'* and the *'jāliyā'* are referred to in medieval Bengali literature from the Arakanese court and because these names appear to be phonetically similar to the *jāli* and the *sulluk*, there can be little doubt that these two operated in Arakan in the 17th century AD. From Sebastien Manrique's evidence there can remain no doubt that this class of vessels operated along the coast of 'Bengal'. Although we do not hear of the *sulluk* from European travelers, the *jāliyā* appears to be very common if we accept – and there is no reason why we should not – Nicholas Pimenta's *jalea* ("the most commonly used vessel in Bengal", 1602), Tibau's *jāliyā* (1605), Manrique's Geliās (1629-35) and Manuci's Julia (1663) to be phonetic derivaties of *jāliyā*. What is striking is that everyone seems to be using it – the Mughals for fetching Portuguese merchants, Manrique for sailing to Dianga from Huglī and Mrauk-U, and the Portuguese and the Arakanese for waging war. Hence we may reasonably assume that the *jāliyā* evolved in the 16th century AD or even earlier.

The *jāliyās* may have evolved from three sources. If we accept the name *jāliyā* to be a derivative of *jalba*, it seems possible that the origin of these vessels lie in Arab Persian *dhows*. The *jalbas* were actually large vessles of Arab-Persian origin that were "made of planks stitched together with coconut fibre". In c. 1330, Ibn Battutā embarked such a vessel at Jeddah and indicates that these vessels also carried camels (Gibb 1986: 106). Unfortunately, we have no pictorial evidence of the *jalbas* to draw a definite conclusion.

The second possible source could be the Portuguese carrack, which, as Moreland (1920: 203) informs us, was one of the four major classes of ships available in South Asia in the second half of the 16th century AD (the other vessels, according to him, were the pilgrim ships sailing to the Red Sea, ordinary sea-going merchant vessels, and small coasting crafts). The carracks, which may have originated in Portugal, were large carvel-built and flat-sterned vessels. They were fitted with three masts with two square sails and a lateen, large fore and aft castles and decks capable of accommodating over a thousand passengers (Angelucci 1970: 26). Unfortunately, as Alves (2003) points out, details of Portuguese ships built before the 17th century are meagre and hence we cannot enter into a comparative study in detail. Nevertheless, even a cursory glance at the visual representations shows that the two vessels are very different in terms of construction. The stempost of the *jāliyā* is by far more diagonally raked than the carracks. Furthermore, the *jāliyā* is fitted with two masts compared to the carrack's three. The *jāliyā* is much smaller in dimension and has only a few diminutive cabins in the aft. Only their carvel-build and flat-sterns can be cited by way of similarity. Because the carracks began venturing in the Bay of Bengal from the beginning of the 16th century, it seems certain that the *jāliyās* could not have evolved directly from them, but may have drawn inspiration from the carracks after the arrival of the Portuguese.

The third possible source for the origin of the *jāliyās* that we may trace is indigenous boat-building tradition. The above-mentioned letter written by Friar Nicholas Pimenta in 1602 testifies that the *jāliyās* (Jaleas) were built from a single tree trunk (Hosten 1925: 55). This leads us to suspect that these were plank-extended dugouts. Our suspicion is confirmed by the *Chittagong Gazetteer* in the mid-20th century, because it describes *jalianao* (i.e., *jāliyā* boat) as a type of *bālām:* a plank-extended dugout with four planks a side. It was used mostly for deep-sea fishing (Greenhill 1971: 114). Because plank-extended dugouts developed locally over a long period of time, it seems more probable that the *jāliyās* originally belonged to this tradition and adopted carvel-build and flat-stern after the arrival of the Portuguese.

Although the maṅgalakāvya corpus confirms the continuance of indigenous tradition of shipbuilding in the medieval period as exemplified in the *bālāms*, the *jālias*, and the *bajarās*, there can be little doubt that junks and *dhows* were the two types of maritime vessels that carried most of the maritime trade. As for the junks, we find confirmation from Tome Pires more than once in his *Suma Oriental*. At the beginning of the Third Book, he says, "[t]he Bengalees are merchants with large fortunes, men who sail in junks" (Pires 1967: 88). In the same chapter, he later repeats, "[a] junk goes from Bengal to Malacca once a year, and sometimes twice" and "[t]hese people sail four or five ships and junks to Malacca and to Pase every year ..." (*ibid.*: 92). Pires' observation is supported by Barbosa, who further clarifies that the "ships" Pires refers to were actually ships of Mekkah build, i.e., *dhows*.

> All of these [i.e., Arabs, Persians, Abexis or Abyssinians and Indians living in the city of Bengala] are great merchants and they possess great ships after the fashion of Meca; others there are from China, which they call "*juncos*", which are of great size and carry great cargoes (Barbosa 1921: 141-142, 145).

It is possible that the sultan's ship at Sonārgāon, compared with small Portuguese ships of the early 16th century by a Portuguese traveller (Ray 1997: 38-39), was actually a *dhow*. Although this reference is vague, we have definite evidence that *dhows* were extensively used and even constructed in medieval 'Bengal'. According to the 17th-century Persian manuscript *The Fathiyah i 'Ibriyah* referred to earlier, Meer Jumla's fleet that invaded Assam in 1662 consisted of 323 ships including 48 jalbahs (Blochmann 1872: 73). According to the Bodleian manuscript, in 1664 Shaistā Khān built an imperial fleet comprising of 288 war ships including 96 *jalbas*, in order to suppress Arakanese-Portuguese piracy. All these were constructed in 'Bengal', possibly at Hughli, Baleswar, Murang, Chilmari, Jessore and Karibari (Sarkar 1907a: 406). The manuscript also shows that the Arakanese navy possessed 67 (or 68?) *jalbas* (*ibid.*: 414). If Meer Jumla and Shaistā Khān could construct the *jalbas* in 'Bengal' in the 1660s, we may confidently believe that the practice of building these vessels in 'Bengal' began much earlier. In fact "the wealthy individuals who build ships" that Ma-Huan (1970: 160) refers to, may actually have built *dhows*. Since we have already examined the *dhow*, we may now concentrate on the junk.

The Junk

Ibn Battutā, who was in China in 1347, provides us with details about contemporary Chinese ships. These he classified in three sizes:

> The Chinese vessels are of three kinds; large ships called *chunks*, middle-sized ones called *zaws*, and small ones called *kakams*. The large ships have anything from twelve down to three sails, which are made of bamboo rods plaited like mats. They are never lowered, but turned according to the direction of the wind; at anchor they are left floating in the wind (Gibb 1986: 235).

Ibn Battutā also adds that each 'large vessel' is followed by three smaller vessels, "which take it in tow and row it forwards" when there is no wind (*ibid.*: 278). As Marco Polo (N.D.: 261) describes, they also served the larger ship "for the purpose of carrying out anchors, for fishing, and a variety of other services". The Venetian gives us further details regarding Chinese junks.

> We shall commence with a description of the ships employed by the merchants, which are built of fir-timber. They have a single deck, and below this the space is divided into about sixty small cabins, fewer or more, according to the size of the vessels, each of them affording accommodation for one merchant. They are provided with a good helm. They have four masts, with as many sails, and some of them have two masts which can be set up and lowered again, as may be found necessary. (...)
>
> Ships of the largest size require a crew of three hundred men; others, two hundred; and some, one hundred and fifty only, according to their greater or less bulk. They carry from five to six thousand baskets (or mat bags) or pepper. In former times they were of greater burthen than they are at present; ...
>
> The vessels are likewise moved with oars or sweeps, each of which requires four men to work it (*ibid.*: 259-260).

Chu Yü, son of a superintendent of merchant shipping in Sung China, confirms in his *Phing-chou Kho Than* ("Table-talk at Phingchow", 1119 AD) Marco Polo's observations about passengers and goods carried by Chinese ships.

> According to the government regulations for sea-going ships, the larger ones can carry several hundred men, and the smaller ones may have more than a hundred on board ... The greater part of the cargo consists of pottery, the small pieces packed in the larger till there is not a crevice left ... (Needham 1971: 462.

About the use of sails, he adds,

> If there is no wind, they cannot move. Their masts are firmly stepped, and the sails are hoisted beside them. One side of the sail is close to the mast, (around which it moves) like a door on its hinges. The sails are made of matting. ... At sea they can use not only a wind from abaft, but winds from onshore or offshore can also be used. It is only a wind (directly) contrary which cannot be used. This is called 'using the winds of the three directions'. When the wind is dead ahead they cast anchor and stop ... (*ibid.*).

Chu Yü's testimony implies that the junks did not usually use oars for motion as indicated by Marco Polo. Regarding the masts, Needham adds that the practice of Sung period junks, which sailed in the Indian Ocean, was quite similar to that of contemporary junks. "All the masts carry balanced lug-sails and some of them have top-masts on which, today as in the Middle Ages, top sails are set under suitable conditions" (*ibid.*: 402). It was usual for the masts to be raked. However,

> The raking is not the same on all ships, but the general tendency is to have the masts radiating like the sticks of a fan. There is also individual variation in the construction of the tabernacles. As in nearly all traditional sea-going ships, the masts are completely devoid of stays (*ibid.*: 401).

Although the Chinese ships were considerably advanced because they were capable of 'using the winds of three direction', there was one weakness: of running aground.

> At sea (the mariners) are not afraid of wind and waves, but of running aground for if this happens there is no way of getting off again. If the ship suddenly springs a leak, they cannot mend it from the inside, but they order their black and moor slaves to take chisels and oakum and mend it from outside, for these men are expert swimmers and do not close their eyes when under water ... (*ibid.*: 462).

We have reliable information regarding the construction of Chinese junks from three sources: Chu Yü, Ibn Battutā and Marco Polo. Let us begin with Chu Yü, who writes about Chinese ships in his *Phing-chou Kho Than*. He clearly states that the junks "are built squarely like rectangular wooden grain-measures" and they are "several tens of fathoms in breadth and depth" (*ibid.*). Ibn Battutā elaborates:

> This is the manner after which they are made: two (parallel) walls of very thick wooden (planking) are raised, and across the space between them are placed very thick planks (the bulkheads) secured longitudinally and transversely by means of large nails, each three ells in length. When these walls have thus been built, the lower deck is fitted in and the ship is launched before the upper works are finished (*ibid.*: 469).

Marco Polo confirms that the hulls of the Chinese ships were built with bulkhead, which created watertight holds. "Some ships of the larger class have, besides (the cabins), to the number of thirteen bulk-heads or divisions in the hold, formed of thick planks let into each other (*incastrati*, mortised or rabbeted)" (Polo N.D.: 259). In case of an accident, if the hull was damaged at any one point, water could not enter other holds. The sailors repaired the particular hold and put the ship back to service without greatly endangering the lives of the passengers or the goods it was carrying.

> The ships are all double planked; that is, they have a course of sheathing-boards laid over the planking in every part. These are caulked with oakum both withinside and without, and are fastened with iron nails. They are not coated with pitch, as the country does not produce that article, but the bottoms are smeared over with the following preparation. The people take quick-lime and hemp, which latter they cut small, and with these, when pounded together, they mix oil procured from a certain tree, making of the whole a kind of unguent, which retains its viscous properties more firmly, and is a better material than pitch (*ibid.*: 260).

Needham adds the information that is missing in Chu Yü's, Ibn Battutā's and Marco Polo's accounts. Reconstructing a picture of junks which journeyed to the Indian Ocean during the Sung (960-1280 AD) period he says,

> These reached in size a length of as much as 170 ft. The pinewood hull is flat-bottomed, the central longitudinal timber being somewhat larger than the others and substituting for a keel. ... Since the curves of the turret-built hull converge at bow and stern, the foremost and after compartments are masterpieces of construction, and the curved deck beams are rabbeted with great ingenuity into the curved frames of the hull. Certain of the stem and stern ribs (longitudinal members) are actually grown to shape. Both bow and stern are bluff and capable of withstanding the worst weather, but abaft the stern a kind of 'false stern' (*tho-lou*) is built on by extending the sides of the hull in a rising curve beyond the final transom, to terminate in a shorter false transom about 7 ft above the water line. The decked surface of this structure prolongs the deckhouses and carries a windlass for hoisting or lowering the rudder which is slung within this enclosed space (Needham 1971: 399).

We need to examine historical accounts in order to ascertain the exact period since when the junks began to venture in 'Bengal'. Although the Chinese had reached the Coromandel Coast by the beginning of the Christian era, these were isolated voyages. It was only in the 9th century AD that the Chinese vessels were beginning to make more frequent voyages in the high seas. The southern Sung dynasty (1127-1279) carried out considerable naval action in Indonesia, which extended into the Bay of Bengal. During the rule of the Mongols (1280-1367 AD), Chinese merchants had established themselves at Kaveripattinam, Quilon and Calicut (Verlinden 1987: 39-40). Hence, it appears probable that Chinese junks began appearing in the Bay after the mid-12th century AD and became a familiar sight by the 13th century AD. However, when we learn from Chinese sources from the 12th century AD that export from China during the century was being made in the ships belonging to Sinhalese and Kling merchants from Coromandel (Ray 1997: 37), it becomes certain that the junks became well-known in the Bay from the 13th century AD. Ibn Battutā further informs us that junks called on the ports of 'Bengal' because he boarded such a vessel at Sonārgāon in 1346 and sailed for Sumatra (Gibb 1992: 271). Thus by the mid-14th century AD, junks must have been frequently used in 'Bengal'. Hence, we may believe with certainty that the Chinese vessel was introduced in 'Bengal' sometime in the 13th century AD.

The tradition of Chinese junk may not have touched India, as Aniruddha Ray (1997: 38) believes, but it certainly touched 'Bengal' – as the *sāmpān* testifies.

The Sāmpān

The most distinguishing feature of a *sāmpān* is its flat (transom) stern with two sternposts (*ārakāṭh*), which curve toward each other like horns. There is no planking across the stern of the boat, but there is a big open space somewhat like a well. This peculiar stern construction can be seen even in Chinese *sāmpāns*. As Andrade (2003) explains, it is thus constructed so as to hold a large volume of water temporarily the instant a wave strikes its stern in turbulent waters. The weight of this water acts as ballast and momentarily holds down the stern and prevents the vessel from lifting unduly. Continuous action of waves striking the stern allows the well to hold uninterrupted supply of water. When the sea calms down, the water runs out of the well, and the boat is left light and free to travel with much greater speed.

The stempost is vertical and rises high curving inward. It is decorated with two eyes incised on its two sides. As in Chinese *sāmpāns*, the stern in the *sāmpāns* of Bangladesh is a little higher than the bow. Although this is not a peculiarity of Chinese construction, it nevertheless gives the *sāmpāns* a number of advantages. Firstly, it offers the steersman a better view; secondly, the vessel can ride head to the wind, if it is forced to drift in a gale; and, thirdly, it minimizes the danger of being swamped by overtaking waves in a heavy sea (*ibid.*).

In the early 70s, Greenhill (1971: 118) had noted that the *sāmpāns* "are the only boats in East Pakistan to have [...] and fixed decks nailed to deck beams". However, today it is usual to see these boats without a fixed deck. Some are partly decked in the aft and covered with a roof of split bamboo, which is used as sleeping and cooking quarters. Like Chinese junks, *sāmpāns* have no longitudinal strengthening member (i.e., keel). The hull is flat bottomed and the sides rise high. The vessel is steered with a fixed stern rudder *(sukān)* which is operated with a tiller. Today, many of the *sāmpāns* use rudders made of iron plates (Fig. 4.19). However, in earlier times, it was common for the blade to be made of wood, as in Chinese *sāmpāns*. Wooden rudders are still seen in a few *sāmpāns* plying on the Caṭṭagrāma coast (Fig. 4.20).

In an ethnographic research carried out by the author in 2001, it was found that *sāmpāns* belong to roughly two groups: (i) the smaller passenger-carrying vessels which are

4 to 5 metres long and (ii) the larger cargo-carrying vessels which are 6 to 11 metres long. The smaller *sāmpāns* are usually rowed by a boatman standing in the stern. He rows facing forward, with two oars crossed in front of him. It is unusual for these vessels to work windward. Among the cargo-carrying *sāmpāns*, the larger are nearly 2.5 metres deep from the sheer strake to the bottom of the hull and 3.5 to 4.5 metres broad. Most of the vessels of this type are equipped with four oars and single mast (fitted amidships), but some have two masts. These are stepped in tabernacles, which are supported by a number of shrouds and backstays. All the masts carry sails that appear to be lateen but are actually settee, because, as Greenhill (*ibid.*: 119) explains, "the foot is in two parts, with a vestigial luff in front of the mast and a vestigial tack line holding down a point on the foot of the sail at the mast". The sail is usually hoisted on the port side of the mast and its aft part is extended with a boom attached to the mast. Some large *sāmpāns* use jib sails, which are set during suitable sailing conditions. However, Rashid (1991: 371) points out that some vessels are seen to use square ribbed sails as seen in Chinese junks. Their carrying capacity varies between 250 *maunds* (about 9 tons) to 2000 *maunds* (about 72 tons).

The crew of larger *sāmpāns* besides the serang, consist of 4 *khālāsīs* (sailors) and one *bhāndārī* (cook). When laden to full capacity, the serang and the *khālāsīs* usually work the vessel to windward. However, when there is no wind, they row the boat with long oars standing on the fore-deck, executing short but deep strokes. The boat is rowed when it is necessary to turn about.

Sāmpāns operate mostly in Caṭṭagrāma and Cox's Bazar districts, and on the Meghnā estuary, where they are engaged for carrying goods, ferrying passengers and unloading cargo from vessels in the deep sea. Sometimes they sail to Khulna, Barisal and Noakhali as well, often carrying Sundari logs from the Sundarbans. The smaller *sāmpāns* are often used for smuggling goods to and from Myanmar.

The construction of the *sāmpān* is different from that of all other boats in Bangladesh. The first stage involves constructing the bottom by joining planks edge to edge with the help of iron nails. The nails are hammered at right angles to the seam and are driven from triangular grooves carved out of the planks. The notches are later clogged with the help of chips of wood. All joining and nailing in *sāmpān* construction follows the same process and no rabbeting is involved in it. When the bottom is assembled, the floor frames are nailed to it and the side planks are built up. The next stage involves inserting the side frames and fitting the deck beams. The deck planks, as separate pieces, are laid at the end.

Fig. 4.19 A sampan fitted with an iron rudder under repair

Fig. 4.20 A sampan fitted with a wooden rudder under repair

The very form of the *sāmpān* testifies Chinese influence. Even the name substantiates Chinese origin because it is believed to have derived from 'San-Pan', a Chinese word. The earliest reference to these vessels that we have from the Bay of Bengal rim is from 17th-century south India. As vouchsafed by an inscription found in the Varadaraja Perumal Temple at Tarangambadi, which records a term "Sampan Suvantiiram" (denoting "the right of trading with Chinese vessels"), we may infer that *sāmpāns* were used in south India, (Ramachandran 1991: 60). We have more detailed information regarding extensive use off *sāmpāns* on the eastern coast of south India from a *Brief Relation of the Trade of the Coromandel Coast* by Antony Schorer (who served in the English East India Company as a factor based at Masulipatnam from 1609 to 1614).

> ... every year many sampans carrying rice, millet, pulse, and other grains, butter and oil, are despatched from the whole coast to Doraspatnam [Dugarazupatnam, at the north end of the Pulicet lagoon], Arianagom, Pulicet, Mylapur [St. Thome], Conlany, Connemont, Tegnapatam, Porto Novo, Altegenampatam. The Portuguese used formerly to come for these provisions with sampans and celytones [possibly *sallittoni*, a type of coastal vessel], as well as foists and ships and carried much merchandise to Cochin; .. (Moreland 1931: 69).

As for *sāmpāns* in 'Bengal', we have conclusive proof of its use in the early 16th century. From the account of Pero Pais who sailed to Martaban on a Malay junk renamed *São João* in

1512, we learn that four or five *sāmpāns* filled with *sanbaf* and other fabrics from 'Bengal' arrived each year at Cosmin in March or April (Bouchon 1984: 100). Hence, we may be certain that the *sāmpān* was one of the maritime vessels that were used in 'Bengal' during the time frame of this research.

****

We may sum up our findings in this chapter by noting the various types of vessels that were used in maritime trade of 'Bengal' during the time frame of the present research. These were as follows:

1. Early Historic Period: plank-extended dugouts (such as the *saraṁgā*), multiple-masted sewn-plank ships (such as the Colandia), single-masted sewn-plank ships (such as the trapyaka) and double-masted sewn-plank ships.
2. Late Historic Period: single-masted sewn-plank ships (such as the trapyaka).
3. Early Medieval Period: the *bālām* and the *dhow*.
4. Medieval Period: the *paṭiyā*, the *bajarā*, the *jāliyā*, the junk and the *sāmpān*.

Among these, the *saraṁgā* must have continued through the early historic, late historic, early medieval and medieval periods because it is still seen in Bangladesh today. For the same reason, the *bālām* must have been prevalent in the medieval period as well. These two types of vessels, having developed out of the dugout tradition of boat-building, can claim to be truly indigenous. They also affirm that sewn-planking was one, if not the only technique of indigenous boat-building tradition in early 'Bengal'. As observed above, the *jāliyās* originally belonged to this tradition and adopted carvel-build and flat-stern after the arrival of the Portuguese. That the *bajarā* was keel-less and sewn-planked indicates that it too developed from the dugout tradition of boat-building. However, we do not have enough information to ascertain this with certainty. The *paṭiyā* belongs to a completely different tradition of reverse-clinker vessels. Since reverse-clinker boats are built in Sylhet, Mymansingh, and Khulna in Bangladesh and clinker-built boats were built in Noakhali, it is very much possible that clinker and reverse-clinker tradition of boats developed in 'Bengal' quite independent of the dugout tradition.

What stands out clearly is that none of these vessels are comparable in size with the Chinese junks. Nevertheless, the diminutive size of the indigenous vessels need not be taken as an indication of inferior skill of the local shipbuilders. As argued at the beginning of this chapter, geography of the local waters is one of the factors that go into determining the development of ships in a region. The geography of the local waters along the coast of 'Bengal', William Metholds observed in the early 17th century, was "too dangerous", so much so that English ships, being large in size, did not dare to adventure "amongst so many shelfes and sands" (Moreland 1931: 40). The indigenous vessels of 'Bengal' were built to sail amongst these "shelfes and sands" and hence their diminutive size. At the same time, this also implies that these ships hardly ever had to sail beyond the Bay of Bengal and were never required to make prolonged trans-oceanic voyages. Perhaps there was never a Sindabad, a Hwang Ho or a James Cook in 'Bengal'.

Our deliberations made in this chapter indicates a pattern which shows (1) continuation of the dugout tradition of boat-building throughout the time-frame of this research and (2) two peaks in the early historic and the medieval periods when quite a few types of non-indigenous vessels were inducted in 'Bengal' in order to meet the requirements of maritime shipping. At the present stage of our knowledge, we are unable to ascertain how and when the reverse-clinker tradition joined the dugout tradition. It may even be that the two are parallel traditions that have existed since proto-historic period.

There is no way of knowing how many of the non-indigenous types of vessels were built in 'Bengal'. We may accept Caesar Frederick's testimony mentioned above that "the Sultan of Constantinople found it cheaper to have his vessels built at [Sandwīp] than at Alexandria" to indicate that many of the non-indigenous vessels may have been built in 'Bengal'. It also indicates a high level of proficiency among Bengali shipwrights to build in accordance with established design (as must have been the case with the *dhow* and the *sāmpān*) or adapt for local use (as the *jāliyā* shows). However, when it came to innovative changes, Bengali shipwrights do not appear to have taken significant initiatives, specially in the medieval period. We may also note that all references to maritime vessels cited above clearly show low level of participation of indigenous vessels in maritime trade of 'Bengal'. This may be seen as a manifestation of Bengal's insignificant control over the Indian Ocean maritime trade network.

Five
Navigational Technique

Having determined the types of sea-going vessels that called on the ports of early 'Bengal', it is now necessary to examine how voyages were conducted from the ports of 'Bengal' through the Bay. Because a voyage from a port is made with the objective of reaching an intended destination, which is another port, it is necessary for the mariners to be able to determine the intended direction of journey and a vessel's position in a vast wilderness of water. This ability is studied under navigation, or "the art and science of deter-mining a vessel's position and of taking her in safety from one place to another" (McGrail 1983: 301) was conditioned further in pre-modern times by seasonal wind and sea current. Hence, it is also necessary to see how the ancient seamen used the wind system and sea currents to conduct their journeys safely. Navigational technique, thus, is organically linked with maritime trade because it considerably determined its characteristic pattern. If, for example, the level of knowledge in these fields is limited, necessitating coastal voyage, a particular port may gain importance because it is on the coastal route. However, if navigational techniques develop to the extent that transoceanic voyage is possible, the importance of the port may fall. The level of attainment in navigational techniques is also indicative of a people's seafaring tradition and control over maritime trade transacted in its littoral. Hence, like other aspects such as history of ports, commodities, ships, etc. navigational technique is an important aspect for maritime studies.

As Arunachalam (1996: 263) reminds us, "[t]he basic nautical parameters that need measurement to aid navigation include depth, time, distance and direction; and these need both units and devices". The three stages in the development of navigational techniques in the world that Needham (1971: 554) has identified, i.e., primitive, quantitative, and mathematical, seek to answer these basic parameters without instruments in the first stage, with instruments in the second stage and with the added application of mathematics in the third stage. Stated differently, primitive navigation, used by early mariners, sought answers to two basic problems when instruments were not available: "(a) how to estimate directions such as courses steered and leeway and drift experienced, and (b) how to estimate speed or distances" (McGrail 1996: 131). Quantitative navigation, in which measurement was the keynote, began with the use of the mariners' compass around 900 AD in the Near East and about 1200 AD in the Mediterranean (although hour-glass, traverse tables, astrolabes, quadrants and rutters were being commonly used only in the 15th century AD). The third stage of mathematical navigation began around 1500 AD. Because the scope of this study covers the period from earliest times to the first half of the 16th century AD, we will need to examine non-instrumental and quantitative stages of navigational technique employed in the Bay of Bengal.

Studies on indigenous navigational techniques of South Asian mariners are very limited. Arunachalam (1987, 1996) and Sarkar (1986) are exceptions as they have dealt with the navigational tradition in India. However, there is hardly any work that deals with indigenous navigational techniques of the mariners of Bangladesh and West Bengal. Archaeological evidence on the subject from the coastal regions of 'Bengal' is also extremely meager. Hence, we will draw on ethnographic evidences of coastal voyages in indigenous vessels collected from field-level research and literary evidences from various sources. Drawing upon these sources, we will attempt to answer three basic questions. How were the ships navigated during coastal voyages? How were they navigated in the high seas? In what way did the climate affect sailing schedule? At the end of the chapter, we will discuss the pattern of change in navigational technology and its consequence in maritime voyages.

NAVIGATION IN COASTAL VOYAGES

Navigational techniques used in conducting a vessel in coastal or cross-channel voyages, within shallow waters restricted by the proximity of land, are essentially based on conditions where mariners are able to determine their whereabouts with the help of recognizable landmarks and identifiable characteristics of the sea. Aided by these indicators, they row or sail from one position to another.

The earliest voyagers in the sea, who always had land in sight as they travelled, knew their way by landmarks. Using reed-built rafts, waterproofed with bitumen, early mariners were already sailing along the coast of Persia and the mouth of the Indus by 3000 BC. For the earliest evidence on coastal voyage along the East Coast of India and 'Bengal', one can cite the *Periplus* (1st century AD), which shows that the route to 'Bengal' via South India was coastal in nature. We may believe that maritime contact between South and Southeast Asia, as indicated by the presence of South Asian artifacts in coastal sites of Myanmar, Thailand, Malaysia and Indonesia (discussed in Chapters One and Two), was established with the help of coastal voyages as early as the 4th century BC. Such voyages continued in the 9th century AD, because we note Ibn Khurdādhbih's *Kitāb* (c. 846-7 AD) describing a route through the Palk Strait and round the shore of the Bay of

Bengal. A scrutiny of the maṅgalakāvya corpus shows that Baṁśīdāsa, Nārāyaṇa Deva, Bijayagupta, Srīrāy Binod and Kavikañkaṇa Mukunda describe, for the most part, coastal voyages. As shown in Chapter Four, travel accounts of Caesar Frederic (who describes his journey from the Port of Pipli to Sātgāon in 1567), Bernier (who voyaged from Pipli to Huglī nearly a century after Frederic), Nicholas Pimenta (who, in 1602, describes quite a few voyages from Dianga and Caṭṭagrāma to Śrīpur, Chandecan, Bacla, Arakan and Pegu, Hosten 1925: 52-73) and Sebastien Manrique (who describes quite a few voyages from and to Caṭṭagrāma/Dianga from 1629-35) all testify that coastal voyages were prevalent in the medieval period. Ralph Fitch actually describes a voyage that he had himself undertaken.

> I went from Serrepore [Śrīpur near the confluence of the Padmā and the Meghnā, long since washed away] the 28 of November 1586 for Pegu, in a small ship or foist of one Albert Caravallos. And so passing downe Ganges, and passing by the island of Sundiva [Sandwīp], Porto Grande, or the countries of Tippera, the kingdom of Recon and Mogen, leaving them on our left side with a faire wind at northwest, our course was south and by east, which brought us to the barre of Negrais in Pegu (Foster 1968: 28-29).

Even today mariners from Cox's Bazar and Teknaf in Bangladesh voyage in *sāmpāns* to Myanmar along the eastern coast of the Bay of Bengal. As reported by the mariners, the *jāli*, the *sulluk*, and the *bālām* also used to ply in this route at earlier times. During these coastal voyages, they carefully observe all landmarks such as beaches, marshes, forest belts, streams, estuaries, shoals etc. and etch them in their memory. These landmarks are their guide throughout the voyage, including entry and exit of ports. Significant physical features of permanent nature are systematically observed and converted into pithy sayings that are orally transmitted to the younger generation of mariners. One such saying in translation may be rendered thus: "From Caṭṭagrāma to Burma, make sure that the coast is always on your left; in reverse direction, do not forget to maintain the shore on your right". We find an echo of this practice in the voyage of Ralph Fitch in 1586, who describes "leaving" Sandwīp, the port of Caṭṭagrāma and the Kingdom of Arakan "on our left side".

In Baṁśīdāsa's *Manasāmaṅgala*, the merchant C̃ād is described sailing past Utkal and Kaliṅga on his right. Nārāyaṇa Deva's *Padmā-purāṇa*, the merchant C̃ād (or Candradhar as the poet prefers to call him) is described sailing along the East Coast, past the estuary of Kāñcan River, and the towns of Haripura, Mahindranagara and Bhabānipura. In his *Padmā-purāṇa*, Bijayagupta describes the Bengali merchant sailing past coastal cities of Mānikyapura (possibly in Orissa or further south) and Bijayārpura (possibly Vijayanagaram in Andhra Pradesh). He also sails past the mouths of a number of rivers, most of that are unidentifiable, except the Godavari. Śrīrāy Binod does not mention any port or city but Kālidaha Sea and a number of "bends" along the coast. In the *Caṇḍīmaṅgala* by Kavikañkaṇa Mukunda, the merchant Dhanapati Datta and his son Śrīmanta are both described sailing past Setubandha-Rāmeśwar and a few islands and mountains. There can be little doubt that the texts reflect the medieval sailing practice of making mental note of all landmarks along the coast. The practices noted above are echoed in 18th century maps that show prominent landmarks such as the banyan tree overlooking a cliff at Ratnagiri, the Narasimha Temple at Bhimunipattanamu on the Andhra Coast, the black pagoda at Konarak in Orissa and groves at the mouth of the Huglī River (Deloche 1994: 199).

One can even discern the practice of noting identifiable characteristics of the sea when all the poets of the maṅgalakāvya corpus noted above describe the merchants encountering marine "creatures of terror" (giant leeches, lobsters, crabs and fishes). A similar practice can be noted in an old Lakshadweep sea manual written in Malayalam, which warns mariners of approaching coral banks of the Coral Island when huge yellow-skinned reptiles, cowries, conches, crabs, sharks, sea-terns and kites are seen (Arunachalam 1996: 270). Arab navigators also recognised that "the surface of the sea possesses several permanent features which can be used to identify one's position" (Tibbetts 1981: 283). In addition, several marine creatures were identified as indicative of approaching land. For example, "the sea-snake was regarded as the first sign of the Indian coast when crossing from Arabia" (*ibid.*: 285).

An important difference between the sailing practices of mariners of Caṭṭagrāma-Cox's Bazar and Barisal-Khulna Coasts is that while the former hug the coast, the latter avoid the coast and cut through estuarine channels. Hence, a vessel travelling from Sandwīp to Barisal would travel across the Hātiyā channel, then sail on the Meghnā River, enter Tetuliyā River on the north of Bhola, and then reach Barisal. This route, it is important to emphasize, does not run south of Hātiyā and Kukri Mukri Char. Similar practice must have been prevalent in the medieval period as Sebastien Manrique's testimony implies.

Most of the indigenous crafts which ply along the coastal routes of Bangladesh still do not carry a compass, for the mariners know the coast like the back of their palm. In the event when the sight of the coast is lost or when they make short cross channel voyages as from Teknaf to the coast of Arakan, they take the help of the sun to determine the direction. Sometimes they also observe the flow of water (which, according to them, always flows from the north to the south), to determine their direction. At night, they have the following stars and constellations to guide them.

Suk Tārā (The Morning Star): It rises in the southeast in the early morning.

Duirā Tārā: It is seen in the south after eight in the evening. While at sea, the mariners maintain the star on the starboard or port side, along an imaginary line running horizontally amidships.

Agni Tārā: A star that rises in the southeast.

Chaghairā Tārā: A star that rises in the west.

Nishi Tārā: A star that rises in the east after mid-night.

Diṅgi or Kisti Tārā (The Big Dipper): It is a constellation composed of seven stars shaped like a ship. It rises in the evening in the northeast and set in the early morning in the northwest. In West Bengal, the constellation is known simply as Sāt Tārā.

Uttarer Tārā (Dhruba Tārā or the North Star): Although this star is not popular among the mariners of Bangladesh, their counterparts in West Bengal often refer to it to determine, if necessary, the north.

Sāt-jāli Tārā: It is the 'V' of the Taurus. The constellation, composed of seven stars, rises in the east around eight in the evening and sets in the early morning in the west. At midnight, it is exactly overhead. The constellation cannot be seen on a full-moon night.

Ādam Surāt: The Orion. Shaped like a human being, the constellation is composed of 11 stars. It rises in the northeast.

The night sky is also an excellent indicator for weather forecasts. For example, a halo around the moon indicates the possibility of rain. On the other hand, if the sky appears to be dotted with myriads of small stars, the sea is sure to turn violent. An approaching storm is foretold by complete stillness in nature – even the wind ceases blowing. During the day, an additional indicator to the stillness is a slightly overcast sky. Black clouds indicate storm while white clouds indicate rain. Mariners in West Bengal interpret wind blowing from the north during the rainy season and that from the east and the south during the winter as an indicator of inclement weather. Like mariners of coastal Bangladesh today, the master mariner Dulāi in Baṁśīdāsa's *Manasāmaṅgala* (composed in the 16th century) is described as navigating with the help of the stars. Hence, there can be little doubt that the practice was prevalent in the medieval period.

Mariners in Bangladesh know that land lies ahead when they notice an increasing frequency of waves striking their vessels from the rear or a change in wave pattern. When navigating in shallow waters, they often use their paddle pole or a bamboo pole to measure depth in terms of a unit known as *bām* (length between two thumbs of outstretched arms are extended sidewise in a straight line). They follow two other practices for determining the depth of water: one, with the help of the colour of the water and the other, with the help of a rope-line. Colour of water is indicative of approximate depth. If the water appears black, the depth is estimated to be between 30 to 20 *bām*; if the water is green, it is 18 to 10 *bām*; if white, it is 10 to 5 *bām*; if it is muddy, the depth is estimated to be less than 5 *bām*. If an accurate depth of water is necessary, they use a rope-line notched in *bām* unit and tied to a *purum* (*baḍā*), a top-shaped iron weight. Those who carry an iron anchor measure the depth not with *purum* but the anchor. They also use lead-line soundings to estimate the topography of the sea floor at shallow depths in order to avoid getting grounded. Thus, position of submerged sandbars, rocks, mud-banks and reeves are determined. In West Bengal, the term *bām* is also used to refer to the depth of water but their name for the depth-measuring instrument is known as *burum*.

The practice of measuring the depth of water by chord was followed in the early 18th century, as the following excerpt from an account by Father Claudius Barbier describing his journey in an Armenian ship from the Coromandel Coast to Huglī testifies. When the ship went aground in a creek near Huglī, Barbier notes that "on one side of the ship there was but a fathom and a half and on the other we paid out six fathoms of chord" (*Bengal Past & Present* 1910: 203). A similar practice must have been followed in the 16th century as well because, as discussed earlier in Chapter Four, Baṁśīdāsa's *Manasāmaṅgala* clearly mentions marking of a bamboo pole for measuring the depth of water.

Navigating in the coastal waters also requires a keen awareness of the rise and the fall of tides, flood and ebb, spring and neap levels. As Arunachalam (1996: 268) informs us,

> All seamen know that the time of the high tide shifts everyday by 48 minutes or two *ghatikas*, and a distinct relation exists between the *tithi* and the height of the tide. High tides in the coastal waters are associated with the period *ekadashi* (11th day) to *chaturthi* (fourth day) through the new or full moon.

However, according to the mariners of the Karṇafulī estuary in Caṭṭagrāma, spring tide takes place during full-moon (*pūrṇimā*) and new-moon (*amābasyā*). The tidal range is minimum during the *daśamī* and the *ekādaśī*. According to the mariners in West Bengal, the tidal range is maximum on the day before the full moon and the day after the new moon.

Acute perception of tidal characteristics is vital in the coastal regions of 'Bengal' because, this belt is highly vulnerable to huge tidal ranges (2 m to 7.9 m high), high amplitude surge waves and tidal bores. In the Sundarbans, all navigators worth their salt know that a tidal bore approaches with a distant low murmur. As the murmur develops progressively into a growl and then into a human cry, all vessels move mid-stream where the bore is less threatening because it does not curl over and break menacingly as it does on the bank (Arunachalam 1996: 268). The tide in the Meghnā estuary approaches the coastal regions of Noakhali with a threatening roar, which the locals call *svar* or the voice of the tide. The ferocity of the tidal range in the Gaṅgā is borne out by Caesar Frederick's testimony made in 1567. He notes that it was possible to row in eighteen hours from the mouth of the Gaṅgā to Sātgāon

> ... with the increase of the water: in which river floweth and ebbeth ..., and when the ebbing water is come, they are not able to rowe against it, by reason of the swiftnesse of the water, ... they cannot prevaile against that Streame, but for refuge must make them fast to the banke of the River until the next flowing water, ... (Purchas 1905b: 113).

It was revealed in the field-level investigation at Sandwīp in 2001 conducted by the author, mariners in the coast of Caṭṭagrāma, Cox's Bazar and offshore islands, sail primarily with the help of tidal flow when the water rushes fast to the south to the Burma Trench. While voyaging south from Sandwīp to Burma in *sāmpāns*, they begin their journey when the ebb tide (*bhāṭā*) commences, which may be at 3 am. They continue as far as the tidal flow will take them and anchor before the high tide (*joyār*) begins, which often is at Kutubdiyā. There they wait for the next ebb tide and commence their journey again when it begins. They anchor again before the next high tide begins, which is often at Cox's Bazar. With the next ebb tide they reach Teknaf by 5 pm of the third day. From Teknaf they sail for Akyab in the Arakan Coast, where they reach by the early morning of the fourth day. Similarly, they return with the help of high tide.

These mariners also take the help of land and sea breeze. Along the Caṭṭagrāma-Cox's Bazar Coast, the land breeze blows in a westerly direction, from the early morning while the sea breeze blows in an easterly direction from the late afternoon. Mariners use the land breeze to blow their lateen sails during their voyages to Caṭṭagrāma and Cox's Bazar from Sandwīp. On the other hand, they use the sea breeze on their return voyage from Cox's Bazar to Caṭṭagrāma or further north. In their voyages to Khulna from Sandwīp, they take the help of sea breeze, which blows in a northerly direction along the Barisal-Khulna Coast. On their return journey, from Khulna to Sandwīp, they take the help of land breeze, which blows in the southerly direction, to move their vessels. However, it must be noted, that land and sea breeze are used only as forces in addition to ebb and high tide. In other words, the tidal flow is the prime mover and the breezes are secondary.

Besides the land and sea breeze, the mariners of Bangladesh also use the monsoon winds. During the summer, they use the southwest monsoon wind (*dakṣinālī bātās*) only to travel to nearby ports because, as they say, "the sea is very hot (i.e., prone to turbulence)". During the winter, they use the northeast monsoon wind (*uttarālī bātās*) for voyaging to Cox's Bazar, Teknaf and Myanmar. Once again, the tidal currents are the prime movers while the winds are secondary. Hence, while travelling from Caṭṭagrāma to Cox's Bazar during the winter, they voyage only with the ebb tide, even if the northeast monsoon is available. On the other hand, while returning from Cox's Bazar to Caṭṭagrāma, they voyage only during high tide. In this case, they use the northeast monsoon to move in a serpentine direction (northeast to northwest) by fore-and-aft sail 'tacking'. Therefore, the journey takes longer.

Mariners in the Caṭṭagrāma-Cox's Bazar Coast prefer to make long distance voyages from the months of Bhādra (mid-August to mid-September) to Māgh (mid-January to mid-February). During this period, i.e., mid-August to mid-February, the sea remains calm and natural calamities such as storms and rains remain minimal. The only calamity is cyclone. Furthermore, the northeast monsoon winds are also favourable. During the remaining six months, the sea is comparatively more turbulent and hence they avoid any trip that necessitates abandoning the coast. Hence routes lying close to the coast i.e., Sandwīp to Caṭṭagrāma and back, Caṭṭagrāma to Kutubdiyā and Maheśkhālī and back, Caṭṭagrāma to Cox's Bazar and back continue to be made. On the other hand, they avoid crossing the Meghnā estuary. Mariners in Barisal and Khulna follow the same schedule as shown above.

The ethnographic findings and literary evidences discussed above are all primitive navigational techniques. These findings and evidences are all that we have to obtain a picture of coastal navigational practice that may have been current among the mariners of the historic and medieval periods. We may corroborate these with a few more literary evidences. Because the Arab-Persians began navigating in the Bay of Bengal since the 9th century AD, and Arab *dhows* frequented littoral 'Bengal' from the same time till the first half of the 19th century, coastal navigational techniques described in Arab-Persian literary sources may be accepted as indicative of similar practices in the 'Bengal' Coast during the medieval period. One of these sources is Muqaddasī, who informs us in his *Aḥsanu 't-Taqāsīm fī Ma'rifati 'l-Aqālīm* (885 AD), how Arab-Persian vessels were navigated in waters where shoals were numerous. Since shoals are quite common in 'Bengal', one may glean a graphic account of an Arab ship negotiating its course near the ports of Sātgāon and Caṭṭagrāma (Samandar).

> On this account the passage is only made by day; in which case the shipmaster takes his stand on the top and steadily looks into the sea. Two boys are likewise posted on his right and on his left. On espying a rock he at once call to either of the boys to give notice of this to the helmsman by a loud cry. The latter, on hearing the cry, pulls one or the other of two ropes he holds in his hand to the right or to the left, according to the directions. If these precautions are not taken, the ship stands in danger of being wrecked against the rocks (Hasan 1928: 111).

An important aid in navigation at night was the lighthouse, definitely introduced by the 8th century AD on the coast of the

Persian Gulf but about which we know very little on the coast of the Bay of Bengal. According to the Chinese sailing directory of Kia Tan, compiled between 785 and 805 AD, the people of the country of Ti-lo-lu-ho (Mekran Coast) had "set up ornamented pillars in the sea, on which at night they place torches so that people travelling on board ships at night shall not go astray" (Hirth and Rockhill 1965: 13). We have further details from Muqaddasī that lighthouses were erected to warn about shoals.

> On the skirts of al-Baṣra, small huts have been erected on palm trunks set in the sea, and people have been stationed there on to keep a fire lighted at night, as a warning to ships to steer clear of these shallow places (Hasan 1928: 111).

One learns about the use of these lighthouses even in the 10th century because Mas'ūdī notes these in his *Murūju 'dh-Dhahab* (947-956 AD). Landmarks were set in the sea below Ubullah and 'Abbādān and people are put in charge to light a fire at night on three stakes, like chairs, in the middle of the sea as a precaution for the ships which come from 'Umān, Sīrāf and elsewhere (*ibid.*: 110).

Similar illuminating devices may have been used on the Tamil Coast since the Sangam literature indicate the practice of lighting a fire on top of the highest building in large ports. Local tradition claims that "the Temple of the Lord of the Oil-measure" at Mamallapuram was a lighthouse (Deloche 1994: 199-200). However, the existence of the above lighthouses is not confirmed by any other sources. Hence, Deloche (*ibid.*: 200) logically observes, "illuminating devices intended to indicate the approaches to the coast had been of an exceptional nature".

Almost nothing is known about lighthouses in 'Bengal' during the historic and medieval periods. However, it may be suggested that the *badarmukāms* (sanctum built in honour of Badar 'Alam) served such a purpose in the Caṭṭagrāma-Cox's Bazar-Arakan Coast. "To the Buddhist" writes Temple (1914: 9), "he is a *nat*, to the Hindus, a *deva* or inferior god, to the Muhammadans a saint, to the Chinese, a spirit". It is no wonder, hence, that *badarmukāms* dotted the entire coast from Assam (here implying Caṭṭagrāma) to the Malay Peninsula. Only one such *badarmukām*, comprised of a mosque and two caves built on a hillock, still exists in south Akyab on the coast of the Bay of Bengal. Known as Pīr Badar to the Muslim mariners of Caṭṭagrāma-Cox's Bazar-Arakan Coast, whose intervention and blessing is sought during all voyages, it is likely that fire lit at the sanctums of the Pīr served as lighthouses even in the early 20th century.

NAVIGATION IN TRANSOCEANIC VOYAGES

Navigational techniques used in transoceanic voyages when the land is out of sight are far more complex than coastal voyages because direction, speed and distance have to be measured without any stationary object as a reference point. In the initial phase when instruments had not developed, mariners had to employ non-instrumental knowledge based on experience and acute perception of the seascape and seamarks, movement of the stellar bodies and behavioral characteristics of natural agents of locomotion (such as the winds and sea-currents). Of all these areas, perhaps the knowledge of seasonal change of winds was decisive in making it possible for early navigators to boldly discard coastal landmarks and embark on transoceanic voyages.

In the Arabian Sea, transoceanic voyages may have been known to Arabian and Dravidian mariners as they had mastered the monsoon winds much before Hippalus, as Schoff (1995: 227) and McPherson (1998: 32) suggest. However, it would be difficult to answer even in the vaguest of terms when such voyages began in the Bay of Bengal, as so little work has been done in this area. As Warren (1987: 146) points out, the commerce during the first few centuries AD "was handled mainly by the Indians and the Malays" but "these people do not seem to have left surviving reports of sailing conditions". Quite justifiably Manguin (1996: 191) laments that "The Bay of Bengal remains .. much a *mare incognitum* when questions of technical nature are raised for the 1st Millennium AD".

The earliest literary evidence of Bengali mariners embarking on transoceanic voyages may be found in the maṅgalakāvya corpus. When Candradhar's uncle Dhonā in Nārāyaṇa Deva's *Padmā-purāṇa* (composed in the beginning of the 16th century) climbs up the mast (*mālum kāṭh)* and sights land at a distance, one gets a distinct impression of such a voyage across the high sea. Sailing with the south wind to reach Laṅkā on his return journey (as in Nārāyaṇa Deva's *Padmā-purāṇa*) and halting at a port because the south wind begins to blow and sailing with a favourable north wind in autumn in the outward journey (as in Sīrāy Binod's *Padmā-purāṇa* composed in the 16th century) reflects knowledge of monsoon wind. As we will show in further detail in Chapter Six, these voyages appear not to reflect a living tradition but events of a dim and half-forgotten past.

Not citing exact references, Arunachalam maintains that the ancient inhabitants of the East Coast of South India knew about the seasonal change of wind. "Though the monsoon was not known by name, literary references in the early Sanskrit and Tamil clearly demonstrate the knowledge of seasonal reversal of winds at least since the beginning of the Christian era" (Arunachalam 1996: 270)[1]. Laying aside these

---

[1] The sources that Arunachalam (1996: 262) states at the beginning of his paper are (1) extensive fieldwork, (2) hand-written sailors' manuscripts in Gujarati-Kutchi and Malayalam dating from the 17th to the early 20th centuries AD and (3) published and unpublished folk documents (in Tamil, Malayalam, Gujarathi and Marathi) related to navigation. No where does he specify his "literary references in early Sanskrit and Tamil".

vague claims, one can only turn to Chinese Buddhist monk Fa-Hien, who voyaged from Tāmralipti to Siṁhala (Sri Lanka) in the early 5th century AD, for the first definite information regarding the knowledge of the monsoon winds in the Bay of Bengal.

> He then shipped himself on board a great merchant vessel. Putting to sea, they proceeded in a south-westerly direction, and, catching the first fair wind of the winter season (i.e., of the N. E. monsoon) they sailed for fourteen days and nights and arrived at the country of the Lions (Siṁhala, Ceylon) (*Fo-kwō-ki*, XXXVII; Beal 1869: 147-48).

His homeward journey from Siṁhala to Yo-po-ti (Java) also proves that by the same period, trans-oceanic voyages were being made across the eastern Indian Ocean. From I-Tsing, who arrived at Tāmralipti in 673 AD, we learn definitely that transoceanic voyages across the Bay had become commonplace.

For the earliest reference to transoceanic voyages across the Bay of Bengal we have to turn to Greco-Roman authors. Ptolemy (Klaudios Ptolemaios) in his *An Outline of Geography* (composed in the mid-2nd century AD) says "[t]he passage across it [i.e., the Gangetic Gulf] from Paloura to Sada in a direct line from west to east is 1,300 stadia. ... The voyage is continued onward from Sada to the City of Tamala, a distance of 3,500 stadia in a south-eastern direction" (Cap. 13, § 7-8; Śāstri 1927: 24). Poloura has been identified by Yule as Jelasur near the mouth of the Suvarṇarekhā in Orissa (*ibid.*: 75) and Tamala as a town, a river and a cape, possibly Cape Negrais as Lassen believes (*ibid.*: 197). However, Sada remains unidentified. It is believed to be a port on the eastern side of the Bay of Bengal, between Pegu and 'Bengal' (*ibid.*: 196-197). We need not be skeptical about the possibility of such trans-oceanic voyages because, as we have already noted, such voyages in the western Indian Ocean were already being made in the 1st millennium BC. Once sailors and navigators had found ways and means to sail across the Bay of Bengal sometime in the 2nd century or slightly earlier, it was inevitable that Tāmralipti in particular and all other ports of 'Bengal' would gradually lose significance unless they could offer competitive market price or unique quality commodities.

All the voyages referred to above were conducted with the help of primitive navigational techniques. Needless to say, the hazards in primitive navigation were great since direction, speed and distance had to be measured mostly with the help of stellar bodies and knowledge of their changing position in the sky was necessary. These uncertainties were mastered with the development of instruments such as the compass, cross-staff or *kamāl,* terrestrial globes and maritime charts. Hence, our investigation into transoceanic voyages to and from the ports of 'Bengal' will be divided into two sections: (1) primitive and (2) quantitative.

Primitive Navigation in Transoceanic Voyages

As part of our investigation into navigational techniques employed in the Bay of Bengal, we may turn to Fa-Hien again. He gives a brief description of his voyage from Siṁhala to Yo-po-ti (Java), which contains indications of what we seek.

> The sea itself is boundless in extent – it is impossible to know east or west, except by observing the sun, moon or stars in their motions. If it is dark, rainy weather, the only plan is to steer by the wind without guide. During the darkness of night, one only sees the great waves beating one against the other and shining like fire, whilst shoals of sea monsters of every description (surround the ship). The merchantmen were now much perplexed, not knowing towards what land they were steering. The sea was bottomless and no soundings could be found, so that there was not even a rock for anchorage (*Fo-kwō-ki*, XL; Beal 1869: 165-172).

There can be no doubt, therefore, that the mariners plying the eastern Indian Ocean in the early 5th century AD, knew how to steer themselves at night by the stars and during the day by the sun. However, they could hardly deal with such situations when the sky was overcast. Fa-Hien's testimony also implies that these ancient mariners took soundings from the sea bottom to ascertain the depth of water. Once again, their problem was when the sea appeared to be "bottomless". A similar practice was also followed by Arab navigators who used the *bild* or plumb line. It was used for measuring depth of water and bringing up specimens of sea-bottom (Tibbetts 1981: 278).

The mark of those highly skilled in their job is well summed up by the qualifications added to master mariner Suparaga in Āryaśūra's *Jātakamālā* (c. 400 AD).

> Knowing the course of the celestial luminaries, he was never at a loss with respect to the regions of the sky; being perfectly acquainted with the different prognostics, the permanent, the occasional, and the miraculous ones, he was skilled in the establishment of a given time as proper or improper; by means of many fold marks, observing the fishes, the colour of the water, the species of the ground, birds, rocks, &c., he knew how to ascertain rightly the part of the sea; further he was vigilant, not subject to drowsiness and sleep, capable of enduring the fatigue of cold, heat, rain, and the like, careful and patient (Speyer 1895: 125).

Suparaga's ability to distinguish the region of the ocean by the colour of the water holds good for South Asian mariners even today. Such observations are based on scientific principles, for the amount of sediment charge and distance from the shore does change the colour of water. Discoloration of water observed at some distance from the shore also helps a keen eye to recognise river mouths.

Even today the mariners of the 'Bengal' Coast measure time by observing the position of the sun during the day, and the moon and specific star positions in relation to the lunar month at night. "The time of rising or setting of the moon is relation to the *tithi* (day reckoned from full/new moon) and the position of the moon in the sky" (Arunachalam 1996:

263) are used as indicators of time at night under clear skies all over South Asia. The sun, the moon and the stars are also used to judge direction. Writing about traditional nautical practice in South Asia, Arunachalam (*ibid.*) says,

> The seamen were aware of the latitudinal shift in the position of the overhead noon sun. Star position at the time of rising and setting are fixed for each star. This knowledge was used practically by identifying and using specific sets of stars on the eastern or the western horizons during their rising or setting for recognising particular direction components. These stellar azimuths or bearing from true north or south thus formed the basis of recognition of the eight major cardinal directions or the 32 points of a nautical compass of true bearings.

Needham (1971: 554-555) observes that a general practice among Asian mariners prior to the introduction of the sextant was to roughly ascertain the latitude by measuring the height of the pole star against their masts and rigging. Similar practices may have been prevalent among South Asian mariners.

In Bangladesh, as revealed in field-level investigation in Caṭṭagrāma Coast, the mariners use the Ādām Surāt and the Sāt Jāli. The mariners of West Bengal and Orissa use the Kālapuruṣa (the Orion and Taurus constellations in combination) for east-west sailing. They use the Polaris (Dhruva Nakṣatra) to determine true north and the octagonal wind rose to ascertain the eight principal directions. When we see that the master mariner Dulāi navigates with the help of the stars and steers C̃ād Saodāgar's ships safely to destination in Baṁśīdāsa's *Padmapurāṇa* (composed in the 16th century), we may logically believe that contemporary practices in the 'Bengal' and Orissa Coast reflect a tradition dating back at least to the medieval period if not earlier times.

Primitive navigation during Fa-Hsien's days could do little to forecast weather, which had a significant effect on navigation, as we see the monk falling a victim of two foul weather periods on his way from Siṁhala to Java. Similarly, I-Tsing himself and many of the 56 monks he writes about, fell frequent victims to storms. We know little of the techniques that the ancient mariners sailing on the Bay of Bengal developed to forecast perilous weather. However, judging by current practices on the eastern coast of South India, one can imagine the strength of ancient wisdom. Mariners of the Coromandel Coast consider bunching and intertwining sea-snakes as a clear sign that a depression is forthcoming. Similarly, when the *konga* (a sea bird) and *karigedu konga* (black sea bird) are seen flying from the north to the south in groups, mariners in the Andhra Coast believe that a cyclone will strike soon. Another danger sign is irregular and rising high waves, for they warn of imminent gale or cyclone. However, if shadow circles are seen around the moon and the sun, mariners all over South Asia are less alarmed for these signs foretell rain (Arunachalam 1996: 268, 270).

Technique of measuring distance, which also plays a significant role in navigation, was crude as we find both Fa-Hsien and I-Tsing counted oceanic distance by number of days' sail, although more accurate measurement of yōjanas was used on land. Today, a practice common in the north Indian Ocean, from Arabia to Indonesia, is measuring distance with units known as *zam*. A single *zam* is "the normal sailing distance under fair sea and weather conditions during a single watch of three hours". Eight *zam* was equal to a day's sailing under favourable conditions (*ibid.*: 263). However, neither is the term known in coastal Bangladesh nor do we find it being used in the maṅgalakāvya corpus.

There is no record to show how the navigators of yore judged current, drift, tide and wave motions. According to Arunachalam (*ibid.*: 264), the traditional practice among South Asian mariners for judging the above with reference to the direction of sailing of the boat is "by throwing a moist ball of coal ash into sea and observing its motion on the water surface. Lateral spread suggests relatively calm sea while flow patterns indicate the direction of flow. In order to determine the speed of the vessel, a heavy wooden plank with metal rims is used as a float. The float is thrown overboard from bow and a standard phrase chanted; the speed is determined by noting the number of times the phrase needs to be chanted for the float to reach the stern" (*ibid.*). Ancient mariners may have used these practices as well.

Although we are uncertain as to when the above practices were introduced, we are certain that the shore-sighting birds were used as an important navigational aid since the 5th century BC, if not earlier, because it has been referred in the *Digha Nikāya* (1. 222) of the *Sutta-Piṭaka*, which T. W. Rhys Davids dates a century after the Buddha's *parinirvana*.

> Long ago ocean-going merchants were wont to plunge forth upon the sea, on board a ship, taking with them a shore-sighting bird. When the ship was out of sight of land they would set the shore-sighting bird free. And it would go to the East and to the South and to the West and to the North, and to the intermediate points, and rise aloft. If on the horizon it caught sight of land, thither it would go. But if not, then it would come back to the ship again (Davids 1899: 432).

Since, as Pliny informs us in his *Natural History* (VI, 24), it was prevalent in Sri Lanka in the 1st century AD, there is no reason why the mariners of the Bay would not have used them as well.

> In making sea-voyages, the Taprobanê mariners make no observation of stars, and indeed the Great Bear is not visible to them, but they take birds out to sea with them which they let loose from time to time and follow the direction of their flight as they make for land. The season for navigation is limited to four months, and they particularly shun the sea during the hundred days which succeed the summer solstice, for it is then winter in those seas (McCrindle 1979: 1[illegible]3).

In Bāveru Jātaka, "some merchants come to the kingdom of Bāveru, bringing on board ship wit them a foreign crow ... perched on top of the mast ..." (Book IV, No. 339; Cowell 1957, III: 83-84). Sarkar (1986: 344-45) believes that Bāveru Jātaka's crow is a *disākāka* (direction giving crow).

The birds were quite definitely used by Arab-Persian mariners of the Bay in the 9th century AD. A Chinese scholar named Tuan Ch'öng-shï (d. 863 AD), has the following to say in his *Yu-Yang Tsa Tsu*:

> On the sea-going ships of the Persians many feed pigeons. These pigeons can fly several thousand *li*, and when let loose, at a single flight they return to their homes, thus serving a letter of good news (Hasan 1928: 109).

Persian nautical treatise, called the *Rahmānī* or the *Rahmānaj*, confirms the use of birds till the 12th century: "when the traveller sails in this sea, seven sorts of birds in the open sea tell him that he is near the island of Socotra" (*ibid.*: 127-28). Archaeological evidence from an excavation at Farz in Iraq, in the form of a seal depicting a boat with a shore-sighting bird, confirms such practice in Arab-Persian sea-going vessels (Sarkar 1986: 344).

Summing up on the mode of primitive navigation in the Bay of Bengal, one can say that basic techniques were comprised of (i) knowledge of the stars, (ii) knowledge of monsoon winds and ocean currents, (iii) use of shore-sighting birds, (v) ability to roughly assess latitude, (vi) ability to take sounding from sea-bottom and (vii) knowledge of various physical properties such as colour of water and samples of sea-bottom. However, it is clear that primitive navigation was gradually giving way to quantitative navigation from the 9th century.

Quantitative Navigation in Transoceanic Voyages

Schoff (1995: 247) believes that the Persians and Arabs visiting China in the 6th and 7th centuries AD were the first to apply the magnetic compass (the "south-pointing chariot") to navigation, having learnt of its use from the Chinese. However, it is more probable that the Chinese were the first to employ the magnetic compass at sea, as Needham (1971: 562-563, 576) argues citing Chinese literary accounts. This was accomplished before 1050, possibly around 850. In all probability, the Chinese compass was a magnetic needle floating on water in a small cup. We have further reference of the use of the "south-pointing chariot" in the *P'ing-chóu-k'o-t'an* by Chu Yü composed in the first quarter of the 12th century (Hirth and Rockhill 1965: 32) and in *Chu-fan-chï* by Chao Ju-kua composed in the mid-13th century (*ibid.*: 176). In the Mediterranean, the magnetic compass became known after about 1185 (Needham 1971: 555) and was perfected in the 14th century by the addition of the compass card, which made possible for mariners to determine bearings at sea (Angelucci 1970: 26). Expressing his skepticism regarding the view that credits the Chinese for introducing the compass in navigation, Angelucci (*ibid.*) argues, "if this is true, it seems strange that Marco Polo found no trace of it on his voyage to Cathay".

The controversy over the use of magnetic compass may become a little clear if we see some reason in Needham's argument. He says, "[f]or the Asian pilot, the needle was only one of his instruments, and the determination of position by star (and possibly even sun) sights was at least equally important" (Needham 1971: 576). This view is further validated by Chu Yü in his *P'ing-chóu-k'o-t'an* (composed in the first quarter of the 12th century) that the Chinese shipmasters combined his knowledge of the coasts, the stars and the sun in the heaven, smell of mud picked up by a hook attached to a line a hundred feet long and the south-pointing needle (Hirth and Rockhill 1965: 32).

In Islamic literature, the navigational use of the compass is mentioned for the first time in *Jāmi' al-Ḥikāyāt* (c. 1232 AD), a collection of Persian stories. It is mentioned again in an Arabic work titled *Kanz al-Tujjar*, composed in 1282, in which the author observes that the ship on which he sailed from Tripoli in Syria to Alexandria in 1242 used a magnetic needle floating in water. Ahmad Ibn Majid, the famous Arab navigator, discusses properties and origin of the loadstone in his *Kitab al-Fawa'id Fi Usul al-Bahar wa'l-Qawa'id* (c. 1489-90 AD). These evidences prove, as Tibbetts (1981: 290-291) argues, that the assertion made by early European travellers in the Indian Ocean that the Arabs never used the compass for sailing were completely wrong. "Either the Europeans were not observant or the Arabs successfully hid their instrument from prying infidel eyes".

A few Indian scholars have tried to show that an "Arabic work on mineralogy (1252 AD) indicate that Indian seamen steered by an iron fish floating in a bowl of oil" (Chattopadhyay 1994: 100). The apparatus is believed to have been called the *Macch Yantra* (a Marathi term derived from Sanskrit *Matsya Yantra* or the "Fish Apparatus"). Sarkar's (1986: 356) attempt to link it with the steering apparatus mentioned in the *Milindapañha* (1st century AD) is too farfetched. Arunachalam (1996: 263), more reasonable and down to the earth, believes that "the mariner's compass was known to the seamen of the northern Indian Ocean since about the 14th century". However, he adds, it is unclear how South Asian seamen used it.

Another important navigational technique was measuring of stellar altitudes. For this purpose, quite a few instruments similar to the sextant had developed in Asia. One of these was the *kamāl* that was introduced to James Prinsep by a navigator from the Maldives in 1835. He describes it thus:

> ... a small parallelogram of horn (about two inches by one) with a string (or a couple of strings, in some instances), inserted in the centre. On the string are nine knots. To use the instrument for taking the height of *polaris*, the string was held between the teeth, with the horn at such a distance from the eye, that while the lower edge seems to touch the oceanic horizon, the upper edge just meets the star: the division or knot is then read off as the required latitude (Prinsep 1836: 785).

Si'di' al-Chelebi describes in the *Mohi't* (composed in 1554) another instrument, more primitive than the Maldivean *kamāl*, called the *loh* or "tablets". The instrument consisted of nine tablets. The first of these was reckoned to be four *isbā* (fingers) wide and each following was one *isbā* wider. All the nine tablets were strung on one string that was as long as the stretch of a man's arms. As Prinsep explains in his note to the above, "that board was selected in applying the instrument to use, which just covered the space between the star and the horizon" (Hammer 1838: 771-772, 778). In the late 15th and the early 16th century, Arab navigators Ibn Majid and Sulaiman al-Mahri mention yet another instrument that was possibly called *khashaba.* Unfortunately, they do not explain its form but leave us with a vague impression that the instrument was some form of wooden tablet (Tibbetts 1981: 317-18).

Although Needham (1971: 574-575) argues that "there is existence of the use of the cross-stuff in China in the 11th century", it is more probable that its use for navigational purpose began in the 15th century when the Chinese pilots were using a device named "guiding star stretch-boards" for observing astral altitude. The device was made by Ma Huai-te and was recorded by Li Hsu (1505-1592) in his *Chieh An Lao Jen Man Pi.* It consisted of twelve ebony tablets ranging gradually from small to large (the largest being seven inches square) plus a small ivory tablet (two inches square). The ebony tablets were held at a fixed distance from the eye and the ivory tablet was used for fine adjustment.

Two early forms of sextants were known in South Asia. One of these was the *yaṣṭhi yantra* which was known since 628 AD, when Brahmagupta mentions it for the first time. The other was the *triphalaka,* a four-feet-high tripod, which was known since 1039 AD when Sripati mentioned it in his *Siddhanta-sekhara* (Sarkar 1986: 358-359). However, there is no indication that the mariners used these instruments for measuring stellar altitude.

As for European use of the cross-stuff (and Jacob's staff), it has been wrongly assumed to have developed from an astronomical and survey instrument described by Levi ben Gerson in 1321. Needham cites Beaujouan and Poulle (I, p. 112) to point out that "no text authorises belief in the use of the cross-stuff for astronomical navigation before the first years of the 16th century" (1971: 557, fn. c). He further shows that the Portuguese cross-stuff or *balestilha* probably did not develop from Gerson's instrument but from the instrument for measuring star altitude developed by the Arabs.

The brief review of development of various instruments for measuring stellar altitude and their application in maritime navigation given above appears to validate Needham's (*ibid.*: 576) opinion that "[b]efore 1300 AD, there is no evidence to prove the existence of instruments such as the cross-staff or *kamāl* by which star altitude was taken at sea, either by the Arab or by South Asian navigators". However, Fatimi (1996: 286, 288) contends that altitude-measuring device must have been known to the Arabs in the late 9th century AD. He substantiates his argument by pointing out that Ya'qub bin Ishaq al-Kindi, well-known as "the Philosopher of the Arabs" (d. 890), composed a treatise on "Finding altitudes by the instrument with two legs", which must have been an astronomical instrument similar to the *kamāl.* Possibly in the early 11th century AD, Abu Ali bin Sina (980-1037) invented the "instrument having sine of arc and azimuth" which must have been another *kamāl*-class instrument. The use of such instruments for navigational purpose is testified by Buzurg bin Shahriyar's *Ajai'ib al-Hind* ("Marvels of India"). In it, Buzurg narrates an anecdote dated to the first half of the 10th century AD and related to Mardanshah, who was one of the master mariners of the "land of peppers". One evening, when he was playing with his son (about 15 months old), a storm arose. Mardanshah asked the child to be taken away and busied himself with "affairs of the ship". Next morning, when the storm had subsided, he asked about the child, only to be informed that it had last been seen with him. In a state of extreme agitation, Mardanshah "plucked his beard and stuck his head with *al-khashab*". Fortunately, the child was found – stuck in the crevice of the rudder after being swept overboard during the storm. Fatimi argues that Mardanshah's *al-khashab* was Ibn Majid's *khashaba.* We may therefore believe that the instrumental measurement of stellar altitude and its application in maritime navigation began with the Arabs, who had already begun using an instrument named *al-khashab* or *khashaba* by the first half of the 10th century.

Although the hour-glass was possibly introduced on Chinese ships towards the end of the 16th century, when it was acquired from the Portuguese and the Dutch, the Chinese may have used burning incense sticks or some form of mechanical clockwork (a development of c. 1370, in which sand was substituted for water in clocks of classic scoop-wheel type) to measure time (Needham 1971: 569-570). At the present state of our knowledge, mariners of South Asia in general and 'Bengal' in particular does not appear to have used any mechanical device for measuring time. During the time frame of this research, they must have depended on primitive method of measuring time that depended on observing the position of stellar bodies.

Terrestrial globes were not used on board Chinese ships. However, it was certainly known in Persian-Arabic tradition. Ahmad Ibn Rustah, a Persian geographer, is known to have given a description of the terrestrial as well as the celestial sphere in 903 AD. A scientific mission from the Persian Ilkhan court headed by Jamāl al-Dīn is known to have travelled to the Chinese court, carrying such a globe or its design (*ibid.*: 585). Thus, it seems possible that the seamen of Arabic tradition may have used terrestrial globes on board their ships anytime after the 10th century.

It is not certain if maritime charts existed on Chinese ships, although its existence is implicit in many Chinese texts. The possibility is further strengthened when one is reminded that the Chinese were capable of producing maps on a scale of 100 *li* to the division by 1137 (*ibid.*: 568). However, the Arab-Persian ships definitely used maritime charts in the 9th century. The geographer Muqaddasī in *Aḥsanu 't-Taqāsīm fī Ma'rifati 'l-Aqālīm* (885 AD) says, "I have also seen in their (crews of Muslim ship) possession charts and sailing directories which they constantly study and follow with implicit confidence" (Hasan 1928: 124). The Arabs and Persians also used nautical treatises, such as the *Rahmānī* or the *Rahmānaj,* since the 12th century or even earlier (*ibid.*: 127-28). It is also known that mariners of the Indian Ocean used navigational charts in the 15th and 16th centuries. Vasco da Gama's Arabian pilot showed him "a chart of the entire Indian coast". Albuquerque sent to the Portuguese king a "document copied from a large map made by a pilot in Java". However, when it comes to producing actual documents showing the use of navigational charts in the Indian Ocean, we can only cite nautical documents (*roz namah*) of the Gujarati sailors from the 17th century, now held by the National Museum in New Delhi (Deloche 1994: 205, 207, fn. 33).

From Si'di' al-Chelebi, who gives detailed navigational instructions to mariners sailing from Diū to Shātijām (Caṭṭagrāma) in the *Mohi't* (Chapter Nine, Section 3, Twenty-eighth Voyage), we get a graphic account of how medieval navigators operated in the Bay of Bengal. Part of the voyage is transoceanic and the remaining is coastal. Because al-Chelebi mentions the use of stellar altitude measuring instrument (he does not name it) and also advises taking soundings and observing colour of the water, the passage is valuable and hence deserves to be quoted in full.

> Leaving *Diū* you first S. S. E. till the pole is five inches, and side then towards the land, till the distance between it and between the ship is six *zams;* from then you steer S. S. E., because in the neighborhood of Ceylon, the sea runs high, the further you keep off the more quiet the sea grow; you must not side all at once but by degrees, first till the *farkadain* (β and γ in the Little Bear) are made by a quarter less than eight inches, from thence to S. E. till the *farkadain* are seven inches and a quarter, from thence true east at a rate of 18 zams, then you have passed Ceylon (Hammer 1836: 465).

> [T]hen you steer N. E. Ceylon remaining on the western side; then N. E. by N. till you come opposite to *Rakanj,* where the pole is made with a quarter wanting to nine, and the *Aselli* scarce with six inches; if in this course you see land it is well; if not, steer E. N. E. till the pole is nine inches and a half so you come to the island of *Dardiw* [probably Nardiel or Narkol deap, off the Teknaf entrance]. If you see it at this time it is well, if not go right east till you see land, but take care of *Fesht Hayumiun* [probably Oyester-island, a barren rock off Arracan, or St. Martin's reef], which is a desert rock, round which the water is twenty fathoms deep; take care also of *Dardiw* where the water is but five fathoms. If *Rakanj* is in sight, go N. N. W. with 25 fathoms of water. At this time *Hayumiun* remains on your right, of which great care is to be taken. After having passed it you approach the land till your soundings give 16 fathoms, and with this course you come to *Dardiw;* after having left it behind you go with 12 fathoms depth N. N. W., there you come to a great *Khur* (?) called *Bakal* [probably *Mascall* island], and then five capes which are taken for islands by those who don't know them; then comes a *Ghobba,* that is to say, a gulph full of shallows, shoals and breakers; this place is called *Kakar Diwa* [Cutub-deep, south of Chittagong], then you come to the island *Zenjilia* [no such islands exist today] which is facing you, your way lies N. N. W. When you approach this island, side to the sea, because its southern cape is *rikk,* that is to say, a shallow, and the colour of the water grows white; meanwhile, on the sea side it is seen green. Hold that course and you'll find better soundings by degrees till you come to 17 and 18 fathoms. Coming to this place you find the water again whitish, these shallows are on the south side of *Fesht Gurian,* which is a desert place; here the sea is noisy, don't keep either too near to the island of *Zenjilia,* nor too far from it but steer a middle course; if the soundings give 18 fathoms or near it, you have passed *Zenjilia;* then you go in the direction of the north pole, and continue to take soundings till you come to seven fathoms; from thence you steer in the direction of the north pole, and to the rising place of the β and γ of the Little Bear, till your soundings are six fathoms but not less. So you come to cape *Khur* which is *Shātijām.* Here you stop till the *rebban* (tide) come, with which you enter the port (*ibid.*: 466-467).

We are now in a position to sum up the state of qualitative navigation in the medieval period by referring to the famous and fateful meeting between Vasco da Gama and Ahmad Ibn Mājid on the East Coast of Africa at Malindi (north of Dar es Salaam).

> Certain it is that when the Portuguese showed him their astrolabes and quadrants in the summer of 1498 Ibn Mājid was not in the least surprised, saying that the Arabs had similar instruments, but the Portuguese were very astonished that he was not surprised (Needham 1971: 567).

Needham (*ibid.*: 576) believes, the meeting clearly shows that in 1498, "fully quantitative navigation was some two or three centuries old 'East of Suez' but hardly one century old in the West". However, when we consider the level of competence of Bengali mariners, we find hardly any achievement in transoceanic voyages, specially in quantitative navigation. Neither contemporary practice nor indications given in the maṅgalakāvya corpus reveal use of compass, instruments for measuring stellar altitude, instrument for measuring time, terrestrial globes and navigational charts.

SAILING SCHEDULE

The *Great Britain*, launched in England in 1844, was the first iron-hulled, double-bottomed, screw-propelled Atlantic liner. The *Clermont,* which steamed up the Hudson River on 7 August 1807, was the first wooden-hulled paddle wheeler to engage in commercial operations (McDowell and Gibbs 1954: 27-28). Till the introduction of such mechanised means of transportation in the 19th century, the energy necessary to set a maritime vessel in motion depended entirely upon wind system and oceanic hydrodynamics. Hence, trade progressed only as humans developed their ability to use natural energy derived from these sources to their advantage.

As Deloche (1994: 209) rightly observes, "[t]he usual textbook explanation that ships sailed in the seas in one direction during the south-west monsoon, and in another during the north-east monsoon, represents an over-simplification". As our examination given below will reveal, wind system and oceanic hydrodynamics gave rise to varied regional conditions. Some of these were feasible for coastal voyages, while others were necessary for transoceanic voyages. Furthermore, neither coastal nor transoceanic voyages continued throughout the year. Specific period/s, when condition of the high sea was inclement, were considered adverse to shipping. Since the sailing schedule of coastal and transoceanic voyages varied because wind system and oceanic hydrodynamics were utilised differently, they are discussed separately.

Sailing Schedule in Coastal Voyages

As already discussed, till the second half of the 2nd century AD, maritime voyages in the Bay of Bengal were essentially coastal. In order to make a successful voyage, the mariners had to have a clear understanding of tidal flow, monsoon winds, land breeze and sea breeze. These were the factors that determined their sailing schedule.

Mariners in the Caṭṭagrāma-Cox's Bazar Coast prefer to make long distance voyages from the months of Bhādra (mid-August to mid-September) to Māgh (mid-January to mid-February). During this period, i.e., mid-August to mid-February, the sea remains calm and natural calamities such as storms and rains remain minimal. The only calamity is cyclone in November. Furthermore, gentle northeast monsoon winds and land breeze are also favourable. During the remaining six months, the sea is comparatively more turbulent and hence they avoid any trip which necessitates abandoning the coast. Hence voyages along routes lying close to the coast i.e., Sandwīp to Caṭṭagrāma and back, Caṭṭagrāma to Kutubdiyā and Maheśkhālī and back, Caṭṭagrāma to Cox's Bazar and back continue to be made. On the other hand, they avoid crossing the Meghnā estuary.

We have good reason to believe that the sailing schedules indicated above were followed in the medieval period and even earlier. Consider, for example, the Touffon (hurricane) that Caesar Frederick's ship came up against when he sailed from Pegu to Caṭṭagrāma in March 1569. "Unfortunate are they", says Frederick, "that are at Sea in that yeere and time of the Touffon, because few are that escape that danger". The hurricane lasted three days and nights, during which time the ship's sails and rudder were lost and the mast had to be cut down. Fortunately for him, Frederick landed at Sandwīp (Purchas 1905b: 135-136). As cited earlier in Chapter Four, we also hear Sebastien Manrique, who was travelling on Geliā from Dianga to Mrauk-U on 2nd July 1630 along the coast, say that it was "dangerous to navigate" because it was the rainy season (Manrique 1927: 94-95).

However, Ralph Fitch reports safe sailing from Śrīpur to Pegu, along the Caṭṭagrāma Coast in November 1586 (Foster 1968: 28-29). We also hear of Friar Melchoir Fonesca, a Jesuit missionary, sailing from Caṭṭagrāma to Bakla in the month of November in 1599 (Hosten 1925: 63). Even Shaistah Khan, the Mughal viceroy of 'Bengal', conducted his naval expedition against the Portuguese-Arakanese forces in Caṭṭagrāma in the month of February of 1667 (Manucci 1907, II: 117, fn. 1).

Sailing between Caṭṭagrāma and Sātgāon must have followed a similar pattern because we find that Sebastien Manrique had departed from Huglī on 11 September 1629 for Dianga. He voyaged on a Geliā "down the Ganges" and reached Dianga in 14 days (Manrique 1927: 83). Although the route of this voyage is not clear, that of a subsequent voyage he made in 1635 is described in greater detail and is hence clearer. This time he commenced his journey on a Geliā from Dianga. The vessel was rowed past Sandwīp Dakṣiṇa Śāhbājpur and Hātiyā, through the estuary of the Meghnā and then through "one of the branches of the mighty and ancient Ganges" till he was captured on one of the channels of the Huglī River (*ibid.*: 394). Thus, it is clear that the coastal route from Sātgāon to Caṭṭagrāma, at least for the smaller crafts, cut through the estuarine rivers of southern Bengal till the mouth of the Meghnā and then voyaged past offshore islands.

Similar or nearly similar sailing schedules must have existed in Contai-Orissa Coast as well because we hear from Father Barbier that during a voyage he undertook in June 1712, from Madras to Huglī, along the coast of Coromandel and Orissa, his ship also met with a violent storm near Balasore (*Bengal Past & Present* 1910: 202). Obviously, June was not the right time to sail in the Contai-Orissa Coast.

Movement of vessels from the mouth of the Gaṅgā to Sātgāon, a distance of hundred miles was difficult because of tidal effect. As Caesar Frederick observed in 1567,

> ... from the mouth of this River [Ganges], to a City called Satagan, where the Merchants gather themselves together with their trade, are an hundred miles, which they rowe in eighteene houres with the increase of the water: in which river it floweth and ebbeth as it doth in the Thames, and when the ebbing water is come, they are not able to rowe against it, by reason of the swiftnesse of the water, yet their barks be light and armed with Oares, like Foistes, yet they cannot prevaile against that Streame, but for refuge must make them fast to the banke of the River until the next flowing water, ... (Purchas 1905b: 113).

Tidal wave at every full and new moon, specially during the equinox, also presented hazards, not only at the mouth of the Gaṅgā-Huglī but also at the mouth of the Meghnā.

Sailing Schedule in Transoceanic Voyages

In the littoral zones of the Arabian Sea, the Bay of Bengal and the South China Sea, the most important component of the wind system was the monsoon winds, which determined the sailing schedule of transoceanic voyages, and which in turn decided the trading season. On the other hand, ocean currents are important because north of 10° S latitude, the monsoon winds cause seasonal change of sea currents, sometimes working as a complementary force of the winds and at other times, as a contradictory force for ships making transoceanic voyages. Because of the monsoon winds, sea currents and the voyaging-time, maritime trade in the littoral regions of Asia developed in three zones. These were,

1. The Arabian Sea Zone, which included countries in northeastern Africa, southern Middle East and the western coast of India.
2. The Bay of Bengal Zone, which included the coasts of Coromandel, Andhra, Orissa, 'Bengal', Myanmar, Tenasserim (Thailand) and the western belt of Malay Peninsula (up to the straits of Malacca).
3. The South China Sea Zone, which encompassed the entire region from Canton in China to the straits of Malacca, including Indo-China, Thailand, the eastern belt of the Malay Peninsula, Sumatra, Borneo and the Philippines (Sarkar 1986: 296).

The skipper of the ancient vessels, in order to ensure favourable wind for his voyage to and from his destination, had to choose his departure dates judiciously. Hence it is necessary to discuss sailing in the three zones separately.

SAILING IN THE ARABIAN SEA

In the Arabian Sea, the southwest monsoon prevails from May to August while the northeast lasts from November to February. Between these two, there are two inter-monsoon periods: (i) September to October and (ii) March to April. During the southwest monsoon regime, the wind generally lies between southwest and west by south and it is accompanied by frequent squalls and heavy rains. The condition of the sea remains turbulent under its influence. The effect of the monsoon weakens in August and in the following month, the weather is much more bearable. During these two months (August and September), the wind blows from the west and west-northwest, occasionally accompanied by heavy rains. The wind is variable in October and November. The northeast monsoon sets in towards the end of October or in the beginning of November, bringing thunder and rain. As the month of November ends, fine weather sets in (*ibid.*: 297-299).

Maritime ports in the north and south Kanara and the Malabar Coast generally remain closed during the southwest monsoon. The Malabar Coast in particular remains a hazardous region for sailing from June to August because of the turbulent condition of the sea. Sailing up the Malabar Coast during the months of October and November is difficult because the wind remains variable and the ocean current flows in the opposite direction. However, voyaging down the coast is comparatively easy (*ibid.*: 298-299).

As recorded in the *Periplus* (§14) the most advantageous time for sailing from Egypt to India in the 1st century AD was in July (Schoff 1995: 27). During this month, the southwest monsoon would attain its peak intensity, providing wind with average velocity of 22 to 33 knots, sometimes rising to gales with average wind velocity of 34 to 47 knots. Braving these fierce winds the ships would arrive on the Indian Coast in September or perhaps early October. The same ships would set sail for their return voyage after the beginning of November and arrive at the entrance of the Red Sea by the winds of the northeast monsoon (Casson 1991: 8).

Nearly a thousand years later, the sailing schedule had changed drastically. As al-Mas'udi informs us, Arab vessels of his time avoided crossing the Arabian Sea in the month of June (Timrah). During this time, he says, "it is impossible to sail from Oman on the sea of India ... except with fast-rate vessels and light cargoes" (Warren 1987: 151). The best time for sailing the sea was when "the Sun was in Sagittarius" (i.e., middle of November to the middle of December). As Sarkar shows, this practice is still followed in contemporary times because the Persian Gulf remains rough during the months of September and October. The northeast monsoon provided favourable wind for sailing between Muscat and the Malabar Coast. Before voyaging across the Bay of Bengal, these ships would usually anchor at Kulam Mali (Quilon), the most important port on the Malabar Coast. Following a similar time schedule, Chinese ships crossed the Persian Gulf before September and October when it remained rough. Then, with the help of the northeast monsoon, they sailed from Muscat and arrived at Kulam Mali a month later, sometime in November or December. Sometime near the end of December or the beginning of January, these ships would set sail for their homeward journey. The northeast monsoon provided the best sailing time from the Gulf of Cambay to Southeast Asia, from January to March. Merchants from the coast of the gulf found it feasible to commence on their return journey from the straits of Malacca and reach home by the end of May before the southwest monsoon set in (Sarkar 1986: 303-304).

From Si'di' al-Chelebi one learns about specific sailing schedules followed by mariners of the West Coast of India in the mid-16th century. The *Mohi't* was written in 1554, but the dates given in the sailing schedule, al-Chelebi informs us, "are ten days later than those given by master Sūleimān Ben Ahmad [Sulaimān b. Aḥmad b. Suleimān al-Mahri]" (Hammer 1834: 553), the Arab mariner whose earliest work was written in 1511.

Si'di' al-Chelebi's schedules as given below in three tables clearly show that sailing from ports on the Arabian Sea to the Bay of Bengal was suspended during the SW monsoon. The Favourable period to sail to the bay was the inter-monsoon period (August-September) between the SW and NE monsoons. On the other hand, sailing from 'Bengal' to the Arabian Sea was favourable during the NE monsoon (November-February) and during the inter-monsoon period (March-April).

SAILING IN THE BAY OF BENGAL

In the Bay of Bengal, the southwest monsoon prevails from the end of May to August while the northeast lasts from November to February. The inter-monsoon periods between these two are similar to those of the Arabian Sea: (i) September to October and (ii) March to April.

The northeast monsoon is often preceded by cyclones and hurricanes, with heavy rains and squalls in mid-October. During this month (i.e., October), which falls in the inter-monsoon period, the wind generally blows from NNE to NE. Cyclones are known to strike even in the first half of November. However, once the northeast monsoon sets in, particularly in December, the weather is settled. During these two months (i.e., November and December), the wind generally prevails from NNE to NE. In January, the winds usually blow from NE to ENE, sometimes even from the east. The wind from northeasterly direction gradually dies down in February. In the coastal regions, wind from ESE, SE and S begins to pick up from the middle of the month. In March and April, the northern zone of the Bay of Bengal experiences strong breeze from SSE to SSW during daytime. However, these are replaced by land breeze from SW to WNW in the evenings. In addition, the month of April experiences squalls from NW. The Coromandel experiences winds from S to SW during the month of May, accompanied by violent squalls and cyclones. Strong wind squalls often strike the Arakan and the 'Bengal' Coast in the month of June. During this period, the winds mostly blow from W to WSW along with heavy rainfall, which make visibility poor. Southwest monsoon attains peak intensity in the months of June and July. The regime of the southwest monsoon begins to slacken in August when winds on the coast blow from WSW to W and NW, which sometimes gives way to sea breezes (Sarkar 1986: 305-307).

In Sri Lanka, the southwest monsoon begins with a brief and mild spell (known as the Little Monsoon) which lasts for a week in the first half of May. Following a fortnight-long break, the Big Monsoon usually arrives normally in the first week of June. Severe monsoon with periodic breaks prevails for three months from June to August. Ships from the southern Coromandel Coast to Sri Lanka stay close to the NE Coast of the island. The severity gradually diminishes in August, ushering in calm weather from 20th October to 10th November. The northeast monsoon sets in by mid-November and continues till mid-February. During this period, the wind blows from the north in the forenoon, changing to NNW in the afternoon and early evening. The end of March and the whole of April see heavy squalls and rain in the surrounding sea (*ibid.*: 307-308).

For the sailors of the Coromandel Coast, the northeast monsoon provides excellent sailing conditions because the Bay remains calm, compared with its turbulent nature during the southwest monsoon. In June and July, when the monsoon attains peak intensity, only occasional vessels sail down the Coromandel Coast from the north to the south, defying the monsoon by keeping close to the shore.

There are but scanty records of sailing across the Bay of Bengal. The earliest of these is from Pliny, who informs us in his *Natural History* (VI, 24) about Sri Lanka in the 1st century AD.

> The season for navigation is limited to four months, and they particularly shun the sea during the hundred days which succeed the summer solstice, for it is then winter in those seas (McCrindle 1979: 103).

Table 5.1:
Beginning of Sailing Season from the Arabian Sea to the Bay of Bengal and Beyond

Port	Destination	From
Aden	Malacca, Sumatra, Tenasserim, Martaban, Bengal and all the ports situated below the wind	12th August
Sheher and Meshkara	Malacca, Sumatra, Tenasserim, Martaban, Bengal and all the ports situated below the wind	22nd August
Gujarat	Sumatra, Tenasserim, Bengal and all the ports situated below the wind	2nd September
Concona (Konkan)	Sumatra, Tenasserim, Bengal and all the ports situated below the wind	6th September
Dībi (the Maldives)	Malacca, Sumatra, Tenasserim, Martaban, Bengal	21st September

(Hammer 1834: 551-552)

Table 5.2:
End of Sailing Season from the Arabian Sea to the Bay of Bengal and Beyond

Port	Destination	From
Gujarat	Malacca, Sumatra (Shomotora), Tenasserim (Tanassari) and Bengal	16th March
Malabar	Malacca, Sumatra, Tenasserim, Martaban, Bengal and all the ports situated below the wind	14th April
Dībi (the Maldives)	Malacca, Sumatra, Tenasserim, Martaban, Bengal and all the ports situated below the wind	14th April
Sheher and Fartak	Malacca, Sumatra, Tenasserim, Martaban, Bengal and all the ports situated below the wind	24th February
Dhofar	Malacca, Sumatra, Tenasserim, Martaban, Bengal and all the ports situated below the wind	24th February
Muscat	Malacca, Sumatra, Siam, Bengal and all the ports situated below the wind	16th March

(Hammer 1834: 549-550)

Table 5.3:
Sailing Schedule from the Bay of Bengal

Port	Destination	Begins	Ends
Bengal	Aden, Mecca (Jedda), Hormūz	25th December	25th January
Bengal	Alinat (Barronat?), Sri Lanka	13th February	Not mentioned
Shomotora	Bengal	13th February	4th April

(Hammer 1834: 552-553)

Table 5.4:
Sailing Schedule across the Bay of Bengal (From Ahmad Ibn Mājid)

From	Destination	Period
Bengal	Hormuz, Yemen, Hijaz	1st January - 31st January
Bengal	Ceylon, Maldives	1st January - 10th February
Malacca, Pegu, Siam	Ceylon, Maldives	1st January - 10th February
Java, Sumatra, Malacca, Tanasari	Bengal	20th February - 11th April (extendable to 1st May)

(Tibbetts 1981: 233)

Table 5.5:
Sailing Schedule across the Bay of Bengal

Source	Origin	Destination	Outward	Return
Methwold	Masulipatam	Achin, Arakan, Pegu, Tenasserim	September	February-April
Schorer	Masulipatam	Bengal, Arakan, Pegu Tenasserim, Achin, Priaman, Queda and Perak (Muslim merchants)	September	-----
Schorer	Masulipatam	Achin, Bantam (English merchants)	May or beginning of June	------
Schorer	Masulipatam	Arrimogam (Armagon), Pulicat, St. Thome, Tegnapatam, Porto Novo, Negapatam, Ceylon, Cochin	January	------
Schorer	Cochin, Negapatam, St. Thome	Bengal, Arakan, Pegu Tenasserim (Portuguese merchants)	August and September	March or April

Pliny's observation tallies with modern observation, for it has been noted above that severe monsoon prevails in Sri Lanka from June to August and the best sailing season is indeed when the northeast monsoon prevails, from mid-November to mid-February. Fa-Hien, who describes briefly his voyage from Tāmralipti to Siṁhala in 411 AD, sailed during this favourable period.

> Putting to sea, they proceeded in a south-westerly direction, and, catching the first fair wind of the winter season (i.e., of the N. E. monsoon) they sailed for fourteen days and nights and arrived at the country of the Lions (Siṁhala, Ceylon) (*Fo-kwō-ki*, XXXVII; Beal 1869: 147-148).

From Siṁhala, Fa-Hien's homeward journey began in September 413 AD (according to calculations made by Sarkar 1986: 310) when he sailed across the Bay of Bengal. On the way his ship encountered a tempest which forced it to sail off course to an unidentified island, possibly in the Andamans. It was beset by foul weather again, when the sky was overcast, making it impossible to get the bearing right. He must have fallen victim to the period preceding the northeast monsoon, which, as noted above, is often beset by cyclones and hurricanes. However, Ibn Battutā's crossing of the bay during his visit to 'Bengal' was unhindered since he sailed during the cold weather of 1345-46 or 1346-47 (Bhattasali 1922: 143-144).

The seventh expedition of Cheng Ho (1431-1433) reached Semudera near Kuala Pasai (northern Sumatra) on 12th September 1432. The fleet sailed for Sri Lanka on 2 November 1432, crossed the Indian Ocean in 26 days and arrived in Sri Lanka on 28 November 1432. On the way from Semudera, a detached fleet with Ma-Huan visited 'Bengal' and rejoined the main fleet at Calicut around 10 December 1432. Obviously, Cheng Ho chose the best time (i.e., November and December) to cross the Indian Ocean and the Bay of Bengal. The fleet, very judiciously decided to stay anchored at Semudera for over six weeks. On the way back home, the fleet re-crossed the Indian Ocean in April, sailing from Calicut on the 9th and arriving at Semudera on the 25th (Mills in Ma-Haun 1970: 17, 19). Similarly, we find from I-Tsing's record of his journey that he embarked on a royal vessel at Ka-cha (Kedah) and sailed for Tāmralipti in the twelfth month (Takakusu 1896: xxx).

From the testimony provided by Tome Pires, we find that trading voyages between Malacca and 'Bengal' in the early 16th century were conditioned by the monsoons. Voyages from Malacca to 'Bengal' were undertaken at the beginning of August and the return voyage from 'Bengal' started at the beginning of February. As Pires (1967: 93) observes "[t]hey leave here at the beginning of August and they reach Bengal in thirty days; they stay there for trading; they leave there on the first of February and they take as long again to Malacca".

The master navigator Aḥmad Ibn Mājid's sailing schedule at the end of the 15th century (Table 5.4) tallies well with the records discussed above, except the schedule from Java, Sumatra, Malacca and Tanasari to 'Bengal'. It is inconceivable that ships could sail in the above direction during the NE monsoon. One suspects some error and the schedule should actually be in the reverse direction, i.e., from 'Bengal' to Java, Sumatra, Malacca, Tanasari: from 20th February-11th April (extendable to 1st May), as Pires' observation suggests. Si'di' al-Chelebi (Table 5.3), copying from Aḥmad Ibn Mājid's sailing schedule, appears to have made the same mistake.

From the early 17th century, we get some more schedules from Europeans for sailing from the eastern coast of peninsular South Asia to ports across the Bay of Bengal and further to the Straits of Malacca. Although these schedules are far outside the time limit of our study, they may help us to understand the sailing schedule of the medieval period since no major change in climatic conditions may have transpired during the intervening centuries. The following table shows sailing schedules as given in William Methwold's *Relations of the Kingdome of Golchonda and Other Neighbouring Nations* and Antony Schorer's *Brief Relation of the Trade of the Coromandel Coast* (Moreland 1931: 37, 61, 64).

The sailing schedules given in Tables 5.4 and 5.5 re-establish our earlier findings from that given by Si'di' al-Chelebi: that the inter-monsoon period between the SW and NE monsoons (August-September) was the favourable time to sail across the bay from the west or south-west to the east or the north-east. On the other hand, return journey was favourable during the NE monsoon (November-February) and the inter-monsoon period (March-April). However, slight difference in dates is also noticeable between the schedules of Aḥmad Ibn Mājid and Si'di' al-Chelebi. These may be taken to indicate climatic variations. For voyages from the southeast to 'Bengal', the favourable time was the inter-monsoon period between the SW and NE monsoons (August-September). For voyages from 'Bengal' to the southeast, the NE monsoon (December-February) and the following intermediary period (March-April) were favourable.

SAILING IN THE STRAITS OF MALACCA AND THE SOUTH CHINA SEAS

Generally stated, the northeast monsoon extends its sway over Southeast Asia (excluding southern Sumatra and parts of Java) from December-January to March. Over the Strait of Malacca it sets in early, by November-December. The eastern coast of Malay suffers much from the fury of the northeast monsoon. As already noted, the northeast monsoon changes into a northwesterly wind as it nears the equator. To the inhabitants of the islands that are located on the south of the equator, specially to the Javanese, the northwesterly wind is known as the 'west' monsoon (because of northwesterly direction it blows from) or the 'wet' monsoon (because it is accompanied by large amount of rainfall). The northeast monsoon is followed by an inter-monsoon period, which extends from April to May.

The regime of the southwest monsoon extends from about June to September, attaining its peak in the month of July. An inter-monsoon period ensues after September for two months. Part of Malay Peninsula from Penang to Singapore does not bear the full brunt of the southwest monsoon because mountains of Sumatra on the southwest and the peninsular cliffs on the east offer protective barriers. This region experiences variable light breeze, which prevails in the Strait of Malacca. Sometimes, the breeze gives way to ferocious southwesterly squalls called the "Sumatras". Consequently, the wind currents are confusing on the southwestern corner of the South China Sea. The tides are strong in some places in this area, as on the Selangor Coast in Malaysia where it rises to a height of 20 feet or more. Besides the monsoon, the seamen of ancient times had also to be cautious while navigating near the west coast of Malaya. Irregular but strong tidal currents, presence of innumerable isles, reefs and submerged rocks, and extreme variability of depth (ranging from 200 m to 30 m) are veritable death traps for unsuspecting seamen.

Besides the two monsoons discussed above, the southern part of Southeast Asia also experiences "southeast monsoon". The reason behind this exception lies in the origin of the southwest monsoon. As noted earlier, it is a continuation of a southeasterly wind in the Southern Hemisphere. It is known as the 'east' monsoon in Java because of its easterly direction, or the 'dry' monsoons because the weather remains comparatively dry.

In Myanmar, Thailand and Indo-China, the northeast monsoon is comparatively dry. However, there is rainfall along coastal Vietnam because the wind bears moisture while travelling over the South China Sea. In northern Vietnam, the season experiences drizzle from heavy overcast sky, a weather condition locally known as *'krachin'.* During the inter-monsoon period, heavy cloudiness and thunderstorms often result in rainfall (known as 'mango rain' in Burma and Thailand). Although the amount varies, the entire region experiences this rainfall. The southwest monsoon is generally weaker than the northeast monsoon. During the inter-monsoon period which follows it, typhoons occur frequently over the South China Sea. Maximum rainfall takes place during this season along the coast of Annam (Nieuwolt 1977: 139-140).

The regime of the northeast monsoon is generally established over northern part of the South China Sea in the month of November. However, south of 5° N latitudes, it is not established before December. The monsoon attains its peak in the months of January and February. During the regime of the southwest monsoon, typhoons are least frequent in the southern half of the South China Sea.

The monsoons determine favourable sailing schedules. A vessel can easily sail past Singapore to Canton in June with the help of the southwest monsoon. On the other hand, December is an excellent month for sailing from Canton to the Musi River past Singapore because the northeast monsoon lends its strength but does not menace with its bite. The northeast monsoon was quite inhospitable to ancient sailing crafts in the South China Seas. The more the monsoon progressed, the more menacing it became for those vessels, making it nearly impossible to sail when it reached its peak. Consequently, the Malays termed it *Musim Tulop Kuala* or "shut-port season", i.e., the shut-down season for small boats. As a rule, indigenous vessels refrain from sailing in the months from October and November to February. On the other hand, the southeastern monsoon is helpful in sailing from the south of the equator.

About sailing schedule in the South China Sea, Chu Yü writes in his *Phing-chou Kho Than* (1119 AD): "Ships sail in the eleventh or twelfth months to avail themselves of the north wind (the north-east monsoon), and return in the fifth or sixth months using the south wind (the south-west monsoon)" (Needham 1971: 462). In the late 15th century,

Aḥmad Ibn Mājid observed similar schedule and noted that "[f]rom Ṣanf (Champa) and China to Malacca, Java, Sumatra, Palimbang and that area they travel in ... the spring of the year, i.e., the first hundred days of the year" [i.e., 21st November - 2nd March] (Tibbetts 1981: 233).

The above schedule was prevalent in the second half of the 7th century, when I-Tsing sailed from Canton to Śrī-vijaya (Sumatra). As he says, "I embarked from the coast of Kwang-chou (Canton), in the eleventh month in the second year of the Hsien Heng period (671 AD), and sailed for the Southern chou (Canton), in the eleventh month in the second year of the Hsien Heng period (671 AD), and sailed for the Southern Sea" (Takakusu 1896: 211). And then he adds "[a]t this time the first monsoon began to blow, when our ship proceeded towards the South, with the ropes a hundred cubits long suspended from above, two by two. ... Before sailing twenty days the ship reached Bhoga, where I landed ... (*ibid.*: xxix-xxx). For his second voyage from China to Śrībhoga in 689 AD, I-Tsing sailed again in the eleventh month (*ibid.*: xxxvi). For his homeward journey, I-Tsing boarded a ship in the middle of the summer and sailed to the north; he reached Kwang-fu (Kwang-tung) "on the twentieth day of the seventh month" in 689 AD (*ibid.*: xxxiv-xxxv).

We find Cheng Ho following a similar sailing schedule. He sailed in his seventh expedition (1431-1433), from Nanking on 19 January 1431 and entered the Min River on 8 April 1431. There he laid anchor for nearly eight months. On 12 January 1432, they sailed south from the Min River with the help of northeast monsoon and arrived at Qui Nhon (in Vietnam) on 27 January 1432. Sailing again on 12 February 1432 from Qui Nhon, he arrived at Surabaja on 7 March 1432. On his return journey, Cheng Ho arrived in Malacca on 9 May 1433 and in the seas around Poulo Condore on 28 May 1433. He arrived at Qui Nhon (Vietnam) on 13 June 1433 and entered T'ai ts'ang (Liu ho) in China on 7 July 1433 (Mills in Ma-Huan 1970: 15, 22-23).

Finally, we need to note that the demarcation line between the Bay of Bengal and the Malay southwest monsoons often lies over the Malay Peninsula and the westernmost part of the Indonesian archipelago. Hence, the ports on this region were important from pre-modern ships sailing from the Arabian Sea and the Bay of Bengal to China.

****

We may sum up our findings in this chapter by noting that in our present state of knowledge, all maritime voyages in the Bay of Bengal were coastal till c. 2nd century AD, when transoceanic voyages began to be made. Furthermore, mariners followed primitive navigational techniques till around 900 AD, after which quantitative navigational techniques began to be introduced. It appears that indigenous navigational techniques in 'Bengal' did not develop beyond a primitive stage during the time frame of this research. However, Chinese and Arab navigators were certainly familiar with most of the quantitative navigational techniques by 1500 AD. Furthermore, mariners from 'Bengal' failed to take advantage of transoceanic voyages and continued with coastal voyages during the entire time frame of this research.

The favourable sailing period for long distance coastal routes is from mid-August to mid-February. For transoceanic voyages across the Bay of Bengal, the following periods were favorable:

1. From Sri Lanka and Coromandel Coast to 'Bengal' and Southeast Asia: the inter-monsoon period between the SW and NE monsoons (August-September).
2. From 'Bengal' and Southeast Asia to Sri Lanka and Coromandel Coast: NE monsoon (November-February) and the inter-monsoon period (March-April).
3. From 'Bengal' to the southeast: the NE monsoon (December-February) and the following intermediary period (March-April).

Six
Trade Routes

Specific geographic, climatic, ecological and economic contexts give rise to a circuit or route that proves to be advantageous for trade. The most important element of a trade route is its recurrent and repetitive use, as against one that is accidental or the result of chance happening. The term *trade route* is used in the sense of a "major channel through which trade flows" (McDowell and Gibbs 1954: 81). Change in number of ships or ports of call on-route do not change or destroy a trade route "so long as a considerable number of ships follow the same track over an appreciable period of time for similar purposes" (*ibid.*: 82).

Trade routes connect 'market places', which can be conceived of as "nodal points" of the routes. Geographical distance or national boundary between nodal points does not need to be a determining factor because trade routes can be extended over long distances or span only a short hop. The nodal points or market places of trade routes connecting 'Bengal' within the time frame established in Chapter One were Tāmralipti, Gaṅgābandar/Chandraketugarh, Wārī-Baṭeśwar, Koṭālipāḍā/Candravarmakoṭa, Sonārgāon, Sātgāon and Caṭṭagrāma.

Besides ports, the other factor that needs to be taken into account for our examination of trade routes are the navigational techniques that have been discussed earlier in Chapter Five. We are now in a position to bring both these factors, along with other archaeological, literary, epigraphic and numismatic evidences, to establish maritime trade routes that connected 'Bengal' from earliest times to the 16th century AD. Not attempting to assimilate mere facts, we will attempt to see the pattern of change in the trade routes and comprehend why they changed.

EARLY HISTORIC PERIOD

Sri Lanka-South India-Orissa-Bengal-Southeast Asia

Most of the archaeological materials discussed in Chapters One and Two indicate the existence of the maritime trade network of 'Bengal'. Among these, Rouletted Ware is a definite indicator of maritime trade between Gaṅgābandar, Tāmralipti and Wārī-Baṭeśwar (in 'Bengal'), Radhanagar, Śiśupālgarh and Manikpatna (in Orissa), Kanchipuram, Karaikadu, Arikamedu, Kaveripattinam, Karur, Manigramam, Uraiyur, Alagankulam and Sengamedu (in Tamil Nadu), and Kantarodai, Mantai, Tissamaharama, Ambalantota and Anuradhapura (in Sri Lanka) from the 3rd century BC to the 3rd century AD. Anuradhapura may have had Rouletted Wares transported from nearby ports on the shore (such as Kantarodai). There can hardly be any doubt that the considerable number of Rouletted Wares found at each of these sites signifies that maritime contact was not accidental but of a "recurrent and repetitive" nature, implying in turn that the transshipment of wares possibly took place along a coastal trade route. This view is further strengthened when we remind ourselves that coastal trade routes were the sole option prior to the 2nd century AD and that such routes continued even in the medieval period. Primitive navigation and sailing schedule determined by monsoon winds, land and sea breeze would make sailing in this route feasible. A vessel could sail from south India during the inter-monsoon period of August-September and sail back any time from November to April. As we shall see below, this was the western segment of the Sri Lanka-South India-Orissa-Bengal-Southeast Asia coastal route.

Among all the port-sites mentioned above, ships sailing from the ports of 'Bengal' (Gaṅgābandar, Tāmralipti and Wārī-Baṭeśwar) must have frequented some ports more than others. This is indicated by NBPW that have been found at Śiśupālgarh, Amaravati, Alagankulam, and Anuradhapura. Another site, which yielded NBPW but is, not mentioned in the above list, is Chebrolu, which may have been a port from where NBP wares were transported to Amaravati. Earthen knobbed ware is another definite indicator of ships sailing between Gaṅgābandar, Tāmralipti and Wārī-Baṭeśwar in 'Bengal', Śiśupālgarh, Jaugada, Manikpatna, Radhanagar in Orissa and Anuradhapura (i.e., Kantarodai) in Sri Lanka. Furthermore, stamped wares indicate transshipment between Gaṅgābandar and Tāmralipti in 'Bengal' with Arikamedu and Alagankulam (in Tamil Nadu) and Anuradhapura and Kantarodai in Sri Lanka. Footed wares indicate sailing between Arikamedu and Gaṅgābandar. As for Indo-Pacific glass beads, its presence at Mahāsthāngarh indicates that there was a trade contact between 'Bengal' (via Gaṅgābandar and Tāmralipti) and Arikamedu, the production centre of the beads (Francis 1996: 140-141). Hence, NBP, knobbed, footed and stamped wares, and Indo-Pacific glass beads, lead us to believe that Wārī-Baṭeśwar, Chandraketugarh, Tamluk, Śiśupālgarh, Manikpatna, Radhanagar, Arikamedu, Alagankulam and Kantarodai were more frequented among all the nodules mentioned in the coastal route connecting 'Bengal' with Orissa, South India and Sri Lanka.

The above-mentioned coastal route extended to ports in Damirica (Lymrike), i.e., Naura, Tyndis, Muziris, Nelcynda (Bacare) and Balita as the following excerpt from the *Periplus* (§ 64) indicates: "... Thinae, from which raw silk and silk yarn and silk cloth are brought on foot through Bactria to

Barygaza, and are also exported to Damirica by way of the river Ganges" (Schoff 1995: 48). The coastal route connected an overland route to China across the Tibetan plateau, through Sikkim (*ibid.*: 272). However, as mentioned earlier in Chapter Two, the land-route was seldom used since it was difficult to access.

Bengal's contact with Sri Lanka, the farthest points on the Bengal-Orissa-South India-Sri Lanka coastal route, must have begun somewhere in the 5th century BC, if we are to credit Vijaya's maritime voyage to the island. By inference we may further believe that contact with the nodules closer to 'Bengal', i.e., those on the Orissa Coast, must have begun much earlier, and were maintained with the help of dugouts. As ports of call began to be more distant and voyages began to require longer time, plank-extended dugouts (such as the *saraṁgā*) and single-masted sewn-planked ships (such as the trapyaka) may have been pressed into service on the Bengal-Orissa-South India-Sri Lanka coastal route.

We may now turn our attention to Southeast Asia. As discussed in Chapters One and Two, archaeological artifacts found in coastal sites of Myanmar, Thailand, Malaysia and Indonesia clearly indicate that maritime contact between these regions and South Asia was established by the 3rd century BC. Among these artifacts, etched semi-precious stone beads indicate definite trade contact between 'Bengal' (Gaṅgābandar, Tāmralipti and Wārī-Baṭeśwar) and Myanmar (Beikthano), Thailand (Ban Chiang, Ban Tung Ketchet, Kok Samrong, U Thong, Krabi, Khao Sam Kao, Ban Kao and Ban Don Ta Phet), Malaysia (Tanjong Rawa, Kalumpang island, Kuala Selinsing), Indonesia (Leang Buidane cave in Salebabu island), the Philippines (Palawan Island) and China (Shi Zhai Shan and Lijiashan in Yunnan province). Rouletted ware is another definite indicator of trade contact between 'Bengal' (Gaṅgābandar, Tāmralipti and Wārī-Baṭeśwar) and Southeast Asia (Bukit Tengku Lembu in Malaysia, Kobak Kendal and Cibutak in north-western Java and Sembiran in north-eastern Bali in Indonesia, and Tra Kieu in Vietnam). We may firmly believe that the considerable number of etched semi-precious stone beads and Rouletted wares found at these sites signify that the maritime contact was not accidental but of a "recurrent and repetitive" nature.

We may logically believe that transshipment of all the commodities mentioned above took place by means of a coastal route since transoceanic routes were not known before the 2nd century AD. It would be possible to sail on this route by monsoon winds by employing primitive navigational techniques. Thus, we may believe that voyages from Malaysia and Indonesia could be undertaken in August or September and return voyage from 'Bengal' could be made from February to April. From May/June to September, one could set sail from Indonesia and Malaysia, and voyage to Vietnam, the Philippines and China with the help of the southwest monsoon. From November to March, one could return from China via Vietnam to Indonesia and Malaysia with the help of the northeast monsoon. One could also make use of land and sea breezes but obviously, the journey would be much slower.

It must have been the above-mentioned coastal route that the *Ch'ien Han-shu* indicates, with the help of which China first came into contact with Gaṅgābandar (Huang-chih) in 'Bengal' during the time of Han Wu-ti (141-87 BC). The text, compiled by Pan Ku in the 1st century AD, contains a description of a voyage by a Chinese mission to Gaṅgābandar, with the objective of obtaining lustrous pearls and live rhinoceroses for Wang Mang, then a regent of the boy-emperor Ping-ti (AD 1-5) who later founded his own Hsin Dynasty (AD 9-23). It took the mission one year to reach Gaṅgābandar following the route described below.

> From the barriers of Jih-nan [Tonkin], Hsü-wen, and Ho-p'u it is about five months by boat to the country Tu-yüan. Further it is about four months by boat to the country I-lu-mo. Again, it is more than twenty days by boat to the country Shen-li. Then it is over ten days by land to the country Fu-kan-tu-lu. From Fu-kan-tu-lu it is over two months by boat to the country Huang-chih (Colless 1980: 164).

The text describes the route as difficult to traverse and time consuming. In its own words, "there are the hazards of tempests and death by drowning in the sea. If these are avoided it takes several years to make the outward and return voyages" (*ibid.*). The length of the journey and the halting points in between confirm that the Chinese mission had arrived in 'Bengal' following the coast.

If the Arakanese chronicle *Ra-dza-weng* (The History of Kings) can be credited with historical accuracy, then we may believe that it was the above-mentioned coastal route that enabled the feudal lord from Magadha, named Sandathuriya (Candra-Sūrya), to establish a kingdom with the help of his Hindu-Buddhist army. He may have sailed from his native land down the Gaṅgā-Padmā and along the coast of Caṭṭagrāma. With Dhānyavatī as its capital, the kingdom of Sandathuriya extended over a territory that included what is now known as the district of Caṭṭagrāma in Bangladesh and the state of Arakan[1] in Myanmar.

If the deliberation made above is acceptable, then we may believe that journey over the entire stretch from 'Bengal' to China, even with the help of monsoon winds would be long and tedious. Commencing a voyage from 'Bengal' to Malaysia or Indonesia anytime from November to April, one could sail from there to China from June to September. The return voyage from China could be made from November to March but then one would have to wait at Malaysia or Indonesia for the following year's inter-monsoon period (August-September)

[1] The boundary of Arakan may be roughly taken to be the Nāf estuary (21° 10' N lat.) in the north, Cape Negrais (16° 2' N lat.) in the south, the Yu-ma mountain range in the east and the Bay of Bengal in the west.

to return to 'Bengal'. Hence, we may logically suspect that because of monsoon winds, voyages from 'Bengal' usually terminated at the western coast of Malay Peninsula or Sumatra. From there, nearby destinations such as Thailand, could be accessed by means of land and sea breezes.

It is possible to substantiate our argument further by pointing out that most of the Rouletted Wares and etched semi-precious stone beads have been found in Thailand, Malaysia and Indonesia. Furthermore, high-tin bronze knobbed wares, stamped wares and north Indian glass beads also lie within the limits of the same zone. High-tin bronze knobbed wares have been found at Wārī-Baṭeśwar in Bangladesh and Ban Don Ta Phet in west-central Thailand; stamped wares at Sembiran in Indonesia and Chandraketugarh and Tamluk in West Bengal; and north Indian glass beads at Prasat Muang Sing and Ban Chi Nam Lai in Thailand and Chandraketugarh and Tamluk in West Bengal. Only seal inscription in Kharoshṭī and Kharoshṭī-Brāhmī reaches out of the zone, although most of these too lie within the zone. The find-spots of this artifact are Chandraketugarh and Tamluk in West Bengal, U Thong in Lop Buri province and Khuan Luk Pat in Krabi province in Thailand, Sembiran in Bali, Indonesia and Oc-Eo in Vietnam. Hence, there can remain little doubt that the coastal route from 'Bengal' extended as far as the West Coast of the Malay Peninsula or Sumatra (Indonesia). We may further believe that dugouts and plank-extended dugouts were employed for traversing shorter distances. For longer distances, as the *Periplus* (§ 60) indicates, the *colandia* voyaged on the Bengal-Southeast Asia route (Schoff 1995: 46).

It is now possible to sum up our argument about the early historic coastal route from 'Bengal' by maintaining that 'Bengal' lay mid-point between the western arm of the route to south India and the eastern arm to Malaysia and Indonesia. It was single route two-ways, necessitating the use of the inter-monsoon period of August-September (for voyages to 'Bengal') and the NE monsoon and the following inter-monsoon period from November to April (for voyages from 'Bengal'). A voyage from Damirica, as a *Colandia* would usually make, could set out in August-September and sail from 'Bengal' for Southeast Asia anytime after November. The same vessel could voyage along the same route again in August-September of the following year and sail to Damirica from 'Bengal' after November.

Tāmralipti-Sri Lanka

The route from 'Bengal' to Sri Lanka must have been discovered accidentally as indicated in the *Mahāvaṁśa,* already cited in Chapter One. The text describes the journey of the banished prince Vijaya, his retinue, their wives and children at a time when journey by sea was unknown to the people of Lala (and by extension, the people of 'Bengal'). Chapter IX of the *Dīpavaṁśa* relates this clearly:

> 13. The ship in which the children had embarked was helplessly driven to an island, the name of which was then called Naggadipa. 14. The ship in which the wives had embarked was helplessly driven to an island, the name of which was then called Mahilarattha. 15. The ship in which the men had embarked went sailing on the sea, losing her way and her bearings, to the port of Suppara (Oldenberg 1982: 160-161).

From Suppara, Vijaya and his men journeyed to Bharukaccha, where they again boarded a ship. Driven by violent winds, they lost their bearings and landed on the shore of Laṅkādvīpa (Sri Lanka), at a place which was later named Tambapanni (copper-palmed) (*Dīpavaṁśa*, IX: 15-31; *ibid.*: 161-162). Vijaya was lucky – in all aspects of the word and as far its value can be stretched, because we hear nothing more of the women and the children.

What is most intriguing about Vijaya's sea voyage, as recounted in the Ceylonese chronicles, is the route. He appears to have journeyed from a sea-coast near Rāḍha, sailed southwest, veered around Sri Lanka without sighting its shore, then sailed in a northerly direction to Suppara. From there to Bharukaccha, they had to sail north again and then in a southerly direction to reach Sri Lanka. In terms of rudimentary navigational practice, Vijaya's route seems absurd and hence must be taken to indicate sailing at a time when the route around Sri Lanka was unknown. Recent archaeological evidence proves beyond doubt that an "Aryan" migration took place about the 6th century BC and the earliest settlement in Sri Lanka grew out of the endeavours of pioneering merchant mariners (Seneviratna 1994: 53). Hence, Vijaya's sea voyage to Sri Lanka need not be taken as a religious fable spun out by devotees.

Three more descriptions of voyages to and from 'Bengal' are recounted in the *Mahāvaṁśa*. These are, (1) the journey of Vijaya's messenger to Sīhapura in Lala ('Bengal'), (2) Paṇḍuvāsudeva's journey to Sri Lanka which ended when he "landed at the mouth of Mahākandara river" (Chapter VIII, verses 1-12; Geiger 1986: 62-63), and (3) the flight of Sakka Paṇḍu's daughter to Sri Lanka which ended when they landed at Goṇagāmaka, at the mouth of the Mahākandara River (Chapter VIII, verses 18- 24; *ibid.*: 63-64). Both Paṇḍuvāsudeva and Sakka Paṇḍu's daughter arrived at the mouth of the Mahākandara river which has been identified as the Mahaveligaṅgā River. The port that stands at the mouth of this river today is Trincomalee. It is worth noting that all these three voyages are made directly from the port of origin to the port of destination. None of these journeys connote trade routes but show that maritime route directly connecting 'Bengal' to Sri Lanka was becoming known.

We are still not dealing with trade but with exchange of gifts between royalty. We now move on to the diplomatic mission sent by Devānaṁpiya Tissa (c. 250-210 BC) to Aśoka. Nevertheless, as argued in Chapter Two, the list of gifts exchanged between Devānaṁpiya Tissa and Aśoka is a valuable document of commodities that we may believe were considered important and luxurious in the kingdoms of the two monarchs. Devānaṁpiya Tissa's envoy embarked on a ship at Jambukola (in north Ceylon, identified as the modern Kankesanturai) and reached Tamlitti (Tāmralipti) in seven days and in the same number of days they reached the capital of Emperor Aśoka in Pataliputta (*Mahāvaṁśa*, XI: 19-26). With the emperor's "gifts of the true doctrine" envoys embarked again at Tamlitti landed at Jambukola (*Mahāvaṁśa*, XI: 38). Then again, Emperor Aśoka sent the Bodhi tree in the 3rd century BC, on a ship down the Gaṅgā from his capital Pataliputra to Tāmralipti (*Mahāvaṁśa,* XIX: 1-8) and then by means of an ocean-going ship to Jambukola (in Sri Lanka) (*Mahāvaṁśa*, XIX, 22-23).

Judging by the description of the transportation of the Bodhi tree, the voyage to Sri Lanka appears to have become quite common and well established by the 3rd century BC. Because we argued in Chapter Two that the gifts exchanged by royalty were an important indicator of trade between Sri Lanka and the Maurya Empire subsequent to, if not before the royal consecration of Devānaṁpiya Tissa, we may logically believe that the direct trade route between Tāmralipti and Sri Lanka was definitely in existence by the second half of the 3rd century BC. Recent archaeological finds in Sri Lanka confirm our view. Most of the finest imported ceramics that belong to the second half of the 3rd century BC to the 3rd century AD were North Indian imports (Bopearachchi 1996: 65). Like Aśoka's Bodhi tree, these north Indian ceramics must have been imported to Sri Lanka via Tāmralipti.

It must have been the above-mentioned direct maritime route connecting Tāmralipti with Sri Lanka that Pliny (23-79 AD) had in mind when he observed in his *Natural History* (VI. 22.24) that "[t]he island [of Taprobanē, i.e., Sri Lanka] in former days... was thought to be twenty days' sail from the country of Prasii, but the distance came afterwards to be reckoned at a seven days' sail ..." (McCrindle 1979: 103). Needless to say, trasnportation by the direct route took much less time in the 1st century AD than before. We may even believe that Pliny is actually referring to sewn-planked extended dugouts such as the *saraṁgā*, in which it took twenty days to voyage from Prasii (Tāmralipti) to Sri Lanka. We have no way to know for sure which vessels took seven days to traverse the same distance.

Tāmralipti/Gaṅgābandar-Chu-li (Takkola)-Fu-nan-Suvaṇṇabhūmi

A Chinese account of South Asia, named *Wān-hëen-t'hung-kaou* ("Deep Researches into Ancient Monuments") by Ma-twan-lin, indicates that direct voyage between 'Bengal' and Southeast Asia already existed in the 3rd century AD. As recorded in the account, King Fan Chān of Fu-nan (Cambodia) sent one of his relations named Soo-wīh as an envoy to South Asia sometime after 280 AD. Sailing from Fu-nan, Soo-wīh crossed the Gulf of Martaban in a northwesterly direction and then coasted along the shore of the Bay of Bengal where he passed "the frontiers of several kingdoms". After about a year, he was able to reach the mouth of the river of India. Soo-wīh then had to sail 7,000 *li* upstream to reach his destination. He returned to Fu-nan by the mouth of the River Irawadi with Scythian horses as gifts for his king (Ma-twan-lin 1837: 64). For ascertaining the identity of "the river of India", we may turn to K'ang T'ai's *Fu-nan-chuan* (composed in the 3rd century AD). According to the *Fu-nan-chuan* (known from a citation in the *Shui Ching Chu*), "the river of India" is the river Gaṅgā and "[a]t the mouth of the river there [was] a kingdom called Tan-mei (Tāmralipti)" (Petech 1950: 53).

The voyage from Fu-nan to the mouth of the Gaṅgā in 'Bengal', as described in *Wān-hëen-t'hung-kaou*, was coastal but does not mention any stopover. But it is likely that all voyages from Southeast Asia to 'Bengal' would have to halt on the West Coast of the Malay Peninsula (or near about) for the monsoon winds, as an account of a voyage given in the *Fu-nan-chuan* clearly shows. Sailing from Fu-nan, the ship halted at Chu-li and then sailing from there it entered the Bay of Bengal. "Travelling straight to the north-west for more than a year, one reache[d] the mouth of the river of India, which is called the river Ganges" (*ibid.*). According to Petech (*ibid.*: 54), Chu-li was situated on the Siamese West Coast of the Malay Peninsula, currently known as Takuapa. It must have been Takkola cited in the *Milindapañha* (VI, 21, 360; Davids 1894: 269), Takkola in the *Mahāniddesa* (Chandra 1977: 129) and Takōla in Ptolemy's *Geography* (VII, 2, 5; McCrindle 1885: 197). The reference to "one year" should not be taken literally but as a considerable period of time because of the stopover at Chu-li for favourable monsoon winds. It should also be noted that the voyage was not coastal any longer, as the direction from Chu-li to the mouth of the Gaṅgā implies.

The *Fu-nan-chuan* also speaks of a Chinese merchant named Chia Hsiang-Li who sailed all the way from China to South Asia (Needham 1971: 449). For reasons stated above, the voyage would also have taken a considerable length of time to complete. K'ang T'ai's *Shui Ching Chu* further informs us that an embassy from the king of Tan Mei (Tāmralipti) was sent to the "Yellow Gate" (the Chinese Court), possibly in the 3rd century AD (Petech 1950: 55). Although the route is uncertain, we may believe it was the same as that described in the *Fu-nan-chuan* and *Wān-hëen-t'hung-kaou.*

All these references clearly indicate the existence of a trade route connecting Tāmralipti or Gaṅgābandar with Southeast Asia via Chu-li (Takkola). From Chu-li, the route must have continued to Cambodia. This must have been the route by which the Kharoshṭī-using merchants exported horses to Southeast Asia. It must also have been possible to sail to

Suvaṇṇabhūmi from Chu-li. The voyages described in the Mahājanaka Jātaka and the Śaṅkha Jātaka, which describe Prince Mahājanaka "sail[ing] on a ship with some merchants bound for Suvaṇṇabhūmi, ..." (Book XXII, No. 539; Cowell 1957, VI: 22) and the Brāhmiṇ named Śaṅkha sailing for Gold Country (Suvaṇṇabhūmi) (Book X, No. 442; Cowell 1957, IV: 10), must have used this route. However, it is quite unlikely that the route extended directly to China. Even though we hear of an occasional merchant and an ambassador sailing from and to China, these may not have been in recurrent and repetitive use and hence may not be considered a trade route. We will find that even in the late historic period, Chinese monks voyaging to South Asia halted at a port in Southeast Asia. In 'Bengal', the route may have connected both Tāmralipti and Gaṅgābandar.

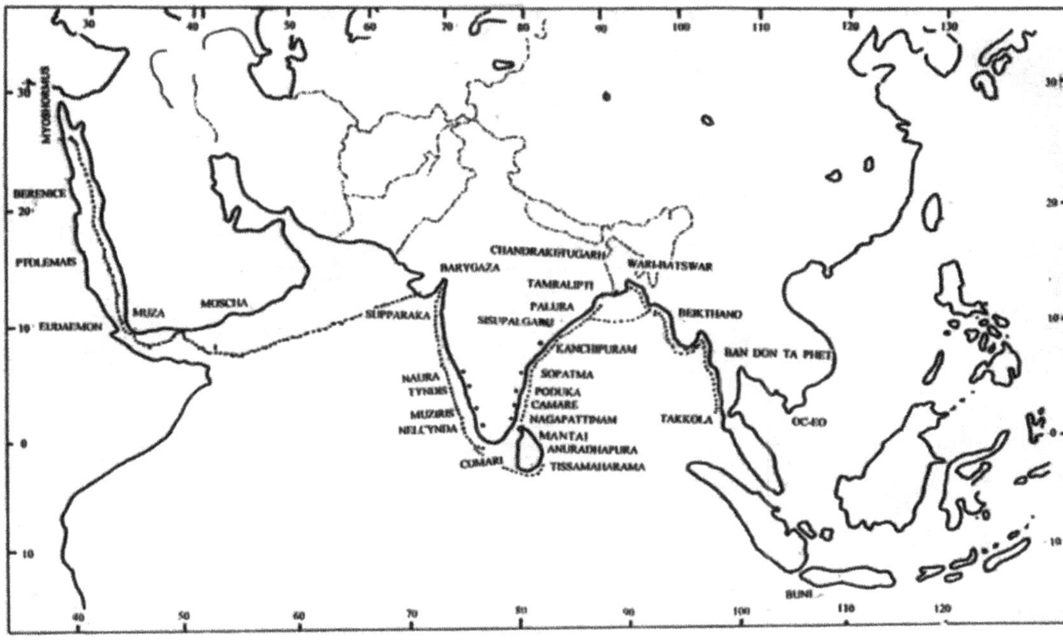

Fig. 6.1 Maritime Trade Routes (Early Historic Period)

The primary reason for the stopover at Chu-li must have been for suitable monsoon winds. It must also have served as a navigation pointer and a stopover for refurbishing provisions before or after embarking on the transoceanic leg of the route across the Bay of Bengal. The western coast of the Malay Peninsula served similar purpose for transoceanic voyages from the western shores of the Bay of Bengal to Southeast Asia. As our examination of later periods will show, the ports of Ka-cha (Kedah) and Malacca successively replaced Chu-li.

Bengal and the (Old) World Maritime Trade Routes

Having ascertained the trade-routes connecting 'Bengal' in the early historic period (Fig. 6.1), it is necessary now to see these in the greater context of contemporary world trade routes. Pliny in his *Natural History* (77 AD) testifies that during his time, there were both overland and sea routes connecting Rome with Asian countries. The land route, (also known as the Silk Route) connected Loyang in China and the two Mediterranean ports of Antioch and Alexandria. At the Chinese end, the route from Loyang bifurcated into the northern and the southern Silk Routes at Dunghuang and crossed in the Taklamakan desert from the north and the south respectively. The northern and the southern branches met again at Kashgarh in Xingchiang (Chinese Turkestan) and the united route crossed Bactria (northeastern Afghanistan) and then Persia (Iran) to arrive at Seleucia and Palmyra, two famous marts. The final part of the route connected these two marts with Antioch and Alexandria. The sea route traversed the Red Sea and the Arabian Sea.

In the 1st century AD, the maritime routes that were in use were (1) from Muziris (Cranganor, about 20 miles north of Cochin) in south India to the ports in the Red Sea; or (2) from Nelcynda, called Bacare (between Kanetti and Kolum in Travancore) to the Red Sea. Sailing in these routes, it was possible for voyages to South Asia to be completed in one year. Red Sea-Muziris voyage could be completed in 40 days but seafarers and traders did not favour the port of Muziris because it could not offer varied merchandise and its vicinity was infested with pirates. Hence, most of the ships sailed to and from Bacare, which was famous for pepper (McCrindle 1979: 110-112).

As indicated in the *Periplus* (Schoff 1995: 44-48) the ports of Malabar (i.e., Naura, Tyndis, Muziris, Nelcynda/Bacare and Balita) served as emporiums for Roman traders, where goods from the further east could be procured. These ports were connected with ports on the East Coast of south India: Comari (Cape of Kumari, 8°5' N & 77°33' E), Colchi (Kolkai, 8°40' N & 78°5' E), Camara (Kaveripattinam on the River Kaveri), Poduca (Arikamedu, Pondicherry, 11°56' N & 79°49' E), Sopatma (Madras, 13°4' N & 80°15' E), Masalia (Masulipatam, 16°11' N & 81°8' E). Then the route went further along the coast to Dosarene (Orissa), Gangê ('Bengal') and Chryse (Myanmar).

Till the 2nd century AD, Gaṅgābandar and Tāmralipti served important functions in the coastal route mentioned above because they served as necessary halting positions for long distance ships whose sailing schedule would have been determined by the monsoon winds. These two ports were also important for all the commodities (such the Gangetic spikenard, malabathrum, muslin, Gangetic pearls and occasionally Chinese silk) that were available there. The commencement of transoceanic voyage in the Arabian Sea did not make significant difference to Gaṅgābandar and Tāmralipti. However, from the 2nd century AD, when transoceanic voyages from Paloura to Sada became possible, Gaṅgābandar and Tāmralipti ceased to be halting positions. With the loss of navigational importance, these two ports continued to be significant so long as Rome existed as the market for the Gangetic spikenard, malabathrum, muslin and Gangetic pearls. Inevitably, these ports began to lose their commercial vitality after the mid-3rd century AD, when Roman trade began to show signs of significant diminution as the Roman Empire began to be beset with legal, agricultural, financial and administrative crises.

From our examination so far, we could not trace any direct Roman contact with 'Bengal'. Those who argue in favour of Roman trade, often attempt to substantiate their argument by referring to Janus (the terracotta double-headed helmet-wearing deity preserved in the Asutosh Museum of Indian Art, Kolkata) and the terracotta votive tablet bearing Greek inscription (found at Tilda in Medinīpur district). It has been claimed that the word *Eurulon* was recognised in the second line of the Tilda votive tablet and has been interpreted as "the East wind that comes with the dawn". Scholars have conjectured that the tablet was possibly in possession of a merchant or sailor of Hellenic origin who had voyaged to the 'Bengal' Coast. Proponents of Roman contact have also pointed to the discovery at Rājbāḍidāṅgā of a seal inscribed 'Horae' (possibly a Greco-Roman deity of the seasons) dated to the 4th century AD (Das 1968: 60) and a clay sealing bearing OABORRA in Roman character (believed to be a personal name), paleographically dated not earlier than the 2nd century AD (*ibid.*: 43). Gupta (1997: 314) believes that the seal and the sealing "could have only belonged to Mediterranean sailors who had voyaged to the Ganga delta". Among other artifacts, one could also mention sherds of Rouletted Ware found at Berenike. As for amphorae, we have already proved conclusively in Chapter Two that they stand little ground as an indicator of Indo-Roman trade operated directly from Tāmralipti.

One suspects that what is at the heart of all these scholars bent on proving "Mediterranean contact" with 'Bengal' is a colonial complex that seeks to elevate the colonised (in this context, 'Bengal') by equating them with the colonisers (the Europeans, by extension in this case, the Romans). By proving Mediterranean contact, it is, as though, maritime trade in 'Bengal' would be elevated to a position of eminence, which otherwise would appear far too insignificant. If we are prepared to recognise that we do not have any hidden agenda derived from a colonial complex, we may proceed logically. To begin with, one may question arguments favouring Mediterranean contact with enough ground by pointing out that "Janus" bears significant Kuṣāṇa influence and that it may have entered 'Bengal' by the land route with the migrant Kharoshṭī-using group of traders from the north-western region of South Asia. As for the fabled Tilda tablet we need to remember that the scholars arguing in favour of Mediterranean contact fail to mention that the tablet was seen only once, and it has disappeared since then. Against the argument of Mediterranean contact, one could justifiably argue that the Tilda tablet came with a merchant of Greek origin from the Bactrian Greek kingdom in the north-western region of South Asia. As for the Rājbāḍidāṅgā seal and sealing, one cannot but agree with Mukherjee (1993-94: 164) that these "could well have been transmitted from the north-west, where in Gandhara art the impact of Hellenistic style had already been well marked". These may have also travelled by land route with merchants from the Kuṣāṇa Empire (c. 1st century BC to AD 262), who had direct contact with the Mediterranean world.

The absence of direct trade contact between 'Bengal' and Rome is further substantiated by the *Periplus* (§ 39; Schoff 1995: 38). Details on sailing schedule given in the text show that ships from Egyptian ports on the Red Sea usually began their voyages for South Asia in July. Sailing with the help of the south-west monsoon winds, they crossed the Gulf of Aden and reached the West Coast ports of South India in September or October. Their return journey, which had to be made with the northeast monsoon winds, began in the month of November (December or January according to Pliny's *Natural History*, Book VI, c. 23.26). Hence, the merchants had one to three months time for transaction of business, which involved selling their merchandise and loading their ships with goods from the local market. Sailing down to Sri Lanka, which offered local goods at cheaper price, was problematic because it entailed the risk of missing the north-east trade winds and spending a year here, waiting for the next north-east trade. Discovery of large number of Roman artifacts at Arikamedu indicates that the port was possibly a Roman emporium, which sent goods to Rome through the West Coast ports, sending its goods either by ships or overland means of transportation.

Clearly, the nautical technology of the 1st century AD that was dependent on the trade winds in the Indian Ocean did not or could not permit direct trade between Rome and 'Bengal'. The absence of direct trade contact between 'Bengal' and Rome is further substantiated by the *Periplus* (sec. 60), which does not mention items of import from the Roman Empire into the Gaṅgā country, though it specifies which items exported from the latter. For die-hard skeptics, one can cite Strabo, who, in his *Geography*, Book XV, Sec. 4 states that "[t]he merchants of the present day, who sail from Egypt to India by the Nile and the Arabian Gulf have seldom made a voyage as far as the Ganges" (McCrindle 1979: 9). Having said that, it would be foolhardy to insist on "no contact ever" and overlook Pliny's "*seldom* made a voyage as far as the Ganges". There may have been an adventurous trader or a wayward traveller who happened to land in 'Bengal'. However, such cases cannot be considered as recurrent and repetitive but accidental or the result of chance happening, and hence need not be considered as indicative of a trade route.

LATE HISTORIC PERIOD

Tāmralipti-Sri Lanka

In the late historic period, regular traffic between Tāmralipti and Sri Lanka appears to have continued, as indicated in two literary sources. The first of these is *Dāthā-dhātu-waṁso* (cited earlier in Chapter One), which indicates that there was a regular intercourse between Tāmralipti and Sri Lanka in 371 AD, when the tooth relic was brought to Sri Lanka. The second source, and by far more important and reliable, is the account provided by Fa-Hien (cited earlier in Chapters One and Four), who sailed from Tāmralipti to Sri Lanka in the early 5th century AD "in a large merchant-vessel". However, even in the first half of the 7th century AD such voyages were extremely perilous, for we learn as much from Hiuen-Tsiang who was advised by a south Indian priest that

> Those who go to the Siṁhala country ought not to go by the sea route, during which they will have to encounter the dangers of bad weather (*winds*), the yakshas, and rolling waves; you ought rather to go from the south-east point of South India, from which it is a three days' voyage. For although in travelling you may have to scale mountains and pass through valleys, yet you are safe (*Life*, Book IV; Beal 1973: 133).

Nevertheless, the Tāmralipti-Sri Lanka sea route must have been very well known because even in the 11th century AD a story is woven with the voyage incorporated as an important factor. In "The King who married his Dependent to a Nereid", a story collected in the *Kathā Sarit Sāgar*, King Chaṇḍasiṁha of Tāmralipti sends his devoted Rājpūt courtier Sattvaśīla to Laṅkā on board a ship, with a marriage proposal for a Laṅkān princess. The Tāmralipti-Sri Lanka route was known even in Tibet, where the legend of the Siṁhalese princess Ratnāvalī recounts "the voyage of the merchants of Srāvastī who were driven down the Bay of Bengal by contrary winds, but who subsequently completed their voyage to Ceylon and back" (Mookerji 1957: 50).

Tāmralipti-Ka-cha (Kedah)

By the second half of the 7th century, when I-Tsing visited South Asia, we are suddenly landed with a profusion of records on maritime contacts between 'Bengal', Southeast Asia and the Far East. As described in the *Nan-hai-chi-kueii-nei-fa* ("A Record of the Buddhist Religion as Practiced in India and the Malay Archipelago"), the monk sailed on a Persian merchant ship from Canton in 671 AD. After crossing the South China Sea, and sailing for twenty days, he arrived at Bhoga (the capital and the country of Śrībhoga, an important intellectual centre under the royal patronage of the Śailendra dynasty, currently known as Palembang and located in southeastern Sumatra). I-Tsing does not catch a ship for Tāmralipti at Bhoga but with assistance from the king, travels to Malayu (eastern coast of Sumatra, Takakusu 1896: appendixed map) and then proceeds to Ka-cha (Kedah, on the western coast of the Malay Peninsula). There, he sailed on board a ship belonging to the king of Bhoga, which, as Takakusu (*ibid.*: xxx, xlvi) points out, may have been dispatched for commerce. His ship sailed via the Nicobar Islands (the country of the Naked People), which were sighted in ten days and finally arrived at Tāmralipti after half a month from the islands (*ibid.*: 211).

On his return journey, I-Tsing embarked on a ship at Tāmralipti and sailed in a southeasterly direction for two months to arrive at Ka-cha, without halting at the Nicobar Islands. From Ka-cha, he says, ships sailed in the southwest direction for Sri Lanka. He, however, boarded a ship sailing south for Bhoga, where he arrived after a month. From Bhoga, ships sailed north for a month to arrive at Kwang-fu (Kwang-tung or Canton) (*ibid.*: xxxiv). Although he does not specifically say so, his manner of description appears to indicate that all these ships were part of regular traffic carrying merchandise and passengers.

Another Chinese monk named Hiuen-ta appears to have accompanied an envoy in a Persian ship to the southern seas. Having arrived at Fo-shai (Śribhōja i.e., Śrī-bhoga), he remained there for six months. He made good use of travelling on board a royal ship dispatched for diplomatic mission to the country of Malayu (eastern coast of Sumatra), where he stayed for some time. He then proceeded to Quēdāh, from where he voyaged on a royal ship bound for 'Bengal'. Sailing north from Quēdāh (Kedah) for about ten days the ship arrived at the country of the naked men (Nicobar Islands). Sailing in the northwesterly direction for half a month the ship arrived at Tāmralipti. On his return, he followed the same route to Quēdāh, from where he proceeded further to Śribhōja (Beal 1973: xxxix-xl).

There can be little doubt that the Tāmralipti-Ka-cha (Kedah) transoceanic route was a continuation of Tāmralipti-Chu-li (Takkola) route. I-Tsing and Hiuen-ta's itineraries clearly show that sea routes from South Asia terminated at Ka-cha, while those from China (mostly from Canton) terminated at Bhoga. Sea-routes from Tāmralipti, south India and Sri Lanka converged at the Nicobars, from where the route to Ka-cha was similar. On the other hand, those from China to Bhoga sometimes touched in Vietnam.

We have the Buddhagupta inscription, the most famous epigraphic evidence that has been cited often to prove maritime trade network of 'Bengal', to vouchsafe that the Tāmralipti-Ka-cha (Kedah) transoceanic route was in operation even in 400 AD. It was discovered in 1834, on the West Coast of Malaysia (Province Wellesley, currently known as Seberang Prai), and is now persevered at the Indian Museum in Kolkata. The inscription is recorded on a stone plaque in the middle of which is carved a Buddhist *stupa*. On its right is inscribed a Buddhist *sutra* which reads "ajñānāc = ciyate karmma janmanaḥ karmma kāraṇa[m]; jñānān = na ciyate [karmma karmmābhāvān = na jāyate]" and a legend "mahānāvikabuddhaguptasya raktamṛttika vās [tavyasya?]"; and on the left is another legend that reads "sarvveṇa prakāreṇa sarvvasmin sarvvatha sa(r)vva ... siddhayāt[r]ā[ḥ] + [:] santu" (Das 1968: 57). The inscription records a prayer for the successful voyage of a *mahānāvika* (master navigator of a ship) named Buddhagupta who was an inhabitant of Raktamṛttikā.

For ascertaining the location of Raktamṛttikā, we may turn to Hiuen-Tsiang. The Chinese monk mentions a monastery called Lo-to-mo-chih (i.e., "Raktamṛta" or "Red-clay") near Karṇasuvarṇa, which may very well have been Buddhagupta's Raktamṛttikā in Chinese corruption (Watters 1905: 191-193). The discovery of archeological remains of an ancient Buddhist monastery at Rājbāḍidāṅgā in Murshidabad district has corroborated Hiuen-Tsiang's testimony. A large number of clay seals have been found at the site, all of which have been dated between the 6th and 8th century AD. One of the seals has inscribed on it a legend in two lines, written in characters of the 7th or 8th century AD. The legend reads, (1) Śrī-Rakta[m]rittikā-ma(mā)havaiha-(2)rik-ārya-bhikshu and may be translated as "[This is the seal] of the community of the noble monks of the great monastery at the illustrious Raktamṛttikā" (Sircar 1967-68: 28). The seal, thus, appears to indicate that *mahānāvika* Buddhagupta hailed from the Murshidabad region in north 'Bengal', who may have sailed from Tāmralipti, a port from where I-Tsing is known to have sailed to Ka-cha in the Malay Peninsula. Hence, the combined evidence of the seal of the Raktamṛttikā Monastery and the dedicatory stone plaque of *mahānāvika* Buddhagupta confirm the existence of a maritime route connecting Tāmralipti with Ka-cha (Kedah).

Harikela-Sri Lanka

During the late historic period, Caṭṭagrāma (known as Harikela in the 7th century) became important enough to feature in the maritime trade routes connecting 'Bengal' to Sri Lanka. In order to prove its existence, we need to turn our attention to I-Tsing's account of Wu-hsing, Prajñādeva and Chih-hung Lu-shih, Mahāprajñā, as narrated in the *Ta-T'ang-hsi-yu-chiu-kao-seng chuan* (or the "Biographies of Eminent Monks").

Wu-hsing, along with fellow-monk Chih-hung Lu-shih, started, on a voyage from China (from Hainan according to Beal 1973: xli) to South Asia. It took them a month to reach Śrī-vijaya (Śribhōja, according to Beal 1973: xli). [Takakusu (1896: Appendixed map) has identified Śrī-bhoga (Śribhōja) in southern Sumatra. Śrī-vijaya, as Hall (1985: 5) reconfirms, was a Sumatra-based state.] From there, they sailed on a royal ship and reached Mo-luo-yu (eastern coast of Sumatra) in fifteen days. They took another fifteen days to reach Kedah. At the end of winter, they embarked on a ship that transported them to Na-chia-po-t'an-na (Nagapattinam) in south India in thirty days, from where they took another ship to reach Sri Lanka in two days. They sailed again from Sri Lanka by ship and after about a month's sail reached O-li-ki-lo (Harikela) in eastern 'Bengal' (Lahiri 1986: 94-96). This account leaves no doubt that Harikela was emerging as a new centre of Buddhist learning in Eastern 'Bengal'.

Harikela-Lang-chia (Pegu or Lower Burma)-Kedah

Valuable indications gleaned from *The Life of Hiuen-Tsiang* may help us ascertain that Harikela maintained contact not only with Sri Lanka but also with ports in Southeast Asia. We need to note that in his account of San-mo-ta-cha [Samataṭa] in eastern 'Bengal', Hiuen-Tsiang is described gathering information from local inhabitants about six kingdoms of Southeast Asia.

> Going from this [Samataṭa] north-east along the borders of the sea, across mountains and valleys we come to the country of Chi-li-t'sa-ta-lo (Śrīkshetra); still going south-east, in a bay of the sea, is the country of Kāmalāṅkā (Pegu); east of this is the country of Dvārapati (Sandoway); east of this is the country of Iśānapura; east of this is the country of Mahāchampā (Siam: also called *Lin-i*); west of this is the country of Yen-mo-lo (*Yamarāja*; but probably a mistake for *Yen-mo-na-chau*, the country of the Yavanas). These six kingdoms are bordered by mountains and the deep sea. Although Hiuen-Tsiang did not enter their territory, he was yet able to gain knowledge of the customs and manners (*of the people*) (*Life*, Book IV; Beal 1973: 132-133).

Watters, disagreeing with Beal (*ibid.*), has identified the six countries as Śrīkshetra or the district of Prome in Burma, Pegu and the Irawadi delta, Dvaravati in Thailand, Kambuja or Cambodia, parts of Vietnam and the island kingdom of Java, respectively (Watters 1905: 188). Even though there exist differences of opinion regarding the identification, what everyone agrees on is that the six countries are "bordered by deep sea" for the text specifically says so. What is most significant about this piece of information is that the people of Samataṭa were well aware of their existence, and more importantly, their geographic location. This could have happened only through maritime contact, which, given the geographic location of Samataṭa and the six countries situated on the coast of "deep sea", could (and still can) be maintained only by means of coastal voyage. Here we have a strong indication of the continuation of the early historic coastal route connecting ports on the Eastern Shore of the Bay of Bengal. Because Harikela lay in Samataṭa, there can be little doubt that the coastal route continued in the late historic period. As observed in Chapter Four, the coastal route from Myanmar to Caṭṭagrāma is still in operation.

A few of the 56 monks described by I-Tsing actually travelled from South Sea region as far as Lang-chia (Pegu or Lower Burma). Consider for example the case of I-lang Lü-shih, Chih-an and I-hsüan, who embarked on a merchant ship at Wu-lei (present Ch'in-hsien in Kuang-tung Island), passed through Fu-nan (Cambodia) and arrived at Lang-chia (Pegu or Lower Burma). From there they sailed for Sri Lanka (Lahiri 1986: 35). A monk named Tao-lin boarded a foreign ship at an unknown port on the South Sea and from there he passed through the copper pillars T'ung-chu and arrived at Lang-chia. From Ling-chia, he sailed to south India via Ho-ling and Luo-kuo (possibly Nicobar Islands) (*ibid.*: 63; Beal 1973: xxxviii). The journey may have taken considerable time because the ships must have availed land-and-sea-breeze for the most of their journey. The objective of the monks mentioned above was not to visit Harikela but Sri Lanka and south India. Hence they must have changed ships at Lang-chia. As for Wu-hsing, we may conjecture that either he failed to avail of a ship sailing on the Southeast Asian coastal route or his initial objective was to visit Sri Lanka. Upon reaching the island, he may have found it necessary to visit Harikela.

Bengal and the (Old) World Maritime Trade Routes

Having ascertained the trade routes connecting 'Bengal' in the late historic period, we may now place these in the greater context of contemporary world trade routes. We may begin by reminding ourselves that although Roman trade began to show signs of significant diminution after the mid-3rd century AD, there is no reason to believe that it had completely ceased. Indeed, the impact of crises in the Roman Empire was less severe in the eastern half that included Egypt, Syria and parts of Mesopotamia. The use of spices from South Asia had actually increased in Egypt in the 3rd and the 4th centuries AD. Suspicion that Roman trade continued, albeit abated, is confirmed by the recovery of a substantial number of Roman bronze coins dated to the 4th century AD and copper coins as well as local imitations dated to the 4th and 5th centuries AD from sites near Sri Lanka and Madras (Basa and Behera: 1999: 25).

Byzantium, surviving the collapse of the Roman Empire in the 5th century AD, began to play an increasingly important role in international commerce after Emperor Justinian succeeded in stabilizing the empire in the 6th century AD. The discovery of Byzantine gold coins in the eastern part of south India and western India proved Byzantine's trade with South Asia. In the 6th and 7th centuries AD, South Asia's exports to Byzantine consisted of iron, ivory, cotton, spices and Chinese silk. Nevertheless, the magnitude of Byzantine's market was significantly smaller than that of Rome and hence South Asia's interest in the western market was significantly reduced.

In the meanwhile (actually from the 3rd or 4th century), the Sassanian Empire began to dominate trade in the Indian Ocean and by the 6th century AD, Persian (Sassanian) merchants monopolized imports to the Middle East, mostly silk from China. Because of their control in trade and because of the shifting of the market to the Byzantine Empire, the ports on the Red Sea lost their importance and in their place, the ports situated on the southern coast of Arabia became important. At the same time, the major centre for trade in the Indian Ocean gradually shifted from the West Coast of south India to Sri Lanka. This is clearly established by Kosmas Indikopleustes, the Alexandrian merchant-turned-monk who wrote *Christian Topography*. He says:

> ... the island is a great resort of ships from all parts of India and from Persia and Ethiopia, and in like manner it dispatches many of its own to foreign ports. And from the inner countries, I mean China and other marts in that direction, it receives silk, aloes, clove-wood, sandalwood, and their other products, and these it again passes on to the outer ports, I mean to Male, where pepper grows, and to Kalliana, where copper is produced, and sesame wood, and materials for dress; for it is also a great mart of trade; and to Sindu also, where musk or castor is got, as well as Androstachus, and to Persia and the Homerite country, and to Adule. Receiving in return the traffic of these marts and transmitting it to the inner ports, the island exports to each of these at the same time her own products (XI, 15; McCrindle 1979: 161).

By the 6th century AD, a considerable number of Persians had settled in Sri Lanka, where they imported, among other items, horses from the Middle East. Persian presence in Sri Lanka can be gauged by thirty-five Persian ships that the South Asian Buddhist monk Vajrabodhi had found in Sri Lankan ports in the 7th century AD. The monk had even travelled by one of these to Sumatra (Siriweera 1990: 126).

With the waning of the Roman market, South Asia's attention was diverted to Southeast Asian gold. "The most visible results of South Asian enterprise in South East Asia", observes McPherson (1998: 76), "were the wider diffusion of South East Asian commodities such as spices, rare timbers and gemstones, as well as the rise of 'Indianized' kingdoms scattered from Burma to Java and southern Vietnam". The Pallavas of south India (3rd century AD to 898 AD, capital, Kañcipuram) were extensively engaged in maritime commerce with Southeast Asia. Influence of Pallava architecture on that of Indonesia and Cambodia clearly bears witness to the extent of their involvement (Antonova, Bongard-Levin and Katovsky 1982: 252). Their trade transactions reached even to Pegu or Lower Burma, as evinced by Tao-lin Fa-shih's voyage from there to South India (Lahiri 1986: 63; Beal 1973: xxxviii).

Bengal's share in this trade must have been minimal, as Kosmas Indikopleustes' list of "the most famous commercial marts" in South Asia shows. The Alexandrian merchant-turned-monk who composed *Christian Topography* some years before the mid-6th century AD, is completely oblivious about any port on the 'Bengal' Coast (Tāmralipti, Gaṅgābandar and Koṭālipāḍā/Candravarmakoṭa) although he gives an accurate description of maritime trade in Sri Lanka and the Malabar Coast.

> Sindus, Orrhotha [a port in the western coast of the Gujarat peninsula], Kalliana, Sibor [seaport, probably Chaul, 23 miles south of Bombay], Male, which has five marts that export pepper, Parti, Mangarouth [Mangalor], Salopatana, Nalopatana, Poudopatana [situated on the coast of Kottonarike- the pepper country]. Then out in the ocean at the distance of five days and nights from the mainland lies Selediba, that is Taprobane [Ceylon]. Then, again, farther away and on the mainland is the mart Marallo, which exports chank-shells, then comes Kaber [emporium, Kaveripattam], which exports alabandēnum, then next is the clove country, then China, which produces silk, beyond which there is no other land, for the ocean encircles it on the east (Book XI; McCrindle 1979: 161-162).

Kosmas Indikopleustes's evidence clearly indicates that none of the ports in 'Bengal' were important enough – at least in trade with Byzantine – to feature in his list of "the most famous commercial marts".

The Qualitative change in the trade network discussed above occurred by the middle of the 7th century AD. As the Middle East united under Islam and Arab armies demolished the Sassanian Empire in the west, the Tang dynasty united China in the east and led the country to fabulous economic growth. Consequently, trade was significantly bolstered. Although the overland routes running through Central Asia were still being used, contemporary literary evidences clearly indicate that most of the commodities of trade were being transshipped by means of maritime mode of transportation (Rougeulle 1996: 159).

The Arab-Persian (Muslim) merchants and navigators had begun to dominate trade-related transactions in the Arabian Sea and began to voyage directly from Siraf on the coast of Fars, via Mascat, Kulam-Malé (Quilon on the Malabar Coast), Kalah (on Malay Peninsula), Pulo Condore to Canton in China. The route was highly profitable but also risky because of frequent shipwrecking and piracy. Because of the length of the voyage, it was necessary for them to set up a colony in Canton. Numerical strength and economic power of the Arab and Persian merchants at the colony must have been substantial because, as T'ang Chronicles reveal, in 758 AD they sacked and burned the city of Canton. The same source reveals the several thousands of Arab and Persian merchants were killed in another uprising at Yang-Chou in 760 AD (Kiribamune 1990: 181). As a result of direct voyage to Canton, the importance of Sri Lanka as an entrepôt was much reduced.

When we consider 'Bengal' in the context of the trade highways of the mid-7th to the mid-8th centuries AD, we are bound to concede that the trade routes leading to and from 'Bengal' were only subsidiary lanes. Even in commodities, as discussed in Chapter Two, we found 'Bengal' re-exporting horses to Southeast Asia (till the 5th century AD) and exporting only rice throughout the period. Among its items of imports, we could trace only cowries and spices. Similarly, w found Wārī-Baṭeśwar had already ceased to function at th end of the early historic period. After the 5th century AD Gaṅgābandar had ceased to function and Tāmralipti was in state of decline. There can be little doubt, therefore, tha maritime trade in the late historic period had undergon significant decline.

EARLY MEDIEVAL PERIOD

Basra-Samandar (Caṭṭagrāma)

Arab and Persian geographers, merchants and traveler provide us with valuable information regarding maritime trad in 'Bengal' from the 9th to the 12th centuries AD. This i particularly important because Arab and Persian merchant were one of the major players in maritime trade of South Asi and Southeast Asia during this period. The information abou the political and economic conditions of Caṭṭagrāma-Araka region (Ruhmi or Rahmi) provided by Sulaiman, Ibn Khur dādhbih, the anonymous author of *Ḥudūd al-'Ālam*, Marva and Idrisi, all of whom lived between the 9th and 12th centuries AD, surely point to the conclusion that the Arab an Persian merchants visited this part of the world.

The most detailed account of trading routes has been give in Ibn Khurdādhbih's *Kitāb al-Masālik wa'l-Mamālik* (the Boo of Roads and Kingdoms) (c. 846-7 AD), which describes th coastal voyage from Basra, along the western coast of India through the Palk Strait and round the shores of the Bay c Bengal. The following is a summary of the route described b him.

The Arab-Persian ships, which must have been *dhows* c smaller tonnage, would begin their voyage from Basra i Mesopotamia at the head of the Persian Gulf. Then the would voyage along the coast making stops at Siraf an Hormuz on the Persian coast. Then, sailing along the Makra Coast, they arrived at Debal in Sindh. Sailing from Debal vi the mouth of the River Mihrān (Indus) to Bakar (the firs place on the border of Hind) was a little less than five days voyage. From Bakar, the vessels sailed via the Meds to Kc (on the Gujarat Coast) and Sindān (north of Bombay). Fror Sindān they arrived at Mali (Malabar) after five days' journey From Mali they sailed through the Palk Strait to Balbu (Nagapattinam on the Tanjore Coast) in two days. At Balbur the route bifurcated, one going to China via the Nicoba Islands and Kedah in the Malay peninsula and the othe following the East Coast of south India to 'Bengal'. Fror Balbun, following the shore, it took two days to reach Bās then on to Sajī (Sandy) and 'Askān. From 'Askān the vessel sailed to Kūra (where several rivers discharge), Kilakān, Lūā and Kanja. Then the route led on to Samundar and then t Urasīr, From Urasīr to Ainā, the last stop was a four-da journey (Ibn Khurdādba 1867: 14-16).

Khurdādhbih's account point to the continuation of the early historic coastal route that connected 'Bengal' with ports on the East Coast of south India. Hence, one may assume that the coastal voyages made by the Arab-Persian merchants from the Persian Gulf to 'Bengal' must have begun much earlier than the mid-9th century AD when Khurdādhbih composed his *Kitāb.* It must have continued at least till the mid-12th century when Al-Idrīsī composed his *Kitāb Nuzhatu-l Mushtāk fi' Ikhtirāqu-l Āfāq* (The Delight of those who seek to wander through the regions of the world) since one may glean the notion of a coastal route from the description he gives of various towns and ports in South Asia. He does not specifically indicate a homeport of the Arab-Persian vessels but one may assume it was on, what he says, "the shores of the Persian Gulf". The ports of call, along the coast of South Asia beginning from the west, may have been as follows: Debal, Kambāya, Barūh (Barūch, Broach), Sindān, Sūbāra (Sopara), Agasha, Bana (Thane), Saimūr (Chaul), Sindābūr, Jirbatan, Fandarīna, Sanji, Kaikasār, Kulam Mali (Malabar), Balbak (Balin), Kilkāyān, Lulu, Kanja and Samandar (Al-Idrīsī 1867: 77-90).

Numismatic evidence, in the form of fifteen Abbasid coins, confirms the existence of trade-route connecting Basra (at the head of the Persian Gulf) and Siraf (an important port in Abbasid Empire situated on the eastern coast of the Persian Gulf) with Samandar in 'Bengal'. Two of these have been found from the Buddhist religious establishments in the Lalmai-Mainamati range, Comilla district, Bangladesh. One is a thin-sheeted gold coin, which, when discovered in the upper level of Kutila Mura, was slightly twisted and broken in two ends. The arrangement on obverse and reverse is similar. "The inscription is arranged within a circle in six lines in the middle and a single line around the margin" (Rashid 1975: 58). The legend in fine Kufic on the reverse side within quatrefoil reads as follows:

> Al-Imam (the Leader). There is no deity except Allah alone. He has no associate with Him. Al-Musta'sim Billah (one firmly depending on the protection of Allah), the Commander of the Faithful. Affairs in the past were in the hands of Allah and will be so in the future and on the day the Believers will rejoice at Allah's help (Qadir 2001: 19).

In the margin of the same side, the date and the place of issue have been stated thus: "The Dinar (gold coin) has been struck in the city of peace and security (Madinatu's Salam-Baghdad) in the year AH 641 (AD 1243-44 or AH 551/AD 1253-54)" (*ibid.*). The second coin recovered from an excavation of a cell at Salban Vihāra is a broken silver piece with legends in Kufic characters belonging to the early Abbasid period (Khan 1963: 27).

Besides these findings in excavations, a set of 12 Abbasid gold coins came to light when the Bangladesh National Museum purchased these from a jeweller's shop at Chandpur in the greater Comilla region. The coins date from the time-bracket of 160 years ending with Khalifah Abu'l Fadl Ja'far Al-Muqtadir Billah (295-320/AD 908-32) (Qadir 2001: 48). Yet another Abbasid coin has been found at Pāhāḍpur in Bangladesh, this time from surface collection. As reported by K. N. Dikshit, it is a thin silver coin of Harunur Rashid, dated AH 172 (788 AD) (Dikshit 1938: 87).

Samandar-Ka-cha-Śrīvijaya

The Nālandā copperplate of the Pāla king Devapāla (821-861 AD), which records the granting of five villages in the *viṣāyas* of Rājagṛha and Gayā. In the copperplate King Devapāla declares, "being requested by the illustrious Mahārāja Bālaputradeva, the King of Suvarṇadvīpa through a messenger, I have caused to build a monastery at Nālandā" (Shastri 1924: 310-327). Bālaputradeva was one of the monarchs of the Śailendra dynasty (c. 750-850 AD) that ruled over Śrīvijaya. There can be little doubt that sending a royal messenger from Śrīvijaya to Pāla Empire in 'Bengal' indicates a well-known and established route of maritime intercourse.

There are a few more epigraphic evidences that substantiate further that the people of 'Bengal' maintained vigorous maritime intercourse with Śrīvijaya for religio-cultural purposes. The clearest indicators are the Kelurak, the Kalasan and the Ratu Boko inscriptions.

The Kelurak inscription was discovered at Kelurak, to the north of Temple Candi Loro-Jonggrang at Prambanan (some 16 km east of Jogjakarta). Dated 782 AD (704 Saka), the inscription is preserved at the Jakarta Museum (accession no. D.44). Incised on a quadrangular stone of dusk-grey, the inscription displays verses composed in Buddhist Sanskrit, written in pre-Nāgarī script. Verse 7 of the inscription refers to "the *guru* (i.e., preceptor), of the land of Gauḍī" ("*Gauḍīdvīpaguru*"). Although his identity is uncertain, Sarkar (1971: 41-43, 45) believes the guru referred to may be Kumāraghoṣa mentioned in later verses, who was the preceptor of the Śailendra king Sangramadhananjaya of Śrīvijaya and who established the image of Mañjuśrī in Kelurak.

The Kalasan inscription, dated 700 Saka (778 AD), was found at Kalasan near Prambanan and is currently preserved in the Jakarta Museum (accession no. D.147). It is beautifully incised in pre-Nāgarī Sanskrit script. According to Bhandarkar, the script not only displays remarkable affinity to northern Indian characters between the 8th and 11th centuries AD, but the execution is also strikingly similar to that of the records found at Ghōsrāwā, near Nālandā (Kielhorn 1888: 307). Another point worth noticing is that the Kalasan inscription opens with a laudatory verse to Tara: "Salutation to the Divine Ārya Tārā" (Sarkar 1971: 34, 37).

The triangular-shaped inscription of Ratu Boko (dated 792 AD, 714 Saka) is also written in pre-Nāgarī script, similar to that of Kalasan. Its earliest fragment was found about 1816 in the Pendava-terrace of the Ratu Boko palace complex (located about three kilometres to the south of Prambanan) and is now preserved at the Jakarta Museum. As Sarkar notes, "palaeography connects the inscription with eastern India and Pāla Bengal" (*ibid.*: 48.i-48.vii).

The significance of all the three inscriptions noted above might be summed up in the following words of Sarkar (*ibid.*: 34-35).

> It is a highly noticeable fact, when we compare Javanese pre-Nāgarī inscriptions with those of India belonging to the same family that these records of Java not only do not betray any archaic form, but on the other hand present some characteristics which were just coming in use or were or in an embryonic stage in Northern India. These phenomena may be attributed to the close cultural connexion that subsisted between India and Indonesia during the period of the Śailendra monarchs.

Sarkar's observation rightly stresses close cultural contact. Furthermore, when Barua (1951: 273) points out that the Nālandā copperplate is actually indicative more of pilgrimage-traffic than maritime trade, we cannot but agree with him and maintain that the same is true of the Kelurak, the Kalasan and the Ratu Boko inscriptions as well. Hence, we need to examine if trade was at all involved in the maritime intercourse between 'Bengal' and Śrīvijaya.

As observed earlier, I-Tsing did not embark on a ship for Tāmralipti at Bhoga but with assistance from the king, travelled to Malayu and then to Ka-cha. In his own words, "[t]he king gave me some support and sent me to the country of Malayu, which is now called Śrībhoga, where I again stayed two months, and thence I went to Ka-cha. Here I embarked in the twelfth month, and again on board the king's ship I sailed to eastern India" (Takakusu 1896: xxx). We may also recall that Wu-hsing, along with fellow-monk Chih-hung Lu-shih also sailed on a royal ship from Śrībhoga (Śrīvijaya) to Malayu. I-Tsing's testimony is important for two reasons. Firstly, it proves that the king of Śrīvijaya, i.e., a Śailendra monarch, possessed ships that sailed to Tāmralipti. From the manner of I-Tsing's description, the sailing of the ships does not appear to have been special events but a regular affair. Such voyages could only be for the purpose of trade. Secondly, I-Tsing could not sail directly to Tāmralipti from Śrīvijaya but had to go to Ka-cha. Hence, we may believe with enough conviction that the Nālandā copperplate, and the Kelurak, the Kalasan, and the Ratu Boko inscriptions not only signify close cultural contact but maritime trade as well.

Bengal's maritime connection with Śrīvijaya must have continued in the 11th century AD for Atīśa Dīpaṅkara Śrījñāna, the renowned Buddhist scholar-monk from 'Bengal' is known to have voyaged from 'Bengal' to Suvarṇadvīpa (Śrīvijaya) sometime after 1011 AD. The objective of Atīśa's journey was not trade but the pursuit of higher studies in Buddhism under the guidance of Candrakīrti, the Buddhist high priest of Suvarṇadvīpa. Details of his journey are not known, except that the journey was strenuous, taking several months. He returned to Magadha via Tāmradvīpa (Sri Lanka), but the port in which he landed is not known (Majumdar and Ganguly 1943: 674). Atīśa's itinerary indicates that by the early 11th century AD, Bengal's trade link with Śrīvijaya was broken.

In the absence of Tāmralipti (which was abandoned as a port in the mid-8th century AD), the port from which the scholars from Gauḍa (north 'Bengal') sailed for Śrīvijaya and the port in 'Bengal' at which the diplomatic mission from Śrīvijaya arrived must have been Samandar. Assuming that the capital of the Pālas was located in northern 'Bengal' (or in localities situated westward from north 'Bengal'), and assuming that the scholars from Gauḍa set off from their homeland, it would be only natural for them to sail down the Gaṅgā-Padmā and board a maritime vessel from Samandar, like Fei Sin and Ma-Huan. Hence, we may conclude our deliberation on trade route linking 'Bengal' and Śrīvijaya in the early medieval period by proposing that it connected Samandar and Ka-Cha, with onward link to various ports in Śrīvijaya. We may further believe the route had declined by the early 11th century AD.

Bengal and the (Old) World Maritime Trade Routes

The most significant feature that distinguishes this period is that links with the Mediterranean world weakened as those with Central Asia and Africa gained importance. The Arab-Persian merchants, who began to gain prominence in the 7th century AD, reached their peak in the 9th century AD when they emerged in a pre-eminent position in maritime trade along the entire circuit from the Persian Gulf to China. While some of their vessels sailed directly from the Persian Gulf (mostly from Siraf) to China (Canton), others found it more feasible to sail segments thereof. In the Arabian Sea, Arab-Persian vessels sailed along routes that were both coastal (along the Persian and Indian West Coast) as well as transoceanic (voyaging directly across the Arabian Sea to the Malabar Coast). While coastal voyages were possible for most months of the year because of land and sea breezes as well as the northeast monsoon wind, the transoceanic voyages were possible only during the north-east monsoon. [Ibn Battutā confirms this when he says, "there is only one season in the year in which the Sea of China is navigable". He had to wait for three months at Calicut for sailing to China (Lee 1829: 172).] From Malabar, these vessels sailed directly or sometimes via Sri Lanka, to Kala on the Malay Peninsula via the Nicobar Islands. Stopover at Sri Lanka often depended on the southeast monsoon that was necessary to sail across Southeast Asia. From Kala, the ships sailed via Qumar (Cambodia), Campa (Vietnam) to Khanfu (Canton). A few ships even sailed up to Zaiton (Quanzhou) and Quinsai (Hanchow). On their return voyage, some ships that required calling on ports in Sumatra, sailed around the island as shown in the itineraries compiled by Kia Tan between 785 and 805 AD. Sailing from Canton, via the Vietnam Coast and Pulo Condore, says Kia Tan, one reached the Strait of Chi (possibly the Singapore Strait) in 20 days, exactly the same as the time taken by I-Tsing. Then the ships sailed to Ho-ling

(Java), crossed the strait (possibly the Strait of Sunda) and sailed via ports on the West Coast of Sumatra and the Nicobar Islands to the country of the Lions (Sri Lanka) (Hirth and Rockhill 1965: 10-14). Suleiman's sailing schedules demonstrates that it was possible to make the entire voyage from the Persian Gulf to China in little over three months. This would involve sailing from Muscat to Quilon in one month, then from Quilon to Kalah within the next month and finally from Kalah to Canton in the third month (Tampoe 1990: 87). As one may recall, in 1980-81 British author-explorer Tim Severin demonstrated the feasibility of sailing in the Persian Gulf-China route by constructing a hand-stitched dhow in Oman and voyaging all the way from Muscat to Canton (Guanzhou) – entirely with the help of monsoon winds (Harris 1999).

Change in the maritime trade route discussed above began in 878 AD as a consequence of the massacre of Canton in which 120,000 foreigners, including Muslims, Christians, Jews and non-Muslim Persians were killed. Consequently, Arab-Persian merchants discontinued their direct voyages to Canton and curtailed their voyages to Southeast Asian ports. By the late 10th century AD, the axes of power in the world maritime trade had decisively taken a new turn. The Abbasids of Baghdad had begun to decline as the domineering power of the Islamic world and their place was occupied by the Fatimids of Egypt (969 AD). Very soon, their capital city Fustat became one of the major political, economic and cultural centres for the Mediterranean world and the Indian Ocean. As a result, the locus of trading activities had shifted from the Persian Gulf to the Red Sea. Another reason that accelerated the shift was the destruction of Siraf, a major port on the Persian Gulf, by an earthquake in 977 AD. Consequently, the maritime trade routes were also changed. Instead of following the coastal line to Gujarat, it became convenient for ships to sail from the Red Sea and Aden, as during the hey-days of Indo-Roman trade, directly across the Arabian Sea to the Malabar Coast in south India. At the other end in China, the Song dynasty had come to power in 960 AD and from the very outset, began to show vigorous interest and implement hegemonic designs in the maritime trade more successfully than any other Chinese dynasties.

As the Arab-Persians began to call on Southeast Asian ports for East Asian commodities following their withdrawal from Canton towards the end of the 9th century AD, Śrīvijaya reassumed their role as intermediate traders – a role that they had to abrogate earlier with the emergence of the Arab-Persians. With the waning of the Arab-Persian pre-eminence by the 10th century AD, the Colas of south India began to follow an aggressive commercial policy and chose the Bay of Bengal as their area of major trading interest since the Arab-Persians tenaciously held on their pre-eminence in the Arabian Sea. Consequently, intense rivalry arose in the bay.

The Colas rose as a splendorous power at a breathtaking speed from 985 to 1025 AD. From their home in the Kaveri delta, King Rājarāja (985-1012) destroyed the Chera (Kerala) navy, conquered the Pandyan kingdom and Vengi, and plundered Sri Lanka and the Maldives. Thus, his sway extended over the whole of south India including the prominent maritime ports on the Coromandel and the Malabar Coasts and the offshore islands of the south. These gains put the Colas in control of the central section of the Indian Ocean trade route. Under Rājarāja's son Rājendra I, Cola expansionist policy was further reinforced. In 1017, Sri Lanka was completely annexed and Polunnaruva was made the new capital of Cola-occupied Sri Lanka. Kerala was subjugated in the next year and the Maldives was attacked again in 1020. In 1022-23, the Cola army marched to Kaliṅga and 'Bengal' and subdued all possible rivals along the Bay of Bengal up to the very apex (i.e., the kingdom of the Candras). Thus had the Colas had turned the Bay of Bengal into the 'Cola Lake'. Then in 1025 it sent a naval expedition against Śrīvijaya and raided fourteen port cities on the Malay Peninsula and Sumatra.

The exact reason for the Cola expedition is still not known. What is clear though is that in 1016 AD, Śrīvijaya had emerged as the sole power in the Malay world by having engineered the sacking of the east Javanese kingdom of Mataram that was its contender for control over the south-eastern section of the Indian Ocean trade route. Kulke (1999: 219) argues that the competition between these two maritime powers "had reached a level where their traditional means of settling conflicts was no longer valid". What was at stake for both Śrīvijaya and the Cola kingdom was the huge profit to be reaped from trade with China and the Fatimids. And the Colas did reap huge profit. By the early 12th century, the ships owned by Kling (Tamil) merchants were handling most of the exports from Java, Sumatra and China. Although large Chinese junks pushed out those of the Klings in the mid-12th century AD, Coromandel ports remained the main entrepôts in the trade between China and the Islamic Near East until the early 15th century AD.

When we consider maritime trade routes leading to and from 'Bengal', we notice that by the early 9th century AD, important changes had taken place. One does not hear of Tāmralipti anymore. Instead, Samandar (Caṭṭagrāma) had established itself as the sole port connecting 'Bengal' with the outside world. It also served besides 'Bengal' (Puṇḍravardhana, Varendra, Samataṭa and Vaṅga) kingdoms such as Laur, Middle Gaṅgā valley, Kāmrūpa and Bhutan. It may be recalled that compared to the late historic period, there was a significant growth in the number of export items (rice, aloes-wood, emery, cotton textile (muslin), Buddhist images, rhinoceros & rhinoceros horns, yak-tails) during the early medieval period. Clearly, the locus of economic activities had shifted eastward: from Fa-Hien's time (early 5th century AD), when he noted the existence only of Tāmralipti, to I-Tsing's time (second half of the 7th century) when he noted ships sailing to Harikela to the early 9th century AD, when Tāmralipti had ceased to function as a maritime port. Recent discovery of Paṭṭikeḍā silver coins of the Devas (c. 720-825 AD) and the Harikela silver coins (second series) of the Candras (c. 900-1050 AD), discussed already in detail in Chapter Three, clearly affirm the rise of eastern 'Bengal' (Samataṭa, Vaṅga and Harikela). In all probability, 'Bengal' was immensely benefited by its direct link with the Abbasid caliphate.

One suspects that eastern 'Bengal' was brutally crushed in the intense maritime rivalry that began in the Bay of Bengal with the waning of Arab-Persian pre-eminence. Rājendra Cola launched the first major offensive sometime between 1021 and 1023 AD and defeated the reigning monarch Govindacandra of Vaṅgāla-deśa (eastern 'Bengal'). Anawrahta (1044-77) of Pagan led the second invasion in 1059 and annexed Caṭṭagrāma. Thus crushed and severed from its sole port, 'Bengal' was sadly out of contention for playing with other elite countries in the maritime super league of the Bay. If we may conjecture that Dīpaṅkara Śrījñāna's visit to Śrīvijaya, said to have taken place sometimes after 1011 AD, actually took place after 1023 AD, we can easily understand why the voyage was so difficult.

MEDIEVAL PERIOD

Sonārgāon-Sumatra

Ibn Battutā sailed from Sunurkāwān (Sonārgāon) on a junk to Sumatra in the mid-14th century AD. After fifteen days, the ship reached the country of Barahnakār (unidentified). Interestingly, he found Muslims from 'Bengal' living there. There is even indication of trade with the natives as Ibn Battutā reports that they "do all the trafficking with the merchants on the shore". We may firmly believe that the junk in which the Moroccan Arab traveller voyaged was on trading mission since he speaks of "merchants who were with us" (Gibb 1992: 271-273).

It must have been on this route that three 'tributary missions' from the sultans of 'Bengal' voyaged to China. As recorded in the *Si yang ch'ao kung tien lu* compiled by Huang Sing-ts'eng (1520 AD), the first of these was sent in 1408 AD by Sultan Ghiyath al-din Azam Shah who reached the Chinese capital in 1411 AD. The second mission was sent in 1414 AD, headed by a minister of the sultan named Pa-yi-tsi (Bayazid). The third embassy was sent in 1438 AD. The gifts sent in these missions included horses, gold and silver ornaments, gold engravings, white porcelain with blue decoration, shawls, *cho-fu-hei-ta-li* cloth, peacock's feathers, unicorn's horn, frankincense, parrots, dragon's blood incense, camphor, ebony wood, pepper, crystallised sugar and aloes wood (Bagchi 1945: 127). Although these voyages do not prove trade routes, we may nevertheless find confirmation of the existence of the route in the early 15th century AD. In the second half of the 15th century, when Sonārgāon ceased to be operational, the route was also discontinued.

Caṭṭagrāma-Sri Lanka

Because Si'di' al-Chelebi has given the sailing schedule from 'Bengal' to Sri Lanka (Hammer 1834: 553), we can firmly believe that there existed a direct maritime route connecting these two countries. Although al-Chelebi does not specifically mention the name of Caṭṭagrāma or Shātijām, we may firmly believe that this was the port he had in mind since in the *Mohit* he mentions no other port of 'Bengal' by name. Ships must have plied on this route in the early 16th century, if not earlier, because we have Barbosa to support our view. In the *Book of Duarte Barbosa* he writes, with "great ships after the fashion of Meca [*dhows*]; others ... from China, which they call '*juncos*', which are of great size and carry great cargoes", Arab, Persian, Abyssinian and Indian merchants from Bengala "sail to Charamandel, Malaca, Çamatra, Peeguu, Cambaya and Ceilam" (Barbosa 1921: 142, 145). As established in Chapter One that Bengala was Caṭṭagrāma.

Caṭṭagrāma-Coromandel Coast

Barbosa's testimony cited above clearly indicates the existence of trade route between Caṭṭagrāma and the Coromandel Coast. This is further confirmed by William Methwold who made the following observation in the early 17th century regarding ships arriving from 'Bengal'.

> For once a yeere there ariveth at Musulipatnam a fleet of small vessels from thence [Bengal], of burden about twenty tunnes, the plankes onely sowne together with cairo [a kind of cord made of the rid of coconuts], and no iron in or about them: in which barkes they bring rice, butter, sugar, waxe, honey, gumme lacke, long pepper, callico, ... (Moreland 1931: 40).

Although Methwold's testimony oversteps the time frame of this research, the manner in which he narrates is indicative of a long-standing practice.

Caṭṭagrāma-Maldives

Ibn Battutā's account of his voyage to 'Bengal' is important because it is the first piece of literary evidence showing a direct trade route between the Maldives and 'Bengal'. As the Moroccan Arab traveller informs us, he arrived at Kannalūs in the Maldives from Cālicūt and sailed from Mahal to Sudkawan (Caṭṭagrāma) in 43 nights (Gibb 1992: 266-267). As mentioned earlier in Chapter Two, trade between Maldives and 'Bengal' consisted of rice and cowries. We have no way of ascertaining the route of trade in the earlier periods. However, there can remain little doubt that by the mid-14th century AD, ships were sailing directly to Maldives with rice and from the islands with cowries. The vessels used in this route were possibly of *dhow* type, built of coconut-palm wood in the Maldives (Digby 1982c: 130). This route must have been operational in the mid-16th century AD because Si'di' al-Chelebi clearly gives dates for beginning and end of the sailing season from Dībi to 'Bengal' (Hammer 1834: 550, 552). Even in 1602, Francois Laval has observed, "yeerly thirtie or fortie ships laden without any other commoditie [save cowry] ... go into Bengala" (Purchas 1905a: 560).

Shātijām-Cochin-Calicut-Goa-Chaul-Dhabol-Cambay-Diū

A number of scattered pieces of literary evidence lead us to believe that a trade route connected Caṭṭagrāma with a number of important ports on the West Coast of India. The first of these is from Si'di' al-Chelebi who gives, as mentioned earlier in Chapter Five, detailed navigational instructions to mariners sailing from Diū to Shātijām (Caṭṭagrāma) in the *Mohi't* (Chapter Nine, Section 3, Twenty-eighth Voyage; Hammer 1836: 466-467). Al-Chelebi also gives schedules for ships sailing from Gujarat, Konkan and Malabar to 'Bengal' (Hammer 1834: 550-551). As observed earlier, Barbosa (1921: 145) also reports ships sailing from Caṭṭagrāma to Cambay. We also hear from Dom Jao do Leyma writing a report to the Portuguese king dated 22 December 1518 that the presence of Gujarati ships in 'Bengal' hampered the mercantile activities of the Portuguese (Ray 1988: 124). The final bit of information comes from Pires (1967: 271) who informs us that merchants from "Chaul, Dhabol and Goa [came] to take up their companies in 'Bengal', and from there they [came] to Malacca; and they [would] also take them up at Calicut". All these pieces of information are enough to establish the fact that the route from Caṭṭagrāma to Diū that al-Chelebi referred to, touched many ports on the West Coast of India such as Cambay, Chaul, Dhabol, Goa and Calicut. We may further believe that the route also touched Cochin since Caesar Frederick's testimony from 1569 shows that ships sailed from Chatigan [Caṭṭagrāma] to Cochin (Purchas 1905b: 135).

As described in the *Mohi't*, the voyage from Shātijām to Diū was coastal till Teknaf and then transoceanic till Sri Lanka. The last leg of the voyage was made around Sri Lanka and then along the West Coast of India till Diū (Hammer 1836: 466-467).

Shātijām-Aden-Jeddah-Sheher (Shihr)-Muscat-Hormuz

Si'di' al-Chelebi gives the sailing schedule from 'Bengal' to Aden, Jeddah, Sheher (Shiḥr) and Muscat (Hammer 1834: 550-553) and Aḥmad Ibn Mājid gives the sailing schedule for Hormuz, Yemen and the Ḥijāz (Tibbetts 1981: 233). It must have been on the route to Aden that Sultan Jalāl al-Dīn Muhammad Shāh of 'Bengal' (1415-1432) sent his diplomatic mission to seek and actually receive the recognition of al-Ashraf Sayf al-Dīn Barsbay (1422-1438), the 9th of the Burjī line of Mamlūk rulers of Egypt ('Abd al-Rahmān al-Sakhāwī, *Al-ḍaw al-lāmi' li-ahl al-qarn al-tāsi'*, Cairo AH 1303, Vol. VIII: 280, cited in Karim 1960: 171). Although this is no evidence for a maritime trade route, it does, nevertheless, confirm the existence of the route in the early 15th century AD.

The route from 'Bengal' must have been from Shātijām (Caṭṭagrāma) since al-Chelebi gives detailed navigational instructions from sailing from this port to the Arabian Coast. The route is described across the Bay of Bengal in a SSW direction, then sailing westward, passing Sri Lanka from its south, till the Maldives. From there, the route lay across the Arabian Sea in WNW direction (siding a little to NW by W) till opposite Kardafun and thence true west till the horn of Africa was reached. Then the vessels crossed the Gulf of Aden to reach the port of Aden (Hammer 1836: 466-467). For onward journey to Jeddah, the vessels sailed up the Red Sea through the Strait of Bab-el-Mandab. For those bound to Sheher and Muscat and Hormuz, the vessels sailed along the southern coast of Arabia and then across the Gulf of Oman.

Jeddah may have been more important for pilgrimage-traffic than maritime trade but Aden was surely important for trade. We learn of merchants from 'Bengal' arriving at Yemen as early as 1381-2 AD. Serjeant (2000: 66) informs us that during the heyday of the sultans belonging to the Rasulid Dynasty of Yemen, merchants from various ports in South Asia presented them with gifts. In 1381-2 and 1391, gifts received from 'Bengal' (al-Banjālah) were mostly textiles. Trade with Aden must have continued throughout the medieval period because, as already observed in Chapter Two, 'Bengal' exported rice to Aden in the early 16th century (Pires 1967: 17). During the same period, as Barbosa (1918: 56) vouchsafes, many ships came from Bengala ('Bengal') bringing abundance of lac, "thin Bengala clothes" (muslin) and sugar. We may believe that the same commodities were also exported to Sheher (Shihr) and Muscat.

Caṭṭagrāma-Mrohaung-Cosmin-Martaban-Tenasserim

South from Caṭṭagrāma lay four important ports of Myohaung (in Arakan), Cosmin and Martaban (in Pegu) and Tenasserim (on the West Coast of the Malay Peninsula). One immediately suspects that a coastal trade route connected all these ports in the medieval period since a similar route linked ports located on the eastern rim of the Bay of Bengal in the early historic period. The following evidence may be produced to confirm the suspicion.

Tome Pires clearly states, "The kingdom of Arakan ... has a good port on the sea, where the Peguans, the Bengalees and the Klings trade, but not much business. The port is called Myohaung (*Mayajerij*)" (Pires 1967: 95). Myohaung should be read as Mrohaung (or Mrauk-U). As pointed out earlier, it was situated on the bank of the Lemru River in Akyab district of Rakhine state in Myanmar and was the capital of the medieval kingdom of Arakan from 1433 to 1785 AD. There can be little doubt that the route to Myohaung originated in Caṭṭagrāma because Arakan occupied the port a number of times during the medieval period and because Sebastien

Manrique describes his voyage from Caṭṭagrāma/Dianga to Mrohaung and back between 1629 and 1635 AD. The itinerary of the Venetian merchant Nicolò de Conti, who visited 'Bengal' between 1419 and 1444 AD, further confirms the above. It appears that after arriving in 'Bengal' from Tenasserim, he visited Cernomen (Sonārgāon) and then traveled to other parts of India. Then he returned to Cernomen and sailed for Arakan via Buffetanya (Mills in Ma-Huan 1970: 65). If Mills' identification of Buffetanya with Chittagong (Caṭṭagrāma) is acceptable, then there can remain no doubt regarding the maritime route connecting the port with Arakan in the first half of the 15th century AD.

The next port on the route was Cosmin, one of the three maritime ports of Pegu (the other two being Dagon and Martaban). Cosmin was situated on the Bassein, a western branch of the Irawadi River. Most of the trade with 'Bengal' and Pegu was carried out at this port (Pires 1967: 97). Hence, Barbosa's (1921: 145) observation cited earlier in this section that ships sailed from Bengala to Peeguu (Pegu) should be taken to indicate voyages between Caṭṭagrāma and Cosmin. Similarly, when Varthema sailed from the port of Banghella (Caṭṭagrāma) to Pegu in c. 1508 (Varthema 1928: 80) and when Caesar Frederick sailed from Pegu for Chatigan (Caṭṭagrāma) in 1569, we may believe with certitude that the port in Pegu was Cosmin. Furthermore, observations made by Pires, Barbosa, Varthema and Frederick should confirm the existence of a maritime route connecting Caṭṭagrāma with Cosmin.

As mentioned earlier in Chapter Four, from the account book of Pero Pais dated 1512 we learn that four or five sampans filled with *sanbaf* and other fabrics from 'Bengal' arrived each year at Cosmin in March or April (Bouchon 1984: 100). The "white cloth from Bengal" that was exported to Burma (Pires 1967: 111) may well have reached its destination through Cosmin. We learn from Tavernier (1889, II: 22) that the kingdom continued to import ready dyed cotton textiles from 'Bengal' even in the second half of the 17th century AD. Caesar Frederick has also informed us that other than victual and ballast, ships sailing on this route from Pegu to 'Bengal' carried only silver and gold (Purchas 1905b: 135-136). Pires (1967: 100) confirms the matter of import of silver and says that a great deal of this metal was taken from Pegu to 'Bengal'. We may remember that two other items of export from Pegu to 'Bengal' were musk and rubies (*ibid.*: 96).

Ralph Fitch's description of his voyage on a small ship from Serrepore (Sripur) to Pegu on 1586 may well give us an idea of the route from Caṭṭagrāma to Cosmin via Mrohaung: "passing by the island of Sundiva, Porto Grande [Caṭṭagrāma], ... the kingdom of Recon and Mogen [Arakan], leaving them on [the] left side with a faire wind at northwest, ... [sailing] south and by east ...". His ship reached the mouth of the Bassein and from there arrived at Cosmin after three more days' journey (Foster 1968: 28-29).

The southern coastal route from Caṭṭagrāma did not terminate at Cosmin but went further east to Martaban on the Sitang estuary, the third port of the medieval kingdom of Pegu. Merchants from 'Bengal' may not have frequented this port because Pires noted that most of the trade with 'Bengal' and Pegu was transacted at Cosmin (Pires 1967: 97). Nevertheless, we hear from Pero Pais that junks from 'Bengal' called at Martaban in the early 16th century (Bouchon 1984: 100). In a letter written by Friar Nicholas Pimenta in 1602, we learn that the Martabanians were still trading with the people of Bengala (Hosten 1925: 69-70). Since it is mentioned that junks called at Martaban while sampans at Cosmin, we may infer that smaller ships (such as the one Ralph Fitch voyaged in) sailed as far as Mrohaung and Cosmin while larger ships such as junks plied to Martaban.

Further south from Martaban lay Tenasserim, which, along with Junkseylon (Juncalom) and Trang, were ports in the kingdom of Siam and lay on the West Coast of the Malay Peninsula. (Junkseylon was actually on an island off the coast). Junks from 'Bengal' must have called at this port since Pires (1967: 105) informs us that Bengalees were living in Siam and that "all the Siamese trade is on the China side, and in Pasé, Pedir and Bengal". He informs us again that "[o]n the Tenasserim side Siam also trades with Pasé, Pedir, with Kedah, with Pegu, with Bengal" (*ibid.*: 109).

Besides Pires, we have Varthema to vouchsafe that ships sailed to and from Caṭṭagrāma and Tenasserim in the early 16th century AD. As mentioned earlier in Chapter One, Ludovico di Varthema arrived at the port of Banghella (Caṭṭagrāma) from Tenasserim in c. 1508 AD. The ship carrying the Italian traveler voyaged for 11 days to traverse the distance (Varthema 1928: 79). Ships may have sailed from Tenasserim even in the first half of the 15th century AD, because Nicolò de Conti arrived in 'Bengal' from there. Although his port of disembarkation in 'Bengal' is not specifically mentioned, Caṭṭagrāma is more likely than Sātgāon because Southeast Asia was a familiar world for eastern 'Bengal' since the times of Hiuen-Tsiang or even earlier.

By the early 18th century, trade with Tenasserim must have slackened substantially. In a letter written to Niccolao Manucci by a friend of his from Siam, we are told that "[n]othing comes here [to Siam] but a few Chinese vessels, or some from 'Bengal' and Surat, and these even, once they have been here, never come back a second time". However, as the same source informs us, in the late 17th century, trade was "very flourishing" (Manucci 1907, III: 506-507).

South from Tenasserim lay Kedah, the port of a kingdom by the same name. In the early 16th century, it was a tributary of Siam (Pires 1967: 104). We have no evidence to prove that ships from 'Bengal' called at Kedah, except Pires' observation that "[w]hen any ship comes to Tenasseerim and to the ports of Siam, it comes to Kedah to sell its merchandise also ..." (*ibid.*: 106). Even if ships from 'Bengal' did not call at Kedah, the port is important because we are at once reminded of the late historic port of Ka-cha from where I-Tsing had boarded a ship for an onward voyage to Tāmralipti.

Further south lay Malacca, possibly the last port of call on the southern coastal route from Caṭṭagrāma. Since ships also voyaged on a direct route from these two ports, we may as well discuss Malacca as a port of call of the direct route.

Caṭṭagrāma-Malacca-Pasé

Malacca, situated near the tip of the Malay Peninsula, served as a flourishing entrepôt from c. 1403 AD. In 1511, the Portuguese admiral Don Alfonse de Albuquerque captured it. Pasé or Samudra-Pasé was a Muslim kingdom in north Sumatra that Ibn Battutā visited in the mid-14th century AD. It was also known as Shumutra. A tiny village called Samoedra still stands on the Pasé river that falls into the sea a little to the east of Lho' Seumawe (Tibbetts: 1981: 493). Tome Pires (1967: 92) provides the most reliable evidence that both of these ports were connected with 'Bengal' by a trade route. He says, "[a] junk goes from Bengal to Malacca once a year, and sometimes twice. ... These people [i.e., merchants from Bengal] sail four or five ships and junks to Malacca and to Pasé every year, and this is still done to a large extent" (*ibid.*). The manner of Pires' observation indicates that sailing in the route was a matter of long-standing practice. Since he also notes that ships took thirty days to sail from the port of origin to destination (*ibid.*: 93), we may firmly believe that ships sailed directly on this route. Since Pires had noted the existence of two ports in 'Bengal' (the City of Bengal or Caṭṭagrāma and Sātgāon) there can remain little doubt that ships sailed from Caṭṭagrāma to Malacca and Pasé. This is further confirmed by Barbosa (1921: 139, 145) who observed that Arab, Persian, Abyssinian and Indian merchants from Bengala (Caṭṭagrāma) sailed to Çamatra (i.e., Pasé), and Malaca (i.e., Malacca). We may further believe in the 16th century AD, that most of the ships sailed to and from Caṭṭagrāma because João de Barros testifies that all merchandise from the east reached Catigao (Caṭṭagrāma) (Ray 1988: 128). The route from Caṭṭagrāma to Malacca and Sumatra may be seen as a continuation of Samandar-Ka-cha-Śrīvijaya route of the early medieval period.

Sātgāon-Malacca-Pasé

It has already been established that trade between Malacca and 'Bengal' was carried out by means of a direct route between Caṭṭagrāma, Malacca and Pasé. Since Pires had noted the existence of two ports in 'Bengal' (the City of Bengal or Caṭṭagrāma and Sātgāon), we may believe that ships plied on another route connecting Sātgāon with the same destinations (i.e., Malacca and Pasé). This route may be seen as an extension of the Tāmralipti-Chu-li (Takkola) transoceanic trade route of the early historic period.

Sātgāon-Sri Lanka-Malabar-Konkan

An important body of literary evidence for ascertaining maritime trade routes in medieval 'Bengal' is the maṅgalakāvya corpus. It is necessary to examine the major texts of the corpus in order to see if any indications of trade routes may be ascertained from them.

Baṁśīdāsa provides quite an elaborate description of the merchant C̃ād Saodāgar's voyage in his *Manasāmaṅgala* (composed in the 16th century). From the city of Campaka, an inland port, the merchant is described setting sail for Dakṣin Pāṭan. After sailing past a number of localities, such as Madhyanagar, Kāmārhāṭi, Pratāpgarh, Gopālpur and Rām-nagar, he crosses the Kālidaha Sāgar (a mythical sea, here used as a poetic expression for deep water) and a few more localities and then reaches the mouth of the Gaṅgā (cited as Gaṅgā-sāgar). Interestingly, there is no mention of any maritime port on or near the mouth of the Gaṅgā. Upon reaching the sea, C̃ād Saodāgar begins his coastal voyage and sails past Utkal and Kaliṅga on his right. Cursed by the serpent goddess Manasā, he has to overcome giant leeches, crabs, lobsters and crocodiles before arriving at "Golden Laṅkā". After a brief halt at Sri Lanka (where he receives permission for further journey), he continues past the Malay Mountains and Bijayanagara, and then visits Parśurāmatīrtha (possibly more for religious merit than trading interest). Till this point, the Bengali merchant and his mariners made a coasting voyage. From Parśurāmatirtha to Dakṣin Pāṭan, their route cut across the high seas, referred in the text as Nīlaccārbānk (literally, "The Bend of the Sea near Nīlaccā", possibly Laccadives). Although the towering waves of the vast sea make the crew giddy, the master mariner Dulāi navigates with the help of the stars and steers C̃ād Saodāgar's ships safely to Pāṭan ruled by King Candraketu. The return journey is roughly similar: they cross the Nīlaccārbānk, pass the Vindhya Ranges, Sri Lanka and Setubandha-Rāmeśwar and finally reach the Kālidaha Sāgar where his ship is sunk by the goddess Manasā (Dasgupta 1935: 31-32).

The route that Baṁśīdāsa describes is clearly coastal along the East Coast of India till Sri Lanka, from where the merchant is described making a transoceanic voyage to Pāṭan. Because there exists a city by that name in Gujarat, we may assume that the poet had Gujarat in mind. However, Tamonash Dasgupta (*ibid.*: 32) identifies the city in question as Somnāth Pāṭan in Gujarat. The matter is a little confusing because at the beginning of the voyage, Baṁśīdāsa describes the merchant setting sail for Dakṣin Pāṭan – a destination that is difficult to locate among known towns and ports in South Asia. This textual problem may be resolved if we recall that the term *'pāṭan'* in Bengali denotes 'city' (such as Gauḍa Pāṭan), 'trade-and commerce', a 'trading place', and even 'sea-trade'. Hence, setting sail for Dakṣin Pāṭan implies setting sail for trade to the south. Arriving at Pāṭan should imply arriving at the 'trading place' of the south, i.e., port of destination. As we will see in the texts discussed below, "Pāṭan" is used indiscriminately, suffixed to a number of locations. In that case, it is possible that Pāṭan is the generic name for city. This view may be substantiated by citing the following names of ports on the East Coast of India, all of which are suffixed by "patna", "patnam" or "pattinam": Manikapatna and Khalkatopatna (in Orissa) Vishakhapatnam and Machilipatnam and Kottapatnam (in Andhra), and Nagapattinam and Devipattinam (in Tamil Nadu). Ibn Battutā vouchsafes that these names were current even in the mid-14th century AD. Not only does he mention names of ports such as Jarafattan and Badafattan in Malabar (Lee 1829: 175) but also two ports named Fattan (Pattan) in Malabar and Coromandel Coasts (*ibid.*: 171, 193). Hence, "Dakṣin Pāṭan" should denote "the City of the South". In Baṁśīdāsa's text, since C̃ād Saodāgar arrives at Pāṭan after crossing Sri Lanka and the Laccadives, we may believe that the poet had the Malabar-Konkan Coast in mind.

Nārāyaṇa Deva also provides an interesting description in his *Padmā-purāṇa* (composed in the beginning of the 16th century). In this version, C̃ād (or Candradhar as Nārāyaṇa Deva prefers to call him) along with his fleet commences his journey from Campaka and sails south down an unspecified river. On the way he crosses Bhabānipura, Kāmanāḍā, Maynābāśu, Kasturipāḍa, Gaḍiyār Thānā, Mahindranagara and a number of other market places and towns. Then, sailing down the Deva and the Suresvari rivers, he reaches the Gaṅgā, where he halts and offers worship to the deities. Then through distributaries of the Gaṅgā, past Hāḍiyākandha, he crosses Tripiṇī (Tribenī?), Saptagrām, Kumārhātī, Mulājoḍā and other localities. As these recede past, Candradhar and his fleet reach the sea and begin coastal voyage. Sailing across a number of lagoons (*daha*), he overcomes obstacles of giant leeches and crabs. In another lagoon, he collects cowries and conch shells. Then he crosses the estuary of Kāñcan River, and the towns of Haripura, Mahindranagara and Bhabānipura. Soon after, Candradhar and his fleet reach the high sea and are overcome with fear by giant waves. Candradhar's uncle Dhonā climbs up the mast (*mālum kāṭh*) and sees land at a distance. Then he informs Candradhar, drawing upon his past experience as a sailor (for he had sailed to these parts once earlier with Candradhar's father), that near these shores lie a number of *pāṭans* or cities (Kaliṅgā, Kinyāt, Laṅkā among others) and kingdoms (Siṁhala Island, Mililā among others). Candradhar decides to sail towards Laṅkā, where he obtains permission to journey further. Sailing thence for three days, he arrives at the Dakṣin Pāṭan. On his return journey, Candradhar is described sailed as with a south wind to reach Laṅkā, from where he sails past a number of "bends" along the coast and across a few lagoons (*daha*), till his ship is sur by the goddess Manasā at Kālidaha (Deva 1942: 188-20 225).

The route that is described in Nārāyaṇa Deva's text is fro 'Bengal' to Dakṣin Pāṭan, i.e., the City of the South. The initi part of the maritime voyage is clearly coastal, where th merchant crosses Kāñcan River, and the towns of Haripura Mahindranagara and Bhabānipura. Among these, Haripur definitely identifiable – on the coast of India, near the bord of Andhra and Orissa. Hence, we may assume that th merchant abandoned the coast after crossing the mouth c the Godavari (where the coast curves inward) and voyage across the high sea to Sri Lanka. Since the merchant described as sailing onward from Sri Lanka, we may assum that Nārāyaṇa Deva's Dakṣin Pāṭan, like Baṁśīdāsa, lay o the Malabar-Konkan Coast.

Bijayagupta's *Padmāpurāṇa* (composed at the end of the 15 century) also describes Cānd (C̃ad in Bijaygupta's tex Saodāgar's journey from Campaka to Dakṣin Pāṭan. H specifically shows the merchant's fleet sailing down th Gaṅgā-Bhāgīrathī. Omitting any reference to any seaport o or near coastal 'Bengal', Bijayagupta describes the Benga merchant sailing past coastal cities of Mānikyapura (possib Manikapatna in Orissa) and Bijayārpura (possib Vijayanagaram in Andhra Pradesh). He also sails past th mouths of a number of rivers, most of which ar unidentifiable, except the Godavari. Instead of Baṁśīdāsa' Parśurāmatīrtha, Bijayagupta's C̃ad Saodāgar pays homage t the gods on the bank of the river Surā. There, the maste mariner Dhonā describe to him the conditions of the fou kingdoms that lie in the east, the west, the south and th north. Although fictitious, Tamonash Dasgupta (1935: 35 believes that these kingdoms actually refer to Myanmar (i the east), China (in the north), Tamil Nadu (in the west) an the fabulous Pāṭan (in the south). (It should be remembere though, that the poet does not mention the names of thes countries.) Having heard Dhonā's advice, C̃ad Saodāga decides to go south to Pāṭan. At the mouth of River Surā, th Bengali merchant abandons the coasting voyage an embarks upon the high seas, sails across Kālidaha Sea Labaṇāmbu Sea and Jamadvip Sea, and overcomes gian leeches and shells. Finally, C̃ad Saodāgar reaches Dakṣi Pāṭan. Bijayagupta does not give details of the return journe but describes in detail the sinking of C̃ad's ships at a unspecified location (Bijayagupta 1962: 235-254).

Bijayagupta does not mention Sri Lanka in C̃ad Saodāgar' voyage from 'Bengal' to Dakṣin Pāṭan. However, it appear that the Bengali merchant's route was coastal till the mout of the Godavari and transoceanic from there to Dakṣin Pāṭa In this respect, there is some similarity with Nārāyaṇa Deva' text. We may assume that Bijayagupta's Dakṣin Pāṭan lay i southern Tamil Nadu (Nagapattinam) or in Sri Lanka sinc the poet does not describe the merchant sailing around the island.

Srīrāy Binod's *Padmā-purāṇa* (composed in the 16th century) describes the journey of C̃ād (or Cāndo as the author prefers to call him) from Campaka not to Dakṣin Pāṭan but to Laṅkā Pāṭan. Reference to past voyages is made not during Cāndo's voyage, as in Nārāyaṇa Deva, but before Cāndo embarks upon his voyage. Here Śṛñgī Paṇdita informs Cāndo that his father had sailed to Dakṣin Pāṭan for trade, from which he had earned fabulous riches. Eliminating all details of riverine journey down the Gaṅgā-Bhāgīrathī, Srīrāy Binod's Cāndo appears to embark directly upon a coastal voyage, sailing on the South Sea. After six month's journey, he has to halt at Śrīnagar for quite some time because south wind begins to blow. When favourable north wind begins in autumn, he sails again, making a brief halt at Tribenī. From there, he sails along the coast. Srīrāy Binod does not mention any port or city but Kālidaha Sea and a number of "bends" along the coast. As he coasts along, he has to overcome giant leeches, fishes and crabs. However, at one bend he is fortunate to collect cowries. As the last "bend" recedes, Cāndo embarks upon the high sea and finally arrives at Laṅkā Pāṭan, or the city of Laṅkā (also referred as Kaṇak Pāṭan or Golden City). Cāndo's return journey is along the same route, briefly touched upon by the poet. His ships are sunk by the goddess at Kālidaha Sea (Binod 1993: 187, 194-208, 221-231).

Srīrāy Binod's text bears a clear indication of the coastal voyage from 'Bengal' to Sri Lanka. Although he makes a brief halt at Tribenī, Saptagrāma is not mentioned at all. What is most striking about Srīrāy Binod's *Padmā-purāṇa* is that the earlier part of Cānd's journey indicates Eastern 'Bengal' (Bangladesh). Not only is the riverine journey (along with localities on riverbank) absent in his account (for C̃ād embarks directly upon the South Sea), but starkly prominent is also the fact that Tribenī comes after sailing on the South Sea. This is possibly because Srīrāy Binod was from Tangail in Bangladesh. Hence, Srīrāy Binod's text may be taken to imply a westward coastal voyage along southern Bangladesh.

Kṣemānanda Dāsa's *Manasāmaṅgala* (end of the 17th and the beginning of the 18th centuries) gives the briefest reference to Cāndo Saodāgar's journey. Omitting all details, he merely states that the merchant sets off for Siṁhala (Sri Lanka) and after sailing swiftly, arrives at Siṁhala Pāṭan (Dāsa 1316: 6).

Caṇḍīmaṅgala by Kavikañkaṇa Mukunda (composed in the mid-16th century) describes two trading voyages – one by the merchant Dhanapati Datta and the other by his son Śrīmanta – from the city of Ujāni (literally, "of upstream") in the kingdom of Gauḍa to Dakṣin Pāṭan (identified in this text as Siṁhala). The king of Ujāni city orders Dhanapati to set sail for Dakṣin Pāṭan (the City of the South) because traders have not been voyaging for quite some time and as a result, his stock of luxury items (such as sandal wood, conch shells, perfume etc) is now nearly empty. Dhanapati reluctantly agrees because other merchants refuse to go. He sets sail with seven ships from the city of Ujāni, down the Gaṅgā. On the way he passes a number of villages and towns such as Lalitapura, Indrani, Navadvīpa, Śāntipura, Halisahara and Tribenī. When he reaches Saptagrāma in Raḍha region he decides to rest for two days. Here he trades, selling articles that he had brought from Ujāni city and buying new items for Dakṣin Pāṭan. Then, sailing past Koñara Nagara, Medana-malla, Birakhānā and other localities, he reaches Magrā River (a distributary of the Gaṅgā), where six of his ships capsize. Sailing further downstream, he reaches the estuary. From there he begins a coastal voyage on the sea, and reaches Purī in Orissa, where he halts to pay homage to the gods. Sailing again, he passes Candrasiddha Island and a lagoon infested with leeches, then Jurgraprastha Island and a lagoon of conch shells and still further, Ramanaka Island and a lagoon of snakes. Overcoming possible calamities by virtue of his intelligence, he sails further on, passes Setubandha-Rāmeśwar and reaches the vicinity of Laṅkā. Then anchoring at a pier near Candracuḍa Mountains, he learns from local people about the location of Laṅkā. Then sailing past Kālidaha, he finally anchors at Ratnamālā port in Siṁhala. There, the king of Siṁhala imprisons him.

Śrīmanta, when he attains maturity, sets off in search of his father. His voyage takes him along the same route down the Gaṅgā, from Ujāni city via Saptagrāma to Magrā River (described in further detail by the poet). Śrīmanta, like his father, also trades at Saptagrāma, where he halts for two days. When he reaches the estuary, he too begins a coastal voyage. On the way, he is assailed by crocodiles and giant fishes but overcomes these impediments. Then he sails past Drāviḍa (Dravidian) kingdom and then halts at Purī to worship the gods. He sails again and is assailed by leeches and snakes in two consecutive lagoons, which he manages to overcome. Sailing further, he crosses Svarṇamaya Island, Harināma Island, Nīlagiri Ranges, Setubandha-Rāmeśwar, Candrakuṭa Mountains (possibly same as Candracuḍa Mountains seen by his father) and Kālidaha. Finally he arrives at Ratnamālā port in Siṁhala. The return journey, after Śrīmanta rescues Dhanapati, is through the same route from Siṁhala to Magrā River, except that the poet mentions a new island – that of Pañcajanya – instead of those mentioned earlier. From Magrā River, when father and son sail upstream on the Gaṅgā, a new city is added – that of Kalikātā – which obviously is a later interpolation (Mukunda 1986: 201-208, 234-252, 297).

If we overlook the anomaly of sailing past Drāviḍa kingdom before Purī and the interpolation of Kalikātā in Śrīmanta's voyage, *Caṇḍīmaṅgala* by Kavikañkaṇa Mukunda clearly describes a coastal voyage from Saptagrāma to Siṁhala (Sri Lanka). However, since Dhanapati had intended to sail for Dakṣin Pāṭan and since Siṁhala is not described as Laṅkā

Pāṭan as Srīrāy Binod does, we may infer that Dhanapati's voyage was actually cut short by the king of Siṁhala.

Let us now consider all the texts together and sift out the trade routes as indicated in the maṅgalakāvya corpus. In both Baṁśīdāsa and Nārāyaṇa Deva's texts, the merchant sails to Dakṣin Pāṭan, halting briefly at Sri Lanka to obtain permission to sail further. Bijayagupta's merchant does not have to halt at Laṅkā but sails directly to Dakṣin Pāṭan, but Srīrāy Binod and Kṣemānanda Dāsa's merchant sails only to Siṁhala or Laṅkā. We may infer from Kavikañkaṇa Mukunda's text that Dhanapati had intended to sail to Dakṣin Pāṭan but was imprisoned on the way at Siṁhala. Hence, if one peels off all the layers of poetic fancy, one may arrive at a core that indicates a trade route linking 'Bengal' with two points – Laṅkā and Dakṣin Pāṭan (Malabar-Konkan Coast) However, the homeport in 'Bengal' is vague. In *Caṇḍīmaṅgala* by Kavikañkaṇa Mukunda, the homeport is the city of Ujāni (literally, "of upstream"). However, in Baṁśīdāsa's *Manasā-maṅgala*, Nārāyaṇa Deva's *Padmā-purāṇa,* Bijayagupta's *Padmāpurāṇa* and Srīrāy Binod's *Padmā-purāṇa* the homeport is the city of Campaka.

Asutosh Bhattacharyya (1989: 291) argues that the fabled Campaka City is Campā described by Fa-Hien (*Fo-kwō-ki*, XXXVII; Beal 1869: 147-48). This may be further substantiated by Hiuen-Tsiang's description of Campā (that was "backed to the north by the river Ganges"; *Si-Yu-Ki*, Book X; Beal 1906: 191) and the *Mahājanaka Jātaka* (that shows us a prince setting out from Campā for Suvarṇabhūmi; Book XXII, No. 539; Cowell 1957, VI: 22)). Ancient Campā is believed to have been the capital of Aṅga and was so named because it was situated on the banks of the River Campā (now called Cāndan) and the River Gaṅgā (Agarwal 1982: 110). It was identified by Cunningham (1871: 477) with Champanagar and Champapur, two modern villages situated 5 km west of Bhagalpur in South Bihar. A comprehensive description of the archaeological aspects of ancient Campā given by B. P. Sinha (in Ghosh 1989, II: 90) indicates the existence of a defensive fortification (of a high brick wall built over an earthen rampart), surrounded by a deep moat and the bed of the Gaṅgā. The earliest phase of the rampart dates from the pre-Śuṅga period (Chakrabarti 1995: 216).

One need not jump to the conclusion that reference to Campā (Campaka) in the maṅgalakāvya corpus and in the *Mahājanaka Jātaka* implies that the site was a maritime port. Significantly, neither Fa-Hien nor Hiuen-Tsiang refers to it as such. Nor have we found any archaeological material indicating maritime activity at the port situated considerably upstream from the mouth of the Gaṅgā. It would be more logical to argue that the ancient legend of Bihar out of which the core narrative of the *Manasāmaṅgala* corpus grew (Bhattacharyya 1989: 290), was built around a merchant of a fabled city of Bihar. Hence, Campaka and Ujāni, very much like Dakṣin Pāṭan, are but figurative expressions, which reflect hazy memory of a time when sailors used to sail from a port, situated upstream from the mouth of the Gaṅgā. Since Baṁśīdāsa, Nārāyaṇa Deva and Bijayagupta describe the voyage of C̃ād Saodāgar down a river which is directly indicated or indirectly implied as the Gaṅgā-Bhāgīrathī, and since Sātgāon was the only port situated upstream of the Gaṅgā-Bhāgīrathī during the medieval period, we may argue that the medieval trade route indicated in the maṅgalakāvya corpus should be read as Sātgāon-Sri Lanka-Malabar-Konkan.

Having put forward our arguments in favour of a trade route that is indicated in the maṅgalakāvya corpus, we must now take cognizance of an underlying implication that can also be sifted from the corpus. From the manner of describing the voyages of Bengali merchants, it is clear that none of these indicate 'trade route' as "recurrent and repetitive"; instead, they are all extraordinary or special ventures. Consider, for example, that the king of Ujāni city orders Dhanapati to set sail because traders have not been voyaging for quite some time and because other merchants refuse to go. Śrīmanta sets off, not for trade but in search of his father. In all the *Manasāmaṅgala* texts, C̃ād Saodāgar has to have his fleet built. Even if Nārāyaṇa Deva's text indicates that his father embarked upon a similar voyage, that too was a special venture which was undertaken "once upon a time". Even when Dhonā narrates what lies ahead, his past experience as a sailor appears to be pitifully limited, for he can actually recall the name of only three cities (Kaliṅgā, Kinyāt and Laṅkā) and two kingdoms (Siṁhala Island and Mililā). Evidently, Dhonā is only a little better than the sailors on the shores of Bangladesh, who can recall only two countries they have voyaged to – Myanmar and India.

Nevertheless, the Sātgāon-Sri Lanka-Malabar-Konkan trade route indicated in the maṅgalakāvya corpus could not have been completely invented since we have ascertained the existence of trade routes connecting Tāmralipti, Sri Lanka and the Malabar Coast both in the early as well as the late historic periods. Hence, we may argue that the maṅgalakāvya corpus is indicative of a maritime trade route that is based on the 'collective memory' of a community with a long-lost tradition amalgamated with their 'lived experience'. In other words, it is a document of what a community remembered of a distant past and what it saw around them in the medieval period. However, the memory was significantly 'rusted' and the 'lived experience' was not their own.

There must have been a significant reason that impelled all those numerous poets of the maṅgalakāvya corpus to write about a rusted 'collective memory' in the medieval period. Surely something was happening during the period when the poets were composing their maṅgalakāvyas, something that the Bengali-speaking Hindu community (for whom the texts were composed) was witnessing that reminded them of their long-lost past. We may believe that this 'something' was intense maritime trade handled by foreign merchants and their factors. In support of our proposition, we may cite Pires' observation that merchants "from Chaul, Dhabol and Goa come to take up their companies in Bengal, and from there they come to Malacca; and they also take them up at Calicut" (Pires 1967: 271). This must be taken to indicate that merchants from Chaul, Dhabol, Goa (all on the Konkan Coast) and Calicut (Malabar Coast) had their factors residing in 'Bengal' and they too voyaged to 'Bengal' and from there, they voyaged to Malabar. Because Pires noted the existence of two ports in 'Bengal', we may justifiably argue that the merchants from the Konkan and the Malabar Coast of India came also to Sātgāon. Furthermore, as pointed out in Chapter One, Kavikañkaṇa Mukunda describes Saptagrāma (Sātgāon) as a port where merchants from Kaliṅga, Telaṅga, Vindhya, Utkala, Drāviḍa, Vijayānagara, Kāñcīpura, Godāvarī (all on the East Coast of India), Karnāṭa, Mahārashṭra, Gujarāt, Dvārikā (all on the West Coast of India), Laṅkā and even Malaya gathered for trading, in their junks (*jaṅga diṅgā*). Surely these reflect the contemporary 'lived experience' of the Bengali-speaking Hindu community of 'Bengal', who witnessed foreign merchants sailing to and from Saptagrāma. It was from these foreign merchants that they must have heard about distant ports, of voyages to Sri Lanka and the Malabar-Konkan Coast. Understandably, the route was vague to them and hence the vagueness has been reflected in the maṅgalakāvya corpus. Perhaps the corpus can be read as a document of a community that relived its rusted 'collective memory' when it saw merchants from abroad doing what they could not do. Perhaps, through Čād Saodāgar, Dhanapati and Śrīmanta, this community relived its 'collective memory' of a distant past.

Hence, even if the maṅgalakāvya corpus is not a valid evidence for ascertaining trade routes, we may surely believe, the very fact that numerous poets were writing about maritime voyages implies the existence of maritime trade in their time. The trade route that they spoke of was in fact the route that the merchants from the Malabar-Konkan Coast used for voyaging to and from Sātgāon. For confirmation of the maṅgalakāvya trade route, Pires' testimony cited above should be good enough. We may further add Caesar Frederick's testimony of voyages he made from Orissa to Sātgāon and Sātgāon to Cochin in 1567 (Purchas 1905b: 115) as another evidence. Actually, Frederick's voyage from Orissa and the presence of merchants from the East Coast of India creates a suspicion that some of the ships plying on Sātgāon-Sri Lanka-Malabar-Konkan route may have touched many ports situated on the Orissa, Andhra and Tami Nadu coasts as well. Although Sebastien Manrique's voyage from Cochin to Huglī was made in 1628 – and hence way beyond the time frame of this research, one may still use this bit of evidence to argue that surely the Portuguese did not invent the route from the mouth of the Gaṅgā to the West Coast of India (Manrique 1927: 7). They as well as the merchants from the Malabar-Konkan Coast were merely continuing on a route that existed from the early historic period.

Bengal and the (Old) World Maritime Trade Routes

Having ascertained the trade-routes connecting 'Bengal' in the medieval period (Fig. 6.2), it is necessary now to see these in the greater context of contemporary world trade routes. As a consequene of changes in the policy of the Southern Sung dynasty (1127-1278 AD) and significant advances in Chinese naval technology, pattern of trade in the Indian Ocean witnessed significant changes by the mid-13th century AD. The changed state policy in China led to the abandonment of 'tributary trading system' and granting of permission for private participation in overseas trade to Chinese merchants (Kiribamune 1990: 186). As a result, Chinese ships, mariners and merchants entered the Indian Ocean trade orbit and their presence could be felt as far as Galle in Sri Lanka and Calicut in southern India. Even the volume and value of imports to China grew, which was compensated by exporting mass-produced ceramics (McPherson 1998: 98-99).

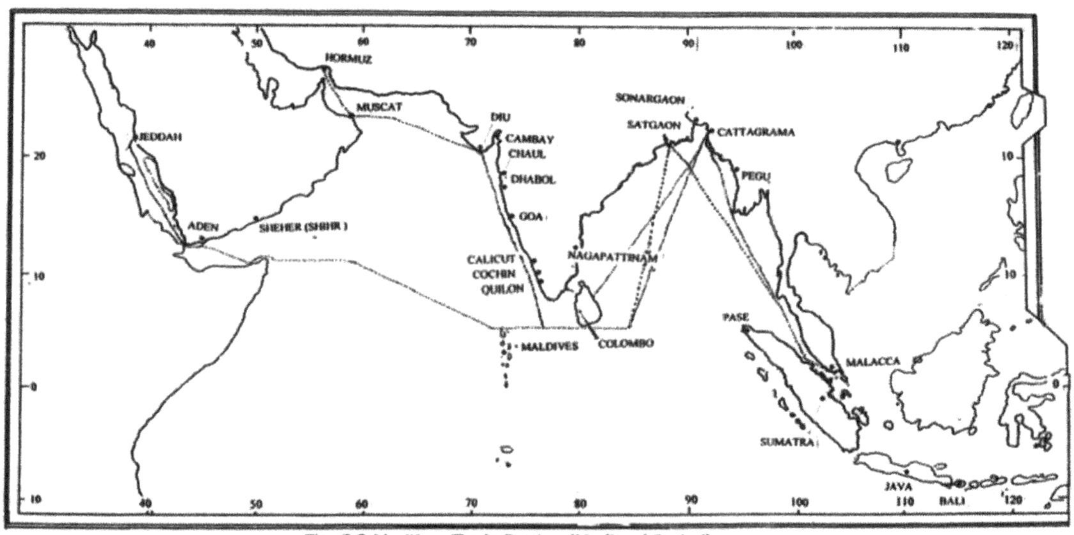

Fig. 6.2 Maritime Trade Routes (Medieval Period)

Although decline in the Abbasid Empire had set in much earlier, its final bells were rung in 1257 with the sacking of Baghdad by the Mongols. Consequently, there was a sharp fall in maritme trade as the hub of activities moved from

Basra (at the head of the Persian Gulf) to Hormuz (at the entrance to the Gulf). From Tabriz, the capital of the newly installed Mongol Il-Khan dynasty, merchandise from Hormuz could be transported via the alternate overland route linking Central Asia and the Mediterranean Sea with the Indian Ocean.

Political changes in China and the Middle East had large-scale repurcussions. In Southeast Asia, Śrīvijaya declined since its role of intermediate trade was taken over by the Chinese merchants. The major entrepôts shifted to Malabar (Elim, Quilon, Calicut, Cochin) and Coromandel (Kayal, Malipatan, Negapatan, and possibly Motupille) in south India. The Arab *dhows* would sail to these ports (in routes described in the earlier section) with their commodities and exchange them with the commodities carried by the Chinese junks that plied on the eastern Indian Ocean. This does not mean that the Arab traders stopped sailing eastward. However, their visits were limited to the Bay of Bengal and the Southeast Asia, where they obtained primary products of these regions as well as east Asian goods (Kiribamune 1990: 186). This pattern in the maritime trade routes stretching from China to the Islamic world and Europe continued until the rise of Malacca in the early 15th century AD.

At the western end of the Arabian Sea, Aden was the point of transshipment of goods bound for the markets of Cairo, Alexandria and Mediterranean Europe. From Aden, these would be transported in smaller vessels up to Aydhab, from there carried by camel to the Nile and then transported up the river (Polo N.D. ii: 282). Hormuz, Kais and Bahrain were the other transshipment points for merchandise marked for the Persian Gulf and the Mediterranean ports via an overland route through Syria. By, the end of the 15th century, when the Turks had practically closed the overland route through Syria (Moreland 1920: 200), trade with Europe became heavily dependent on Aden. At the eastern end, Canton was replaced by Zayton (Ch'uan-chou, situated on the Taiwan Strait) as the main port of China, where a sizeable and influential Muslim trading community composed mostly of merchants from the northern side of the Persian Gulf maintained links with ports on the coast of western India and 'Bengal'.

The first half of the 15th century (between 1404 and 1433) saw mammoth maritime expeditions of the Chinese across the Indian Ocean under the Muslim admiral Zheng He ('Cheng Ho'). These expeditions, actually state-sponsored trading missions with the auxilliary function of enhancing the prestige of Emperor Yung-lo, may have led to disruption of regular trade – as numerous prohibitions against foreign trading attest (Digby 1982c: 138). After the seventh voyage returned home in 1434, the Ming emperors gradually closed Chinese ports for foreign visitors and prohibited overseas trade of Chinese merchants. Consequently, the role of the large Chinese junks as the principal means of maritime transportation between the Chinese ports, Southeast Asia and south India eventually ceased. McPherson (1998: 112) has identified the following reasons behind the move: xenophobia, the expulsion of the Chinese army from Vietnam in 1427, suspicion of the loyalty of southern Chinese merchants, and poor returns on maritime trade. However, a considerable amount of contemporary Chinese porcelain found in India, 'Bengal', the Maldives and the Middle Eastern countries indicate that the state-imposed prohibition could not stop smuggling of merchandise by Chinese merchants via the Philippines, Tongking and Malacca.

With the decline of the Chinese imperial interest in maritime trade, the hub of transshipment shifted eastward again – this time to Malacca. It is possible that Chinese support extended through admiral Cheng Ho played decisive role in establishing a Muslim ruler (Sultan Iskandar) at the Southeast Asian entrepot. Changes had taken place at the Arabian Sea as well. Ports in Gujarat, such as Surat, Broach, Cambay and Diū, turned into the hub of maritime activities in the Arabian Sea, because West Asian merchant found it more convenient to halt there before the onward journey to Malacca. The reason is well-explained by Tome Pires (1967: 269):

> Because those from Cairo and Mecca and Aden cannot reach Malacca in a single monsoon, as well as Parsees and those from Ormuz, and *Rumes*, Turks and similar peoples such as Armenians, at their own time they go to the kingdom of Gujarat, bringing large quantities of valuable merchandise; and they go to the kingdom of Gujarat to take up their companies in the said ships of that land, and they take the said companies in large numbers.

The Gujarati merchants had turned out to be the most dominant in the trade networks of the Bay of Bengal as they controlled all direct sea routes. They had substantial control over those of East Africa and the Middle East as well. Since our informant is Tome Pires, we can believe that the change had taken place by the early 16th century AD. However, they may have assumed the pre-eminent position a century earlier because it is generally believed that the presence of West Asian Muslims in South Asian trade gradually diminished from the 13th century AD, as South Asian Muslim merchants increasingly took over the shipping of commodities from the east.

The Asian maritime trade witnessed another change that began with Vasco da Gama's "discovery" of the maritime trade route to south India in 1498. Subsequently, with the capture of Diū in 1508, Goa in 1510 (afterwards the Portuguese capital of their far-flung commercial empire) and Malacca in 1511, the Portuguese emerged as a key player in pre-modern Asian maritime trade. The most distinguishing feature of their activities in the 16th century AD was a "combination of religion with commercial motives" (Moreland 1920: 200). The effect of Portuguese involvement does not lie within the scope of this research. Nevertheless, it is important to note, as we verge at the end of our period of study, that the entry of the Portuguese "does not mark the beginning of a new epoch in the commercial and political history of the area" (McPherson 1998: 138). As recent research has revealed, "the Portuguese compet[ed] with only qualified success for a share of the country's trade and indeed reach[ed] accommodations with other holders of power as to how large that share should be" (Digby 1982c: 150). As McPherson (1998: 165) observes, even with control over Hormuz and Diū, their "exercise of power was restrained by the knowledge that their prosperity depended on the access to hinterland markets which were controlled by strong Muslim dynasties".

The Portuguese first appeared in 'Bengal' in 1518, when Joao Coelho landed in Caṭṭagrāma as a passenger on a Moorish boat. By that time, 'Bengal' was well entrenched in its trade with Malacca and its textiles had a firmly established market in Southeast Asia. In the Arabian Sea, Bengal's trade had reached Hormuz and Aden. After the Gujaratis, the Bengali merchants, along with those from the Malabar and the Coromandel Coasts, were the lesser partners in the vast network of trade in the Bay of Bengal. Compared to the previous era, the medieval period was one of revival of Bengal's fortune in maritime trade. The trade routes identified during the medieval period further confirm this view.

Dasgupta (1973: 142-143) finds a direct relation between the revival of Bengal's fortune and the spread of Islam. He argues,

> ... the spread of Islam along the sea-routes of Asia had a direct relation with the revival of Bengal's commerce and overseas contacts in the 14th century. The eastward spread of Islam in the 13th and 14th centuries worked as a stimulant of Asia's maritime commerce. Consequently, the isolation of Bengal was ended and once again the country was linked up with the major east-west sea-route passing through western Indonesia.

The stimulation of Asian maritime commerce and revival of Bengal's fortune in maritime trade could happen not so much because Islam had created social attitudes conducive to trade. Rather, Islam *reflected* social attitudes within a fraternity that was conducive to creating trade networks. Consequently, there prevailed a "remarkable uniformity ... in nautical matters right round the shores of India Ocean" (Moreland 1920: 199).

The fraternity in South Asia was not only sizeable in numerical terms, but also possessed a long history of mercantile acumen. "The Turkish Muslim invasion led to the conversion of large numbers of merchants and artisans, particularly in the ports of Gujarat and Bengal" (McPherson 1998: 109). Among the large numbers of Muslims engaged in maritime trade eastward from India into insular Southeast Asia, "the greater number were from maritime mercantile areas of South Asia, and were drawn from convert communities whose ancestors, as Hindus or Buddhists, had long been engaged in commerce between the Middle East and South and South East Asia" (*ibid.*: 109-110). Kiribamune (1990: 188) echoes a similar view. "Muslim rule extended throughout northern India and the Deccan by the middle of the 14th century and many Gujerati and Bengali merchants seem to have embraced Islam. This in turn led to strengthening of the Muslim trading communities of the Coromandel and Malabar Coasts" (*ibid.*). Instead resistence as in the early medieval period, the converted merchants of 'Bengal' must have found easy access to the maritime trade network that the Muslim merchants had already established by then.

****

We may sum up our findings in this chapter by noting that the following maritime trade routes connected 'Bengal' with a number of overseas destinations during four successive periods. It should be evident that all the nodal points in 'Bengal' in the routes given below served as feeder ports.

Early Historic Period:

1. Sri Lanka-South India-Orissa-Bengal-Southeast Asia
2. Tāmralipti-Sri Lanka
3. Tāmralipti/Gaṅgābandar-Chu-li (Takkola)-Fu-nan-Suvaṇṇa-bhūmi.

Late Historic Period:

1. Tāmralipti-Sri Lanka
2. Tāmralipti-Ka-cha (Kedah)
3. Harikela-Sri Lanka
4. Harikela-Lang-chia (Pegu or Lower Burma)-Kedah.

Early Medieval Period:

1. Basra-Samandar (Caṭṭagrāma)
2. Samandar-Ka-cha-Śrīvijaya.

Medieval Period:

1. Sonārgāon-Sumatra
2. Caṭṭagrāma-Sri Lanka
3. Caṭṭagrāma-Coromandel Coast
4. Caṭṭagrāma-Maldives
5. Shātijām-Cochin-Calicut-Goa-Chaul-Dhabol-Cambay-Diū
6. Shātijām-Aden-Jeddah-Sheher (Shihr)-Muscat-Hormuz
7. Caṭṭagrāma-Mrohaung-Cosmin-Martaban-Tenasserim
8. Caṭṭagrāma-Malacca-Pasé
9. Sātgāon-Malacca-Pasé
10. Sātgāon-Sri Lanka-Malabar-Konkan.

Seven

Merchants and Mercantile Operative Milieu

As discussed in the Introduction, maritime trade is a "reciprocal traffic, exchange, or movement of materials or goods through peaceful human agency" (Renfrew 1969: 152) by means of maritime mode of transportation. What is important in Renfrew's definition is the human agency. However, detailed is any discussion and analysis of the determinants of maritime trade, i.e., ports, commodities in relation with the hinterlands, media of exchange, ships and shipbuilding, navigational techniques and trade routes, they remain disparate and disfunctional till the human agency is brought in. Who were the maritime merchants in 'Bengal' during the time frame of this investigation? What was the nature of mercantile operative milieu? It is only when we know the answer to these questions that we may begin to perceive the salient characteristics of the maritime trade in pre-modern 'Bengal' – not as an un-varying mechanical quantum but as pulsations of flux operating within the parameters set by all the determinants.

As Chakravarti (2001: 13) shows, "the trader functions as a vital link between the actual producer and the actual consumer/user of a product. He [sic.] is, strictly speaking, neither a direct producer nor a consumer and engages in trade for profit". Unfortunately, very little is known regarding the role of the merchant in 'Bengal' prior to the mid-16th century AD. A crucial thesis, which J. C. van Leur builds in his seminal work *Indonesian Trade and Society* (1955), is that "for at least two thousand years up to and into the seventeenth century", two factors always determined the patterns of early Asian trade – "the wealthy money-holders on the one hand and the travelling peddlers on the other" (Van Leur 1955: 60). The wealthy money-holders were the monarchical or aristocratic regimes that not only levied tolls on trade but also carried on trade and shipping of their own, regulated prices, claimed the right to pre-emption and acted as the financiers of the trade. Allied to them, there was often "an urban patriciate on a level with the politically dominant group as far as the size of possessions was concerned" (*ibid.*: 66). So far as international trade was concerned, the two above-mentioned groups performed as 'passive' partners, i.e., they were its financiers and they invested occasionally in *commenda* and bottomry (*ibid.*: 67).

> The 'active' ones were the handicraft traders undertaking journeys with *commenda* money or *commenda* merchandise, and, alongside them, the independent handicraft traders, among them pedlars travelling with packs on their backs, journeying individually or in company as pedlar caravans. Shipping, too, manifested the same forms, the commander and crew carrying on trade on their own account alongside the transport of people and goods (*ibid.*: 67).

Arguing against Van Leur's unchanging character of Asian traders, Ashin Dasgupta (2001: 32) convincingly shows that in the early 17th century, maritime merchants at Surat were anything but peddlers. Further challenging the hackneyed image of the petty peddler in early South Asian trade, Ranabir Chakravarti (2001: 31) shows that "[t]he immense wealth of the *seṭṭhī*, [or *śreṣṭhī*, very rich merchant or financier], the influence exerted by the *rājaśreṣṭhī* [royal merchant] and the impressive financial gains made by the *nauvittikas* [ship-owning merchants] are well documented and one cannot reduce them to the position of trivial peddlers".

The pre-modern South Asian merchant, as a category, has also suffered from a blanket generalisation in the hands of conventional historiography of early South Asian trade. It is important to re-examine early literary texts with care, as Chakravarti (*ibid.*: 25) has done, to identify different categories and levels in addition to the three mentioned above. These were *vaṇik* (petty merchant), *vaidehaka* (petty merchants), *bānjārā* (itinerant pedlar), *āpaṇika* (shopkeeper engaged in retail trader), *sārthavāha* (caravan trader) etc. One can add another category, *sādhu* or *sāhā* (a merchant), from current titles among traders in 'Bengal' (Chakravarti and Sinha 1985: 46).

To these observations, it is necessary to add that of Chaudhuri (1985: 16), who maintains, "in Asia commercial traffic was in the hands of highly skilled professional merchants, who operated as private individuals with little substantive state support". This was unlike Christian Mediterranean Italian City states, such as Genoa and Venice (and later replicated in Seville, Lisbon, Amsterdam and London) where the state provided substantive support. However, there were exceptions too because sometimes the ruling elite participated in "shorter commercial voyages when opportunities for making profits were clearly visible. Ships were fitted out either in their names or often in partnership with a wealthy and prominent merchant" (*ibid.*). Taking up a similar position with Dasgupta, Chakravarti and Chaudhuri, this chapter attempts to break away from the hackneyed image of the petty peddler and proceeds to identify different categories of merchants in 'Bengal' and their modes of operation.

The transaction of the merchant needs to be examined in his/her operative milieu, i.e., the market and the mechanism of trade. As Neale (1957: 357-358) reminds us, from the point of view of an economist, the market is a specific institution with a mechanism that produces prices. "The function of market prices is to regulate the supply of goods in relation to the demand, and to channel the demand for goods in relation to the available supply. Hence the market may be called a supply-demand-price mechanism" (*ibid.*: 365). Exchange in a self-regulating market system is determined by the above mechanism. Furthermore, it is not imperative for a market to be physically located at a given place. However, from the point of view of a historian or an anthropologist, the market is often the 'market place', i.e., a meeting place with a specific location where goods are transferred from one set of hands to another. Moreover, the supply-demand-price mechanism is not imperative in a market place. The latter has nothing in common with a self-regulating market, "except that goods move from person to person" (*ibid.*: 365-366). Most importantly, self-regulating market systems have existed "in a workable approximation to the ideal type during the latter part of the 19th and the early part of the 20th centuries" (*ibid.*: 370). In order to prove the substantial existence of a pre-modern market place, we will use the term 'exchange centres' and bear in mind that these did not necessarily operate within a self-regulating market system.

In our inquiry, we also need to guard against the tendency of lumping together varied types of exchange centres. Chakravarti (2001: 24) goes back to ancient literary texts to show that a wide spectrum of such physical locations existed all over South Asia. At one end were rural level exchange centres, which were known as *haṭṭa/haṭṭika* and *yātrā* (*hāṭ* and *melā*, respectively, in contemporary Bangladesh). At the other end were large exchange centres in urban locations (*nagara/pura*) and those in or close to harbours (*velākula*). Since the 5th-4th centuries BC, there also appeared the *puṭabhedana*, i.e., marketplaces where exchangeable commodities could be stored. From the post-Gupta onwards (600-1300 AD), there also appeared the intermediate category of exchange centres known as *maṇḍapikā*, *peṇṭhā* and *nagaram*, which served to link the rural-level and urban-level categories.

The operation of any merchant implicitly implies a mechanism of trade, i.e., instruments and personnel involved in delivery of the commodity from the producer to the merchant and from the merchant to the consumer. How was the commodity produced? How was it transported to the exchange centres? How many stages did it cross before it reached the maritime merchant? How did the merchant arrange his/her finance? A clear picture of the operation of a merchant can emerge when we can formulate the mechanism of trade. Unfortunately it is not always possible to make a complete formulation because data from pre-modern 'Bengal' is extremely sparse.

Having thus detailed the framework of our examination, we will now proceed to investigate the merchants and their operative milieu (exchange centres and mechanism of trade) during the time frame of this research. The analysis will be presented chronologically which, it needs to be stressed, does not imply linear development.

EARLY HISTORIC PERIOD

The Pre-Maurya Era (c. 600 BC to 325 BC)

Absence of data constrains us to ascertain who may have been the merchants and what may have been the operative milieu in 'Bengal' during this era. It may be suggested that inter-tribal barters took place in great fairs, festivities and feasts. The *Periplus* (§ 65) informs us about such an annual festival of an ethnic community called Besatæ (a Tibeto-Burman tribe allied to the Kiratas, Kuki-Chin, Naga and Garo), who met "in a place between their own country and the land of This" (possibly Gangtok in Sikkim) (Schoff 1995: 48-49; 278-79). It may not be illogical to assume that the Besatae people held similar festivals in the early historic times in other places between their own land (i.e., what today is known as Assam, Meghalaya and Sylhet-Mymansingh region) and Puṇḍravardhana-Vaṅga regions of 'Bengal'.

If, following Ray's (1993: 31) argument, we may believe that the people of the Nicobar Islands belonged to the same Negrito stock as those who lived in 'Bengal' in the early historic time, then we have at hand a 'living' example of how trade may have actually been conducted during this period in the following excerpt of I-Tsing's account of his voyage to South Asia in the 7th century AD.

> When the natives saw our vessel coming, they eagerly embarked in little boats, their number being fully a hundred. They all brought cocoa-nuts, bananas, and things made of rattan-cane and bamboos, and wished to exchange them. What they are anxious to get is iron only; for a piece of iron as large as two fingers, one gets from them five to ten cocoa-nuts (Takakusu, 1896: xxx).

The findings from archaeological excavations at 32 known early historic sites in West Bengal and Bangladesh prove that by the second half of the 4th century BC the people of Vaṅga, Puṇḍra, Bajja and Subbha/Suhma were well-acquainted with sedentary cultivation as well as a number of crafts based on which they could manufacture iron and copper products and earthen wares (red-slipped, black-slipped and coarse grey wares). To this we may add the evidence of the *Mahābhārata*, which speaks of the kingdoms and tribes of the Eastern Regions paying tributes to Bhima. The items included in the list of tribute imply the existence of craft specialisation related to sandalwood, aloes, textiles, gems, pearls, valuable corals, blankets, gold and silver (*Mahābhārata*, Sabhā Parva, Section XXIX; Ganguli 1990: 61-62). Each of these crafts implies the existence of other levels of craft production. For example, various types of metallic weapons that must have been manufactured for the armies of the kingdoms and tribes of the Eastern Region imply the existence of a whole range of craft specialisation related to metallurgy and black-smithy.

Corals and pearls (cited above), harpoon with incised boat-motif, fishhooks (cited in Table 1.1 in Chapter One) and dugouts (discussed in Chapter Four) all imply existence of various crafts related to maritime activities. Gems, gold and silver suggest the existence of jewelry-related crafts. It would be reasonable to assume that the manufacturing centres where the craftsmen operated were located in some of the early historic sites noted above. We may believe that a society that has a range of specialized craftsman would also have a group of traders to facilitate exchange in the manner of the Tibeto-Burman and Negrito peoples described above.

Although our state of current knowledge does not permit us to make further deductions, we may infer that some of the traders mentioned above must have been involved in maritime trade because the existence of coastal voyages has already been established by the 5th century BC. Further, the distribution pattern of the early historic sites in West Bengal and Bangladesh show that half (i.e. 16 out of 32) of are located near the seacoast and along the courses of the Rūpnārāyaṇ and the Huglī (in Medinīpur and 24-Parganas districts, respectively), while others are spread inland. This is definitely indicative of the importance of maritime activities in the life of the people who inhabited the sites. The significance is further accentuated when one is reminded that of the eighty-eight Chalcolithic sites identified in the entire region of 'Bengal', only seven are located in the coastal region, along the lower Rūpnārāyaṇ valley (Ray 1998: 28). Thus, one notes a clear shift to coastal regions from after the 6th century BC. The implication, once again, is that maritime activities must have gained considerable importance during this time. In these mature conditions, there can be little doubt that maritime traders must have appeared on the scene. However, we have to wait for further research before we can suggest a clearer picture.

The Maurya Era (c. 324 to 187 BC)

By the 4th century BC, Magadha had risen as the dominant state and in the fourth quarter of the 4th century BC, Candragupta Maurya had established the first South Asian imperial dynasty of the Mauryas. Mahāsthān stone inscription and the discovery of Northern Black Polished Ware (henceforth referred to NBPW) and imperial series of punch-marked coins at Tamluk, Chandraketugarh, Bāngarh, Mahāsthāngarh and Wārī-Baṭeśwar indicate that the authority of the Mauryas was acknowledged in northern and deltaic 'Bengal' at least by the 3rd century BC if not earlier.

The distribution pattern of NBPW indicates that the influence of the second urbanization in South Asian history (alternatively called the Gaṅgā valley civilisation) reached Vaṅga, Rāḍha Suhma and Puṇḍra by the late 4th century BC. As a consequence, flourishing urban centers such as Puṇḍranagara, Gaṅgābandar and Tāmralipti developed in the above regions. Archaeological evidences discussed earlier in Chapters One and Two clearly point to the existence of craft industries manufacturing terracotta and semi-precious stone beads, Rouletted Wares, NBPW, stamped wares etc. It is also clear from the preceding chapters that by the 3rd century BC, the maritime ports of Tāmralipti, Gaṅgābandar and Wārī-Baṭeśwar had already been integrated into the Indian Ocean trade network. Hence there can remain little doubt that craft specialisation, trade and markets had grown at the above-mentioned urban centres. Since these ports served, among other hinterlands, the middle Gaṅgā valley (as established in Chapter Two), it can also be reasonably assumed that there existed close economic contacts between the above ports and the urban centres of the middle Gaṅgā valley. In such a context it is but reasonable to posit that the economic milieu, as projected in Buddhist canonical literature and Kauṭīlya's *Arthaśāstra*, were not too distant from that of Tāmralipti, Gaṅgābandar and Wārī-Baṭeśwar.

One receives an impression of a lively merchant community from Buddhist canonical literature in Pāli. The merchants are mostly referred to as *vāṇijja* and *vesso* in the *Majjhimanikāya* II (Chalmers 1898: 150, 232). Others were known as the *apaṇika* (shopkeeper), the *krayavikrayika* (retail dealer) and the *vasanika* (investor of money) (Thapar 1984: 100-101). Loan (Pāli *iṇa*, Sanskrit, *ṛṇa*) may have been indispensable for these merchants because the *Dīghanikāya* (Davids and Carpenter 1890: 71-72) makes such indications. Mercantile venture must have been highly profitable since the *Majjhimanikāya* (II, Chalmers 1898: 198) considers trading (*vaṇijjā*) to be "an occupation where there is not a great deal to do", and one that involved "few duties, a small administration, [and] small problems". If a venture failed, it bore "small fruit" but if it succeeded, bore "great fruit" (Horner 1957: 387-388). The *Aṅguttaranikāya* (Woodward 1936: 59-60) helps us get an idea of the range of financial return these petty traders and merchants may have generated from their business ventures. A clever and energetic trader, if luck was favourable, could have expected from half a *kāhāpaṇa* (Sanskrit *kārṣāpaṇa*, a silver coin of 32 *ratis*) to fifty *kāhāpaṇas* a day. Merchants with great wealth could expect one hundred *kāhāpaṇas* to a thousand *kāhāpaṇas* a day.

That a very complex structure of economic organisation had grown during the Maurya era is amply proven by the existence of guilds (*śreṇīs*). These were industrial and mercantile bodies under which many of the professions were organised. The guilds also functioned as banks. Investments were made in these institutions, which generated favourable profit. The guilds in turn invested in business ventures including overseas trade. The guilds were considerably important as the ruler also respected the opinion of the guild-heads (Chopra *et al.* 1974: 128).

Sanskrit Buddhist literature and the *Jātakas* give a list of eighteen guilds, such as that of the gold-smiths (*sauvarṇikas-hiraṇyakas*), jewel splenderers (*mani-prastarakas*), perfumers (*gandhikas*), oil millers (*tailikas*), makers of pots for storing ghee (*ghritakundikas*), makers of molasses (*golikas*), makers of cotton cloth (*karpasikas*), makers of candied sugar (*khand-akarakas*), sweetmeat confectioners (*modaka-karakas*), wheat-flour dealers (*samita-karakas*), fruit-dealers (*phala-vanijas*), dealers in roots (*mulevanijas*), dealers in perfumed oil (*gandhatailikas*) and others. One need not accept the 'eighteen guilds' as constant because its number and organisational structure varied from region to region (*ibid.*: 127). As we shall observe later, in the early medieval period many of these guilds were transformed into rigid occupational castes.

The guilds were headed by *jethakas* or *mukhyas*, who had to be obeyed by the members and were responsible for them. A small council of senior members assisted him. Kauṭīlya's reference to *śreṇī-bala* indicates that the guilds maintained their private armies. In order to keep these armies under control, he also suggests that they were provided with land that was constantly threatened by an external enemy (Lahiri 1972: 67). Kauṭīlya's *Arthaśāstra* contains numerous references to guilds relating to their responsibilities and privileges (including executive and judicial powers) and also specifies punishment should there be an infringement. Judging by his reference to the Superintendent of Accounts who was to regularly register various professions and corporations and three commissioners who were to receive deposit of guilds (*ibid.*), it appears that the state attempted to maintain considerable supervision over the guilds.

The *Arthaśāstra* insists that commodities should not be sold at their production centres and prescribes "fines for purchasing metals etc. directly from mines, or flowers, fruits etc. directly from the gardens, or grains directly from the fields" (2.22.9-13; Kangle 1963: 167-168). Hence, it is arguable that commodities would be available at large exchange centres in urban locations at Tamluk, Chandraketugarh, Wārī-Baṭeśwar, Mahāsthāngarh, Bāngarh and Maṅgalkoṭa. The *Arthaśāstra* stipulates that goods produced by state-managed industries (such as forest products, metal products or textiles) were to be sold in one place (2.16.4; *ibid.*: 146), which possibly implies an exchange centre situated at the capital where all state-run stores may also have been located.

It may not be too difficult to reconstruct a sketch of the maritime merchants and their operative milieu from the Jātaka tales. Consider, for example, the case of Prince Mahājanaka as described in Mahājanaka Jātaka (Book XXII, No. 539; Cowell 1957, VI: 19-37). Having been deposed from his rightful inheritance to the throne because of fratricide committed by his uncle, the prince, at the age of sixteen, decided to "go to Suvaṇṇabhūmi on a merchant venture, get riches there and then seize his father's kingdom". After persuading his mother to give him half the number of jewels she had smuggled out from Mithilā and "having got together his stock-in-trade he put it on board a ship with some merchants bound for Suvaṇṇabhūmi, ...". Clearly, the decision of the prince to embark on "a merchant venture" in order to seize his father's kingdom appears striking. A similar striking situation is also to be seen in the Śaṅkha Jātaka (Book X, No. 442; Cowell 1957, IV: 9-13), where a pious Brāhmīn named Śaṅkha, after exhausting his wealth on account of almsgiving, sets sail for the Gold Country to earn more in order to continue his virtuous acts. Such examples of members of the priestly class and the royalty engaging in maritime trade clearly indicate social mobility and absence of rigid classes. Similar to situations where rich landowners could invest in trade, members of royalty and priestly classes could also occasionally set off on a maritime voyage for trade. These indicators speak not only of lucrative prospects (notwithstanding the dangers involved) in maritime trade but also of mobility in a society burdened with a lesser degree of caste-bound rigidity. More importantly, as Ray (1998: 36) points out, "maritime ventures (..) involved a range of groups in society at different hierarchical level".

The manner in which Prince Mahājanaka raises his capital also deserves attention because he does it by selling half of his mother's jewels. Investing capital in trade by selling one's possessions may have been a common practice as well. Finally, it is worth noting that his commodity for trade appears to have been no more than a bundle (he "got together his stock-in-trade" and "put it on board a ship"). It may not therefore be far fetched to deduce that Mahājanaka's stock-in-trade was low volume and high value goods, such as semi-precious stone beads and ceramic wares. The other merchants "bound for Suvaṇṇabhūmi" also appear to have been carrying similar bundles since the prince is described to have put his commodities together with theirs. These indicators all point to petty traders (*vaṇija*). However, such does not appear to be the case with Śaṅkha because there is no mention of "some merchants or stock-in-trade". He does not appear to have possessed much wealth for he is reported to journey by foot all the way from Benares. When he reached the harbour, the Brāhmīn simply took a ship and sailed. In such a case, it would possibly be assumed by contemporary readers that he borrowed his capital from a guild or a *vasanika* – a considerable sum – and sailed, if not alone in a ship entirely hired by him, at least in some condition of affluence. Surely Śaṅkha was not a petty trader.

At this point we may as well try to examine a nagging question: how many of the traders that we have been discussing were from Puṇḍravardhana, Rāḍha, Suhma and Vaṅga? According to Ray (1994: 571-572) it seems that "the region and its people did not in those times have a very big share in the trade and commerce of north India". He may be quite correct. As the Jātaka tales indicate, neither Prince Mahājanaka nor the Brāhmīn Śaṅkha was from 'Bengal'.

The most striking character of trade in the Maurya era appears to be state control – if the authority of the *Arthaśāstra* is to be trusted as reflecting an accurate picture of trade related activities in Puṇḍravardhana, Rāḍha, Suhma and south-western Vaṅga where the authority of the Mauryas was acknowledged. However, given the likelihood that these territories were peripheral to the Maurya Empire and that the *Arthaśāstra* possibly reflects an ideal condition (which is also clear in the voice of the author making suggestions in all his formulations), it is best to see the following references to Kauṭīlya's text as possibilities and not actualities.

At the very outset, three important indicators need to be borne in mind. Firstly, as Thapar (1961: 93) shows, "the Mauryan period was one of an expanding economy". Secondly, agricultural sector was the backbone of Maurya economy. Although *vanijya* (trade) is recognised in the *Arthaśāstra* (1.4.1) as one of the three principal vocations, the most important of the three is *kṛsi* or agriculture (the other vocation being *pasupālya* or cattle-tending) (Kangle 1963: 10 and 1965: 166-167). Thirdly, Kauṭīlya believed that the land-route is to be preferred to a water-route, arguing, "the former is open in all seasons and is fraught with comparatively fewer danger, which, moreover, can be easily overcome" (7.12.18-20; Kangle 1963: 416). Hence, when referring to the *Arthaśāstra* as a source-material, one needs to bear in mind that it was the product of a land-bound culture, which suspected maritime trade as unsafe. If trade was important for Kauṭīlya, it was because of the additional revenue it fetched over and above the agricultural sector (in which the share of the king was ¼ or more). However, revenue from overland trade must have been significantly more than maritime trade.

The most important state official whose role needs to be examined for an understanding of state control in maritime trade is the *paṇyādhyakṣa* 'the superintendent of trade'. The *Arthaśāstra* suggests that "all trade is to be under state control" with him in charge. He is given the authority to fix prices of various commodities after taking all factors related to investment into consideration (4.2.36; *ibid.*: 303) and allowing ten percent profit on foreign goods (4.2.28-30; *ibid.*). He is even authorized to centralize sale of a commodity should there be a glut of that commodity (4.2.33-35; *ibid.*). According to Kangle (1965: 176), "this means that the entire supply [was] purchased and its sale carried out through the agency of the state at the fixed price". However, this is to be seen as an extreme measure in the event of a glut of a particular commodity. Apart from private traders, the state, through the *paṇyādhyakṣa*, was also to engage in trade quite extensively because this was seen as a source of revenue (2.16-1-3; Kangle 1963: 145). The state could have directly engaged in import and export of commodities, again under the *paṇyādhyakṣa* (2.16.11-13 and 2.16.18; *ibid.*: 146-147). Interestingly, Kauṭīlya also saw the possibility of barter for the *paṇyādhyakṣa*, who is advised to investigate into such possibilities (2.16.24; *ibid.*: 148). There was also to be a *saṁsthādhyakṣa*, 'the superintendent of markets', whose duty was to ensure that traders and artisans refrained from fraudulent practices in weight or quality (4.2.1-20; *ibid.*: 300-302).

It appears from evidence provided by Strabo (XV, 46) that shipbuilding was a state monopoly because he says, "shipbuilders receive wages and provisions from the king for whom they work alone (McCrindle 1979: 53). However, Kauṭīlya maintains that merchants and fishermen could own their own vessels. All state-owned maritime vessels would have been maintained under the *navādhyakṣa* (the superintendent of ships). Merchants as well as fishermen could hire these vessels for their use (2.28.3-4 and 2.28.21; Kangle 1963: 186, 189). Foreign ships arriving with merchants and their commodities at the three ports would have to pay duty because Kauṭīlya stipulates, "[w]hen goods are brought along water-ways, they are to pay the duty and other charges at the ports" (2.28.3; Kangle 1965: 179). These ports must also have had a customhouse with a *śulkādhyakṣa*, 'the superintendent of custom' and four or five subordinate officials because the *Arthaśāstra* (2. 21.1-2; Kangle 1963: 162) suggests such a measure. He would have collected *praveśya* and *niṣkrāmya śulka* (import and export duties) from all imported and exported commodities.

In detailing the manner in which duties were to be collected, Kauṭīlya speaks only of merchants "who would mostly be coming in caravans" (Kangle 1965: 178). Nevertheless, the same mechanism can have been applicable for maritime merchants as well. First of all, they were required to obtain an entry permit at the port (2.21.24-26; Kangle 1963: 165). The *Arthaśāstra* warns the merchants not to make false declarations about their commodities, or try to bypass the customhouse (2.21.3-6; *ibid.*: 162-163). This obviously indicates, goods were occasionally smuggled. The duty imposed varied from one-sixth to one-twenty-fifth of the value of the commodity (2.22.3-8; *ibid.*: 166-167). Almost every commodity was dutiable – "from flowers, vegetables, fruits etc. on the one hand to diamonds, pearls and other precious stones on the other" (2.22.4-7; *ibid.*: 166-167; Kangle 1965: 178). However, in cases where merchandise was spoilt or damaged by water, duty was either halved or waived completely (2.28.8; Kangle 1963: 187). Our shrewd author must have been aware that prices of commodities may rise due to heavy demand and competition among native traders. In such a case, he stipulates, "the state is to receive the excess over the declared price along with the duty" (2.21.7-9; *ibid.*: 167).

However, one can hardly overlook that the Jātaka tales present a remarkably different milieu from that which one can read in Kauṭīlya. Merchants are shown "to journey about trading with, five hundred carts, travelling now from east to west and now from west to east" (as in Apaṇṇaka Jātaka, Book I, No. 1; Cowell 1957, I: 4), but there is not the slightest indication of any state official described in the *Arthaśāstra*. Similarly, one comes across detailed accounts of how merchants with their caravans fell prey to goblins' tricks and perished (Apaṇṇaka Jātaka, Book I, No. 1; *ibid.*: 1-8), journeyed across sandy wilderness and suffered for want of water (Vaṇṇupatha Jātaka, Book I, No. 2; *ibid.*: 10) and hired wood-cutters to lead them through forests infested with robbers (Khurappa Jātaka, Book II, No. 265; Cowell 1957, II: 232) but there is absolutely nothing about all the king's men one would logically expect to encounter – having read Kauṭīlya.

The Jātaka stories indicate absence of state control in other domains of trade as well. Consider, for example, that in the Taṇḍulanāli Jātaka (Book I, No. 5; Cowell 1957, I: 22), the king's valuer decides the price of 500 horses offered to the king for sale by a horse-dealer from the North Country. In the Makasa Jātaka (Book I, No. 44; *ibid.*: 116), a trader goes directly to a carpenter. Although not clearly stated, it is implied that the trader's objective for the visit was for procuring manufactured goods (in this case, furniture). In the Guttila Jātaka (Book II, No. 243; Cowell 1957, II: 172), when traders from Benares arrive at Ujjeni for trade, they club together and procure their required commodities. In the Sussondī Jātaka (Book V, No. 360; Cowell 1957, III: 124), a minstrel requests some merchants of Bharukacca, who were about to set sail for the Golden Land, to be pardoned from paying his passage money and promises to act as their minstrel during the trip. Akataññu Jātaka (Book I, No. 90; Cowell 1957, I: 220-221) clearly shows that trans-border overland trade was conducted with the help of merchants, who may have never met personally, acting as each other's correspondent. A merchant would send his/her caravan of carts loaded with goods attended by his staff to his correspondent in a neighbouring kingdom. The latter would barter the merchandise and hand over to the attending staff the goods received in exchange.

As Ray (1998: 40) correctly points out, "there is no evidence to suggest that the ruling dynasties of the early historic period maintained an elaborate bureaucratic infrastructure to monitor and control trade". It is also important to remember that Puṇḍravardhana, Rāḍha, Suhma and Vaṅga were peripheral territories in the Maurya Empire. Thus it is possible that the Maurya state could never fully actualize Kauṭīlya's rigid state control. Further, as Thapar (1961: 79) observes, "the picture presented by Kauṭīlya is that of the ideal state". It was an ideal, which monarchs sought to actualise to the degree of their authority. For example, one would hardly expect that maritime merchants would find it feasible to import a commodity form abroad entertaining all possible risks on the high seas for a profit of only ten-percent. "It is more probable" as Thapar (*ibid.*: 80) notes, "that the officers may have been bribed and the matter of profits privately settled between the superintendents and the merchant". On the other hand, the Jātakas may not also be taken as a comprehensive and 'authentic' documentation of life during the Maurya rule because its dating is not beyond question. Further, materials from varied times and places must have got rolled into these tales of religious edification. What may have existed was a system that was neither "predominantly under private control" as Ray (1998: 40) would have us believe, nor completely under state control as Kauṭīlya would want the Mauryas to practice. It was possibly a halfway house – betwixt and between the two.

The Post-Maurya Era (c. 186 BC to 320 AD)

As discussed earlier, a large number of terracotta plaques, seals and seal impressions, clay pots and sherds with Kharoshṭī-Brāhmī inscriptions have been discovered in lower West Bengal. Explaining the presence of Kharoshṭī-Brāhmī inscriptions in Vaṅga and Rāḍha, Mukherjee (1990: 14) argues with enough reason that they were introduced sometime between the late 1st and the 2nd century AD by a people from the northwestern region of South Asia (i.e., northwestern Pakistan, parts of Kashmir, Punjab, Himachal Pradesh and Hariyana in India today) who used the Kharoshṭī script and may have been related to the Kuṣāṇa ruling class. The Kharoshṭī using emigrants began to use the 'Mixed' Kharoshṭī-Brāhmī script in order to facilitate transactions with the local inhabitants of Vaṅga and Rāḍha, who used Brāhmī script during this era. As the distribution pattern of the Kharoshṭī-Brāhmī inscribed objects indicate, the settlements of the Kharoshṭī-using people were concentrated in Chandraketugarh (the emporium of Gaṅgā) and Tamluk (Tāmralipti). Their initial objective was trade but they gradually "became owners of vast agricultural lands, large-scale traders in corn and horses, and even rulers of the land, at least in the territory now included in the district of 24 Parganas (north)" (*ibid.*: 24).

Two of the Kharoshṭī-Brāhmī inscribed objects, both discovered at Chandraketugarh and dated to the 2nd century AD, speak of two wealthy grain-merchants named Devajñātamitra and Aja. The impression on the obverse of one of these (Asutosh Museum of Indian Art, Kolkata, Acc. No. T.4312) is in Brāhmī. The legend appears to be decorated with ears of paddy. It reads, in translation, as follows: "grains [of the value of] 90 *kārṣāpaṇas*". The impression of the reverse displays a vessel with stalks of grain, flanked by two auspicious symbols. A marginal legend, in translation, reads as follows: "[issued] by [the] wise [councilors] from Tirajachata". Another inscription incised on the edge reads: "of Devajñātamitra, the wealthy (or old, i.e., senior) carrier [of merchandise]" (*ibid.*: 48). The impression on the obverse of the other terracotta object (Asutosh Museum of Indian Art, Kolkata, Acc. No. 6) shows a Yupa-like device and an inscription, which reads: "grains [of the value of] 90 *kārṣāpaṇas*". One of the inscriptions on the reverse is not legible but the other can be read as follows: "of Aja, the wealthy (or old, i.e., senior) leader" (*ibid.*: 49). Mukherjee (*ibid.*: 48-49) shows that both the objects under review were sale and/or transport permits, each carrying "a royal seal, a seal of a local authority and the name of a trader". These merchants may have possessed their own means of transportation such as bullock-carts or riverine boats. This is indicated by a terracotta object (Asutosh Museum of Indian Art, Kolkata, Acc. No. 1035), which is believed to have been a trader's identification ticket. It displays a boat containing stalks of grain, a conch and taurine symbol. The Kharoshṭī-Brāhmī inscription, which the ticket bears, has been translated as follows: "a vessel containing grain" (*ibid.*: 44-45). It is possible to believe that the ticket was attached to a boat sealed with grains meant for merchants such as Devajñātamitra and Aja. Since the ticket was found at Bāngarh, it may be suggested the boat carrying consignments of grain was meant to be transported from Bāngarh (which may have been a regional exchange centre), where local agents of the merchants would have attached such tickets after loading the boat with grains. The find-spot of the ticket also indicates that Vaṅga and Rāḍha maintained trade links with Puṇḍravardhana. We may hence believe that local agents in regional exchange centres acted as representatives of affluent merchants who operated from large urban exchange centres.

The traders in Vaṅga and Rāḍha possibly operated under some form of organised structure. A terracotta object from the 3rd century AD that has been discovered at Chandraketugarh (Asutosh Museum of Indian Art, Kolkata, Acc. No. T 5140) indicates this. The obverse of the object shows the impression of a matrix with a boar (or a bull) and marginal legends. The legend on top can be read as "grains [of the value of] 90 *kārṣāpaṇas*" and that of the bottom as, "this is the eternally known [seal] of the persons having the grain [of wealth] as (their) conveyance" (*ibid.*: 54-55). Along with a taurine symbol, the name, 'Vamaka' has been stamped twice. The "persons" cited in the seal refer to an organised structure, possibly a guild, which existed during the Maurya era (and as will be shown later, even during the Gupta and the Pāla eras). It is possible that Vamaka was a trader and a member of the guild. The terracotta object serving as an identification ticket may have been attached to Vamaka's grains loaded in a bag or sack containing 90 *kārṣāpaṇas*. If this is acceptable, it may also be suggested that Vamaka paid some form of tax or membership fee to the guild. All these merchants not only traded grains and paddy but as shown in Chapter Two, horses and pottery as well.

A terracotta administrative seal of semi-circular shape with an oval-shaped flat top bears the following inscription: "from [*i.e.*, of] the Gaṇarājya" (*ibid.*: 48). The prefix *gaṇa* deserves special attention. As Lahiri (1972: 63) reminds us, the term is found in the *Ṛgveda* and in later times, often signified corporate bodies of merchants. Going by its use in the *Sūtra* literature, it is possible to believe that the term definitely signified any kind of corporate body – political, religious or industrial.

Having arrived at a picture of internal trade, we may now focus our attention on maritime trade. The first evidence that we may examine is a seal impression (c. 2nd century AD) that was discovered somewhere in the district of 24-Parganas (South). It shows a boat or a ship with two long masts, with a hanging ladder from one of these. The inscription on the seal has been translated thus: "[The seal of] Dhe(or Dhai) jula, (who is) being in water" (Mukherjee 1990: 61). The pictorial and written signs have been read to indicate that the person mentioned in the impression, Dhejula or Dhaijula, was connected with maritime trade in any of the following capacities: a seafarer, a manufacturer, an owner or a middleman in the shipping business. Although the seal impression is vague regarding the occupation of Dhejula or Dhaijula, three more terracotta objects that we have as evidence, are more specific.

One of the terracotta objects is a trader's identification ticket from the 3rd century AD that was discovered at Chandraketugarh (and is now held by the Department of Archaeology, West Bengal bearing Accession No. CKG184). It displays a masted ship flying a banner, a stalk of grain and a taurine symbol. The inscription in Kharoshṭī-Brāhmī has been translated as follows: "the journey to (or in) three directions of (i.e. by) Yasoda, who has earned food-wealth (i.e., whose wealth is earned by selling food)" (*ibid.*: 45). There can remain little doubt that Yasoda was a trader in food-grains. However, the ship fitted with a mast implies that he was a different type of trader from Devajñātamitra whose ticket displays a Yupa-like device. Whereas Devajñātamitra and Aja are described as "the wealthy (or old, i.e., senior) carrier [of merchandise]" and their merchandise possibly were transported in sacks containing "grains [of the value of] 90 *kārṣāpaṇas*", Yasoda's ship fitted with a mast may be read to imply that he was a trader who exported grains abroad by means of maritime vessels.

Two additional trader's identification tickets, both from the 3rd century AD, may further confirm the above. One of the tickets, found in Chandraketugarh area (and is now held by the Indian Museum, Kolkata bearing Accession No. 90/181), shows a sea-going vessel fitted with a mast flying a banner and carrying a basket with stalks of grain. The Kharoshṭī-Brāhmī inscription impressed on it has been rendered as "[the ship called] jaladhiśakra (lit. "Indra of the ocean") of [i.e., belonging to] Dvijanma, who is famous as very wealthy" cited earlier in Chapters Two and Four. We now have the name of a ship! Obviously Dvijanma, described as famous for his wealth, was a ship-owner. He may also have been a grain exporter like Yasoda, for his ship is shown carrying stalks of grain. If not, he was at least the owner of one or more grain-carrying ships. The second ticket was found at Chandraketugarh (and is now held by the Directorate of Archaeology, West Bengal bearing Accession No. CKG180/T.687). It too displays a ship fitted with a mast. A marginal legend in Kharoshṭī-Brāhmī has been rendered in English as follows: "of [the ship of the class of] trapyaka, belonging to (i.e., owned by) the power-conquering (i.e., powerful) Tasvodaja family" (*ibid.*: 47). Although the name of the ship is not mentioned, we now have a wealthy family of ship-owners named the Tasvodajas. Absence of grains in the ticket may imply that the family business of the powerful Tasvodajas rested entirely on hiring out ships.

We have definite evidence regarding the existence of exchange centres during this era from the *Periplus* (§ 63). The oft-quoted passage reads: "On its bank is a market-town which has the same name as the river, Ganges" (Schoff 1995: 47). Tāmralipti also could have been an exchange centre if we may take available archaeological evidences into account. We have no further details, but abundance of coins and other trade-related objects (NBPW, RW, semiprecious stone beads, glass beads etc.) discovered from Wārī-Baṭeśwar, Mahāsthāngarh, Bāngarh, Harinārāyaṇpur, Deulpota clearly indicates that there must have been many more exchange centres.

One may believe that the merchants in Rāḍha and Vaṅga paid some kind of tax or revenue to obtain permits from the state in order to engage in trade. If one is not stretching one's imagination too far, it may also be safe to believe that the traders were private operators, from whom the state levied revenues. The "office of receipts and expenditure" inscribed on a seal-impression from Chandraketugarh dated to the 2nd century AD (Mukherjee 1990: 50) might actually have been the royal treasury that collected these revenues. These assertions may be amply substantiated with the help of two sale and/or transport permits cited earlier that bear the names of Devajñātamitra and Aja. Devajñātamitra and Aja must have obtained these permits to transport grain carried in bags, each of which was worth 90 *kārṣāpaṇas*. All the evidences discussed above indicate that trade must have been predominantly under private control of merchants such as Devajñātamitra and Aja.

LATE HISTORIC PERIOD

The Gupta Era (c. 320 AD to the mid-6th century AD)

We hear the names of quite a few Gupta era merchants operating in 'Bengal'. Consider, for example, the four Dāmodarpur copperplate landgrants published by Mukherji and Maity (1967: 45-49, 61-64, 70-74). *Nagaraśreṣthī* Dhṛtipāla (the chief merchant of Koṭivarṣa), *sārthavāha* Bandhumitra (the leader of the caravan traders of the same city) and *prathamakulika* Dhṛtimitra (the chief artisan of the same city) are mentioned by name in two landgrants issued during the reign of Kumāragupta I in 444 AD and 448 AD. They may have been representatives of local guilds (*śreṇīs*) of merchants. Again, in the landgrant issued during the reign of Budhagupta (476-95 AD), *nagaraśreṣthī* Ribhupāla of Koṭivarṣa, *sārthavāha* Vasumitra and *prathamakulika* Varadatta of the same city. Another *nagaraśreṣthī* named Ribhupāla, along with *sārthavāha* Sthāṇudatta and *prathamakulika* Matidatta, are mentioned in the landgrant issued in 543 AD. If Kosambi's (1970: 197) argument that "sale of land for cash ... implies rich trade in the neighbourhood" is acceptable, then it is possible to believe that the Gupta copperplates, as records of sale transactions of land in exchange of gold coins, indicate the existence of a prosperous mercantile community.

There is very little information on the maritime merchants of 'Bengal' from the Gupta era. We have some more seal-impressions, all inscribed with Kharoshṭī-Brāhmī inscriptions, which definitely indicate that the Kharoshṭī-using mercantile community were present in the early 5th century AD. One of the seal impressions from Chandraketugarh, dated to the 4th century AD (preserved at the Asutosh Museum of Indian Art, Kolkata, Acc. No. T.8906) shows a yupa-like device and was cited earlier in Chapter Two. It bears traces of Brāhmī legend and a marginal inscription in Kharoshṭī-Brāhmī. The second is a seal-impression possibly from Chandraketugarh area, dated to the 4th century AD (held by the State Museum, Kolkata, Acc. No. 04-294), which shows a boat, a shield with crossed swords and a bird in the upper field and a Kharoshṭī-Brāhmī inscription, which, in translation, reads *Deava'ura* or *Dedhtha'ura* (Mukherjee 1990: 61). Another seal impression from Chandraketugarh (c. early 5th century AD and held by the Department of Archaeology, West Bengal, Acc. No. CKG181/T.732) shows a woman (possibly a deity) standing beside a seated man with an elephant head and holding a mace. A Kharoshṭī-Brāhmī inscription on the seal read "Laḍhapeya, the Sustaining Elephant" and a marginal legend in Brāhmī reads, "water was used by mixing with boiled rice" (*ibid.*: 49). Although these artifacts signify the presence of the Kharoshṭī-Brāhmī users in Gaṅgābandar during the Gupta rule, nevertheless, because the number of artifacts with Kharoshṭī-Brāhmī inscriptions found at Chandraketugarh dwindle to a noticeable degree from that of the Kuṣāṇa era, one is inclined to believe that their influence may have been on the decline. Finally, all their signs cease to exist after the 5th century AD. The reason behind this may be the rise of the Huns, who occupied Kabul and Persia sometime before 458 AD and towards the end of the 5th century, captured Punjab and established an independent Huna kingdom (Bhattacharjee 1979: 292-293). With the fall of the north-western part of South Asia, not only was the power-base of the Kharoshṭī-users lost but also the source of the supply of horses on which their fortunes in trade rested was snapped. Hence, emigrant traders must have left 'Bengal' by the end of the 5th century AD.

As for the exchange centres, it is possible that the city of Koṭivarṣa was one of the most prominent, if we may draw such an inference from the presence of *nagaraśreṣthīs*, *sārthavāhas* and *prathamakulikas* in the city (as mentioned in the copperplates cited above). Similar exchange centres may have existed in other administrative centres such as Puṇḍra-nagara (from where the Pāhāḍpur copperplate of 479 AD was issued), Pañcanagarī (from where the Baigrām copperplate of 448 AD was issued) and Krīpura (from where the Gunaighar copperplate of 507 AD was issued). As for exchange centres at the village level, we hear of one in the Dāmodarpur copperplate of the time of Kumāragupta I (448 AD). Line 10 of the inscription speaks of a *haṭṭa* lying to the west of the Airāvata-Gorājya village in the district of Koṭivarṣa (Mukherji and Maity 1967: 48-49). For maritime trade, the ports of Tāmralipti and Gaṅgābandar must have served as the two most important exchange centres.

In all probabilities, the merchant community paid *śulka* (custom duties and sale tax) (Maity 1975: 159; Chowdhury 1983: 191); in return they must have received security under a firm and stable administration because Fa-Hien testifies that the people enjoyed peace and freedom to a considerable extent, there was prosperity and the administration was relatively lenient (Legge 1886: 42-43). The merchants must have enjoyed considerable freedom, as may be evinced by the existence of powerful guilds. Furthermore, because the Guptas did not attempt to intervene in the market dynamics by exerting state control over the prices of commodities, the mercantile community enjoyed greater economic freedom than those of the Maurya age.

The guilds within which the merchants of the Gupta era operated were very powerful. Indeed, the economic strength and all-pervading trust commanded by some of the guilds had become so strong that "even some of the Gupta emperors deposited money with them to run charitable institutions out of interest paid on the deposits" (Maity 1975: 167). The very detailed treatment of the guilds in the *Nāradasmṛti* and the *Bṛhaspatismṛti* compared to scant references in the law books of the previous age, indicate their rise in importance. Whereas the law-givers of the previous era, Gautama (in *Gautama Dharmasutra* 2.2: 21-22; Kale and J. P. 1966: 86) and Manu (*Manusmṛti* VIII, 41, 48; Panshikar 1933: 276-277), charge the reigning monarch to be respectful to the customs of the guilds, ... the law-makers of the Gupta era, Yajñavalkya (*Yajñavalkyasmṛti* II, 192; Acharya 1949: 277) and Nārada (*Nāradasmṛti* X, 2; Jolly 1885: 163), direct the reigning monarch to enforce prevalent customs in the guilds. Bṛhaspati (*Bṛhaspatismṛti* XVII, 18; Aiyangar 1941: 152-153) clearly decrees that the heads of guilds are appointed managers of affairs and hence if any one of them, in his dealings with other people, acts in any manner that is not contrary to prescribed regulations, such actions must be approved by the reigning monarch. He further cautions that if the customs of localities, castes and families are not sustained, there will be discontent among the people and wealth will languish (*Bṛhaspatismṛti* I, 126; Aiyangar 1941: 21).

These indications, as R. C. Majumdar (1969: 58-60) observes, show that during the time frame represented by the later *Dharmaśāstras* (4th and 5th century AD), the guilds held enormous authority and bound the reigning monarch to abide by their decision. This is not to say that the rulers were impoverished in their administrative role. Nevertheless, one does not fail to notice a threat to their authority. For instance, we find that Nārada (*Nāradasmṛti* X, 4-7; Jolly 1885: 163-164) prescribes that the guilds may not be armed without adequate reason and should be prevented from merging with one another and charges the reigning monarch to ensure that they do not launch any anti-state, profligate or unlawful action. These regulations clearly indicate that during the Gupta era, the guilds not only "functioned as independent units of production" but were also "considered capable of threatening the authority of the state" (Sharma 1966: 85).

Having noted the power of guilds, we must be aware of falling into the trap of assuming prosperous mercantile trade during this era. It has already been shown that out of approximately 250 or more Gupta coins found in 'Bengal', only eight have been recovered from maritime port sites. We must also remember that because Roman trade began to show signs of significant diminution after the mid-3rd century AD, South Asian maritime trade with the western world as a whole had fallen considerably during the Gupta era. It is no coincidence that the master mariner Buddhagupta had sailed to the Malay Peninsula.

In addition to the guilds, Buddhist monasteries of the period may also have been involved in the organisation of maritime trade. Consider, for example, that Raktamṛttikā Monastery in Rājbāḍidāṅgā, from the neighbourhood of which *mahānāvika* Buddhagupta hailed, has yielded a seal inscription, part of which reads "*vanijah Varendrasya*", i.e., "the merchant of Varendra" (Mukherjee 1991: 39). If one may add the Buddhagupta inscription with the seal inscription, then it becomes possible to agree with the thesis presented by Kosambi (1955: 60) and supported by Ray (1998: 149-50) that the Buddhist monasteries may have provided the capital to merchants at an interest. It may even be suggested that Buddhist monastic establishments in South and Southeast Asia facilitated maritime trade network. However, we do not have enough data from Buddhist monastic establishments in 'Bengal' to enter into a discussion on the acceptability of Kosambi's thesis. Nevertheless, because excavations at the

Raktamṛttikā Monastery have also yielded a large number of charms and sealing, we may believe with some degree of confidence that many of the maritime mariners and merchants were Buddhists by faith and hence, monasteries such as the Raktamṛttikā Vihāra provided the charms to protect the lay devotees of the faith from dangers of the ocean.

As demonstrated by the four Dāmodarpur copperplate landgrants cited above, the local governments during Gupta rule included representatives of mercantile community although they were in no way state functionaries. For anyone familiar with the history of the Gupta rule, this is not news. Indeed, much has been said, closely reflecting the standard but repetitious formula of the copperplates, regarding the pres-tige and prominence of the mercantile community enjoyed during the Gupta rule and the consequent prosperity of 'Bengal'. In this vein Ray (1994: 302) reads the presence of the mercantile community noted above as indicative of "[a] system of mercantile capitalism" and an economy "that was under the control of the business community, and [a] government [that] was sustained by its wealth". He even goes to the extent of declaring that "the pinnacle of ancient Bengal's commercial prosperity" (*ibid.*) was reached during this era.

The problem in Ray's reading is that it is based on only four out of eleven copperplates issued by the Guptas. There is no mention of a mercantile community in the remaining seven copperplates. Of course, one may smile and add that they are not mentioned because most of the others are regarding grants made in villages. Accepting such a hypothetical correc-tion, one would still be in a position to point out that when seven out of eleven documents of financial transaction do not mention the business community, the economic system under which these transactions took place can hardly claim to be a mercantile capitalist system. It is also indicative that the government was *not* under the control of the business community, and was *not* sustained by its wealth. Rather, it must have been that the wealth produced by the rural economy was more important.

Two other points may be worth noting. First, all the four copperplates, that Ray refers to, reflect the structure of *only* one city – Koṭivarṣa. The sole copperplate issued by the Puṇḍravardhana City Council (Pāhāḍpur copperplate Land-grant of 479 AD) makes no mention of mercantile commu-nity. This is striking, given the fact that Puṇḍravardhana was one of the most important urban centres in 'Bengal' under the Gupta rule. Secondly, there is no indication of maritime trade or traders in all the 11 Gupta copperplates from 'Bengal'. The *sārthavāhas* mentioned in the plates were caravan traders. This, too, is striking, given the expectation that during "the pinnacle of ancient Bengal's commercial prosperity" when prosperity is believed to have been achieved by "commerce ... conducted by way of both water and land routes" (Ray 1994: 120), some reflection should have been there in the copperplates.

We need to remember that for the Gupta state, "[l]and was by far the most important of all the sources of revenue" (Maity 1975: 158). As sources of Gupta wealth indicates, its opulence was begotten more from earnings related to agrarian productions than from trade, lesser still from maritime trade. The peasants in the regions outside the core of the empire (the Madhyadeśa) paid one-sixth of the produce of the land. The king also had sole ownership over the mines. "The real profit", reminds Kosambi (1975: 300), came from conquered tribes and kings outside what had been prime Magadhan territory." He further adds "[t]he accu-mulated surplus looted from the numerous defeated prince-lings helped maintain a luxurious but cultured court and powerful army for a long time, yet with the quite low taxes commented upon by the Chinese pilgrims and attested by the charter of these Gupta kings" (Kosambi 1970: 192-193).

As Kosambi (*ibid.*: 193-196) shows, the contribution of the Gupta era was double-edged: "immediately very profitable for all; eventually fatal to the advance of a powerful and cultured society". He argues with enough reason that the "double-edged" contribution "which accounted at once for initial Gupta prosperity and later decline lay at the village level". With the expansion of the Gupta Empire, innumerable forest chiefs were subdued and the Gaṅgā heartland was cleared for peaceful agricultural production. Consequently, there was a sudden spurt in village settlements. "Traders profited from the increased production, as the crown did from the augmented revenue; but the towns and cities could not meet the demand for village essentials". Neither was the transportation system conducive to large-scale centralised production that would match the demands of innumerable village settlements, nor was the total amount of silver and lower denomination coins in circulation sufficient to support such large-scale commodity production. Hence, it became impossible for the guilds to supply all village needs regularly and ensure profit for themselves. "This problem was solved", says Kosambi, "by the system of village artisans". Provision was made so that each village could support its blacksmith, carpenter, potter, priest, skinner of dead cattle, tanner, barber, etc. These village artisans became an integral part of the village system with duties fixed by custom. Consequently, by the end of the 6th century AD, feudalism began to set in, the cities declined rapidly and the guilds began to break up. Other than occasional fairs and visits by poor caravaneers for bartering salt and metals, the villages became relatively insular.

Kosambi's thesis is amply supported by urban decay noticeable at Tāmralipti and Gaṅgābandar. The case of Gaṅgābandar may be conveniently presented by referring back to Chapter One, Table 1.2 (Archaeological findings from the explorations and excavations of Chandraketugarh).

Comparing all antiquities recovered from the Maurya, Śuṅga, Kuṣāṇa and Gupta eras it becomes apparent that the port was most prosperous during the Kuṣāṇa era, after which it gradually began to decay. However, the structural remains present a different picture. Although habitation at the site began during the pre-Maurya era, there is no structural remain from the era. From Maurya era, decomposed wood and bamboo, pottery drain made of pipes and a reservoir have been found. Śuṅga era shows wattle-and daub structures with tile roofs, earthen rampart, the basal layer of which was composed of *surkhi*, brickbats and potsherds. Remains from Kuṣāṇa era were house complexes of wattle-and-daub type with tile roofs, mud floors, grain storage enclosures and ring-wells. Remains recovered from the Gupta era are remnants of brick house structure and a ring-well made of thick and large terracotta rings, *Sarvato-bhadra* type polygonal brick temple, square brick temple, two miniature brick shrines and a flight of twenty steps. The post-Gupta phase shows a small brick temple (5.94 m square), circular brick basements believed to be remains of the votive *stupas* and remains of the plinth of a huge brick-built temple (15.75 m x 29.58 m) with three distinct construction phases (the earliest of which is believed to have been c. 7th-8th century AD). By the Pāla-Sena phase, for we note only the renovation work of the upper part of the massive rampart wall and the remains of a few structures.

As the review given above shows, Gaṅgābandar's greatest structural prosperity came during the Gupta era but in terms of antiquities, the highest level was attained during the Kuṣāṇa era. However, if one examines the list of structural remains more closely, some striking features begin to emerge clearly. First, the post-Gupta and Pāla-Sena structures at Chandraketugarh area were limited only to Khana-Mihirer-Dhipi, which is clearly indicative of urban decay. Secondly, temple building at Khana-Mihirer-Dhipi began during the Gupta era, reached its peak during the post-Gupta era (when two new temples were built and the square temple of the Gupta era was renovated twice) and ceased completely in the Pāla-Sena era. Thus, the Gupta era stands out as the beginning of a new direction in the life of the inhabitants and that was centered on religious activities.

If one bears in mind that the antiquities are mostly the indicators of non-food producing activities of a community requiring specialist craftsmen, merchants and administrative officers, and their greatest find during the Kuṣāṇa era indicates maximum level of such activities at Chandraketugarh then it become clear that the reason for structural prosperity during the Gupta era was the building of temples. There can thus remain do doubt that trade and commerce had declined during the Gupta era.

The case of Tāmralipti may be presented by referring back to Chapter One, Table 1.1 (Archaeological findings from the explorations and excavations of Tamluk). Comparing the antiquities recovered from the Maurya, Śuṅga, Kuṣāṇa and Gupta eras, it becomes apparent that Tāmralipti flourished most during the Kuṣāṇa era, after which decay sets in. In terms of structural remains, one can easily see indications of rise to prosperity from the Maurya era (represented by a burnt floor) to the Kuṣāṇa era (a brick-built stepped tank, a ring-well, and a soak-pit) and then decline to the Gupta era (with no structural remains).

Since excavations at Tamluk and the adjoining area were not conducted at the same scale as those at Chandraketugarh, one may question if the evidence of structural remains is conclusive. However, one may recollect that Fa-Hien who visited Tāmralipti in the early 5th century AD, noted the existence of 24 monasteries at Tāmralipti but mentions no merchant or mercantile activity in the port-city (*Fo-kwō-ki*, XXXVII; Beal 1869: 147). At the same time, he did not fail to take note that the "[m]erchants of different countries resorted here [Siṁhala] to trade". If one may be permitted to read between the lines, then the signs are clear: Sri Lanka was prosperous in maritime trade while Tāmralipti was declining. Clearly, Tāmralipti, like Gaṅgābandar, had transformed from an important maritime port into an important religious centre with subsidiary functions as a maritime port.

This is not to argue that the Gupta state was adversely inclined to maritime trade. Indeed, Samudragupta's westward drive, "completed successfully by Chandragupta II, was largely inspired by the desire to occupy the coastal region of Saurastra, which had grown rich from trade with the west" (Maity 1975: 165). However, by that time, Indo-Roman trade was on the decline. By the 5th century AD, the Gupta contact with central Asia and western Asia was completely destroyed as a consequence of the Huna invasions. Hence, it was inevitable that Southeast Asia and China would appear more lucrative. As discussed in Chapter Six, Sri Lankan ports were the entrepôts of this trade. None of the ports under the Gupta domain, including Tāmralipti and Gaṅgābandar, lay on the Asian highway of maritime trade in the late historic period. Whatever share South Asia had of the trade, was not so much in the hand of the Gupta Empire but various south Indian kingdoms such of the Vakatakas, Pallavas, Colas, Cheras and Pandyas. Bengal's share in this trade must have declined considerably, as Kosmas Indikopleustes' account cited earlier in Chapter Six shows. Surely "the pinnacle of ancient Bengal's commercial prosperity" was not achieved in the Gupta era. As Kosambi (1975: 313) argues, the 'golden age' of the Guptas was more of a nationalist construction of the nascent Indian bourgeoisie, who had seized Prinsep's translations of Gupta inscriptions in the 19th century in order to resist British hegemony. "Far from the Guptas reviving nationalism, it was nationalism that revived the Guptas" (*ibid.*).

The Post-Gupta Era (c. 525 to 750 AD)

What is striking in the Vaṅga of the 6th century AD is that the *nagaraśreṣṭhīs*, the *sārthavāhas* and the *prathamakulikas* appear to have entirely disappeared. In all the five copperplates of Gopacandra (Mallasarul regnal year 3 and Faridpur regnal year 18), Dharmāditya (Faridpur undated and Faridpur 3rd regnal year) and Samācāradeva (Ghugrāhāti), village heads or elders are mentioned by name. Only the Faridpur copperplate of Gopacandra mentions "principal traders" (*pradhāna-vyāpāriṇa*) (Mukherji and Maity 1967: 83-85) and the Ghugrāhāti Grant of Samācāradeva mentions "principal men of business" (*pradhānā-vyavahā(ri)ṇa*) (Pargiter 1911: 476, 485). In neither case are any traders named in particular although some of the village heads are named.

An interesting transition appears to have taken place in Navyāvakāśikā from the time of Gopacandra (c. 525-540 AD) to the time of Dharmāditya (c. 540-560 AD). The grant issued during the reign of Gopacandra names the viceroy Nāgadeva as simultaneously holding the post of the customs officer (*vyaparaṇda*) of Navyāvakāśikā (Mukherji and Maity 1967: 83-85). The Faridpur copperplate issued during the reign of Dharmāditya (undated), when Nāgadeva was still the viceroy, names the administrative officer Gopālasvamin as simultaneously in charge of customs (*viṣayadhiniyuktak vyapara-karaṇḍaya*) of Vārakamaṇḍala *viṣaya* under Navyāvakāśikā (*ibid.*: 79-81). The Faridpur copperplate issued during the reign of Dharmāditya (3rd regnal year), which deals with landgrants made in the same Vārakamaṇḍala, does not even mention a customs officer. In the first two cases, a separate official did not hold the office of customs. However, there is an important difference. While Nāgadeva was the customs officer and also the viceroy of Navyāvakāśikā (a higher position in the state hierarchy) during the reign of Gopacandra, he appears to have relinquished the office of customs during the reign of the next monarch Dharmāditya. Consequently, Gopālasvamin, a lower official in the state hierarchy, concurrently held the offices of customs and administration of a *viṣaya*. In the third case, the office of customs appears to have been abolished.

That the state maintained the office of customs officer (*vyaparaṇda*) implies that it considered trade to be of some importance. However, the diminishing stature of the functionary leading to the total abolishment of the post indicates the state was increasingly less involved in the mercantile operative milieu because of the insignificant financial gain from the sector. Although material evidences pertaining to this era are scanty, numismatic evidences show that Gupta coins were prevalent during the reigns of Gapacandra and Dharmāditya but Samācāradeva introduced his own coins. Introduction of gold coins and mentioning of merchants in his copperplate (Ghugrāhāti) may be taken as indicators that the state was attempting some measures to revive maritime trade. However, we have very little data to even hazard a guess. Nevertheless, all the evidences cited above might easily lead to the conclusion that in the post-Gupta era, the merchants of Vaṅga had lost much of their prominence they had enjoyed during the Gupta era.

Neither of the two copperplates issued during Śaśāṅka's regnal years 8 and 19 (Majumdar 1945: 1-9) contain any information regarding mercantile community or trade. It is specially noteworthy that Tāvīra, from where both the above mentioned copperplates were possibly issued, lay in Medinīpur district and hence may not have been very far from the port of Tāmralipti. Judging by the second copperplate (issued during Śaśāṅka's regnal year 8), which speaks of "[t]he administrative office of Tāvīra, full of eminent Brāhmaṇas"(*ibid.*: 9), one is led to infer that the maritime mercantile community, even in this coastal district, was not important enough to be included in administration. Similarly, the Nidhanpur inscription of Bhāskaravarman (Gupta 1967: 32-38) issued from Karṇasuvarṇa in Murshidabad district and the Vappaghosavata Grant of Jayanāga (Barnett 1925-26: 60-64), are both silent about the mercantile community in Gauḍa and Rāḍha. Hence, the importance of the merchants of Gauḍa in the first half of the 7th century appear to have diminished even further from that of Vaṅga of the 6th century. Such a condition can be expected from the political turmoil that raged in north India and Gauḍa during this time because of expansionist designs of three great empire builders, Śaśāṅka, Harṣavardhana and Bhāskaravarman.

The situation is hardly different in Samataṭa. Of the five copperplates of the Khaḍgas, three (of Devakhaḍga, an unnamed Khaḍga monarch and Balabhaṭṭa, all found at Salban Vihāra) are badly corroded. The last of the three plates (i.e., of Balabhaṭṭa) has been partially read by Kamalakanta Gupta (1979: 141-144) but there is little to be inferred about the mercantile community. The two Ashrafpur copperplates of Devakhaḍga (Laskar 1907: 85-91) are also silent regarding the merchants. Of the four Rāta copperplates (one discovered at Kailan and three others at Urisvara, all in Comilla district), only the Kailan plate of Śrīdhāraṇa Rāta (Sircar 1947: 211-241) has been read. This too is silent about merchants and mercantile activities. The Kālāpur copperplate of Maruṇḍanātha has only been partially read owing to its badly corroded state. Whatever information is available from the copperplate (Gupta 1967: 66-80), there is no mention of mercantile community. However, in the Tipperah copperplate grant of Lokanātha, we note the presence of merchants among a host of other state officials for whom the content of the grant acts as a notification. The hierarchical order is worth noting because the businessmen have been placed on the second last step of the hierarchy: "the present and future feudatories (*mahāsāmantas*) ... and *viṣayapatis* (district officers), headed by Brāhmaṇas and Āryas, with their staffs and with chief businessmen [(*pra)dhāna-vyavahāri*] and people of the country" (first side, lines 1-2; Basak 1919-20: 310). Hence, we notice the presence of the mercantile community in only one of the six copperplates that have been fully or partially read.

Analysing the copperplate landgrants made after the 6th century AD, Toshio Yamazaki (1982: 17-36) argues that the exclusion of artisans and merchants in the landgrants demonstrates sharp decline of trade and urbanisation. He also points out that for several decades in the 6th century, the price of land did not change in Vārakamaṇḍala (four *dināras* per *kulyavapa* as mentioned in the Dharmāditya's copperplate regnal year 3; Dharmāditya's copperplate undated; Gopacandra's copperplate regnal year 18). Evidently the presence of artisanal, mercantile, and trading elements in the headquarters of Vārakamaṇḍala did not alter land prices in the countryside. This clearly indicates that the district remained economically closed and there seems to have been very little mercantile transactions between different areas. Echoing a similar opinion, Sharma observes:

> Till the end of the Gupta period artisans and traders were active in some parts of the country. In subsequent centuries the role of those who exchanged goods between one area and the other was reduced to the minimal, and the importance of the trading, mercantile and artisanal elements was very much eroded. This seems to have been the general situation between 650 and 950 in the major portion of the country (Sharma 1987: 109).

Although Yamazaki and Sharma's analyses carry enough weight, we must be cautious about drawing definitive conclusion regarding Samataṭa because out of the 11 copperplates discovered so far, five have not been deciphered at all and two have only been partially read.

Besides the copperplates, we have only one inscription, the Dudhpani Rock Inscription of Udayamana found in Hajaribagh district and assigned to the 8th century AD, which sheds some light on the mercantile community of Tāmralipti. According to the Dudhpani inscription, three merchant-brothers named Udayamana, Śrīdhautamana, and Ajitamana went on business from Adodhya to Tāmralipti, where they appear to have made plenty of money (Kielhorn 1894: 344). Obviously Tāmralipti still maintained contacts with the Middle Gaṅgā plains and served the business interest of Ayodhya as well. One may reasonably assume that like the brothers from Ayodhya, traders from other kingdoms of South Asia must have visited Tāmralipti as well, creating something of a cosmopolitan atmosphere in the port city. Since (i) the inscription mentions Adisiṁha as the king of Bihar, (ii) it makes no mention of Gopāla (750-770 AD) who is believed to have extended his domain over most of 'Bengal' and (iii) Dharmapāla (770-810 AD) is known to have extended his domain over Magadha, it is likely that the Dudhpani inscription belongs to the first half of the 8th century AD. The business of the brothers is not mentioned, but because they visited a maritime port, one can reasonably assume that maritime trade-related activities at Tāmralipti had not entirely disappeared. This is significant, especially because the first half of the 8th century was not a very stable time politically. Unfortunately, nothing more can be ascertained about the nature of trade that the merchants conducted.

Literary sources of the era, provided by Hiuen-Tsang and I-Tsing, hardly contribute any information regarding trading community. I-Tsing speaks of Sheng-che, one of the fifty-six Buddhist monks from China, identifies Rājabhaṭa of the Khaḍga dynasty in his *Biography of Eminent Monks* (Lahiri 1986: 84-86) but hardly provides any glimpse of mercantile activities of Samataṭa during this time. Nevertheless, we are grateful to him for informing us that the Chinese monk Wu-hsing sailed from Sri Lanka and reached the port of Haikela in a month's time (*ibid.*: 95).

As discussed earlier in Chapter Six, Hiuen-Tsang's account provided in the *Life* gives the impression that Samataṭa ("whose frontiers border on the great sea") maintained maritime intercourse with southeast Asia (Śrīkshetra, Pegu, Dvarapati, Isanpura, Siam and the country of the Yavanas) since the Chinese monk was "able to gain knowledge of the customs and manners" of the people of the above mentioned kingdoms from Samataṭa (Beal 1973: 132-133). Nevertheless, there is no direct reference to a mercantile community. Among all the places he visited in 'Bengal', only Tāmralipti shows some indications of their existence. He observes, "[t]he country formed a bay where land and water communication met; consequently rare valuables were collected in it and so its inhabitants were generally prosperous" (Watters II, 1973: 190). However, compared to his comments on Charitra (a town on the southeastern frontiers of Orissa), which he describes as "a rendezvous for merchants who embark on the sea" (Beal 1973: 134) or on Surat, which he describes as a "country on the highway to the sea" in which all the inhabitants "were traders by profession" (Watters II, 1973: 248), Tāmralipti does not appear to show very bright signs. Archaeological materials unearthed from the site that date from the era under review (shown in Table 1.1) are only potteries, plaques and clay tablets. No coins or structural remains datable to the post-Gupta era have been recovered. Clearly, Tāmralipti had declined greatly from what it was even during the Gupta era.

Compared to Tāmralipti, Candraketugarh has more to offer in terms of archaeological remains. These are terracotta spindle-whorl and beads, beads of semiprecious stone and bone, and conch-shell bangles. None of these are definite indicators of trade since they may have been used locally. The rest, including structural remains, are all of religious nature: a mutilated bust of Viṣṇu in sandstone, black basalt *cakra* of Viṣṇu, a stone Viṣṇu plaque and remains of the votive *stupas*, a small brick temple and remains of the plinth of a huge brick-built temple. These signs, as discussed in Chapter One, indicate that during the post-Gupta age, Gaṅgābandar had turned into a religious centre and ceased operating as a port.

Summing up on our deliberations on epigraphic, archaeological and literary sources, we can deduce the existence of quite a few exchange centres during this era.

Testimonies provided by Hiuen-Tsang and I-Tsing as well as the Dudhpani inscription may be added up to infer that Tāmralipti continued to be an exchange centre till the end of the late historic period. However, Gaṅgābandar had ceased operating as a maritime port. We hear of two urban centres during the era of Gopacandra and his successors: Savar and Koṭālipāḍā (Candravarmakoṭa). Both of these were administrative centres. In addition, the first was a riverine and the second, a maritime port. The findings of quite a few coins in the vicinity of both the sites indicate mercantile activities. Hence we may believe that both of these were exchange centres of no slight importance. Discovery of the coins of ŚrīKumāra and Vāsuvarman at Savar indicate that during the 7th century AD, it was possibly an important transit port between Kāmrūpa and Samataṭa.

As the Kailan copperplate of Śrīdhāraṇarāta testifies, Devaparvata (Mainamati in Comilla) emerged as an administrative centre with a hill-fort and a riverine port during the rule of the Rātas. Since the fort has been described as a *sarvatobhadraka*, we may assume that it was encircled by a wall with four gateways in the east, north, west and south. The port was situated on the bank of the river Ksiroda. The river, which encircled the city like a moat, is said to have been adorned by clusters of boats (Sircar 1947: 225). During Balabhaṭṭa's reign, as his Mainamati copperplate informs us, Devaparvata was his capital and was adorned with "wonderful *Mahabhogasrama*, eight vihāras adorned with large number of white coloured *Caityas*" (Gupta 1979: 143). The city also had large water-tanks, a *rāja-mārga* (Royal Avenue, possibly the main thoroughfare) and the royal palace (Rashid 1997a: 263). These references to the city of Devaparvata as an administrative centre and a riverine port imply that it was an important exchange centre in Samataṭa of the 7th century AD.

The epigraphic and literary sources also indicate that during the era under review, the mercantile community maintained a low profile. We learn of "principal traders" (*pradhāna-vyāpāriṇa*) during the reign of Gopacandra (c. 525-540 AD) and principal men of business" (*pradhānā-vyavahā(ri)ṇa)* during the reign of Samācāradeva (c. 560 AD). After a period of silence, we encounter mercantile community again in Samataṭa in c. mid-7th century AD, when the Tipperah copperplate grant of Lokanātha speaks of "chief businessmen" *[(pra)dhāna-vyavahāri]*. Around the same time, Hiuen-Tsiang indicates maritime contact of Samataṭa with Southeast Asia and some maritime trade-related activity in Tāmralipti. Around a quarter of a century later, I-Tsing indicates maritime contact of Harikela with Sri Lanka. After another black hole of silence, the merchant community surfaces again in the Dudhpani inscription, where we hear of three merchant-brothers from Adodhya travelling to Tāmralipti and making a fortune. Hence it would appear that there was a mercantile community in 'Bengal' that was engaged in maritime trade. However, their activities appear to have diminished tremendously from the Gupta era.

Numismatic evidences belie, at least partly, the picture drawn by the epigraphic sources. As already discussed in Chapter Three, most of the post-Gupta coins of post-Śaśāṅka era have been found in the regions of Faridpur (including Koṭālipāḍā), Dhaka (including Savar), Bogra, Jessore, Comilla (including Mainamati) in Bangladesh and the state of Tripura in India. Most importantly, the presence of Harikela silver coins, a high value and low volume medium of exchange that carried value because of its intrinsic metal content and not the issuing authority, clearly indicates the prevalence of foreign trade. To this, we must not forget to add Hiuen-Tsiang's testimony, which indicates trade contact with Southeast Asia. Hence, one can convincingly argue in favour of a rise in trade, not decline, in Vaṅga and Samataṭa during the post-Śaśāṅka era. However, we must wait for further information before drawing a definitive conclusion.

EARLY MEDIEVAL PERIOD

The trade guilds that flourished during the Gupta age appear to have completely disappeared in the Pāla and the Sena kingdoms. Raṇaka Śūlapāṇī, described as *vārendraka-śilpigoṣṭhī-cūḍāmaṇī* (Mukherji and Maity 1967: 249), in the Deopara inscription of Vijayasena should be understood as "the foremost of the association (or body or society) of artists of Varendra" rather than "the foremost of the guild of artists of Varendra" as translated by Mukherji and Maity (*ibid.*: 258). It is likely that in place of the trade guilds, Brāhmaṇical caste system began to appear during the Pāla era in "liberal and flexible" form and as a result of "the active and deliberate efforts of the Senas and the Varmanas it became inflexible and rigidly defined" (Ray 1994: 184). At this point, it may be worthwhile to be reminded, "Aryanization of Bengal had not been in accordance with Ṛgvedic social organisation, and therefore, the *caturvarṇa* society of Brāhmaṇas, Kṣatriyas, Vaiśyas and Śudras did not apply here" (*ibid.*: 176). As Ray (*ibid.*) further elaborates that the "Bengal caste pattern comprises Brāhmaṇ and Śudra castes, as well as Antyaja classes and outcastes".

Acknowledging that the *Vṛhaddharma purāṇa* (composed not before the 12th and not after the 14th century) does not provide an authentic account, Ray (*ibid.*: 162) nevertheless cites the text because it provides "some picture of the caste structure in the last stage of the Hindu era" [i.e., the rule of the Senas]. The *Vṛhaddharma purāṇa* (*ibid.*: 195) lists 41 sub-castes of the Śudras (divided into three groups of descending social prestige). Of all the sub-castes (*upa-varṇas* or *jātis* i.e., occupational castes or occupationally differentiated endogamous groups) mentioned, the following were traders: the *gandhika-vaṇika* (perfume merchants), *tailika* (traders in betel nut), *tambali* (*pān* vendors), *suvarṇavaṇika* (traders in gold), *saundika* (wine merchants) and *dhivara* (fishmongers). That the above sub-castes are mentioned by their trade may indicate that their members were the most numerous in 12th century Vaṅga, Rāḍha and Puṇḍravardhana (the regions under Sena domain). All of them, except the *suvarṇavaṇika*, were possibly petty traders. Some of the sub-castes of artisans mentioned in the *Vṛhaddharma purāṇa* were *tantravaya* (weavers), *karmakara* (blacksmiths), *kumbhakara* (potters), *śaṁkhika* (workers and dealers in conch-shells), *modaka* (confectioners), *suvarṇakara* (goldsmiths and makers of ornaments), *tailakara* (oilmen), *jalika* (fishermen), *carmakara* (tanners) etc. As mentioned earlier, many of these sub-castes arose out of the guilds that operated in the early and late historic periods. Although the above list should give an idea of the major occupational groups of manufactures of Vaṅga, Rāḍha and Puṇḍravardhana in the 12th century AD, the situation in Samataṭa, as argued later in this section, may have been entirely different.

We hear of three types of merchants during this period, as three image inscriptions and a copperplate testify. These three types were: the *vaṇik*, the *sārtha(vāha)* and the *vyavahāriṇ*. The first of these evidences is the Mandhuk inscription from the era of Gopāla III (c. 952-972 AD), which records the installation of an image of Ganeśa by a *vṛddha sārtha(vāha)* (i.e., senior or old itinerant trader) named Jambhalamitra (Sircar 1952: 55-57). He further adds that the phraseology of the inscription and the name suggest that the merchant was a Buddhist. The second is the Bāghāurā image inscription from the era of Mahipāla I (c. 977-1027 AD), which records the installation of the image of Nārāyaṇa by the *vaṇik* (merchant) Lōkadatta, son of Vasudatta, hailing from a village named Bilakīndaka (Bhattasali 1923-24b: 255). The third is the Narayanapur inscription from the era of the same monarch and it describes the person who installed the image as "the merchant *(vaṇik)* Buddhamitra, son of the illustrious merchant *(vaṇik)* and great householder (?) Jambhalamitra, and an inhabitant of Bilakīndaka in Samataṭa" (Sircar 1942: 125). Sircar (1952: 57) believes that these two merchants belonged to a Buddhist family, although it is possible that this religion was gradually merging with Brāhmaṇical faith. The fourth, a general reference to "tradesmen" (*vyavahāriṇ*), is found in the Irdā copperplate of the Kamboja king Nayapāla (Majumdar 1933-34: 155, 158).

The very act of installation of the images by all the four merchants cited by name in the three image inscriptions suggests that they were very affluent, well known and/or renowned. Their village of origin is stated to have been situated in Samataṭa, which, during the period of installation of the images, was under Pāla domain. Interestingly, Lokadatta (of Bāghāurā inscription) hailed from the same village in Samataṭa as Buddhamitra and Jambhalamitra (of Narayanapur inscription). It is possible that Jambhalamitra of the Mandhuk inscription was also from Samataṭa since the image was installed at Mandhuk, described as an "ancient place under Barura police station and about 24 kilometres south-south-west of Lalmai railway station" (Zakariah 1997: 225).

It may be useful to return to the Vallālasena-Vallabhānanda legend by Ānandabhaṭṭa (the first part of which was recounted in Chapter Three), to glean further information regarding the merchants of the Sena kingdom. After Vallālasena's confiscation of the merchants' wealth, they refused to attend a royal banquet where they were to dine with members of lower *jātis*. At the same time, an intelligence report reached Vallālasena that Vallabhānanda was conspiring with the Pālas against him. Driven by fury, the Sena monarch reacted by demoting the caste position of the *suvarṇavaṇikas* from the first to the second group of Śudras. The merchants reacted by buying all the slaves at twice or thrice the market price. Hence, Vallālasena was forced to promote members of lower groups to the first group of Śudras. As a consequence of the acrimonious relations, many merchants reportedly migrated away from the Sena kingdom (Ray 1993: 212).

Even if we discount the details of the legend as fabricated, we cannot fail to read the implication that there may have been powerful merchants in the Sena kingdom who also operated as bankers for the royalty. Further, the interest of the affluent section of the mercantile community may have been in conflict with the state. Nevertheless, Ray (1994: 225-226) reads the same legend to arrive at the conclusion that the mercantile community had completely lost its position of pre-eminence, ridden as it was by dissent arising from caste distinction. He cites Govardhanacarya, a court poet of Lakṣmanasena, who, as he says, gives as an apt summary of the prevailing situation:

> O Indra! Where are those merchants who one day held you above all others? Nowadays men have harnessed you to the plough and with your rod have yoked the oxen (*ibid.*: 226).

Scholars including Ray (1993: 132-169, 1994: 99-129) and Chakravarti (1943: 642-669) have gone over in detail the prevailing economic condition of the Pāla and Sena eras and have argued that the period saw the complete entrenchment of feudalism and urban decay in 'Bengal'.

There can be little doubt that by the 8th century AD, agriculture had become the mainstay of the economy of Puṇḍravardhana, Rāḍha and Vaṅga. The copperplate inscriptions of the Pālas (for example the Khalimpur plate of Dharmapāla, Kielhorn 1896-97: 254), the Candras (the Rāmpāl grant of Śrīcandradeva, Basak 1913-14a: 141), the Varmans (the Belava copperplate of Bhojavarman, Basak 1913-14b: 43) and the Senas (the Barrackpur plate of Vijayasena, Majumdar 1929: 66), in which the cultivators have been mentioned as a class apart, indicate that agriculture was the primary source of wealth of the period under study. As Ray (1994: 225) observes, "from about the eighth century the Bengali economy had become dependent on agriculture and that cultivators had developed as a distinct class". The rise of the cultivators is seen in relation to the complete silence about the mercantile community in all the copperplates from this period (except the Irdā copperplate). This is taken to indicate further decline of their importance. However, as argued later, Samataṭa deserves separate examination.

We may now turn our attention to exchange centres, which quite a few copperplate landgrants indicate to have existed during the period under review. The Khalimpur copperplate of Dharmapāla is one of these. It mentions *haṭṭika* (Kielhorn 1896-97: 254), i.e., a small-scale exchange centre. *Haṭṭa* (exchange centre) is mentioned in the Irdā copperplate of the Kamboja king Nayapāladeva (Majumdar 1933-34: 155, 158) and the Rāmganj copperplate of Isvaraghosa (Majumdar 1929: 154, 156). The copperplate issued by Laḍahacandra (6th regnal year) refers to the *haṭṭa* of Dhritipura at Sripattikeraka in Samataṭa (Zakariah 1997: 224). The Bhaṭerā plate of Govinda Keśavadeva (11th century) refers to a large-scale exchange centre *(haṭṭa-vara)* in the kingdom of Srihatta (Gupta 1967: 170).

Haṭṭa has also been mentioned in other plates. Nalanda had at least two exchange centres named after reigning monarchs. These were *Śrī-Dhamra-haṭṭe* [sic. should be read as *Dharma-haṭṭa*] (Shastri 1942: 103) and *Devapāladeva-haṭṭa* (Mitra, D 1978: 149; Ghosh 1939-40: 334). We also hear of an exchange centre named after Nalanda. It was called the *Śrī-Nālandāyā(yāṅ)talahaṭṭakē,* as evinced from an inscription on a votive statue found at Nalanda (Shastri 1942: 113). The same name appears on a stone image of Avalokiteśvara that was found at Nalanda, this time as *Nālandā-tala-haṭaka* (Ghosh 1939-40: 334, fn. 3).

Clearly, one can infer a graded hierarchy from the terms applied to indicate the exchange centres. This may be formulated as (i) the *haṭṭika,* where commodities produced in a small locality were exchanged, (ii) the *haṭṭa,* where commodities produced in a large region were exchanged and (iii) the *haṭṭavara,* which were essentially wholesale exchange centres. We may believe that cowries were mostly used in *haṭṭikas*, and gold dust or bullion in *haṭṭas* and *haṭṭavaras* of the Pāla kingdom. We may further infer that the *vṛddha sārtha(vāha)* cited in the Mandhuk inscription must have been an itinerant trader who transacted business at levels one and two, i.e., he must have bought commodities from *haṭṭas* and sold them at *haṭṭikas* and vice versa. In the same manner, Lokadatta, Buddhamitra and Jambhalamitra may have dealt at levels two and three. We have almost no information regarding the nature of the organisation of labour and capital necessary for producing manufactured goods that were bought and sold in these exchange centres.

The exchange centres of the Pāla kingdom must have been controlled, to some extent at least, by the Pāla state. This is evident from the reference to "guardians of weight" in every selling-centre *(pratyāpaṇamānapaiḥ)* in the Khalimpur copperplate inscription of Dharmapāla (Kielhorn 1896-97: 248, 252). The same must have been true of the kingdom of Īśvarghoṣa (c. 1040-1080 AD), located somewhere in the Bardha-mān, Jalpaiguri-Cooch Behar or Kāmrūpa-Goalpara region, because his Rāmganj copperplate mentions *haṭṭapati* or "superintendent of markets" (Majumdar 1929: 153, 156).

We can trace the existence of at least two riverine ports in eastern Bengal during this period, both of which emerged during the Khaḍga era. One of these was Savar, as testified by the Madanpur copperplate of Śrīcandra (Basak 1949-50: 57). The port is mentioned as a 'sambhāṇḍāriyakē', which possibly means that it offered storing/warehousing facilities. The other port was at Devaparvata, as the Devaparvata inscription of Bhavadeva indicates. Both these ports must have facilitated movement of goods to the maritime port of Samandar and must also have functioned as *haṭṭavaras*. It may be worth noting that both Savar and Devaparvata were flourishing Buddhist centres.

The *haṭṭas, haṭṭikas* and *haṭṭavaras* discussed above must have been exchange centres for internal trade. We must look elsewhere for information regarding exchange centres dealing with external trade. As already discussed in Chapter One, Samandar came into prominence in the 8th century AD after the decline of Tāmralipti. Description of the port, available in testimonies of Arab-Persian geographers and traders such as al-Idrisi's *Kitāb Nuzhat al-Mushtāk fi'Khtirāq al-Āflāq* (composed sometime in the mid-12th century AD) may be cited at this point to help us ascertain the nature of exchange centres for external trade. According to al-Idrisi (1867: 90), "Samandar is a large town, commercial and rich, where there are good profits to be made. ... Rice and various grains, especially excellent wheat, are to be obtained here". The Arab geographer's description has all indicators necessary for Samandar to be an exchange centre: it was a town where commercial transactions were made involving substantial sums of money (hence it was rich). The transactions involved not only grains as al-Idrisi indicates but also, as discussed in Chapter Three, cotton-textiles (including Muslin), Cāmara (yak-tails), horses, aloes-wood, emery, cowries, swords, spices, sugar and molasses, camphor, silver and pearl.

The Arab geographer goes on to make a curious statement. He says, "One day's sail from this city there is a large island well peopled and frequented by merchants of all countries" (al-Idrisi 1867: 90). Doubtless, the large island was Sandwīp. However, what is surprising is that al-Idrisi makes a specific note of the island's visitors ("merchants of all countries") while he is silent about their visit to Samandar. One could hazard a guess that Sandwīp was a colony of foreign traders where existing laws of the land were much relaxed. There may be no way of knowing what was in the geographer's mind who never visited the site he described but for our purpose, we may, without committing any gross mistake, assume that these "merchants of all countries" must have visited Samandar as well (how else would they arrive there in the first place?). These considerations made Samandar the most important exchange centre in entire 'Bengal' during the period under study.

In the mercantile operative milieu of the Pāla kingdom, one must not forget the presence of the *śaulkika* (the officer charged with collecting customs and tolls), whose presence is declared in a number of copperplates. These are the Khalimpur copperplate inscriptions of Dharmapāla (Mukherji and Maity 1967: 100), the Monghyr copperplate inscription of Devapāla (*ibid.*: 118), the Bhagalpur copperplate inscription of Nārāyaṇapāladeva (*ibid.*: 167), the Bānagaḍa copperplate inscription of Mahipāla I (*ibid.*: 202) and the Manahali copperplate grant of Madanapāla (*ibid.*: 215). The same functionary was present also in the kingdom of Īśvarghoṣa, as Rāmganj copperplate testifies (Majumdar 1929: 153). The *śaulkikas* of the Kamboja kingdom also had some role to play in working with the tradesmen *(vyavahāriṇ)* cited in the Irdā copperplate of King Nayapāla.

Nevertheless, the role of the *śaulkika* in general may be inferred from the manner the official is mentioned in the copperplates. Two officials called the *dāśāparādhika* ("a high official in charge of detection of ten crimes") and *cauroddharaṇika* ("the head of a department entrusted with the charge of collecting taxes necessary for prevention of theft") (Maity and Mukherji 1967: 129) are mentioned before the *śaulkika* in the Monghyr, the Bhagalpur and the Bānagaḍa copperplates. In the Manahali and the Rāmganj copperplates, the *dāśāparādhika* is forgotten but the *cauroddharaṇika* is not. The implications are clear. Theft must have been rampant and considerable revenue was collected for catching thieves! The state even attempted to probe into the minds of the subject since we have *dāśāparādhika*, who was supposed to detect the crime of "bad thought" (*ibid.*). One is tempted to infer that the importance of the *śaulkika,* and by implication, the importance of trade as far as the state exchequer was concerned, must have been less important than that of the *dāśāparādhika* and the *cauroddharaṇika*.

The Sena copperplate landgrants clearly state the revenue yield of precise measures of land. Hence one may deduce "that a careful system of public accounting and a tax system based upon a precise knowledge of average annual yields existed" during their rule (Morrison 1980: 99). That the state devised such a strict measure of revenue accounting must be seen in relation to the complete silence in the copperplates regarding traders and trade-related activities. Hence, one may deduce that the revenue yielded by land had become the most important source of wealth for the state exchequer of the Senas and that trade-related activities enjoyed very little prominence. Nevertheless, some activities must have prevailed because not only do we stumble across a literary account of Vallabhānanda but also we find the mention of a state functionary in copperplates who may have been in charge of collecting taxes from the traders in the Sena kingdom. This functionary, called the *gaulmika* or the "custom receiver", is cited in the Naihati copperplate of Vallālasena (Mukherji and Maity 1967: 262), the Govindapur (*ibid.*: 273), the Madhainagar (*ibid.*: 281), the Sundarban (*ibid.*: 291) and the Anulia copperplates of Lakṣmaṇasena (*ibid.*: 305), the Madanpāḍā (*ibid.*: 316) and the Calcutta Sāhitya Parishad copperplates of Visvarupasena (*ibid.*: 325), and the Edilpur copperplate of Keśavasena (*ibid.*: 337). In all these plates, the *cauroddharaṇika* precedes the *gaulmika* and we immediately sense a repetition of the pattern set by the Pālas.

The Rāmpāla (*ibid.*: 224), the Dhullā (Sircar 1959a: 139) and the Pascimbhag (Gupta 1967: 91) copperplates of Śrīcandra mention the *śaulkika* again followed by *cauroddharaṇika*, echoing the trend set by the Pālas. Hence, one may reasonably assume that the relative importance of trade in the kingdom of the Candra was also not much different from the Pālas. The Belava copperplate of Bhojavarman is much less specific as regards the officers of the state and the specificities of revenue income. Although it is generally accepted that "the Varmanas ... maintained the administrative pattern of the Pāla period" (Ray 1994: 282-283), it would be unwise to draw a conclusion till further material evidence is available.

In the copperplate landgrants of the Devas, only a small number of courtiers and officers of the state are mentioned. The Mainamati copperplate of Anandadeva mentions only the *mahapratihara* who was also the *dutaka* of the grant. For the grant of Bhavadeva, which is inscribed in the same plate, the *mahāsāmantādhipati* was the *dutaka*. Other state officials mentioned are *viṣayapatis* and *adhikaranas* (Gupta 1979: 147-148). The Devaparvata copperplate landgrant of Bhavadeva mentions only the *mahāsāmantādhipati* (who was the *dutaka* of the grant) and the *viṣayapatis* (Sircar 1951: 93-94). These copperplates appear to be silent about any officer who may have been charged with the duty of collecting customs and tolls. As a matter of fact, there is no reference to revenue accounting, trade or agriculture.

At this point, one could sum up the matter of trade in the period under review had not the Paṭṭikeḍā, the Harikela (Series II) and the Harikela (Associate Series) coins been found. As mentioned earlier in Chapter Three, none of the Harikela (Series II) and the Harikela (Associate Series) coins has been found in Mainamati. Since these coins have only been found in southern Tripura, it is hard to believe that they circulated in the whole of 'Bengal'. Since no monarch has been named on these coins as the issuing authority and since they have been found only in southern Tripura, it is likely that the coins were issued by local authorities or guilds which functioned, for some unknown reason, only in the Harikela region. If guilds were the issuing authority, they must have been very powerful. Since the copperplate inscriptions do not speak of state officials in charge of trade, it would appear that the state did not directly manage the organisation of trade as the suggestions made in the *Arthaśāstra*. Hence, we may tentatively assume that trade in Harikela was largely controlled by the merchant class organised under powerful guilds or by local authorities.

Let us now consider the Paṭṭikeḍā coins. Because these have been found in hoards in ruined Buddhist monasteries at Mainamati, one may conjecture that the Buddhist religious establishments were linked with the traders. The absence of the names of the royalty also indicate, as in the case of the Harikela (Series II and the Associate Series) coins, that these were issued by local authorities or the guilds of Paṭṭikeḍā. It also appears that trade was by no means state-controlled since the copperplate inscriptions of the Devas do not speak of state officials in charge of trade. Hence it may not be illogical to assume that trade in the kingdom of the Devas may have been controlled by the merchant class organised under powerful guilds or by local authorities. However, we must acknowledge that the Harikela and Paṭṭikeḍā coins remain unresolved pieces of a jigsaw puzzle. We must await further discoveries before drawing anything of a definitive conclusion.

One of the methodological problems of the scholars noted above was that they have considered the whole of 'Bengal' as a composite and homogeneous geographical unit (instead of separate sub-units of Vaṅga, Puṇḍravardhana /Varendra, Rāḍha and Samataṭa). Consequently, epigraphical, literary and archaeological data from one sub-unit was applied as equally relevant for all others. Our deliberation till now should have already proved that Samataṭa deserves separate examination. Not only had it developed, during the period under review, a complex monetary system and at least one prosperous exchange centre for international commerce, but also an affluent community of merchants such as Lokadatta, Buddhamitra and Jambhalamitra. Perhaps, Govardhanacarya would not have lamented had he been born in Samataṭa!

Analysing the copperplate landgrants of 'Bengal', Morrison (1980: 153) shows that, Samataṭa was perhaps the only area in 'Bengal' delta where Buddhism was firmly rooted. It is perhaps no coincidence that Bhāskaravarman (in the Nidhanpur copperplate), Śrīcandra (in the Paścimbhāg copperplate) and Govinda Keśavadeva (in the Bhaṭerā copperplate) should have made extraordinarily large donations of land in the same trans-Meghnā region of Samataṭa where the Lalmai-Mainamati complex containing over fifty sites was also situated, – the most extensive brick-built remains of the 'Bengal' delta. In sharp contrast to the landgrants made to individual Brāhmaṇas mostly for maintaining domestic rituals (as in the Bhāgīrathī-Huglī area), more endowments were made to collectives (institutions and groups) in Samataṭa. This may certainly be taken as "an index to the difference between these parts of the Delta". The index that Morrison refers to distinguishes Samataṭa so much so that one begins to suspect that the caste-bound social practices that were beginning to emerge in Varendra and Rāḍha during the Pāla reign may have been largely absent in Samataṭa during the reign of the Devas and the Candras. As a consequence of Buddhist predominance, what may have existed was a system akin to the guilds that emphasised occupational division among the people. It appears that Samataṭa, where sedentary cultivation and urbanisation possibly began with the inception of Gupta rule, witnessed an unprecedented expansion of maritime trade from the post-Gupta era that culminated in the Candra era. However, it is acknowledged that the above is but a tentative formulation and needs to be rigidly tested against further research on socio-economic conditions in early medieval Samataṭa.

MEDIEVAL PERIOD

Although an agrarian-feudal economic pattern was the primary characteristic of Sultanate Bengal, by the early 15th century it also showed signs that were distinctly different from the previous period. Tarafdar (1995: 70) succinctly sums up the distinction thus: "The growth of a money economy, urbanisation, the production of the commodities that could be exported to foreign countries and the expansion of inland and foreign trade distinguished the medieval period from the previous Pāla-Sena period dominated by a form of agriculture-based economy". It is in this distinct economic environment that we shall strive to locate the medieval maritime merchants and their mercantile milieu.

In sharp contrast to the early medieval period, when one has to probe with diligence and patience for evidences on maritime trade, the medieval period offers a sudden profusion of literary evidences. Even in the distant empire of Kublai Khan (1272-1291 AD), the news reached Marco Polo that 'Bengal' was a land of flourishing trade and that "merchants from various parts of India resort[ed] thither" in order to purchase commodities such as spikenard, galangal, ginger, sugar, cotton and many kinds of drugs (Polo N.D.: 204). Unfortunately, the Venetian traveller does not provide details.

For the details, we need to examine Fei Sin's testimony, who visited Sultanate Bengal between 1412 and 1414 AD and again between 1415 and 1418 AD. He gives a brief but clear description of the merchants he must have met during his visit.

> The men wear a white cotton turban and a long white cotton shirt. On their feet they wear low sheep-skin shoes with gold thread. The smarter ones think it is correct to have designs on them. Every one of them is engaged in business, the value of which may be ten thousand pieces of gold ... (Bagchi 1945: 122).

Obviously the merchants that Fei Sin describes were very affluent. It may have been the people of same ethnic background that Ma-Huan met during his sojourn in Gauḍa in

1432 AD because his description of their clothing, as in the following excerpt, is remarkably similar.

> The men all shave the hair of the head and use a white cloth to bind around it. On the body they wear a long round-collared garment which is slipped down over the head; round the lower [part of the body] they wear a broad multi-coloured kerchief; [and] on the feet they wear leather shoes with a shallow face (Ma-Huan 1970: 160).

Their complexion is described as black ["brown pear colour" according to another manuscript of the same text], "with but an occasional white person" and by faith they were all Muslims (*ibid.*). As for their language, Ma-Huan says "they all adopt Pang-ko-li [presumably Bengali], which constitutes an independent tongue, though there are also some people who speak the Pa-erh-his [Persian] language" (*ibid.*: 161). Among these people, the wealthy are described as maritime merchants "who build ships and go to various foreign countries to trade" and they are said to have been numerous. He also speaks of another group of people, "who go abroad to hire themselves out as servants". They are also said to have been "numerous" (*ibid.*). It is possible that these numerous "people who hired themselves out" were agents of the wealthy maritime merchants.

The affluent merchants that the Chinese diplomat speaks of were all Muslims by faith, whose clothing, we may presume, followed the practice of the Indo-Turkish ruling classes. However, it is curious that Ma-Huan describes the complexion of most of the merchants as black (or brown pear) with only an occasional white person. Further, they all are described as having adopted Bengali and only a few are described as speaking Persian. This could mean that the Bengali-speaking black/pear-brown men were natives and only a few among them were Arab-Persians. If we remember that the time of the visit of the Chinese diplomats matches exactly with the rise of Rājā Ganeśa and the reign of his dynasty (1415-1433 AD)[1], it may not be too difficult to imagine that the affluent merchants were indeed Bengalis. They may have converted to Islam and adopted the clothing of the Indo-Turkish ruling elites, very much like Rājā Ganeśa's son Jadu, who accepted Islam and reigned as Jalal al-Din Muhammad Shah (1415-1432 AD).

About three-quarter of a century later (in 1518 to be precise), Duarte Barbosa presents a picture of the elite residents of the city of Bengala cited below that agrees to a great extent with the Chinese accounts cited earlier.

> The respectable Moors walk about clad in white cotton smokes, very thin, which come down to their ankles, and beneath these they have girdles of cloth, and over them silk scarves, they carry in their girdles daggers garnished with silver and gold, according to the rank of the person who carries them; on their fingers many rings set with rich jewels, and cotton turbans on their heads. They are luxurious, eat well and spend freely, and have many other extravagancies as well. They bathe often in great tanks which they have in their houses (Barbosa 1921: 147).

However, the 'Moors' that Barbosa speaks of are described more elaborately in the following passage, in which it becomes apparent that they were of non-indigenous stock.

> The inhabitants there of are white men, well-built; and there dwell there as well strangers from many lands, such as Arabs, Persians, Abexis [Abyssinians], and Indians. And this by reason that this land is large, fruitful and healthy. All of these are great merchants and they possess great ships after the fashion of Meca; others there are from China, which they call *"juncos"*, which are of great size and carry great cargoes. With these they sail to Charamandel, Malaca, Çamatra, Peeguu, Cambaya and Ceilam, and deal in goods of many sorts with this country and many others (*ibid.*: 137-142, 145).

The Italian trader Varthema, who is said to have arrived in the city of Banghella in c. 1508, further confirms the affluence of the Arab, Persian, Abyssinian and Indian merchants. He saw in the city, in his own words, "the richest merchants I have ever met with". The most affluent among these were possibly the "very great merchants in jewels" because Varthema names their trade in particular. Although he identifies only the Nestorian Christians from Sarnav (in Siam) and the Persians with whom he sailed to Pegu, his account leaves no doubt that the city of Banghella was alive with numerous foreigners (Varthema 1928: 79-80). The memoir of an anonymous interpreter who visited Gauḍa with a Portuguese mission in 1521 speaks of Turkish, Arab and Persian merchants in 'Bengal' but does not mention the Abyssinians and the Indians (Ray 1997: 52).

We hear about some of the Arab merchants by their names. According to the *'Ahādis ul-Khawānin* (or *'Tārīkh i Hamīdī*) by Maulawi Hamidullah Khan Bahadur (1871), a great merchant from Baghdad named Alfā Husainī, who owned 14 ships and repeatedly sailed to the port of Caṭṭagrāma, helped Sultan Nusrat Shah in one of his military expeditions in the district of Caṭṭagrāma with sea-going vessels. Alfā Husainī was well recompensed for his invest-ment. Not only did he enjoy greater benefit under the sultan than the Arakanese monarch, he also became the sultan's son-in-law (Blochmann 1872: 337). In 1517, we hear of a merchant named Gromalle (Gulam Ali), a relative of the then governor of Caṭṭagrāma, whose two ships sailing to Cambay were captured in the high sea by a Portuguese agent named Dom João de Silveira (Campos 1919: 28). From 1526, we hear of another rich merchant from Persia named Khājeh Shiāb-ud-din (Khajah Shihab-ud-din) whose galleot was captured in Caṭṭagrāma by a Portuguese commander named Ruy Vaz Pereira (*ibid.*: 30-31). These, of course, are only two among numerous instances of Portuguese piracy.

The memory of the Arab merchants still lives in local traditions. According to one tradition current in Malda, quite a few Arab merchants settled at Gauḍa for the purpose of commerce. In an old but unnamed Bengali manuscript, a

[1] Rājā Ganeśa, described in a contemporary letter as "a landholder of four hundred years' standing" (cited in Eaton 1994: 51), was a Hindu feudal lord of great power and prominence. Because of his political maneuverings, he succeeded in installing his son in the throne of Bengal sultanate.

merchant from Baghdad named Chamban Ali is said to have given a vivid description of the port of Gauḍa busy with countless ships (Mookerji 1957: 158-159). In yet another story it is recounted that sometime in the second half of the 16th century, "one Shaikh Bhik, who used to trade in Maldehi cloths, such as *kātār* and *musri,* set sail for Russia with three ships laden with silk cloths, and that two of his ships were wrecked somewhere in the neighbourhood of the Persian Gulf" (Hunter 1876b: 95). In Noakhali and Caṭṭagrāma coasts today, memory of Arab *saodāgars* (affluent maritime merchants) of bygone days still command respect and reverence. It may be worthwhile to note that all the sources mentioned above are entirely silent about the Bengali-speaking black/pear-brown merchants that the Chinese diplomats had met in 'Bengal'.

However, merchants similar to those described by the Chinese diplomats appear again in another literary account of nearly the same time as Barbosa and Varthema: Tome Pires' *Suma Oriental* (completed between 1512-1515 AD). As the Writer and Accountant of the Portuguese factory in Malacca writes from his personal observations at Malacca, it may be worthwhile to examine his testimony in detail. "The Bengalees are great merchants and very independent, brought up to trade" and that they "are merchants with large fortunes, men who sail in junks" (Pires 1967: 88). Although he does not identify the religious faith of the Bengalees, Pires clearly distinguishes between them and the foreigners for he says "[a] large number of Parsees, *Rumes*, Turks and Arabs, and merchants from Chaul, Dhabol and Goa, live in Bengal" (*ibid.*). In addition, we also learn that merchants from Aden visited 'Bengal' and those merchants from Ormuz and adjoining the Persian Gulf area maintained factors in 'Bengal' (*ibid.*: 17, 45).

As for the 'Bengalee' merchants, Pires seems to have possessed mixed feelings. Apart from their domestic nature, he also says they are all "false" (*ibid.*: 88). Later he seems to be admiring them: "Most of the Bengalees are sleek, handsome, black men more sharpwitted than the men of any other known race" (*ibid.*). But finally he comes down with a curious observation: "When they want to insult a man they call him a Bengalee" (*ibid.*: 93). It appears that many of these 'Bengalees' had settled in Malacca. "There are a large number of Bengalees, men and women, in Malacca. The men are fishers and tailors – most of them – and some of the workmen do very bad work" (*ibid.*). It is this bit of information that Meilink-Roelofsz (1970: 144) stresses and chooses to overlook those described by Pires specifically as merchants. Let us not commit the same mistake and examine the condition of these merchants.

Among the four thousand Bengalees, Persians and Arabs residing at Malacca, some are specifically described as rich merchants and factors (Pires 1967: 255). Besides, there must have been those visiting from 'Bengal' who are described as "great merchants and very independent", "with large fortunes, men who sail in junks". Even if they lacked business ethics, one must also remember that Pires also found them "more sharpwitted than the men of any other known race".

There is an obvious implication in Pires' usage of the term "Bengalee": that they were Bengali merchants not because they were from 'Bengal' since there were others from 'Bengal' who were referred to as foreigners; they must have been Bengalis because they spoke Bengali. Pires' description of the Bengalis as sleek, handsome and sharp-witted black men clearly indicate that they were natives of 'Bengal'.

At this point, it may be valuable to examine contemporay literary works in Bengali to see what local poets have to say about the Bengali maritime merchants of the period under review. Bāsudeva Ghoṣa, in his *Kaḍcā*, has devoted an entire chapter on the merchants of Sātgāon (Saptagrāma). Among the residents of Saptagrāma, he speaks of shopkeepers, merchants and traders. The Hindu merchants belonged to three *jātis*: *gandhavaṇik* or the spice merchants, the *śaṅkhavaṇik* or the dealers in conch-shells, and the *suvarṇavaṇik* or the gold merchants (Ray 1999: 157). The maṅgalakāvya corpus employs quite a few appellations to denote a merchant, such as *sādhu*, *saodāgar*, *baṇik*, *bāniyā*, *bānyā* and *bene*. For example, Kavikaṅkaṇa Mukunda (1986: 158) describes Dhanapati as a *sādhu* as well as a *saodāgar* in the *Caṇḍīmaṅgala*. The last-mentioned text, where the poet describes numerous *jātis* in an idealised Bengali city of his time (discussed earlier in Chapter One), is often cited as an index of occupations of members of the Hindu community in the mid-16th century AD. Among all the *jātis* that the poet mentions, only the *gandhabānyā*, the *śaṅkhabānyā*, the *maṇibānyā* (the jeweller) and the *suvarṇabānyā* (*ibid.*: 82) can fit into the category of maritime merchants.

However, scholars such as Aniruddha Ray (1997: 34) believe that the external trade at maritime ports such as Sātgāon (Saptagrāma) was mainly in the hands of foreign merchants including the Indians. The internal trade is believed to have been controlled by Bengali-speaking Hindu merchants, who used to carry merchandise from different parts of 'Bengal' to Sātgāon. This impression is confirmed by the description of Saptagrāma that Mukunda (1986: 237-38) provides. As discussed in Chapter One, our poet informs us that merchants (*sadāgar*) from numerous kingdoms and ports visited Saptagrāma but merchants (*baṇik)* of Saptagrāma never sailed from their homeport. Furthermore, as Digby (1982b: 159) argues, there is very little evidence that Hindu merchants participated in overseas trade across the Arabian Sea.

Nevertheless, both Dhanapati and Srimanta (the legendary maritime merchants around whose exploits Mukunda has composed his *Caṇḍīmaṅgala*) describe themselves as a *gandhavaṇik* (Mukunda 1986: 209, 254, 286). In *Manasā-purāṇa* by Tantrabibhūti (1980: 246) merchant Candrapati's son Lakṣmīndar describes himself as a "*gandhabānyā-*

nandari' (son of a *gandhabānyā*). In Vipradāsa Pipilāi's *Manasā Vijaya*, Čādo does not mention his *jāti* but proudly declares that he was born in a family of merchants and that his father was Koṭīśvar (the name literally denotes a multimillionaire) (Sen 1953: 147). Clearly, the *gandhavaṇik* or *gandhabānyā* is shown in the maṅgalakāvya corpus as a *jāti* that ventured in maritime trade implies that overseas voyage was known in their tradition.

The impression of Sātgāon (Saptagrāma) created by Kavikañkaṇa Mukunda in his *Caṇḍīmaṅgala*, Vipradāsa Pipilāi in his *Manasā Vijaya,* Bāsudev Ghoṣa in his *Kaḍcā*, Bṛndābana Dāsa in his *Śrīśrīcaitanya Bhāgabata* and Jayānanda in his *Caitanya-maṅgala* reflects a picture accurate enough. All these poets could not have been falsifying social condition of 'Bengal'. Hence, Aniruddha Ray's view, that the Bengali-speaking Hindu merchants controlled the internal trade, is perfectly acceptable. What he and others of similar view overlook is the strong possibility that, as McPherson (1998: 109-110) and Kiribamune (1990: 188) have suggested (and cited earlier in Chapter Six), many Bengali merchants embraced Islam by the middle of the 14th century. If we remind ourselves that Rājā Ganeśa's period in the first half of the 15th century "was a turning point in Bengali history" because following this time, [a]t both royal and popular levels, Bengalis were gradually accommodating themselves to Muslim rule" (Eaton 1994: 55-56) and that Rājā Ganeśa's son is an example of how that accommodation was taking place, then it may not be inconceivable that the Bengali-speaking black/pear-brown merchants of the Chinese diplomats and the "Bengalee merchants" of Tome Pires were Bengali-speaking Hindu merchants of *gandhavaṇik jāti* who had converted to Islam. Medieval Bengali literature does not refer to them because they were not Hindus.

Even if the conclusion made above is unacceptable to the sceptic, so much is clear that Tarafdar (1999: 171) was wrong in devaluing the Bengali merchants as "junior partners of the Gujarati and the Coromandel merchants" and as "a body of speculators and peddlers that grew as a by-product of the international trade". This further implies, Tarafdar's sweeping observation that "the sea-borne trade of Bengal had completely gone out of the reach of the local traders and it was being thoroughly controlled by the Arabs, Persians, Gujarati and Coromandel merchants" (*ibid.*: 152-153) does not appear to be an accurate reflection of the contemporary operative milieu of maritime merchants. Bengali merchants must have had a share – and that share, if the testimony of Tome Pires cited above is acceptable, may not have been very small compared to the rest.

Our examination of the merchants made above indicates that maritime trade was largely in the hands of private entrepreneurs during the period under review. However, we also have enough evidence to believe that the sultans also found maritime trade lucrative enough to venture into it occasionally. As Ma-Huan (1970: 165) testifies, "[t]he king also sends men to travel on board ship to the various foreign countries to trade; [and] he procures and buys local products, pearls, and precious stones, which were presented as tribute to the Central Country." It is also possible that the ambassadors sent to China from 'Bengal' sailed in ships owned by the sultans. According to un-named Portuguese travellers, the sultan's ships that they saw at Sonārgāon in the early 16th century were small compared to those of the Portuguese. The same source testifies that a ship owned by Sultan Ala al-Din Husain Shah that sailed to Malacca, was burnt by the Portuguese (Ray 1997: 38-39). We also have in our knowledge that two ships of Nusrat Shah, valued at 250,000 Cruzades, were seized by the Portuguese (Bouchon and Thomaz 1988: 332). Even down to the first half of the 18th century we learn of the mercantile marine of the *nawab* of 'Bengal' from Bowrey who reports that about 20 sail of ships annually sailed from Dacca, Balesore and Pipli, to Ceylon and Tenessarim to fetch elephants and six or seven sailed to the Maldives to fetch cowries and coir (Bowrey 1905: 180). Although the mercantile marine of the *nawab* of 'Bengal' is way beyond the time frame of this research, it indicates the prevalence of a continued tradition of the sultans and *nawabs* of 'Bengal' participating in maritime trade, at least from the 15th to the 18th century AD.

The participation of the sultans in the maritime trade need not surprise us since we are informed of similar practice all over South Asia during the medieval period. As Ibn Battutā informs us, the Sultan of Delhi, the Sultan of Maabar, the king of Ceylon and Prince of Jurfattan (a vassal of the Kolathiri of Eli) all possessed ships of their own which were used in maritime trade. He even mentions that the Sultan of Delhi had placed three ships "with complete equipment and full pay and provisions for the crew" at the disposal of a merchant named Shihab al-Din, who sailed in them from Cambay to Hormuz (Gibb 1992: 201). Like the sultans of Delhi, those of 'Bengal' may also have placed their ships at the disposal of influential merchants.

The involvement of the sultans in maritime trade may have led to occasional acrimony between the merchants and the state. This is evident in Tome Pires' description of how the custom officials dealt with merchants at the maritime ports of 'Bengal'. "They say that ten or twelve people collect the dues, each one his own, and they are the officials for this, and when they take their tithe they wrong the merchants and tyrannise over them greatly" (Pires 1967: 95). The condition may have worsened to such a degree during the reign of Husain Shah, that Pires (*ibid.*) makes the following observation: "The Bengalee merchants say that the king of Bengal, who is called Vçem Xaa [Husain Shah], is not benevolent to the merchants, and that many of them are going to other places". Pires' observation may not have been entirely fictitious. Citing an indigenous source, Ray (1999: 157) shows that the sultan tortured Hindu merchants belonging to *suvarṇavaṇik jāti* in 1514-15 AD. We may recall quite a similar situation in the Sena kingdom as recounted in the Vallālasena-Vallabhānanda legend by Ānandabhaṭṭa. It is not impossible that the *suvarṇavaṇiks*, like their forefathers, were also the bankers of the state and acrimonious relationship between them and Husain Shah may have arisen from circumstances similar to those recounted in the Vallālasena-Vallabhānanda legend.

Having discussed the merchants, let us now turn our attention to the exchange centres. Literary sources from the period under review inform us of three types of exchange centres in 'Bengal'. In all probabilities, those who frequented these exchange centres were essentially peddlers *(bepārī)* and traders *(pasārī)*. Some of these exchange centres were known as *hāṭs* as mentioned in the *Padmā-purāṇa* (1494-95 AD) by Bijayagupta (1962: 309, 312), the *Gorkha-vijay* (16th century AD) by Shaikh Faiḍullāh (1356: 40) and the *Caṇḍīmaṅgala* (mid-16th century AD) by Kavikañkaṇa Mukunda (1986: 157-159, 214). These were weekly or bi-weekly gatherings where the residents of the neighbouring villages would buy their daily necessities and sell their commodities. Interestingly, Mukunda (*ibid.*: 157) uses another term, *bājār* (bazar) synonymously with *hāṭ*. Viṣṇu Pāla's *Manasāmaṅgala* (composed in the later half of the 17th century) speaks of both *hāṭ* and *bājār* in urban setting (Sen 1953: xl). Mukunda further shows that wholesale markets were known as *golā-hāṭ* (Mukunda 1986: 67).

The Venetian merchant Caesar Frederick possibly referred to these *hāṭs* established in villages on the banks of the Gaṅgā during his visit to Sātgāon. As described in his account, he along with other foreign merchants went "up and downe the River of Ganges to Faires [in boats], buying their commoditie with a great advantage, because that every day in the weeke they have a Faire, now in one place, and now in another, ..." (Purchas 1905b: 114). Ralph Fitch confirms Caesar Frederick.

> Here in Bengala they have every day in one place or other a great market which they call Chandeau, and they have many great boats which they call pericose [possibly a corruption of the Portuguese *barca;* 'porgos' or 'purgoos' of the later writers], wherewithal they go from place to place and buy rice and many other things; ... (Foster 1968: 26).

If contemporary practice in rural Bangladesh may be accepted as ethnographic evidence, one may add that seasonal *hāṭs* were held to transact specific commodities. For example, during the harvesting season of paddy, *hāṭs* may have been established specifically to buy and sell paddy in paddy-growing areas, which provided easy communication. Similar *hāṭs* may also have been established for buying and selling of cattle, vegetables or even manufactured products.

The *hāṭs* and *bājārs* are still seen in Bangladesh and West Bengal. Not seen, though is the *vikrayasthānas* [literally, place for selling (goods)] which Śrīnātha Ācāryacūḍāmaṇi speaks of in his *Vivāha-tattvārṇava* (Bandyopadhyay 1368 BS: 55). It may be added here that an interesting type of balance, known as the *ḍālā*, may have been used for weighing commodities during this period. "This is a branch of wood without scales, and they tie the goods to the ends, and it is done like that. And with the merchants, if you take a balance, they work out the accounts, and so you do your trading" (Pires 1967: 95). In contemporary Bengali, a balance is known as *pāllā*.

Apart from rural areas, exchange centres were also established in cities such as Gauḍa, Pāṇḍua, Sātgāon, Caṭṭagrāma and Sonārgāon, where volume of mercantile transactions was considerable. *Si yang ch'ao kung tien lu* by Huang Sing-ts'eng (1520), which observes that "[t]here are in the country [of Bengal] ... all kinds of artisans who are skilful in hundreds of crafts" and that "[t]hey gather in the market and hold different shops there" (Bagchi 1945: 124), indicates the possibility of the existence of other centres besides those in the above mentioned cities. In all probability, the people who frequented most in these exchange centres were *pasārī* (trader), *baṇik* (merchant), *sādhu* and *saodāgar*.

Pāṇḍuā (the capital of Sultanate Bengal from c. 1342 to 1432) was situated twenty miles to the northeast of Gauḍa at the confluence of the Mahānandā and a former course of the Gaṅgā. It was well connected by river and land routes leading to various towns in north Bengal and Bihar. Of Pan-tu-wa (Pāṇḍuā), Fei Sin made the following observation during his visit in the early 15th century: "The city walls are very imposing, the bazars well arranged, the shops side by side, the pillars in orderly rows, they are full of every kind of goods" (Bagchi 1945: 121).

The commercial area in Gauḍa (the capital of Sultanate Bengal from 1432) was situated in the northern part of the city (Abid Ali cited in Tarafdar 1999: 133). Ma-Huan (1970: 161) testifies, in the first half of the 15th century "[t]he market-streets [of Gauḍa used to] contain all kinds of shops – bathing establishments, wine-shops, food-shops, sweetmeat-shops ...". Memoirs of the anonymous interpreter who visited the city with a Portuguese mission in 1521 shows that Gauḍa was very large, "stretching for four leagues along the river. (...) The streets and lanes [were] paved with bricks like the Lisbon New Street. The market [was] everywhere and everything – food and other goods alike – [was] in plentiful supply and very cheap" (Bouchon and Thomaz 1988: 323). Tome Pires' (1967: 91) observation, that one of the chief "trading cities in Bengal" was the City of Bengal (Gauḍa in this context), confirms the Portuguese account of 1521.

When Fei Sin reached Suo-na-eul-kiang (Sonārgāon) in the early 15th century, he found the city to be "a walled place with tanks, streets, bazars and which carries on business in all kinds of goods..." (Bagchi 1945: 121). *Si yang ch'ao kung tien lu* compiled by Huang Sing-ts'eng (1520) confirms that the city of Sonārgāon was an exchange centre (Bagchi 1945: 123). *Shu yu chou tseu lu* compiled by Yen Ts'ong-kien (1574) also speaks of the existence of an exchange centre in Sonārgāon and adds that all kinds of goods were brought and distributed from here (Bagchi 1945: 130). Sonārgāon must have been noted for cotton cloth and rice because even at the end of the 16th century, Ralph Fitch observed that "[g]reat store of cotton cloth goeth from hence, and much rice, wherewith they serve all India, Ceilon, Pegu, Malacca, Sumatra, and many other places" (Foster 1968: 28).

Sadegam (Sātgāon) must have been a flourishing centre of trade and commerce in the early 16th century because, according to Tome Pires (1967: 91), it was one of the two chief "trading cities in Bengal" inhabited by ten thousand people, many of whom were merchants. Caesar Frederick, who arrived in 'Bengal' possibly in 1565, speaks of "Merchants gather[ing] themselves together with their trade" in the port-town (Purchas 1905b: 113). As mentioned earlier in Chapter One, Kavikaṅkaṇa Mukunda in his *Caṇḍīmaṅgala*, Vipradāsa Pipilāi in his *Manasā Vijaya*, Bāsudeva Ghoṣa in his *Kaḍcā*, Bṛndābana Dāsa in his *Śrīśrīcaitanya Bhāgabata* and Jayānanda in his *Caitanya-maṅgala* offer a picturesque view of Sātgāon (Saptagrām) as a busy urban trading centre. These evidences from the end of the 15th to the mid-16th century and slightly beyond certainly indicate, alongwith Pires' observation, that as a centre of commercial transactions, Sātgāon held an important position during the 15th-16th centuries. Caṭṭagrāma must have been an important centre for bullion trade. Frederick testifies that a great deal of silver and gold was imported from Pegu to the port (Purchas 1905b: 136). The account of Vincent la Bleau, the French merchant and traveller who arrived in Caṭṭagrāma (Castigan or Shatigan) in 1575 with a group of merchants, confirms Caesar Frederick's information that Caṭṭagrāma was indeed a centre for bullion trade because he (la Bleau) writes of making profit by trading in gold and silver (Ray 1999: 364).

Because both the prime "trading cities in Bengal" were also maritime ports, the state maintained customhouses in these cities, in order to collect custom duties from maritime merchants. Barbosa (1921: 148) and Castanheda (quoted by Campos 1919: 46) confirm the existence of such customhouses under the supervision of a custom-chief who was directly designated by the sultan. The mechanism of collecting custom duties must have been prevalent not only in the early 16th century, as observations made by Pires, Barbosa and Castanheda show but even earlier. In the early 15th century, Fei Sin noted the existence of a customhouse at Ch'a-ti-kiang (Caṭṭagrāma) where "certain duties [were] collected" (Bagchi 1945: 120). There is actually no reason to believe that such a mechanism did not exist throughout the medieval period.

Besides all the exchange centres discussed above, we come to learn of a number of other centres from Ralph Fitch (Foster 1968: 24, 28). These were Tanda, Bacola (Bakerganj) and Serrepore (Śrīpur). Since we do not hear of these exchange centres before the late 16th century, we cannot say definitely whether they existed in the first half of the 16th century. Hence, these must be excluded from the purview o this research.

Caesar Frederick described two interesting exchange centre specially set up for foreign merchants, one of which was regular yearly event at Buttor, the other, an impromptu affai at Sandwīp. Let us hear from him the description of th yearly exchange centre established at Buttor.

> Every yeere at Buttor they make and unmake a Village, wit Houses and Shops made of straw, and with all things necessari to their uses, and this Village standeth as long as the Ships rid there, and till they depart for the Indies, and when they depart everie man goeth to his plot of Houses, and there setteth fire o them, which thing made me to marvaile. For as I passed up t Satagan, I saw this Village standing with a great number o people, with an infinite number of Ships and *Bazars*, and at m returne comming downe with my Captaine of the last Ship, fo whom I tarried, I was all amazed to see such a place so soon razed and burnt, and nothing left but the signe of the burn Houses (Purchas 1905b: 113-114).

The impromptu exchange centre at Sandwīp was set up whe the same merchant was caught in a *Touffon* (*tūfan*, cyclone while sailing to Chatigan (Chāṭgāon) from Pegu, and wa driven to the island located 120 miles from Chatigan.

> And when the people of the Iland saw the ship, and that w were coming a-land: presently they made a place of *Bazar* o Market, with Shops right over against the ship with all manner o provision of victuals to eate, which they brought downe in grea abundance, and sold it so good cheape, that we were amazed a the cheapnesse thereof (*ibid.*: 137).

Caesar Frederick's observations slightly exceed the limit o this research. Nevertheless, his account shows that exchange centres in 'Bengal' need not be seen as rigidly bound to a definite space. Rather, these could be established whereve demand for commodities existed. Not only did the maritime merchants go to the exchange centres, the exchange centre also "came" to the merchants.

As for mechanism of trade in Sultanate Bengal, existin information is extremely vague. Nevertheless, from scan references available and from our deliberations made above it may be possible to reconstruct a working hypothesis.

No foreign travel account speaks of bankers as a separat group or community. Ma-Huan (1970: 160) speaks only o "[w]ealthy individuals who build ships and go to variou foreign countries to trade", Barbosa of "great merchants" Varthema, of "the richest merchants [he] ever met with" an Pires of "merchants with large fortunes". These indicator produce the impression that the merchants, such a Vallabhānanda of the Sena kingdom cited earlier, were thei own bankers. This impression is further strengthened by Zi u-d din Barnī's testimony that in 14th-century Delhi, the rulin class often borrowed large sums of money from Multan merchants (money-lenders and traders who were mostl Hindus) and the *sāhus* (Hindu merchants and bankers) (Ra 1997: 33-34). Although we do not hear of the Multan merchants, the *sāhus* or their compatriots in Sultanate Bengal, it is possible that the *sādhus* of 'Bengal' (merchant and/or moneylenders) actually functioned like the *sāhus*

(Even, the two terms, *sādhus* and *sāhus* appear to be phonetically close to each other.) It is not unlikely that the local ruling class of 'Bengal', dependent on land revenue like their brethren in Delhi, may have found the service of *sādhus* useful and necessary for tiding over lean periods between harvesting seasons when liquidity must have been hard-pressed.

Despite the black hole regarding the bankers of the urban elite residing in Lakhnauti, Pāṇḍua and Gauḍa, we find oft-repeated mention of the *potdār* (a moneychanger, pawnbroker and moneylender roled into one) and *mahājan* (a whole-sale dealer and moneylender) in medieval Bengali literature such as the *Caṇḍīmaṅgala* (Mukunda 1986: 66). One may also refer to a popular tradition of Malda that ascribes the Dhanchak Mosque in Firozpur (Malda) to a Dhanapat Saodāgar (Lambourn 1918: 91). The tradition identifies him and his brother C̃ād Saodāgar, who lived near the small Sāgardīghi east of the Lotan Mosque, as the bankers of Gauḍa in the 16th century. The names of these merchants, it hardly needs to be pointed out, is clearly reminiscent of our oft-cited maritime merchants Dhanapati and C̃ād Saodāgar in the *Caṇḍīmaṅgala* and numerous *Manasāmaṅgala*. That Dhanapat Saodāgar and C̃ād Saodāgar are identified as brothers in the popular tradition of Malda actually seems to say that in the medieval period, the merchant and the banker were closely related as brothers – more possibly as twin brothers – so much so that the merchant was always his double, the banker. The existence of *potdār*s and *mahājan*s clearly prove the point. If near-contemporary practice is of any use as corroborative evidence, it may be helpful to remember that the Marwaris and the Kabulis, who are still remembered for their usurious transactions in 19th century 'Bengal', were primarily merchants.

By the early 16th century, some important changes had taken place in the mechanism of trade, about which we only have scant information from Pires (1967: 17, 45). As our Portuguese source informs us, merchants from Ormuz and the adjoining Persian Gulf maintained factors in Sultanate Bengal. The same source also indicates that the merchants from Chaul, Dhabol and Goa had organised themselves into companies in the country (*ibid.*: 270-271). We have no indication regarding the existence of the *hundi* system or the convention of remitting money by bills of exchange that Jaen-Baptiste Tavernier refers to in his account of 'Bengal' based on his visit in 1666 (Tavernier 1889, I: 130). Nevertheless, since a few trading companies had already been formed in the early 16th century, it is not unlikely that a system akin to *hundi* may have existed as well.

There can be no doubt that there were numerous foreign merchants who ventured into maritime trade in medieval 'Bengal'. Some of them were ship-owners (as Ma-Huan testifies). There must have been others who did not own ships like the merchants of Malacca that Tome Pires (1967: 283-284) describes. They booked "cabins" (the division or partition in the hold of a ship) to transport their merchandise and employed two or three men to look after and manage it (perhaps like the "people who hired themselves out" as described by Ma-Huan). Within 44 days of the return of the ship, the merchant paid the ship-owner a certain percentage of the profit made. In another arrangement, the merchant handed over his merchandise to the ship-owner and received a higher percentage when the ship returned. For vessels bound for 'Bengal', the ship-owner's share was 80%-100% because the merchant who "load[ed] up" for 'Bengal' often made 300% profits. Although is not clear if the merchants' representatives accompanied the merchandise or those were directly handed over to the ship-owner, we may believe both modes of operation were followed.

We have very little information regarding the system of procurement of exportable commodities. As Prakash (1985) shows, from 1630 to 1720, the Dutch East India Company procured cotton and silk textiles through *dālāls* (brokers), usually a native salaried employee who possessed in-depth knowledge of local market and merchants. According to Streynsham Master, the English East India Company operating in Dhaka in the 17th century would appoint *dālāls* (brokers) who would take the money from the Company and deliver it to the *pāikar*s (local stockists) who in turn would travel from town to town and deliver it to the weaver. However, as Master clearly states, the merchants could also purchase the commodities directly from the producers (Raychaudhuri 1982: 344-45).

Dālāls must have existed in Delhi sultanate since we hear Barnī praising Ala al-Din Khalji for the harsh measures he had taken in order to control them. Even though they were non-existent in pre-Muslim South Asia, the *dālāls* must have emerged, argues Ray (1997: 96), as facilitators of transaction between merchants and traders in the expanding market of Sultanate Bengal. However, contemporary Bengali literature appears to be silent about them, implying their non-existence in 'Bengal' during the period under review. Since all foreign accounts on exchange centres cited above appear to have been based on first-hand knowledge of the market, it is probable that the merchants procured their exportable commodities from urban exchange centres. By the 1560s, foreign merchants may even have visited rural exchange centres, as the following account provided by Caesar Frederick testifies.

> I was in this Kingdome foure moneths, whereas many Merchants did buy or freight boates' for their benefits, and with these Barkes they goe up and downe the River of Ganges to Faires, buying their commoditie with a great advantage, because that every day in the weeke they have a Faire, now in one place, and now in another, and I also hired a Barke and went up and downe the River and did my businesse, ... (Purchas 1905b: 114).

As for the mode of production of the commodities, we may turn to Irfan Habib (1978: 293) who has proposed that "a process of enslavement of very large numbers of people, so as to provide cheap reserves of labour" was at work in the Delhi sultanate. These slaves were trained by skilled artisans who had migrated to South Asia from West Asia and then were employed in industrial concerns *(kārkhānās)* owned by the sultans and other members of the aristocracy to produce industrial goods. In support of his view, Habib has cited the case of Firuz Tughlaq who employed 180,000 slaves of whom 12,000 were skilled artisans and 40,000 labourers. Some of them were engaged for carding and spinning in his palace.

Tarafdar (1995: 78) summarily dismisses Habib's view as baseless. "During the period under review" [i.e., the Sultanate period], he says, "commodities were generally produced by artisans in their own houses in collaboration with the family members, not in big factories or industrial organisations which developed at a later period of time". Tarafdar's view, as far as 'Bengal' is concerned, appears plausible because references to industrial goods produced by slave-labour scarcely appears anywhere in medieval Bengali literature. In Śukur Māhmud's *Gopīcāder Sannyās* (composed in 1705), we see slaves engaged in household activities such as fetching water, cutting logs etc. (Sharif 1977: 402). Ālāul's *Tohfā* (composed in 1664) creates a similar impression although the poet does not specify the activities of slaves (*ibid.*: 181). The most note-worthy appointment of slaves in 'Bengal' was in the military and the civil services in the 1460s and the 1470s, which actually led to a *coup d'état* in 1486 and the end of the restored Ilyas Shahi dynasty.

Bearing Tarafdar's opinion in mind, it may be more helpful to turn to Prakash's study on the Dutch East India Company's mode of operation from 1630 to 1720. The following excerpt explains the mode of production of weavers, whose textile products were the most important exportable commodity of Sultanate Bengal. As Prakash shows, the weavers operated as independent artisans. They procured cotton yarn from spinners and raw silk from silk reelers to produce

> standardized varieties of textiles for traditional markets (...) on the basis of the weavers' own resources and at their own risk. These goods were then transported to urban centres and sold to merchants. Some of these merchants might themselves be engaged in trade in these goods, while others bought them on inventory for sale to other merchants (Prakash 1985: 98).

The mode of production and marketing of commodities described above, however, accounted for only a small percentage of the total output of textile goods from 1630 to 1720. Most of the production was organised in *dādani* (from the Persian word *dādan* or "advance") system. Under this system, the weavers agreed to supply specified quantity and stipulated quality of textile within an agreed date of delivery in exchange for an advance provided by the merchants (often a substantial part of the total value of the commodity to be supplied). The merchants providing the advance were known as the *dādandār*, the *dādani*-merchants or *pāikars* (local stockists) who received the money from the Dutch and the English trading companies. The weaver used the *dādan* (advance) for his family's subsistence and procurement of raw materials. In this system, the artisan retained his independent status and remained a "price worker". It is estimated that "[a]bout two-thirds of the price obtained by the weaver covered the costs of the raw material, and the remainder was the reward for his labour" (*ibid.*: 99).

> Clearly, the three key elements in this system were the weavers' need of finance, their relative lack of access to the [international] market, and a desire on their part to avoid risks arising out of their inability to forecast correctly the behaviour of the demand for a given variety of textiles. If finance alone were needed, the weavers could have borrowed from professional moneylenders by pledging the final product to them. But the merchant was the only agency that simultaneously provided the credit and guaranteed the purchase of the product (*ibid.*: 98).

Tarafdar is uncertain if the *dādani* system was operating even towards the end of the period under study (Tarafdar 1999: 153) and he is quite justified in his uncertainty since we do not hear of the system anywhere in contemporary literary sources. Rather, as the following excerpt from the *Gorkha-vijay* (16th century) by Shaikh Faiḍullāh (1356: 40) indicates, the artisans themselves sold their products in the markets.

> I will spin the thread in the dark
> You will weave the *dhūti* (loin cloth)
> Selling them in the *hāṭ* will fetch [us] cowries
> Day by day [we] will flourish
> Our wealth will increase
> Then our tattered sheet and bag will be no more.

Although Shaikh Faiḍullāh is actually speaking of the Tantric practice of a yogi and his female consort, the use of the image – of a weaver and his wife producing textile piece goods and selling them in the market – clearly indicates the general practice of production and marketing during the period under review.

No trade guild is known to have existed in the Sultanate Bengal. Kavikaṅkaṇa Mukunda (1986: 81-83) in his *Caṇḍī-maṅgala* and Bijaygupta (1962: 368-369) in his *Padmā-purāṇa* describe various *jātis*, which, as discussed earlier, were occupationally differentiated endogamous groups. From their descriptions, the following may be identified as the occupational groups of Hindu artisans which existed towards the end of the period under review: iron smiths (*kāmāra*), potters (*kumbhakāra*), weavers (*tantravāya* or *tãti* or *kuri*), confectioners (*modak*), brass smiths (*kãsāri*), oil pressers (*teli*), goldsmith (*paśyatohar*), umbrella makers (*doma*), manufacturers of *ciḍā* and *muḍi* (*chuthār*), carpenters (*chutar*), sawyers (*karati*), handicraftsmen (*karikar*), and leatherworkers (*cāmāra*). The same sources inform us about the following endogamous communities (*jāti*) of Muslim artisans: weavers (*jolā*), loom makers (*sānākar*), paper-makers (*kāgāti* or *kāgāji*), molasses makers (*śiuli*), and arrow makers (*tirakar*) (Mukunda 1986: 78-79; Bijaygupta 1962: 135-139; Cūḍāmaṇidāsa 1957: 30-31).

Repeated reference to weavers in contemporary Bengali literature (Mukunda 1986: 78; Das 440: 278; Bijaygupta 1962: 135-139; Sen (Vipradas Pipilai) 1953: 80) indicates that the majority of Muslims in rural 'Bengal' were members of this occupational group. This group, along with the loom makers, the tailors (*darji*), the weavers of thick ribbon, and the dyers served the textile industry, which was the most important industry of the period. However, as Eaton (1997: 101) reminds us, the Muslim artisans were "[s]ocially distinct from the *ashraf*" (Muslim elite). Similarity in social organisation between them and the Hindus suggest that Muslim artisans were converted from Hinduism.

****

We may now sum up our findings in this chapter by making the following observations:

During the entire time frame of this research, maritime trade was privately controlled with varying degrees of state control. At one end of an imaginary scale, we find the Maurya state attempting to exert some amount of control with the *paṇyādhyakṣa* ('the superintendent of trade'), the *saṁsthādhyakṣas* ('the superintendent of markets'), the *navādhyakṣas* ('the superintendent of ships') and customhouses with *śulkādhyakṣas* ('the superintendent of custom') in charge for collecting *praveśya* and *niṣkrāmya śulka* (import and export duties). In some cases, such as in the Sultanate of 'Bengal', the sultans themselves participated in maritime trade. At the other end of the imaginary scale, powerful guilds operated in the Khaḍga and the Deva kingdoms with very little state control.

Non-native maritime merchants who operated in Vaṅga and Suhma or southern Rāḍha from the 1st century AD to the early 4th century AD were predominantly the Kharoshṭī-using immigrants and in Sultanate Bengal, they were foreigners of various nationalities such as Arabs, Persians, Abyssinians, Turks and Indians. Only in the medieval period we hear of merchants whom we can identify with certitude as a breed of maritime merchants with indigenous roots. There may have been others, such as the maritime merchants who must have accompanied or followed Vijaya in the early historic period, unnamed maritime cousins of Dhṛtipālas and the Ribhupālas of the Gupta era, Jambhalamitra Lōkadatta and Buddhamitra of the Pāla era, and anonymous merchants from Samataṭa. However, we have no definite information about them.

We have a relatively complete picture of the mechanism of trade only from the medieval period. During this period, the artisans themselves manufactured specific commodity in their own houses in collaboration with the family members, on the basis of their own resources and at their own risk. Instead of guilds, they operated under different occupational castes or occupationally differentiated endogamous groups. The artisans themselves sold their commodities in the nearest exchange centre (*bājār*, *hāṭ* or *melā*). *Byāpārīs* (small-scale traders or a dealers) and *pasārīs* (traders) procured these and sold them in *golā-hāṭs* (wholesale markets) to *baṇiks*, *bāniyās*, *bānyās*, *benes* (merchants) in urban areas (Gauḍa and Pāṇḍua) or maritime ports (such as Sātgāon, Caṭṭagrāma and Sonārgāon). From them the *saodāgars* (affluent maritime merchants), who were their own bankers, procured the commodities. Then they freighted the commodities in their own vessels, or booked a division in the hold of the ship. In the latter case, they either handed their commodities to the captain or sent their representatives with the commodities. The emergence of trading companies by the early 16th century indicates that maritime trade operations may have begun to acquire a multi-national and corporate character.

In the early medieval period, we hear of the *vaṇik* (merchant) and the *sārtha(vāha)* (itinerant trader) in Samataṭa and the *vyavahāriṇ* (tradesmen) in the Kamboja kingdom (Southwest Bengal). Exchange centres such as *haṭṭika* ("petty market"), *haṭṭa* (market) and *haṭṭa-vara* (large market) may have existed all over 'Bengal'. Savar, Devaparvata and Samandar were large exchange centres. Hence, the mode of operation in the early medieval period, from the first to the third level of exchange centres may have been similar to that of the medieval period. We may hazard a guess that merchants belonging to the powerful guilds of Harikela obtained their commodities from the *sārtha(vāha)* (itinerant trader) and that Buddhist religious establishments may have been linked with the guilds.

Because of paucity of information, we can only suggest that during the reign of Gopacandra and Samācāradeva, the mode of operation of the "principal traders" (*pradhāna-vyāpāriṇa*) and "principal men of business" (*pradhānā-vyavahā(ri)ṇa)* in urban exchange centres of Savar and Candravarmakoṭa may have been similar to that of the *baṇiks, bāniyās, bānyās* and *benes* of the medieval period. During the Gupta era, the mechanism of trade by which the *nagaraśreṣṭhīs* (the chief merchants) and the *prathamakulikas* (the chief artisans), along with other merchants and artisans and their powerful guilds operated in exchange centres at Koṭivarṣa, Puṇḍranagara and Pañcanagarī (in Puṇḍravardhana), Krīpura (in Samataṭa), Tāmralipti (in Suhma) and Gaṅgābandar (in Vaṅga), may have been rigidly structured and custom-bound. We may also add that Buddhist monastic establishments may have facilitated the maritime trade network. Beyond this we have very little data to show how exactly the mechanism of maritime trade functioned.

From the Post-Maurya era, we may derive a not-too-distinct image of the affluent Kharoshṭī-using merchants such as Devajñātamitra and Aja procuring grains and other commodities from inland urban centres such as Puṇḍranagara (Mahāsthāngarh) and Koṭivarṣa (Bāngarh) with the help of local agents. These merchants may have transported their commodities in their own means of transportation such as bullock-carts or riverine boats to Tāmralipti and Gaṅgābandar. There, maritime merchants such as Yasoda may have procured their commodities and exported them abroad on ships hired from ship-owners such as the Tasvodajas. Others, such as Dvijanma, may have exported his commodities in his own ships. All these merchants operated under some form of organised structures similar to guilds.

Perhaps the most distinguishing aspect of the mechanism of trade in the Maurya era was that wide-ranging social groups at different hierarchical levels were involved in a manner that reflects the bustling activities of a time when the mechanism was yet to become rigidly structured and custom-bound as it did in the Gupta era. The state may have had a monopoly in producing some commodities and occasionally intervened in setting the price and may even have imported and exported some commodities. Nevertheless, the state must have operated in a complementary relationship with the private merchants operating under various guilds.

Conclusion

It may be recalled that in the **Introduction**, the problem for this research was identified thus: absence of a logically developed chronological overview of maritime trade focussed on the entire region of 'Bengal', with clear enumeration of all major aspects that any kind of maritime trade entails. The examination undertaken by this research traverses a period of over two thousand years, and identifies the maritime port sites of 'Bengal', the hinterlands of these ports, the exported and imported commodities, the media of exchange, the types of ships, the navigational techniques employed in coastal and transoceanic voyages, the sailing schedules, the trade routes and the merchants involved in the maritime trade and their mercantile milieu.

In our pursuit of answers to the problems we have been able to prepare a strong and reliable empirical base and chronological framework that may lead to problem-oriented perusal of future research on maritime trade in 'Bengal'. We have also been able to present the findings at the end of each chapter. We may now sum up these findings in order to arrive at a comprehensive picture of maritime trade in early 'Bengal'.

1. Bengal's maritime trade continued uninterruptedly from the 3rd century BC to the first half of the 16th century AD.

2. A total of seven maritime ports operated in the region of 'Bengal'. These were: Tāmralipti (c. 3rd century BC to the mid-8th century AD), Gaṅgābandar (c. 3rd century BC to the 5th century AD), Wārī-Baṭeśwar (c. 3rd century BC to the 3rd century AD), Koṭālipāḍā/Candravarmakoṭa (c. 2nd century AD to the early 8th century AD), Sonārgāon (early 14th century to the second half of the 15th century AD), Sātgāon (early 14th century to 1632 AD) and Caṭṭagrāma (prior to the second century AD to the present). Four of the seven ports were located in eastern 'Bengal' (known at present as Bangladesh).

3. The importance of these ports lay not so much as entrepôts in Indian Ocean trade network. They were more important for their hinterland since they provided vital economic links to landlocked regions lying in the north-west (Central Asia and Bactrian Greek kingdom), the north (kingdoms in the eastern Himalayas and Cooch Behar), the north-east (Kāmrūpa, Tripura and China) and the east (Tripura). In terms of area, the total hinterland was largest in the early historic period, followed by the medieval period.

4. 'Bengal' exported predominantly agricultural products (rice, sugar and edible items) and manufactured goods (cotton, textiles, pottery and beads). In return, it mostly imported mineral products, spices and cowries. It appears that Bengal's basket of exported commodities was filled with most numerous items in the medieval period, followed by the early historic period. The items in the basket had shrunk to its lowest number in the late historic period.

5. Among all the media of exchange that prevailed in 'Bengal', cowries appear to have persisted right from the Maurya era to the first half of the 16th century. It is not unlikely that barter also persisted, albeit in varying degree of puissance. Bullion money has been used from the 4th century BC to the 12th century AD except the Maurya and the Gupta eras. Continued use of coins may be seen from the Maurya to the Gupta era and the Sultanate era and intermittent use may be seen in the post-Gupta era. All coins were issued by ruling authorities (i.e., states) except in Puṇḍravardhana, Rāḍha, Suhma, and in the south-westernmost area of Vaṅga during the reign of the Mauryas, and Samataṭa and/or Harikela during the reign of the Khaḍgas, the Devas and the Candras.

6. Maritime shipbuilding industry evolved in 'Bengal' in the early historic period. Two indigenous traditions of shipbuilding may be identified. These are (1) the dugout and sewn-planking tradition (in which belong the *Saraṁgā*, the *bālām*, and the *bajrā*) and (2) the reverse-clinker tradition (in which belongs the *paṭiyā*). Quite a few types of non-indigenous vessels were inducted in the maritime shipping of 'Bengal'. These were the multiple-masted sewn-plank ships (such as the Colandia), the single-masted sewn-plank ships (such as the Trapyaka and other) and the double-masted sewn-plank ships (in the early historic period), the *dhow* (in the early medieval period) and the *sāmpān* and the junk (in the medieval period).

7. It appears that indigenous navigational techniques followed by the mariners of 'Bengal' had much in common with the techniques followed all over South Asia. However, the mariners in 'Bengal' did not develop beyond the primitive stage. Furthermore, they failed to take advantage of transoceanic voyages and continued with coastal voyages during the entire time frame of this research.

8. The maritime trade routes connected 'Bengal' with major ports in South Asia and Southeast Asia and the Red Sea. The farthest extent eastward was Fu-nan and westward was Jeddah. It was never directly linked with Rome or China.

9. Non-native maritime merchants played dominating role in maritime trade of 'Bengal' and the share of native merchants in the trade has mostly been insignificant or low. Maritime trade has always been privately controlled with varying degree of state control. The greatest degree of state control existed in Maurya Bengal and the least in the Khaḍga and the Deva kingdoms. In some cases, such as in the Sultanate Bengal, the sultans themselves participated in maritime trade.

10. Bengal's control over Indian Ocean maritime trade networks, as manifested by indigenous vessels, development of navigational techniques and participation of maritime merchants does not appear ever to have been significant.

References

Acharya, N.R. (Ed.) 1860. *Suśruta-samhita*. Bombay: Nirnay Sagar Press.

Acharya, N.R. (Ed.) 1949. *Yajñavalkyasmṛti with Mitaksara*. Bombay: Nirnay Sagar Press.

Agarwal, R.S. 1982. *Trade Centres and Routes in Northern India (c. 322 BC-AD 550)*. Delhi: B.R. Publishing Corporation.

Ahmad, S. Maqbul 1960. *India and the Neighbouring Territories in the Kitāb Nuzhat al-Mushtāq Fi'khtirāq al-Āfāq of al-Sharīf al-Idrīsī (a translation with commentary)*. Leiden: E.J. Brill.

Ahmad, S. Maqbul 1989. *Arabic Classical Accounts of India and China: Book One Al-Masalik wa'l-Mamalik and BookTwo Akhbar Al-Sin wa'l-Hind,* translated from the original Arabic with commentary. Shimla: Indian Institute of Advance Studies in association with Ṛddhi-India, Calcutta.

Ahmed, Nazimuddin 1975. *Pāhāḍapur* (in Bengali). Dhaka: Department of Archaeology and Museums, Government of the People's Republic of Bangladesh.

Ahmed, Nazimuddin (Ed.) 1979. *Bangladesh Archaeology*, Vol. 1, No. 1. Dacca: Department of Archaeology and Museums, Government of the People's Republic of Bangladesh.

Ahmed, Noazesh 2003. Indigo, *Banglapedia: National Encyclopedia of Bangladesh*, Volume 5 (Sirajul Islam chief editor), p. 251, Dhaka: Asiatic Society of Bangladesh.

Ahmed, Shamsuddin 1936. Note on a Unique Copper Coin of Barbak Shah, *Journal of the Royal Asiatic Society of Bengal, Letters* II (Numismatic Supplement No. XLVI): 111-112.

Ahmed, Wakil 1990. *Bāṅglāy Bideshi Parjatak* (Foreign Travellers in Bengal; first published in 1968; in Bengali). Dhaka: Anisur Rahman.

Ahmed, Zia Uddin 2003. Cotton, *Banglapedia: National Encyclopedia of Bangladesh*, Volume 3 (Sirajul Islam chief editor), pp. 140-141, Dhaka: Asiatic Society of Bangladesh.

Aiyangar, K.V. Rangaswami (Ed.) 1941. *Bṛhaspatismṛti*. Baroda: Oriental Institute.

Alam, Mahbubul 1965. *Caṭṭagrāmer Itihās: Purānā Āmal* (History of Chittagong: Ancient Period, in Bengali). Chittagong Nayalok Prakashani.

Alam, Md. Shafiqul, M.M.A. Bashar, M.A. Bakar Siddique, M. Majibar Rahman, A. Abdullah, and Md. Sadequzzaman 2004. Wārī-Baṭeśware Sāmpratik Pratnatāttvik Khanan, a seminal paper presented at the national seminar titled *Sāmpratik Pratnacarcā* organised by the Department of Archaeology, Government of Bangladesh and Bangladesh Itihās Parishat (Department of Islamic History and Culture, University of Dhaka), held on May 28, 2004 at Lalbagh Fort, Dhaka.

Ali, A.K.M. Yaqub 1989. *Muslim Mudrā O Hastalikhan Śilpa* (in Bengali). Dhaka: Bangla Academi.

Ali, Syed Murtaza 1964. *History of Chittagong*. Dacca: Standard Publishing Ltd.

Allaby, Michael 1996. *The Concise Oxford Dictionary of Botany*. Oxford: Oxford University Press.

Allan, John 1975. *Catalogue of the Coins of the Gupta Dynasties and of Śaśāṅka, King of Gauḍa* (originally published in 1914). New Delhi: Oriental Books reprint Corporation.

Alves, Francisco 2003. Geneaology and Archaeology of Portuguese Ships at the Dawning of the Modern World, http://www.abc.se/~m10354/publ/gen_port.htm, site accessed on 22 September 2003.

Andrade, C. Jr 2003. Chinese Sampan Teaches Much to Designers, http://www.friend.ly.net/~dadadata/ junk/sampan.html, originally published in *The Rudder,* July 1917. Site accessed on 22 September 2003.

Angelucci, Enzo 1970. *Encyclopaedia of Ships*. London: Odhams Books.

Annual Report of the Archaeological Survey of India (Eastern Circle) 1906-07: 12.

Antonova, K., G. Bongard-Levin, and G. Kotovsky 1982. *Bhāratbarṣer Itihāsa* (*History of India,* in Bengali), translated by M. Chattopadhayaya and D. Sharma. Moscow: Progressive Publishers.

Arasaratnam, Sinnappah 1994. *Maritime India in the Seventeenth Century*. Delhi: Oxford University Press.

Ardika, I. Wayan & Peter Bellwood 1991. Sembiran: the Beginnings of Indian Contact with Bali, *Antiquity* 65 (247): 221-232.

Ardika, I. Wayan, Peter Bellwood, R.A. Eggleton and D.J. Ellis 1993. A Single Source for South Asian Export Quality Rouletted Ware, *Man and Environment* 18 (1): 101-109.

Arunachalam, B. 1987. The Haven-finding Art in Indian Navigational Traditions and Cartography, *The Indian Ocean Explorations in History, Commerce and Political* (Satish Chandra Ed.), pp. 191-221, New Delhi: Sage Publications.

Arunachalam, B. 1996. Traditional Sea and Sky Wisdom of Indian Seamen and Their Practical Applications, in *Tradition and Archaeology: Early Maritime Contacts in the Indian Ocean* (Himanshu Prabha Ray & Jean-Francois Salles Eds.), pp. 261-281, New Delhi: Manohar Publishers.

Askari, S.H. 1956. The Correspondence of Two 14th Century Sufi Saints of Bihar with the Contemporary Sovereigns of Delhi and Bengal, *The Journal of the Bihar Research Society* XLII (II): 177-195.

Aung, Maung Htin 1967. *A History of Burma*. New York: Columbia University Press.

Aung, Myint 1970. The Excavations at Halin, *Journal of Burma Research Society* LIII (ii): 55-61.

Aung, San Tha 1997. *The Buddhist Art of Ancient Rakhine* (second edition, first edition published in 1979). Insein: U Ye Myint.

Aung Thaw 1968. *Report on the Excavations at Beikthano*. Rangoon: Ministry of Union Culture, Revolutionary Government of the Unio of Burma.

Bag, A.K. 1988. Ships and Ship-building Technology in Ancient and Medieval India, in *Marine Archaeology of Indian Ocean Countries Proceedings of the First Indian Conference on Marine Archaeology of Indian Ocean Countries-Oct 1987* (S.R. Rao Ed.), pp. 8-11 Goa: National Institute of Oceanography.

Bagchi, Prabodh Chandra 1943. Development of Religious Ideas, in *The History of Bengal*, Volume 1: Hindu Period (R.C. Majumda Ed.), pp. 394-428, Dacca: The University of Dacca.

Bagchi, Prabodh Chandra 1944. *India and China: A Thousand Years of Sino-Indian Cultural Contact*. Calcutta: China Press Limited.

Bagchi, Prabodh Chandra 1945. Political Relations between Bengal and China in the Pathan Period, *Visva-Bharati Annals*, Vol. I (P.C Bagchi Ed.), pp. 96-134, Calcutta: Visva-Bharati.

Bagchi, Prabodh Chandra 1981. India and *China: A Thousand Years of Cultural Relations*. Calcutta: Saraswat Library.

Bāṇabhaṭṭa 1897. The *Haṣra-carita* (E.B. Cowell and F.W. Thomas Eds.). London: Royal Asiatic Society.

Bandyopadhyay, S.C. 1368 BS. *Smrti Sastre Vāṅgāli*. Kolikata.

Banerji, Adris 1951. Kushanas in Eastern India, *Journal of the Numismatic Society of India* XIII (I): 107-109.

Banerji, R.D. 1911. *Descriptive List of Sculptures & Coins in the Museum of Baṅgīya Sāhitya Parishad*. Calcutta: *Baṅgīya Sāhity Parishad*.

Banerji, R.D. 1917a. The Naihati Grant of Vallāl-sena: The 11th Year, *Epigraphia Indica* XIV: 156-163.

Banerji, R.D. 1917b. The Bangarh Grant of Mahi-Pāla I: The 9th Year, *Epigraphia Indica* XIV: 324-330.

Banerji, R.D. 1919-20. Barrackpur Grant of Vijayasena: The 32nd Year, *Epigraphia Indica* XV: 278-286.

Banerji, R.D. 1920. Unrecorded Kings of Arakan, Numismatic Supplement XXXIII, *Journal and Proceedings of the Asiatic Society c Bengal* (New Series) XVI: 85-87.

Baṅśīdāsa, Dvija 1357 BS. *Śrīśrī Padmapurāṇa* (Pūrṇacandra Cakravartī Ed.). Kolikata: Victoria Library.

Barbosa, Duarte 1918. *The Book of Duarte Barbosa: An Account of the Countries Bordering on the Indian Ocean and Their Inhabitant* (Mansel Longworth Dames edited and annotated), Vol. I. London: Hakluyt Society.

Barbosa, Duarte 1921. *The Book of Duarte Barbosa: An Account of the Countries Bordering on the Indian Ocean and Their Inhabitant* (Mansel Longworth Dames edited and annotated), Vol. II. London: Hakluyt Society.

Barnett, Lionel D. 1925-26. Vappaghoshavata Grant of Jayanāga, *Epigraphia Indica and Record of the Archaeological Survey of Indi* XVIII: 60-64.

Barnī, Zīāu-d dīn 1871. Tārikh-I Fīroz Shāhī, in *The History of India, as Told by Its Own Historians: The Muhammadan Period*, vol. II (John Dowson edited from the Posthumous papers of the late Sir H.M. Elliot), pp. 93-268, London: Trubner & Co.

Barua, Birinchi Kumar 1951. *A Cultural History of Assam (Early Period)*, Volume 1. Nowgong (Assam): Shri K.K. Barooah.

Barua, B.M. 1934. The Old Brāhmī Inscription of Mahāsthān, *Indian Historical Quarterly* X: 57-66.

Barua, B.M. and Pulin Behari Chakravarti 1947-48. Mehar Plate of Damodardeva, *Epigraphia Indica* XXVII: 182-191.

Baruah, S.L. 1985. *A Comprehensive History of Assam*. New Delhi: Munshiram Manoharlal Publishers.

Basa, Kishor K. and Karuna Sagar Behera 1999. Indo-Roman Trade, in *Maritime Heritage of India* (K.S. Behera Ed.), pp. 15-28. New Delhi: Aryan Books International.

Basak, Radhagovinda 1913-14a. Rampal Copper-plate Grant of Srichandradeva, *Epigraphia Indica* XII: 136-142.

Basak, Radhagovinda 1913-14b. Belava Copper-plate of Bhojavarmandeva, the Fifth Year, *Epigraphia Indica* XII: 37-43.

Basak, Radhagovinda 1915-16.The Silimpur Stone-slab Inscription of the Time of Jayapāla-deva, *Epigraphia Indica and Record of the Archaeological Survey of India* XIII: 283-295.

Basak, Radhagovinda 1919-20. Tipperah Copper-plate Grant of Lokanatha: The 44th Year, *Epigraphia Indica and Record of the Archaeological Survey of India* XV: 301-315.

Basak, Radhagovinda 1923-24. Dhanaidaha Copper-plate Inscription of the Time of Kumaragupta I: The Year 113, *Epigraphia Indica* XVII: 345-348.

Basak, Radhagovinda 1949-50. Madanpur Plate of Srichandra, Year 44. *Epigraphia Indica* XXVIII: 51-58.

Basham, A.L. 1964. *Studies in Indian History and Culture*. Calcutta: Sambodhi Publications.

Basham, A.L. 1985. *The Wonder that was India: A Survey of the History and Culture of the Indian Sub-continent Before the Coming of the Muslims* (1st edition published in 1954). Calcutta: Rupa & Co.

Beal, Samuel (Tr.) 1869. *Travels of Fah-hian and Sung-yun, Buddhist Pilgrims from China to India (400 AD and 518 AD)*. London: Trubner and Co.

Beal, Samuel (Tr.) 1906. *Si-Yu-Ki: Buddhist Records of the Western World*. Vol. II. London: Kegan Paul, Trench, Trubner & Co.

Beal, Samuel (Tr.) 1973. *The Life of Hiuen-Tsiang by Shaman Hwui Li with an introduction containing an account of the works of I tsing* (second edition, first published by Kegan Paul, Trench, Trubner & Co, London in 1911). New Delhi: Munshiram Manoharlal Publishers Pvt. Ltd.

Begley, Vimala 1983. Arikamedu Reconsidered, *American Journal of Archaeology* 87 (4): 461-481.

Begley, Vimala 1988. Rouletted Ware at Arikamedu: A New Approach, *American Journal of Archaeology* 92 (3): 427-440.

Begley, Vimala 1991. Ceramic Evidence for Pre-*Periplus* Trade on the Indian Coasts, in *Rome and India: The Ancient Sea Trade* (Vimala Begley and Richard Daniel De Puma Eds.), pp. 157-196, Madison: The University of Wisconsin Press.

Bengal Past and Present 1910. The Earliest Recorded Episcopal Visitation of Bengal 1712-1715, *Bengal Past and Present* VI (July-December): 200-215.

Bennett, Anna and Ian Glover 1992. Decorated High-Tin Bronze Bowls from Thailand's Pre-history, in *Southeast Asian Archaeology 1990* (Ian Glover Ed.), University of Hull: Centre for Southeast Asian Studies, pp. 187-208.

Bernier, François 1968. *Travels in the Mogul Empire (AD 1656-1668)*. A revised and improved edition based upon Irving Brock's translation by Archibald Constable (first published in 1891). New Delhi: S. Chand & Co.

Bhaduri, Rina 1992. Madhyayuge Bāṅglāy Nagarbinyāser Dhārā (Sultānī Āmal), in *Madhyayuge Bāṅglār Samāj O Saṁskṛti* (Society and Culture in Medieval Bengal: A Collection of Articles in Bengali) (Aniruddha Ray and Ratnavali Chattopadhyaya Eds.), pp. 31-59, Calcutta: K.P. Bagchi & Co.

Bhandare, Shailendra 1999. Ship-Type Satavahana Coins - An Examination, a paper presented at the Second International Conference on Marine Archaeology, 8th to 10th January 1999 at "Shivshakti" Dr Bedekar's Hospital, Naupada, Thane 400 602.

Bhandarkar, D.R. 1921. *The Carmichael Lectures on Ancient Indian Numismatics*. Calcutta: University of Calcutta.

Bhattacharjee, Arun 1979. History *of Ancient India*. New Delhi: Sterling Publishing Pvt. Ltd.

Bhattacharya, Bijanbihari (Selected and Edited) 1961. *Manasāmaṅgala* (A Selection from Ketakadasa Kshemananda's works). New Delhi: Sahitya Akademi.

Bhattacharya, Gouriswar 1992. The New Pāla Ruler Mahendrapāla, *Pratna-Samiksha* 1: 165-170.

Bhattacharya, Padmanath Vidyavinod 1920. To the East of Samatata (on the six countries mentioned but not visited by Yuan Chwang), *Journal of the Royal Asiatic Society* I: 1-19.

Bhattacharyya, Amitabha 1977. *Historical Geography of Ancient and Early Medieval Bengal*. Calcutta: Sanskrit Pustak Bhandar.

Bhattacharyya, Asutosh 1989. *Vangala-Mangal Kavyer Itihas* (A History of Medieval Bengali Narrative Poetry). Calcutta: A. Mukherjee & Co. Pvt. Ltd.

Bhattacharyya, Dhires 1973. *Understanding India's Economy: A Course of Analysis*, Volume 1. Calcutta: Progressive Publishers.

Bhattacharyya, Dinesh Chandra 1933. The Maināmati Copperplate of Raṇavaṅkamalla Harikāladeva (114 Śaka), *Indian Historical Quarterly* IX: 282-289.

Bhattacharyya, P.N. 1935-36. Nalanda Plate of Dharmapaladeva, *Epigraphia Indica and Record of the Archaeological Survey of India* XXIII: 290-292.

Bhattasali, Nalini Kanta 1922. *Coins and Chronology of the Early Independent Sultans of Bengal*. England: W. Heffer & Sons.

Bhattasali, Nalini Kanta 1923-24a. The Kedarpur Plate of Sri-Chandra-Deva, *Epigraphia Indica* XVII: 188-192.

Bhattasali, Nalini Kanta 1923-24b. Some Image Inscriptions from East Bengal, *Epigraphia Indica* XVII: 349-355.

Bhattasali, Nalini Kanta 1925-26. The Ghugrahati Copper-Plate Inscription of Samachara-Deva, *Epigraphia Indica and Record of the Archaeological Survey of India* XVIII: 74-86.

Bhattasali, Nalini Kanta 1943. The New Kailan Plate of Sridharana Rata, *Indian Historical Quarterly* XXII (3): 169-171.

Bhattasali, Nalini Kanta 1954. Two Grants of Varmans of Vanga, *Epigraphia Indica* XXX: 255-263.

Bhattasali, Nalini Kanta 2001. *Iconography of Buddhist and Brahmanical Sculptures (in the Dacca Museum)*. Reprinted, originally published in 1929 from Dacca. New Delhi: Aryan Books International.

Bhowmik, S.K. 1988. Examples of Fine Art Connected with Ancient Maritime Activities in Gujarat, in *Marine Archaeology of Indian Ocean Countries: Proceedings of the First Indian Conference on Marine Archaeology of Indian Ocean Countries-Oct 1987* (S.R. Rao Ed.), pp. 97-98, Goa: National Institute of Oceanography.

Bijayagupta 1962. *Padmā-purāṇa* (Jayantakumar Dasgupta Ed.). Calcutta: University of Calcutta.

Bijaygupta, No Date. *Padmāpurāṇa bā Manasāmaṅgala* (Paṇḍiit Kālīkiśor Bidyābinod Ed.). Kolkata: Benimadhab Sheel's Library.

Binod, Srīrāy 1993. *Padmā-purāṇa* (Muhammad Shahjahan Miah Ed.). Dhaka: University of Dhaka.

Bird, J.H. 1963. *The Major Seaports of the United Kingdom*. London: Hutchinson and Co.

Blochmann, H. 1870. Notes on Arabic and Persian Inscriptions in the Hūglī District, *Journal of the Asiatic Society of Bengal* XXXIX (IV): 280-303.

Blochmann, H. 1872. Koch Bihar, Koch Hajo, and Asam, in the 16th and 17th centuries, according to the Akbarnamah, Padishahnamah, and the Fathiyah i Ibriyah, *Journal of the Asiatic Society of Bengal* XLI, part I (I): 49-101.

Blochmann, H. 1968. *Contributions to the Geography and History of Bengal (Muhammedan Period)* (originally published in the Journal of the Asiatic Society in 1873, 1874 and 1875). Calcutta: Asiatic Society.

Blue, Lucy, E. Kentley, S. McGrail and U. Mishra 1997. The Patia Fishing Boat of Orissa: A Case Study of Ethnoarchaeology, *South Asian Studies* 13: 189-207.

Bopearachchi, Osmund 1996. Seafaring in the Indian Ocean: Archaeological Evidence from Sri Lanka, in *Tradition and Archaeology: Early Maritime Contacts in the Indian Ocean* (Himanshu Prabha Ray & Jean-Francois Salles Eds.), pp. 59-77, New Delhi: Manohar Publishers.

Bose, A.N. 1967. *Social and Rural Economy of Northern India*. In two volumes. Calcutta: Firma K.L.M.

Bose, P.N. 1893. Notes on the Geology of a part of the Tenasserim Valley with special reference to the Tendau-Kamapying Coal-field, *Records of the Geological Survey of India*, XXVI (4): 148-164.

Bouchon, Genevieve 1984. Trade Routes to Pasai and Pegu at the Beginning of the 16th century, in *Trade and Shipping in the Southern Seas* (selected readings from Archipel 18 <1979>), pp. 93-121, Bangkok: SPAFA Co-ordinating Unit.

Bouchon, Genevieve 2000. A Microcosm: Calicut in the Sixteenth Century, *Asian Merchants and Businessmen in the Indian Ocean and the China Sea* (Denys Lombard and Jean Aubin Eds.), pp. 40-49. Oxford: New Delhi.

Bouchon, Genevieve and Luis Filipe Thomaz 1988. *Voyage Dan Les Deltas Du Gange Et De L'irraouaddy: Relation Portugaise Anonyme (1521)*. Paris.

Bowen, Richard LeBaron, Jr. 1960. Egypt's Earliest Sailing Ships, *Antiquity* XXXIV: 117-131.

Bowrey, Thomas 1905. *A Geographical Account of Countries Round the Bay of Bengal 1669 to 1679*, Part 1, (Richard C. Temple Ed.). Cambridge: Hakluyt Society.

Brahma, Tripti 1989. *Lokojībane Bāṅglār Loukik Dharmasaṁgīt O Dharmīya Melā*. Kolkata: Firma K.L.M.

Briggs, John 1910. *History of the Rise of the Mahomedan Power in India till the Year AD 1612* (translated from the original Persian of Mahomed Kasim Ferishta), Vol. IV. Calcutta: R. Cambray & Co.

Bronson, Bennett 1990. Glass and Beads at Khuan Lukpad, Southern Thailand, in *Southeast Asian Archaeology 1986* (Ian Glover and Emily Glover Eds.), pp. 213-230, Oxford: Bar Internationals.

Cakravartī, Nāgendranath 1960. *Rājaśekhara O Kāvyamimāṁsā* (containing Bengali translation of Rājaśekhara's *Kāvyamimāṁsā*). Santiniketan: Visvabharati.

Campos, J.J.A. 1919. *History of the Portuguese in Bengal*. Calcutta: Butterworth & Co.

Casson, Lionel 1973. *Ships and Seamanship in the Ancient World*. Princeton: Princeton University Press.

Casson, Lionel 1989. *The Periplus Maris Erythraei*. Princeton: Princeton University Press.

Casson, Lionel 1991. Ancient Naval Technology and the Route to India, in *Rome and India: The Ancient Sea Trade* (Vimala Begley and Richard Daniel De Puma Eds.), pp. 8-11, Madison: The University of Wisconsin Press.

Chakrabarti, Dilip K. 1992. *Ancient Bangladesh: A Study of the Archaeological Sources*. Dhaka: University Press Ltd.

Chakrabarti, Dilip K. 1996. Two Examples of Mauryan Art from Bengal, *Journal of Bengal Art* 1: 77-80.

Chakrabarti, Dilip K., N. Goswami and R.K. Chattopadhyay 1994. Archaeology of Coastal West Bengal: Twenty-four Parganas and Midnapur Districts, *South Asian Studies* 10: 135-160.

Chakraborti, H.P. 1966. *Trade and Commerce of Ancient India (c. 200-c.650 AD)*. Calcutta: Academic Press.

Chakraborty, Sharmi 2000. *Chandraketugarh: A Cultural and Archaeological Study (500 BC to 500 AD)*. Unpublished Ph. D. Dissertation, Deccan College Post-Graduate and Research Institute, Pune.

Chakravarti, P.C. 1943. Economic Conditions, *The History of Bengal*, Vol. 1: Hindu Period (R.C. Majumdar Ed.), pp. 642-669, Dacca: University of Dacca.

Chakravarti, Rajkumar and Anangamohan Dasa 1330 BS. *Sandwīper Itihāsa*, Sandwīp: Jayakumar Chakravarti.

Chakravarti, Ranabir 1992. Maritime Trade in Horses in Early Historical Bengal: A Seal from Chandraketugarh, *Pratna-Samiksha* 1: 155-160.

Chakravarti, Ranabir 1992-93. Maritime Trade and Voyages in Ancient Bengal, *Journal of Ancient Indian History* XIX: 145-171.

Chakravarti, Ranabir 1995. Merchants and Other Donors at Ancient Bandhogarh, *South Asian Studies*, 11: 33-41.

Chakravarti, Ranabir 1996. The Putabhedana as a centre of Trade in Early India, *South Asian Studies* 12: 33-38.

Chakravarti, Ranabir 1998. Vangasagara and Other Related Terms: An Examination, in *History and Archaeology of Eastern India* (Asok Datta Ed.), pp. 254-264, New Delhi: Books & Books.

Chakravarti, Ranabir (Ed.) 2001. *Trade in Early India*. New Delhi: Oxford University Press.

Chakravarti, Ranabir & Gopal Chandra Sinha 1985. A Note on the Tumain Inscription of Kumāragupta I, G.E. 116, *Indian Museum Bulletin* XX: 46-48.

Chakravortty, Surendra Kisor 1932. Kapardaka Purāṇa, *Indian Historical Quarterly* VIII: 595-599.

Chalmers, Robert (Ed.) 1898. *The Majjhima-Nikāya*, Vol. II. London: Luzac & Company.

Chandra, Moti 1977. *Trade and Trade Routes in Ancient India*. New Delhi: Abhinav Publications.

Chattopadhyay, Bhaskar 1994. *An Introduction to the Maritime History of India (With Special Reference to the Bay of Bengal): Pre-Modern Period*. Calcutta: Punthi Pustak.

Chattopadhyaya, B.D. 1977. *Coins and Currency Systems in South India c. AD 225-1300*. New Delhi: Munshiram Manoharlal Publishers Pvt. Ltd.

Chaudhuri, K.N. 1985. *Trade and Civilisation in the Indian Ocean: An Economic History from the Rise of Islam to 1750*. Cambridge: Cambridge University Press.

Chaudhuri, Mamata 1990. Glass – An Archaeological Specimen of Some Sites of Southern India (circa 2560 BC-1600 AD), in *Historical Archaeology of India: A Dialogue Between Archaeologists and Historians* (Amita Ray and Samir Mukherjee Eds.), pp. 217-225, New Delhi: Books and Books.

Chaudhury, Nalini Ranjan Roy 1983. *Tripura Through the Ages: A Short History of Tripura from the Earliest Times to 1947 AD*. New Delhi: Sterling Publishers Pvt. Ltd.

Chimpa, Lama and Alaka Chattopadhyaya (Translated) 1970. *Tāranātha's History of Buddhism in India* (Debiprasad Chattopadhyaya Ed.). Delhi: Motilal Banarsidass.

Chitnis, Cmde Ajay H. 1999. Navigation in the Indian Ocean - A Comparative Study of European and Indian Maritime Techniques in the Medieval Period, in *Proceedings of Twentieth Anniversary Seminar on European Influence in the Shaping of Maritime India*, pp. 21-28, Mumbai: Maritime History Society.

Chittagong Port Authority 1998. *Year Book 1996--98*. Chittagong: Bandar Bhaban.

Chopra, P.N., B.N. Puri and M.N. Das 1974. *A Social, Cultural and Economic History of India*. Delhi: Macmillan Company of India.

Chowdhury, Abdul Hoque 1994. *Prachin Arakan Rowainga Hindu O Barua Bouddha Adhibashi* (in Bengali, Rowainga, Hindu and Barua Buddhist Inhabitants of Ancient Arakan). Dhaka: Bangla Academy.

Chowdhury, Kamalakanta Gupta 1966. Paśchimbhāg copperplate of Mahārājā Śrīchandradeva in *Nalini Kanta Bhattasali Commemoration Volume*. Dacca: Dacca Museum.

Chowdhury, Kiranchandra 1983. *Bhārater Itihāskathā*, Vol.1. Calcutta: Modern Book Agency.

Christie, Anthony 1957. An Obscure Passage from the *Periplus: ΚΟΛΑΝΔΙΟΦΩΝΤΑ ΤΑ ΜΕΓΙΣΤΑ*, *Bulletin of the School of Oriental and African Studies* XIX (2): 345-353.

Clark, Grahame 1977. *World Prehistory: In New Perspective* (third edition). Cambridge: Cambridge University Press.

Colless, Brian 1980. Han and Shen-tu: China's Ancient Relations with South Asia, *East and West*, New Series 30 (1-4): 157-177.

Comfort, Howard 1991. Terra Sigillata at Arikamedu, in *Rome and India: The Ancient Sea Trade* (Vimala Begley and Richard Daniel De Puma Eds.), pp. 134-150, Madison: The University of Wisconsin Press.

Cortesao, A 1945. The 'City of Bengala' in Early Reports, *Journal of the Royal Asiatic Society of Bengal, Letters* XI (1): 10-14.

Cowell, E.B. (Ed.) 1957. *The Jātaka or Stories of the Buddha's Former Births* (translated from the Pāli by various hands), Six volumes. London: Luzac and Co.

Cūḍāmaṇidāsa 1957. *Gaurāṅgabijay* (Sukumar Sen Ed.). Calcutta: Asiatic Society.

Cunningham, Alexander 1871. *The Ancient Geography of India: The Buddhist Period including the Campaigns of Alexander, and the travels of Hwen-Thsang*. London: Trubner and Co.

Cunningham, Alexander 1967. *Coins of Mediaeval India from the Seventh Century down to the Muhammadan Conquests*. Varanasi: Indological Book House.

Cunningham, Alexander 1969. *Report of A Tour in Bihar and Bengal in 1879-80 from Patna to Sunargaon*. Delhi: Indological Book House.

Dani, Ahmad Hasan 1952. The House of Rājā Ganeśa of Bengal, *Journal of the Asiatic Society, Letters* XVIII (2): 121-170.

Dani, Ahmad Hasan 1962. Coins of the Chandra Kings of East Bengal, *Journal of the Numismatic Society of India*, XXIV (I): 141-142.

Dani, Ahmad Hasan 1963. *Indian Palaeography*. Oxford: Clarendon Press.

Dāsa, Bṛndābana 440 Gaurābda. *Śrīśrīcaitanya Bhāgabata*. Kolkata: Mṛṇālakānti Ghoṣ.

Dāsa, Kṣemānanda 1316 BS. *Manasā Maṅgala;* Calcutta: (name of publisher not available).

Das, S.C. 1965. *Indian Pandits in the Land of Snow*. Calcutta: Firma K.L. Mukhopadhyay.

Das Sudhir Ranjan 1968. *Rājbāḍīdāṅgā: 1962 (Chiruṭī: Jadupur): An Interim Report on Excavations at Rājbāḍīdāṅgā and Terracotta Seals and Sealings*. Published as the Asiatic Society Monograph Series, Volume XIV. Calcutta: The Asiatic Society.

Dasgupta, Arun 1973. Aspects of Bengal's Sea-Borne Trade in the Pre-European Period, *Proceedings of Third History Congress*, pp. 143-153, Dacca.

Dasgupta, Ashin 2001. The Maritime Merchant and Indian History, in *The World of the Indian Ocean Merchant 1500-1800: Collected Essays of Ashin Das Gupta* (Uma Das Gupta Compiled), pp. 23-33 (first published in *South Asia*, New Series, Vol. 7, No. 1, 1984), New Delhi: Oxford University Press.

Dasgupta, Paresh Chandra 1975. *The Archaeological Treasures of Tamralipta*. Tamluk: Tamralipta Museum & Research Centre.

Dasgupta, Tamonash. Chandra 1935. *Aspects of Bengali Society from Old Bengali Literature*. Calcutta: University of Calcutta.

Dastidar, A.G. and P.K. Ghosh 1964. A Study of Subsoil Conditions of Calcutta, *Proceeding of the Symposium on the Study of Soil Properties in Calcutta Region*, September 18-19: 37-64.

Datta, Asok 1995. *Black and Red Ware Culture in West Bengal*. Delhi: Agam Kala Prakashan.

Datta, Asok 1999. Bengal and South East Asia – Early Trade and Cultural Contacts. *Journal of Bengal Art* 4: 49-60.

Datta, Asok 2000. Geographical Location of Ancient Tamralipta Port, *Journal of Bengal Art* 5: 129-136.

Davids, T.W. Rhys (Tr.) 1894. *The Questions of King Milinda*, Part II. Oxford: Clarendon Press.

Davids, T.W. Rhys 1899. Early Commerce between India and Babylon, *Journal of the Royal Asiatic Society* 51: 432.

Davids, T.W. Rhys and J. Estlin Carpenter 1890. *The Dīgha Nikāya*. London: Oxford University Press.

De, Bijan Behari 1970. Epigraphic Accounts of the Numismatic History of Bengal, in *Early Indian Indigenous Coins* (D.C. Sircar Ed.), pp. 141-146, Calcutta: University of Calcutta.

De, Gourisankar 2001. Ship Motif on Ancient Indian Coins, in *Hakim Habibur Rahman Khan Commemoration Volume* (Enamul Haque Ed.), pp. 145-148, Dhaka: The International Centre for Study of Bengal Art.

Deba, Nārāyaṇa and Jānakī Nātha 1382 BS. *Padma-purāṇa (Manasaāmaṅgala)* (5th edition). Dhaka: New Age Publcations.

Deloche, Jean 1991. Boats and Ships in Bengal Terracotta Art, *Bulletin de l' École Française d' Extréme-Orient* LXXVIII: 2-49.

Deloche, Jean 1994. *Transport and Communications in India Prior to Steam Locomotion, Vol. II: Water Transport* (Translated from the French by James Walker). Delhi: Oxford University Press.

Deloche, Jean 1996. Iconographic Evidence on the Development of Boat and Ship Structures in India (2nd cent. BC-15th cent. AD): A New Approach, in *Tradition and Archaeology: Early Maritime Contacts in the Indian Ocean* (Himanshu Prabha Ray & Jean-Francois Salles Eds.), pp. 199-224, New Delhi: Manohar Publishers.

Deo, S.B. 1989. Beads, in *An Encyclopedia of Indian Archaeology*, Vol. 1 (A. Ghosh Ed.), pp. 216-221, New Delhi: Munshiram Manoharlal.

Deraniyagala, S.U. 1986. Excavations in the Citadel of Anuradhapura: Gedige 1984, A Preliminary Report, *Ancient Ceylon* 6: 39-48.

Deraniyagala, S.U. 1990. The Proto-and-Early Historic Radiocarbon Chronology of Sri Lanka, *Ancient Ceylon* 12: 251-292.

Deva, Narāyaṇa 1942. *Padmā-purāṇa* (Tamonash Chandra Dasgupta Ed.). Calcutta: University of Calcutta.

Digby, Simon 1982a. Economic Conditions before 1200, in *The Cambridge Economic History of India, Volume I: c. 1200-c. 1750* (Tapan Raychaudhuri and Irfan Habib Eds.), pp. 45-47, Cambridge: Cambridge University Press.

Digby, Simon 1982b. The Currency System, in *The Cambridge Economic History of India, Volume I: c. 1200-c. 1750* (Tapan Raychaudhuri and Irfan Habib Eds.), pp. 93-101, Cambridge: Cambridge University Press.

Digby, Simon 1982c. The Maritime Trade of India, in *The Cambridge Economic History of India, Volume I: c. 1200-c. 1750* (Tapan Raychaudhuri and Irfan Habib Eds.), pp. 125-159, Cambridge: Cambridge University Press.

Dikshit, K.N. 1921-22. Notes of Places Visited by Mr. Dikshit, *Annual Report of the Archaeological Survey of India:* 1921-22: 74-87.

Dikshit, K.N. 1922-23. *Annual Report of the Archaeological Survey of India* 1922-23: 109-110.

Dikshit, K.N. 1938. Excavations at Paharpur, Bengal, in *Memoirs of the Archaeological Survey of India*, No. 55. Delhi: Archaeological Survey of India.

Dikshit, Moreshwar Gangadhar 1969. *History of Indian Glass*. Bombay: University of Bombay.

Dutt, M.N. 1988. *The Mahābhārata,* vols. I and VI, translated literally from the original Sanskrit text. Delhi: Parimal Publications.

Dutt, Manmatha Nath (Ed.) 1904. *A Prose English Translation of Agni Puranam*, Vol. II. Calcutta: M. N. Dutt.

Dvivedi, Mahāmahopādhyaya Sudhākara 1897. *The Bṛihat Saṃhita by Varāhamihhira with the Commentary of Bhaṭṭotpala*, Vol. X, Part II. Benares: E. J. Lazarus & Co.

Eaton, Richard M. 1997. *The Rise of Islam and the Bengal Frontier 1204-1760*. Delhi: Oxford University Press.

Edye, John 1834. Description of the Various Classes of Vessels Constructed and Employed by the Natives of the Coasts of Coromandel, Malabar, and the Island of Ceylon, for their Coasting Navigation, *Journal of the Royal Asiatic Society* I: 1-14.

Faiḍullāh, Shaikh 1356 BS. *Gorkha-vijay* (Panchanan Mandal Ed.), Calcutta: Vishvabharati Publications.

Fatimi, S.Q. 1996. History of the Development of the *Kamāl*, in *Tradition and Archaeology: Early Maritime Contacts in the Indian Ocean* (Himanshu Prabha Ray & Jean-Francois Salles Eds.), pp. 283-292, New Delhi: Manohar Publishers.

Fergusson, James 1971. *Tree and Serpent Worship or Illustrations of Mythology and Art in India in the First and Fourth Centuries after Christ from the Sculptures of the Buddhist Topes at Sanchi and Amravati*. Delhi: Oriental Publishers.

Fergusson, James and James Burgess 1880. *The Cave Temples of India*. London: W. H. Allen & Co.

Fitch, Ralph 1905. The Voyages of Master Ralph Fitch Merchant of London to Ormus, and so on to Goa in the East India, to Cambaia, Ganges, Bengala, in *Hakluytus Posthumus, or Purchas his Pilgrims,* by Samuel Purchas (1625), 20 vols. Vol. 10, pp. 165-204. Glasgow: James MacLehose & Sons.

Foster, William (Ed.) 1968. *Early Travels in India*. Rreprint, no date is available of the original publication. Delhi: S. Chand & Company.

Francis, Peter Jr. 1986. Bead Report XVIII: The Asian Bead Study Tour, part iv: a little tube of glass, *Ornament* 10 (1): 54-57 and 74-78.

Gait, Edward 1926. *A History of Assam*. Calcutta: Thacker, Spink & Co.

Ganguli, D.C. 1938. The Early Home of the Imperial Guptas, *The Indian Historical Quarterly* XIV (3): 532-535.

Ganguli, Kisari Mohan 1990. *The Mahābhārata of Krishna-Dwaipayana Vyasa*, Vol. II, translated into English prose from the original Sanskrit text. New Delhi: Munshiram Manoharlal Publishers Pvt. Ltd.

Gaur, A.S., Sundaresh and Sila Tripati 2005. Marine Archaeological Investigations along the Saurashtra Coast, West Coast of India, *Journal of the Asiatic Society of Bangladesh* (Humanities) 50: 159-195.

Geiger, Wilhelm 1986. *The Mahāvaṃsa or the Great Chronicle of Ceylon*. New Delhi: Asian Educational Services.

Gerini, G.E. 1909. *Researches on Ptolemy's Geography of Eastern Asia (Further India and Indo-Malay Archipelago)*. New Delhi: Oriental Books Reprint Corporation.

Ghosh, A. 1939-40. A Bronze Image Inscription from Nalanda, *Epigraphia Indica* XXV: 334-335.

Ghosh, Ishan Chandra (translated and edited) 1323 BS. *Jātaka* (Volumes I-VI). Calcutta: Prakashani (1381 BS reprint).

Ghosh, N.C. 1986. Excavations at Satanikota (1977-80), *Memoirs of the Archaeological Survey of India*, No. 82. New Delhi: Archaeological Survey of India.

Ghosh, R.N. 1998. Post-Neogene Lithostratigraphy of Bengal Basin and Orissa Plains: A Prelude for Archaeological Studies, in *History and Archaeology of Eastern India* (Asok Datta Ed.), pp. 1-22, New Delhi: Books & Books.

Ghosh, R.N. and S. Majumder 1991. Geology and Morphostratigraphy of West Bengal: A Database for Archaeological Exploration, in *Studies in Archaeology: Paper presented in Memory of P.C. Dasgupta* (Asok Datta Ed.), pp. 7-40, New Delhi: Books and Books.

Ghoshal, U.N. 1967. Industry, Trade and Currency, in *Age of the Nandas and Mauryas* (K.A. Nilakanta Sastri Ed.), pp. 260-283, Delhi: Motilal Banarsidass.

Gibb, H.A.R. (translated and selected) 1986. *Ibn Battuta: Travels in Asia and Africa (1325-1354)*. New Delhi: Oriental Books Reprint Corporation.

Gibb, H.A.R. (translated and selected) 1992. *Ibn Battūta: Travels in Asia and Africa (1325-1354)*. New Delhi: Asian Educational Services.

Giles, H.A. (re-translated) 1972. *The travels of Fa-hsien (399-414 AD), or Record of the Buddhistic Kingdoms*. Varanasi: Indological Book House.

Glover, Ian C. 1989. *Early Trade between India and Southeast Asia: A Link in the Development of a World Trading System*. Occasional Papers no. 16, University of Hull: Centre for South-East Asian Studies.

Glover, Ian C. 1990. Ban Don Ta Phet: The 1984-85 Excavation, in *Southeast Asian Archaeology 1986: Proceedings of the First Conference of the Association of Southeast Asian Archaeologists in Western Europe* (Ian and Emily Glover Eds.), pp. 139-184, Oxford: BAR International series -561.

Glover, Ian C. 1996a. Recent Archaeological Evidence for Early Maritime Contacts between India and Southeast Asia, in *Tradition and Archaeology: Early Maritime Contacts in the Indian Ocean* (Himanshu Prabha Ray & Jean-Francois Salles Eds.), pp. 129-158, New Delhi: Manohar Publishers.

Glover, Ian C. 1996b. The Southern Silk Road: Archaeological Evidence for Early Trade between India and Southeast Asia, in *Ancient Trades and Cultural Contacts in Southeast Asia* (Amara Srisuchat Ed.), pp. 57-94, Bangkok: The Office of the National Culture Commission.

Gogte, Vishwas D. 1997. The Chandraketugarh-Tamluk Region of Bengal: Source of the Early Historic Rouletted Ware from India and Southeast Asia, *Man and Environment* XXII (1): 70-85.

Gogte, Vishwas D. 2001. XRD Analysis of the Rouletted Ware and Other Fine Grey Ware from Tissamaharama, in *Ancient Ruhuna: Sri Lankan-German Archaeological Project in the Southern Province*, Volume 1 (Hans-Joachim Weisshaar, Helmut Roth and W. Wijeyapala Eds.), pp. 197-202, Mainz Am Rhein: Verlag Philipp Von Zabern.

Goodal, George (Ed.) 1952. *The Mercantile Marine Atlas*. London: George Philip & Sons Ltd.

Gopal, Lallanji 1965. *The Economic Life of Northern India c. AD 700-1200*. Varanasi: Motilal Banarsidass.

Goswami, Kunja Gabinda 1948. *Excavations at Bangarh (1938-41)*. Asutosh Museum Memoir No. 1. Calcutta: University of Calcutta.

Goswami, Kunja Gabinda 1966. Chandraketugarh and its Archaeological Importance, *Indian Museum Bulletin* 1(2): 42-46.

Greenhill, Basil 1971. *Boats and Boatmen of Pakistan*. Newton Abbot: David & Charles (Publishers) Limited.

Greenhill, Basil and John Morrison 1995. *The Archaeology of Boats and Ships: an Introduction*. London: Conway Maritime Press.

Greeshmalatha, A. P. and G. Victor Rajamanickam 1993. An Analysis of Different Types of Traditional Coastal Vessels along the Kerala Coast, *Marine Archaeology* 4: 36-50.

Griesbach, C. L. 1892. Geological Sketch of the Country North of Bhamo, *Records of the Geological Survey of India*, XXV (3): 127-130.

Griffiths, John 1983. *The Paintings in the Buddhist Cave-Temples of Ajanta, Khandesh, India*, Volume 1 (originally published in 1896). Delhi: Caxton Publications.

Guṇasēkara (Ed.) 1900. *The Rājavaliya or A Historical Narrative of Sinhalese Kings from Vijaya to Vimala Dharma Surya II*. Colombo: George J.A Skeen.

Gunawardana, R.A.L.H. 1987. Changing Patterns of Navigation in the Indian Ocean and Their Impact on Pre-colonial Sri Lanka, in *The Indian Ocean: Explorations in History, Commerce and Politics* (Satish Chandra Ed.), pp. 54-89, New Delhi: Sage Publications.

Gunawardana, R.A.L.H. 1990. Seaways to Sielediba: Changing Patterns of Navigation in the Indian Ocean and Their Impact on Precolonial Sri Lanka, in *Sri Lanka and the Silk Road of the Sea* (Senake Bandaranayake, Lorna Dewaraja, Roland Silva and K.D. G. Wimalaratne Eds.), pp. 25-43, Colombo: The Sri Lanka National Commission for UNESCO and the Central Cultural Fund.

Gupta, Kamalakanta 1979. Two Mainamati Copper-plate Inscriptions of the Khadga and Early Deva Times (7th & 8th Centuries AD), in *Bangladesh Archaeology*, Number 1 (Nazimuddin Ahmed Ed.), pp. 141-148, Dacca: The Department of Archaeology and Museums, Government of the People's Republic of Bangladesh.

Gupta, Kamalakanta (edited with translations, notes, etc.) 1967. *Copperplates of Sylhet*, Volume I (7th-11th century). Sylhet: Lipika Enterprise.

Gupta, K.M 1927-28. The Bhatera Copper-plate Inscription of Govinda Kesavadeva (c. 1049 AD), *Epigraphia Indica* XIX: 277-286.

Gupta, Parmeshwari Lal 1975-76. The Date of Bakhtiyar Khilji's Occupation of Gauda, *Journal of the Varendra Research Museum* 4: 29-34.

Gupta, Parmeshwari Lal 1996. *Coins* (originally published in 1969). New Delhi: National Book Trust.

Gupta, Sunil 1997. *Roman Egypt to Peninsular India: Archaeological Patterns of Trade 1st century BC to 3rd century AD*. Unpublished Ph. D. Dissertation, Poona University.

Gupta, S.P. 1987. Sanghol: The Meeting Place of Works of Art of Gandhara and Mathura Schools, in *Investigating Indian Art* (M. Yaldiz and W. Lobo Eds.), pp. 89-104, Berlin.

Gupta, Vijaya No Date. *Manasāmaṅgala* (Basanta Kumar Bhattacharya Ed.), 3rd edition. Barisal: Vaniniketan.

Guy, John 1997. A Sculptural Boat Model from Eastern India, *South Asian Archaeology 1995*, Vol. 2 (Raymond Allchin and Bridget Allchin Eds.), pp. 769-778, New Delhi: Oxford and IBH Publishing Co.

Habib, Irfan 1978. Economic History of the Delhi Sultanate – An Essay in Interpretation, *Indian Historical Review* IV (2): 287-303.

Habib, Irfan 1982a. Agrarian Economy, in *The Cambridge Economic History of India, Volume I: c. 1200-c. 1750* (Tapan Raychaudhuri and Irfan Habib Eds.), pp. 48-76, Cambridge: Cambridge University Press.

Habib, Irfan 1982b. Non-Agricultural Production and Urban Economy, in *The Cambridge Economic History of India, Volume I: c. 1200-c. 1750* (Tapan Raychaudhuri and Irfan Habib Eds.), pp. 76-93, Cambridge: Cambridge University Press.

Habibullah, A.B.M. 1948a. Later Ilyas Shahis and the Abyssinians (1442-1498), in *The History of Bengal, Volume II: Muslim Period, 1200-1757* (Jadu-Nath Sarkar Ed.), pp. 130-141, Dacca: University of Dacca.

Habibullah, A.B.M. 1948b. Husain Shahi Dynasty (1493-1538), in *The History of Bengal, Volume II: Muslim Period, 1200-1757* (Jadu-Nath Sarkar Ed.), pp. 142-165, Dacca: University of Dacca.

Habibullah, A.B.M. 1991. Takar Itihas, in *Abu Mohamed Habibullah Smarakgrantha* (in Bengali) (Salahuddin Ahmed, Momtazur Rahman Tarafdar and Ajoy Roy Eds.), pp. 431-442, Dhaka: Bangladesh Itihas Parishad.

Hammer, Joseph von (Tr.) 1834. Account of the Mohi't: A Nautical Work in Arabic, by Sidi Ali Capudān, *Journal of the Asiatic Society* III: 545-553.

Hammer, Joseph von (Tr.) 1836. Extracts from the Mohi't (*the Ocean*): A Turkish Work on Navigation in the Indian Seas, *Journal of the Asiatic Society* V: 441-468.

Hammer, Joseph von (Tr.) 1838. Extracts from the *Mohit* (the Ocean): A Turkish Work on Navigation in the Indian Seas, *Journal of the Asiatic Society of Bengal* VII: 767-780.

Haque, Enamul 1996. Chandraketugarh: A Resume of Excavation Reports (1956-67), *Journal of Bengal Art* 1: 39-75.

Haque, Enamul, S.S. Mostafizur Rahman & S.M. Kamrul Ahsan 2000. A Preliminary Report on Wari-Bateshwar Trial Excavation by ICSBA, *Journal of Bengal Art* 5: 283-315.

Hardy, E. (Ed.) 1900. *The Aṅguttara-Nikāya*, Part V: Dasaka-Nipāta, and Ekadasaka-Nipāta. London: Luzac & Company.

Harris, Jeff 1999. The Dhow of Racing, *Saudi Aramco World*, Vol 50, N0 3, <http://www.saudiaramcoworld.com/issue/199903/the.dhow.of.racing.htm>, accessed on May 20, 2006.

Harvey, G.E. 1967. *History of Burma: From the Earliest Times to 10 March 1824, The Beginning of the English Conquest.* London: Frank Cass & Co. Ltd.

Ḥasan, Hādī 1928. *A History of Persian Navigation.* London: Methuen and Co. Ltd.

Hasan, Mahmudul (compiled and edited) 1983. *Bāṅglādeśer Lokaśilpa.* Sonargaon, Dhaka: Bangladesh Folk Art and Crafts Foundation.

Heeley, W.L. 1875. Extracts from Taranatha's History of Buddhism in India, *Indian Antiquary* IV: 101-104.

Heeren, A.H.L. 1846. *Historical Researches into the Politics, Intercourse, and Trade of the Principal Nations of Antiquity*, Vol. 1 (translated from the German). Delhi: Daya Publishing House.

Hirth, Friedrich and W.W. Rockhill 1965. *Chau Ju-Kua: His Work on the Chinese and Arab Trade in the Twelfth and thirteenth Centuries, entitled Chu-fan-chi* (originally published in St Petersburg by the Printing Office of the Imperial Academy of Sciences in 1911). Taipei: Literature House Ltd.

Hoernle 1882. Coins found at Toomluk, *Proceedings of the Asiatic Society of Bengal* (August, 1882): 111-115.

Hornell, James 1920. The Origins and Ethnological Significance of Indian Boat Designs, *Memoirs of the Asiatic Society of Bengal* VII (3): 139- 256.

Hornell, James 1923. Survivals of the Use of Oculi in Modern Boats, *The Journal of the Royal Anthropological Institute of Great Britain and Ireland* LIII: 289-321.

Hornell, James 1924. The Boats of the Ganges, *Memoirs of the Asiatic Society of Bengal* VIII (3): 173-198.

Hornell, James 1970. *Water Transport: Origins and Early Evolution* (originally published in 1946 by Cambridge University Press, Cambridge). Newton Abbot: David & Charles.

Horner, I.B. (Tr.) 1957. *The Collection of the Middle Length Sayings (Majjhima-Nikāya)*, Vol. II: The Middle Fifty Discources (Majjhimapaṇṇāsa). London: Luzac & Company.

Horner, I.B. (Tr.) 1959. *The Collection of the Middle Length Sayings (Majjhima-Nikāya)*, Vol. III: The Final Fifty Discources (Uparipaṇṇāsa). London: Luzac & Company.

Hoskins, K.F.G. 1969. Aspects of the Geology of the Tin-field of South East Asia, *Second Technical Conference on Tin.* Bangkok: International Tin Council.

Hossain, Anwar 2003. Wind Energy in Bangladesh, http://www.sdnbd.org/wind.htm, accessed on 23 March 2003.

Hussein, Asiff 2006. The Durava – toddy tappers or royalty? WWW Virtual Library - Sri Lanka, <http://www.lankalibrary.com/cul/durava.htm>, accessed on 20 May 2006.

Hosten, H. (Tr.) 1925. Jesuit Letters from Bengal, Arakan & Burma (1599-1600), *Bengal Past and Present* XXX: 52-76.

Hourani, G.F. 1951. *Arab Seafaring in the Indian Ocean in Ancient and Early Medieval Times.* Princeton: Princeton University Press.

Hoyle, B.S. 1967. *The Seaports of East Africa.* Nairobi: East African Publishing House.

Hughes, T.W.H. 1893. Report on the Prospecting Operations, Mergui District, 1891-92, *Records of the Geological Survey of India,* XXVI (1): 40-53.

Hultzsch, E. 1901. Plates of the Times of Saasankaraja, Gupta-Samvat 300, *Epigraphia Indica and Record of the Archaeological Survey of India*, Vol. VI, pp. 143-146.

Hultzsch, E. 1907-1908. Tirumalai Rock Inscription of Rajendra-chola I, *Epigraphia Indica* IX: 229-233.

Humphrey, Caroline 1985. Barter and Economic Disintegration, *Man* 20 (1): 48-72.

Hunter, W.W. 1876a. *A Statistical Account of Bengal*, Volume III: Districts of Midnapur and Hughli (including Howrah). Delhi: D.K. Publishing House.

Hunter, W.W. 1876b. *A Statistical Account of Bengal*, Volume VII, Districts of Maldah, Rangpur and Dinajpur. London: Trubner & Co.

Hunter, W.W. 1877. *A Statistical Account of Bengal, Volume IV: Districts of Bardwān, Bānkurā and Bīrbhūm.* London: Trubner & Co. (Delhi: D. K. Publishing House, 1973 reprint.)

Hunter, W.W. 1973. *A Statistical Account of Bengal*, Vol. VI: Chittagong Hill Tracts, Chittagong, Noakhali, Tipperah, Hill Tipperah (first Indian reprint, originally published in 1876 by Trubner & Co, London). Delhi: D. K. Publishing House.

Huntingford, G.W.B. (Tr. & Ed.) 1980. *The Periplus of the Erythraean Sea by an Unknown Authour with Some Extracts from Agatharkhidēs 'On the Erythraean Sea*. London: The Hakluyt Society.
Husain, Mahdi 1953. *The Rehla of Ibn Baṭṭūṭa (India, Maldive Islands and Ceylon)*. Baroda: Oriental Institute.
al-Idrīsī. 1867. Nuzhatu-l Mushtak, in *The History of India as Told by Its Own Historians*, edited from the posthumous papers of the late Sir H.M. Eliot by Professor John Dowson, Vol. I, pp. 74-93, London: Trubner & Co.
Ibn Battūta 1983. *Travels in Asia and Africa (1325-1354)*. London: Routledge & Kegan Paul.
Ibn Khurdadba 1867. Kitabu-l Masalik Wa-l Mamalik, in *The History of India as Told by Its Own Historians* (Professor John Dowson edited from the posthumous papers of the late Sir H.M. Eliot), Vol. I, pp. 12-17, London: Trubner & Co.
Imam, Abu 2000. *Excavations at Mainamati: An Exploratory Study*. Dhaka: The International Centre for Study of Bengal Art.
Indian Archaeology – A Review: 1954-55: 19-20, 1955-56: 61-62, 1956-57: 29-30, 81, 1957-58: 51-53, 1958-59: 55-56, 1959-60: 50-52, 1960-61: 39-40, 1961-62: 62-63, 1962-63: 46-47, 1963-64: 59, 63-65, 1964-65: 52-53, 1965-66: 59-60, 1966-67: 48, 1967-68: 50 and 1973-74: 33. New Delhi: Department of Archaeology, Government of India.
Islam, Kamrunnesa 1984. *Aspects of Economic History of Bengal, c. 400-1200 AD*. Dhaka: Asiatic Society of Bangladesh.
Islam, M. Shahidul 2001. *Sea-level Changes in Bangladesh: The Last Ten Thousand Years*. Dhaka: Asiatic Society of Bangladesh.
Jagajjiban 1984. *Manasāmaṅgala* (Ashutosh Das and Sureshchandra Bhattacharya Eds.). Calcutta: Calcutta University.
Jahan, Shahnaj Husne 1999. Wari-Bateshwar: An Important Centre of Maritime Activities in Ancient Bengal, *Journal of Bengal Art* 4: 207-216.
Jahan, Shahnaj Husne 2000. Samandar: An Important Centre for Maritime Activities in Bengal, *Journal of Bengal Art* 5: 223-243.
Jahan, Shahnaj Husne 2002. Early Maritime Trade Network of Bengal, *Man and Environment* XXVII (1): 127-138.
Jahan, Shahnaj Husne 2003. Examining Possible Existence of a Maritime Port at Koṭālipāḍā, *Journal of the Bengal Art* 8: 251-263.
Jahan, Shahnaj Husne 2004. Of Gangê and Gaṅgābandar: Location of the Port and Condition of the Harbour, *Man and Environment*, XXIX (2): 90-101.
Jahan, Shahnaj Husne 2005a. State's Role in the Maritime Trade of Early Historic Bengal, *Man and Environment* XXX (2): 74-82.
Jahan, Shahnaj Husne 2005b. The Port of Tāmralipti in Early Bengal, *Journal of the Indian Ocean* Archaeology (2): 115-135.
Jahan, Shahnaj Husne 2005c. The Operative Milieu of Merchants and the Role of the State in Gupta Bengal, *Journal of the Asiatic Society of Bangladesh (Humanities)* 50: 196-217.
Jahan, Shahnaj Husne (forthc.). Re-examining 'Borobudur Ships' as Evidence of Maritime Contact with South Asia, in *Vanamala: Festschrift Adalbert J. Gail* (Gerd J.R. Mevissen and K. Bruhn Eds.), Berlin.
Jana, Rangan Kanti 1998. Ships on Seals from Chandraketugarh, in *History and Archaeology of Eastern India* (Asok Datta Ed.), pp. 242-253, New Delhi: Books & Books.
Jarrett, H.S. 1891. *The Ain I Akbari by Abul Fazl Allami* (translated from the original Persian). Calcutta: Asiatic Society of Bengal.
Jayānanda 1971. *Caitanya-maṅgala* (Bimanbehari Majumdar and Sukhamay Mukhopadhyay Eds.). Calcutta: Asiatic Society.
Joseph, Charles 1881. Notes on the Right Bank of the Hooghly (executed in 1841 and first published in *The Calcutta Review*, Vol. IV, Dec. 1845), in *Selections from the Calcutta Review*, Nos. I-IV, Vol. I, May-Dec 1844-45. Calcutta: Thomas S. Smith.
Jolly, Julius (Ed.) 1885. *Institutes of Narada: Together with copious extracts from the Naradabhāshya of Asahāya and Other Standard Commentaries*. Calcutta: Asiatic Society.
Kale, Gangadhara V.R. and J.P. (Eds.) 1966. *Gautamapraṇīta Dharmasutraṇi with the Commentary Mitaksara-vṛtti of Haradatta*. Pune: Anandasrama Mudranalaya.
Kale, M.R. 1966. *Daśakumāracharita of Daṇḍin*. Delhi: Motilal Banarsidass.
Kangle, R.P. 1963. *The Kauṭilīya Arthaśāstra, Part II: An English Translation with Critical and Explanatory Notes*. Bombay: T. V. Chidambaran, Registrar, University of Bombay.
Kangle, R.P. 1965. *The Kauṭilīya Arthaśāstra, Part III: A Study*. Bombay: T. V. Chidambaran, Registrar, University of Bombay.
Karim, Abdul 1960. *Corpus of the Muslim Coins of Bengal down to AD 1538*. Dacca: Asiatic Society of Pakistan.
Karim, Abdul 1967. Two Hitherto Unnoticed Sultanate Mosques of Chittagong, *Journal of the Asiatic Society of Pakistan* XII (3): 321-331.
Karim, Abdul 1987. *Bāṅglār Itihās: Sultānī Āmal* ((History of Bengal: Sultanate Period, in Bengali). Dhaka: Bangla Academy.
Karim, Abdul 1994. *Muslim Bāṅglār Itihās O Oitihya* (History and Tradition of Muslim Bengal, in Bengali). Dhaka: Bangla Academy.
Karim, Mohammad Rezaul 1399 BS. Wārī-Baṭeśwarer Chāpāṅkita Raupya Mudrā: Ekti Prastābanā (in Bengali), *Itihāsa* 26 (1-3): 5-10.
Karunatilaka, P.V.B. 1990. Journeys to the Diamond Throne: Sri Lankan Buddhist Monks and Pilgrims at Buddhagaya, in *Sri Lanka and the Silk Road of the Sea* (Senake Bandaranayake, Lorna Dewaraja, Roland Silva and K.D.G. Wimalaratne Eds.), pp. 141-146, Colombo: The Sri Lanka National Commission for UNESCO and the Central Cultural Fund.
Kasinathan, Natana 1997. Antiquity of Sea Voyage in Tamil Nadu, in *Abstracts of Papers presented at the First International Conference on Marine Archaeology of Indian Ocean Countries February, 22-23, Chennai*, pp. 19-20, National Institute of Oceanography, Goa: Society for Marine Archaeology.
Kennedy, J. 1898. The Early Commerce of Babylon with India, 700 BC-300 BC, *Journal of the Royal Asiatic Society* 50: 241-288.
Kentley, Eric, Sean McGrail and Lucy Blue 1999. Further Notes on Patia Fishing Boats in the Bay of Bengal, *South Asian Studies* 15: 151-158.
Khan, Daulat Wazir Bahram 1958. *Lailee-Majnu* (edited with an introduction and a glossary by Ahmed Sharif). Dhaka: Bangla Academy.

Khan, F.A. 1963. *Mainamati: A Preliminary Report on the Recent Archaeological Excavations in East Pakistan.* Department of Archaeology: Government of Pakistan.

Khan, F.H. 1991. *Geology of Bangladesh.* Dhaka: The University Press Ltd.

Kidwai, Atiya Habeeb 1992. Conceptual and Methodological Issues: Ports, Port Cities and Port-Hinterlands, *Ports and Their Hinterlands in India (1700-1950)* (Indu Banga Ed.), pp. 7-43, New Delhi: Manohar Publications.

Kielhorn, F. 1888. A Buddhist Stone-inscription from Ghosrawa, *The Indian Antiquary* XVII: 307-312.

Kielhorn, F. 1894. Dudhpani Rock Inscription of Udayamana, *Epigraphia Indica* II: 343-347.

Kielhorn, F. 1896-97. Khalimpur Plate of Dharmapāladeva, *Epigraphia Indica* IV: 243-254.

Kiribamune, Sirima 1990. Muslims and the Trade of the Arabian Sea with Special Reference to Sri Lanka from the Birth of Islam to the Fifteenth Century, in *Sri Lanka and the Silk Road of the Sea* (Senake Bandaranayake, Lorna Dewaraja, Roland Silva and K.D.G. Wimalaratne Eds.), pp. 179-190, Colombo: The Sri Lanka National Commission for UNESCO and the Central Cultural Fund.

Knox, R. 1985. Jewellery from the Nilgiri Hills: A Model of Diversity, in *South Asian Archaeology 1983* (J. Schotsmans and M. Taddei Eds.), pp. 523-534, Naples: Istituto Universitario Orientale.

Kosambi, Damodar Dharmanand 1955. Dhenukakata, *Journal of the Asiatic Society of Bombay* XXX: 50-71.

Kosambi, Damodar Dharmanand 1970. *The Culture and Civilisation of Ancient India in Historical Outline.* New Delhi: Vikash Publishing House.

Kosambi, Damodar Dharmanand 1975. *An Introduction to the Study of Indian History* (first published in 1956). Bombay: Popular Prakashan.

Krishnaswamy, S. 1972. *India's Mineral Resources.* New Delhi: Oxford and IBH Publishing Co.

Kulke, Hermann 1999. Trade and Politics in Eleventh Century Bay of Bengal in *Maritime Heritage of India* (K.S. Behera Ed.), pp. 214-224. New Delhi: Aryan Books International.

Lahiri, Bela 1972. Guilds in Ancient India and the Evidence of Coins, *Early Indian Trade and Industry*, (D.C. Sircar Ed.). Calcutta: University of Calcutta.

Lahiri, Bela 1981-82. A Survey of the Pre-Muhammadan Coins of Bengal, *Journal of Varendra Research Museum* 7: 69-86.

Lahiri, Latika 1986. *Chinese Monks in India: Biography of Eminent Monks Who Went to the Western World in Search of the Law during the Great T'ang Dynasty.* Delhi: Motilal Banarsidass.

Lahiri, Nayanjot 1992. *The Archaeology of Indian Trade Routes upto c. 200 BC: Resource Use, Resource Access and Lines of Communication.* Delhi: Oxford University Press.

Lal, B.B. 1949. Śiśupālgarh 1948: an Early Historical Fort in Eastern India, *Ancient India* 5: 62-105.

Lal, B.B. 1954-55. Excavation at Hastinapura and Other Explorations in the Upper Ganga and Sutlej Basins 1950-52, *Ancient India* 10-11: 5-151.

Lal, Hira 1907-08. Ragholi Plates of Jayavardhana II, *Epigraphia Indica and Record of the Archaeological Survey of India* IX: 41-47.

Lal, Makkhan 1984. *Settlement History and Rise of Civilization in Ganga-Yamuna Doab (from 1500 BC to 300 AD).* Delhi: B.R. Publishing Corporation.

Lambourn, G.E. 1918. *Bengal District Gazetteers: Malda.* Calcutta: The Bengal Secretariat Book Depot.

Laskar, Ganga Mohan 1907. Ashrafpur Copper-Plate Grants of Devakhaḍga, *Memoirs of the Asiatic Society of Bengal* I (6): 85-91.

Legge, James (Tr.) 1886. *A Record of Buddhistic Kingdoms being an Account by the Chinese Monk Fā-Hien of His Travels in India and Ceylon (AD 399-414) in Search of the Buddhist Books of Discipline.* Oxford: Clarendon Press.

Lee, Samuel 1829. *The Travels of Ibn Batūta; translated from the abridged Arabic manuscript copies, preserved in the Public Library of Cambridge, with notes, illustrative of the History, Geography, Botany, Antiquities, etc., occurring throughout the work.* London: The Oriental Translation Committee of the Royal Asiatic Society (1968 reprint).

Ma-Huan 1970. *Ying-yai Sheng-lan* (The Overall Survey of the Ocean's Shores, 1433) (J.U.G. Mills translated and edited). London: Cambridge University Press (for the Hakluyt Society).

Maite, Dilip Kumar 1993. *Atīt Āloke Chandraketugarh* (first published in 1974). Beracampa: Chandraketugarh Saṁgrahaśālā.

Maity, Sachindra Kumar 1970. Currency and Exchange in Ancient India, in *Early Indian Indigenous Coins* (D.C. Sircar Ed.), pp. 11-20, Calcutta: University of Calcutta.

Maity, Sachindra Kumar 1975. *The Imperial Guptas and Their Times (cir. AD 300-550).* New Delhi: Munshiram Manoharlal Publishers Pvt. Ltd.

Majumdar, Nani Gopal 1929. *Inscriptions of Bengal*, Vol. III. Rajshahi: Varendra Research Society.

Majumdar, Nani Gopal 1932. Three Kushan Coins from North Bengal, *Journal of the Asiatic Society of Bengal* N.S. XXVIII: 127-129.

Majumdar, Nani Gopal 1933-34. Irda Copperplate of the Kamboja king Nayapaladeva, *Epigraphia Indica* XXII: 150-159.

Majumdar, R.C. 1927. *Ancient Indian Colonies in the Far East, Vol. I: Champa.* Lahore: The Punjab Sanskrit Book Depot.

Majumdar, R.C. 1937. *Ancient Indian Colonies in the Far East, Vol. II: Suvarnadvipa, Part I: Political History.* Dacca: Asoke Kumar Majumdar.

Majumdar, R.C. 1938. *Ancient Indian Colonies in the Far East, Vol. II: Suvarnadvipa, Part II: Cultural History.* Dacca: Asoke Kumar Majumdar.

Majumdar, R.C. 1940a. Physical Features of Ancient Bengal, in D.R. Bhandarkar Volume (Bimala Churn Law Ed.), pp. 341-364, Calcutta: Indian Research Institute.

Majumdar, R.C. 1940b. Lama Taranatha's Account of Bengal, *Indian Historical Quarterly* XVI (2): 219-238.

Majumdar, R.C. 1941-42. Chittagong Copper-plate of Kantideva, *Epigraphia Indica* XXVI: 313-318.

Majumdar, R.C. 1943a. Rise of Gauḍa and Vaṅga, in *The History of Bengal*, Vol. 1: Hindu Period (R.C. Majumdar Ed.), pp. 47-76, Dacca: University of Dacca.

Majumdar, R.C. 1943b. Minor Ruling Dynasties during the Sena Period, in *The History of Bengal*, Volume 1: Hindu Period (R.C. Majumdar Ed.), pp. 253-262. Dacca: The University of Dacca.

Majumdar, R.C. 1943c. The Pālas, in *The History of Bengal*, Volume 1: Hindu Period (R.C. Majumdar Ed.), pp. 96-191, Dacca: The University of Dacca.

Majumdar, R.C. 1943d. Minor Independent Kingdoms during the Pāla Period, in *The History of Bengal*, Volume 1: Hindu Period (R.C. Majumdar Ed.), pp. 192-204, Dacca: The University of Dacca.

Majumdar, R.C. 1943e. Political Disintegration after Śaśāṅka, in *The History of Bengal*, Volume 1: Hindu Period (R.C. Majumdar Ed.), pp. 77-95, Dacca: The University of Dacca.

Majumdar, R.C. 1945. Two Copper-Plates of Śaśāṅka from Midnapore, *Journal of the Royal Asiatic Society of Bengal, Letters* XI (1): 1-9.

Majumdar, R.C. 1960. *The Classical Accounts of India*. Calcutta: Firma K.L. Mukhopadhyay.

Majumdar, R.C. 1963. *Ancient Indian Colonization in Southeast Asia*. Baroda: Oriental Institute, The Maharaja Sayajirao University.

Majumdar, R.C. 1969. *Corporate Life in Ancient India* (3rd edition, first published in 1918). Calcutta: Firma K.L. Mukhopadhay.

Majumdar, R.C. 1971. *History of Ancient Bengal*. Calcutta: G. Bharadwaj & Co.

Majumdar, R.C. and D.C. Ganguly 1943. Bengalis Outside Bengal in *The History of Bengal*, Vol. 1: Hindu Period (R.C. Majumdar Ed.), pp. 670-689, Dacca: University of Dacca.

Majumdar, R.C. and Basak, Radhagovinda 1943. Administration in *The History of Bengal*, Volume 1: Hindu Period (R.C. Majumdar Ed.), pp. 263-289. Dacca: The University of Dacca.

Manguin, Pierre-Yves 1996. Southeast Asian Shipping in the Indian Ocean during the First Millennium AD, in *Tradition and Archaeology: Early Maritime Contacts in the Indian Ocean* (Himanshu Prabha Ray & Jean-Francois Salles Eds.), pp. 181-198, New Delhi: Manohar Publishers.

Manrique, Fray Sebastien 1927. *Travels of Fray Sebastien Manrique 1629-1643: A Translation of the* Itinerario des las Missiones Orientales *with an introduction and notes by C. Eckford, assisted by Father H. Hosten*, Volume I: Arakan. Oxford: Hakluyt Society.

Manucci, Niccolao 1907. *Storia Do Mogor or Mogul India 1653-1708*, Vol. II and III (translated by William Irvine). London: John Murray.

Marshall, John 1951. *Taxila*. Vol. II. Cambridge: Cambridge University Press.

al-Ma'sūdī 1867. Murūju-l Zahab, in *The History of India as Told by Its Own Historians* (Professor John Dowson Ed. from the posthumous papers of the late Sir H.M. Eliot), Vol. I, pp. 18-25, London: Trubner & Co.

Mathew, K.S. 1999. Portuguese and Shipbuilding in India in the Sixteenth and Seventeenth Centuries, in *Proceedings of Twentieth Anniversary Seminar on European Influence in the Shaping of Maritime India*, pp. 95-98, Mumbai: Maritime History Society.

Ma-twanlin 1837. Chinese Account of India, translated from the Wan-heen-t'hung-kaou, or 'Deep Researches into Ancient Monumants', Book 338, fol. 14 (tanslator's name is not mentioned), *Journal of Asiatic Society of Bengal*, VI (1): 61-75.

McCrindle, John W. 1885. *Ancient India as Described by Ptolemy*. Calcutta: Thacker, Spink & Co.

McCrindle, John W. 1897. *The Christian Topography of Cosmas, an Egyptian Monk* (translated from the Greek and edited with notes and introduction by John W. McCrindle). London: Hakluyt Society.

McCrindle, John W. 1926. *Ancient India as Described by Megasthenēs and Arrian*. Calcutta: Chuckervertty, Chatterjee & Co.

McCrindle, John W. 1979. *Ancient India as Described in Classical Literature* (reprinted from Westminister 1901). New Delhi: Oriental Books Reprint Corporation.

McDowell, Carl E. and Helen M. Gibbs 1954. *Ocean Transportation*. New York: McGraw-Hill Book Company Inc.

McGrail, Sean 1983. Cross-Channel Seamanship and Navigation in the Late First Millennium BC, *Oxford Journal of Archaeology* 2 (3): 299-337.

McGrail, Sean 1984. Maritime Archaeology – Present and Future, in *Aspects of Maritime Archaeology and Ethnography* (Sean McGrail Ed.), pp. 11-40, Greenwich: National Maritime Museum.

McGrail, Sean 1996. Prehistoric Water Transport in N.W. Europe, in *Marine Archaeology: The Global Perspectives*, Vol. I (G. Kuppuram and K. Kumudamani Eds.), pp. 121-135, New Delhi: Sundeep Prakashan.

McGrail, Sean, Lucy Blue and Eric Kentley 1999. The Reverse-Clinker Boats of Bangladesh and Their Planking Pattern, *South Asian Studies* 15: 119-158.

McPherson, Kenneth 1998. *The Indian Ocean: A History of People and The Sea*. Delhi: Oxford University Press.

Meilink-Roelofsz, M.A.P. 1962. *Asian Trade and European Influence in The Indonesian Archipelago between 1500 and about 1630*. Martinus Nijhof: The Hague.

Meilink-Roelofsz, M.A.P. 1970. Trade and Islam in the Malay-Indonesian Archipelago Prior to the Arrival of the Europeans, in *Islam and the Trade of Asia* (D.S. Richards Ed.), pp. 137-157, Oxford: Bruno Cassirer.

Michael, Rice 1985. *Search for the Paradise Land*. London: Longman.

Minhāju-s Sirāj 1869. Tabakāt-i Nāsirī, in *The History of India as Told by Its Own Historians: The Muhammadan Period* (Professor John Dowson edited from the posthumous papers of the late Sir H.M. Eliot), Vol. II, pp. 259-383, London: Trubner & Co.
Minorsky, V. (translated and explained) 1937. *Ḥudūd al-'Ālam. 'The Regions of the World': A Persian Geography*. London: Luzac and Co.
Mishra, Umakanta 2000. An Ethnographic Study of Fishermen and Their Boats: Its Importance in the Maritime Archaeology of Ancient Orissa, in *Archaeology of Orissa*, Vol. II (Kishor K. Basa and Pradeep Mohanty Eds.), pp. 613-634, Delhi: Pratibha Prakashan.
Mitra, Debala 1971. *Buddhist Monuments*. Calcutta: Sahitya Samsad.
Mitra, Debala 1978. *Bronzes from Achutrajpur, Orissa*. Delhi: Agam Kala Prakashan.
Mitra, D.B. 1978. *Cotton Weavers of Bengal 1757-1833*. Calcutta: Firma KLM.
Mitra, Rājendralāla 1852. Note on Three Ancient Coins Found at Muhammadpur, in the Jessore district, *Journal of the Asiatic Society of Bengal* XX (5): 401-402.
Mitra, Rājendralāla 1961. *The Antiquities of Orissa*, Vol. I. Originally published under orders of the Government of India, Calcutta in 1875, Reprint, Calcutta: Indian Studies: Past & Present.
Mookerji, Radha Kumud 1957. *Indian Shipping: A History of the Sea-borne Trade* and *Maritime Activity of the Indians from the Earliest Times* (originally published in 1912 by Longmans, Green and Co, London). Calcutta: Orient Longmans Private Ltd.
Moreland, W.H. 1920. *India at the Death of Akbar*, London: Macmillan and Co.
Moreland, W.H. (Ed.) 1931. *Relations of Golconda in the Early Seventeenth Century*. London: Hakluyt Society.
Morgan, J.P. and W.G. McIntire 1959. Quaternary Geology of the Bengal Basin, East Pakistan and India, *Bulletin of the Geological Society of America* 70: 319-342.
Morris, Richard (Ed.) 1885. *The Aṅguttara-Nikāya*, Part I: Ekanipāta, Dukanipāta, and Tikanipāta. London: Luzac and Company.
Morrison, Barrie M. 1974. *Lalmai, a Cultural Center of Early Bengal: An Archaeological Report and Historical Analysis*. Seattle: University of Washington Press.
Morrison, Barrie M. 1980. *Political Centers and Cultural Regions in Early Bengal*. Delhi: Rawat Publications.
Muckelroy, Keith 1978. *Maritime Archaeology*. Cambridge: Cambridge University Press.
Mukherjee, Amitabha (Ed.) 1999. *Studies in India's Maritime Trade*. Calcutta: Institute of Historical Studies.
Mukherjee, B.B. No Date. *An Economic and Commercial Geography of India* (5th edition). Calcutta: Kamala Book Depot. Limited.
Mukherjee, B.N. 1975-76. Some Observations on the Coins of Paṭṭikeḍā (Paṭṭikeḍa or Paṭṭikera), *Journal of Varendra Research Museum* 4: 19-28.
Mukherjee, B.N. 1981-82. Place of Harikela Coinage in the Archaeology of Bangladesh, *Journal of Varendra Research Museum* 7: 59-68.
Mukherjee, B.N. 1982. Commerce and Money in the Western and Central Sectors of Eastern India (c. AD 750-1200), *Indian Museum Bulletin* XVII: 65-83.
Mukherjee, B.N. 1988. *The Rise and Fall of the Kushana Empire*. Calcutta: Firma KLM Private Limited.
Mukherjee, B.N. 1990. *Kharoshṭī and Kharoshṭī-Brāhmī Inscriptions in West Bengal (India)*. Published as the *Indian Museum Bulletin*, Vol. XXV. Calcutta: Indian Museum.
Mukherjee, B.N. 1991a. Trade, Traders and Media of Exchange in Pre-Gupta Vanga, in *Coinage, Trade and Economy: 3rd International Colloquium* (Amal Kumar Jha Ed.), pp. 46-51, Nashik: Indian Institute of Research in Numismatic Studies.
Mukherjee, B.N. 1991b. A Sealing in the Lopburi Museum (Thailand), *Journal of the Asiatic Society* XXXIII (3-4): 85-86.
Mukherjee B.N. 1991c. Coins in Pre-Gupta Bengal, in *Studies in Archaeology: Papers Presented in Memory of P.C. Dasgupta* (Asok Datta Ed.), pp. 281-308, New Delhi: Books & Books.
Mukherjee, B.N. 1992a. *Coins and Currency System in Gupta Bengal (c. AD 320-550)*. New Delhi: Harman Publishing House.
Mukherjee, B.N. 1992b. *External Trade of Early Northeastern India*. New Delhi: Har-Anand & Vikas.
Mukherjee, B.N. 1993. *Coins and Currency Systems of Post-Gupta Bengal (c. AD 550-700)*. New Delhi: Munshiram Manoharlal Publishers Pvt. Ltd.
Mukherjee, B.N. 1993-94. Early Maritime Trade of Vanga – A Review of the Data, *Pratna Samiksha* 2 & 3: 164-168.
Mukherjee, Chhanda 1991. Gupta Coinage from Bengal and Contemporary Trade & Commerce, *Indian Museum Bulletin* XXVI: 36-41.
Mukherji, Ramaranjan and Sachindra Kumar Maity 1967. *Corpus of Bengali Inscriptions bearing on History and Civilization of Bengal*. Calcutta: Firma K.L. Mukhopadhyay.
Mukherji, S.C. 2000. Two New Copper Plates of King Gopala II of the Pala Dynasty of Bengal and Bihar, Regnal Year 4 (c. 877 AD), *Journal of Bengal Art* 5: 61-65.
Mukhopadhyay, Samir Kumar 1993. Routes from Chinese Accounts and Chinese Travellers in India up to 550 AD, *Indian Museum Bulletin* XXVIII: 33-36.
Mukunda, Kavikaṅkaṇa 1986. *Caṇḍīmaṅgala* (Sukumar Sen Ed.). Calcutta: Sahitya Academy.
Mukundaram 1974. *Kavikaṅkaṇa Caṇḍī* (Srikumar Bandyopadhyay and Visvapati Chaudhuri Eds.). Calcutta: University of Calcutta.
Mulvaney, D.J. 1975. *The Prehistory of Australia*. Revised edition. London: Penguin Books.
Nandargikar, Gopal Raghunath (Ed.) 1982. *The Raghuvaṃśa of Kālidāsa, with commentary of Mallinātha* (5th edition). Delhi: Motilal Banarsidass.
Naravane, M.S. 1998. *The Maritime and Coastal Forts of India*. New Delhi: APH Publishing Corporation.

Neale, Walter C. 1957. The Market in Theory and History, in *Trade and Market in the Early Empires: Economies in History and Theory* (Karl Polanyi, Conrad M. Arensberg and Harry W. Pearson Eds.), pp. 357-372, Glencoe (Illinois): The Free Press and the Falcon's Wing Press.

Needham, Joseph 1971. *Science and Civilisation in China,* volume 4 Part III, pp. 379-699, Cambridge: University Press.

Nieuwolt, S. 1977. *Tropical Climatology: An Introduction to the Climates of the Low latitudes.* London: John Wiley and Sons.

Nigam, Shyamsunder 1975. *Economic Organisation in Ancient India (200 BC-200 AD).* New Delhi: Munshiram Manoharlal Publishers.

Niharika 1993. *A Study of Stone Beads in Ancient India.* Delhi: Bharat Kala Prakashan.

Nilakanta Sastri, K.A. 1938. The Beginnings of Intercourse between India and China, *The Indian Historical Quarterly* XIV (2): 380-387.

Niyogi, Puspa 1967. *Brahmanic Settlements in Different Subdivisions of Ancient Bengal.* Calcutta: R.K. Maitra on behalf of Indian Studies: Past and Present.

Olchiski, Leonardo 1960. *Marco Polo's Asia: An Introduction to His "Description of the World" Called "Il Milione".* Barkley: University of California.

Oldenberg, Hermann 1982. *The Dipavamsa: An Ancient Buddhist Historical Record.* New Delhi: Asian Educational Services.

O'Malley, L.S.S. 1910. *Bengal District Gazetteers: Santhal Parganas.* Calcutta: The Bengal Secretariat Book Depot.

O'Malley, L.S.S. 1925. *Bengal District Gazetteers: Faridpur.* Calcutta: Bengal Secretariat Book Depot.

Oung, Mg. May 1912. The Chronology of Burma, *Journal of the Burma Research Society* II (I): 8-29.

Panshikar, V.L. (Ed.) 1933. *Manusmṛti.* Bombay: Nirnay Sagar Press.

Panikkar, K.M. 1947. *A Survey of Indian History.* Bombay: The National Information & Publications Ltd.

Paranavitana, S. 1970. *Inscriptions of Ceylon*, Vol. 1. Colombo: Department of Archaeology.

Paris, Pierre 1951. A Note on Two Passages from Strabo and Pliny Concerning Taprobana, *The Ceylon Historical Journal* 1 (4): 293-300.

Pargiter, F.E. 1911. The Ghāgrahāṭi (Koṭwālipāṛā) Grant and Three Other Copper-Plate Grants, *Journal of the Asiatic Society of Bengal,* New Series VII (8): 475-502.

Paul, Ashis Kumar 1995. Tidal Landforms of the Coast of West Bengal, in *Indian Geomorphology: Landforms and Process* (S.R. Jog Ed.), pp. 195-224, Jaipur: Rawat Publications.

Pearson, M.N. 1916. *Merchants and Rulers in Gujarat: The Response to the Portuguese in the Sixteenth Century.* New Delhi: Munshiram Manoharlal.

Penzer, N.M. 1924. *The Ocean of Story being C.H. Tawney's translation of Somadeva's Kathā Sarit Sāgar,* Vol. II. London: Chas. J. Sawyer Ltd.

Penzer, N.M. 1925. *The Ocean of Story being C.H. Tawney's translation of Somadeva's Kathā Sarit Sāgar,* Vol. III. London: Chas. J. Sawyer Ltd.

Penzer, N.M. 1926. *The Ocean of Story being C.H. Tawney's translation of Somadeva's Kathā Sarit Sāgar,* Vol. VI. London: Chas. J. Sawyer Ltd.

Perera, B.J. 1951. The Foreign Trade and Commerce of Ancient Ceylon: I The Ports of Ancient Ceylon, *The Ceylon Historical Journal* I (2): 109-119.

Petech, L. 1950. *Northern India According to the Shui/Ching/Chu.* Roma: Istituto Italiano Per Il Medio Ed Estremo Oriente.

Phayre, Arthur P. 1844. On the History of Arakan, *Journal of the Asiatic Society of Bengal* 13 (145): 23-52.

Phayre, Arthur P. 1884. *History of Burma including Burma Proper, Pegu, Taungu, Tenasserim, and Arakan from the Earliest Time to the End of the First War with British India.* London: Trubner &Co.

Pires, Tome 1967. *The Suma Oriental of Tome Pires: An Account of the East from the Red Sea to Japan, Written in Malacca in 1512-1515,* two volumes, translated by Arman-do Cortesao, Nendeln, Liechtenstcin: Kraus Reprints.

Pliny (Plinius Secundus C.) 1962. *Natural History with an English Translation in Ten Volumes* (D.E. Eichholz Tr.), Vol. X. London: William Heinemann Ltd.

Polanyi, Karl 1957. The Economy as Instituted Process, in *Trade and Market in the Early Empires: Economies in History and Theory* (Karl Polanyi, Conrad M. Arensberg and Harry W. Pearson Eds.), pp. 243-270, Glencoe (Illinois): The Free Press and the Falcon's Wing Press.

Polo, Marco No Date. *The Travels of Marco Polo.* New York: The Orion Press.

Pradhan, Debaraj, Pradeep Mohanty and Jitu Misra 2000. Manikapatana: An Ancient and Medieval Port on the Coast of Orissa, in *Archaeology of Orissa*, Vol. II (Kishor K. Basa and Pradeep Mohanty Eds.), pp. 473-494, Delhi: Pratibha Prakashan.

Prakash, Om 1985. *The Dutch East India Company and the Economy of Bengal, 1630-1720.* Princeton: Princeton University Press.

Prasad, Prakash Charan 1977. *Foreign Trade and Commerce in Ancient India.* New Delhi: Abhinav Publications.

Prinsep, James 1836. Notes on the Nautical Instrument of the Arabs, *Journal of the Asiatic Society of Bengal* V: 784-794.

Purchas, Samuel 1905a. Account of Francois Pyrard de Laval in *Hakluytus Postumus or Purchas His Pilgrims Contayning a History of the World, in Sea Voyages and Lande Travells by Englishmen and others,* Vol. IX, pp. 503-570. Glasgow: James Maclehose & Sons.

Purchas, Samuel 1905b. Account of Caesar Frederick in *Hakluytus Postumus or Purchas His Pilgrims Contayning a History of the World, in Sea Voyages and Lande Travells by Englishmen and others,* Vol. X, pp. 88-143. Glasgow: James Maclehose & Sons.

Purchas, Samuel 1906a. Account of Marco Polo in *Hakluytus Postumus or Purchas His Pilgrims Contayning a History of the World, in Sea Voyages and Lande Travells by Englishmen and others,* Vol. XI, pp. 188-309. Glasgow: James Maclehose & Sons.

Purchas, Samuel 1906b. The Voyage of Nicolo di Conti a Venetian, to the Indies, Mangi, Cambalu and Quinsal, with Some Observations of Those Places, Vol. XI, 394-400. Glasgow: James Maclehose & Sons.

Qadir, Muhammad Abdul 1980. *A Guide of Paharpur.* Dhaka: Department of Archaeology, Government of the People's Republic of Bangladesh.

Qadir, Muhammad Abdul 2001. Al-Musta-Ṣim Billāh's Gold Coin from Bangladesh, in *Hakim Habibur Rahman Khan Commemoration Volume* (Enamul Haque Ed.), pp. 17-49, Dhaka: The International Centre for Study of Bengal Art.

Qanungo, Kalika Ranjan 1948a. Muslim Conquest of Bengal (Sections 1, and 3-6), in *The History of Bengal, Volume II: Muslim Period, 1200-1757* (Jadu-Nath Sarkar Ed.), pp. 1-5, 8-29, Dacca: University of Dacca.

Qanungo, Kalika Ranjan 1948b. Bengal under the House of Balban, in *The History of Bengal, Volume II: Muslim Period (1200-1757)* (Jadu-Nath Sarkar Ed.), pp. 58-91, Dacca: University of Dacca.

Rahim, Muhammad Abdur 1963. *Social and Cultural History of Bengal, Vol. I (1201-1576).* Karachi: Pakistan Historical Society.

Rahim, M. Abdur, A.M. Chowdhury, A.B.M. Mahmood and Sirajul Islam 1981. *Bangladesher Itihas* (History of Bangladesh). Dacca: Nawroze Kitabistan.

Rahula, Walpola 1956. *History of Buddhism in Ceylon: The Anuradhapura Period 3rd Century BC-10th Century AC.* Colombo: M.D. Gunasena & Co. Ltd.

Ramachandran, S. 1991. Ships of Tarangambadi, *Journal of Marine Archaeology* 2: 60-61.

Ramachandran, T.N. 1951. Tāmralipti (Tamluk), *Artibus Asiae* XIV: 226-239.

Ramachandran, T.N. 1946. Recent Archaeological Discoveries along the Mainamati and Lalmai Ranges, Tippera District, East Bengal, in *B.C. Law Volume. Part II* (D.R. Bhandarkar, K.A. Nilakanta Sastri, B.M. Barua, B.K. Ghosh and P.K. Gode Eds.), pp. 213-231, Poona: The Bhandarkar Oriental Research Institute.

Rao, Nalini N. 1988. Marine Art in India, in *Marine Archaeology of Indian Ocean Countries: Proceedings of the First Indian Conference on Marine Archaeology of Indian Ocean Countries-Oct 1987* (S.R. Rao Ed.), pp. 93-96, Goa: National Institute of Oceanography.

Rashid, Haroun Er. 1991. *Geography of Bangladesh* (Second Revised Edition). Dhaka: University Press Ltd.

Rashid, M. Harunur 1974. Pāla Rule in South-East Bengal, *Journal of the Varendra Research Museum* 3: 27-47.

Rashid, M. Harunur 1975. The Mainamati Gold Coins, *Bangladesh Lalit Kala* 1 (1): 43-58.

Rashid, M. Harunur 1975-77. The Candra Rulers of Bengal: History and Chronology of the Dynasty in the Light of Recent Discoveries, *Journal of the Varendra Research Museum* 5: 31-56.

Rashid, M. Harunur 1997a. The City and Its Environs, *Mainamati-Devaparvata: A Survey of Historical Monuments and Sites in Bangladesh* (A.B.M. Husain Ed.), pp. 233-275. Dhaka: Asiatic Society of Bangladesh.

Rashid, M. Harunur 1997b. Site and Surroundings, *Mainamati-Devaparvata: A Survey of Historical Monuments and Sites in Bangladesh* (A.B.M. Husain Ed.), pp. 1-75. Dhaka: Asiatic Society of Bangladesh.

Rawlinson, H.G. 1916. *Intercourse between India and the Western World from the Earliest Times to the Fall of Rome.* Cambridge: Cambridge University Press.

Ray, Aniruddha 1997. *Sultani Amoler Arthanaitik Itihas: Ekti Samiksha* (in Bengali). Calcutta: Firma KLM.

Ray, Aniruddha 1999. *Madhyayuger Bhāratīya Śahar* (Medieval Cities in India, in Bengali). Kolkata: Ananda Publishers Private Ltd.

Rāy, Asīm Kumār 1988. *Baṅga Bṛttānta: Bideśīi Paryaṭakder Lekhāy, Bāṅgālār Kathā [pancam Theke Saptadas Satabdi].* Calcutta: Ṛddhi India.

Ray, Himanshu Prabha 1998. *The Winds of Change: Buddhism and the Maritime Links of Early South Asia* (1st published in 1994). Delhi: Oxford University Press.

Ray, Himanshu Prabha and Jean-Francois Salles (Ed.) 1996. *Tradition and Archaeology: Early Maritime Contacts in the Indian Ocean.* New Delhi: Manohar Publishers.

Ray, Indrani 1992. Pharāsī Compāni O Bāṅglār Baṇik (1680-1730), in *Madhyayuge Bāṅglār Samāj O Saṁskriti* (Aniruddha Ray and Ratnavali Chattopadhyaya Eds.), pp. 109-122, Kolkata: K.P. Bagchi & Co.

Ray, Niharranjan 1979. Tamralipta and Gange – The Two Port Cities of Ancient Bengal and Connected Consideration, *Geographical Review of India* 41 (3): 205-222.

Ray, Niharranjan 1993. *Bangalir Itihas: Adiparba* (in Bengali). (First published in 1356 BS) Calcutta: Dey's Publishing.

Ray, Niharranjan 1994. *History of the Bengali People (Ancient Period)* (translated with an introduction by John W. Hood). Calcutta: Orient Longman Ltd.

Raychauchuri, H.C. 1943a. Physical and Historical Geography, in *The History of Bengal*, Volume I: Hindu Period (R.C. Majumdar Ed.), pp. 1-34, Dacca: The University of Dacca.

Raychaudhuri, H.C. 1943b. The Legendary Period, in *The History of Bengal*, Volume I: Hindu Period (R.C. Majumdar Ed.), pp. 35-40, Dacca: The University of Dacca.

Raychaudhuri, H.C. 1943c. Early History from 326 BC to 320 AD, in *The History of Bengal*, Volume I: Hindu Period (R.C. Majumdar Ed.), pp. 41-46, Dacca: The University of Dacca.

Raychaudhuri, Tapan 1982. Inland Trade, in *The Cambridge Economic History of India, Volume I: c. 1200-c. 1750* (Tapan Raychaudhuri and Irfan Habib Eds.), pp. 325-359, Cambridge: Cambridge University Press.

Renfrew, Colin 1969. Trade and Culture Process in European Prehistory, *Current Anthropology* 10 (2-3): 151-169.

Renfrew, Colin 1975. Trade as Action at a Distance: Questions of Integration and Communication, in *Ancient Civilisation and Trade* (Jeremy A. Sabloff and C.C. Lamberg-Karlovsky Eds.), pp. 3-59, Albuquerque: University of New Maxico Press.

Rizvi, S.N.H. (General Editor) 1970. *East Pakistan District Gazetteers: Chittagong.* Dacca: East Pakistan Government Press.

Rougeulle, Axelle 1996. Medieval Trade Networks in the Western Indian Ocean (8-14th centuries): Some Reflections from the Distribution Pattern of Chinese Imports in the Islamic World, in *Tradition and Archaeology: Early Maritime Contacts in the Indian Ocean* (Himanshu Prabha Ray & Jean-Francois Salles Eds.), pp. 159-180, New Delhi: Manohar Publishers.

Roy, Nirod Bhusan 1948. Rise of the Ilyas Shahi Dynasty (Sections 2-6, and 8), in *The History of Bengal, Volume II: Muslim Period, 1200-1757* (Jadu-Nath Sarkar Ed.), pp. 97-114 and 116-119, Dacca: University of Dacca.

Rudra, Kalyan 1990. Tamralipta and its Locational Problem, in *Historical Archaeology of India: A Dialogue Between Archaeologists and Historians* (Amita Ray and Samir Mukherjee Eds.), pp. 245-254, New Delhi: Books and Books.

Rudra, Kalyan and M.K. Mukherjee 1986. Locational Dispute over Two Ancient Ports of Bengal, *Geographical Review of India* 48 (1): 32-37.

Salim, Ghulām Husain 1904. Riyazu-s-Sal*ātīn (A History of Bengal).* Translated into English from original Persian with notes by Maulavi Abdus Salam. Calcutta: Asiatic Society.

Sandhyākara Nandī 1910. *Rāmacarita* (Mahāmahopādhāya Haraprasād Sāstrī Ed.). Calcutta: Asiatic Society.

Sangermano, Father 1969. *A Description of the Burmese Empire: Compiled Chiefly from Burmese Documents by Father Sangermano,* translated by William Tandy (first edition, Rome, 1833). New York: Augustus M. Kelly Publishers.

Sankalia, H.D. and M.G. Dikshit 1952. *Excavation at Brahmapuri (Kolhapur),1945-46.* Poona: Deccan College.

Sanyal, Niradbandhu 1955-56. Sultanpur Copperplate Inscription, *Epigraphia Indica* XXXI: 57-66.

Sargent, A.J. 1938. *Seaports and Hinterlands.* London: Adam and Charles Block.

Sarkar, Jadunath 1906. Shaista Khan in Bengal (1664-66), *Journal & Proceedings of the Asiatic Society of Bengal,* New Series II (6): 257-267.

Sarkar, Jadunath 1907a. The Conquest of Chātagāon, 1666 AD", *Journal & Proceedings of the Asiatic Society of Bengal,* New Series III (6): 405-417.

Sarkar, Jadunath 1907b. The Feringi Pirates of Chātagāon, 1665 AD", *Journal & Proceedings of the Asiatic Society of Bengal,* New Series III (6): 419-425.

Sarkar, Himansu Bhusan 1937. The Cultural Contact between Java and Bengal, The Indian Historical Quarterly XIII (4): 589-599.

Sarkar, Himansu Bhusan 1971. *Corpus of the Inscriptions of Java upto 928 AD,* Vol. 1, Calcutta: Firma K.L. Mukhopadhyay.

Sarkar, Himansu Bhusan 1972. Bengal and Her Traffic-routes in the Bay of Bengal and Southeast Asia (c. 300 BC to 300 AD), *Journal of the Asiatic Society* XIV (2-4): 74-90.

Sarkar, Himansu Bhusan 1973. Export and Import Trade of Bengal (c. 300 BC to c. 800 AD), *Journal of the Asiatic Society* XV (1-4): 177-198.

Sarkar, Himansu Bhusan 1974. Bengal and Her Overland Routes in India and Beyond, *Journal of the Asiatic Society* XVI (1-4): 92-119.

Sarkar, Himansu Bhusan 1986. Trade and Commercial Activities of Southern India in the Malayo-Indonesian World (up to 1511), Vol. 1, Calcutta: Firma KLM.

Sarkar, Jagdish Narayan 1975. Studies *in Economic Life in Mughal India.* New Delhi: Oriental Publishers and Distributors.

Sarmadhikari, Rajib Kanti 1984. Some Observations on the Coins of Early Bengal, *Indian Museum Bulletin* XIX: 38-47.

Sastri, K.A. Nilakanta (Ed.) 1957. *A Comprehensive History of India, Vol. II: The Mauryas & Satavahanas 325 BC- AD 300.* Bombay: Orient Longmans.

Sastri, K.A. Nilakanta (Ed.) 1967. *Age of the Nandas & Mauryas* (2nd edition). Delhi: Motilal Banarsidass.

Sastri, K.A. Nilakantha 1935. *The Colas.* Vol. I: To the Accession of Kulottunga I. Madras: University of Madras.

Sastri, K.A. Nilakantha 1937. Rajendra Cola I and Mahipala of Bengal, *The Indian Historical Quarterly* XIII (I): 149-152.

Śāstrī, Surendranath Majumdar 1927. *McCrindle's Ancient India as Described by Ptolemy,* a facsimile reprint edited with an introduction, notes and an additional map. Calcutta: Chuckervertty, Chatterjee & Co.

Schlingloff, Dieter 1988. *Studies in the Ajanta Paintings: Identifications and Interpretations.* Delhi: Ajanta Publications.

Schoff, Wilfred H. 1995. *The Periplus of the Erythraean Sea: Travel and Trade in the Indian Ocean by a Merchant of the first Century.* (1st published in 1912 by Longmans, Green and Co., London.) New Delhi: Munshiram Manoharlal Publishers.

Sen, Benoychandra 1942. *Some Historical Aspects of the Inscriptions of Bengal.* Calcutta: University of Calcutta.

Sen, P.K. and M. Banerjee 1988. Palaeoenvironment of Bengal Basin during the Holocene Period, *Geographical Review, India* 50 (4): 21-38.

Sen, Sukumar 1398 BS. V*angala Sahityer Itihas,* Volume II (The History of Bengali Literature). Calcutta: Ananda Pubishers Limited.

Sen, Sukumar (Ed.) 1953. *Vipradāsa's Manasā-vijaya.* Calcutta: Asiatic Society.

Sen, Surendra Nath 1948. The Portuguese in Bengal, in *The History of Bengal, Volume II: Muslim Period (1200-1757)* (Jadu-Nath Sarkar Ed.), pp. 351-370, Dacca: University of Dacca.

Seneviratna, Anuradha 1994. *Ancient Anuradhapura: The Monastic City.* Colombo: Archaeological Survey Department.

Sengupta, Gautam 1996. Archaeology of Coastal Bengal, in *Tradition and Archaeology: Early Maritime Contacts in the Indian Ocean* (Himanshu Prabha Ray & Jean-Francois Salles Eds.), pp. 115-128, New Delhi: Manohar Publishers.

Serjeant, Robert Bertram 2000. Yemeni Merchants and Trade in Yemen, in *Asian Merchants and Businessmen in the Indian Ocean and the China Sea* (Denys Lombard and Jean Aubin Eds.), pp. 53-78. Oxford: New Delhi.

Sharif, Ahmad 1375 BS. *Caṭṭagrāmer Itikathā Adiyuga Itihāsa*. Dhaka.

Sharif, Ahmad 1977. *Madhyajuger Sahitye Samaj-o-Sanskritir Rup* (Society and Culture in Medieval Bengali Literature). Dacca: Muktadhara.

Sharma, Ram Sharan 1966. *Light on Early Indian Society and Economy*. Bombay: P.C. Manaktala and Sons.

Sharma, Ram Sharan 1983. *Material Culture and Social Formations in Ancient India*. Delhi: MacMillan India Ltd.

Sharma, Ram Sharan 1987. *Urban Decay in India (c. 300-c. 1000)*. New Delhi: Munshiram Manoharlal Publishers Pvt. Ltd.

Sharma, Y.D. 1953. Exploration of Historical Sites, *Ancient India* 9: 116-169.

Shastri, Hirananda 1924. The Nalanda Copperplate of Devapaladeva, *Epigraphia Indica* XVII: 310-327.

Shastri, Hirananda 1928. Sanskrit Epigraphy, *Annual Report of the Archaeological Survey of India 1925-26*: 131-150.

Shastri, Hirananda 1942. Nalanda and Its Epigraphic Material, in *Memoirs of the Archaeological Survey of India*, No. 66. Delhi: Archaeological Survey of India.

Sheel, Benimadhava (Ed.) No Date. *Baish Kavi, Sree Sree Padmāpurān ba Manasā Punthi*. Calcutta: Akshaya Library.

Singh, A. K. 1988. *Indo-Roman Trade: An Archaeological Perspective*. New Delhi: Janaki Prakashan.

Singh, Jai Prakash (Ed.) 1980. *Coinage of Bengal and Its Neighbourhood*. Varanasi: The Numismatic Society of India, Benaras Hindu University.

Singh, Madan Mohan 1961. India's Overseas Trade as Known from the Buddhist Canons, *The Indian Historical Quarterly* XXXVII (2 & 3): 177-182.

Singh, M.P. 1985. *Town, Market, Mint and Port in the Mughal Empire (1556-1707): An Administrative-cum-Economic Study*. New Delhi: Adam Publishers and Distributors.

Singh, Ravindra N. 1980-81. The Antiquity of Gold-Glasses in India, *Puratattva* 12: 157-159.

Singh, Ravindra N. 1989. *Ancient Indian Glass: Archaeology and Technology*. Delhi.

Sircar, D.C. 1942. Narayanpur Vinayaka Image Inscription of King Mahipala-Regnal Year 4, *Indian Culture* IX (1): 121-125.

Sircar D.C. 1943. Kalaikuri Copper-plate Inscription of the Gupta Year 120 (=AD 439), *The Indian Historical Quarterly* XIX (1): 12-26.

Sircar, D.C. 1947. The Kailan Copper-plate Inscription of King Śrīdhāraṇa Rāta of Samataṭa, *The Indian Historical Quarterly* XXIII (3): 221-240.

Sircar, D.C. 1949-50. Epigraphic Notes: Madanpur Plate of Srichandra, Year 46, *Epigraphia Indica* XXVIII: 337-339.

Sircar, D.C. 1950. Udamāna in Bengal Epigraphs, *The Indian Historical Quarterly* XXVI (4): 309-313.

Sircar, D.C. 1951. Copper-plate Inscription of King Bhvadeva of Devaparvata, *Journal of the Asiatic Society, Letters* XVII (2): 83-94.

Sircar, D.C. 1951-52. Alagum Inscription of Anantavarman; Regnal Year 62, *Epigraphia Indica* XXIX: 44-48.

Sircar, D.C. 1952. Pala Rule in the Tippera District, *Indian Historical Quarterly* XXVIII (1): 51-57.

Sircar, D.C. 1953-54. Mehār Plate of Dāmodardeva: Saka 1156, Regnal Year 4, *Epigraphia Indica* XXX: 51-58.

Sircar, D.C. 1957-58. Inscriptions of Chandras of Arakan, *Epigraphia Indica* XXXII: 102-109.

Sircar, D.C. 1959a. Dhulla Plate of Srichandra, *Epigraphia Indica* XXXIII: 134-140.

Sircar, D.C. 1959b. Bhaturiya Inscription of Rajyapala, *Epigraphia Indica* XXXIII: 150-154.

Sircar, D.C. 1960. Madanapada plate of Visvarupasena, *Epigraphia Indica* XXXIII: 315-326.

Sircar D.C. 1963-64. Three Pala Inscriptions, *Epigraphia Indica* XXXV: 225-238.

Sircar, D.C. 1967-1968. Inscribed Clay Seal from Raktamṛttikā, *Epigraphia Indica* XXXVII: 25-28.

Sircar, D.C. 1968. *Studies in Indian Coin*. Delhi: Motilal Banarsidass.

Sircar, D.C. 1971. *Studies in the Geography of Ancient and Medieval India*. Delhi: Motilal Banarsidass.

Sircar, D.C. 1972-73. Three East Indian Inscriptions of the Early Mediaeval Period, *Journal of the Ancient Indian History* VI (1-2): 39-59.

Sircar, D.C. 1973. *Epigraphic Discoveries in East Pakistan*. Calcutta: Sanskrit College.

Sircar, D.C. 1974. *Studies in the Political and Administrative Systems in Ancient and Medieval India*. Delhi: Motilal Banarsidass.

Sircar, D.C. 1977. *Early Indian Numismatic and Epigraphical Studies*. Calcutta: Indian Museum.

Sircar, D.C. 1982. *Pala-Sena Yuger Vaṁśanucarit*. Calcutta: Sahityalok.

Sircar, D.C. 1983. *Select Inscriptions bearing on Indian History and Civilization*. Vol. 2: from the sixth to the eighteenth century AD. Delhi: Motilal Banarsidass.

Sircar, D.C. 1986. *Select Inscriptions bearing on Indian History and Civilization*. Vol. 1: from the sixth century BC to the sixth century AD. (Originally published by the University of Calcutta, 1942.) Third edition, Delhi: Asian Humanities Press.

Siriweera, W.I. 1990. Pre-colonial Sri Lanka's Maritime Commerce with Special Reference to Its Ports, in *Sri Lanka and the Silk Road of the Sea* (Senake Bandaranayake, Lorna Dewaraja, Roland Silva and K.D.G. Wimalaratne Eds.), pp. 125-133, Colombo: The Sri Lanka National Commission for UNESCO and the Central Cultural Fund.

Slane, Kathleen Warner 1991. Observations on Mediterranean Amphoras and Tablewares Found in India, in *Rome and India: The Ancient Sea Trade* (Vimala Begley and Richard Daniel De Puma Eds.), pp. 204-215, Madison: The University of Wisconsin Press.

Snead, Rodman E. 1982. *Coastal Landforms and Surface Features: A Photographic Atlas and Glossary*. Stroudsburg: Hutchinson Ross Publishing Company.

SPARRSO 1986. *Report on the Pilot Project on Remote Sensing Applications to Coastal Zone Dynamics in Bangladesh.* Dhaka.

Speyer, J.S. (Tr.) 1895. *The Jātakamālā or Garland of Birth-Stories of Āryaśūra.* Indian reprint 1982. Delhi: Motilal Banarsidass.

Srinivasan S. and S. Ranganathan 2003. Wootz Steel: An Advanced Material of the Ancient World. http://metalrg.iisc.ernet.in/~wootz/heritage/WOOTZ.htm (site accessed in March 25 2003).

Srinivasan, Sharada (2005). Megalithic high-tin Bronzes: Athno-Archaeological and Archaeological Insights on Manufacture and Possible Artistic and Musical Significance, a seminal paper presented at the Conference of Indian Society for Prehistoric and Quaternary Studies, organized by M.H. Krishna Institute of Indology, Bangalore, Department of Sanskrit, Bangalore University and Directorate of Archaeology and Museums, Government of Karnataka, held at Central College Campus, Bangalore on 15-18 December, 2005.

Srivastava, Balram 1968. *Trade and Commerce in Ancient India (From the earliest times to AD 300).* Varanasi: The Chowkhamba Sanskrit Series Office.

Strickland, C. 1940. *Deltaic Formation, with Special Reference to the Brahmaputra.* Calcutta.

Sulaiman 1867. Salsilatu-t Tawarikh, with additions by Abu Zaidu-l Hasan of Siraf, in *The History of India as Told by Its Own Historians,* edited from the posthumous papers of the late Sir H.M. Eliot by Professor John Dowson, Vol. I, pp. 1-11, London: Trubner & Co.

Takakusu, J. (Tr.) 1896. *A Record of the Buddhist Religion as Practised in India and the Malay Archipelago (A.D. 671-695) by I-tsing.* Oxford: Clarendon Press.

Tampoe, Moira 1990. Tracing the Silk Road of the Sea: Ceramic and Other Evidence from the Partner Ports of the Western Indian Ocean (8th-10th c. AD), in *Sri Lanka and the Silk Road of the Sea* (Senake Bandaranayake, Lorna Dewaraja, Roland Silva and K.D.G. Wimalaratne Eds.), pp. 85-103, Colombo: The Sri Lanka National Commission for UNESCO and the Central Cultural Fund.

Tantrabibhūti 1980. *Manasāpurāṇa* (Aśutoṣ Dās Ed.). Calcutta: Calcutta University.

Tarafdar, Mamtazur Rahman 1991. Tome Pireser Bibaraṇe Bangladesh, *Abu Mohamed Habibullah Smarakgrantha* (in Bengali) (Salahuddin Ahmed, Momtazur Rahman Tarafdar and Ajoy Roy Eds.), pp. 184-213, Dhaka: Bangladesh Itihas Parishad.

Tarafdar, Mamtazur Rahman 1995. *Trade, Technology and Society in Medieval Bengal.* Dhaka: International Centre for Bengal Studies, University of Dhaka.

Tarafdar, Mamtazur Rahman 1999. *Husain Shahi Bengal, 1494-1538 A.D.: A Socio-Political Study.* Dhaka: University of Dhaka.

Tavernier, Jean Baptiste 1889. *Travels in India* (V. Ball translated from the original French edition of 1676 with a biographical sketch of the author, notes and appendices, etc.), in two volumes. London: Macmillan and Co.

Taw-Sein-ko 1894. Some Remarks on the Kalyani Inscription, *Indian Antiquary* XXIII: 100-103, 222-224 and 255-259.

Taylor, James 1840. *Topography and Statistics of Dacca, Volume I.* Calcutta: Mann, Military Orphan Press.

Taylor, James 1847. Remarks on the Sequel to the Periplus of the Erythrean Sea, and on the Country of the Seres, as described by Ammianus Marcellinus, *Journal of the Asiatic Society of Bengal* XVI, New Series (1): 1-78.

Temple, Richard Carnac (Ed.) 1914. *The Travels of Peter Mundy in Europe and Asia 1608-1667,* Vol. II. London, Hakluyt Society.

Thakur, Upendra 1970. The First Coins: A Study in Evolution and Growth, in *Early Indian Indigenous Coins* (D.C. Sircar Ed.), pp. 21-47, Calcutta: University of Calcutta.

Thakur, Upendra 1972. *Mints and Minting in India.* Varanasi: The Chowkhamba Sanskrit Series Office.

Thakur, Upendra 1980. Source of Gold for Early Gold Coins of India, *East and West,* New Series 30 (1-4): 99-115.

Thapar, Romila 1961. *Aśoka and the Decline of the Mauryas.* Delhi: Oxford University Press.

Thapar, Romila 1984. From Lineage to State: Social Formations in the Mid-First Millennium BC in the Ganga Valley. Bombay: Oxford University Press.

Thaplyal, Kiron Kumar 1993. India as seen by Hiuen-Tsang, *Indian Museum Bulletin* XXVIII: 37-46.

Thivakaran, G.A. and Victor Rajamanickam 1993. Traditional Boat-Building in Andhra Pradesh, *Marine Archaeology* 4: 12-28.

Thomaz, Luis Filipe F.R. 2000. Melaka and Its Merchant Communities at the Turn of the Sixteenth Century, *Asian Merchants and Businessmen in the Indian Ocean and the China Sea* (Denys Lombard and Jean Aubin Eds.), pp. 25-39. Oxford: New Delhi.

Tibbetts, G.R. 1981. *Arab Navigation in the Indian Ocean Before the Coming of the Portuguese, being a translation of Kitāb al-Fawā'id fī uṣūl al-baḥr wa'l-qawā'id of Aḥmad b. Mājid al-Najdī.* London: The Royal Asiatic Society of Great Britain and Ireland.

Tripathi, Rama Shankar 1937. *History of Kanauj: To the Moslem Conquest.* Benares: Indian Book Shop.

Tomber, Roberta 2000. Indo-Roman Trade: The Ceramic Evidence from Egypt, *Antiquity* 74: 624-631.

Umitsu, M 1993. Late Quaternary Sedimentary Environment and Landforms in the Ganges Delta, *Sedimentary Geology* 83: 177-186.

Van Leur, J. C. 1955. *Indonesian Trade and Society: Essays in Asian Social and Economic History.* The Hague: W. van Hoeve Ltd.

Van Schendel, Willem (Ed.) 1992. *Francis Buchanan in Southeast Bengal (1798): His Journey to Chittagonfg, the Chittagong Hill Tracts, Noakhali and Comilla.* Dhaka: University Press Limited.

Vanaja, R. 1983. *Indian Coinage.* New Delhi: National Museum.

Varthema, Ludovico di 1928. *The Itinerary of Ludovico di Varthema of Bologna from 1502 to 1508 as Translated from the Original Italian Edition of 1510, by John Winter Jones, F.S.A. in 1863 for the Hakluyt Society with A Discourse on Varthema and his Travels in Southern Asia by Sir Richard Carnage Temple.* London: The Argonaut Press.

Venis, Arthur 1894. Copperplate Grant of Vaidyadeva, King of Kāmarūpa, *Epigraphia Indica* II: 347-358.

Verlinden, Charles 1987. The Indian Ocean: The Ancient Period and the Middle Ages, in *The Indian Ocean: Explorations in History, Commerce and Politics* (Satish Chandra Ed.), pp. 27-53, New Delhi: Sage Publications.

Vipradas 1953. *Manasa-Vijaya* (Sukumar Sen Ed.). Calcutta: Asiatic Society of Bengal.

Vitharana, V. 1992. *The Oru & The Yatra: Traditional Out-rigger Water Craft of Sri Lanka*. Dehiwela.

Wadia, D.N. 1961. *Geology of India* (third edition, revised; originally published in 1919). London: Macmillan and Co.

Walker, Francis A. 1886. *Money*. London: Macmillan and Co.

Walker, Michael J. & S. Santoso 1977-78. Romano-Indian Rouletted Pottery in Indonesia, *Puratattva* 9: 104-108.

Warmington, E.H. 1974. *The Commerce between the Roman Empire and India* (first published in 1928 by Cambridge University Press) Delhi: Vikas Publishing House Pvt. Ltd.

Warren, Bruce A. 1987. Ancient and Medieval Records of the Monsoon Winds and Currents of the India Ocean, *Monsoons* (Jay S. Feir and Pamela L. Stephens Eds.), pp. 137-158, New York: John Wiley and Sons.

Watt, Sir George 1908. *The Commercial Products of India*. London: His Majesty's Secretary.

Watters, Thomas 1905. *On Yuan Chwang's Travels in India*, Vol. II. London: Royal Asiatic Society.

Watters, Thomas 1973. *On Yuan Chwang's Travels in India (AD 629-645)* (T.W. Rhys Davids and S.W. Bushell Eds.). (Second Indiar edition, originally published by Royal Asiatic Society, London in 1904-05.) New Delhi: Munshiram Manoharlal Publishers.

Weigend, G.G. 1958. Some Elements in Port Geography, *Geographical Review* XL (viii): 185-200.

Weisshaar, Hans-Joachim, Heidrun Schenk and W. Wijeyapala 2001. Excavations in the Citadel at Akurugoda: The Workmen's Quarter (Tissa 1) and the Court's Garden (Tissa 2), in *Ancient Ruhuna: Sri Lankan-German Archaeological Project in the Southern Province*, Volume 1 (Hans-Joachim Weisshaar, Helmut Roth and W. Wijeyapala Eds.), pp. 5-39, Mainz Am Rhein: Verlag Philipp Von Zabern.

Wheatley, Paul 1961. *The Golden Khersonese: Studies in the Historical Geography of the Malay Peninsula before AD 1500*. Kuala Lumpur: University of Malaya Press.

Wheeler, R.E. Mortimer 1947-1948. Brahmagiri and Chandravalli 1947: Megalithic and Other Cultures in the Chitaldrug District, Mysore State, *Ancient India* 4: 180-310.

Wheeler, R.E. Mortimer 1955. *Rome beyond the Imperial Frontiers*. Harmondsworth: Penguin.

Wheeler, R.E. Mortimer 1976. *My Archaeological Mission to India and Pakistan*. London: Thames and Hudson.

Wheeler, R.E.M., A. Ghosh & Krishna Deva 1946. Arikamedu: an Indo-Roman Trading-station on the East Coast of India, *Ancient India* 2: 17-124.

Wilford, Francis 1799. On the Chronology of the Hindus, Asiatic Researches V: 241-295.

Wilford, Francis 1822. On the Ancient Geography of India, *Asiatic Researches* XIV: 373-470.

Wilhelm, G. Solheim II. 1965. A Preliminary Report on a New Pottery Complex in Northeastern Thailand, in *Felicitation Volumes of Southeast Asian Studies*, Vol. II, pp. 249-254, Bangkok: The Siam Society.

Will, Elizabeth Lyding 1991. The Mediterranean Shipping Amphoras from Arikamedu, in *Rome and India: The Ancient Sea Trade* (Vimala Begley and Richard Daniel De Puma Eds.), pp. 151-156, Madison: The University of Wisconsin Press.

Winternitz, M. 1978. *A History of Indian Literature* Volume I, Part II: Epics and Purāṇas. Calcutta: University of Calcutta.

Wise, James 1874. Notes on Sunārgāoṇ, Eastern Bengal, *Journal of the Asiatic Society of Bengal* XLIII (I): 82-96.

Wolters, O.W. 1967. *Early Indonesian Commerce: A Study of the Origins of Śrīvijaya*. Ithaca, New York: Cornell University Press.

Woodward, F.L. (Ed.) 1936. *The Book of the Gradual Sayings (Aṅguttara-Nikāya) or More Numbered Suttas*, Vol. V: The Book of the Tens and Elevens). London: Luzac and Company.

Yamazaki, Toshio 1982. Some Aspects of Land-Sale Inscriptions in Fifth and Sixth Century Bengal, *Acta Asiatica*, 43 (Japanese Studies in Ancient and Medieval Indian History, Tokyo): 17-36.

Yule, Henry (Tr. and Ed.) 1903. *The Book of Ser Marco Polo the Venetian Concerning the Kingdoms and Marvels of the East*. In two volumes. London: John Murray.

Yule, Henry (Tr. and Ed.) 1866. *Cathey and the Way Thither; being a Collection of Medieval Notices of China*. Vols. 1 and 2. London: Hakluyt Society.

Yule, Henry and A.C. Burnell 1903. *Hobson-Jobson: A Glossary of Colloquial Anglo-India Words, and Phrases, and of Kindred Terms, Etymological, Historical, Geographical and Discursive* (William Crooke Ed.). London: John Murray.

Zakariah, A.K.M. 1984. *Bāṅglādeśer Pratnasampad* (in Bengali). Dhaka: Bangladesh Shilpakala Academy.

Zakariah, A.K.M. 1997. Inscriptions, in *Mainamati-Devaparvata: A Survey of Historical Monuments and Sites in Bangladesh* (A.B.M. Husain Ed.), pp. 207-231. Dhaka: Asiatic Society of Bangladesh.

Zaki, Muhammad (Ed.) 1981. *Arab Accounts of India during the Fourteenth Century*. Delhi: Idarah-i Adabiyat-i Delhi.

Index

SOUTH ASIAN ARCHAEOLOGY SERIES

EDITED BY ALOK K. KANUNGO

SAA No 1. Kanungo, Alok Kumar 2004 *Glass Beads in Ancient India: An Ethnoarchaeological Approach* (*British Archaeological Reports, International Series* S1242) Oxford. ISBN 1 84171 364 3.

SAA No 2. Kanungo, Alok Kumar (Ed) 2005 *Gurudakshina: Facets of Indian Archaeology, Essays presented to Prof. V.N. Misra* (*British Archaeological Reports, International Series* S1433) Oxford. ISBN 1 84171 723 1.

SAA No 3. Swayam, S. 2006 *Invisible People: Pastoral life in Proto-Historic Gujurat* (*British Archaeological Reports, International Series* S1464) Oxford. ISBN 1 84171 732 0.

SAA No 4. Mushrif-Tripathy, Veena & Walimbe S.R. 2006 *Human Skeletal Remains from Chalcolithic Nevasa: Osteobiographic Analysis (British Archaeological Reports, International Series* S1476) Oxford. ISBN 1 84171 737 1.

SAA No 5. Jahan, Shahnaj Husne 2006 *Excavating Waves and Winds of (Ex)change: A Study of Maritime Trade in Early Bengal (British Archaeological Reports, International Series* S1533) Oxford. ISBN 1 84171 753 3.

www.ingramcontent.com/pod-product-compliance
Ingram Content Group UK Ltd.
Pitfield, Milton Keynes, MK11 3LW, UK
UKHW061846041026
15591UKWH00015B/944

9 781841 717531